HANDBOOKS

D1035985

MONTRÉAL & QUÉBEC CITY

SACHA JACKSON

Contents

Montréal Maps

Québec City Maps

SEE MAP 2

Station
Square Victoria

Station
Place-d'Armes

AVE VIGER

720

RUE VIGER

JEAN-PAUL RIOPELLE

720

RUE SAINT ALEXANDRE

RUE SAINT URBAIN

RUE CLARK

BLVD SAINT LAURENT

RUE SAINT ANTOINE

RUELLES DES FORTIFICATIONS

RUELLES DES FORTIFICATIONS

Quartier
International

RUE SAINT JACQUES

SQ VICTORIA

RUE McGILL

RUE BLEURY

RUE DOLLARD

RUE SAINT JACQUES

CÔTE DE LA PLACE D'ARMES

PLACE D'ARMES

Place
d'Armes

SEE MAP 2

RUE NOTRE DAME

Basilique Notre-
Dame-de-Montréal

RUE DE L'HÔPITAL

RUE SAINT ALEXIS

RUE SAINT JEAN

RUE SAINT FRANÇOIS XAVIER

RUE SAINT SULPICE

VIEUX-MONTRÉAL

Rue
Saint-Paul

RUE RÉCOLLETS

RUE SAINTE HÉLÈNE

RUE SAINT SACREMENT

RUE SAINT NICOLAS

RUE SAINT PAUL

RUE SAINT JEAN

56

RUE SAINT MAURICE

RUE DE LONGUEUIL

RUE LEMOYNE

RUE SAINT PIERRE

RUE SAINT JEAN

47

48

49

RUE SAINT HENRI

PLACE ROYALE

RUE CAPITALE

Place Royale

RUE DE LA COMMUNE

Pointe-à-Callière
Musée d'Archéologie
et d'Histoire

PLACE D'YOUVILLE

RUE WILLIAM

PLACE D'YOUVILLE

RUE DU PORT

RUE DE LA COMMUNE

46

Centre des
Sciences de
Montréal

RUE NORMAND

RUE MARGUERITE D'YOUVILLE

To 25
Darling Foundry

RUE WELLINGTON

RUE McGILL

RUE SOEURS GRISES

RUE KING

RUE QUEEN

Quai
Alexandria

RUE DE LA COMMUNE

0   200 yds

0   200 m

DISTANCE ACROSS MAP
Approximate: 1 mi or 1.6 km

© AVALON TRAVEL

⑤ SHOPS

19	CLUSIER HABILLEUR	36	REBORN
31	ESPACE PEPIN	45	SCANDINAVE
32	MICHEL BRISSON		LES BAINS
34	ZONE ORANGE		VIEUX-MONTRÉAL

Ⓗ HOTELS

2	W HOTEL	39	LE PETIT HÔTEL
4	HÔTEL LE ST-JAMES	44	HÔTEL NELLIGAN
7	L'HOTEL MONTREAL	52	AUBERGE DU
9	PLACE D'ARMES		VIEUX-PORT
	HÔTEL AND SUITES	65	PIERRE DU CALVET
13	HÔTEL GAULT	67	L'HÔTEL
21	HÔTEL ST-PAUL		CHAMPS-DE-MARS

Station Champ-de-Mars

Square Vigor

SEE MAP 3

RUE SAINT ANTOINE

720

RUE SAINT ANTOINE

RUE SAINT LOUIS

67 H

RUE DU CHAMP DE MARS

Place Vauquelin

RUE NOTRE DAME

59 A
61 ✪ **Hôtel de Ville**
60 R **Musée du Château Ramezay**
62 R
58
✪ **Place Jacques-Cartier**
57 R
55
Marché Bonsecours
66 A
65
RUE SAINT PAUL
RUE FRIPPONNE
64
63
Chapelle Notre-Dame-de-Bon-Secours and the Musée Marguerite Bourgeoÿs

RUE DE LA COMMUNE

53 N 54
51 N 52

VIEUX-PORT

50 **Vieux-Port**

RUE DE LA COMMUNE

Bonsecours Basin

72 A

73 ✪ **Tour de l'Horloge**

68 A
69 A
71 A

Quai Jacques-Cartier

70 N

Quai King-Edward

AVE PIERRE DUPUY

74 ✪ **Habitat 67**

✪ SIGHTS

5	QUARTIER INTERNATIONAL	42	PLACE ROYALE	63	MARCHÉ BONSECOURS
10	PLACE D'ARMES	48	RUE SAINT-PAUL	64	CHAPELLE NOTRE-DAME-DE-BON-SECOURS AND THE MUSÉE MARGUERITE BOURGEOYS
12 ◖	BASILIQUE NOTRE-DAME-DE-MONTRÉAL	50	VIEUX-PORT		
40 ◖	POINTE-À-CALLIÈRE MUSÉE D'ARCHÉOLOGIE ET D'HISTOIRE	58	PLACE JACQUES-CARTIER	73	TOUR DE L'HORLOGE
		60	MUSÉE DU CHÂTEAU RAMEZAY	74	HABITAT 67
		61	HÔTEL DE VILLE		

R RESTAURANTS

3	TOQUÉ!	24	SOUPESOUP	35	GANDHI
14	CAFÉ TITANIC	26	BENIAMINO MARKET	37	STASH CAFÉ
17	BORIS BISTRO	27	MUVBOX	38	GARDE MANGER
18	BRIT AND CHIPS	28	DNA	57	JARDIN NELSON
22	GRAZIELLA	29	GIBBY'S	62	LE CLUB CHASSE ET PÊCHE
23	LE CARTET	33	OLIVE & GOURMANDO		

N NIGHTLIFE

1 ◖	WUNDERBAR	20	LE CONFESSIONAL	54	PUB ST-PAUL
6	BAINS DOUCHES	43	VERSES SKY	56	LE VELVET
8	LE TERRASSE SUITE 701	51	NARCISSE BAR À VIN	70	TERRASSES BONSECOURS
		53	LES DEUX PIERROTS		

A ARTS AND LEISURE

11	CALÈCHES-PLACE D'ARMES	46	CENTRE DES SCIENCES DE MONTRÉAL AND IMAX TELUS THEATRE	66	SIR GEORGE-ÉTIENNE CARTIER NATIONAL HISTORIC SITE OF CANADA
15 ◖	DHC/ART				
16	CENTAUR THEATRE	47	GALERIE PANGÉE	68	CIRQUE DU SOLEIL
25	DARLING FOUNDRY	49 ◖	ÇA ROULE MONTRÉAL	68	JACQUES-CARTIER PIER
30	CENTRE D'HISTOIRE DE MONTRÉAL	55	GALERIE ORANGE	68	LE BATEAU-MOUCHE
41	LACHINE CANAL BIKE PATH	59	CALÈCHES-PLACE JACQUES-CARTIER	69	BONSECOURS BASIN
				71	CIRQUE ÉLOIZE
				72	SAUTE MOUTONS

☼ SIGHTS

1	GRAND SÉMINAIRE DE MONTRÉAL	20	MCGILL UNIVERSITY	57	CATHÉDRALE MARIE-REINE-DU-MONDE
10	CENTRE CANADIEN D'ARCHITECTURE	22	MUSÉE MCCORD		
		56	DORCHESTER SQUARE	59	PLACE VILLE-MARIE
15	MUSÉE DES BEAUX-ARTS DE MONTRÉAL			64	CENTRE BELL

ℝ RESTAURANTS

3	QING HUA DUMPLING	25	BOUSTAN	55	QUEUE DE CHEVAL
5	AVESTA	26	CAFÉ NESPRESSO	72	LIVERPOOL HOUSE
8	KAZU	28	M:BRGR	73	BURGUNDY LION
9	LE PARIS	32	CAFÉ MYRIADE	74	JOE BEEF
23	LA TROÏKA RESTAURANT	34	LE GOURMET BURGER	75	MCKIERNAN
				81	BONNY'S
24	BURRITOVILLE	49	DUNN'S FAMOUS DELI	83	GRIFFINTOWN CAFÉ

Square Cabot

Strathcona Parc

Centre Canadien d'Architecture
10

Grand Séminaire de Montréal
1

RUE SHERBROOKE OUEST

Station Guy-Concordia

3

BLVD DE MAISONNEUVE OUEST

RUE SAINTE CATHERINE OUEST

RUE TUPPER

RUE BAILE

BLVD RENÉ LÉVESQUE OUEST

To Parisian Laundry
69
70

RUE SAINT ANTOINE OUEST

Station Georges Vanier

AVE BLANCHARD

RUE COURSOL

Square Richmond

RUE BLAKE

RUE QUESNEL

RUE SAINT JACQUES

AVE LIONEL GROULX

ℕ NIGHTLIFE

33	UPSTAIRS JAZZ BAR AND GRILL	36	LA TERRASSE MAGNÉTIC	40	BRUTOPIA	60	ALTITUDE 737
				41	CLUB 1234	68	LE BAR SOLEIL
35	NEWTOWN	39	HURLEY'S IRISH PUB	50	DOMINION SQUARE TAVERN	84	TIME SUPPER CLUB

Ⓐ ARTS AND LEISURE

4	AMC	19	REDPATH MUSEUM OF NATURAL HISTORY	51	MANSFIELD ATHLETIC CLUB	65	MONTRÉAL CANADIENS
11	CANADIAN GUILD OF CRAFTS	45	YMCA	67	LE ATRIUM 1000	85	MONTRÉAL PLANETARIUM
		48	CINEMA BANQUE SCOTIA	69	PARISIAN LAUNDRY		

Ⓢ SHOPS

7	MEDIAPHILE	29	BLEU COMME LE CIEL	47	RUE SAINTE-CATHERINE	76	GRAND CENTRAL
12	LIBRISSIME	30	CHEAP THRILLS			77	BEIGE
13	MONA MOORE	38	LA MAISON OGILVY	52	LA MAISON SIMONS	78	RUE NOTRE-DAME WEST
14	LES CRÉATEURS	43	STUDIO BEAUTÉ DU MONDE	53	EATON CENTER		
16	HOLT RENFREW			61	MURALE	79	L'ÉCUYER ANTIQUES
21	PARAGRAPHE	44	BROWNS	70	HARRICANA	80	ORIENTAL TREASURES
27	MARIE SAINT PIERRE	46	LES COURS MONT ROYAL	71	RETRO-VILLE	82	ERA VINTAGE

RUE NOTRE-DAME OUEST
72 75 76
71 73 74

RUE FAUTEUX

RUE VINET

RUE CHARLEVOIX

RUE DUVERNAY

BLVD GEORGES VANIER

78

RUE NOTRE-DAME OUEST
79 80
81 82

RUE SIMPSON

RUE REDPATH

RUE DU MUSÉE

PL DE RICHELIEU

PL ONTARIO

RUE DE LA MONTAGNE

RUE DRUMMOND

RUE STANLEY

PL MOUNTAIN

RUE PEEL

RUE MCTAVISH

RUE MCGILL COLLEGE

RUE UNIVERSITY

19 Ⓐ

20 ✪
McGill University

Musée des Beaux-Arts de Montréal ✪

11 Ⓡ Ⓡ Ⓢ Ⓢ Ⓡ
12 13 14

15 ✪

16 Ⓢ

17 Ⓝ

18
RUE SHERBROOKE OUEST

Musée McCord

RUE VICTORIA

21 Ⓢ

22 ✪

23 Ⓡ

24 Ⓡ

25 Ⓡ

26 Ⓡ

27 Ⓢ

28 Ⓡ

29 Ⓢ

30 Ⓢ

RUE METCALFE

31 Ⓝ

RUE MANSFIELD

AVE DU PRÉSIDENT KENNEDY

SEE MAP 3 ▶

32 Ⓝ

RUE MACKAY

RUE BISHOP

34

RUE CRESCENT

35 Ⓝ

36 Ⓝ 37 Ⓡ

38 Ⓢ

42 Ⓝ

43 Ⓢ

44 Ⓢ

45 Ⓝ

46 Ⓢ

BLVD DE MAISONNEUVE OUEST

Ⓜ **Station Peel**

PL MONT ROYAL

47 Ⓢ

48 Ⓢ

52 Ⓢ

53 Ⓢ

Station McGill

La Centre Commercial
Eaton de Montrèal

RUE SAINTE CATHERINE OUEST ▶▶

33 Ⓝ

41 Ⓝ

39 Ⓝ

40 Ⓝ

Ⓡ 49

Ⓝ 50

51 Ⓐ

RUE PALACE

RUE CATHCART

CENTRE-VILLE

54 Ⓝ

55 Ⓡ

PL DOMINION

RUE CYPRESS

56 ✪
Dorchester Square

RUE METCALFE

59 60 61
Ⓡ Ⓝ Ⓢ
Place Ville-Marie

BLVD RÉNE LÉVESQUE OUEST

62 Ⓗ

AVE OVERDALE ▶▶

63 Ⓗ

Station Lucien l'Allier
Ⓜ

RUE LUCIEN L'ALLIER

RUE DE LA MONTAGNE

RUE DRUMMOND

RUE STANLEY

RUE PEEL

Place
du
Canada

57 Ⓡ
Cathédrale Marie-Reine-du-Monde

58 Ⓡ

RUE CATHEDRALE

RUE BELMONT

RUE UNIVERSITY

SEE MAP 1 ▶

AVE ARGYLE

AVE DES CANADIENS DE MONTREAL ▶▶

64 65
Ⓝ Ⓐ
Centre Bell

66 Ⓗ

67 Ⓝ

Station Bonaventure

RUE DE LA GAUCHETIÈRE OUEST

68 Ⓝ

AVE BEXHAM

RUE LUSIGNAN

RUE VERSAILLES

RUE TORRANCE

RUE TORRANCE

RUE SAINT FÉLIX

RUE SAINT JEAN D'ESTREES

RUE DES RIVIERES

RUE MANSFIELD

RUE SAINTE CECILE

RUE CATHEDRALE

RUE SAINT ANTOINE OUEST

RUE VIGER OUEST

84 Ⓝ

85 Ⓐ

720

RUE SAINT JACQUES OUEST ◀◀

Ⓝ **HOTELS**

2 CHÂTEAU VERSAILLES
6 L'HÔTEL DU FORT
17 🅒 RITZ-CARLTON
18 SOFITEL MONTREAL
31 🅒 HÔTEL LE GERMAIN

37 L'HÔTEL DE LA
   MONTAGNE
42 LOEWS VOGUE HOTEL
54 L'HÔTEL LE CRYSTAL

58 🅒 FAIRMONT
   QUEEN ELIZABETH
62 L'HÔTEL ESPRESSO
63 LE PETIT PRINCE
66 MARRIOTT CHÂTEAU
   CHAMPLAIN

RUE NOTRE DAME OUEST

83 Ⓡ

RUE BARRE

RUE WILLIAM

0   200 yds

0   200 m

DISTANCE ACROSS MAP
Approximate: 1.4 mi or 2.2 km

✪ SIGHTS

14	MUSÉE D'ART CONTEMPORAIN	15	PLACE DES ARTS	27	CHINATOWN

🍴 RESTAURANTS

13	BRASSERIE T!	26	MAISON KAM FUNG	30	CHEZ BONG
25	NUI KEE	28	PÂTISSERIE HARMONIE		

🌙 NIGHTLIFE

2	VINYL LOUNGE	10	NYKS	21	LES FOUFOUNES ELECTRIQUES
6	JELLO MARTINI LOUNGE	18	KATACOMBS	23	LE STE-ÉLISABETH
				17	CLUB SODA

🎭 ARTS AND LEISURE

4	CABARET JUSTE POUR RIRE	16	LES GRANDS BALLETS CANADIENS DE MONTRÉAL	17	CLUB SODA
9	BELGO BUILDING	16	OPÉRA DE MONTRÉAL	19	SAT
11	GESÙ CENTRE DE CRÉATIVITÉ	16	L'ORCHESTRA SYMPHONIQUE DE MONTRÉAL	20	MÉTROPOLIS
12	L'ASTRAL			24	THÉÂTRE STE-CATHERINE

🛍 SHOPS

1	THE WORD	5	EVA B	8	LA BAIE
		7	BIRKS	22	HENRI HENRI

🏨 HOTELS

3	OPUS MONTRÉAL	29	HOLIDAY INN SELECT

SEE MAP 4 ▷

RUE SANGUINET
RUE ÉMERY
RUE SAINT DENIS
AVE SAVOIE
RUE BERRI
RUE DE LA PROVIDENCE
RUE SAINT HUBERT
RUE SAINT CHRISTOPHE

Station Saint Laurent Ⓜ
BLVD DE MAISONNEUVE EST
Station Berri-UQAM Ⓜ

Square Berri

RUE DE BOISBRIAND
RUE DE BOISBRIAND

20 21 22 23

RUE SAINTE CATHERINE EST
RUE DUFAULT
24

Université du Québec á Montréal

17
18
19

RUE BERGER
RUE CHARLOTTE

RUE CHRISTIN
RUE SAVIGNAC

PLACE PASTEUR

RUE LABELLE
RUE SAINT CHRISTOPHE
RUE SAINT ANDRE

BLVD RENE LEVESQUE EST

Hôpital Saint Luc

BLVD SAINT LAURENT
RUE SAINT DOMINIQUE
AVE DE L'HOTEL DE VILLE
RUE DE BULLION
RUE SAINTE ELIZABETH
RUE SANGUINET
RUE SAINT DENIS
RUE NOTRE DAME DE LOURDE
RUE BERNADETTE
RUE BERRI
RUE DE LA GAUCHETIÈRE
RUE SAINT HUBERT
RUE ROULIER

30

AVE VIGER EST

Station Champ-de-Mars Ⓜ

Square Vigor

720

Square
St Louis

RUE RIGAUD

RUE BERRI

RUE SAINT DENIS

SEE MAP 5

RUE SHERBROOKE EST

RUE SAINT ANDRÉ

RUE SAINT HUBERT

20 **S**

CAR AMHERST

21 **A**

22 **R**

1 **S**

2 **S**

THE VILLAGE

3 **N**

4 **N**

RUE ONTARIO EST

19 **N**

RUE DUCLOS

RUE LABRECQUE

5 **R**

RUELLE DE LA PROVIDENCE

24 **S**

RUE SAINT DENIS

6 **N**

AVE SAVOIE

RUE ROBIN

25 ✪ **Rue Amherst**

7 **N**

RUE LAFAYETTE

RUE SAINT CHRISTOPHE

RUE SAINT TIMOTHÉE

RUE AMHERST

RUE WOLFE

RUE MONTCALM

26 **N**

9 **R**   **8** **N**

RUE EMERY

27 **S**

10 **R**

11 **R**

13 ✪ **La Grande**
        Bibliothèque

RUE LABRECQUE

28 **N**

12 **A**

BLVD DE MAISONNEUVE EST

M *Station*
        Berri-UQAM

29 **R**

30 **M**

Université
du Québec
á Montréal

Square Berri

31 **N**

34 **N**

37 **N**

38 **N**

SEE MAP 3

PL PASTEUR

RUE SAINTE CATHERINE EST

S
14

15 ✪ **UQÀM**

RUE BERRI

RUE LABELLE

RUE SAINT HUBERT

RUE SAINT CHRISTOPHE

32 **N**

35 **A**

36 **N**

16 **H**

RUE CHRISTIN

RUE SAINT DENIS

33 **N**

**QUARTIER
LATIN**

18 **H**

RUE RENÉ LÉVESQUE EST

© AVALON TRAVEL   17 **H**

QUARTIER LATIN AND THE VILLAGE

✪ SIGHTS
13 LA GRANDE BIBLIOTHÈQUE	41 ❖ RUE SAINTE-CATHERINE EST
15 UQÀM	45 ÉGLISE ST-PIERRE-APÔTRE
25 RUE AMHERST	

ⓡ RESTAURANTS
5 LA PARYSE	23 AU PETIT EXTRA
9 CAMELLIA SINENSIS	29 CHIPOTLE AND JALAPENO
10 JULIETTE ET CHOCOLAT	42 LE MIE MATINALE
11 LA BRIOCHE LYONNAISE	46 KITCHENETTE
22 SPIRITE LOUNGE	

ⓝ NIGHTLIFE
3 L'AMÈRE À BOIRE	34 CIRCUS
4 CAFÉ CHAOS	36 PARKING
6 L'ABSYNTHE	37 CABARET CHEZ MADO
7 LE SAINT-SULPICE	38 CLUB UNITY
8 LES TROIS BRASSEURS	39 ❖ CLUB DATE
19 LE CHEVAL BLANC	43 LE DRUGSTORE
26 GOTHA	44 SKY PUB CLUB
32 STEREO	

ⓐ ARTS AND LEISURE
12 CINÉMATHÈQUE QUÉBÉCOISE	21 ÉCO MUSÉE DU FIER MONDE
12 DAZIBAO	35 L'OLYMPIA
	40 LE NATIONAL

ⓢ SHOPS
1 ATOM HEART	20 SPOUTNIK BOUTIQUE
2 RUE SAINT-DENIS	24 CITÉ DÉCO
14 DESERRE	27 SECONDE CHANCE

ⓗ HOTELS
16 L'HÔTEL ST-DENIS	30 SIR MONTCALM
17 CELEBRITIES LOVELY HOTEL	31 L'HÔTEL GOUVERNEUR PLACE DUPUIS
18 L'HÔTEL LORD BERRI	33 L'HÔTEL MANOIR DES ALPES
28 LA LOGGIA	

DISTANCE ACROSS MAP
Approximate: .9 mi or 1.5 km

BLVD SAINT JOSEPH

To Ⓐ 81 Sir Wilfred-
Laurier Pool
Ⓡ 80

Ⓡ 82
RUE GILFORD
RUE MENNAIS

85 Ⓐ

RUE GÉNÉREUX

AVE DU MONT ROYAL EST

79 Ⓝ

Ⓡ 83
84 Ⓝ
RUE SIMARD

RUE LATREILLE

RUE MARIE ANNE EST

RUE COURVILLE

SEE MAP 4

113 Ⓡ

114 Ⓡ   Ⓡ 115   Ⓝ 116
AVE BUREAU
RUE RACHEL EST

Parc   Lafontaine

120 121
Ⓐ
Parc
Lafontaine

© AVALON TRAVEL

DISTANCE ACROSS MAP
Approximate: 2.6 mi or 4.2 km
0 — 200 yds
0 — 200 m

✪ SIGHTS

24 THE MAIN	95 RUE SAINT-DENIS	120 PARC LAFONTAINE
77 AVENUE DU MONT-ROYAL	105 CARRÉ SAINT-LOUIS	

Ⓝ RESTAURANTS

2 COCOA LOCALE	29 CHEZ JOSÉ	83 SALLE À MANGER
3 KAZA MAZA	31 CAFÉ SANTROPOL	92 CHUCHAI
7 LA SALA ROSA	38 MOISHES	94 L'ACADEMIE
9 Ⓒ AUX VIVRES	41 Ⓒ SCHWARTZ'S	98 L'EXPRESS
10 MEATMARKET	48 EURO DELI	103 PINTXO
13 CLUB ESPAGNOL DE QUÉBEC	60 ISAKAYA	104 LALOUX
14 CHEZ DOVAL	67 LA CANTINE	110 LES INFIDELES
19 CRUDESSENCE	69 PATISSERIE KOUIGN AMANN	112 L'ANECDOTE
20 ROTISSERIE ROMADOS	71 AU CINQUIÈME PÉCHÉ	113 AU 917
21 CAFÉ NÉVÉ	75 LE BARBARE	114 Ⓒ LA BANQUISE
23 PATATI PATATA	80 LE QUARTIER GÉNÉRAL	115 LE POISSON ROUGE
28 RÉSERVOIR	82 Ⓒ LE CHIEN FUMANT	117 Ⓒ AU PIED DU COCHON
		119 LA COLOMBE

Ⓝ NIGHTLIFE

1 BUVETTE CHEZ SIMONE	45 TOKYO BAR	65 LE SALON DAOMÉ
5 Ⓒ CASA DEL POPOLO	46 BIFTEK	70 BAR PLAN B
17 DIVAN ORANGE	47 GO-GO LOUNGE	72 Ⓒ BILY KUN
27 BARFLY	51 CAFÉ CAMPUS & PETIT CAMPUS	74 O PATRO VYS
34 BLUE DOG MOTEL	58 BUONANOTTE	79 BRASSERIE CHEZ BAPTISTE
36 BLIZZARTS	62 Ⓒ PULLMAN	86 L'ESCOGRIFFE
39 KOROVA	63 GLOBE	90 BAR BAROUF

Ⓐ ARTS AND LEISURE

4 LA SALA ROSSA	40 LES ALOUETTES DE MONTRÉAL	54 CINEMA DU PARC
16 LA CENTRALE GALERIE POWERHOUSE	42 MOKSHA YOGA	81 SIR WILFRED-LAURIER POOL
22 PARC JEANNE-MANCE	44 MUSÉE DES HOSPITALIÈRES DE L'HÔTEL DIEU	85 LA TULIPE
33 CINEMA L'AMOUR	52 MAI	108 AGORA DE LA DANSE
35 MAINLINE THEATER	53 CLUB LACITÉ	121 PARC LAFONTAINE

Ⓢ SHOPS

8 ESPACE NOMAD	50 SCANDALE	88 Ⓒ DUBUC
11 LE CANARD LIBÉRÉ	55 DUO	89 ZONE
12 SABOR LATINO	56 MULTIMAGS	91 RIEN À CACHER
15 INTERVERSION	57 M0851	96 OZ BIJOUX
18 BUMMIS	59 LOLA & EMILY	97 ARTHUR QUENTIN
25 BOULEVARD SAINT-LAURENT	61 NOTA BENE	99 COULEURS
26 LUSTRE	64 MASKARAD	100 JOHN FLUEVOG
30 Ⓒ LA GRANDE OURSE	66 PAUL'S BOUTIQUE	101 Ⓒ PRIMITIVE RECORDS
32 Ⓒ KITSCH 'N' SWELL	68 OLD GOLD	102 BEATNICK MUSIC
37 FRIPERIE ST-LAURENT	73 FOLLES ALLIÉES	109 KANUK
43 LA VIEILLE EUROPE	76 3 FEMMES ET 1 COUSSIN	111 A LA TRICOTEUSE
49 U&I	78 CHEZ FARFELU	118 Ⓒ LES CHOCOLATS DE CHLOÉ
	87 DEUXIÈME PEAU	

Ⓗ HOTELS

6 PENSIONE POPOLO	
84 LE PLUMARD	
93 ANNE MA SŒUR ANNE	
106 GINGERBREAD MANOR	
107 Ⓒ L'HOTEL DE L'INSTITUT	
116 Ⓒ AUBERGE DE LA FONTAINE	

MAP 6

DISTANCE ACROSS MAP
Approximate: 2.2 mi or 3.6 km

0   300 yds
0   300 m

RUE DE CASTELNAU OUEST

Station de
Castelnau

RUE JEAN TALON ES
PLACE DE
MARCHE DE NORD
Marché
Jean-Talon
PLACE DU
MARCHE DU NORD

AVE OGILVY

RUE DE GASPE
DE HENRI JULIEN

AVE MONMOUTH
BLVD DE L'ACADIE SUD

RUE JEAN TALON OUEST

AVE ALEXANDRA

AVE MOZART OUEST
AVE MOZART EST

RUE BELANGER

Station
Acadie

AVE BEAUMONT

AVE BEAUMONT

Chiesa Della
Madonna
Della Difesa

RUE DANTE

RUE SAINT ZOTIQUE OUEST

RUE SAINT ZOTIQUE OUEST

PETITE
ITALIE

Parc
Martel

RUE BEAUBIEN OUEST

RUE BEAUBIEN EST

RUE BURELLE

RUE HENRI IV

AVE DUCHARME

AVE VAN HORNE

AVE VAN HORNE

RUE DE BELLECHASSE

Station
Outremont

RUE DE L'ARCADE

BLVD ROSEMONT

RUE MARMIER

RUE MARMIER

AVE BERNARD

RUE BERNARD OUEST

Parc
St Viateur

MILE END

Parc
Beaubien

Church of
Saint-Michael and
Saint-Anthony

Parc
Outremont

RUE SAINT VIATEUR OUEST

RUE SAINT VIATEUR EST

RUE GROLL

RUE MAGUIRE

CHEMIN DE LA CÔTE SAINTE CATHERINE

AVE ELMWOOD

AVE FAIRMOUNT EST

Parc de
St Michel

AVE FAIRMOUNT OUEST

RUE LABADIE

AVE CLERMONT

Parc
Lahaie

AVE LAURIER OUEST

AVE LAURIER EST

RUE CHARLES

BLVD SAINTE JOSEPH OUEST

BLVD SAINTE

© AVALON TRAVEL

Parc le Provost
Parc Turin
Hôpital Jean-Talon Ⓜ
Station Fabre

Station Jean-Talon Ⓜ

RUE BELANGER

Parc St Edouard

RUE SAINT-ZOTIQUE EST

Station Beaubien Ⓜ

RUE BEAUBIEN EST

RUE DE BELLECHASSE

Station Rosemont Ⓜ

BLVD ROSEMONT

Parc des Carrières
RUE DES CARRIÈRES

RUE SAINT GREGOIRE

Parc Sir-Wilfred Laurier

RUE MASSON

Parc de Lorimier

Station Laurier Ⓜ
AVE LAURIER EST

☉ SIGHTS

6	MARCHÉ JEAN-TALON	47	CHURCH OF SAINT-MICHAEL AND SAINT-ANTHONY
13	CHIESA DELLA MADONNA DELLA DIFESA		

Ⓡ RESTAURANTS

3	KITCHEN GALERIE	40	CAVA
4	LE PETIT ALEP	42	MILOS
7	DÉPANNEUR LE PICK-UP	43	CLUB SOCIAL
9	CAFÉ ITALIA	44	LES DEUX SINGES DE MONTARVIE
10	LUCCA	46	CAFÉ OLIMPICO
12	PIZZERIA NAPOLETANA	48	LE PANTHÈRE VERTE
14	BOTTEGA PIZZERIA	51	LE CAGIBI
18	VIEUX VÉLO	55	LA CROISSANTERIE FIGARO
24	LE BILBOQUET	57	LEMÉAC
25	LE PETIT ITALIEN	66	WILENSKY'S LIGHT LUNCH
26	CAFÉ SOUVENIR		
27	LA MOULERIE	73	LAWRENCE
33	LA LUMIÈRE DU MILE END	74	LA MONTÉE DE LAIT
		77	CHEZ CLAUDETTE

Ⓝ NIGHTLIFE

2	IL MOTORE	54	SPARROW
17	VICES ET VERSA	65	BALDWIN BARMACIE
30	HELM	69	DIEU DU CIEL
39	WHISKY CAFÉ	71	BU

Ⓐ ARTS AND LEISURE

1	BATTAT CONTEMPORARY	31	RIALTO THEATRE
20	GALERIE YVES LAROCHE	53	GALERIE SIMON BLAIS
		56	ARTICULE
29	THEATRE OUTREMONT	68	LE YETI

Ⓢ SHOPS

5	FROMAGERIE HAMEL	41	S.W. WELCH
8	MILANO	45	GENEVIEVE GADBOIS
11	QUINCAILLERIE DANTE	49	GENERAL 54
15	SAVON POPULAIRE	50	THE ANNEX
16	FOUNDERIE	52	MONASTIRAKI
19	LA GUILDE CULINAIRE	58	GOURMET LAURIER
21	BELLE ET REBELLE	59	BILLIE
22	EFFILOCHÉ	60	LYLA
23	LOZEAU	61	LISE WATIER INSTITUT
28	AUX PLAISIRS DU BACCHUS	62	LA CANADIENNE
32	DRAWN & QUARTERLY	63	BOUTIQUE CITROUILLE
34	PHONOPOLIS	64	LES TOUILLEURS
35	ARTERIE	67	AU PAPIER JAPONAIS
36	STYLE LABO	70	LES ÉTOFFES
37	LOCAL 23	72	CO
38	BODYBAG BY JUDE	75	JAMAIS ASSEZ
		76	UNICORN

SEE MAP 5

Prairie River

To 1 Club de Golf
Sainte-Rose

Parc
Marcelin-
Wilson

Aéroport
International
Pierre-Elliot-
Trudeau
de Montréal

13

AUTOROUTE CHOMEDEY

AUTOROUTE TRANSCANADIENNE

BLVD. MARCEL LAURIN

BLVD. DE LA CÔTE-VERTU

Saint-Laurent

15

AUTOROUTE DES LAURENTIDES

BLVD. DE L'ACADIE

40

AUTOROUTE CÔTE DE LIESSE

To 2 Dorval Municipal
Golf Club and 3 Meadowbrook
Golf Club

520

40

13

Hampstead

15

5 S

Mont-Royal

20

Outremont

8
A
9

CHEMIN DE LA CÔTE SAINTE CATHERINE

Université de
Montréal

Montréal-Ouest

AUTOROUTE DÉCARIE

AVENUE VICTORIA

10 St-Joseph's
Oratory

Cimetière Notre-
Dame-des-Neiges

11

Cimetière
Mont-Royal

12

13

15

Parc du
Mont-Royal

14

Concordia
University

Lac aux
Castors

RUE SHERBROOKE

138

Westmount

Chalet du
Mont-Royal

16

17

Croix du
Mont-Royal

18 S

Universit
McGill

108

AUTOROUTE JEAN LESAGE

15

20

19 S

RUE SHERBROOKE

CENTRE-VILLE

Lasalle

BLVD. NEWMAN

720

20 S

21

Marché Atwater
A

22

Parc
Angrignon

20

23

BLVD. DE LA VERENDRYE

RUE WELLINGTON

Verdun

10

AUTOROUTE BONVENTURE

24 S

Île de
Soeurs

PONT
CHAMPLAIN

© AVALON TRAVEL

Heron
Island

Île aux
Chèvres

St. Lawrence River

SIGHTS

10	ST-JOSEPH'S ORATORY	13	LAC AUX CASTORS	17	CROIX DU MONT-ROYAL
11	CIMETIÈRE NOTRE-DAME-DES-NEIGES	14	PARC DU MONT-ROYAL	21	MARCHÉ ATWATER
12	CIMETIÈRE MONT-ROYAL	16	CHALET DU MONT-ROYAL	26	CASINO DE MONTRÉAL
				27	BIOSPHÈRE

29	PARC JEAN-DRAPEAU	35	TOUR OLYMPIQUE
30	LA RONDE	37	BIODÔME
31	MUSÉE STEWART	38	INSECTARIUM DE MONTRÉAL
33	JARDIN BOTANIQUE		
35	STADE OLYMPIQUE		

ARTS AND LEISURE

1	CLUB DE GOLF SAINTE-ROSE	7	TOHU	15	PARC DU MONT-ROYAL
2	DORVAL MUNICIPAL GOLF CLUB	8	MONTRÉAL HOLOCAUST MEMORIAL MUSEUM	15	BEAVER LAKE
3	MEADOWBROOK GOLF CLUB	9	SEGAL CENTRE FOR THE PERFORMING ARTS	22	H2O ADVENTURES
6	ROGERS CUP			22	MY BICYCLETTE

23	MAISON SAINT-GABRIEL	32	LE MUSÉE CHÂTEAU DUFRESNE
25	CANADIAN GRAND PRIX	34	JARDIN BOTANIQUE AND PARC MAISONNEUVE
28	JEAN-DRAPEAU AQUATIC COMPLEX	36	OLYMPIC POOL
		39	MONTRÉAL IMPACT

SHOPS

5	ABE & MARY'S	20	LA GAILLARDE
18	ENVERS	24	STROM SPA NORDIQUE
19	OINK OINK		

MILE END

PETITE ITALIE

Montréal

PLATEAU MONT-ROYAL

QUARTIER LATIN

CENTRE-VILLE EST

VIEUX MONTRÉAL

Parc Maisonneuve

Jardin Botanique 33 34

Stade Olympique/ Tour Olympique 32 38 39 36 35 37 Biodôme

Insectarium de Montréal

THE VILLAGE

Île Sainte-Hélène

St. Lawrence River

31 Musée Stewart
La Ronde 30
Biosphère 27 28
Parc Jean-Drapeau 29

Île Notre-Dame 25 Casino de 26 Montréal

PONT VICTORIA

Longueuil

Lemoyne

Saint-Lambert

RUE JEAN TALON
BLVD. BEAUBIEN
BLVD ROSEMONT
RUE SHERBROOKE
RUE NOTRE-DAME EST
AUTOROUTE MÉTROPOLITAINE
BLVD SAINT-LAURENT
BLVD SAINT MICHEL
BLVD PIE-IX
RUE VIAU
BLVD LOUIS H. LAFONTAINE

DISTANCE ACROSS MAP
Approximate: 12.6 mi or 20 km
0 — 1 mi
0 — 2 km

✪ SIGHTS

31	PARC DE L'ARTILLERIE	66	PLACE D'ARMES
33	◀ LES FORTIFICATIONS	67	TERRASSE DUFFERIN
49	SÉMINAIRE DE QUÉBEC	68	◀ CHÂTEAU FRONTENAC
50	MUSÉE DE L'AMÉRIQUE FRANÇAISE	73	MUSÉE DES URSULINES
51	BASILIQUE-CATHÉDRALE NOTRE-DAME-DE-QUÉBEC	79	PARC DU CAVALIER-DU-MOULIN
		84	LA CITADELLE

🍴 RESTAURANTS

2	CHEZ TEMPOREL	39	LE SAINT-AMOUR
6	LES FRÈRES DE LA CÔTE	41	APSARA
9	◀ CHEZ ASHTON	53	CAFÉ BUADE
11	CASSE-CRÊPE BRETON	56	LE PAIN BÉNI
14	CAFÉ-BOULANGERIE PAILLARD	60	LA CRÉMAILLÈRE
18	LE PATRIARCHE	69	LE CHAMPLAIN
21	CHEZ SOI LA CHINE	70	◀ LE CAFÉ DE LA TERRASSE
25	LE PETIT COIN LATIN	74	LE CONTINENTAL
30	IL TEATRO	75	CONTI CAFFE
		76	AUX ANCIENS CANADIENS

🌙 NIGHTLIFE

3	L'OSTRADAMUS	26	LE CHANTAUTEUIL
4	PUB ST-PATRICK	63	LE CHARLES BAILLAIRGÉ JAZZ BAR
12	LES YEUX BLEUS		
17	PUB ST-ALEXANDRE	70	ST-LAURENT BAR AND LOUNGE
24	◀ BAR STE-ANGÈLE		

🎨 ARTS AND LEISURE

1	MUSÉE BON PASTEUR	38	PARC DE L'ESPLANADE
29	LE CAPITOLE	58	QUÉBEC EXPERIENCE
32	GOLF TOURISTIQUE DE QUÉBEC	61	CROISIÈRE DUFOUR
34	PATINOIRE DE LA PLACE D'YOUVILLE	65	MUSÉE DU FORT
35	PALAIS MONTCALM	77	GALERIE D'ART BROUSSEAU AND BROUSSEAU
36	MORRIN CENTRE	80	◀ GLISSADES DE LA TERRASSE DUFFERIN

🛍 SHOPS

5	◀ MAGASIN GÉNÉRAL P.L. BLOUIN	44	ZIMMERMANN
7	CANDEUR	45	BOUTIQUE ARTISANS CANADA
8	INSPIRATIONS SPA	46	LA MAISON SIMONS
13	CONFISERIE C'EST SI BON	47	AU ROYAUME DU PÈRE NOËL
15	LIBRAIRIE PANTOUTE	48	BOUTIQUE CLAUDE BERRY
16	ARCHAMBAULT	52	LA BOUTIQUE DE NOËL
19	BOUTIQUE CANADEAU	54	BOUTIQUE LE SACHEM
20	MAISON DE LA PRESSE INTERNATIONALE	59	LA MAISON DARLINGTON
22	LES DÉLICES DE L'ÉRABLE	64	ARTISANS DE LA CATHÉDRALE
23	BOUTIQUE L'ÉCHELLE	72	GALERIE D'ART LES TROIS COLOMBES
27	PREMIÈRE ISSUE	78	LAMBERT & CO.
43	◀ BIBI ET COMPAGNIE		

🏨 HOTELS

10	HÔTEL MANOIR VICTORIA	55	HÔTEL STE-ANNE
28	LE CAPITOLE DE QUÉBEC	57	◀ AUBERGE PLACE D'ARMES
35	◀ AUBERGE INTERNATIONALE DE QUÉBEC	62	HÔTEL CLARENDON
		71	◀ FAIRMONT LE CHÂTEAU FRONTENAC
37	HÔTEL LE CHAMPLAIN	81	MANOIR SAINTE-GENEVIÈVE
40	CHEZ HUBERT	82	LA MARQUISE BASSANO
42	HÔTEL LE CLOS SAINT-LOUIS	83	HÔTEL CAP DIAMANT

MAP 8

SEE MAP 9

QUAI SAINT AANDRÉ

RUE BIOUX

RUE SAINT PAUL

CÔTE DE LA CANOTERIE

RUE SAINT-PIERRE

RUE DALHOUSIE

RUE DES REMPARTS

RUE DE LAVAL

RUE HÉBERT

RUE DU SAULT AU MATELOT

RUE DE LA BARRICADE

RUE MABEL

1 A

RUE COUILLARD

RUE SAINT-FLAVIEN

RUE FERLAND

RUE SAINTE-FAMILLE

RUE DE LA VIEILLE UNIVERSITÉ

49

Séminaire de Québec

RUE SAINT ANTOINE

E COUILLARD

2 R

RUE CHRISTIE

43

RUE GARNEAU

RUE DES REMPARTS

44 S   45 S

CÔTE DE LA FABRIQUE

46   47 48
S   S S

Musée de l'Amérique Française

50

Parc Montmorency

CÔTE DE LA MONTAGNE

CÔTE DU PORCHE

RUE SAINT-PIERRE

RUE DALHOUSIE

Basilique-Cathédrale Notre-Dame-de-Québec

51

RUE DE BUADE

52 53   58   59   S
55   56 57
R   R R
54 S

RUE DU TRÉSOR

RUE DU FORT

60 R   A H N
61 62 63

RUE DES JARDINS

64 S

RUE SAINTE-ANNE

65 A

Cathedral of the Holy Trinity

66

Place d'Armes

67

funicular

Terrasse Dufferin

RUE DU PETIT CHAMPLAIN

BLVD CHAMPLAIN

Musée des Ursulines

73

RUE DONNACONA

76   78

RUE SAINT-LOUIS

69 70
R N
68   71

75   R
74   R

RUE DU CARMANO

RUE DES CARRIÈRES

Château Frontenac

72 S

77 A

St. Lawrence River

RUE CORPS-GARDE

79

RUE MONT-CARMEL

Jardin des Gouverneurs

80 A

42

Parc du Cavalier-du-Moulin

82

RUE DES BISSONS

RUE DE LA PORTE

AVE SAINTE-GENEVIÈVE

H 81

PLACE TERASSE DUFFERIN

RUE DE BERGEL

83

AVE SAINT-DENIS

Parc de l'Esplanade

La Citadelle

84

SEE MAP 10

DISTANCE ACROSS MAP
Approximate: 1.1 mi or 1.7 km

0   100 yds
0   100 m

© AVALON TRAVEL

To R **1** Café Riviera

SEE MAP 11

SEE MAP 8

Hôtel-Dieu de Québec

Parc de l'Artillerie

RUE DE LA GARE DU PALAIS
RUE SAINT PAUL
CÔTE DINAN
CÔTE DE LA CANOTERIE
RUE DES REMPARTS
BLVD JEAN LESAGE
RUE SAINTE MARGUERITE
BLVD CHAREST EST
RUE DES PRAIRIES
RUE SAINT VALLIER EST
CÔTE DE LA POTASSE
RUE CARLETON
CÔTE DU PALAIS
RUE DE L'ARSENAL
RUE DICKMAHON
CÔTE CHARLEVOIX
RUE COLLINS
RUE PIERRE OLIVIER CHAUVEAU
RUE SAINT JEAN
RUE COOK
RUE DAUPHINE
RUE SAINTE ANNE
RUE SAINTE URSULE
RUELLE LÉPISOTTE
RUE SAINT LOUIS
RUE D'AUTEUIL
RUE ABRAHAM MARTIN
RUE SAINT NICOLAS
RUE SAINT PAUL
RUE SAINTE VALLIER EST
RUE DES REMPARTS

SIGHTS
2 LE MOULIN À IMAGES
19 VIEUX-PORT DE QUÉBEC
32 MUSÉE DE LA CIVILISATION
36 RUE SOUS-LE-CAP
48 LA FRESQUE DES QUÉBÉCOIS
50 PLACE ROYALE
51 ÉGLISE NOTRE-DAME-DES-VICTOIRES
56 FUNICULAIRE DU VIEUX-QUÉBEC
68 QUARTIER DU PETIT-CHAMPLAIN

RESTAURANTS
1 CAFÉ RIVIERA
9 BRYND SMOKED MEAT
10 PIZZA MAG
13 LA PIZZ
18 POISSON D'AVRIL
21 LES CAFÉS DU SOLEIL
23 BUFFET DE L'ANTIQUAIRE
26 SSS
28 LE 48 ST-PAUL
29 LAURIE RAPHAËL
31 CAFÉ DU MONDE
37 L'ÉCHAUDÉ
38 CAFÉ BISTRO DU CAP
42 PANACHE
43 TOAST!
46 RESTAURANT L'INITIALE
57 MARIE-CLARISSE
61 LAPIN SAUTÉ
66 LE COCHON DINGUE

NIGHTLIFE
14 TAVERNE BELLEY
47 L'ONCLE ANTOINE
54 LE PAPE-GEORGES

ARTS AND LEISURE
3 MUSÉE NAVAL DE QUÉBEC
4 CROISIÈRES COUDRIER
5 ÉCOLOCYCLO
7 PLANÈTE FITNESS GYM
8 GALERIE TZARA
12 CYCLO SERVICES
16 GALERIE MADELEINE LACERTE
30 L'AGORA DU VIEUX-PORT
33 LA CASERNE DALHOUSIE
35 ATELIER GUY LÉVESQUE
45 GALERIES D'ART BEAUCHAMP AND BEAUCHAMP
52 CROISIÈRE AML
60 MAISON CHEVALIER
67 LE THÉÂTRE DU PETIT CHAMPLAIN
73 CORRIDOR DU LITTORAL

SHOPS
6 LE MARCHÉ DU VIEUX PORT
11 FOURRURES RICHARD ROBITAILLE
17 MACHIN CHOUETTE
20 MAISON DAMBOURGÈS
22 RUE ST-PAUL
24 BOUTIQUE AUX MÉMOIRES ANTIQUITÉS
25 ANTIQUITÉS BOLDUC
49 BOUTIQUE DES MÉTIERS D'ART
53 ATELIER LA POMME
55 LA FUDGERIE
58 POT EN CIEL
59 PAULINE PELLETIER
62 PONT BRIAND JOALLIER
63 LE CAPITAINE D'ABORD
64 OCLAN
65 O PETITES DOUCEURS DU QUARTIER
69 QUARTIER DU PETIT-CHAMPLAIN
70 MADAME GIGI CONFISERIE
71 SOIERIE HUO
72 LA PETITE CABANE À SUCRE DE QUÉBEC

HOTELS
15 HÔTEL BELLEY
27 HÔTEL PORT-ROYAL
34 HÔTEL LE GERMAIN-DOMINION
39 AUBERGE SAINT-PIERRE
40 HÔTEL 71
41 AUBERGE SAINT-ANTOINE
44 HÔTEL LE PRIORI

To
Le Moulin à Images

Vieux-Port
de Québec

19

18 Ⓡ

QUAI SAINT ANDRÉ

RUE RIOUX

22 Ⓢ

RUE SAINT PAUL

20 Ⓢ

21

23 24 Ⓢ
25 Ⓢ 26 Ⓡ

RUE DES REMPARTS

35 Ⓐ
36
Rue Sous-le-Cap
37 Ⓡ
38 Ⓡ

RUE DE LAVAL

RUE HÉBERT

RUE COUILLARD

RUE DE LA VIEILLE UNIVERSITÉ

RUE SAINTE FAMILLE

RUE FERLAND

RUE GARNEAU

FABRIQUE

29 Ⓡ

28 Ⓢ
27 Ⓡ

34

33

RUE BELL

RUE DE LA BARRICADE

30 Ⓐ

VIEUX-
QUÉBEC

RUE DALHOUSIE

31 Ⓡ
32

Musée de la Civilisation

39 Ⓑ
40 Ⓗ

RUE SAINT ANTOINE

43 Ⓡ
Ⓗ
44

45 Ⓐ 46 Ⓡ

RUE DE LA MONTAGNE

41 42 Ⓡ

RUE DU SAULT AU MATELOT

Parc
Montmorency

RUE PORT DAUPHIN

RUE DE BUADE

RUE SAINTE ANNE

RUE DU TRÉSOR

CÔTE DE LA MONTAGNE

RUE DU FORT

La Fresque des
Québécois
48 Ⓢ
49

47 Ⓝ

50 Ⓢ Place Royale

51

Ⓢ Église Notre-Dame
-des-Victoires

RUE SAINT PIERRE

RUE DU PORCHE

RUE NOTRE DAME

RUE DALHOUSIE

St. Lawrence River

Cathedral of
the Holy
Trinity

RUE DES JARDINS

RUE SAINT LOUIS

54 53
funicular
56 Ⓐ
55 Ⓢ
Funiculaire du
Vieux-Québec
57 Ⓡ

58 Ⓢ

52 Ⓐ

RUE SOUS LE FORT

RUE DU CUL DE SAC

Le Château
Frontenac

RUE SAINT LOUIS

RUE DU PETIT CHAMPLAIN

59 Ⓢ
61 Ⓡ
60 Ⓐ
62 Ⓢ

63
64
65 Ⓢ
66

Quartier du
Petit-
Champlain

67 Ⓐ
Ⓗ 69
68

70 Ⓐ
72 Ⓢ

71 Ⓢ

RUE DES TRAVERSIERS

Jardin des
Gouverneurs

RUE MONT CARMEL

RUE DE LA PORTE

RUE DES CARRIÈRES

PLACE TERRASSE DUFFERIN

AVE SAINTE GENEVIÈVE

AVE SAINT DENIS

RUE DALHOMAND

BLVD CHAMPLAIN

73 Ⓐ

SEE MAP 8

DISTANCE ACROSS MAP
Approximate: 4.2 mi or 6.9 km

0   100 yds
0   100 m

© AVALON TRAVEL

SEE MAP 11

Parc de l'Amérique Française

Parc des Champs-de-Bataille

Musée National des Beaux-Arts du Québec

SEE MAP 8

1 Fontaine de Tourny

2 Hôtel du Parlement
*Parlement du
Québec*

Observatoire
de la Capitale
3

*Parc
de la
Francophonie*

9 N
La Grande-Allée
8

Plains of Abraham
and Battlefield Park
4 A 5

12
R 10
11

7

6
Manège Militaire

13
R 14

15 H 16

PARLIAMENT HILL

Tour Martello 2
18

LA GRANDE-ALLÉE EST
RUE DE SENÉGERGUES

RUE PL. MONTCALM

AVE GEORGE VI
AVE TACHÉ

Parc des Champs-de-Bataille

Tour Martello 1
17

*Parc de
l'Esplanade*

AVE DU CAP DIAMANT

BLVD CHAMPLAIN

RUE DES SAPEURS

St. Lawrence River

AVE ONTARIO

RUE PETIT CHAMPLAIN

RUE GARNEAU

BLVD CHAMPLAIN

DISTANCE ACROSS MAP
Approximate: 1.2 mi or 1.9 km

0   100 yds
0   100 m

© AVALON TRAVEL

SAINT-ROCH

☺ SIGHTS

30	RUE SAINT-JOSEPH
51	JARDIN SAINT-ROCH
58	ST-MATTHEW CHURCH AND CEMETERY
73 ◖	RUE SAINT-JEAN
77	ÉGLISE SAINT-JEAN-BAPTISTE

☺ RESTAURANTS

1	LA PETITE BOÎTE VIETNAMIENNE
9	TAVERNE STEAKHOUSE LE TONNEAU
12	CAMELLIA SINENSIS
14	LES BOSSUS
23	VERSA
24	YUZU SUSHI BAR
32 ◖	BRÛLERIE ST-ROCH
34	LA BOÎTE À PAIN
37	NEKTAR
39 ◖	LE CERCLE
40 ◖	LE CLOCHER PENCHÉ
43	PAPILLES ET POÊLON
44	PAIN ET PASSION
45	CAFÉ BABYLONE
49	JOE SMOKED MEAT
60	TUTTO GELATO
66	LE MOINE ÉCHANSON
68	LIBRAIRIE ST-JEAN-BAPTISTE
69 ◖	CRÊPERIE LE BILLIG
72	LA TAVERNA
75	LE SULTAN
79	LE CARTHAGE
81	LE PAIN GRÜEL
82	AU BONNET D'ÂNE
85	CHEZ VICTOR

☺ NIGHTLIFE

4	LA BARBERIE
6	MO
13	LE LARGO
22 ◖	LE BOUDOIR
42 ◖	TAVERNE JOS DION
46 ◖	LA CUISINE
47	LES SALONS D'EDGAR
48	SCANNER
54 ◖	LE DRAGUE
55	LA NINKASI
61	BAR LE ST-MATTHEW
63	LE TEMPS PARTIEL
70	FOU-BAR
76 ◖	LE SACRILÈGE

Rue Saint-Joseph ◖S 30

R 32

A 33

A 35

R 34

39 R

S 38 R 37 S 36

R 40

41 S

440

175

BLVD CHAREST EST

RUE NORTE DAME DES ANGES

RUE SAINTE HÉLÈNE EST

RUE SAINT VALLIER EST

N 48 R 49

N 47

42 N

R 43

440

440

R 44

R 45 N 46

RUE DEMERS

RUE CHRISTOPHE COLOMB EST

Ⓐ ARTS AND LEISURE

2	LE LIEU
3	MORGAN BRIDGE
5 ◖	LES CHEMINS INVISIBLES
28	CENTRE MATERIA
33	THÉÂTRE LA BORDÉE
35	IMPÉRIAL DE QUÉBEC
52 ◖	MÉDUSE

Ⓢ SHOPS

7	CHAMPAGNE LE MAÎTRE CONFISEUR
8 ◖	TOHU BOHU
10	FANAMANGA
11	LA QUINTESSENS
15	LALIBERTÉ
16	LA GODASSE
17 ◖	BENJO
18	MADEMOISELLE B
19	PHILIPPE DUBUC
20	FLIRT
21	COSMÉTIQUES BLOOMI
25	BALTHAZAR
27 ◖	MOUNTAIN EQUIPMENT CO-OP
31	RUE ST-JOSEPH
36 ◖	L'ARTISAN ET SON PAYS
38	BLANK
41	BOUTIQUE LUCIA F.
53 ◖	ESTHER P
56 ◖	JUPON PRESSÉ
57	POINT D'EXCLAMATION
59	SCHÜZ
64	CHOCO-MUSÉE ERICO
65	CODE VERT
67	EPICERIE EUROPÉENNE
71	LOBO LAVIDA
74	RUE ST-JEAN
80	ROSE BOUTON
83	CD MÉLOMANE

Ⓗ HOTELS

26 ◖	HÔTEL PUR
29 ◖	AUBERGE L'AUTRE JARDIN
50	AUBERGE LE VINCENT
62 ◖	AUBERGE J.A. MOISAN
78	LE CHÂTEAU DU FAUBOURG
84	CHÂTEAU DES TOURELLES

R 85

© AVALON TRAVEL

SEE MAP 10

To N 4 La Barberie

440

SEE MAP 9

SEE MAP 8

175

RUE SAINTE MADELEINE

St-Matthew
Church and Cemetery

SAINT-JEAN-
BAPTISTE

Église Saint-
Jean-Baptiste
77
Rue Saint-Jean

Jardin
Saint-Roch
51

RUE DE LA REINE
RUE DE LA SALLE
RUE DU ROI
RUE SAINT FRANÇOIS EST
RUE SAINT JOSEPH EST
RUE SAINTE HÉLÈNE EST
RUE FLEURIE
RUE SAINT VALLIER EST
CÔTE D'ABRAHAM
RUE SAINT RÉAL
RUE DE LA COURONNE
RUE VICTOR REVILLON
RUE DU PARVIS
RUE SAINTE MARGUERITE
RUE SAINTE CLAIRE
RUE SAINTE-MARIE
RUE RICHELIEU
RUE SAINT OLIVIER
RUE DE LA TOURELLE
RUE LAVIGUEUR
CÔTE SAINTE GENEVIÈVE
RUE SAINT AUGUSTIN
RUE D'AIGUILLON
RUE SAINT JEAN
RUE SAINT JOACHIM
RUE SAINT GABRIEL
RUE SAINT PATRICK
RUE JEAN JACQUES BERTRAND
BOULEVARD RENÉ LÉVESQUE EST
RUE LOUIS ALEXANDRE TACHEREAU
RUE DE COME
RUE BERTHELOT
RUE SCOTT
RUE PREVOST
RUE DU RON PASTEUR
RUE BERTHELO
RUE LOCKWELL
RUE SAINT JEAN
RUE SUTHERLAND
RUE D'AIGUILLON
RUE DU ROY
AVENUE HONORÉ MERCIER
RUE SAINT DOMINGUE
RUE DU PONT
RUE DE LA CHARLE
RUE RICHARD

0   100 yds
0   100 m
Approximate: .8 mi or 1.3 km

⊙ SIGHTS
24 AQUARIUM DU QUÉBEC

⑩ NIGHTLIFE
18 LE PUB DE
   L'UNIVERSITÉ LAVAL
20 L'OZONE LAURIER

ⓐ ARTS AND LEISURE
1 MEGA PARC
  DES GALERIES
  DE LA CAPITALE
3 REMPARTS
  DE QUÉBEC
4 ROC GYMS
5 BAIE DE BEAUPORT
6 DOMAINE
  MAIZERETS
7 PARC
  CARTIER-BRÉBEUF
8 PARC LINÉAIRE DE LA
  RIVIÈRE ST-CHARLES
9 POINTE-AUX-LIÈVRES
10 PARC VICTORIA
11 LES CAPITALES
   DE QUÉBEC
12 CORRIDOR DES
   CHEMINOTS
14 ⓒ PARC DU
   BOIS-DE-COULONGE
15 LES KEBS DE QUÉBEC
16 LE CLAP
17 LE ROUGE ET OR
23 PARC DE LA PLAGE
   JACQUES-CARTIER
25 LE CHAMPLAIN AND
   LE PYLÔNE
27 LA TEMPÊTE

ⓢ SHOPS
2 GALERIES DE LA
  CAPITALE
2 UNIVERS TOUTOU
13 LATULIPPE
19 LA MAISON
   ANGLAISE
19 LAURIER QUÉBEC
19 PLACE DE LA CITÉ
19 PLACE STE-FOY
19 HOLT RENFREW

ⓗ HOTELS
21 ⓒ HÔTEL SÉPIA
22 CHÂTEAU
   BONNE ENTENTE

573

L'ANCIENNE-LORETTE

ROUTE DE L'AÉROPORT

358

Québec City
Jean Lesage
International Airport

✈

136

LA SUETTE

Lac
Laberge

540

AUTOR...

Le Grand-Village

367

40

138

40

Lac
St-Augustin

Le Faubourg - L'Erpinière

138

Club de Golf
de Cap Rouge

SAINT AUGUSTIN

St. Lawerence River

132

Saint-Nicolas

CHEMIN SAINT JOSEPH

171

CHEMIN AUBIN

20

© AVALON TRAVEL

138
5
6
LAIRET
3
4
973
LEBOURGNEUF
1 2
40
VIEUX-LIMOILOU
73
VANIER
7
8
9
AUTOROUTE DUFFERIN MONTMORENCY
10
11
Lauzon
SAINT-ROCH
12
132
Lévis
SAINT-
JEAN-BAPTISTE
175
VIEUX-
QUÉBEC
13
Québec City
Club de Golf
Lévis
PARLIAMENT
HILL
Battlefields
Park
440
16 15
14
740
17
St. Lawerence River
18
N
SILLERY
PLACE-DU-
VIEUZ-MOULIN
SAINTE-FOY
19
136
S
N
20
132
CHEMIN-DES-ILES
20
ST LOUIS
DUPLESSIS
H
21
22
24
H
23
Aquarium du Québec
25
SAINT-ROMUALD
20
73
132
SAINT-JEAN-CHRYSOSTOME
Place-
Normandie
116
175
RUE DE L'EGLISE
275
Moulin-Gosselin
73
27

0   1.5 mi
0   1.5 km
DISTANCE ACROSS MAP
Approximate: 18.7 mi or 30 km

Discover Montréal & Québec City

The province of Québec is a place all its own: It's a country within a country with its own traditions, architecture, and language. Its two major cities, Montréal and Québec City, illustrate the diverse character of the province.

Montréal has been shaped by Franco-Anglo tensions and an ever-changing wave of immigrants. Because of this, the city is unbelievably diverse and dynamic. Known for its laissez-faire and hedonistic attitude, the city is one of the most artistic and culturally rich places in the country – and can throw a hell of a good party. From the vine-covered alleys to the corkscrew staircases, Montréal should be discovered by foot or bike. Take your time exploring its nooks and crannies, stopping for a coffee in a cozy café or a drink in one of its historic taverns along the way.

Perched on a cliff above the St-Lawrence River, Québec City is the soul of the province: the first city to be founded in Canada, the seat of the Québec government, and the self-proclaimed "Capitale Nationale." You can still walk the narrow, cobblestone streets of Vieux-Port or pose next to one of the many cannons that line the city's walls. But a youthful revolution in the old working-class neighborhoods is bringing a daring new quality of art and culture to this historic city.

In both cities the historic landmarks and 17th-century architecture are captivating. But what will impress you the most is the infectious energy that people exude here. Temperatures drop below freezing in winter but bars and restaurants are still packed, with windows steaming with that unmistakable joie de vivre.

Planning Your Trip

▶ WHERE TO GO

Montréal

VIEUX-MONTRÉAL

You'll be captivated by the heart of the city's historical district, with cobblestone streets, early–New France architecture, regal Beaux Arts buildings, and the grandeur of the Basilique Notre-Dame-de-Montréal. It's here that you'll also find some of the city's trendier restaurants, shops, and hotels. In the south end, a gradual slope leads to the converted warehouses and green spaces of the Vieux-Port and the St-Lawrence River.

CENTRE-VILLE

The downtown core is the city's main commercial district. Rue Ste-Catherine is lined with everything from historical department stores to trendy boutiques, while rue Crescent is popular for clubbing. South of the shopping area is the Centre Bell, home of the popular hockey team Montréal Canadiens, and to the north, the Musée des Beaux-Arts de Montréal sits among other stately Belle Époque buildings. In cold weather, enjoy the shelter of the Underground City.

CENTRE-VILLE EST

The main cultural district is home to the Belgo Building, an arts hub, and the Place des Arts, where you can catch the symphony, ballet, and opera and check out the Musée d'Art Contemporain next door. In summer, the streets are taken over by the Festival International de Jazz and the Just for

Located in the Vieux-Port, Montréal's Pointe-à-Callière Musée d'Archéologie et d'Histoire features archaeological treasures of the city's past.

Built for the 1976 Olympics, Montréal's Olympic Stadium (Stade Olympique) has become an iconic building.

Laughs festival. South of the cultural district is Chinatown, the place to find the best dim sum in the city.

QUARTIER LATIN AND THE VILLAGE

Centered around UQÀM, this is the stomping ground of Francophone university students. The city's main library, La Grande Bibliothèque, is a masterful piece of contemporary architecture, and lively and boisterous bars and restaurants can be found on rue St-Denis. To the east is the Village, Montréal's gay neighborhood, a mecca for late-night partying, karaoke bars, and antiques shopping on rue Amherst.

PLATEAU MONT-ROYAL

This charming artistic enclave features tree-lined streets, cozy neighborhood bistros, and 100-year-old townhouses. The best restaurants in the city are located here, and the

bars that line the historic Main have secured Montréal's place as a nightlife destination, while the bars, cafés, and boutiques on rue St-Denis are a quintessential part of the Francophone community.

MILE END AND PETITE ITALIE

Populated by hipsters and artists, the Mile End is also home to a large Orthodox Jewish population. This mix of cultures is part of the neighborhood's DNA, as witnessed in the Italian cafés, Greek restaurants, and famous bagel shops, which mix well with the chic stores on avenue Laurier and rue Bernard in Outremont. North of Mile End is Little Italy, with its pre-fascism Mussolini fresco at Chiesa della Madonna della Difesa and the sprawling farmers market Marché Jean-Talon.

GREATER MONTRÉAL

Parc du Mont-Royal is a haven for recreation,

Vieux-Québec's Upper Town

and it provides the best views of the city. To the east of the park are the buildings for the 1976 Olympics, including the breathtaking Stade Olympique. Île Sainte-Hélène and Île Notre-Dame make up Parc Jean-Drapeau, a great place for biking, outdoor concerts, and exploring the Biosphère.

EXCURSIONS FROM MONTRÉAL
Montréalers typically head north into the Laurentian mountains for skiing and cottaging and south to the Cantons de l'Est for the picturesque villages and antiquing—though a bit of each can be done in both.

Québec City
VIEUX-QUÉBEC'S UPPER TOWN
Les Fortifications surround Vieux-Québec's Upper Town, a 400-year-old neighborhood where the history of the winding streets and original architecture remains safe from the ravages of time. Protected by these walls is the Château Frontenac, Québec City's most famous sight, and the Séminaire de Québec, one of the city's oldest sights.

VIEUX-QUÉBEC'S LOWER TOWN
The stone Norman-style buildings and cobblestone streets of Place Royale mark the country's birthplace. History is unavoidable here, from the narrow lanes of Quartier du Petit-Champlain to the historic Vieux-Port, with its converted warehouses, antiques shops, and trendy hotels.

PARLIAMENT HILL AND THE PLAINS
Outside of the walls are the Plains of Abraham and Battlefield Park, the site of France's historic defeat by the British. The seat of the provincial government is to its north, housed in Hôtel du Parlement. Running alongside the government building are the nightclubs and bars of La

the countryside on Île d'Orléans, near Québec City

Grande-Allée, the city's nightlife destination. Also in the Plains is Musée National des Beaux-Arts du Québec, which holds the largest existing collection of Québec art.

SAINT-JEAN-BAPTISTE AND SAINT-ROCH
Once working-class neighborhoods, Saint-Jean-Baptiste and Saint-Roch are now trendy, bohemian neighborhoods home to the city's coolest kids, and the area where you'll find the best bars, browse independent boutiques, and catch the latest bands. It's also a major arts hub, and the contemporary arts complex Méduse is located here.

GREATER QUÉBEC CITY
In the areas surrounding the center of the city, find kid-friendly destinations like the Aquarium du Québec and the water park Village Vacance Valcartier. The slopes of Mont-Sainte-Anne are fun for the whole family.

EXCURSIONS FROM QUÉBEC CITY
Just a half-hour drive from the city are the picturesque towns of Île d'Orléans and Côte-de-Beaupré, while an hour north, the Charlevoix region has some of the most spectacular scenery in the region.

► WHEN TO GO

Though summer is the busiest time to visit, it's also the best time to explore the cities' neighborhoods, and you'll get to experience fun summer festivals like Montréal's Festival International de Jazz and Quebec's Festival d'Été.

It's no surprise that prices drop considerably October–April, so if you can handle a bit of cold your pocketbook will thank you. Plus, the cold isn't so bad when it's hockey season and 98 percent of the people—and you—are crowded into bars watching the game. Québec City winters can be particularly freezing, but December–March is an ideal time to visit if you love skiing or other winter recreational activities. October is particularly pretty thanks to the changing fall foliage, and even February has a couple of bright spots with Le Festival Montréal en Lumière's all-night art party and the Carnaval de Québec's unadulterated celebration of snow.

The Just for Laughs festival in Montréal, which takes place in July, is one of the biggest comedy festivals in the world.

▶ BEFORE YOU GO

Passports and Visas

All visitors must have a valid passport or other accepted secure documents to enter the country; even those entering from the United States by road or train must have these documents.

Citizens of the United States, Australia, New Zealand, Israel, Japan, and most Western European countries don't need visas to enter Canada for stays up to 180 days. U.S. permanent residents are also exempt.

Nationals from South Africa, China, and about 150 other countries must apply for a temporary resident visa (TRV) in their home country. Full details can be found at Citizen and Immigration Canada. Single-entry visitor visas are valid for six months and cost $75, while multiple-entry visas cost $150 and last for two years, as long as a single stay doesn't last for longer than six months. A separate visa is required if you intend to work in Canada.

Transportation

Visitors arriving by air will arrive at Montréal's Pierre Trudeau International Airport, the main hub for both national and international air travel to the province. It's about 21 kilometers from downtown, and shuttles and public transport are available. Direct flights are also available to Quebéc City's Aéroport International Jean-Lesage de Québec. It's about 15 kilometers from Quebéc City's downtown, but there are no shuttles to downtown from this airport.

If you're arriving by train you'll arrive at Montréal's Gare Centrale in the downtown core, or Québec City's Gare du Palais near the Vieux-Port.

Those arriving by bus in Québec City will also arrive at the Gare du Palais. In Montréal buses arrive at the main bus terminal, Gare d'Autocars, in the Quartier Latin.

The Montréal public transit system is run by STM, and it includes both the Métro (subway) and buses. Pay-as-you-go public bike rentals, otherwise known as Bixis, are available between April and November, and navigating the city's streets by car is fairly simple, though parking can be a pain and expensive.

Québec City's transit system is limited to buses, but they are fast and efficient in getting you up those steep hills. Taxis are useful when the winter hits, though they can be hard to flag down, depending on the area. Although driving the city streets is straightforward enough, if you're not used to ice and snow, it's better to leave it to the pros.

Explore Montréal & Québec City

► THE BEST OF MONTRÉAL AND QUÉBEC CITY

Ten days is the perfect length of time to visit both Montréal and Québec City, allowing you to dedicate enough time to experience Montréal's legendary nightlife and Québec City's historic center, with a few side trips.

Day 1

Arrive in Montréal and head to your hotel in Vieux-Montréal. Drop your bags and head out to grab a coffee and a light bite at Olive & Gourmando. Then stroll down rue St-Paul, the oldest street in the city, and do a little browsing.

Head to the Pointe-à-Callière Musée d'Archéologie et d'Histoire to brush up on your Québec history. Kitty-corner to the museum is Place Royale, the first public square in Ville-Marie. Walk down to the Vieux-Port and stroll along the waterside promenade and check out Habitat 67 and Chapelle Notre-Dame-de-Bon-Secours, the oldest church in the city.

In the late afternoon head out onto Jacques-Cartier Quay to Terrasses Bonsecours for a drink on the patio and a great view of the skyline as the sun begins to dip down. Head past the artists and street vendors on Place Jacques-Cartier and up to Basilique Notre-Dame-de-Montréal for the nightly light show.

Try local French favorite Le Club Chasse et Pêche for dinner. After the meal head to Place d'Armes Hôtel and Suites for a night-cap and a view of the city's twinkling lights at rooftop bar La Terrasse Suite 701. If you're not ready to head back to your hotel, there's always a chance to make a few late-night dance moves at dance club Wunderbar.

Day 2

After breakfast at Le Cartet rent a Bixi from the closest stand and head down to the river and along the Lachine Canal. Hook a right and cross the bridge at Marché Atwater; leave the bike there and head along rue Notre-Dame West to dig for treasures in the numerous antiques shops. Stop for lunch at McKiernan for their classic oysters and toast before hopping back on a bike or walking up to the Centre Canadien d'Architecture.

the interior of Basilique Notre-Dame-de-Montréal

COLD COMFORTS, WINTER PURSUITS

Life in Montréal and Québec City completely changes once winter hits. And though it might seem like the perfect season to hibernate, the mounting snow is no excuse to stay indoors. Whether you're in the city or the country there's a ton of different things to do when the mercury drops.

MONTRÉAL

• Even the most reformed of mall-rats will enjoy shopping and exploring the linked walkways in Montréal's **Underground City.** Running 32 kilometers long from the Place des Arts Métro station in the east to Peel in the west, its size and diversity make it more than just a shopper's paradise

• Winter means hockey, and hockey means the **Canadiens.** Grab tickets to a game at the **Bell Centre** (which can involve some finagling) or head to a local bar to catch the game on a big screen. Either way the action both on and off the ice will warm you up.

• Ice-skating is the ultimate Canadian pastime, and the open-air rink in **Parc Lafontaine** is large enough to accommodate hockey players, wannabe figure skating stars, and those just finding their skating legs.

ice-skating, Mont-Royal

• There are few things in the world as decadent as real hot chocolate. Warm up and indulge in cup of the good stuff at **Juliette et Chocolat.**

• "If you can't beat 'em join 'em." That's the Montréaler's attitude to winter, and most of them join by hopping on toboggans and sliding down **Mont-Royal** to avenue du Parc.

• See a different side of the city and **cross-country ski** along the historic **Lachine Canal.** The old, converted warehouses and views of the downtown skyline will give you a whole new perspective.

QUÉBEC CITY

• Drive an hour north to **Le Massif,** the highest ski mountain in the province. The ski runs offer 49 different trails of varying levels and have the most breathtaking views of the St-Lawrence River.

• Bundle up and head to **Château Frontenac** for some serious winter sledding down the **Glissades de la Terrasse Dufferin.**

• The sweet treat known as *tire sur la neige* (maple syrup frozen on snow) can be found at just about every corner come winter.

• A typical après-ski meal of **raclette** is the perfect end-of-the-day fare. It can be procured in the cozy confines of restaurant **Le Petit Coin Latin.**

• **Carnaval de Québec,** which takes place between the end of January and early February, is two weeks of mostly free outdoor fun, from dog-sled races and ice canoeing to outdoor dance parties and snow sculpture competitions.

Lachine Canal in Montréal

From there head along rue Ste-Catherine for some retail therapy, making sure to stop into classic Montréal department stores Holt Renfrew and La Maison Ogilvy, as well as designer Marie Saint Pierre's eponymous boutique. Grab dinner at the Dominion Square Tavern and sip on a Canuck cocktail.

Catch a dance production at the Place des Arts or see an old art house film or foreign flick at the Cinémathèque Québécoise, before walking back to your hotel through Chinatown and picking up a slice of Japanese cheesecake at Pâtisserie Harmonie.

Day 3

Take the Métro to rue Sherbrooke and walk north on rue St-Denis, taking as many side streets as possible to explore the neighborhood's true character. Grab breakfast at French bistro L'Express and keep your eyes peeled for the cobblestone avenue Duluth and, farther north, avenue Marie Anne, Leonard Cohen's old haunt. Explore a bit of the French side of avenue Mont-Royal before heading back west.

Take advantage of one of the best lunch deals in the city at Au Cinquième Péché and then head for boulevard St-Laurent. Browse the shops and take in the street's history as you head south. Stop in at Kitsch 'n' Swell and La Centrale Galerie Powerhouse. Have a microbrew at Réservoir and get a thick, smoked-meat sandwich at Schwartz's. Catch an up-and-coming band or dance the night away to the city's most eclectic DJs at Casa del Popolo.

Day 4

Go for breakfast at Beniamino Market before heading to the latest exhibit at the Musée d'Art Contemporain. Then lunch at Brasserie T! next door. Hop on the bus 80 up avenue du Parc,

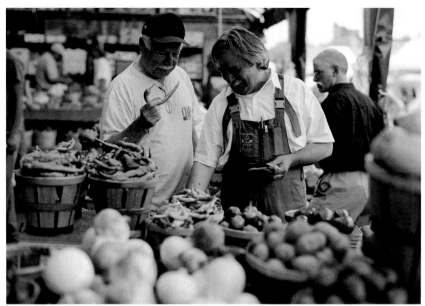

Open year-round, Marché Jean-Talon in Montréal's Petite Italie has thrived since the days of the Great Depression.

getting off at the George-Étienne Cartier statue, and follow the signs to the top of Mont-Royal for a spectacular view of the city. Take your time coming back down, and head north on avenue du Parc toward Mile End.

Browse the chic boutiques on avenue Laurier, then make your way to St-Viateur Bagel and eat your hot-from-the-oven treat with a coffee from Café Olympico. Check out the vintage stores on rue St-Viateur and avenue Bernard. Comic fans should hit up Drawn & Quarterly.

Walk north into Petite Italie on St-Laurent and pop into Café Italia for a shot of espresso, then over to Marché Jean-Talon for some local Québec goods. Keep dinner simple but chic at Bottega Pizzeria and then hop a cab to Baldwin Barmacie for a little nightlife.

Day 5

Head to the Village, get goodies to go from Le Mie Matinale, and make your way to the Pont Jacques-Cartier. Built over the St-Lawrence River, the bridge has spectacular panoramic views of the city, and it's a unique way to get to Parc Jean-Drapeau. Once on the island you can head off for a day of rides at La Ronde or just ogle the awe-inspiring wonder that is Buckminster Fuller's Biosphère.

Have a picnic on the shores of the river, wander the gardens, then hop the Métro back for a simple bistro meal at Boris Bistro and an evening performance at Cirque du Soleil.

Day 6

Throw your hiking boots in a bag and leave Montréal on the first bus to Mont-Tremblant National Park for a day in the rugged outdoors. At the largest and oldest park in the province you can hike, swim, canoe, and kayak here till your heart's content. For something a little less taxing head to Mont-Tremblant Resort for some alpine luging

MONTRÉAL ON THE CHEAP

Montréalers are all about having the highest standard of living on the smallest possible budget. That's part of what makes Montréal such an attractive city in the first place. Sure, you can still enjoy exclusive shops and four-star restaurants, but you don't need a bank loan to do it. Here are a few tips to get the most from your travel budget.

RESTAURANTS

When downtown, Asian eateries are often a budget-friendly choice. Try **Qing Hua Dumpling** and **Kazu.**

The best burger in town costs a little over $6 at **La Paryse,** and **Patati Patata**'s mini-burgers and fries are the ultimate takeout, especially for an alfresco dinner at Parc Jeanne-Mance.

A number of upscale restaurants offer affordable lunchtime meals. Some of the best include **Kitchenette, DNA,** and **Graziella.**

Diners in the know cart their own bottle to **Pizzeria Napoletana** and **Le Quartier Général.**

The king of upscale late-night dinners is the classic French bistro **Leméac,** where they serve a table d'hôte special for $22 after 10 P.M.

Vegans and vegetarians should head to the Mile End for some of the best and most affordable vegetarian in the city. Top spots include **Le Cagibi, La Lumière du Mile End, Le Panthère Verte,** and **Dépanneur le Pick-Up.**

NIGHTLIFE

Most bars have nightly music and impromptu dancing for the price of a drink. Check the listings at **Bar Plan B, Korova, Casa del Popolo, L'Escogriffe,** and **Brutopia.**

MUSEUMS AND GALLERIES

Most of the city's independent galleries are free and host weekly or monthly vernissages (exhibition openings) with complimentary drinks. Top spots include **Belgo Building, DHC/ART,** and **Parisian Laundry.**

At the **Musée des Beaux-Arts de Montréal**

The Musée des Beaux-Arts de Montréal was designed by famous architect Moshe Safdie.

many exhibits can be viewed free of charge, and the museum offers half-price admission on Wednesday nights.

Admission is free on Wednesday nights after 5 P.M. at **Musée d'Art Contemporain.**

HOTELS

Vieux-Montréal is the ideal place to stay, but the prices can be polarizing. If you're on a budget try the welcoming hostel **Auberge Alternative de Vieux-Montréal,** which offers private rooms, or the affordable and charming bed-and-breakfast **Le Petite Prince.**

Or move away from the tourist areas and stay in the residential neighborhood Plateau Mont-Royal at bed-and-breakfasts like **B&B Le Plumard** and **Pensione Popolo.**

The ruins of Château St-Louis in Québec City were found in the shadow of Château Frontenac, under the Terrasse Dufferin.

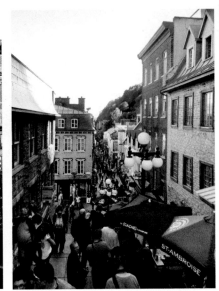
L'Escalier du Casse-Cou connects Québec City's Upper Town and Lower Town.

and pedal-boating. Spend the night in Mont-Tremblant's Auberge la Porte Rouge and have dinner at Seb l'Artisan Culinaire.

Day 7

Get up early for the drive to Québec City. Check into your hotel in Vieux-Québec's Upper Town then head directly to Café-Boulangerie Paillard for some fresh croissants. Browse the shops and historic buildings on Côte de la Fabrique till it brings you to Terrasse Dufferin in the shadow of Château Frontenac. Snack on a beaver tail pastry as you stroll the promenade and look out over the St-Lawrence, then head into the chateau for a guided tour.

Tour the historic Citadelle and then wander through the winding streets and alleys of Upper Town.

For dinner take your pick of the restaurants along rue St-Louis or splurge at Le Patriarche. After dinner walk along Les

Fortifications and find a comfortable nook in which to watch the Le Moulin à Images.

Finish the night at a *boîte à chansons,* such as Le Pape-Georges, or with a cocktail at the cozy Bar Ste-Angèle.

Day 8

After breakfast at Crêperie le Billig take the L'Escalier du Casse-Cou or ride the Funiculaire du Vieux-Québec down to one of the oldest streets in North America, rue du Petit-Champlain. Browse the independent boutiques and follow the cobblestone lanes that will eventually lead you to Place Royale. Take a peek at La Fresque des Québécois and see if you can point out the famous characters. Whether you fail the test or not, head to the Musée de la Civilisation and brush up on your history.

After visiting the museum, head west along rue St-Paul to browse antique stores. Or skip the stores and take the well-hidden

Musée National des Beaux-Arts du Québec

rue Sous-le-Cap till it brings you to Galerie Madeleine Lacerte. Check out the latest exhibit and then cross the street for a drink at Taverne Belley.

On your way to Saint-Roch, stop to admire the graffiti murals on the highway overpass, then head for a bistro dinner at Les Bossus. Cap the night off with a show at Le Cercle and a bit of dancing at La Cuisine.

Day 9

Have a hearty breakfast among the neon trees at Le Cosmos, then head to the Fontaine de Tourny and a take a trip around the statues at the Hôtel du Parlement. Stroll the rolling hills of the Plains of Abraham and make a stop at Tours Martellos. Continue through the park all the way to the Musée National des Beaux-Arts du Québec. After seeing the latest exhibit grab a sandwich from Le Fastoche on avenue Cartier.

Follow Cartier south, down the sloping hill, and take a right on rue St-Jean, where you can spend the rest of the afternoon, popping in and out of stores and drinking coffee at the many cafés. Don't miss J.A. Moisan, the oldest grocery store in North America, or the quiet shade of St-Matthew Church and Cemetery.

While you've got the European vibe going why not continue with a French wine and regional cuisine at Le Moine Échanson. After your meal head over to La Grande-Allée for a taste of sophisticated nightlife at Le Charlotte Ultra Lounge.

Day 10

Head down to Cyclo Services and rent bikes for the day. Pack your bags with sandwiches and goodies from the Marché du Vieux-Port and then take the Corridor du Littoral heading west. Ride about three kilometers and make a stop at the historic park Domaine Maizerets. After a wander among the ancient trees and lily-pad ponds get back on your bike and ride another nine kilometers to the impressive park Chute Montmorency.

Leave your bike and follow the path closest to the falls and cool off in the mist. If you have any energy left, climb the stairs to the top for a view of the falls and mythic Île d'Orleans.

After you've taken in the view go for a well-earned dinner at L'Aventure, then get back on your bikes and return to the city. Once there leave the bikes at the rental place and head for a late-night stroll around the Vieux-Port, grabbing a treat at Marché de Vieux-Port along the way.

Head back to your hotel for a good night's rest and an early drive back to Montréal in the morning before heading home.

► ROMANTIC WEEKEND GETAWAYS

For a short, romantic getaway Montréal offers the perfect balance of sightseeing and nightlife. Whether it's a moonlit walk along the Vieux-Port or a dinner at one of the city's best restaurants, couples can't help but be intoxicated by the city's French charm.

Québec City meanwhile is considered one of the most romantic cities in North America. The winding cobblestone streets, classic New France architecture, and overall charming ambience has a tendency to bring out the amorous side in visitors. But nothing seems forced about it—instead it carries its romantic status quite naturally.

Montréal
DAY 1
After you check into the sumptuous Pierre du Calvet, stroll through Vieux-Montréal. Go for lunch at Toqué!, then take in the latest exhibit at DHC/ART and check out some local talent at Marché Bonsecours. In the Vieux-Port climb the steps to the top of the Tour de l'Horloge for a magnificent view of the river and skyline.

As the stars start to come out get a cozy booth in Le Confessional and an enjoy a pre-dinner drink before your reservations at the inviting Le Club Chasse et Pêche. Head back to your hotel or hire a calèche to take you for a horse-drawn carriage tour, and take in the scenery as you snuggle up.

DAY 2
Head straight to the Plateau for brunch at Réservoir. Afterwards hop on the Métro and

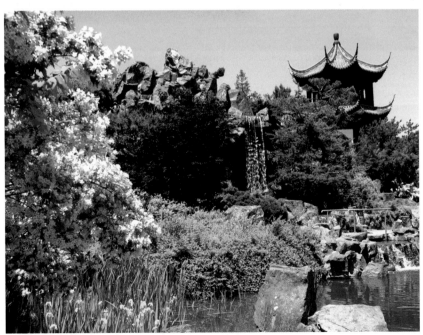
the Chinese Garden at Jardin Botanique in Montréal

a quaint staircase in the historic Quartier du Petit-Champlain in Québec City

head out to Jardin Botanique, Montréal's botanical gardens, and explore the 30 different gardens and get an up-close look at the Stade Olympique. Head back toward the city on a Bixi and stop off in Parc Lafontaine to leave the bikes and pick up some chocolate at Les Chocolats de Chloé.

Head south on rue St-Denis and stop in at Juliette et Chocolat for lunch as you browse the shops. Farther north, on St-Laurent check out casually cool designer pieces at Les Étoffes, then head up the road into BU for an early evening drink.

Cut across avenue Laurier and nab a cozy table for two at Buvette Chez Simone for dinner. When the meal's over head for a walk under the stars to Pullman and finish the night off with a delicious cocktail.

DAY 3

Hop in the car and head to La Croissanterie Figaro for breakfast with a French flavor. Afterwards leave the city behind for a day in the country; take Route 20 out to the Eastern Townships and follow La Route des Vins (The Wine Route), going for tastings at Vignoble Les Pervenches and Domaine Vitis and finishing off with some of Québec's ice wine at Vignoble Chapelle Ste-Agnès.

Head to the town of Knowlton to check out the quaint English-influenced architecture and antiques shops, then go for dinner and have the local specialty Lac Brome duck at Knowlton's Le Relais. After dinner drive back into the city and relax with a glass of wine at Narcisse Bar à Vin before calling it a night.

Québec City

DAY 1

Check into your suite at the plush Auberge Saint-Antoine and then go exploring along the cobblestone streets of Quartier du Petit-Champlain. Stop for a coffee or a cool drink on the corner terrace of Lapin Sauté and be charmed the by traditional music of the street performers. Head to Place Royale and check out the small but beautiful chapel in Église Notre-Dame-des-Victoires.

Browse antiques and galleries on rue St-Pierre and rue St-Paul. Stroll among the boats and quays of the Vieux-Port, then head to Quai Chouinard and board the Louis Jolliet.

Enjoy views of Chute Montmorency, Île d'Orleans, and the illuminated city on this four-hour boat cruise as you dine on a five-course meal.

DAY 2

Breakfast at Panache and then take the Funiculaire du Vieux-Québec to Terrasse Dufferin. Snap the requisite shots of Château Frontenac before taking the stairs at the far end to the Parc des Plaines d'Abraham. Stroll through the park to the Musée National des Beaux-Arts du Québec. After browsing the largest existing collection of Québec art, pick up some gourmet treats at Les Halles du Petit Quartier on Cartier, then grab a cab to Parc du Bois-de-Coulonge. Picnic overlooking the St-Lawrence River then wander the grounds, and don't miss the arboretum close to the shore.

Hail a cab back to Upper Town and shop the independent boutiques along rue St-Jean. Freshen up back at the hotel and cab it to your reservation in the glass dining room at Le Saint-Amour. After dinner take a moonlight tour through the streets in a calèche, stopping to admire the view at the Parc du Cavalier-du-Moulin. Then grab a cozy nook at Pub St-Alexandre for a nightcap.

Lapin Sauté's sidewalk terrace, Québec City

DAY 3

Rise early and drive to La Malbaie, about 90 minutes north of Québec City. Take in the stunning views of the Charlevoix region, stopping off at points along the way. Head into Baie-Saint-Paul and stop for lunch and a local microbrew at Le Saint-Pub.

Explore the city's rich cultural heritage at the many galleries and artisanal shops, then get back in the car and head to the majestic Fairmont le Manoir Richelieu for an overnight stay. Located on the banks of the river, it's one of the prettiest spots in the region and a perfect place to kick back for the night. When you're settled in your room, relax next to the outdoor pool and get a massage at the in-house spa.

In the evening have dinner at the Fairmont's Le Charlevoix Restaurant, overlooking the river.

▶ EDIBLE QUÉBEC: A FOODIE FRENZY

Québec has a food culture all its own, from such low-brow culinary accomplishments as cheese curds to some world-renowned restaurants. High- or low-brow, one thing is for certain; what you'll eat here is unlike food anywhere else, and you don't have to be a connoisseur to enjoy these offerings.

Montréal
DAY 1
Drop your bags at your downtown hotel and head out to grab a coffee at Café Myriade, where beans from Canada's top roaster, 49th Parallel, are run through a Mirage coffee machine for the most perfect latte. From there browse the stores along rue Ste-Catherine before heading for the best dumplings in town at Qing Hua Dumpling.

After lunch head east toward the Plateau, along rue Sherbrooke, then north on Peel, and take the steps to the top of Mont-Royal, where you can admire the view from the Belvedere Kondiaronk and get a cold drink at the snack bar.

Follow the winding path down the mountain, then walk along avenue du Parc and pop into Cocoa Locale for a sweet treat, and then keep walking till you get to avenue Fairmount, where you can get a fresh, hot bagel at Fairmount Bagel or at St-Viateur

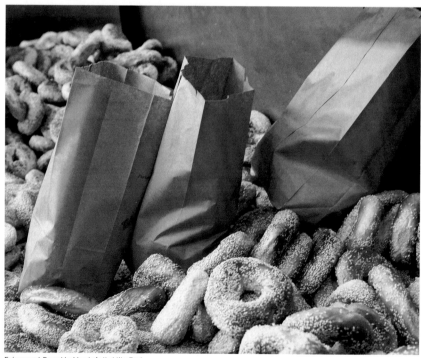
Fairmount Bagel in Montréal's Mile End

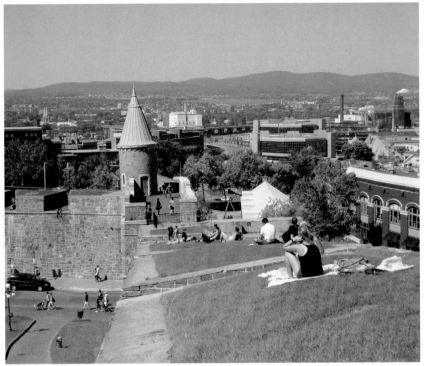

Québec City's Les Fortifications is a popular place for a picnic or just to admire the view of the city and the Laurentian mountains.

Bagel on rue St-Viateur for tomorrow's breakfast. Since you're in the neighborhood, you have to try a famous fried bologna sandwich from Wilensky's Light Lunch and wash it down with a hand-mixed soda pop.

Down the block, at Dieu du Ciel, go for a midafternoon beer-tasting and try some of the microbrews. Then head down to rue Rachel and get in line at Rotisserie Romados for some of the best Portuguese chicken in town. Beeline it with your chicken and wine for Parc Lafontaine and enjoy your dinner while the light fades in the sky. When the sun's gone down, finish the night off with a pint of Cheval Blanc at tavern Le Cheval Blanc, the first microbrewery in Montréal.

DAY 2

Get up and take bus 55 north on St-Laurent; jump off in Petite Italie, get a cappuccino to go at Café Italia, and browse the stores until you can no longer ignore your rumbling stomach. Grab a front row seat at Dépanneur le Pick-Up and order their ricotta crêpes for breakfast or their pulled pork sandwich. Afterwards peruse the goodies at Marché Jean-Talon.

After you've picked up some Québec cheeses and birch syrup, take a Bixi bike to rue Mont-Royal. Look for kooky housewares in Chez Farfelu and then go to Patisserie Kouign Amann for a sticky, sweet treat from Brittany.

Hop back on the Bixi, ride to Vieux-Montréal, and spend a few hours popping

Try an Italian gelato in Québec City.

into the neighborhood's cafés and specialty boutiques, like Le Cartet, for perfect foodie gifts. Make a stop at Verses Sky for a pre-dinner drink and then take a cab up to Au Pied du Cochon for foie gras *poutine* and foie gras pizza.

If you're feeling ambitious after the meal, walk off some of those calories and head to Outremont for some ice cream at Le Bilboquet before calling it a night.

Québec City

DAY 1

Take the early train from Montréal and head directly to Buffet de l'Antiquaire and fill up on some serious Québécois grub before carting your bags to Vieux-Québec's Upper Town. After you've checked into your hotel head right back out for a walk along Les Fortifications. Take in the views of the city, and when you start to get peckish get a few macaroons and a coffee from Café-Boulangerie Paillard or a maple-flavored gelato from Les Délices de l'Érable. Keep exploring Upper Town and don't forget to pop into Confiserie C'est si Bon for some hand-made chocolates and old-timey sweets; they are great gifts to bring home with you.

Stroll along the Terrasse Dufferin and then head into the Château Frontenac for drinks overlooking the river at Le Café de la Terrasse.

Take the Funiculaire du Vieux-Québec to Laurie Raphaël, where the meal is all about the aromas and local ingredients. After dinner take a stroll along the Vieux-Port and stop in for a nightcap at SSS.

DAY 2

Skip the hotel breakfast and opt instead for a hearty breakfast at Le Clocher Penché. Afterwards stroll along St-Joseph and get some Québec cheeses and charcuterie at L'Artisan et Son Pays. Follow rue St-Paul all the way to Vieux-Port. Check out the antique stores, then get into the heart of Vieux-Québec's Lower Town.

Dig into the fudge and nougat at La Fudgerie and stock up on maple syrup at La Petite Cabane à Sucre de Québec. Climb L'Escalier du Casse-Cou to Upper Town and explore rue St-Jean outside of the walls, where you can stand in awe at the old-time grocery store J.A. Moisan and learn about the history of chocolate at Choco-musée Erico.

Enjoy French wine and Québécois cuisine at Le Moine Échanson and finish off the night with an Italian gelato from Tutto Gelato.

MONTRÉAL

SIGHTS

Modern and historic, Montréal is one of the most distinctive cities in Canada. Old Montréal, Notre-Dame Basilica, Olympic Stadium, the Biosphère, even its legendary Underground City are all part of what makes the city so unique. It is home to both French- and English-speakers and has a large immigrant community; these cultures have inspired and left their marks on the various neighborhoods, and their history is reflected in the sights.

Montréal may have the second-largest population in the country, but geographically it is tiny, making it ideal to navigate by foot, bike, or Métro (the subway system). Many of the sights, like the Musée d'Art Contemporain, Chinatown, and Basilique Notre-Dame-de-Montréal, are concentrated in the downtown and Vieux-Montréal areas, so even when temperatures drop, you can stroll from one to the next—plus that's what the Underground City is for.

Spend a day wandering the historic Vieux-Montréal (Old Montréal), brush up on your Canadian history at Musée d'Archéologie et d'Histoire Pointe-à-Callière, then stroll along the waterfront and stop in at the Chapelle Notre-Dame-de-Bon-Secours. While you're there take a peek at Hôtel de Ville (city hall) and catch an evening light show at the Notre-Dame Basilica. If you're not worn out yet, an after-dark calèche ride is a romantic end to the day.

In the western part of downtown there's the Centre Canadien d'Architecture; check out the post-modernist facade and then head north and see the latest exhibit at the Musée des Beaux Arts on rue Sherbrooke, which is famous for its stately buildings. From there it's an easy walk to the Musée McCord, or if you're all museumed out,

© SACHA JACKSON

HIGHLIGHTS

LOOK FOR **(** TO FIND RECOMMENDED SIGHTS.

(**Most Beautiful Church:** The iconic **Basilique Notre-Dame-de-Montréal** has the most stunning interior decoration (page 52).

(**Best History Museum:** Learn about Montréal's history at **Pointe-à-Callière Musée d'Archéologie et d'Histoire,** the site where the city was officially established (page 58).

(**Best Contemporary Art Museum:** **Musée d'Art Contemporain** features the work of some of the world's most well-known contemporary artists (page 66).

(**Most Pedestrian-Friendly Street:** Closed to traffic in the summer, **rue Sainte-Catherine Est** turns into one long street party, with sidewalk cafés, street sales, and impromptu drag shows (page 68).

(**Best Public Market:** Marché Jean-Talon is a year-round farmers market that offers some of the most diverse and delicious food in the city (page 71).

(**Best Architecture:** Buckminster Fuller's geodesic dome, the **Biosphère,** hovers in the distance like a great architectural puzzle (page 73).

(**Best Views: Parc du Mont-Royal** offers amazing vantage points of the city and tons of places to stop off and admire the view (page 77).

(**Most Miraculous Sight:** Built to honor Brother André Bessette and his chosen saint, **St-Joseph's Oratory** is a place of pilgrimage for those looking to be healed (page 77).

(**Most Spectacular Botanical Garden:** Wander for hours through 20 different gardens at **Jardin Botanique** (page 78).

(**Most Iconic Sight:** Built for the 1976 Olympics, the **Stade Olympique** has since become an internationally recognized building (page 79).

© TOURISME MONTREAL

The Biosphère is one of the biggest architectural attractions in the city.

take a tour of McGill University. Afterwards, walk through the campus and head up avenue du Parc to Mont-Royal; it's only a few hundred steps up to a beautiful night view of the city.

Ride the Métro to Marché Jean-Talon and from there make your way through Little Italy to see a fresco of Italian dictator Benito Mussolini at the Chiesa della Madonna della Difesa. Continue south and grab a bagel and a coffee with the locals in Mile End, then keep heading south along St-Laurent to suck up the history of the Main.

Sights that are farther away, like the Stade Olympique and the Jardin Botanique, are easily accessible by Métro. Plan to dedicate a day to exploring the area, especially if you have the kids in tow, since the Biodôme and Insectarium de Montréal are all found in the same old Olympic grounds.

Marché Atwater southwest of downtown is best explored on bike—or cross-country skis in the winter—since it backs directly onto the Lachine canal. Make a morning out of it and head to rue Notre-Dame for breakfast and antiquing, then grab lunch from the market and follow the canal back downtown. Watch a Canadiens game at the Centre Bell or visit the Hall of Fame. Montréal may just be an island, but its sights are varied and they pack a punch.

Vieux-Montréal   Map 1

Old Montréal is the city's historic center and remains one of its most charming neighborhoods. It's here that you'll find the Basilique Notre-Dame-de-Montréal and rue St-Paul, the oldest street in the city. Strolling round the area it's difficult not to swoon at the cobblestone streets, narrow, tin-roofed boutiques, and converted warehouses. All this history, however, means that when you buy anything here, whether it's a lunchtime snack or a drink at a bar, you're paying, in part, for the ambience.

◖ BASILIQUE NOTRE-DAME-DE-MONTRÉAL

110 rue Notre-Dame W., 514/842-2925, www.basiliquenddm.org
HOURS: Mon.-Fri. 8:30 A.M.-4:30 P.M., Sat. 8 A.M.-4 P.M., Sun. 12:30-4 P.M.; tours daily every hour on the hour and half hour Mon.-Fri. 9 A.M.-4 P.M., Sat. 9 A.M.-3:30 P.M., Sun. 12:30-3:30 P.M.
COST: $5 adult, $4 child
Presiding over Place d'Armes, the Basilique Notre-Dame-de-Montréal is in the heart of Old Montréal. It's here that thousands of fans lined the streets to celebrate Celine Dion's wedding and paid their respects to the funeral processions of former prime minister Pierre Elliot Trudeau and hockey legend Maurice Richard. The basilica is not only in the heart of historic Montréal—in many ways it represents the heart of the city.

As you approach the basilica you get a feel for its grandness; its tall bell towers rise high, and on the building's facade there are three statues looking out over the growing metropolis: Virgin Mary (representing Montréal), St-John the Baptist (representing Québec), and St-Joseph (representing Canada).

Completed in 1830, the Gothic Revival church, the first of its kind in Canada, is set back from the site of the original Notre-Dame parish church, a baroque-style chapel built by the Roman Catholic Sulpician Order in 1672. By 1800, the original chapel was too small to accommodate the population and plans were underway for the basilica. It was designed by James O'Donnell, an Irish-American Protestant who eventually converted to Catholicism and is buried in the crypt.

Specially ordered and designed by Father Olivier Maurault to celebrate the church's centennial in 1929, the stained-glass windows are entirely unconventional. Depicting the religious and social life of the early Ville-Marie settlement, they show the city's strong ties to the Catholic religion. The deep blue and gold of the ceiling is both particularly striking and unusual. The basilica was viewed as too grandiose for such common events as weddings

THE UNDERGROUND CITY

Montréal's Underground City has turned from legendary to legend. Though it is true that below the city's streets and skyscrapers there are 32 kilometers of underground tunnels to explore, it is not true that that there are entire apartment buildings that exist exclusively within this subterranean matrix. Or that the city's inhabitants never have to go outdoors.

Urbanist Vincent Ponte was the first to envision this underground metropolis when, in 1957, his underground pedestrian walkways were included in developer William Zeckendorf's plans for Place Ville-Marie. At the time the plan only covered seven acres, but Harvard-educated Ponte's self-sufficient pedestrian complex would soon lead to his nickname as the "multilevel man." What started as a solution to cover old railway tracks soon became an integral part of the city's urban planning.

Since Ville-Marie opened in 1962, the subterranean city has grown to include 120 exterior access points and over 12 square kilometers.

Universities, banks, museums, Métro stations, condos, and hotels are all accessible through the underground complexes, but its most important and obvious function is as a huge underground mall. Linking three major shopping tunnels, it is the bloodline of winter commerce, allowing consumers to browse and buy in a temperature-controlled environment. Exploring the many tunnels and passageways can be interesting – especially when you realize just how far you can go – but the main draw of Montréal's underworld is that it allows you to avoid the bitter, freezing cold. In fact, for many Montréalers figuring out how to get from point A to point B without going outside has become something of an art.

and funerals, so a second, smaller chapel, Notre-Dame du Sacré-Cœur, was completed in 1891—only to be destroyed by arson nearly 100 years later in 1978. The restoration that took place shortly after drew from original drawings for inspiration, but the vault and altar were given a new, modern twist.

Today, the basilica is a site for many high-profile events. Daily mass continues to be held in French at the basilica, and a 20-minute tour is free with entry. If you're interested in classical and religious music, the basilica plays host to concerts throughout the year.

CHAPELLE NOTRE-DAME-DE-BON-SECOURS AND THE MUSÉE MARGUERITE BOURGEOYS

400 rue St-Paul E., 514/282-8670,
www.marguerite-bourgeoys.com
HOURS: Mar.-Apr. Tues.-Sun. 11 A.M.-3:30 P.M.,
May-Canadian Thanksgiving Tues.-Sun.
10 A.M.-5:30 P.M., Canadian Thanksgiving-mid-Jan.
Tues.-Sun. 11 A.M.-3:30 P.M., mid-Jan.-end of Feb. closed
COST: $8 adult, $4 child, $5 senior and student
Marguerite Bourgeoys was 33 years old when

she arrived in Montréal in 1653, recruited by Paul de Chomedey de Maisonneuve, founder of Montréal, to teach school and religion classes. By 1658, she had traded her skills teaching, mending, and sewing in return for a stone chapel, the first of its kind in the colonial outpost and the only one dedicated to the Virgin Mary, Our Lady of Perpetual Help. It's over the ruins of this original church that the existing Chapelle Notre-Dame-de-Bon-Secours was built in 1771.

With its soft pastels and trompe-l'œil effect, the arched vault of the chapel, a 1886 addition, gives the space a distinctly feminine feel, one that's juxtaposed by a number of ex-votos (a votive offering to a saint) of ships that hang above the pews. Dating back to 1872, the ex-votos give thanks to Mary for a safe passage, a tradition that continues to this day as every September 21 descendants of those who sailed on these ships return to the chapel to pay thanks. Given that the chapel went through a number of different incarnations, the final effect is an eclectic mishmash. One permanent fixture, however, is a wooden

© SACHA JACKSON

Chapelle Notre-Dame-de-Bon-Secours

statuette of Notre-Dame-de-Bon-Secours, brought from France by Marguerite Bourgeoys in 1672, which miraculously survived the fire of 1754. The chapel also includes artwork by Québécois painters Théophile Hamel and Ozias Leduc.

From the chapel climb the 69 steps up to the tower and the remaining 23 to the belvedere for two great views of the Old Port (Vieux-Port). Then head down to the crypt. Once used as a school rec room, it now houses treasures that the museum uncovered while excavating the original site of the chapel, which was discovered in 1996.

Much smaller than the chapel itself, the Marguerite Bourgeoys Museum is housed on the third floor of what was once an adjacent schoolhouse. Famous for founding the Sisters of the Congregation of Notre Dame, Bourgeoys's order still exists today, and the nuns have made a charming history of her life in doll form. Tours of varied length and focus are available, designed to suit visitors' interests and time constraints.

HABITAT 67

2600 ave. Pierre-Dupuy,
www.habitat67.com
COST: Free

Architect Moshe Safdie was only 24 years old when his master's thesis for McGill University was chosen to be constructed as part of Expo 67. An architectural marvel, Habitat 67 sits on a thin peninsula in the St-Lawrence just south of the Old Port. Loosely based on the idea of a kibbutz, 158 interlocking concrete forms are the basis of the experimental housing complex, which was supposed to reflect cities of the future, a time when the population would outgrow urban space. Contrary to the original aim of affordable housing, it's one of the most sought-after addresses in Montréal today and is home to the city's rich and cultured elite. This is a private residence, so no one can actually go inside.

HÔTEL DE VILLE

275 rue Notre-Dame E., 514/872-0077,
www.ville.montreal.qc.ca
HOURS: Mon.-Fri. 8 A.M.-5 P.M.; tours daily 10 A.M.-4 P.M.
COST: Free

Hôtel de Ville stands outside the business center, aligning itself with the provincial courts and overlooking the historic port. Its green copper roof and stoic facade may lend it an air of old-world nostalgia, but even after 130 years it retains a youthful vitality as the city's political hub. Housing the offices of the mayor and city councillors, it remains the site of countless protests and speeches. It was from its famous balcony in 1967 that French president Charles de Gaulle shouted to a frenzied crowd "Vive le Québec libre!" (Long live a free Québec!), further fanning the flames of bilingual unrest.

Built 1872–1878 the original building was gutted by a fire in 1922. The roof collapsed, the interior was destroyed, and the city's records turned to ash. With only the exterior wall left standing, architect Louis Parant rebuilt from the inside out, reinforcing the building with a self-supporting steel structure from behind the ruins. Taking inspiration

EXPO 67 AND THE 1976 OLYMPICS

There are a number of reminders that Montréal was once hoisted onto the world stage as an example of the "City of the Future." Hosting both the World's Fair and the Olympics within 10 years of each other catapulted the city into the 20th century and gave it a futuristic look, one that continues to resonate. What turned out to be one of the most popular world exhibitions in history rightfully put the spotlight on the city. Mayor Jean Drapeau was instrumental in securing the city was given the attention it deserved and with amazing results. Montréal had so impressed the world that it won the bid for the 1976 Summer Olympics, an event that would also leave a lasting impression but in a much different way.

What started as an already ambitious project became too much for the city to handle, and partway through preparations the provincial government had to take over, something they were reluctant to do. Bad management and planning led to a loss of three years worth of building, and by 1973 the project was already behind. Though the Olympics themselves went off without a hitch, they left the city and its citizens reeling from a massive deficit, one that isn't altogether the fault of the Games.

Drapeau famously said that the Olympics could no more incur a deficit than a man could have a baby and in some ways he was right. What he did wrong, however, was to include the costs of basic infrastructure improvements with that of the Olympic construction. Though the final bill was $1.3 billion, much of that went into the roads and Métro system still in use today.

from the city hall of Tours in France, he remodeled the roof in a Beaux Arts style, swapping its slate-tiled roof for the existing copper one.

Inside, you're greeted by the Hall of Honour, an open space full of marble and gold embellishments. Just off the hall is the council room, adorned with five stained-glass windows by John Patrick O'Shea. Installed in 1926, they depict the fundamental aspects of the city: religion, agriculture, the port, commerce, and finance. Open to visitors year-round, the hall plays host to a number of exhibits throughout the year. Free, hour-long tours are offered throughout the day, though certain areas, such as the protocol room and the mayor's office, are off-limits.

Behind city hall is a wide swath of land known as the Champ-de-Mars. Used for military maneuvers and parades, it was once the site of Montréal's fortifications. Buried under a municipal parking lot for a good portion of the last century, it was returned to its former incarnation in the 1980s, and remnants of the original city walls are now integrated into the landscape of the park.

MARCHÉ BONSECOURS
350 rue St-Paul E., 514/872-7730,
www.marchebonsecours.qc.ca
HOURS: Jan.-May 3 daily 10 A.M.-6 P.M.; May 4-June 22 Sun.-Thurs. 10 A.M.-6 P.M. and Fri.-Sat. 10 A.M.-9 P.M.; June 23-Sept. 7 daily 10 A.M.-9 P.M.; Sept. 8-Nov. 1 Sun.-Wed. 10 A.M.-6 P.M., Thurs.-Fri. 10 A.M.-9 P.M., and Sat. 10 A.M.-7 P.M.; Nov. 1-Dec. 31 daily 10 A.M.-6 P.M.
COST: Free

When the city of Montréal decided to build a structure to house an indoor market in the 19th century, the site on which Marché Bonsecours now sits was an ideal choice. Since the early days of Nouvelle France, many prominent Montréalers made their home on the site, including François Bigot, last Intendant of Nouvelle France, and John Molson, founder of the popular Canadian brewery. Charles Dickens and his group of amateur actors even performed on this very site during its incarnation as the Théâtre Royal, whose ruins are buried underneath the existing structure's foundations.

Designed by architect William Footner in 1844, the building was inaugurated with its first public market in January 1847 and remained the city's main agricultural market for over a century. With its tin-plated dome and neoclassical style it's considered one of the 10 major achievements in the history of Canadian architecture.

From 1852 to 1878 it served as city hall and as such demanded specialized banquet and dining halls to accommodate the social demands of the city. Though no longer a public market, the spirit remains, with exclusive boutiques selling everything from authentic Canadian crafts to jewelry, leather, and hand-blown glass, all of which is designed and made in Québec. Cafés and restaurants line the facade of the building, and it remains a center for gatherings and currently hosts Montréal's biannual Fashion Week.

MUSÉE DU CHÂTEAU RAMEZAY

280 rue Notre-Dame E., 514/861-3708,
www.chateauramezay.qc.ca
HOURS: June-Canadian Thanksgiving daily
10 A.M.-6 P.M.; Canadian Thanksgiving-May Tues.-Sun.
10 A.M.-4:30 P.M.
COST: $10 adult, $5 child, $7 student, $8 senior
When the governor of Montréal, Claude de Ramezay, started work on his house in 1704, Montréal was a mere colonial outpost home to approximately 1,500 inhabitants and barely 200 buildings. Choosing a plot of land at the edge of the fortified city (it now sits across the street from city hall), he was obsessed with having a home that matched his perceived importance. He paid for the construction of the property out of his own pocket and promptly went into debt, though not before becoming the envy of the city's residents. The house has gone through many incarnations in its 300-year history, including head offices for the French West India Company (1745–1764), the base for American Revolutionaries including Benjamin Franklin (1775–1776), and a university (1884–1889).

Little of the original structure remains inside the house, though, so if you're expecting a trip back in time, you'll be a little disappointed. Though multimedia displays take you through the building's evolution, the real focus is on the history and progression of the city itself. One of the highlights includes the Salle de Nantes, a dark-wood paneled room from 1725 that is thought to have been carved by Germain Boffrand, chief architect to Louis XIV and XV. The room was part of the French pavilion at the 1967 Expo and donated to the museum shortly after. Of the entire house, the basement feels the most preserved, with vaulted ceilings and authentic fireplaces that still smell of freshly burned wood. It's also where the life of Montréal's 18th-century inhabitants is depicted, with recreations of one-room homes, mannequins in traditional dress, examples of farming material, and a room dedicated to the furniture found in homes during the period. From May to October, the museum also boasts an outdoor café that looks out over the house's gardens and that is, in a genius move, catered by the renowned restaurant Le Club Chasse et Pêche.

PLACE D'ARMES

Corner of rue St-Jacques W. and Côte-de-la-Place d'Armes
As early as 1720, citizens of the Ville-Marie settlement would gather on this site to watch military maneuvers on the "Place d'Armes," a French name for the area where a city's defenders would congregate. After the Notre-Dame church was demolished and replaced by the basilica, Place d'Armes became a public square, the site of hay and wood markets and, later, of a Victorian garden and tramway hub.

The site's real significance, however, comes not so much from the spot itself as from what surrounds it. Located in the heart of historic Montréal, it's bordered on all sides by structures that define Montréal's diverse heritage. Directly to the right of Notre-Dame Basilica is the Séminaire de Saint-Sulpice, the city's oldest building. It was constructed in a U shape by the Sulpician priests in 1684. The building's clock, built in 1701, is the oldest of its kind in North America, and the gardens are said to be among the oldest on the continent. It's still owned and run by the Compagnie des Prêtres de Saint-Sulpice.

Erected in 1888, the New York Life building on the northeast corner of the square became the city's first skyscraper, a whole eight floors up and furnished with an elevator. Kitty-corner to New York Life, the Royal Trust Building and the Duluth Building (to the left of the basilica) are two early-20th-century skyscrapers. They represent a distinct architectural shift around the square, one that is cemented with the arrival of the art deco Aldred Building in 1931. A glass and steel structure, now known as the National Bank Tower, completed the square's architectural timeline in 1968.

The newly refurbished square still features the de Maisonneuve monument depicting the founders of Montréal: Paul de Chomedey de Maisonneuve, Charles Lemoyne, Lambert Closse, Jeanne Mance, and an Iroquois warrior, but it has since been made more pedestrian friendly with cobblestone streets one either side and park benches for a rest.

PLACE JACQUES-CARTIER

Btwn. rue Notre-Dame E., rue de la Commune E., and Place Jacques-Cartier

Lined with restaurants, inns, and cafés and populated by street artists and seasonal fruit stalls, Place Jacques-Cartier, sloping down toward the St-Lawrence River, remains true to its roots as a natural meeting place. An archaeological dig in 1991 uncovered remains of a First Nations campsite in this exact spot. By the early 1800s, it had become the site of the New Marketplace, surrounded by wooden stalls, inns, and stores. With the creation of Marché Bonsecours the "New Marketplace" was no longer needed but it remained the market's outdoor extension and started its transformation into a center for hotels and restaurants.

At the north end of the square you'll find Nelson's Column, erected in 1809. The second monument to be built in the city—the first was a bust of King George III, which stood for five years before it was mutilated in 1775—and

© MADE IN MONTRÉAL

The art deco Aldred Building on Place d'Armes was the first skyscraper in Montréal.

the first monument in the British Empire to be dedicated to the admiral, famous for defeating Napoleon during the Seven Years' War. As in Nelson's Column in London's Trafalgar Square (which was built 31 years after its Montréal counterpart), Nelson faces away from the banks of the river, allegedly to combat his seasickness. The monument was highly controversial, and in 1930, Montréal's Francophone population erected a statue in honor of French naval officer Jean Vauquelin, who fought against the British before being subsequently captured and released. Waging an eternal personal battle, their statutes now stare at each other from across rue Notre-Dame.

PLACE ROYALE
Corner of rue de la Commune and Place Royale
This flat square of concrete tiles might not be much to look at, but it represents one of the most important places in all of Old Montréal. From the early days of the Ville-Marie settlement this was the spot where inhabitants would gather to hear royal orders and decrees read out. Between 1642 and 1676, this was the location of the annual fur-trading fairs where the First Nations would bring their pelts to be traded for various goods from the French.

The most important event to have taken place on this spot, however, is the signing of the Great Peace Treaty of Montréal in 1701 between the French, their native allies, and the Five Nations Iroquois, ending nearly a century of war.

◖ POINTE-À-CALLIÈRE MUSÉE D'ARCHÉOLOGIE ET D'HISTOIRE
350 Place Royale, 514/872-9150, www.pacmusee.qc.ca
HOURS: Tues.-Fri. 10 A.M.-5 P.M., Sat.-Sun. 11 A.M.-5 P.M.; tours Mon.-Fri. 12:30, 2:30, 3:30, and 4:30 P.M. and Sat.-Sun. 12:30, 2:30, and 3:30 P.M.
COST: $15 adult, $6 child, $8 student, $10 senior
It was on this site on May 17, 1642, that Montréal was established. Founding members of the colony Paul de Chomedey de Maisonneuve, Jeanne Mance, and Father Vimont were on hand to mark the occasion at what was then a small point of land that jutted

out into the St-Lawrence and St-Pierre Rivers. By 1688 the site was home to Louis Hector de Callière, third governor of Montréal and the museum's namesake. When the settlement began to build fortifications in 1716, the point fell outside of those boundaries, making it an invaluable archaeological site. Dedicated to the various people—native, French, and English—that make up the city's past, Pointe-à-Callière is Canada's only sizable archaeology museum and the quintessential museum on Montréal.

Opened in 1992 as part of the celebrations for the city's 350th anniversary, the museum's architecture is distinctly contemporary, standing out in the historic port and disguising the rich history that sits within and beneath its walls. Don't be fooled by the modern reception area: Historic artifacts and archaeological finds confront you at every turn throughout the six distinct buildings, which include Montréal's first custom house (Ancienne-Douane Building) and first electrically operated wastewater pumping system (Youville Pumping Station). The most fascinating exhibit, however, remains the museum's own archaeological site.

Below the ground level of the main Éperon building, you'll discover traces of Montréal's (then Ville-Marie) first Catholic cemetery. Burial plots of both French colonists and First Nations show the unique reality of the early days of the settlement, when French and First Nations were encouraged to live and mix harmoniously.

Montréal's oldest collector sewer is also on display here: completed in 1838, it canalized the St-Pierre River underground into one of the first sewer pipes, one that remained in use until 1989.

The number of yearly visitors to the museum has hit the 350,000 mark, so you can almost always expect to find a crowd, especially during the high season of June through August.

QUARTIER INTERNATIONAL
Corner of rue St-Jacques and rue de Bleury
Linking Old Montréal and downtown, the newly designated Quartier International is the

© MADE IN MONTRÉAL

Place Royale is the site of the first settlement in Montréal.

result of one of the city's most extensive redevelopment projects. Inaugurated in 2004, the centerpiece of the area is Place Jean-Paul-Riopelle, a fountain and public square flanked on one side by the newly developed Palais des Congrès (Montréal's convention center). On the other side, you'll find the sleek glass headquarters of Caisse de Dépôts et Placements du Québec, new home of Montréal's renowned restaurant Toqué!

Riopelle, who died in 2002, was a seminal Québécois artist and member of the Automatistes movement, whose works was influenced by surrealism and similar to abstract-expressionism. The fountain at the center of the square incorporates his 1969 sculpture *La Joute,* a tribute to the hockey heroes of his youth, which originally stood in the Parc Olympique.

RUE SAINT-PAUL
Btwn. rue McGill and rue Berri
Winding and narrow rue St-Paul lives up to its name as the oldest street in Montréal.

Designed by priest, historian, and urban planner François Dollier de Casson, who created the majority of the street layout of what is now Old Montréal, rue St-Paul was originally paved in 1672 under the direction of city founder Paul de Chomedey de Maisonneuve, whose home, conveniently enough, was also on the same road. Linking Fort Ville-Marie with the Hôtel Dieu (the hospital), it was the settlement's main thoroughfare and remained a vital part of the historic center until the 20th century.

Many of the buildings that line the street date back to the 19th century but now house some of the city's most modern and contemporary stores and restaurants. Between June and September, it is partially closed to traffic.

TOUR DE L'HORLOGE
Clock Tower Quay
HOURS: May 6-Sept. 8 daily 10 A.M.-7 P.M.
COST: Free
Jutting out into the St-Lawrence, the Montréal Clock Tower marks the entry to the Port of Montréal. Built 1919–1922 in the Beaux Arts

© SACHA JACKSON

The Tour de l'Horloge keeps watch over the Vieux-Port.

style, the 45-meter-high tower commemorates the merchant navy seamen who lost their lives during World War I and II. It is fitted with a clock face that looks out over four directions of the port and that was built in London, England, by Gillett and Johnson. It is a replica of the one that sits atop London's Big Ben. It also served as a lighthouse, guiding ships into shore.

You're invited to climb up the tower's 192 steps and look out over the St-Lawrence for an unparalleled view.

VIEUX-PORT

For centuries after the first explorers arrived, Montréal was the final destination of hundreds of thousands of immigrants who made their way for the first time onto Canadian shores. Until 1948, when a series of locks finally connected the St-Lawrence with the Great Lakes, Montréal was the disembarkation point for both trans-Atlantic ships and trains from all over North America. Between 1896 and 1930, Montréal was the major distribution point for merchandise both into and out of the country. At the west end of the Old Port, grain elevator

no. 5, which closed for good in 1995, is one of its grandest monuments.

The sheds, grain elevators, and quays that line the port are relics from its heyday, but a major revamp in the 1980s transformed the port into today's booming district. Converted warehouses are now quay-side restaurants, cafés, and boutiques. You'll find a labyrinth in shed 16, the Montréal Science Center and IMAX on King Edward Pier, and Cirque du Soleil one pier over.

A single park runs the entire length of the Old Port Promenade, offering tourists and locals an ideal spot to relax and catch a cool breeze off the water. If being in the water is more to your liking you can dock your boat in the many marinas, take a boat cruise on the St-Lawrence, or hire pedal boat for a trip round the Bonsecours basin.

The port is bordered on the north by railway tracks, and you'll occasionally find yourself caught waiting for a passing cargo train, a reminder that this was once a bustling commercial port. Though not with the same frequency as in the past, international cruise and cargo ships still dock here throughout the year.

Centre-Ville
Map 2

CATHÉDRALE MARIE-REINE-DU-MONDE

1085 rue de la Cathédrale, 514/866-1661,
www.cathedralecatholiquedemontreal.org

HOURS: Mon.-Sat. 7 A.M.-7 P.M., Sun. 9 A.M.-6 P.M.

COST: Free

After St. James Cathedral burnt down in 1852, Ignace Bourget, the first bishop of Montréal, decided he wanted to recreate a smaller version of Rome's St-Peter's Basilica. After drawing up the plans architect Victor Bourgeau quit, saying he could not replicate St-Peter's on a smaller scale. The project went ahead without him (though he subsequently returned), and the first cornerstone for the existing church was laid in 1870. It opened to the public in 1894 and became a cathedral in 1919. Bourget got his wish, though he wasn't around to see it; the sizable church is a perfect replica, right down to the red copper baldachin that was hand-carved in Rome.

Unsurprisingly, the cathedral appears older than its years; behind the facade the limestone on the outer part of the nave of the church looks distinctly aged. In a delightfully modern move, however, the wrought iron and glass front doors open automatically, sweeping out and ushering you into the narrow narthex. Columns with gilded crowns and the otherwise modest ceiling moldings inlayed with gold support the high, arched ceilings of the nave. Hues of soft green and blush decorate the cathedral, giving it a gentle and slightly feminine touch. Rising 80 meters in height, the cupola is surrounded with stained-glass windows. Similar to Notre-Dame Basilica, the cathedral's main works of art are dedicated to the city's devout Catholics and include depictions of Marguerite Bourgeoys teaching native children and Grey Nun founder Marguerite d'Youville aiding the sick. Bourget's remains are buried beneath one of the pillars,

LOOK UP: ARCHITECTURAL MONTRÉAL

Structures from Expo 67 and the 1976 Olympics stand out as some of the best architecture in the city, but there are also a number of buildings worth a look.

- **Aldred Building:** Completed in 1931 in the art deco style, this stands as an ode to the arcditectural style that once dominated the cityscape (507 Place d'Armes).

- **École de Musique Schulich:** McGill University's latest addition is sleek, with black cladding and dark windows. It also has an acoustically perfect auditorium (555 rue Sherbrooke W.).

- **Gare Windsor:** Headquarters of the Canadian Pacific Railway, this Romanesque Revival building was completed in 1889, and you can still visit its old arrival terminal (1100 ave. des Canadiens-de-Montréal).

- **L'ITQ:** L'Institut de Tourisme et D'Hotellierie du

Québec was once a mass of brown, corrugated siding but is now a glamorous glass building with lots of light and glimmer (3535 rue St-Denis).

- **Palais des Congrès:** Mario Saia's kaleidoscopic extension has put a new, colorful twist on what could have been another concrete slab (159 rue St-Antoine W.).

- **Tour de la Bourse:** Erected in 1964, this is the home of the Montréal stock exchange and an example of the international style (800 Place Victoria).

- **Université de Montréal:** The main building, designed by Ernest Cormier, was finished in 1943 and is situated on the northern slope of Mont-Royal (2900 blvd. Edouard-Monpetit).

- **Westmount Square:** Designed by Mies van de Rohe, this is one of the preeminent examples of international style in the city (1 Square Westmount).

but there is a mortuary chapel in his honor; the floor and walls are covered in Italian marble, and his tomb takes center stage.

Like St-Peter's, the cathedral has 13 statues that adorn the facade, but breaking with tradition they do not represent Jesus and the 12 apostles. Instead they represent the patron saints of parishes that offered them to the diocese and include Saint Hyacinth, Saint Francis of Assisi, and Saint John the Baptist.

CENTRE BELL

1250 rue de la Gauchetière W., 514/932-2582, www.centrebell.ca
HOURS: Tues.-Sat. 10 A.M.-6 P.M., Sun. noon-5 P.M.; tours daily 11:15 A.M. and 2:45 P.M.
COST: $10 adult, $7 child and senior

Even those who know little about Montréal have probably heard of the city's passionate relationship with their beloved Montréal Canadiens. Partially hidden on the southern edge of downtown, the enormous red-brick and concrete Centre Bell (Bell Center) building is not the most inspired of sports arenas—at least not from the outside. Home of the Canadiens since 1996, it replaced the history-laden Montréal Forum (now a movie theater) and seats 21,273 fans, alternately olé-ing and booing.

Originally called the Molson Centre—the area changed hands and names in 2002, though Molson still owns the team—it is the largest hockey arena in North America. The interior is exclusively dedicated to Canadiens history and features team photographs and bronze busts of many players. History continues outside the area with statues honoring the team's four greatest players: Howie Morenz, Guy Lafleur, Maurice "Rocket" Richard, and Jean Béliveau.

Below street level you'll find the Montréal Canadiens Hall of Fame, inaugurated as part of the centennial celebrations. It features memorabilia from throughout the team's 100-year-old history, including Jacques Laplant's original goalie mask, which was the first of its kind in 1959. You can also visit a replica of the 1976–1977 Canadiens dressing room (luckily without the smell), and interactive features invite you to play the hockey journalist—a favorite pastime of many Montréalers. Proceeds from the Hall of Fame go toward helping retired players—many of whom did not profit from the game as much as the owners.

When not packing the house with hockey fans, the center hosts stars of a different kind; entertainers from U2 to Celine Dion and from Lady Gaga to Justin Timberlake have performed here.

CENTRE CANADIEN D'ARCHITECTURE

1920 rue Baile, 514/939-7026, www.cca.qc.ca
HOURS: Wed.-Sun. 11 A.M.-6 P.M., Thurs. 11 A.M.-9 P.M.
COST: $10 adult, $7 senior, child and student free

Unique in aim and design, the Centre Canadien d'Architecture (CCA) is the only cultural institution of its kind in Canada. Founded in 1979 by architect Phyllis Lambert, the aim of the institution is to expand the public's awareness of the role architecture plays in our lives, and to act as a research center for scholars.

Lambert, who convinced her father, Samuel Bronfman, to hire Mies van de Rohe to design the famous Seagram's building in New York, later studied architecture at the Illinois Institute of Technology before going on to design Montréal's Saidye Bronfman Centre for the Arts, which is named after her mother. It was Lambert's vast collection of architectural drawings, photographs, and books that became the founding objects of the center's research collection.

Designing the museum to incorporate a Victorian mansion, the 1872 Shaughnessy House, Lambert stayed true to her vision of modern architecture, one that focused on both preservation and progress. Built 1985–1989 by Montréal-born Peter Rose (Lambert was consulting architect), the CCA is a perfect example of post-modern architecture. The new wings of the center attach themselves seamlessly to the existing structure, and elements such as the color of limestone, the bay windows, and the windows' placement mimic those of the mansion, preserving and simultaneously mixing the two distinct styles.

From the entrance, however, none of this is visible. Instead you have a view of a thoroughly modern building; it's not until you're inside and past the entrance stairs that you really understand the extent that these two visions have been fused. The fully restored Victorian Devencore Conservatory is one of the museum's highlights and offers a glimpse of the home's past glory.

The center houses exhibits each year that examine the effects of modern living on our surroundings, our environment, and ourselves. It also hosts interesting talks throughout the year as well as family-friendly workshops.

Across the busy boulevard René-Lévesque and just above the highway, you'll find the institute's unconventional garden. Designed by artist and architect Melvin Charney, its use of concrete and unique statues is a comment on the city's architectural and cultural history, and most importantly it offers a great view of the CCA's post-modern facade.

DORCHESTER SQUARE

Corner of blvd. René-Lévesque and rue Peel

Inaugurated in 1878, Dorchester Square became a central meeting point and a prestigious address for a number of large companies. The largest was Sun Life Insurance, whose Sun Life Building continues to preside over the east side of the square. Completed in 1931, after 24 years of on and off construction, its architectural presence is rivaled only by the Dominion Square Building at the north end. Designed as both a shopping arcade and an office tower, it opened in 1930 and now houses the offices of the Montréal *Gazette,* the city's only English-language newspaper and one of Canada's oldest.

Recently renovated, the square's four monuments honoring the Boer War, Canadian prime minister Sir Wilfrid Laurier, Scottish poet Robert Burns, and Queen Victoria were refurbished and have kept their positions on the square's pathways, which form a five point equilateral cross.

Though it is now surrounded by some of the most interesting architecture in the downtown area, between 1799 and 1854 the square was the site of a Catholic cemetery, an ideal burial spot at the end of the 18th century when it would have been situated in open countryside. And it is the final resting place of many victims of the 1832 cholera epidemic. During the renovations, archaeologists examined the remains before exhuming the bodies and moving them to Notre-Dame-des-Neiges Cemetery on Mont-Royal. To honor those who were laid to rest in this spot, 60 crosses have been installed in the brickwork of the walkways.

Across the street you'll find Place du Canada, inaugurated at the same time. It too was the site of cemeteries until the late 1800s. Today, it's one of a few green spaces in the downtown core and home of the Macdonald Monument, honoring Canada's first prime minister, John A. Macdonald. It was here in 1995 that 100,000 Canadian citizens gathered as part of the Unity Rally, to protest Québec's referendum and persuade the province to vote against separating from the rest of Canada.

GRAND SÉMINAIRE DE MONTRÉAL

2065 rue Sherbrooke W., 514/935-1162, www.gsdm.qc.ca

HOURS: Tours July-Aug. Tues.-Sat. 1 and 3 P.M.

COST: Free

Barricaded by two stone turrets and a high stone wall, the Grand Séminaire de Montréal is well hidden from the busy stretch of Sherbrooke. Built in 1840 as a place to train priests, it is the second seminary to be built in the city—the first is next door to Notre-Dame Basilica—and stands on the same site as the Fort de la Montagne.

Constructed in 1685, the purpose of the fort was to help ward off attacks from the native population; today only the turrets and fieldstone walls remain and are some of the oldest structures in Montréal. Along with the towers the priests built a series of canals that run along Mont-Royal. The first of these was built in 1675 and remains in use today. It also houses a Romanesque chapel, which boasts hand-carved oak stalls, and is one of the best examples of the Beaux Arts style in the city.

Now the home of a private college, it continues to educate future priests.

MCGILL UNIVERSITY

845 rue Sherbrooke W., www.mcgill.ca

COST: Free

Built on the southern slope of Mont-Royal on ground that was once owned by James McGill, McGill is one of the oldest universities in Canada, predating confederation by 46 years.

Born in Glasgow, McGill immigrated to Canada, where he became a successful merchant. Upon his death in 1813 he donated his Burnside summer estate to the Royal Institution for the Advancement of Learning, and by 1829, classes were being held in his former home. McGill University granted its first medical degree in 1833, which remained the school's only faculty until 1843, with the addition of the faculty of arts.

Between 1880 and 1920 the university experienced a huge amount of expansion thanks in large part to the financial backing of the city's wealthiest men—William Molson (beer), Sir Peter Redpath (sugar), Lord Strathcona (Hudson's Bay Company), and Sir William Macdonald (tobacco). Much of the architecture from this time still exists today, including the Arts Building, which sits as the focal point of the university's campus looking north from rue Sherbrooke. The Roddick Gates, which so nicely frame the entrance, are themselves a gift, donated by Lady Amy Redpath Roddick in memory of her doctor husband in 1924.

The campus with its sprawling tree-lined lawns is an ideal place to take a rest from the downtown, and it also offers an ideal shortcut to the Plateau Mont-Royal, which is reached by wandering through McGill Ghetto, a nice quiet neighborhood full of gorgeous townhouses and university students.

Historical tours covering the rise and development of the university and campus are provided to the general public but require an email request at least a week in advance at welcome@mcgill.ca, or you can download your own self-guided tour on the website. Visitors can pass through the campus any time of day, but the Welcome Center, which offers tours, is only open Monday–Friday 9 A.M.–5:30 P.M.

MUSÉE DES BEAUX-ARTS DE MONTRÉAL

1380 rue Sherbrooke W., 514/285-2000, www.mbam.qc.ca

HOURS: Tues. 11 A.M.-5 P.M., Wed.-Fri. 11 A.M.-9 P.M., Sat.-Sun. 10 A.M.-5 P.M.

COST: $15 adult, $10 senior, $7.50 student; Wed. 5-8:30 P.M. $7.50

Framed in white marble, Musée des Beaux-Arts' Jean-Noël Desmarais Pavilion stands out among the limestone and columns of rue Sherbrooke's Golden Square Mile. Designed by Moshe Safdie of Expo 67 fame, and inaugurated in 1991, the modern building stands in contrast to the museum's original Beaux Arts structure by William Sutherland Maxwell, which faces it from across the street.

In 1860 a group of art-loving Montréalers convened to create the Art Association of Montréal, with the aim of spreading the arts with exhibitions and art classes. Little was done, however, until 1879, when the association finally got its first building, at the time the only one in the country specifically designed to exhibit and house works of art. By 1909, the association was financially stable enough to live up to its aspirations and built the Beaux Arts building, which still exists today.

The two pavilions (which are connected through underground walkways), with their distinct designs, speak volumes about the museum's collections and exhibitions. The modern Jean-Noël Desmarais Pavilion is filled with light, the space open and the floors a beautiful black slate. The majority of the museum's permanent collection is found here and includes religious pieces, works by First Nations, and a number of recent acquisitions, contemporary pieces by young Canadian and international artists. Spread throughout the building's four floors, the collection takes you on a perfectly balanced art-history tour.

The Beaux Arts building instead houses many of the temporary exhibits. With its sweeping marble staircase, maple woodwork, and Victorian light-fixtures, it's the perfect environment for viewing exhibits like Tiffany

Glass, Van Dongen, and the ground-breaking show Yves Saint-Laurent.

The recently converted Erskine and American United Church, which opened in late 2010, is the museum's Canadian pavilion, and the building itself is a national historic site.

MUSÉE MCCORD

690 rue Sherbrooke W., 514/398-7100, www.mccord-museum.qc.ca

HOURS: Mon.-Tues. and Thurs.-Fri. 10 A.M.–6 P.M., Wed. 10 A.M.–9 P.M., Sat.-Sun. 10 A.M.–5 P.M.

COST: $13 adult, $10 senior, $7 student, $5 child; Wed. 5-9 P.M. free

Even before David Ross McCord began trolling the country for historical artifacts in 1878, his family, who had been collecting since their arrival in Canada around 1760, had done a good deal of the work for him. By 1921, when the McCord Museum was finally established, his collection contained 15,000 objects.

Since then the collection has grown, and the museum now has nearly 1.5 million objects, all of which are housed in a classic Arts and Crafts building adjacent to McGill University. Designed by Percy Erskine Nobbs in the early 20th century, it has been the museum's home since 1971. The facade leads to a modern interior—in fact the original structure is almost completely unrecognizable once you pass through the foyer.

The three floors of exhibition space house two temporary exhibits and the permanent collection Simply Montréal, an exciting exhibit of artifacts that traces the history of the area from the early days of discovery.

Anyone who enjoys looking at stuff will enjoy the McCord. The ephemera from bygone eras allows the viewer to understand the cultural and social aspects of the city's life. And much of its life is represented here, from crossbows, helmets, and armor from the explorer days to the Montréal of the 1920s–1940s, when American Prohibition turned it into a swinging hot spot—the cocktail napkins and menus are here to prove it.

Interactive multimedia features can be found throughout the museum and offer a unique way to look at the exhibitions. To the left of the entrance is a charming café; the intimate Salle des Amis (Friends' Room) is particularly welcoming.

PLACE VILLE-MARIE

1 Place Ville-Marie, www.placevillemarie.com

HOURS: Stores Mon.-Wed. 9:30 A.M.–6 P.M., Thurs.-Fri. 9:30 A.M.–9 P.M., Sat. 9:30 A.M.–7 P.M., Sun. noon–5 P.M.

COST: Free

One of the most controversial projects the city has ever encountered, Place Ville-Marie was part of Mayor Jean Drapeau's plan to create a new, modern metropolis. Designed by I. M. Pei (who would go on to become one of the most recognized architects of the 20th century) and Henry N. Cobb, the international-style tower was completed in 1962. Originally the head offices of the Royal bank, its construction marked the move of the city's financial district from Old Montréal's rue St-Jacques to downtown. Rising 47 stories, the four cross-shaped towers made up the world's largest and most complex office building—indeed, the complex itself has 52 different postal codes.

Though no longer the only skyscraper in the downtown core, it remains one of the most breathtaking. Inside, over 80 stores and boutiques connect the tower to the central railway station and Métro lines. This is the starting point of the mythical and complicated Underground City. Since it allows access to the Métro and a club, the concourse is open later than the shops.

High above is Altitude 737, a panoramic restaurant and one of the city's hottest clubs, whose revolving lights sweep over the city and can be seen from 50 kilometers away.

Centre-Ville Est Map 3

CHINATOWN
Bordered by blvd. René-Lévesque, ave. Viger, blvd. St-Laurent, and rue Jeanne-Mance

With the railroad boom of the 1800s came a wave of Chinese immigration to the city. Dating back to the 1860s, Montréal's Chinatown is far smaller than many of those found in other parts of North America but, perhaps because of its size, it remains a vital and culturally important neighborhood. The center of traditional festivals and holidays for the city's Asian communities, it also has its own Chinese hospital and community center.

An exquisite red arch on the corner of St-Laurent and René-Lévesque marks the entrance to Chinatown, which borders downtown and the Quartier International and sits just north of Vieux-Montréal. Originally a residential neighborhood, it is now a mainly commercial district with restaurants, bakeries, stores, and traditional crafts—this is the place to pick up authentic Japanese and Chinese china—many of which are concentrated on rue de la Gauchetière. In the summertime this pedestrian-only street fills up with a number of outdoor markets.

Though established by the Chinese immigrants who came to Canada to work on the railway and to the mines, there was also an influx of Vietnamese-Chinese refugees, many of them French-speaking because Vietnam was under French colonial rule until 1941. As a result there are now many Vietnamese restaurants throughout the area and it's a great place to pick up some of the best bánh mì sandwiches in the city.

A Holiday Inn at the edge of Chinatown designed in the style of a pagoda is a slightly kitschy but nonetheless sweet homage to the community and culture.

◖ MUSÉE D'ART CONTEMPORAIN
185 rue Ste-Catherine W., 514/847-6226, www.macm.org
HOURS: Tues.-Sun. 11 A.M.-6 P.M., Wed. 11 A.M.-9 P.M.
COST: $10 adult, $8 senior, $6 student; free Wed. 5-9 P.M.

Established in 1964 at the height of Québec's Quiet Revolution and abstract art boom, the Musée d'Art Contemporain (MAC) had various homes before settling into its own modern building in 1992. Part of the Place des Arts, Canada's only cultural complex devoted to both visual and performing arts, the MAC's subtle concrete facade is the perfect foil for the columns and glass of Salle Wilfrid Pelletier next door.

Entering through the unassuming door, you're bathed in light from a domed skylight around which the museum's restaurant is placed. With over 7,000 works in the permanent collection, including works by some of the biggest names in Québéc art—like Paul-

LE QUARTIER DES SPECTACLES

Le Quartier des Spectacles is the center of attention during festival season. From Les Franco-Folies de Montréal in early June to the Montréal World Film Festival in late August this square kilometer of the city has been the hub for shows and performances for over a century. Revamped, revitalized, and newly christened, Le Quartier des Spectacles has over 80 cultural venues, from performance halls to art galleries. The area stretches between rue City Councillors, boulevard St-Laurent, rue Sherbrooke, and boulevard René-Lévesque. The **Place des Arts** complex remains the centerpiece with the addition of a brand-new concert hall (**L'Adresse Symphonique**), and the new area encompasses many existing venues, like the **Cabaret Juste pour Rire,** the **Monument-National,** and the **SAT,** as well as new buildings like sleek new arts hub **Le 2-22,** with galleries, radio stations, arts associations, and a bookstore.

Émile Borduas, Claude Tousignant, and Jean-Paul Riopelle—it also hosts some of the most exciting, interesting, and boundary-pushing exhibits by Canadian and international artists, such as Marcel Dzama and Bruce Nauman. Grab a drink, catch a live up-and-coming local act, and see the latest exhibit the first Friday of every month at Friday Nocturnes. Or relax in the cool of the museum while watching an artistic version of MTV at their summer-long Music Video projection series.

PLACE DES ARTS

175 rue Ste-Catherine W., 514/842-2112, www.laplacedesarts.com

HOURS: Vary

Taking up an entire block of the downtown core, Place des Arts is a multi-venue arts center and the home of four of the city's largest production companies—the Orchestre Symphonique de Montréal, the Opéra de Montréal, Les Grands Ballets Canadiens de Montréal, and the Jean-Duceppe theater company. The Musée d'Art Contemporain is right next door. The site recently underwent major reconstruction in order to include a sixth concert hall, L'Adresse Symphonique, dedicated to musical performances by the Montréal Symphony and to remodel the Grand Foyer, which greets visitors to the complex.

Opening in September 1963, just four years shy of Expo 67, at the height of Montréal's construction and architectural boom, the inauguration concert featured Canadian conductor Wilfrid Pelletier and Indian conductor Zubin Mehta.

Running along rue Ste-Catherine, the Esplanade is the site of many of the city's outdoor cultural happenings. It is here that you'll find the International Jazz Festival's main stage, free movie screenings during the Montréal World Film Festival, and a host of other free summer festival events. Indeed, the block in front of the Esplanade is virtually shut down to regular traffic and even bikes from June to September. The Esplanade's stairs are a choice spot for a meeting point or to simply sit and people-watch, and the fountain at the top is often surrounded by office workers and visitors alike cooling off, their feet dangling in the basin.

Quartier Latin and the Village — Map 4

ÉGLISE ST-PIERRE-APÔTRE

1201 rue de la Visitation, 514/524-3791, www.stpierrapotre.org

HOURS: Mon.-Fri. 10:30 A.M.-4 P.M., Sat. noon-5 P.M., Sun. 9:30 A.M.-4 P.M.

COST: Free

With its flying buttresses, stained-glass windows, and open nave, this neo-Gothic church constructed in 1851 is one of the most traditional in the city. Inspired by Brooklyn's Holy Trinity, it was the first church to be designed by Victor Bourgeau—who would go on to become one of the most prolific church architects in Québec. It is still considered his masterpiece.

Bourgeau's materials were unusual; he used stone throughout, and even the pillars are made of limestone. Step inside, however, and you realize just how nontraditional this church really is. Decorated with rainbow banners, it's known for its gay-friendly Sunday services as well as its overall support of the gay community. Set alight in July 1996, a flame burns permanently in the Chapel of Hope, the first chapel in the world dedicated to memory of victims of AIDS.

LA GRANDE BIBLIOTHÈQUE

475 blvd. de Maisonneuve E., 514/873-1100, www.banq.qc.ca

HOURS: Tues.-Fri. 10 A.M.-10 P.M., Sat.-Sun. 10 A.M.-6 P.M.

COST: Free

One of the most interesting buildings in the city, La Grande Bibliothèque (the National Library) was completed in 2005. Set on the former site of the Palais de Commerce, a serious concrete eyesore, the library invigorated the area and gave it a much-needed boost of elegance.

Designed by the architectural team of Patkau from Vancouver and Croft-Pelletier/ Gilles Guité from Québec City, the two architectural studios beat out 36 other international firms to win the contract. The 6,000 U-shaped plates of frosted glass create the glacial green color seen on the outside of the building, which is reminiscent of the glacial ice found in the far north. It was the first time this type of glass was used in North America.

Light filters into the great hall, which is supported by three concrete pillars and runs the length of the structure. From the great hall you enter into the working area of the library, featuring sleek, glass elevators and elongated stairs that are the centerpiece of a the building. Yellow birch wood, one of Québec's official emblems, is used throughout to separate areas and diffuse sound. It is complemented by the classic yet modern library desks by Michel Dallaire Design.

With close to three million users, it's one of the most popular libraries in the French-speaking world and regularly hosts art exhibitions. Ninety-minute tours are available free of charge, but check before you go since the schedule changes monthly. Self-guided tours are also available for download from the library's website.

RUE AMHERST

Btwn. blvd. de Maisonneuve E. and rue Ontario E.

In the heart of the Village this delightful street is an excellent place to browse and grab a bite. The finds in the antiques stores here span from the 1930s to the 1960s and are sure to turn your head. Fans of mid-century modern design, beware; there's an assortment of it here and at some of the best prices you'll find on the East Coast. Sputnik and Cité Déco top the lists for best kitsch and mid-century modern respectively, but for old rotary phones, stackable cafeteria chairs, and Expo 67 memorabilia—the

perfect gift for any fan of design—Seconde Chance is unrivaled.

Alongside the antiques you'll find stores featuring up-and-coming designers; Québécois designer Dinh Bà's store can be found on this strip. Follow the street all the way south toward the port and be sure to check out the 200-year-old walls of the Molson Brewery, which look sturdy enough to defend an entire city, let alone a beer factory.

◖ RUE SAINTE-CATHERINE EST

Btwn. rue Berri and Papineau

This is the heart of one of the largest gay villages in North America, the center of the week-long pride celebration Divers/Cité, and overall life of the party. People of all sexual orientations flock to the bars and clubs along Ste-Catherine Est, making it one of the liveliest nightlife spots in the city.

Occupying what was once a poor, working-class neighborhood, the Village first started to grow during the late 1960s and early '70s, with the opening of many gay-owned and gay-friendly businesses. At the time, however, it was kept rather discreet, and in the lead-up to Expo 67 and the 1976 Olympic Games, Mayor Jean Drapeau conducted raids on bath houses and saunas, further relegating the gay community to the margins—or at least out of the public eye.

By the early 1980s, though, things started to change, with gay bars opening up and drawing a new generation of gays to the neighborhood. It's now an active community, one whose importance is recognized by all levels of government—former provincial leader for the Parti Québécois, André Boisclair, is openly gay—and a newly refurbished Beaudry Métro station, the Village's main stop, is adorned with rainbow pillars.

Though gays and lesbians live in every corner of the city—Montréal is known for and proud of its accepting attitude—the Village remains the center of activity for the LGBTQ community. Between June and September Ste-Catherine is closed to traffic, becoming one long pedestrian-only strip.

UQÀM

Various locations, www.uqam.ca

COST: Free

Architect and urban designer Dimitri Dimakopoulous was one of the most sought after architects in the country, having designed award-winning buildings from coast to coast. In 1974, along with his ACORP associates, he undertook the project to create an urban campus for the relatively new Université du Québec à Montréal (commonly referred to as UQÀM). It subsequently won the city's Prix d'Excellence award in Architecture for that year.

Situated in what is now the Quartier Latin (the Latin Quarter), the campus Dimakopoulous created is an urban one, seamlessly integrated into the city's existing architecture. As such, the school features two former churches that have been incorporated into the design. Vastly different in styles and even materials, they add a unique twist to the modern brick structures and can be seen and explored on Ste-Catherine and St-Denis.

Established in 1969, UQÀM is the product of a merger between the fine-arts-focused École des Beaux-Arts de Montréal and the classics college Collège Sainte-Marie. It continues to be the preeminent Francophone arts university in the province, with special schools in fashion, feminist studies, and environmental studies.

Plateau Mont-Royal · Map 5

AVENUE DU MONT-ROYAL

Btwn. ave. du Parc and ave. Papineau

By the end of the 1800s, avenue du Mont-Royal was a bustling thoroughfare linking two smaller villages, De Lorimier and Coteau-Saint-Louis. Marked only with nine homes, including two dairies, a cart-maker, and a cobbler, today it's the main, and hippest, artery of the Plateau, lined with trendy bars, restaurants, and boutiques.

Made famous by novelist and playwright Michel Tremblay and his depiction of the area as a mostly working-class French-Canadian neighborhood, it has maintained a Francophone population but is no longer as working-class as it once was. Residents today are sometimes chided for being "bobo," a sort of French hipster, both bourgeois and bohemian. The population, however, likely has a lot to do with the impeccably preserved traditional houses and the area's numerous great restaurants.

At the far east end of the street you'll find the Stade Olympique, whose gleaming white tower is an impressive view, jutting into the air over the avenue. It can be seen from just about any point.

To help visitors explore, free bicycles are

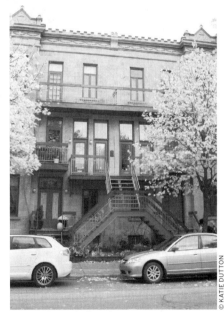
avenue du Mont-Royal
© KATIE DUTTON

available from early June to late August. You can find them at Place Gérald-Godin, just in front of the Mont-Royal Métro station.

CARRÉ SAINT-LOUIS

Bordered by rue St-Denis, ave. Laval, and rue du Square Saint-Louis

Found at the end of the pedestrian-only Prince Arthur, this square links St-Laurent and St-Denis streets and is bordered by a number of grandiose 19th-century houses. During that period, the area attracted wealthy French-Canadian families, a legacy that remains today—the majority of the Second Empire homes around the square are beautifully kept up and retain much of their charm even 200 years later.

Artists were also drawn here, including important French-Canadian poet Émile Nelligan, who was influenced by French Symbolists like Charles Baudelaire and Paul Verlaine, who made his home here.

Though not a destination on its own, the square has a nice fountain and a number of pathways lined with trees and park benches. In the summer, the kiosk on the west side of the square sells ice cream and other refreshments, making it a great place to stop and take in the scenery.

THE MAIN

Blvd. St-Laurent btwn. blvd. René-Lévesque and blvd. St-Joseph

Affectionately called the Main by locals, boulevard Saint-Laurent was first cobbled together from streets that were established by both the French and the British regimes. When Montréal was still a fortified city the Main was located inside the walls; it was only with the advent of the Grand Porte Saint-Laurent, which provided a single route out of the walled city, that it became known as Saint-Laurent road. In 1792, it became the official division between east and west—a division it still marks today—and the street was renamed as Saint-Laurent du Main.

Though it is the physical division of east and west, historically, it has also divided the city by language—French to the east, English to the west. Over 11 kilometers long, it runs nearly the entire width of the island of Montréal, which is 14 kilometers from north to south, and it is to this long street that waves of immigrants have flocked.

From the mid-1900s onward the Main became the home of the Jewish community, which migrated north from what is now Chinatown. Waves of more immigrants followed, including Italians, Portuguese, Poles, Greeks, Chinese, Latin Americans, and most recently Africans and people from the Caribbean, all of whom have left a distinct mark on the strip.

Once the center of industry, with factories and retail businesses lining the Main from one end to the other, today this national historic site is best known for its restaurants, bars, clubs, and live venues.

PARC LAFONTAINE

Corner of rue Sherbrooke and ave. Parc LaFontaine

HOURS: Daily 6 A.M.–10 P.M.

COST: Free

An oasis in the middle of the Plateau, Parc LaFontaine's 40 hectares have everything from tennis to *pétanque* courts, outdoor skating to baseball fields. Bordering the Village in the south and directly in the middle of the quarter, the park draws people from all over the city no matter the season.

The houses that border the park might look fancy, but most of them, and indeed most of the buildings in the city, don't have gardens, so Montréalers flock, or more precisely, bike to the green space to picnic with friends, catch a performance at the outdoor theater, jog along its shaded path, or come simply to be outdoors.

Old maps of the park have suggested that it was once used as a shooting range, but by 1909 the city had turned the land into a public park that looked not unlike the one that exists today. It was named after Louis-Hippolyte Lafontaine, a politician and the first prime minister of the United Province of Canada, whose writings would help lead to the founding of the confederation.

RUE SAINT-DENIS

Btwn. rue Sherbrooke and ave. du Mont-Royal

A few blocks east of the Main is Saint-Denis, a largely Francophone street that traverses virtually the whole north–south length of the island. It is filled with restaurants, independent boutiques, and cafés, and the vibe here is undoubtedly French-Canadian. Hang out in this area for any length of time and you're sure to start to feel the English and French differences.

Though only a few blocks apart, the architectural contrast between Saint-Laurent and Saint-Denis is vast. Where Saint-Laurent's buildings have been informed by immigration and industry, Saint-Denis's remains relatively unchanged and stereotypically Montréal. Limestone buildings with steep, outdoor staircases and peaked roofs make Saint-Denis feel much more residential than Saint-Laurent.

This street is the center for performing arts in the French-language community. You'll find some of the biggest theaters here, including Theatre Rideau Vert and, farther north, the renowned National Theatre School.

Mile End and Petite Italie — Map 6

CHIESA DELLA MADONNA DELLA DIFESA
6800 ave. Henri Julien, 514/277-6522
HOURS: Daily 10 A.M.-6 P.M.
COST: Free

Built in 1919 by Italian immigrants from Molise, in the southern part of Italy, the Madonna della Difesa (Our Lady of Protection) commemorates a miracle said to have occurred in Casacalenda, Italy, at the end of the 19th century. The creation of the church, built in a Romanesque style and in the shape of a Greek cross, was instrumental in centering the Italian community closer to rue Jean-Talon.

The design of the church, a designated national historic site of Canada, was based on drawings by artist Guido Nincheri. It was built by architect R. Montbirant. Inside, the church is decorated with Nincheri's frescoes, one of which features a pre-World War II Benito Mussolini signing the Lateran Accords. The church is central to the Italian community in the area; even those who have moved away return occasionally for mass.

Next door to the church is Dante Park, dedicated to the 14th-century *Divine Comedy* poet. It features a bocce court, where you'll often find groups of older Italian men playing from noon to midnight.

CHURCH OF SAINT-MICHAEL AND SAINT-ANTHONY
5580 rue St-Urbain
HOURS: Daily 10 A.M.-6 P.M.
COST: Free

The most prominent landmark in Mile End, this Byzantine-style Roman Catholic church stands out thanks to its unique architecture. Inspired by Istanbul's Hagia Sophia (though now a mosque, it was originally a Greek Orthodox basilica), architect Aristide Beaugrand-Champagne integrated many different styles, including Roman and Gothic elements into the design and topping it off with a dome and a minaret-style tower typical of Islamic mosques.

Steps lead up to the front door, and inside the dome is decorated with a Guido Nincheri fresco, depicting St-Michael watching the fall of the angels.

Built in 1915 for the large Irish Catholic population, it was originally called Saint-Michael's; by the mid-1960s, however, the Mile End's Polish population had grown so large that it merged with the existing congregation and Saint-Anthony was added to the name to mark this change. Today, the church is mainly frequented by the area's Polish, Italian, and Greek community, and services are given in a number of languages. Standing on the corner of St-Urbain and St-Viateur streets, it's commonly, though incorrectly, called St-Viateur church by the locals.

◖ MARCHÉ JEAN-TALON
7070 ave. Henri Julien, www.marche-jean-talon.com
HOURS: Mon.-Wed. 7 A.M.-6 P.M., Thurs.-Fri.
7 A.M.-8 P.M., Sat. 7 A.M.-6 P.M., Sun. 7 A.M.-5 P.M.
COST: Free

Constructed in the 1930s as a make-work project during the Depression, the market is

fruit stands at Marché Jean-Talon

© SACHA JACKSON

as busy and central nowadays as it was then. Open seven days a week and nearly 365 days a year, this farmers market goes way beyond expectations. Surrounded by a number of permanent stores (among them a fishmonger, two bakeries, a cheese shop, a wine store, and numerous specialty shops), you barely need to do your shopping anywhere else.

It's an ideal place to browse in the summer; you can snack as you pass by the various stands, tasting many of the fruits and vegetables before you buy. If you're looking to sample locally grown produce, pick up some Québec sausage or ice wine, or buy some goat cheese off the back of someone's truck—and trust me it's worth it—this is the place to do it. Come winter the market moves indoors but stays just as busy. At the start of sugaring-off season in early March the crowds are out in droves drinking in the sunshine, listening to a few street performers, and happily eating maple syrup on a stick.

Greater Montréal
Map 7

ÎLE SAINTE-HÉLÈNE AND ÎLE NOTRE-DAME
◖ BIOSPHÈRE

160 chemin Tour-de-Isle, Île Ste-Hélène, 514/283-5000, www.biosphere.ec.gc.ca

HOURS: Nov.-May Tues.-Sun. 10 A.M.-6 P.M., June-Oct. daily 10 A.M.-6 P.M.

COST: $12 adults, $8 student and senior, free 17 and under

Designed by visionary architect R. Buckminster Fuller, this geodesic dome is the most iconic structure left from Expo 67. Fuller was seen as an eccentric for his philosophical approach to design and his views on creating a synergy between the environment and technology, but his works were beyond their time. Because he had successfully built a few geodesic domes across the United States, when he approached the American government in 1963 with his plans for the American Pavilion for the 1967 World's Fair, they immediately responded.

With the invention of the geodesic dome Fuller created the most efficient structure ever, using one-fiftieth of the materials normally used in conventional architecture. This perfect form would become one of the biggest attractions at the fair—a futuristic monorail that originally passed through it also added to its appeal—and is still one of the most breathtaking sights in the city. It was originally covered in thin acrylic panels, but repairs to the structure in 1976 set the whole of the skin ablaze in a matter of minutes. It was never replaced.

Popular with architecture buffs and kids alike, the 20-story-high building remained empty until 1995, when a new structure was built inside the Biosphère that would become an environmental museum of the same name. The only one of its kind in North America, this unique museum, which caters to children, is aimed at raising awareness for environmental issues such as air and water quality, biodiversity, and sustainable

Casino de Montréal glimmers in the middle of the St-Lawrence River.

development. The structure itself uses sustainable energy resources, such as solar panels, wind turbines, and a geothermal heating system.

CASINO DE MONTRÉAL

1 ave. du Casino, Île de Notre-Dame, 514/392-2746, www.casinosduquebec.om

HOURS: Daily 24 hours

COST: Free

If you happen to catch a glimpse of the casino at night, you're in for a treat. Bathed in a golden light it's a sparkly mirage in the St-Lawrence. Housed in the former French and Québec Expo 67 Pavilions, the casino is the largest in Canada, with over 3,000 slot machines and 120 gaming tables.

Modeled after sculpture, the French Pavilion was criticized for its numerous tall fins, accused of being merely tacked on. The Québec Pavilion meanwhile was made of glass, and by night acted as an illuminated display case. Today it is these exact traits that contribute to the casino's impressive exterior. The interior, though, is atypical for a casino and features lots of windows and low ceilings.

If you get tired of the game of chance there are plenty of other things to keep you occupied, including four restaurants, three bars, and a cabaret. The eatery Nuances is the casino's top dining spot and a regular award winner. For a bit of Vegas in Montréal, take in a show at the cabaret with 500 seats and regular musical and dance performances.

MUSÉE STEWART

Vieux Fort, Île Ste-Hélène, 514/861-6701, www.stewart-museum.org

HOURS: May–Oct. daily 10 A.M.–5 P.M., Oct.–May Wed.–Mon. 10 A.M.–5 P.M.

COST: $10 adult, $7 student, children under 7 free

This former garrison belonging to the British Army now serves as a museum dedicated to Canada's past. Built in 1820, the fort is the most important historical military site in Montréal. During the summer months daily military parades are given on the fort's grounds, and in a nod to both French and English heritage, both the Franche de la Marie and Olde 78th Fraser Highlanders are represented.

The collection attempts to draw a picture of the Old and New Worlds by establishing links in technological and societal advances with events in early Canada. Using artifacts like sedans, compasses, traveling ensembles, and baby rattles, the museum also tells us of our ancestors daily lives. Guides in period costume reenact daily life and role-play in order to give a full view of life during that era.

Founded in 1955, the museum recently underwent a major reconstruction, reopening in late 2010.

PARC JEAN-DRAPEAU

Île Ste-Hélène and Île Notre-Dame, 514/872-6120, www.parcjeandrapeau.com

HOURS: Daily 6 A.M.–11 P.M.

COST: Free

Named after the mayor who turned Expo 67 into a reality, Parc Jean-Drapeau consists of two islands, Île Sainte-Hélène and Île Notre-Dame; the second was built using rock excavated to make way for the Montréal Métro.

A green paradise just southeast of the city, it was the site of Expo 67, and though you'll find some relics remaining—like Buckminster Fuller's geodesic dome and the Québec and French Pavilions now Casino de Montréal—most of the pavilions were destroyed in the 1970s to make room for a large basin used for the 1976 Olympics. Today it still exists and is a great place try your hand at rowing, canoeing, and dragon boating. Just beside the Jean-Drapeau Métro station you'll find the Jean-Drapeau Aquatic Complex with an Olympic-size pool and diving board to match. They're open for public swims from May–September. Or, if open water is more your thing the park also has a beach, which includes boat rentals, beach volleyball, and the like. Between all the outdoor sports you'll also find 25 hectares of gardens, originally created for 1980's Floralies Internationales horticultural fair. The grounds were designed by some of the world's best landscape architects and boast

5,000 rose bushes. Not a bad place to stop and smell the flowers.

LA RONDE
22 chemin Macdonald, Île Ste-Hélène, 514/397-2000, www.laronde.com
HOURS: Mid-May–Oct., hours vary
COST: $40 adult (taller than 54 inches), $26 child (shorter than 54 inches), $26 senior, 2-year-olds and under free

Situated on the far eastern tip of Île Sainte Hélène, La Ronde opened as part of Expo 67 and has since grown to become the second-largest amusement park in Canada. Previously owned by the City of Montréal, it was bought by Six Flags in 2001. Though little of the quaint, original park remains, the frontier town of "Fort Edmonton" is still in use and is now the entrance to le Monstre (the Monster), the highest double wooden roller coaster in the world.

Throughout June and August the park plays host to an international fireworks competition with countries from all over the world competing for top spot, as judged by a public jury. Though you don't have to be at the park to see the fireworks—anywhere near the water will do—it's still a nice place to sit on the Ferris wheel as you watch the colorful explosions.

As at most amusement parks, much of the food is overpriced, and though it's close to downtown and easily reached by public transport, there are no food options in the area.

MONT-ROYAL
CHALET DU MONT-ROYAL
1196 chemin Camillien-Houde, 514/872-3911
HOURS: Daily 10:30 A.M.–4 P.M.
COST: Free

Sitting on the top of Mont-Royal and looking out over downtown, this structure was a make-work project during the Depression. Commissioned by then-mayor Camillien Houde, the chalet was inaugurated in 1932 and is decorated with paintings tracing the history of the city. The impressive artworks, along with the chalet's spacious interior and exposed wood beams, make it look more like a vast dining hall than a mountaintop chalet.

A small café serving light refreshments inside the chalet is a nice place to pause with a hot chocolate or a cold drink and take in the view after the long climb to the top.

Just in front of there's the Belvedere Kondiaronk, named after a Huron First Nations chief who signed the Great Peace Treaty. It is the biggest lookout on the mountain, with sweeping views of downtown and beyond. On a clear day, you can see parts of Old Montréal, the bridges that traverse the St-Lawrence, and the mountains southeast of the city, including Mont-Saint-Bruno and Mont-Saint-Grégoire.

CIMETIÈRE MONT-ROYAL
1297 chemin de la Forêt, 514/279-7358, www.mountroyalcem.com
HOURS: Daily 8:30 A.M.–4:30 P.M.
COST: Free

One of the first rural cemeteries in North America, Mont-Royal Cemetery was incorporated in 1847. Though the first burial took place here in 1852, two years before the opening of its Catholic counterpart, Mont-Royal is the smaller of the two, taking up 165 acres of the mountain. In 1901 it became the site of Canada's first crematorium.

Predominantly Protestant, it is the final resting spot of many of the city's English-speaking founding fathers, including John Molson and John Redpath. Other famous Canadians, including hockey player Howie Morenz and author Mordachai Richler, are also buried here. One of the more famous graves is that of Joe Beef—now the namesake of a popular restaurant—otherwise known as Charles McKiernan, who owned a canteen on the port and was known for giving food to the homeless and housing them in his 100-bed dorm. He died in 1889.

Though distinctly different, you can access both Notre-Dame-des-Neiges and Mont-Royal Cemetery through a small path found behind the war monument and marked with two cannons. It's a particularly popular spot for joggers as well as those delving into their family's past.

CIMETIÈRE NOTRE-DAME-DES-NEIGES
4601 chemin de la Côte-des-Neiges, 514/735-1361,
www.cimetierenotredamedesneiges.ca
HOURS: Apr.-Oct. daily 8 A.M.-7 P.M., Nov.-Mar. daily
8 A.M.-5 P.M.
COST: Free

Covering a fair portion of the Mont-Royal
and following the mountain's natural landscape is Notre-Dame-des-Neiges Cemetery,
the biggest in Canada and the third largest
in North America. It is traditionally Catholic
and Francophone, while its smaller counterpart, Mont-Royal Cemetery, is Protestant and
Anglophone. It was founded in 1854, and
more than one million people have been in-
terred here.

Because of its garden-like character, it is a
great place to have a stroll, be it on a hot summer day or on freshly fallen snow. You can
enjoy the flora (it has almost 6,000 trees), the
fauna (squirrels, groundhogs, raccoons, foxes,
and more) and, of course, the quietness of the
dwellers. Among them, you'll come across the
tombs of various prominent Montréalers, from
doomed poet Émile Nelligan to hockey star
Maurice Richard and some of the most important Canadian politicians.

The direction of the main chapel and office
is indicated by the white dots on the ground
from three access points: entrance Côte-des-
Neiges, entrance Decelle (by the university)
and entrance Camillien-Houde (the other side
of Beaver Lake). There you can get maps and
information.

CROIX DU MONT-ROYAL
East side of Parc du Mont-Royal

On the eastern side of the mountain in Parc
du Mont-Royal is a large, illuminated cross.
If you'd forgotten about the city's Catholic
roots, this acts as a pretty good reminder. It's
no coincidence that the cross faces east, either.
It symbolizes the appropriation of the area by
the French-speaking population, who historically, and even today, live in the east.

In December 1642, the city, then Ville-
Marie, a small, fortified settlement on the
banks of the St-Lawrence, experienced what

could've been a disastrous flood. To ward
off disaster, founder Paul de Chomedey de
Maisonneuve and others prayed to the Virgin
Mary, pleading with her to make it stop and
promising to erect a cross in her honor if she intervened. Divine or not, the flood receded and
the settlement was saved. Keeping his word,
de Maisonneuve carried a large wooden cross
from the settlement all the way to the top of
Mont-Royal, where it was erected on January
6, 1643.

In 1924, Sulpician priest Pierre Dupaigne
decided to re-create the cross and designed
one that included an observation platform.
The arms and base of the cross are cut in stone
and illuminated with lightbulbs. The cross
today is illuminated by LED lights that glow
in a range of colors, signifying such events
as the death of the Pope, Saint-Jean-Baptiste
Day (Québec's national holiday), and even
AIDS awareness.

Rising 251 meters above sea level, the cross
is made of 26 tons of steel and is visible from
80 kilometers away.

LAC AUX CASTORS
Chemin Remembrance, 514/849-2002
COST: Free

Near the top of Mont-Royal, you'll find Lac
aux Castors (Beaver Lake), a manmade watering hole perfect for winter skating and summer pedal-boating. Facing the lake is a pavilion
built in 1961 by architects Hazen Size and Guy
Desbarats. It was seen as one of the most innovative buildings in the province. Its zigzagged
roof and glass facade make it a modern-day
landmark, one that stands in stark contrast to
the bucolic surroundings.

Newly revamped, with a fancier cafeteria
and a casual fine-dining restaurant on the second floor, it is no longer just the place where
you rent skates in the winter and boats in the
summer. Though the public is still encouraged to bring their own snacks, the various
food options are a plus, especially if you've just
walked all the way up. The addition of the restaurant also makes Beaver Lake an ideal winter date spot.

☑ PARC DU MONT-ROYAL

From east via Camillien Houde Pkwy., from west via rue Remembrance, access by foot available along ave. du Parc, 514/843-8240, www.lemontroyal.qc.ca
HOURS: Daily 6 A.M.-11 P.M.
COST: Free

Montréal's namesake and an integral part of city life, Mont-Royal rises out of the heart of the metropolis. It was first climbed by French explorer Jacques Cartier, with the help of the Hochelaga First Nations tribe, in 1535. When writing about it to the king of France he referred to it as Mount Royal and the name stuck. Though it was often used as a spot for recreation, it wasn't until 1876, after a mass culling of trees for firewood outraged citizens, that the area was finally designated a park.

Consisting of 200 hectares and 234 meters tall at its highest point, the park was designed by famous American landscape architect Frederick Law Olmsted, who also designed New York's Central Park. Inaugurated on Queen Victoria's birthday, May 24, 1876, with the shot of a cannon, the celebration continued with a parade through the city's streets. In the late 1880s the Mount Royal Funicular Railway carried sightseers to the top and continued to do so until 1920. What was once the site of the old track is now a popular lookout spot—Belvédère Camillien-Houde. Known as "Lovers Lookout," this place is a popular stop for couples, who like to canoodle here once the sun sets. Looking out east over the city it gives a view of both Olympic Stadium and the oil refineries in Anjou—it might not be romantic but it's true.

Crisscrossed by a number of trails, the mountain is frequented by runners, bikers, dogwalkers, and, in winter, cross-country skiers. It's also a popular sledding place, and stacks of hay line the base along avenue du Parc come winter. The Sunday Tam-Tam is a tradition that started in the late 1970s with an African drumming workshop that is still going strong. In the summer the public congregates weekly at the base of the Sir George-Étienne Cartier statue, near avenue du Parc and Duluth, to drum, dance, and generally indulge their inner hippie—pot will be smoked.

☑ ST-JOSEPH'S ORATORY

3800 chemin Queen Mary, 514/733-8211, www.saint-joseph.org
HOURS: Daily 7 A.M.-9 P.M.; tours summer daily and Sept.-Oct. Sat.-Sun. at 10 A.M. and 2 P.M.
COST: Free

Set into the northern slope of Mont-Royal, this Roman Catholic basilica can be seen from various points in the city, though it stands out the most when you catch it from the window of an airplane. The largest church in Canada, it was built by the recently sainted Brother André Bessette, whose healing powers he attributed to St-Joseph.

Frail all his life, Brother André always believed in the healing and aiding power of the saint and soon recommended others to pray to him when they fell ill. Wanting to honor St-Joseph, Brother André began building a small chapel in 1905. It was soon too small for the number of visitors that came, so they started work on a second, larger chapel, which was completed in 1917, and today it is still part of the basilica and is known as the Crypt. Somehow, though, the Crypt was not enough, and in 1924, work on the basilica was officially underway. It was completed over 40 years later in 1967.

Built in the Italian Renaissance style, its dome was modeled on the Duomo in Florence. It's 233 steps from the gates to the doors of St-Joseph's Oratory—shuttles are available for those who are unable to make the journey themselves. As you enter at crypt level you'll find the Votive Chapel, lined with the wooden crutches of those that Brother André healed. The Crypt Church itself features low, arched ceilings and a statue of Joseph instead of a cross over the altar. Above, the basilica is stark compared to most, with the dome rising 195 feet and adorned with stained-glass images depicting events in Canada's religious history in which St-Joseph is thought to have intervened.

Out back you'll find Oratory Gardens, with oversized Stations-of-the-Cross and a lush green surrounding. Brother André's wooden chapel is still on the premises, on the other side of what is now a parking lot, and is open to the public. In 1910 the chapel underwent renovations and a room was added on top that would become Brother André's living quarters; they are today as he left them.

Ninety-minute guided tours are offered in several languages; call for times.

HOCHELAGA-MAISONNEUVE

BIODÔME

4777 ave. Pierre-du-Coubertin, 514/868-3000, www.biodome.qc.ca
HOURS: June-Sept. daily 9 A.M.-6 P.M., Sept.-May daily 9 A.M.-5 P.M.
COST: $16.50 adult, $12.50 senior and student, $8.25 child 5-17, $2.50 child 2-4

Part of the former Olympic complex, the Montréal Biodôme is housed in the old velodrome, where cycling and judo events took place in 1976.

Designed by French architect Roger Taillibert, who designed the entire plan for the massive Olympic park, from above the shape is reminiscent of a stingray with its flat, aerodynamic shape.

Opened in 1992, it re-creates four ecosystems found in the Americas: the tropical and Laurentian forests, the St-Lawrence marine system, and the polar regions of the Arctic and Antarctic. In these re-created environments the animals live in partial freedom, adding a dimension of reality that you don't always find in a zoo. The ecosystems also blend into one another so that you slowly migrate from one area to the next—from the hottest to the coldest—as you explore the ecosystems. The Laurentian forest, in particular, is worth visiting as it represents the diverse vegetation and wildlife that surrounds Montréal. Unlike the other ecosystems it also changes with the seasons.

INSECTARIUM DE MONTRÉAL

4581 rue Sherbrooke E., 514/872-1400, www.ville.montreal.qc.ca/insectarium
HOURS: Nov.-May 14 Tues.-Sun. 9 A.M.-5 P.M., May 15-Sept. 9 daily 9 A.M.-6 P.M., Sept. 10-Oct. 31 daily 9 A.M.-9 P.M.
COST: $14 adult, $10.50 senior and student, $7 child 5-17, $2 child 2-4

Founded by retired notary, George Brossard,

the insectarium has a unique history. Obsessed with insects even as a child, Brossard studied law, eventually working as a notary, making a decent living and retiring in his late 30s in order to travel the world as an insect hunter. Before the museum existed the majority of the collection was housed in Brossard's basement.

Established in 1990, directly inside the city's Jardin Botanique (Botanical Garden), it is the largest insectarium in North America and among the largest in the world. Appealing to a certain kind of kid who's enthralled by, instead of creeped out by, creepy-crawlies, the collection features both live and mounted insects. Observe a live insect community in the Busy Bodies exhibit, and go inside the nests of ants, bees, and termites. Bugs from Africa; Australia; North, South, and Central America; and Asia, including spiders, walking sticks, and beetles can be observed in the Live Collection room, and a number of butterflies are displayed among the Mounted Collection. Entrance to the Jardin Botanique is free with the ticket to the Insectarium.

◖ JARDIN BOTANIQUE

4101 rue Sherbrooke E., 514/872-1400, www.ville.montreal.qc.ca/jardin
HOURS: Nov.-May Tues.-Sun. 9 A.M.-5 P.M., May 15-Sept. 9 daily 9 A.M.-6 P.M., Sept. 10-Oct. 31 daily 9 A.M.-9 P.M.
COST: $14 adult, $10.50 senior and student, $7 child 5-17, $2 child 2-4, free admission to the outdoor gardens Nov. 1-May 14

Facing Montréal's Olympic Park is the Jardin Botanique, 185 acres of outdoor gardens. Founded in 1931, at the height of the Great Depression, by Mayor Camillien Houde, it was the brainchild of Brother Marie-Victorin, a De La Salle brother and noted botanist who established the Botanical Institute at the Université de Montréal in 1920—he's also a relative of writer Jack Kerouac and was born Conrad Kirouack. After years of tirelessly campaigning, Marie-Victorin got his garden and Houde used out-of-work Montréalers to make the garden a reality. Designed by Henry Teuscher, a Berlin-born landscape architect and horticulturalist, it consists of 30 thematic gardens and 10 exhibition greenhouses. Its goal is to educate the general public as well as students of horticulture and to conserve endangered plant species. To aid in the education of the public the outdoor parks are free for Quebec residents and to anyone at all between six in the evening and nightfall from May to September.

Though all the gardens are worth a visit, the most popular are the Chinese and Japanese gardens, both of which were designed by architects from their respective countries. In the case of China, pieces used in the garden were even shipped over and carefully reassembled.

STADE OLYMPIQUE
4141 ave. Pierre-du-Coubertin, 514/252-4737, www.rio.gouv.qc.ca
HOURS: Nov.-May Tues.-Sun. 9 A.M.-5 P.M., May 15-Sept. 9 daily 9 A.M.-6 P.M., Sept. 10-Oct. 31 daily 9 A.M.-9 P.M.
COST: $8 adult, $16 senior and student, $4 child 5-17, free child 2-4

Built as the main stadium for the 1976 Olympics, it hosted both the opening and closing ceremonies as well as equestrian and athletic events. The structure, designed by French architect Roger Taillibert, is one of the most impressive sights in the city and considered one of the best examples of organic architecture in the world. As impressive as it is, however, it doesn't quite erase the fact that its construction put the city into some serious debt.

With its saucer-like shape and swooping roof, the stadium is a looming reminder of the problems that plagued its construction and the debt the city incurred in the process. Its nickname, The Big O, refers not only to the stadium's doughnut-like shape but also to the amount of money it cost the city. In fact, the city didn't pay off its stadium debt until 2006, but even that didn't stop people from referring to it as The Big Owe.

The former home of the much-missed Montréal Expos baseball team, the stadium now stands mainly empty, hosting the occasional concert or sporting event when they city's smaller stadiums cannot accommodate the crowds. On the cheerier side, the aquatic pavilion is still in use and has regular free swims; check the website for times. Guided tours of the stadium are also available.

TOUR OLYMPIQUE
4141 ave. Pierre-du-Coubertin, 514/252-4737, www.rio.gouv.qc.ca
HOURS: June-Sept. daily 9 A.M.-7 P.M., Sept.-mid-June daily 9 A.M.-5 P.M. (closed Jan.-Feb.)
COST: $15 adult, $11.25 senior and student, $7.50 child 5-17, free child 2-4

The Olympic tower with its moving funicular and observation deck didn't open until 1987, 11 years after the Olympic Games. At the time the malfunctioning only added to the city's Olympic hangover, but today it's a unique way to see the city. Built at a 45-degree angle, the tower is 175 meters high and accessible only by a two-level funicular that rides the rails to the top at 2.8 meters per second and works using hydraulics. Once you get to the top, you enter the observatory, the exhibition hall, and the reception hall, which occupied the three upper floors of the Tower. The view from the observation deck is unique, offering a near-panoramic view of the city and its surroundings; on a clear day you can see as far as 80 kilometers away, even catching sight of the Laurentians.

Though the stadium and tower are connected, they operate as separate entities, which means admission to one won't get you into the other.

LACHINE CANAL
MARCHÉ ATWATER
138 rue Atwater, www.marche-atwater.com
HOURS: Mon.-Wed. 7 A.M.-6 P.M., Thurs.-Fri. 7 A.M.-8 P.M., Sat.-Sun. 7 A.M.-5 P.M.
COST: Free

A public market since it opened in 1933, the art deco building designed by Ludger Lemieux is one of the most striking in the area. Located on the Lachine canal, the two-floored market is home to butchers, general-food stores, and fresh produce stalls that migrate outside during the summer. Though it has long been the community's home for daily staples, it's also been the site of social and sporting events, including wrestling, as well as political speeches. Mayor Camillien Houde and Québec premier Maurice Duplessis both spoke here to roaring crowds. In fact, a large room on the second floor, which seats up to 1,000 people, can still be rented.

RESTAURANTS

Montréal is full of culinary delights, with more ethnic and rough-and-tumble options than Québec City. Strong ties to French cuisine remain, so many eateries offer a table d'hôte, and a café is a place where you can drink your espresso standing up or sit down with a café au lait and a bite to eat.

Boundaries are blurred between café, bar, and restaurant with most places serving all three functions, depending on the time of day. Most cafés follow the French model and serve breakfast, lunch, and dinner, so don't be surprised if you find a place that makes a great cappuccino and croissant in the morning and duck confit at night. Liquor licensing can be bizarre in the city; some restaurants serve full meals but not alcohol, while other places can only serve alcohol as a long as it's accompanied by a snack, like nachos or nuts. Many restaurants also have a bring-your-own policy, which allows diners to bring their own store-bought vintage to the table.

Ethnic food is available throughout the city and is often your best late-night bet—that or fast food. Some areas are obviously ethnic, like Little Italy (Petite Italie) and Chinatown, but a Koreatown and a second Chinatown are growing in the western part of downtown. The best Indian and Pakistani food can be found in Park-Ex, west of Little Italy, while Greek is a Mile End staple. Some ethnic food, though, can be hard to find; good Mexican and Japanese options are few and far between, and don't go looking for a cheap but decent slice of pizza or staples like chicken wings for that matter. You might never find them.

HIGHLIGHTS

LOOK FOR ◖ TO FIND RECOMMENDED RESTAURANTS.

◖ **Best Japanese:** Stepping into **Kazu,** a downtown *izakaya,* is like stepping into a tiny back-alley eatery in Shibuya, complete with soju cocktails and cramped seating (page 88).

◖ **Most Worthwhile Splurge:** Classy without being stuffy, **Joe Beef**'s rustic cuisine and fresh oysters make this one of the best places to empty your wallet (page 89).

◖ **Best Deli:** Schwartz's is the oldest deli in Canada, and their smoked meat and fries are the stuff of legend (page 95).

◖ **Best Late-Night Eats:** After a night of dancing nothing recharges you like a *poutine* from **La Banquise** (page 99).

◖ **Coziest Dinner Spot:** Grab a seat at the bar, knock back a special cocktail, and let the folks at **Le Chien Fumant** make you a good home-cooked-style meal (page 100).

◖ **Best Nouveau Québécois:** Chef Martin Picard's **Au Pied du Cochon** has almost single-handedly changed the entire culinary landscape of the city (page 100).

◖ **Best Place to Eat Healthy:** The chapatis and vegan butter at **Aux Vivres** are out of this world; nothing here sacrifices taste (page 102).

◖ **Best Neighborhood Café:** Do like the locals do: Get a paper and get in line for the city's best espresso at **Café Olimpico** (page 105).

◖ **Best Brunch:** The line at **Lawrence** starts even before the doors open, but it is one of the most satisfying and hearty weekend brunches in the city (page 106).

© TOURISM MONTTRÉAL/PIERRE-LUC DUFOUR

the smoked meat sandwich at Schwartz's, the oldest deli in Canada

◖ **Most Distinct Setting:** Literally a diner in a corner store, **Dépanneur le Pick-Up** will change the way you feel about pulled-pork sandwiches, which are also available in a vegetarian option (page 107).

◖ **Best Sandwich:** The timeless and iconic **Wilensky's Light Lunch** is the only place to get a hand-mixed soda pop along with their signature double-grilled salami and bologna sandwich with mustard (page 107).

RESTAURANTS

RESTAURANTS

PRICE KEY

$ Entrées less than CAN$10

$$ Entrées CAN$10-20

$$$ Entrées more than CAN$20

What Montréal does do well, however, is rustic Québécois-influenced fare in an exciting, boisterous atmosphere. There is a real emphasis on fresh in the city, and though it can sometimes translate to higher prices, it's worth it. At times it seems Montréal suffers from a lack of good midrange restaurants, but that's not exactly true. Many neighborhood bistros—or bars for that matter—offer delicious and affordable meals that are likely to exceed your expectations.

Though menus are often written in French, they are usually accompanied by an English translation, and if there's something that needs clarifying servers will gladly translate anything on the menu. Keep in mind that although you might originally be greeted by the waitstaff in French, it is perfectly fine, and normal, to switch to English. If you're comfortable, adding a French word here or there, like *merci,* is always welcomed.

Many restaurants are closed earlier in the week, on Mondays and/or Tuesdays. Diners start late, especially later in the week or on weekends; it's not unusual to sit down to a meal at 10 o'clock at night. In fact, some restaurants keep their kitchen open past midnight. There's no smoking in restaurants or cafés, though it is fair game if you are sitting on an outdoor terrace.

The food choice is Montréal is expansive, and as you get to know the city you'll recognize a few of its own chain restaurants, as well as international ones, but the real culinary wizardry is found in the neighborhood bistros. Take a chance on smaller, intimate eateries; you won't be disappointed.

Vieux-Montréal   Map 1

CAFÉS
BENIAMINO MARKET $$
32 rue McGill, 514/284-1711
HOURS: Mon.-Fri. 7:30 A.M.-11 P.M.,
Sat.-Sun. 10 A.M.-9 P.M.

Fresh Italian fare is this café's specialty. Choose from a selection of fresh antipastos, satisfyingly huge sandwiches with fillings like prosciutto and fig or hot selections like meatballs, scaloppini, and eggplant parmesan. Chic, minimal decor is accented by shelves full of foodstuffs from hard-to-find Italian and European brands. It's packed with office workers during the week, and there are always a few regulars sipping espressos and chatting with staff, no matter when you go. Don't be surprised if they boast about their cappuccino while you order. If you're in the mood, take them up on the offer and judge for yourself.

CAFÉ TITANIC $$
445 rue St-Pierre, 514/849-0894,
www.titanicmontreal.ca
HOURS: Mon.-Fri. 8 A.M.-4:30 P.M.

Once you step foot into this bustling café filled with dark wood, exposed brick walls, and upcycled metro chairs, you'll be hungry if you weren't already. Serving the 9–5 crowd, it's especially busy between noon and 1:30 P.M. Go later to avoid the hubbub and enjoy your lunch in a more laid-back atmosphere. True to its name, the sandwiches are "titanic," so bring your appetite or a friend. They're on view in a huge, open display case; you can choose from a lineup of rich but satisfying flavors. "Bacon Butty," anyone? For something lighter, try the soup of the day, often served with a crispy oil-drenched baguette. Coffee here is some of the best in the area and always elegantly served. Treat yourself to a slice of decadent-but-worth-it carrot cake.

MONTRÉAL TAKEOUT

On warm summer nights there's nothing better than eating alfresco. But dining outdoors doesn't mean you have wait in line at the hottest restaurant hoping to nab a table on the cramped, sidewalk terrace. In Montréal, smart diners take their meal to go. The reason? Parks.

The city is full of large, beautiful parks just begging for you to spread out a checkered tablecloth, pop open a bottle of white, and chow down. As soon as the warm winds begin to blow, picnicking becomes its very own pastime, with diners covering the city parks. City bylaws allow alcohol, as long as it is enjoyed as part of a bona fide picnic (once the food is gone be sure to put the alcohol away to avoid getting stung with a ticket), so other than the table service you sacrifice nothing. Packing your own picnic, even if it's as simple as a baguette, a roast chicken, and a bottle of your favorite wine, is a great, affordable way to enjoy an evening.

LE CARTET $$
106 rue McGill, 514/871-8887
HOURS: Mon.-Fri. 7 A.M.-7 P.M., Sat. 9 A.M.-4 P.M.

This open-concept dining hall offers a great selection of hot (grilled salmon, seafood lasagna) or cold (salade niçoise, salmon tartare, grilled chicken sandwiches) lunches. Take-out or eat in at one of their long, inviting communal tables. The ambience is one of urgency and fever pitch during the week, when business deals are going down and office workers come to get their needed morning coffee. The weekend crowd is much more diverse, with locals and family and friends meeting up before an afternoon in Vieux-Montréal. Since many places in the neighborhood are closed on weekends, the popular brunch features mimosas and dishes like the hearty country breakfast, which comes in a skillet. The walls are lined with local and international

fine foods, making it a perfect spot to grab a gift for your favorite foodie. If you like your coffee with a bit of kick, however, make sure to ask for a double shot.

OLIVE & GOURMANDO $$
351 rue St-Paul W., 514/350-1083,
www.oliveetgourmando.com
HOURS: Tues.-Sat. 8 A.M.-6 P.M.

To enter Olive & Gourmando is to enter a lunchtime institution. From the fresh-from-the-oven bread to the array of mouthwatering goodies (the Valhorna chocolate brioche is divine) that greet you at the front counter, this place has the title of best lunch in Old Montréal on lockdown. It was started by two former chefs from Toqué!, and the atmosphere is casual but chic, with heavy wood tables, comfy seats with leather accents, and deep red walls. The dining room is always packed with tourists, office workers, and locals. In fact, on weekdays just getting takeout can be chaotic—but the food is worth the wait. With many of the dishes incorporating vegan and organic ingredients, you know exactly what you're getting in your grain-fed chicken sandwich.

COMFORT FOOD
BRIT AND CHIPS $$
433 rue McGill, 514/840-1001,
www.britandchips.com
HOURS: Mon.-Sat. 8 A.M.-11 P.M.

With its old-school stools, blackboard menu, and white-shirted, bow-tied staff, Brit and Chips oozes the charm of a lost era. This tiny neighborhood chip shop, which has only six tables and counter space for about 20, serves five different kinds of fish, everything from cod to salmon, as well as English staples like steak and kidney pie and Scotch eggs. This is comfort food at its most authentic. Takeout is wrapped in newspaper-print wax paper, and no matter the hour of the day, you'll find construction and office workers alike chowing down on the fries and fish straight from the fryer. Of course they also have salads, but really what's the point?

RESTAURANTS

SOUPESOUP ❸

649 rue Wellington, 514/759-1159,
www.soupesoup.com

HOURS: Mon.-Fri. 11 A.M.-4 P.M., Sat.-Sun. 11 A.M.-4 P.M.

A few steps up into this dining room just off McGill you'll find an open-concept space decorated with simple wooden tables, old movie posters, and chairs reminiscent of your high school cafeteria. This Montréal-based chain now has six establishments around the city, but for a simple, cost-effective lunch in Old Montréal you can't do better than a hearty soup (especially come mid-January). Eat-in or take-out, the menu changes daily and offers a variety of seasonal soups, salads, and sandwiches. Those with a smaller appetite take note: A single order of soup is served with a generous slice of bread.

FRENCH
BORIS BISTRO ❸❸❸

465 rue McGill, 514/848-7595,
www.borisbistro.com

HOURS: Mon.-Fri. 11:30 A.M.-11 P.M., Sat.-Sun. noon-11 P.M.

Housed in a nondescript office building—through whose foyer you walk to access the restaurant and the bathroom—the setting isn't ideal. But come the warmer months (mid-May–mid-October) the outdoor terrace is a great place for alfresco dining. Wood tables, bistro chairs, and beige umbrellas give the restaurant (partially hidden behind the ruins of an old storefront) a relaxed elegance. Weekdays the place is packed with diners on a business lunch, but it calms down on weekends and is the perfect place to bring a large group—though those under 18 aren't allowed on the terrace after 8 P.M. Classic French dishes like duck *magret,* beef tartare, and shoestring fries are a good bet, and the vibe, even inside on a cold winter day, is always lively.

LE CLUB CHASSE ET PÊCHE ❸❸❸

423 rue St-Claude, 514/861-1112,
www.leclubchasseetpeche.com

HOURS: Mon.-Fri. 11:30 A.M.-2:30 P.M.,
Tues.-Sat. 6-10:30 P.M.

Set on an unassuming side street in Old Montréal with its rounded and tiled doorway, Le Club Chasse et Pêche looks more like a forgotten Portuguese diner than one of the best restaurants in the city. All that changes, however, when you enter its warm, cavernous, and clubby interior with quasi-famous animal-inspired lighting fixtures by Antoine Laverdière. Attracting young professionals and foodies into a splurge, the ambience is decidedly grown up and sophisticated with a boys' club edge. The menu changes weekly but there are a few constants, such as scallops and risotto (though the manner in which they're prepared never stays the same).

JARDIN NELSON ❸❸❸

407 Place Jacques-Cartier, 514/861-5731,
www.jardinnelson.com

HOURS: May-Canadian Thanksgiving Mon.-Fri. 11:30 A.M.-10 P.M., Sat.-Sun. 10 A.M.-11 P.M.

Conveniently located on Place Jacques-Cartier in a historic building that dates back to 1812, this seasonal restaurant's real gem is its courtyard. Enormous parasols save diners from the occasional rain shower and, along with the overflowing gardens and nightly live jazz, heighten the restaurant's intimate atmosphere. The menu offers everything from crêpes to pizzas, osso bucco to salmon lasagna, but the ambience and surroundings remain the real draw.

INDIAN
GANDHI ❸❸❸

230 rue St-Paul W., 514/845-5866,
www.restaurantgandhi.com

HOURS: Mon.-Fri. noon-2 P.M., daily 5:30-10:30 P.M.

There's a refinement to these classic Indian dishes that makes you wonder whether there's a little French mixed in with the curry powder. Traditional Far East fare is the restaurant's specialty. Tandoori chicken, lamb tikka, and the homemade chutney are particular stand-outs. Quiet and relaxed, Gandhi is perfect for couples craving a romantic Indian meal. Carved Hindu statues reveal themselves throughout the restaurant, but there's nothing kitschy here, just bistro-style seating, lots of natural light, and white, sparsely decorated walls. Gandhi gives off an air of easy comfort.

ITALIAN
DNA ⑤⑤⑤
355 rue Marguerite D'Youville, 514/287-3362, www.dnarestaurant.com
HOURS: Tues.-Fri. 11:30 A.M.-2:30 P.M., Tues.-Sat. 6-10:30 P.M.

Having worked as chef de cuisine at Jamie Oliver's restaurant Fifteen in London, Chef Derek Dammann returned to Canada to open DNA with sommelier Alex Cruz. Hip and young—both Dammann and Cruz are in their early 30s—the restaurant has an effortlessly cool vibe. In a nod to this youthful irreverence, the seats in the lounge are covered in basketball material. The restaurant is situated on the ground floor of a historic building overlooking the Old Port. Part lounge, part restaurant, the two halves of DNA have their own distinct personalities, cleverly divided by a shimmery, see-through wall. Using fresh and local products, Dammann's menu is constantly evolving though the Italian-influence remains. Even those on a budget can partake in this foodie's dream: A weekday table d'hôte lunch will set you back a mere $20 before tax and tip.

GRAZIELLA ⑤⑤⑤
116 rue McGill, 514/876-0116, www.restaurantgraziella.ca
HOURS: Mon.-Fri. noon-2:30 P.M., Mon.-Sat. 6-10 P.M.

Chef and owner Graziella Baptista creates memorable northern Italian dishes in her namesake restaurant on the west extremity of Old Montréal. Simple, honest, and prepared to perfection, the house specialties include the osso bucco, red wine risotto, and the (totally potato-free) gnocchi. The dining room itself is light-filled and airy with modern minimalist decor, appealing to mature diners and those looking for a quiet, refined meal Keep an eye on your spending and skip dinner in favor of the reasonably priced lunchtime table d'hôte. But no matter when you dine, cap the meal off with what might be the best cannoli in the city.

POLISH
STASH CAFÉ ⑤⑤
200 rue St-Paul W., 514/845-6611, www.stashcafe.com
HOURS: Mon.-Fri. 11:30 A.M.-11 P.M., Sat. noon-11 P.M.

If it's stick-to-your-ribs comfort food you're after, look no further than Stash Café. Since opening over 30 years ago, it's become a veritable Montréal institution and the only place to get your fill of borscht, pierogies, and *wódka*. For those unfamiliar with Polish cooking there's the "primer," a table d'hôte menu that'll introduce you to the basics of the hearty cuisine. The exposed stone walls, bench seating, Polish theater posters, and live pianist give the space a homey feel—the perfect setting for filling up on a cold winter night.

QUÉBÉCOIS
TOQUÉ! ⑤⑤⑤
900 Place Jean-Paul-Riopelle, 514/499-2084, www.restaurant-toque.com
HOURS: Tues.-Fri. 11:30 A.M.-2 P.M., Tues.-Sat. 5:30-10:30 P.M.

Since opening in 1993, Normand Laprise's Toqué! has almost single-handedly changed the culinary landscape of Montréal. Known around the globe for his use of Québécois ingredients, partnerships with local producers, and boundary-pushing creations, Laprise's restaurant should not be missed if you're a fool for new culinary experiences. The menu includes such notable dishes as pork shoulder with black pudding, foie gras with wild mushrooms, and beet mousse with caramel sorbet.

It's situated on the cusp of Old Montréal and the Quartier International, and the subtle and minimalist decor only adds to the overall sophistication of the atmosphere. The website may note attire as casual but ignore it; if you rarely get the chance to dress up, this is your opportunity. Reservations are a must.

SEAFOOD
GARDE MANGER ⑤⑤⑤
408 rue St-Francis-Xavier, 514/678-5044
HOURS: Tues.-Sun. 6 P.M.-3 A.M.

A former sailor's bar, this restaurant/hotspot/makeshift nightclub retains its working-class charm with manly, shabby-chic decor and a rough-and-tumble menu that includes such culinary classics as the fried Mars bar. Since opening in 2006, it has maintained its reputation as one of the wildest restaurants in the city—so no matter when you go, expect a rowdy crowd and come expecting to join them. Reservations are a must, and so is a stab at the seafood platter, if you can convince your dining companions over the raucous crowd.

MUVBOX $

Place du Génie, www.muvboxconcept.com
HOURS: May–Oct. daily 11:30 A.M.–9 P.M. weather permitting
Muvbox brings new meaning to the word snack cart. This ex-shipping container transforms into a solar-powered seasonal restaurant complete with seating, counter space, and a stone oven with the flip of a switch. It's a sight to behold and would be worth checking out even if they didn't serve some of the best lobster pizza and lobster rolls you've likely ever tasted. Everyone flocks here, from office workers to tourists, and its location next to the water gives it an easy, breezy vibe. Local artists Seripop were commissioned to design the outside of the container, which means Muvbox is eye-catching even when it's closed up.

STEAKHOUSE
GIBBY'S $$$

298 Place d'Youville, 514/282-1837, www.gibbys.com
HOURS: Mon.-Fri. 5:30-10 P.M., Sat.-Sun. 5-10:30 P.M.
Located in the Youville Stables, which once belonged to the Sisters of Charity, the setting for this classic Montréal steakhouse dates back to 1740. Stone walls, original beamed ceilings, and numerous fireplaces are dotted throughout the six separate dining rooms, which include a cocktail lounge and a secluded outdoor courtyard. If your preference is for surf, not turf, they've also got an excellent seafood selection. And though the steak is said to be the best in the city, their prices, reminiscent of expense-account heydays, tend to keep more discerning diners away. There is something about the atmosphere that makes it particularly attractive for special family get-togethers—it's a popular wedding spot—and romantic dinners. Chalk it up to the cozy fireplace classic fine-dining service.

Centre-Ville   Map 2

AMERICAN
DUNN'S FAMOUS DELI $$

1249 rue Metcalfe, 514/395-1927, www.dunnsfamous.com
HOURS: Daily 24 hours
Opened in 1927, Dunn's is a Montréal staple. The long narrow dining hall, banquette seating, and wood ceiling beams give the place the feel of an old ski chalet—confusing for a smoked meat joint. Open 24 hours, seven days a week, this is a late-night or early-morning staple. A favorite with downtown shoppers, pre- or post-movie diners, and those just leaving the bars, Dunn's has a no-nonsense staff; they can be a little short at times. The deli counter selections offer a great choice of classic deli fare, and you can't go wrong with any one of their five club sandwiches.

LE GOURMET BURGER $

1433B rue Bishop, 514/435-3535, www.legourmetburger.com
HOURS: Daily 11 A.M.–1 A.M.
Perfect for a quick pit stop, this burger joint lets you build your own from the patty up, with freshly baked bread, organic herbs and spices, and homemade sauces like wasabi mayo. Everything is grilled on wood charcoal. Toppings range from coleslaw to pickled beets and truffle oil, and they make a mean, juicy veggie burger and old-fashioned floats. Despite the all-American toppings, the place itself feels a little antiseptic with white walls and modern bright-green chairs at odds with the meaty menu. A popular student hangout—it's right next to Concordia University—it's a great place to grab a bite before or after the bar.

M:BRGR $$

2023 rue Drummond, 514/906-2747, www.mbrgr.com
HOURS: Mon.-Thurs. 11:30 A.M.–11 P.M., Fri.-Sat. 11:30 A.M.–midnight, Sun. noon–9 P.M.
Past meets present at this gourmet burger restaurant with sleek banquettes running along a backdrop of old sepia photos of Montréal.

GIBEAU ORANGE JULEP

For Montréalers there's nothing quite like the Orange Julep (7700 Décarie, 514/738-7486, daily 24 hours, hours limited in winter), a huge, two-story orange ball that sits near the Décarie highway and serves classic fast food. You can't go wrong with the standard club sandwich, as well as the world-famous orange drink. It was started in 1932 by Hermas Gibeau, and he constructed the orange itself in 1945. Rumor has it he wanted to move both his business and his family into it (who wouldn't want to grow up in a giant ball?). A symbol to many Montréalers, it draws the curious and long-time residents. Open 24 hours in the summer, there's no better place to grab a late-night bite.

Created by Moishes, an upscale steakhouse, M:brgr is its cosmopolitan offspring. Choose from a list of truly gourmet burgers—Kobe beef, tuna—and keep piling on the gourmet with toppings like smoked gouda, grilled asparagus, caramelized onions, and foie gras. Hamburgers are the focus but they also have gourmet mac 'n' cheese, Michigan hot dogs, and an assortment of salads. Despite the messy nature of the food, however, diners here usually come dressed to be seen, and the music can sometimes make you feel as though you're dining in a club.

MCKIERNAN ⓢⓢ
2485 rue Notre-Dame W., 514/759-667, www.joebeef.ca
HOURS: Tues.-Fri. 11:30 A.M.-3 P.M., Sat. 11 A.M.-3 P.M., Wed.-Sat. 6:30 P.M.-close

This luncheonette and wine bar is Joe Beef's pint-sized little brother. With only 12 seats the place is perfect for a quick lunch; it attracts the 9–5ers and after-work crowd. There's an emphasis on finger food, like smoked oysters on toast, and sandwiches. The chicken tikka is out of this world, but there are also daily specials as well as wine, available by the glass or bottle and stacked casually in crates. They also serve a mean chowder, and a great brunch on Saturdays. If you're planning on visiting during a weekday evening, call ahead; hours vary.

BREAKFAST
GRIFFINTOWN CAFÉ ⓢ
1378 rue Notre-Dame W., 514/931-5399, www.griffintowncafe.com
HOURS: Tues.-Fri. 11:30 A.M.-10 P.M., Sat. 10 A.M.-10 P.M., Sun. 10 A.M.-3 P.M.

Serving lunch, brunch, and dinner, and with live music Tuesday through Saturday evenings, the Griffintown Café attracts families, artists, and music lovers. Situated on a newly revitalized strip of Notre-Dame West, this is a great place for the first meal of the day since they offer an eclectic brunch selection that includes mac 'n' cheese, crab cakes, and a breakfast burger with a beef, duck, and lamb patty topped with a fried egg and aged cheddar.

CAFÉS
CAFÉ MYRIADE ⓢ
1432 rue Mackay, 514/939-1717, www.cafemyriade.com
HOURS: Mon.-Fri. 8 A.M.-8 P.M., Sat. 9 A.M.-8 P.M., Sun. 10 A.M.-6 P.M.

Coffee lovers take note: This is without doubt the best coffee you'll find in downtown Montréal. Serving blends from Canada's top roaster, 49th Parallel, and using a Mirage coffee maker—the only one of its kind in Canada—they take their coffee seriously, but in taste, not pretension. The decor too is well thought out, with lots of wood and large, open windows letting in a ton of light, which is needed in the winter months. During the summer there's a small terrace out front. The vibe is friendly and the baristas eager to please. As it's surrounded by Concordia University, expect to find yourself among students during the school year.

CAFÉ NESPRESSO ⓢ
2045 rue Crescent, 514/939-1717, www.nespresso.com
HOURS: Mon.-Wed. 9 A.M.-6:30 P.M., Thurs.-Fri. 9 A.M.-9 P.M., Sat. 9 A.M.-6 P.M., Sun. 10 A.M.-5 P.M.

Sleek and modern, this two-floor café and store

RESTAURANTS

is the only place in Montréal to relax with a cup of one of Nespresso's premium blends or pick up a supply of their coffee pods. Barely half a block from the Musée des Beaux Arts, it attracts a mature, adult crowd. This is not the kind of place where children run around, and the atmosphere can be a bit cold at times. If you're familiar with the brand, however, you'll know what you're getting here—perfectly delicious coffee in an upscale surrounding.

CHINESE
QING HUA DUMPLING ❸
1676 ave. Lincoln, 438/288-5366
HOURS: Daily 11 A.M.-11 P.M.

People from the Asian community and Chinese food fans in general have been raving about this hole-in-the-wall ever since its doors opened. Situated on small street—south of rue Sherbrooke and north of boulevard de Maisonneuve—this Chinese eatery whose main decorative element is a window into the kitchen—is worth seeking out, especially if you're in the mood for a mind-altering meal. With the restaurant's owner hailing from the port city of Dalian, known for its dumplings, you know you're getting the real goods when you step inside this unassuming restaurant. They're fried or boiled and stuffed with just about any combination you can imagine—the classic pork and cabbage ones are still some of the best.

FRENCH
LE PARIS ❸❸❸
1812 rue Ste-Catherine W., 514/842-7128
HOURS: Mon.-Thurs. noon-3 P.M. and 5:30-10:30 P.M., Fri.-Sat. noon-3 P.M. and 5:30-11 P.M., Sun. 5:30-10:30 P.M.

Open since 1956, this French bistro in the middle of downtown Montréal has changed little over the years, while the surrounding area has changed a lot. With its striped white and burgundy awning and simple, cursive sign, Le Paris is a bit of old world charm in the center of a modern city. The red banquettes and simple decor only add to the pleasure of the food, which includes classics like beef bourguignon and *poule au pot* (chicken in a pot). Many of

the clientele are older French patrons, so you know this place serves great French food and has been doing it for years.

ITALIAN
LIVERPOOL HOUSE ❸❸❸
2501 rue Notre-Dame W., 514/313-6049, www.liverpoolhouse.ca
HOURS: Tues.-Sat. 6:30 P.M.-close

The only thing that marks the spot at this restaurant, which forgoes a sign, is a large, glowing L. This unaffected atmosphere is reflected inside with original moldings, antique hooks on which to hang your coat, and old brass lighting fixtures. The second venture by the people who brought us Joe Beef, Liverpool House, despite the name, serves a good amount of Italian fare, like veal scaloppini and traditional pasta dishes.

JAPANESE
❰ KAZU ❸❸
1862 rue Ste-Catherine W., 514/937-2333
HOURS: Daily noon-3 P.M. and 5:30-9:30 P.M.

Montréalers are virtually starving for authentic Japanese food, so when this place popped up in 2010 it was no surprise to learn it was an automatic hit. Anyone who has eaten in an authentic Japanese *izakaya*—or visited a reasonable facsimile—knows there's nothing quite like it. From the hurried pace of the staff to the cold beers and hamburger patty, Kazu is a little slice of Japan in the heart of Montréal, and that includes the limited seating. Because it has only three tables and a handful of stools, you may be forced to wait in line, along with a sizable portion of the city's Japanese population, before sitting down and digging into your 48-hour pork and ramen bowl.

LEBANESE
BOUSTAN ❸
2020 rue Crescent, 514/843-3576, www.boustan.ca
HOURS: Daily 11 A.M.-4 A.M.

There are a lot, and I mean *a lot* of Lebanese restaurants in Montréal, but nothing comes close to Boustan, smack-dab in the center of downtown barely a block from Concordia

University and on the main clubbing strip. You'll find everyone from students to office workers and late-night revelers stopping into this fluorescently lit, three-table fast-food counter. The stand-bys like falafel, shawarma, and shish kebabs are all tasty as the next; even the vegetarian pita is worth a try. But no matter what you order, make sure you say "yes please" to the secret sauce. If you want to look like a local, get it to go.

PUB GRUB
BURGUNDY LION ☺☺
2495 rue Notre-Dame W., 514/934-0333, www.burgundylion.com
HOURS: Mon.-Fri. 10 A.M.-8 P.M., Sat. 11 A.M.-5 P.M.

A classic-style British pub—it even has popular Brit-Pop nights—the people here are always warm, welcoming, and drinking a pint. Typical public house grub like Lancashire pot, bangers and mash, fish and chips, and the requisite Sunday roast are all on the menu. But as at modern British counterparts, it's gastro-pub fare: less grease, more cuisine. The weekend brunch is also a treat and can be served with a choice of English muffins or crumpets and even a serving of Scotch eggs (a hard-boiled egg rolled in sausage and deep fried). The decor tends toward dark wood, exposed brick, and a fire in winter.

QUÉBÉCOIS
☪ JOE BEEF ☺☺☺
2491 rue Notre-Dame W., 514/935-6504, www.joebeef.ca
HOURS: Tues.-Sat. 6:30 P.M.-close

Named after Charles "Joe Beef" McKiernan, a popular 19th-century innkeeper, today's Joe Beef is one of the hottest places to dine in Montréal, and with good reason. Its name has become synonymous with fresh, hearty fare. The oysters are popular, as are dishes like lobster pasta, when it's available—regional ingredients mean the menu often changes. Co-owners Allison Cunningham Frédéric Morin and David McMillan have since gone on to conquer the rest of the strip with Liverpool House and McKiernan. The atmosphere is casual chic—brick walls, simple dark-wood tables, and a huge blackboard menu.

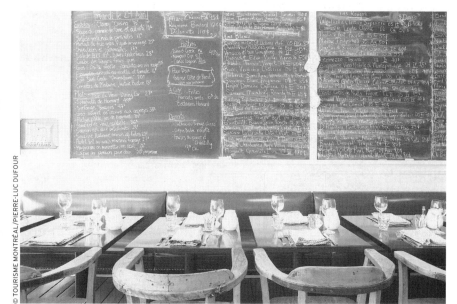

© TOURISME MONTRÉAL/PIERRE-LUC DUFOUR

RESTAURANTS

Rustic yet classy, Joe Beef is a local favorite.

RUSSIAN
LA TROÏKA RESTAURANT ⑤⑤⑤
2171 rue Crescent, 514/849-9333,
www.restauranttroika.com
HOURS: Mon.-Thurs. 5 P.M.-1 A.M., Fri.-Sat. 5 P.M.-3 A.M.

It would be easy to miss Troïka, situated on the bottom floor of a grand-looking Victorian townhouse. Smothered in luxury—from the golden rooster to the opulent fabrics—the restaurant remains true to its Russian roots and offers extensive vodka and caviar menus. Many come later in the night to sip vodka and enjoy the elegant but lively atmosphere. Those looking for more traditional fine dining will find it in dishes like Peter the Great (a rib-eye steak), or wild boar cooked in a red wine reduction.

STEAKHOUSE
QUEUE DE CHEVAL ⑤⑤⑤
1221 blvd. René-Lévesque W., 514/390-0090,
www.queuedecheval.com
HOURS: Mon.-Fri. 11:30 A.M.-2:30 P.M., Sun.-Wed. 5:30-10:30 P.M., Thurs.-Sat. 5:30-11:30 P.M.

Top 40 hits and techno blare out of the speakers at this steakhouse, which is easily one of the most expensive in the city. But if you love steak and enjoy a good splurge once in a while, this is an ideal place. A little ostentatious at times, the vibe is lively, young, and oddly masculine, but the staff are always attentive and knowledgeable. From its downtown location you have a view of the Bell Centre, so it's a perfect spot before or after catching a Canadiens game. The lunchtime table d'hôte is also a prefect time to get a taste.

TURKISH
AVESTA ⑤⑤
2077 rue Ste-Catherine W., 514/937-0156,
www.restoavesta.com
HOURS: Daily 11 A.M.-11 P.M.

The first thing you'll notice about this restaurant is a woman methodically rolling out dough in the storefront window. What she's rolling, and what features in almost all of the dishes, is lavash, a thin, doughy flatbread that'll just about melt in your mouth. Dip this bread into any of a large selection of *mezzes* (small dishes) or try it folded around some spinach and feta in *gozleme* (Turkish crêpes). West of the regular tourist path, Avesta is full of locals in the know, and the service couldn't be more accommodating. The atmosphere here is casual, comfortable, and inviting, with traditional crafts accenting the seating and walls. Relax after your meal with a strong Turkish coffee and some baklava.

VEGETARIAN
BONNY'S ⑤
1748 rue Notre-Dame W., 514/931-4136,
www.bonnys.ca
HOURS: Mon.-Fri. 11:30 A.M.-3 A.M., Sat.-Sun. 9 A.M.-3 A.M.

Dedicated to organic, vegetarian meals, this eatery also caters to vegans and those with other similar dietary restrictions. Seating composed of church pews, an open kitchen, and a wall covered with logs adds to its charm. The soup of the day is served in a giant teacup. Burgers, sandwiches, and salads make up the majority of the menu, but there are also daily specials for more dinner-like fare. Their desserts tend to be simple but no less inviting, and the crispy rice square in particular tastes like a healthier version of your mom's recipe. They also have a takeout counter for those on the run.

BURRITOVILLE ⑤
2055 rue Bishop, 514/286-2776,
www.burritoville.ca
HOURS: Mon.-Sat. 11 A.M.-11 P.M.

Serving the most basic of Mexican fare—quesadillas, tacos, and, uh, burritos—this vegetarian restaurant is a downtown haven of sorts for non-meat eaters. In an old townhouse, the dark wood accents make it look more like a pub than Mexican place, but it does have an inviting, relaxed vibe. Across from Concordia University, it's an ideal spot for students or those looking for a simple and healthy bite to eat. Offering organic and locally grown ingredients, it's also environmentally friendly, and if you pop in for a bite later in the night you might also catch some live music, throughout the week.

Centre-Ville Est

Map 3

CHINESE
MAISON KAM FUNG ⑤⑤

1111 rue St-Urbain, 514/878-2888,
www.restaurantlamaisonkamfung.com

HOURS: Daily 7 A.M.-3 P.M. and 4:30-10 P.M.

Hidden in a nondescript all-purpose complex on the edge of Chinatown, Maison Kam Fung is the go-to place for dim sum but they also offer Cantonese and Sichuan dishes. Maison Kam Fung takes up prime real estate on the corner unit, and you can often see the packed house before you even step in the building. No matter the time this place is always bustling, so expect a line for Sunday morning dim sum. Evenings are when you can grab an authentic Cantonese and Sichuan meal, and though there'll still be a crowd, this one will be full of community locals.

NUI KEE ⑤⑤

1163 rue Clark, 514/868-1866

HOURS: Mon.-Fri. noon-11 P.M., Sat.-Sun. 11:30 A.M.-11:30 P.M.

Nui Kee, a local favorite, is brightly lit, teeny tiny, and concealed on the second floor of an nondescript building. But the northern Chinese dishes will make your mouth water for days after. The key to many of these dishes is the out-of-this-world spice; those who like it hot, like it here. The kung pao chicken is one of the spiciest. If you've got a delicate palate, come prepared and order the dumplings, garlic eggplant, or sizzling beef. The crispy spicy garlic fish, however, can and should be enjoyed by everyone. Ordering can be a bit confusing, however, if you don't speak Mandarin; luckily, the menu has photos.

DESSERT
PÂTISSERIE HARMONIE ⑤

85 rue de la Gauchetière W., 514/875-1328,
www.patisserieharmonie.com

HOURS: Daily 8 A.M.-9 P.M.

Fifty different kinds of sweets are on offer at this Chinese bakery. It's an ideal spot to pop in and grab a mango cake, a few rounds of egg custard, or a deliciously moist slice of Japanese cheesecake. Buns are their hallmark, though, so be sure to sample both the savory (barbecue pork, curried beef) and the sweet (red bean cake, taro, and sesame). With no seats and no counter space this is a take-away place, and you'll see recent shoppers, from tourists to the local Chinese community, digging in to their sweet as they wander the streets.

FRENCH
BRASSERIE T! ⑤⑤

1425 rue Jeanne-Mance, 514/282-0808,
www.brasserie-t.com

HOURS: Daily 11:30 A.M.-midnight

Opened in the brand-new Quartier des Spectacles, Brasserie T! is the bistro brainchild of Toqué!'s Normand LaPrise. Housed in a sleek all-glass corridor-like building, it cozies up to the Museum of Contemporary Art and looks out onto the sleek low fountains of the new *quartier*. Serving dishes like burgers and Montréal sausage, this place has been packed with businessmen and -women during lunch hours, curious tourists, and young professionals since it opened. It provides an excellent alternative to Laprise's super good and super expensive usual fare. Reservations, no matter the time of day, are recommended.

KOREAN
CHEZ BONG ⑤⑤

1021 blvd. St-Laurent, 514/396-7779

HOURS: Tues.-Sun. 11 A.M.-9 P.M.

Half a flight of stairs leads down to this eatery in the heart of Chinatown. You'll find a menu full of Korean cuisine. The modest decor consists of a few long, communal tables, wood-paneled walls, and lighting that gives the place a yellowish hue. It is usually packed with locals, and the atmosphere is decidedly relaxed. Though it's not exclusively Korean barbecue, you can still get your fill here and cook your marinated beef or chicken to your desired degree right at your table. Other dishes, however, like the seafood omelet, kimchi pork stir-fry with tofu, and, of course, a big old bowl of classic *pho* all go down a treat.

Quartier Latin and the Village   Map 4

AMERICAN
KITCHENETTE $$$

1353 blvd. René-Lévesque E., 514/527-1016,
www.kitchenetterestaurant.ca
HOURS: Mon. 11 A.M.-3 P.M., Tues.-Fri. 11 A.M.-11 P.M.,
Sat. 5-11 P.M.

This family-run bistro—owner and chef Nick
Hodge is from Texas; his wife and her parents
are Québécois—mixes both backgrounds and
cuisines with gratifying results. The relaxed atmosphere and minimal and welcoming decor—
dark wood bar, antique white columns, and lots
of windows—are the backdrop for dishes like
beer-braised short ribs, smoked organic chicken
pot pie, and sourdough grilled cheese. Though
both lunch and dinner can draw a crowd, from
those on a business lunch to foodies on a budget
taking advantage the lunch special, the menus
vary. Drop in at lunch and try the fish tacos,
rumored to be the best in the city.

LA PARYSE $

302 rue Ontario E., 514/842-0204, www.laparyse.com
HOURS: Tues.-Fri. 11 A.M.-11 P.M., Sat. noon-10:30 P.M.,
Sun. noon-10 P.M.

If you come across this tiny restaurant by accident, you're likely to notice it because of the line.
La Paryse, open since 1980, attracts burger lovers from all walks of life, and the ambience here
ranges from tense (when you're in the line-up)
to boisterous and lively (when you've finally sat
down). La Paryse's burgers are the best in town, so
it's no surprise that the tiny, neo-retro diner is almost always packed. The classic burger with fries
is the way to go, but if you're vegetarian (or even
if you're not), opt for the nut burger, a perfectly
delicious alternative. Go later (around 9:30 P.M.)
or earlier (5 P.M.) to avoid the crowds.

BAKERIES
LE MIE MATINALE $

1371 rue Ste-Catherine E., 514/529-5656,
www.lamiematinale.ca
HOURS: Tues.-Sat. 8:30 A.M.-7 P.M., Sun. 9 A.M.-5 P.M.

This artisanal bakery, whose name means

morning bread, offers everything from muffins
to croissants, and since the owners are originally
from France, you know they're going to be good.
This cozy spot also serves homemade soups. At
Christmastime, stop by the café, with its exposed brick walls, bistro chairs, and welcoming staff, for some of their Stollen, a German
Christmas cake. It's so popular with the local
community, you can order it online. One quirk
about this place, however, is their dedication to
Dalida, a popular French singer from the early
1960s; her image completely fills one long wall,
and her music is on heavy rotation.

CAFÉS
LA BRIOCHE LYONNAISE $

1593 rue St-Denis, 514/842-7017,
www.labriochelyonnaise.com
HOURS: Sun.-Thurs. 8 A.M.-10 P.M., Fri.-Sat.
8 A.M.-midnight

The crêpes in this stone-walled bistro are the prefect dish, no matter the time of day. With a selection of both savory (*sarrazin*) and sweet (*froment*),
they range from the simple (ham and cheese) to
the gourmet (smoked salmon and pesto). Filled
with bistro tables and chairs and with a big, green
backyard terrace, this is a popular place for studying students or hungry movie- and theater-goers—a French cinema and playhouse are across
the street. The ambience is decidedly Franco,
with patrons lingering over espressos and dipping
pastries into bowls of café au lait. They also serve
a number of quiches, sandwiches on baguettes,
and homemade gelato.

DESSERT
JULIETTE ET CHOCOLAT $

1615 rue St-Denis, 514/287-3555,
www.julietteetchocolat.com
HOURS: Sun.-Thurs. 11 A.M.-11:30 P.M.,
Fri.-Sat. 11 A.M.-midnight

There's a bit of a joke surrounding Juliette et
Chocolat, that the place is filled 90 percent
of the time with 90 percent women. And it's
partly true, but only if you fill the remaining

10 percent up with men on dates or digging into a hearty, homemade crêpe. The main draw, though, is the chocolate, which can be ordered in an array of ways—shots, milkshakes, cocktails—and from an array of places—Madagascar, Ecuador, Ghana. The decor too is like a warm, chocolate-y hug with dark walls, low lighting, and intimate tables. Started by the sweet-loving Juliette of the title, the St-Denis location is the original, but you can now find two more locations, one in Outremont (377 Laurier W., 514/510-5651) and one on the Plateau (3600 St-Laurent, 438/380-1090).

FRENCH
AU PETIT EXTRA $$$
1690 rue Ontario Est., 514/527-5552,
www.aupetitextra.com
HOURS: Mon.-Fri. 11:30 A.M.-2:30 P.M.,
Mon.-Sat. 6-10 P.M., Sun. 5:30-9:30 P.M.

Chef Natalie Major's classic French dishes are always a crowd pleaser. Though the menu varies depending on the season, it always features staples like steak frites, *foie de veau,* and *magret canard.* The atmosphere is casual but elegant and often full of lively clientele; it has the feel of a great neighborhood bistro, which is exactly what it is. If you're in the mood for a full meal opt for the table d'hôte, available at either lunch or dinner, and always a great deal.

MEXICAN
CHIPOTLE AND JALAPENO $
1481 rue Amherst, 514/504-9015,
www.chipotleetjalapeno.com
HOURS: Sun.-Wed. 10 A.M.-6 P.M.,
Thurs.-Sat. 10 A.M.-9 P.M.

With an on-site store, a score of waiters, and a resident cockatoo presiding over the space, Chipotle and Jalapeno has all the bases covered. Simple and delicious Mexican food is served, and the pared-down presentation doesn't diminish the dishes' flavors. Favorites like *queso fundido, nopales,* and pozole soup give it an authentic Mexican kick, as does the fact that most of the diners are Spanish-speaking. The Cuban sandwich, with no less than three kinds of meat, is a standout both in taste and size.

TEA
CAMELLIA SINENSIS $
351 rue Emery, 514/286-4002, www.camellia-sinensis.com
HOURS: Daily noon-10 P.M.

Started by four men who, quite simply, just loved tea, the aim of Camellia Sinensis was to bring quality teas from all over the world to tea lovers in Montréal. Each year the four head off to different corners of the world to find the best tea there is, and each year, the menu changes accordingly. The salon in the Quartier Latin is a cozy spot full of red cushions on which to sit cross-legged and enjoy a pot of one of the 10 types of teas available.

VEGETARIAN
SPIRITE LOUNGE $$
1205 rue Ontario, 514/522-5353
HOURS: Tues.-Sun. 6-11 P.M.

Until recently, the Spirite Lounge was best-known for charging diners a fine if they couldn't finish their meal. And though you can now leave a bite on your plate without the shaming process of having your picture tacked up on the wall and being blacklisted, that won't stop you from wanting to eat every last morsel. Spirite is kookily decorated with tinfoil, lava lamps, Christmas lights, and other weird but wonderful things. The vegan meal, a set menu that changes daily, is served in small and large portions. It's popular with the queer community, and many of the servers have quite a bit of sass, so don't be afraid to sass back—in a light-hearted way. This place is popular so reservations are highly recommended. Bring cash.

RESTAURANTS

Plateau Mont-Royal Map 5

AMERICAN
L'ANECDOTE ⑤
801 rue Rachel E., 514/527-7697
HOURS: Mon.-Fri. 7:30 A.M.-10 P.M.,
Sat.-Sun. 9 A.M.-10 P.M.

This all-purpose diner is a cute place full of mismatched chairs, checkerboard floors, and old-style counter seating. It's open from breakfast to dinner, seven days a week. The menu is extensive, offering everything from filling and delicious crêpes and omelets to fried fish and fancier dishes like ravioli. And though the fancier dishes can be tempting, what's really worth it here is classic diner grub, like the club sandwich or a burger and fries. Frequented by locals, especially those with kids, the atmosphere is one of a typical diner, inviting and unpretentious.

LE BARBARE ⑤⑤
4670 rue St-Denis, 514/288-8377
HOURS: Mon.-Fri. noon-midnight, Sat. 9 A.M.-3 P.M. and 5:30-10:30 P.M., Sun. 9 A.M.-3 P.M.

The microbrew beers and killer weekend brunches make this a worthwhile stop, morning, noon, or night. The open, rustic interior is welcoming, as is the large front window that's open late into the night when it's warm enough. A gathering spot for a young, fun-loving Francophone crowd, it can get rowdy on weekends. The brunches feature the usual savory and the sweet suspects, and the evening menu offers hearty fare.

BE YOUR OWN SOMMELIER

Unique to Montréal are BYOBs, otherwise known as Bring Your Own Bottle restaurants, where diners are invited to bring their own wine instead of choosing from the restaurant's wine list. These restaurants are popular with groups and, it has to be said, young university students. But it doesn't have to be a rowdy night; many BYOBs have some of the best chefs in the city, and depending on where you go the atmosphere can be either casual or refined. No matter where you end up dining, however, it's a great way to enjoy a meal without the sometimes-pricey wine lists.

Though you might find this elsewhere (Toronto for one has recently caught on), in Montréal you won't be charged a corking fee, so your $12 bottle of wine will only cost you $12. Bring-your-owns can be found around the city, but Duluth and Prince Arthur, both charming cobblestone streets, have the highest concentration. Duluth has the most choices in the city, but some options are mediocre. One standout is **La Colombe**, a great, elegant corner bistro, and if you are with a group the three-story **L'Academie** is always accommodating.

Prince Arthur has a number of different restaurants serving various cuisine – though Greek is the most popular – for you to choose from. Though none of it will reach the apex of culinary experiences, the restaurants at least offer good value for a decent meal, and sidewalk dining in the summertime is hard to beat.

Farther north on Rachel, you'll find small, Parisian-esque bistro **Au 917,** seafood restaurant **Le Poisson Rouge,** and **Les Infideles** (771 Rachel E., 514/528-8555, www.lesinfideles.ca, Wed.-Fri. 11:30 A.M.-2 P.M., daily 6-10 P.M.), probably one of the most refreshing and interesting restaurants in the neighborhood.

Up in the Plateau, Gilford is a picturesque street full of irresistible BYOBs: **Le Quartier Général** is one of the newest and chicest on the scene, while **Le Pégase** (1831 Gilford, 514/522-9487, Tues.-Sun. 5:30-11 P.M.) is perfect for a romantic meal. **Chez Doval** serves, simple, classic Portuguese fare and has a dedicated fan base. One of the most popular with locals and visitors alike is **Pizzeria Napoletana,** a lively, busy pizza parlor and Italian eatery in Little Italy. They don't take reservations, however, so you might be in for a wait.

© KATIE DUTTON

The always-packed Patati Patata is one of the smallest restaurants in the city.

MEATMARKET $$

4415 blvd. St-Laurent, 514/223-2292,
www.meatmarketfood.com

HOURS: Mon. 11 A.M.-3 P.M., Tues.-Sat. 11 A.M.-11 P.M.

Despite the name, this is not a sleazy pickup joint, but an inviting, casual restaurant that just happens to serve some of the best ribs in town. Montréal is seriously lacking when it comes to restaurants with midrange prices, so luckily there's MeatMarket, barely a block south of Mont-Royal. The concrete floor, wood tables, and refurbished chairs give it a retro-chic feel. Though meat dishes are their forte, there's also a great selection of vegetarian salads. The perfect place for a relaxed meal with friends.

PATATI PATATA $

4177 blvd. St-Laurent, 514/844-0216

HOURS: Mon. 9 A.M.-11 P.M., Sat.-Sun. 11 A.M.-11 P.M.

With only 13 seats at windows and the serving counter this could be the smallest restaurant in the city, and yet somehow they manage to serve what seems like a bazillion people a night. Seriously. This is one of the hottest restaurants on the strip, and the lineup, especially in the summer, is usually out the door with everyone from students to families and intrigued tourists. If you're lucky enough to grab a seat, get one at the counter and watch the cooks/waiters as they flip mini burgers, stir up tofu stir-frys, and load the toppings on one of their huge *poutines*. Service is brisk, and when it's busy even the stools feel cramped. If it's nice out, skip the seat and take your order to the nearby Parc Jeanne-Mance instead. Cash only.

(SCHWARTZ'S $

3895 blvd. St-Laurent, 514/842-4813,
www.schwartzsdeli.com

HOURS: Sun.-Thurs. 8 A.M.-12:30 A.M.,
Fri. 8 A.M.-1:30 A.M., Sat. 8 A.M.-2:30 A.M.

This is the oldest deli in Canada, so when the term "Montréal institution" is used to describe this place, it is warranted. Opened in 1928, Schwartz's Hebrew Delicatessen remains largely unchanged, right down to its location, placemat menus, banquette seating, gruff waiters, fast service, and fluorescent lighting. Using tried and true methods, the cooks smoke the meat daily in a special blend of spices to give it that Schwartz's taste. The basic smoked-meat sandwich, cole-slaw, and fries combination is the only way to go. You should, however, expect to wait, no matter the weather: Be it -30 below or 30 above, there is always a lineup down the block.

CAFÉS
CAFÉ NÉVÉ $
151 rue Rachel E., 514/903-9294, www.cafeneve.com
HOURS: Mon.-Thurs. 8 A.M.-10 P.M., Fri. 8 A.M.-9 P.M., Sat. 9 A.M.-9 P.M.

Taking over the corner spot that used to belong to a bike repair shop, Café Névé is a great addition to this strip of Rachel, linking St-Laurent and St-Denis. The large, open space is sparsely decorated with shabby-chic decor and a couple of well-placed flatscreens (prefect for watching the game). Run by three young guys, the vibe is youthful and cool, but it's also a favorite for families—no one's going to be uptight about your tantrum-throwing four-year-old. Everything is reasonably priced, from the eggs Benedict to the lattes. The place is also open late, for those wanting a quiet place to grab a light dinner. The one drawback? The bicycle seat stools may look cool but they are decidedly difficult to sit on.

CAFÉ SANTROPOL $$
3990 rue St-Urbain, 514/842-3110, www.santropol.com
HOURS: Daily 10:30 A.M.-10 P.M.

Renowned for serving some of biggest sandwiches and milkshakes in the city, Cafè Santropol is a laid-back place that's always welcoming. Started in 1976, in an attempt to save a derelict building from being torn down, it has become a staple in the city and caters to everyone from students to aging hippies. In the summer, prime seating is in their quaint backyard with views of Mont-Royal. The coffee here is fair-trade organic, and it's so popular, you can now pick up a pound or two on your way out the door, or at the local grocery store.

CHEZ JOSÉ $
173 ave. Duluth E., 514/845-0693
HOURS: Mon.-Fri. 7 A.M.-6 P.M., Sat. 8 A.M.-6 P.M., Sun. 9 A.M.-6 P.M.

Small and ambitiously decorated—hey, at least you're not bored waiting for your order—this tiny café, serves up sandwiches, soups, salad, smoothies, homemade pastries, and an affordable and great weekend brunch. Students, artists, and neighborhood locals pop in for a coffee and the laid-back atmosphere and service. Found on Duluth, which is rife with BYOBs but not many café's, José's is a multi-colored café-serving haven. Grab a latte to go, or sit by one of the open windows and people watch as you sip.

DESSERTS
COCOA LOCALE $$
4807 ave. du Parc, 514/271-7162, www.cocoalocale.com
HOURS: Wed.-Sun. noon-6 P.M.

Reema Singh is the one-woman show behind this sweet boutique cake shop. Stepping in here feels like you've just stepped into your friend's kitchen, which is exactly the idea. A display counter at the front full of cakes (chili chocolate is popular), cupcakes, and brownies is the only thing that separates customers from Singh, who bakes her goodies right there in the shop. Touches here and there, like a mint-green rotary phone and the pink walls, give it a nostalgic feel. Since it's such a small operation it's first-come, first-served for everything, so those wanting a cake for a special day should order ahead.

PÂTISSERIE KOUIGN AMANN $
322 ave. du Mont-Royal E., 514/845-8813
HOURS: Mon.-Wed. 7 A.M.-7 P.M., Thurs.-Fri. 7 A.M.-8 P.M., Sat. 7 A.M.-6 P.M.

This bakery specializes in *kouign amann,* a hard-to-pronounce treat from Brittany in northern France. Like all good things it consists largely of butter and sugar and tastes so good you'll want to eat two. This is a teeny-tiny place that seats about six on a good day. Weekend strollers pop in to warm up or grab a treat to go. Known among locals, its cuteness also attracts tourists. Cozy and welcoming, it also serves coffee, sandwiches, croissants, and quiches, and is a great place for a light lunch. The whole operation takes place directly behind the counter, so you can watch the chefs work as you bite into your little piece of French heaven.

FRENCH

L'ACADEMIE ⑤⑤⑤

4051 rue St-Denis, 514/849-2249, www.academie.ca

HOURS: Daily noon–10 P.M.

This is the place to go if you're dining in a large group. It's three stories high and located on the corner of Duluth and St-Denis, and it's not unusual for this BYO to have a line around the corner. Decorated with subtle earthy tones like gray and beige, it feels and looks more upscale than you'd expect. It serves grilled meats and fish with an array of pastas.

AU CINQUIÈME PÉCHÉ ⑤⑤⑤

330 ave. du Mont-Royal E., 514/286-0123, www.aucinquiemepeche.com

HOURS: Tues.-Wed. 5:30–10 P.M., Fri. 11:30 A.M.-2:30 P.M., Thurs.-Sat. 5:30–11 P.M.

When a restaurant's name is "Fifth Sin," you know you're heading into gluttonous territory. A French bistro to a T, its walls are adorned with black-and-white photos of early-20th-century Paris, and the vibe is refined, sophisticated, and unpretentious. Chef Benoit Lenglet serves up contemporary French cooking with a twist of nouvelle cuisine. Everything they serve is worth tasting—which says a lot because they change their menu regularly. Locals love this place for its value and atmosphere. A tip for frugal travelers: The end-of-the-week lunchtime table d'hôte offers three dishes at a fraction of the regular cost.

LA COLOMBE ⑤⑤⑤

554 ave. Duluth E., 514/849-8844

HOURS: Tues.-Sat. 5:30–10 P.M.

Located on the end of a busy restaurant strip, this bring-your-own-wine restaurant is both romantic and elegant. Popular with both gourmet and classical diners, it serves French fare with a North African flavor. Dishes like venison in blueberry sauce, lamb shank, and escargots are favorites. Most mains come as a table d'hôte with soup, appetizer, and dessert for approximately $50. With exposed brick walls, low

lighting, and seating topping out at 45 people it's a small restaurant with a neighborhood feel. Open since 1990, it is starting to look a little tired, but the service is still attentive, and the dining room is often packed.

L'EXPRESS ⑤⑤

3927 rue St-Denis, 514/845-5333

1251 rue Gilford, 514/658-1839

HOURS: Mon.-Fri. 8 A.M.-2 A.M., Sat. 10 A.M.-2 A.M., Sun. 10 A.M.-1 A.M.

If L'Express isn't the best French bistro in the city, then it is somewhere close. From the unnamed facade—look down, the restaurant's name is spelled out in the sidewalk tiles in front—to the floor-to-ceiling front window, it looks exclusive and inviting all at once. Inside, the tables are populated with regulars giving the place a jovial, comfortable atmosphere. Chef Joel Chapoulie, who has presided over the kitchen for close to 20 years, is renowned for dishes like his fish soup with Gruyère croutons and veal liver with tarragon. Top off the meal with a *île flottante,* a meringue and custard delight.

LES INFIDELES ⑤⑤⑤

771 rue Rachel E., 514/528-8555, www.lesinfideles.ca

HOURS: Wed.-Fri. 11:30 A.M.-2 P.M., daily 6-10 P.M.

Things here are kept simple, from the white walls and low gray banquettes to the French menu inspired by local ingredients. Venison medallions with poached pear, maple pork loin, and goat cheese cheesecake feature on chef Louis Legault's menu, all to be paired with a wine of your own choosing at this bring-your-own restaurant. One of the more upscale places in the category, it's a huge hit with locals. The ambience is subtle and romantic, and the service always hits the mark. With a four-course tasting menu at around $50 you can't go wrong.

LALOUX ⑤⑤⑤

250 ave. des Pins E., 514/297-9127, www.laloux.com

HOURS: Mon.-Fri. 11:30 A.M.-2:30 P.M., Sun.-Thurs. 5:30-10:30 P.M., Fri.-Sat. 5:30-11:30 P.M.

A young, ambitious staff handles the kitchen at

RESTAURANTS

this casual but elegant bistro. Chef du Cuisine Seth Gabrielse's menu is focused on Québécois and Montréal flavors, using local produce and artisanal suppliers for creations like veal sweetbreads, lobster salad, and duck *magret*. Pastry chef Michelle Marek is well-regarded for her sinfully delicious creations, which include a chocolate pot-de-crème with Maldon salt and caramel. The staff are young and so are many clients—many of whom dine before hitting up Pop!, the wine bar next door. Located off the beaten path, it's a neighborhood staple, appealing mostly to those with discerning palates. Their midday table d'hôte is a great deal.

AU 917 $$$

917 rue Rachel E., 514/524-0094, www.au917.com

HOURS: Daily 5 P.M.-midnight

Established in 1985, this bring-your-own restaurant is one of the best in the city. With its authentic French bistro fare—beef bourguignon, grilled sole, duck à l'orange, and chocolate-covered profiteroles for dessert—it's been attracting Plateau locals with refined palates since it first opened its doors. Dark wood interior, cozy banquette seating, and a single wall lined with mirrors—everything stays true to its French aesthetic, including the white-shirted, mostly Francophone waiters who serve you with an air of nonchalance. Though often packed, things stay relatively calm and low-key.

RÉSERVOIR $$

9 ave. Duluth E., 514/849-7779, www.brasserie-reservoir.ca

HOURS: Mon. 3 P.M.-3 A.M., Tues.-Fri. noon-3 A.M., Sat. 10:30 A.M.-3 A.M., Sun. 10:30 A.M.-3 A.M.

Conveniently located, this restaurant and bar helmed by Dany Bolduc is known for its exquisitely put together plates and fantastic microbrews. The basic principles are locally sourced ingredients and unique pairings. It's fairly small, with the entire front made up of window; you can see the vats from the street. An early proponent of Montréal chic, with a chalkboard menu and casual wooden seating, it draws a diverse crowd from Plateau-ites to young professionals. It's a popular brunch spot, and you won't find anything like it in the city,

with choices like seared halibut over polenta and chorizo. In the evenings stop in for a drink and something from the snack menu, which includes everything from olives and mixed nuts—perfect with a microbrewed blanc beer—to fried cod and Gruyère grilled cheese.

SALLE À MANGER $$$

1302 ave. du Mont-Royal E., 514/522-0777, lasalleamanger.ca

HOURS: Tues.-Sat. 6 P.M.-2 A.M.

Specializing in market-fresh French cuisine with a twist, with dishes like scallop ceviches and venison tartare, Salle à Manger is spacious, light-filled and, as the name suggests, has the atmosphere of an upscale cafeteria. Whether you're dining with a small or large group, prepare to share (an entire roasted suckling pig serves 12). With the menu divided in three sections—appetizers, mains, and deluxe mains—picking off of each other's plate is expected. But don't let the cafeteria analogy fool you: Set in the heart of the Plateau with floor-to-ceiling front windows, this is a place to be seen, and the young and hip flock here for late-night meals and chic, unpretentious atmosphere.

JAPANESE
ISAKAYA $$$

3469 ave. du Parc, 514/845-8226, www.bistroisakaya.com

HOURS: Tues.-Fri. 11:30 A.M.-2 P.M., Tues.-Thurs. 6-9:30 P.M., Fri. 6-10:30 P.M., Sat. 5:30-11 P.M., Sun. 5:30-9 P.M.

Chef Shinge Minagawa stays true to his Japanese roots with classic dishes like soba and ramen noodles and calf's liver, which you'll be hard-pressed to find elsewhere in the city. He's known for hand-picking his seafood; the fish is fresh and perfect in either a roll or as tartare. The appetizer menu is a filled with distinctly authentic fare like *yakitori, gyoza,* and *chawanmuhi*. Long and narrow—a bit of a trend in Montréal—the decor is minimal with a sushi bar running the length of one wall and bistro-style seating the other. The relaxed decor with low lighting attracts an eclectic clientele, from university students and office workers to the artistically minded.

LATE-NIGHT EATS
◖ LA BANQUISE ⓢ
994 rue Rachel E., 514/525-2415,
www.restolabanquise.com
HOURS: Daily 24 hours

Poutine capital of Montréal, La Banquise serves 25 different kinds of *poutine,* 24 hours a day, seven days a week. For the uninitiated, *poutine* (fries smothered in gravy with cheese curds) is the unofficial food of the province. Initially opened in 1968 as an ice cream shop, La Banquise soon started to serve typical *crasse croute* fare (junky snack food in Québec) and stared dishing out *poutine* in the '80s. Brightly painted walls, wooden banquettes, and boisterous company is what you'll find, no matter the time of day. Since it's open all night, this place is busiest at four in the morning with revelers enjoying a *poutine* of their choice and maybe a hot dog before finally heading home.

EURO DELI ⓢ
3619 blvd. St-Laurent, 514/843-7853
HOURS: Daily 11 A.M.-midnight

This bustling Italian eatery with exposed brick walls, standard restaurant seating, and long order counter is dedicated to fast food with a homemade twist. It's situated just north of Prince Arthur, and regulars can be found on the steps outside, sipping their *allongés* or eating a slice. The coffee is some of the best in the area and their pizza is tops. Locals pop in to grab an easy dinner, and students love it for their filling, affordable meals. Staples like their eggplant parmesan and caesar salad are perfect for lunch or a casual, quick dinner. Open late, it's a great place for a quick bite on your way back from the bar.

MIDDLE EASTERN
KAZA MAZA ⓢⓢ
4629 ave. du Parc, 514/844-6292, www.kazamaza.ca
HOURS: Tues.-Thurs. 5 P.M.-midnight, Fri. 5 P.M.-2 A.M., Sat. 11 A.M.-2 A.M., Sun. 11 A.M.-midnight

On the first floor of what was once a residential building, Kaza Maza is a comfortable, low-key eatery that also doubles as a performance space. Open and sparsely decorated, it serves up some of the best simple and yummy Middle Eastern food in the area. Tapas-style *mezzes* are their forte, with a selection of both hot and cold,

classic *poutine* at La Banquise

though the *basturma mezze* and the thick *muhammara* are standouts. For something a bit different try the pistachio *kefta*, which mixes the nut with minced beef, lamb, and pine nuts.

PORTUGUESE
CHEZ DOVAL ❸❸
150 rue Marie-Anne E., 514/843-3390,
www.chezdoval.com
HOURS: Daily 11:30 A.M.-midnight

This is traditional Portuguese cooking in a traditional Portuguese barebones atmosphere; decor here passes for wainscoting on the walls and burgundy tablecloths. Satisfying customers since 1974, this bring-your-own-wine restaurant is a neighborhood staple with diehard regulars from all walks of life. The specialty here is the grill, so no matter what you get—sardines, octopus, chicken—it's infused with a char-grilled flavor and it is going to be delicious. The simply prepared seafood, like the clams and mussels, is a standout, as is the Portuguese troubadour who serenades the diners on most nights.

ROTISSERIE ROMADOS ❸
115 rue Rachel E., 514/849-1803
HOURS: Daily 11 A.M.-8 P.M.

The lineup here is usually out the door with locals and for a good reason. Rotisserie Romados serves the best grilled chicken in town, and that's about all they serve. It's cooked just right—salty, spicy, and juicy—and you can smell the tastiness all the way down the block. There are only three seats, so the best deal is to get your half chicken, fries, rice, and salad—which will likely be a soggy mess buried under the perfect fries—to go and head to Parc Jeanne-Mance for some alfresco dining. The atmosphere is best summed up by one word: smoky. Hot as Hades in the summer, the interior is all white, with a Virgin Mary or a painted Portuguese folk-chicken here and there.

QUÉBÉCOIS
LA CANTINE ❸❸
212 ave. du Mont-Royal E., 514/750-9800,
www.lacantine.ca
HOURS: Tues.-Fri. 5:30-10:30 P.M., Sat. 9 A.M.-3 P.M. and 5:30-10:30 P.M., Sun. 9 A.M.-3 P.M.

It doesn't get kitschier than La Cantine, where the velour upholstery and psychedelic patterns give the space a '70s vibe. Serving weekend brunch and dinner throughout the week, it takes classics like a burger, only to turn it on its head with a Québécois twist of minced deer and bison. If you're in the mood get the appetizer sampler (*un p'tit peu de tout*); though they're named after trashier treats—la Pop Tart, les Pogos, les Trous d'Beignes (donut holes)—they're much tastier, and healthier than they sound. The clientele matches the decor; young with a thing for nostalgia, with an equal mix of French and English.

❰ LE CHIEN FUMANT ❸❸❸
4710 rue de Lanaudière, 514/524-2444,
www.lechienfumant.com
HOURS: Tues.-Sat. 6 P.M.-2 A.M., Sun. 10 A.M.-2 P.M. and 6 P.M.-2 A.M.

Started by three young culinary whiz kids, this is one of the best new restaurants in the city. Situated on the corner of a quiet street, the long, narrow restaurant is virtually all windows, but it stays cozy even in the deepest of winter with hearty fare like flat iron steak, fried chicken, and stewed rabbit. Using local, market-fresh ingredients the menu changes regularly. The youthful atmosphere invites a youthful crowd, and most nights it's full of late-20-somethings eating at the bar, but it's also a popular family spot for brunch. Start your meal with one of the cocktails—the bar is artfully hung from the ceiling. Make reservations.

❰ AU PIED DU COCHON ❸❸❸
536 ave. Duluth E., 514/281-1114,
www.restaurantaupiedducochon.com
HOURS: Tues.-Sun. 5 P.M.-midnight

Since opening in 2001, this bustling Plateau bistro specializing in a uniquely meaty, hearty Québécois fare hasn't been quiet since. Chef Martin Picard and his restaurant are now household names in the province thanks to outrageous dishes like Foie Gras Poutine, Duck in a Can, and Stuffed Pied du Cochon with Foie Gras, which cater to a carnivorous crowd. The name, by the way, means "the pig's foot." The open, warmly lit restaurant with an open kitchen down one side, wood tables, and counter seating piques the interest of even the least carnivorous. Always lively, it's a popular place for group get-togethers and riotous dinners. It gets full, however, so plan ahead.

LE QUARTIER GÉNÉRAL ⬤⬤⬤
1251 rue Gilford, 514/658-1839
HOURS: Tues.-Sat. 6-11 P.M.

Putting a new spin on the tried-and-true bring-your-own-wine model, Quartier Général offers a menu full of originality and quality. On a quiet, residential street in the Plateau, there's no better setting for the food than this minimal and chic restaurant. Ingredients tend toward local with Stanstead rabbit and venison steak, written up on the blackboard menu. But no matter your order the generous mains come with a choice of soup or salad. It's popular with couples and groups wanting a nice dinner without breaking the bank, and the atmosphere is warm and welcoming. Call ahead for reservations.

SEAFOOD
LE POISSON ROUGE ⬤⬤⬤
1201 rue Rachel E., 514/522-4876,
www.restaurantlepoissonrouge.com
HOURS: Tues.-Sat. 5-10 P.M.

True to its name the interior of this bring-your-own-wine restaurant is a rich, deep red, with banquette seating and mirrors along one wall to make the cozy dining room seem all that much bigger. Specializing in seafood—the name means "red fish"—they offer dishes like scallops in coconut milk, grilled tuna steak, and lobster bisque, as well as some turf selections. The intimate setting, relaxed familiar ambience, and attentive staff will make you feel like you've been going here for years.

SPANISH
CLUB ESPAGNOL DE QUÉBEC ⬤⬤
4388 blvd. St-Laurent, 514/842-6301
HOURS: Tues.-Sun. 11 A.M.-1 A.M.

As the name suggests this is a place to congregate for the city's Spanish population, but that doesn't mean you're not invited to join in the festivities. On the second floor of what looks like

a rather official storefront, an unassuming door leads you upstairs, where the decor is about as relaxed as you'd expect. Large tables usually filled with groups of family and friends take up the main dining area, but just in front of the windows there's a small enclave perfect for smaller groups. In keeping with the community atmosphere, tapas are the menu's main feature and should be shared among dining companions.

PINTXO ⬤⬤
256 rue Roy E., 514/844-0222, www.pintxo.ca
HOURS: Wed.-Fri. noon-2 P.M., Mon.-Sat. 6-11 P.M., Sun. 6-10 P.M.

"Pintxo" is the basque word for bite-size food, which is what this restaurant does best. The subdued setting—white tablecloths, exposed brick walls, large works of art—makes it an ideal place for a leisurely meal, but things get lively later in the evening—it's a Spanish resto after all. Though they serve a variety of mains, consider making a meal out of the *pintxos* themselves. The *pintxo de foie con su cebolla confitada* is a perfect example: set on tiny circles of bread it's a mixture of foie gras, raisins, honey, and onion confit. Popular with groups who are ready to share, it attracts young professionals and mature diners.

LA SALA ROSA ⬤⬤
4848 blvd. St-Laurent, 514/844-4227,
www.lasalarosa.com
HOURS: Tues.-Sun. 5-11 P.M.

Frequented by hipsters and elders of the Spanish community alike, this trendy restaurant represents the diversity of the neighborhood. Tapas are the main draw, though they also make a mean paella, or opt for the chorizo, garlic shrimp, or grilled sardines. Their sauce is perfect for dipping the endless bread. Diners should not miss out on the fried goat cheese with honey and caramelized onions. Every Thursday diners are treated to a live flamenco performance.

STEAKHOUSE
MOISHES ⬤⬤⬤
3961 blvd. St-Laurent, 514/845-3509, www.moishes.ca
HOURS: Mon.-Fri. 5:30-11 P.M., Sat.-Sun. 5-11 P.M.

Enjoying a long history, Moishes was started in

1938, by Moishe Lighter, a Jewish-Romanian immigrant. Lighter was part of the immigrant community that helped shape the Main, and his tradition of smoked meat would turn Moishes into one of the best steakhouses in Montréal. Its position in the community means it's *the* place for important family celebrations. The menu is heavy on the meat—from filet mignon to sweetbreads—and the atmosphere is just as elegant and inviting as you'd expect. The upscale prices mean men, wear a dinner jacket; ladies, wear your pearls.

VEGETARIAN

CHUCHAI 🟢🟢🟢

4088 rue St-Denis, 514/843-4191, www.chuchai.com
HOURS: Mon.-Wed. and Sun. 5-10 P.M., Thurs.-Sat. 5-11 P.M.

ChuChai is the grand dame of vegetarian and vegan restaurants in the city, specializing in vegetarian Thai cuisine. There's nothing you can get here that you couldn't in any regular Thai resto, and with about triple the taste. Fake duck, chicken, and shrimp are all on the menu and supremely delicious, same goes for the melt-in-your-mouth fried spinach. The choice of diehard vegans wanting to indulge in a refined meal, it also appeals to all Thai-food lovers, since, meat or not, they serve some of the best Thai in the city. The vibe here is fine dining, so if you want casual head next door (4094 St-Denis) to their sister restaurant, Chuch Végéthaïexpress.

CRUDESSENCE 🟢

105 rue Rachel W., 514/510-9299, www.crudessence.com
HOURS: Sun.-Wed. 11 A.M.-9 P.M., Thurs.-Sat. 11 A.M.-10 P.M.

The first living food restaurant in Québec, Crudessence's menu fuses Latin, Asian, and Mediterranean flavors to create unique dishes that include ingredients like blue-green algae and hemp seed. Located in a narrow storefront on a sleepy strip of Rachel, its summer terrace is a great place to enjoy your quinoa salad and a cup of Kombucha, fizzy living tea. Since they specialize in health food, it's not unusual to see

© CRUDESSENCE

raw goodness at Crudessence

the place full of diners in workout gear, always flanked by a local in the mood for something healthy. A stone's throw from Parc Jeanne Mance and with prepared foods available for takeout, this is a great option for a midsummer picnic meal.

🌙 AUX VIVRES 🟢🟢

4631 blvd. St-Laurent, 514/842-3479, www.auxvivres.com
HOURS: Daily 11 A.M.-11 P.M.

Since its humble beginnings as a tiny hole-in-the-wall, Aux Vivres has been praised for its unique take on vegan dining. Now located in a bright, open space on the Main—they even have a nice backyard terrace—it serves the most wholesome and filing vegan food, at brunch, lunch, and dinner, that you'll find in the city. It's not just vegans and vegetarians that frequent the joint, however; those craving a healthy, satisfying meal are regulars. Everyone will enjoy the Dragon Bowl, while reluctant vegetarians should go for the BLT. Save room for dessert and try a slice of their uncheesecake.

Mile End and Petite Italie   Map 6

BELGIAN
LA MOULERIE $$
1249 rue Bernard W., 514/273-8132,
www.lamoulerie.montrealplus.ca
HOURS: Mon.-Fri. 11:30 A.M.-11 P.M., Sat.-Sun.
10 A.M.-11 P.M.

Decor-wise this place is definitely past its prime, but if you can ignore the mid-'90s hunter-green banquettes—or better yet nab a seat outside on the lively sidewalk terrace—this is a great place to fill up on mussels. A staple in the neighborhood, it's the go-to place of young folks, families, and mature diners. It's one of the few places in the city that specialize in the Belgian dish, *moules-frites* (mussels and fries). You've got 10 different flavors of *moules-frites* to choose from here, all well worth a taste, especially ones like *les gaspésiennes* with smoked salmon, cream, and white wine or *les flamandes* with leeks, *lardons,* and beer. Creamy, calorie-heavy, and great for baguette dipping.

BREAKFAST AND BRUNCH
CAFÉ SOUVENIR $$
1261 rue Bernard W., 514/948-5259,
www.cafesouvenir.com
HOURS: Daily 7 A.M.-11 P.M.

This neighborhood bistro is a stylish and comfortable place to grab a bite. An eclectic clientele fills the barstools, the banquette seating, and the sidewalk terrace—posh older women from the neighborhood, young professionals, families of all ages. Open for breakfast seven days a week, it has an assortment of dishes including eggs, pancakes, or a simple croissant. The menu stays casual for lunch and dinner, with hearty salads, burgers, couscous dishes, and lasagna available.

LA CROISSANTERIE FIGARO $
5200 rue Hutchison, 514/278-6567,
www.lacroissanteriefigaro.com
HOURS: Daily 7 A.M.-midnight

Full of round, marble-topped tables, gilded light fixtures, and wrought-iron chairs, this corner café and bistro is a little bit of Paris in Outremont. The long, wooden counter adds to the art deco interior and old world feel, and the menu too is decidedly Parisian, offering homemade croissants, coffees, and a reasonably priced lunch and dinner table d'hôte with selections like quiche Lorraine and roast beef. The spacious, leafy outdoor terrace is a great place to meet friends for drinks in the evening.

VIEUX VÉLO $$
59 rue Beaubien E., 514/439-5595
HOURS: Tues.-Fri. 8:30 A.M.-4 P.M., Sat.-Sun. 9 A.M.-4 P.M.

This tiny place spruced up with Formica-topped tables, old wooden school chairs, and '70s hanging lamps has a lived-in feel to matched its relaxed attitude. Located between Mile End and Little Italy, it serves breakfast and brunch all day every day—and what a brunch it is. With simple egg, toast, and hash-brown combinations as well as some absolutely killer Benedicts—like the bacon, brie, avocado—their menu attracts everyone from early-risers to home-office workers. It you're in the mood for something heartier, they have a selection of homemade pizzas, made on a thin, whole-wheat crust.

CAFÉS
CAFÉ ITALIA $
6840 blvd. St-Laurent, 514-495-0059
HOURS: Daily 6 A.M.-11 P.M.

If you grew up in a boisterous family—especially an Italian one—you'll feel right at home here. Waiters and baristas banter back and forth to each other and the customers at this always-busy spot. The no-frills decoration and relaxed serving ethos allow for more focus to be put on the coffee, which is always perfect. If you're lucky enough to grab a seat, get one of their sandwiches, made on a hearty bun with meat, tomatoes, and roasted mushrooms. The place also has a couple of TVs, usually showing the latest sports, but if Italy's playing, grab a coffee to go.

BAGEL WARS

Mile End is known for two things: indie musicians and bagels. Once the home of the Jewish community, their legacy continues with the existence of two iconic bagel shops, **St-Viateur Bagel Shop** (263 rue St-Viateur, 514/276-8044) and **Fairmount Bagel** (74 Fairmount W., 514/272-0667, www.fairmountbagel.com), both of which continue to operate 24 hours a day and seven days a week. With only a single city block between them, these two shops have a similar history, one that includes a wood-burning oven and a hand-rolled tradition.

Founded in 1957 by Myer Lewkowicz, who brought his recipe with him when he immigrated from Eastern Europe, St-Viateur has since expanded to include two cafés and a second bakery on the small strip.

The origins of Fairmount Bagel, however, go much farther back. Opened in 1919 by Isadore Shlafman, off a back alley on the Main, it was the first bagel bakery in Montréal. When it moved to its current location on Fairmount in 1949, it was renamed "The Original Fairmount Bagel Bakery." The Shlafman family continues to run the business to this day.

Unlike the big, doughy New York bagel, Montréal bagels are smaller, denser, and covered in sesame seeds. There's no everything, no cinnamon raisin – the only choice you get here is plain, poppy, or sesame – and that's on the days when there is a choice. Made round the clock, using a wood-fired oven and hand-rolled dough, they are always hot and delicious and are best dipped in whipped cream cheese. Since the early days there has been a silent, but ongoing competition between the two shops, and both have their diehard customers. To an outsider the differences between the two are negligible, but ask any Montréaler and they'll likely have a preference.

St-Viateur Bagel Shop

© KATIE DUTTON

© KATIE DUTTON

Join the locals for a coffee at Café Olimpico.

■ CAFÉ OLIMPICO ⑤

124 rue St-Viateur W., 514/495-7046

HOURS: Daily 7 A.M.-midnight

The line at this neighborhood café can sometimes look intimidating, but it moves fast thanks to the no-nonsense staff who bark at you from their post at the espresso machine. Everybody comes here, from local hipsters to local cops, and on weekends it's taken over by young families who come to socialize. Dedicated to coffee, the place sells a few extras like cold drinks, biscotti for dipping, and slices of lemon cake, and they don't mind a bit if you bring in a hot bagel or two to enjoy with your latte. Don't expect a large cup of joe, however; this place exclusively serves espresso and its derivatives.

CLUB SOCIAL ⑤

180 rue St-Viateur W., 514/495-0114

HOURS: Daily 7 A.M.-midnight

Originally a private club, Club Social opened to the public back in the late-1990s, but a host of men from the Old Country still occupy most of the tables. Just a few doors down from Café Olympico, the baristas here are often young women from the neighborhood who politely ask for your order instead of barking. Both Café Olympico and Club Social are usually packed with locals, and most have an allegiance to one or the other, though their menus are about the same. See which ambience suits you best.

DESSERT

LE BILBOQUET ⑤

1311 rue Bernard W., 514/276-0414

HOURS: Mar.-Dec. daily 11 A.M.-midnight

Quite possibly the best ice cream shop in the city. The line here is down the street on hot summer nights. A couple of park benches are scattered outside and there are a few counter stools and wrought-iron tables inside, but for the most part the interior is taken up with ice cream cases. A chalkboard menu gives you the list of flavors and the (mostly) teenage staff will let you try a few until you find one you like. Unique flavors like King Kong (banana and chocolate), Cacophonie (white chocolate and

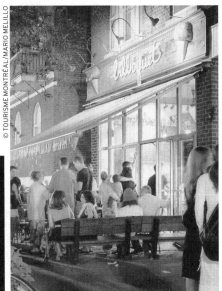

© TOURISME MONTRÉAL/MARIO MELILLO

There are usually lines down the block on summer evenings at Le Bilboquet, an ice cream shop in Outremont.

cashew nuts), and Brouhaha (brownie bits and two types of caramel) are enough to keep you coming back again and again. They also carry other sweets, including cookies, cakes, and cupcakes, and make a mean banana split.

FRENCH

LES DEUX SINGES DE MONTARVIE $$$

176 rue St-Viateur W., 514/278-6854

HOURS: Mon.-Wed. 11 A.M.-2 P.M. and 6-10 P.M., Thurs.-Sat. 11 A.M.-2 P.M. and 6-11 P.M., Sun. 9 A.M.-2 P.M.

On summer evenings the floor-to-ceiling windows of this tiny bistro are rolled wide open, letting the life of the street mingle with the lively diners inside. There's something decidedly quirky about this resto that gives it vibrant atmosphere. This vibrancy translates to the food as well, like the lobster sausage main, which tastes every bit as unique and complex as it sounds. Every wine listed by the bottle is also available by the glass—a nice touch you don't always find.

KITCHEN GALERIE $$$

60 rue Jean-Talon E., 514/315-8994, www.kitchengalerie.com

HOURS: Tues.-Sat. 6-11 P.M.

Just west of Marché Jean Talon, along a boring strip of the busy avenue, is Kitchen Galerie, anything but a boring restaurant. Simply decorated with white walls and black and red accents, it's run by two co-owners who bustle around the restaurant as chefs, maître d's, sommeliers, waiters, busers, and dishwashers. And yet they find the time to create some of the freshest and most unique dishes, which attract adventurous palates. Taking advantage of their location, the evening's dishes are based on the market's deals, and the menu changes accordingly. But they always offer a choice of two appetizers, six mains, and three desserts, as part of their table d'hôte, which is always affordable. The small space fills up fast so call ahead.

◖ LAWRENCE $$

5201 blvd. St-Laurent, 514/503-1070

HOURS: Wed.-Fri. 11:30 P.M.-3 P.M. and 5:30-11 P.M., Sat. 10 P.M.-3 P.M. and 5:30-11 P.M., Sun. 11 A.M.-3 P.M.

At Lawrence, chef Marc Cohen adds to the restaurant's casually chic atmosphere with his simple and delicious dishes and a classic brunch on weekends. The evening and lunch offerings feature everything from seared mackerel to beef-and-bone marrow pie, but the menu changes often. Lawrence is ideally located in a cozy corner spot, with windows on both sides of the restaurant, allowing light to come in at all times of the day. Inside, plaid banquettes and long wooden tables compliment the soft gray walls.

LEMÉAC $$$

1045 ave. Laurier W., 514/270-0999, www.restaurantlemeac.com

HOURS: Mon.-Fri. noon-midnight, Sat.-Sun. 10:30 A.M.-midnight

Open and spacious, this is one neighborhood bistro that can, and does, accommodate a crowd. Built on great bistro fare like steak frites, *foie de veau*, and blood pudding, Leméac goes just that little bit farther with homemade desserts and Québec specialties like local cheese. Depending on when you go the clientele varies from ladies who lunch to young professionals having a late bite before heading out on the town. The atmosphere is always a little reserved, however, in that classic French way. A little on the pricier side, it's popular for its $22 après 22 ($22 after 10 P.M.) table d'hôte.

LA MONTÉE DE LAIT ❸❸❸
5171 blvd. St-Laurent, 514/273-8846,
www.lamonteedelait.com
HOURS: Mon.-Fri. 11:30 A.M.-11 P.M., Sat.-Sun. 11 A.M.-11 P.M.

When this place opened on a small side street in the Plateau in the 2000s, it was an instant hit, such a hit in fact that its small surroundings couldn't accommodate the demand. After a short stint downtown it has settled back into its roots in the Plateau and has recaptured its original magic. The high, red banquettes, a (usually) crowded bar, and the open kitchen give the whole place an exciting atmosphere in which to enjoy dishes like halibut with sausage and glazed pork belly. It's known for an excellent imported wine list; selections can be pricey.

GREEK
CAVA ❸❸❸
5551 ave. du Parc, 514/273-7772,
www.cavarestaurantmontreal.com
HOURS: Mon.-Sat. 5:30 P.M.-midnight

In Greek, *cava* means either land or earth, so it is no surprise that just about everything on the menu here is meat. Opened by the owners of Milos, Cava is opulence, with a dark-wood bar, aging cured meats and cheeses displayed in the wall-to-wall fridge, and a waitstaff dressed in pin-striped aprons over white shirts and jeans. The opulence matches its expensive menu. The crowd here follows suit—always chic and well-put-together. The swank but chic surroundings translate to the ambience, and everything has an expensive air. Menu standouts include the slow-cooked veal shank, the lamb chops, and the sirloin.

MILOS ❸❸❸
5357 ave. du Parc, 514/272-3552, www.milos.ca
HOURS: Mon.-Fri. noon-3 P.M. and 5:30 P.M.-midnight,

Sat. 5:30 P.M.-midnight, Sun. 5:30-11 P.M.

Serving what is considered by some to be the best seafood in the city, Milos is ubiquitous for its pricey dishes and cool surroundings. It's on a strip of avenue du Parc that, despite the name, doesn't quite fit with the dishes' price tags. Milos's sleek black exterior stands out, and so do dishes like the wine-marinated octopus, crab cakes, and *tsipoura,* fresh from the Aegean Sea. Super-affordable lunch and after 10 P.M. specials are also available.

LUNCH COUNTERS
🅲 DÉPANNEUR LE PICK-UP ❸
7032 rue Waverly, 514/271-8011,
www.depanneurlepickup.com
HOURS: Mon.-Wed. 7 A.M.-7 P.M., Thurs.-Fri.
7 A.M.-9 P.M., Sat. 9 A.M.-7 P.M., Sun. 10 A.M.-6 P.M.

If you're up for a food adventure find your way to Dépanneur le Pick-Up. In Québec a *dépanneur* is a corner store, and that's exactly what this place is: a corner store with a food counter and outdoor seating in the summer. A little off the beaten path, tucked away on a residential street, Le Pick-Up is known for their amazing pulled pork sandwiches—both vegetarian and regular style—and their weekend brunches. Hipsters rub elbows with old-time regulars who frequented the place when it just did coffee and eggs over easy. Now, it's the site of some of the best culinary events in the city.

🅲 WILENSKY'S LIGHT LUNCH ❸
34 ave. Fairmount W., 514/271-0242
HOURS: Mon.-Fri. 9 A.M.-4 P.M.

Not much has changed since Moe Wilensky opened this lunch counter in 1932, housed in the current location since 1952. You'd be forgiven for thinking its origins were earlier. Nine counter stools make up the only seating in the place, and the decor can only be described as nonexistent. If timelessness were an ambience they'd have it in spades. Act like a regular and get the house special, a double grilled salami and bologna sandwich with mustard—mustard is compulsory, as a sign inside makes clear—on a kaiser bun, which tastes as delicious as it sounds. Immortalized

Step back in time with a trip to Wilensky's.

by Mordecai Richler in *The Apprenticeship of Duddy Kravitz,* the sodas here are all old-fashioned and mixed by hand.

ITALIAN
BOTTEGA PIZZERIA $$
65 rue St-Zotique E., 514/277-8104, www.bottega.ca
HOURS: Tues.-Sun. 5 P.M.-midnight

Located on a side street in Petite Italy (Little Italy), this modern upscale setting is welcoming, with the heat of a real wood fireplace burning in the background. Using traditional Neapolitan methods—which attracts lots of traditional Italians—Bottega makes some of the most authentic pizza in the city, and their wine list is exquisite. Following tradition they offer a number of *sfizis,* typical Neapolitan appetizers—try the giant meatball, you won't be disappointed. For dessert go for a gelato, the perfect cap to a Neapolitan meal.

LUCCA $$$
12 rue Dante, 514/278-6502
HOURS: Mon.-Fri. noon-3:30 P.M., Mon.-Sat. 6-10:30 P.M.

Italians love Italian food, and they're often the majority at this neighborhood staple. Classy and rustic all at once, this is the swankiest of restaurants in the area with the prices to prove it. Lucca might not be the cheapest Italian in town but it is one of the best. Their deceptively simple cuisine is what customers come back for, such as the seafood linguine with clams, shrimp, and fish. Because they use market-fresh ingredients, dishes often change, but staples like risottos, pasta, and meat dishes are always available, as is their heavenly tiramisu for dessert.

LE PETIT ITALIEN $$
1265 ave. Bernard, 514/278-0888, www.lepetititalien.com
HOURS: Mon.-Wed. 11:30 A.M.-10 P.M., Thurs.-Fri. 11:30 A.M.-midnight, Sat. 9:30 A.M.-midnight, Sun. 9:30 A.M.-11 P.M.

This busy neighborhood restaurant is a saving grace on nights when you simply don't feel like cooking. One wall is filed with jars of tomato sauce while the other is mirrored, to give the allusion that this tightly packed restaurant is bigger than it looks. Casual fine dining is the aim and it hits the mark every time. Their homemade pastas are a great choice on a bitterly cold winter night—the gorgonzola linguine is especially satisfying—but they also have a great selection of meat and fish and a reasonably priced table d'hôte. In summer there's an outdoor sidewalk terrace.

PIZZERIA NAPOLETANA $$
189 rue Dante, 514/276-8226, www.napoletana.com
HOURS: Daily 11 A.M.-11 P.M.

Located in the heart of Little Italy since 1948, Pizzeria Napoletana is everyone's favorite bustling, boisterous, bring-your-wine pizza joint. They don't take reservations and there's usually a line but things move quickly inside. Although it's quirkily decorated—there's a fake tree with sprawling branches and a thick trunk in the middle of the room—they serve 34 different types of pizza and pasta, including their signature Napoletana with anchovies. Service is fast and efficient if not totally attentive, though they'll happily uncork two bottles of wine at once.

LATE-NIGHT EATS

CHEZ CLAUDETTE ⓢ
351 ave. Laurier E., 514/279-5173

HOURS: Sun.-Wed. 10 A.M.-midnight, Thurs.-Sat. 24 hours

There's nothing quite like Chez Claudette, a 24-hour diner that caters to late-night revelers of any persuasion, and that includes vegans. This old-style diner tucked away on a quiet part of one of the city's fancier strips is so perfectly timeless you'll forget you're feeding your face at four in the morning. Their menu is extensive and includes the regular greasy spoon breakfast, but you can never go wrong with their *poutine* and a club sandwich, either the regular or vegan kind.

MIDDLE EASTERN

LE PETIT ALEP ⓢⓢ
191 rue Jean-Talon E., 514/270-9361

HOURS: Tues.-Sat. 11 A.M.-11 P.M.

Simply delicious. There's no better way to describe the food on the menu here, from their coffee to their meats, which are always tender and juicy, to the *fattouch* salad that comes with a nice bit of kick. The relaxed atmosphere is reflected in the magazines that hang on the wall and the newspapers nearby that invite you to bring them along to your table while you dig into a filet brochette. If you're feeling fancy pop next door to big Alep (199 rue Jean-Talon E., 514/270-6396) and enjoy your Syrian meal in slightly more romantic and upscale surroundings.

VEGETARIAN

LE CAGIBI ⓢ
5490 blvd. St-Laurent, 514/509-1199, www.lecagibi.ca

HOURS: Mon. 6 P.M.-midnight, Tues.-Fri. 9 A.M.-1 A.M., Sat. 10:30 A.M.-1 A.M., Sun. 10:30 A.M.-midnight

Situated on the corner of St-Laurent and St-Viateur, Le Cagibi is in the heart of hipsterville. But don't let that put you off; it is also one of the coziest cafés in the area, serving affordable vegetarian meals and good coffee all day long. At night the back room transforms into a performance space with everything from live shows to standup comedians and public talks. If you drink, however, you must eat, so make sure to bring an appetite. Though Montréal is queer-friendly, Le Cagibi is especially so, though for a younger LGBT crowd. Cash only.

LA LUMIÈRE DU MILE END ⓢ
214 rue Bernard W., 514/585-7453

HOURS: Daily 11 A.M.-8 P.M.

This tiny restaurant with bench seating, lots of light, and a café ambience caters to vegans with a number of delicious options on the menu, including black bean and quinoa burgers and the Whoa Black Betty wrap with olive tapenade and roasted red peppers. Though the fare here is modest, everything is fresh and usually served with nacho chips and a side salad. There's a small garden out back open in the summer months, and the place also serves a great vegan brunch on the weekend.

LE PANTHÈRE VERTE ⓢ
66 rue St-Viateur W., 514/903-7770, www.lapanthereverte.com

HOURS: Mon.-Fri. 11 A.M.-8 P.M., Sat. 11 A.M.-5 P.M.

Falafels, falafels, falafels. Sure, this place does other stuff like tofu steak, tempeh, and a veggie burger, but their falafels reign supreme—or your money back. Owner Chaim, an Israeli native, gives it a traditional twist that adds up to a fresh and healthy sandwich. Maybe it's the whole-wheat pita or the fact that you can get a shot of wheat grass with your meal, but no matter what it is the food here is both delicious and good for you. The decor is low-key, with a few tables cut out into funny, not-so-practical shapes, and a clientele that ranges from new-age hippies to tired out parents grabbing a quick dinner for the fam.

RESTAURANTS

NIGHTLIFE

Montréal is known for its nightlife, whether it's catching the latest emerging bands, dancing till the early morning, or sharing drinks with friends on a *terrasse* (otherwise known as a patio to non-Montréalers), there's no shortage of places or things to keep you busy.

Cafés, restaurants, live venues—many of them double as nightlife hotspots when the sun goes down. It might be hard to wrap your head around the idea that the place where you ate lunch is the same place you're headed to dance, but just go with it. If you're looking for something unpretentious and fun, these are the kinds of joints you'll want to seek out.

Those looking for a flashy night out at the club should head directly to St-Laurent; the lower part of this strip on the boundary of downtown and the Plateau has long been one of the top places to see and be seen. Restaurants that double as nightlife hotspots are especially popular in this area; servers are even known to get in on the party at these types of venues.

Chockablock with bars and nightclubs, rue Crescent may be enticing but should be avoided—unless you're an 18-year-old out-of-towner enjoying your first taste of freedom, in which case, party on. As in any popular strip there are definitely some more sophisticated and worthwhile spots, like Newtown, but migrating farther east to St-Laurent will give you a more authentic Montréal experience.

Legal drinking age in Québec is 18; kids who are from the province are usually well behaved, but because the drinking age is much lower than that in the States or even neighboring provinces, many teenagers come to

HIGHLIGHTS

LOOK FOR 🌙 TO FIND RECOMMENDED NIGHTLIFE.

🌙 **Most Likely to Transport You to Paris: Bar Barouf**'s red-hued lighting, Francophone staff, and bistro chairs will trick you into thinking you're in the City of Light in no time (page 113).

🌙 **Unique Decor:** At **Bily Kun,** the Czech-influenced decor is unlike you've ever seen, with mounted ostrich heads and tiles reminiscent of an old public pool (page 114).

🌙 **Best Microbrews:** Taste real Québécois beer at **Dieu du Ciel,** an unpretentious neighborhood staple (page 115).

🌙 **Best Gastro-Pub: Dominion Square Tavern** is one of the oldest taverns in the city. It has now been renovated into a sleek gastropub that serves a great mix of food and drink (page 115).

🌙 **Best Beer Garden:** Surrounded by immense, ivy-covered walls, **Le Ste-Élisabeth**'s majestic beer garden is always packed (page 117).

🌙 **Best Dance Club:** Sleek design, good-looking people, and the city's top DJs have made the W Hotel's **Wunderbar** one of the best places to go dancing in the city (page 120).

🌙 **Best Karaoke Bar:** Karaoke reigns supreme nightly at **Club Date,** a popular Village bar with a diverse list of songs and a great crowd (page 121).

🌙 **Most Versatile Venue:** Drink, dance, and catch the latest bands at **Casa del Popolo,** where there is always something happening and it's always fun (page 122).

🌙 **Best Cocktails:** A former pharmacy, **Baldwin Barmacie** has a cocktail menu that continues the theme with drinks like the "Pharmacien." Its white, retro-chic interior is a great place to kick back with a fancy drink (page 125).

🌙 **Best Wine Bar: Pullman**'s stunning interior and extensive wine list featuring 300 wines, with 50 wines by the glass, make this the best spot in the city for a classy but laid-back night out (page 128).

NIGHTLIFE

© ALEXANDRE CHABOT

Casa del Popolo

Montréal for the clubs, especially during New Year's and spring break. They tend to stick to the same area, however, like the aforementioned rue Crescent, so if you head off the beaten path you'll soon lose them.

Live music is a big part of going out, especially in a city known for its indie rock scene. Whether you're into minimal electro, hiphop, metal, or even bluegrass, there's a club or a DJ night for you. The Plateau is best area to catch emerging or lesser-known bands, both Canadian and international. If you're wandering the area at night you'll likely come across a show or three; most

venues have a small cover charge, under $20, so if you like what you hear it is usually worth it.

Since it is such a nightlife spot, Montréalers tend to go out late. It's not unusual to head out for an evening at midnight, or even later. That being said, Montréalers also love a good after-work drink. Happy hour is referred to as a 5 à 7, meaning cheaper drinks between five and seven in the evening.

No matter what you're up for—a quiet night sipping scotch, or hitting the clubs until the wee hours of the morning—Montréal has you covered.

Bars

L'ABSYNTHE
1738 rue St-Denis, 514/285-1738,
www.myspace.com/labsynthe
HOURS: Daily 3 P.M.-3 A.M.
COST: No cover
Map 4

A small, outdoor terrace invites patrons inside, where the crowd is invited to lounge in easy chairs and stare at the banister that leads to nowhere. This is, of course, after you've had a drink of the green fairy, the absinthe of the bar's name. The bartenders are adept

at pouring the infamous stuff, which comes in a variety of choices. Music here tends toward hippie-er sounds like world, electronic, and late-'60s.

L'AMÈRE À BOIRE
2049 rue St-Denis, 514/282-7448,
www.amereaboire.com
HOURS: Mon.-Sun. 2 P.M.-3 A.M., Thurs.-Sat. noon-3 A.M.
COST: No cover
Map 4

Three stories tall, this artisanal microbrewery

MONTRÉAL, ORIGINAL SIN CITY

Only a few hours from the American border, Montréal has always had a tortured history with its neighbors to the south. For generations, out of work Quebeckers would head across the border, looking for work in any number of small New England towns close to the frontier. After World War I, however, roles reversed and it was the Americans who came north, though they were seeking something different.

Between 1920 and 1933, Prohibition turned Montréal into a paradise for many Americans who came north in search of alcohol and found the jazz clubs, burlesque shows, gambling rooms, and brothels that went along with it.

With this kind of "entertainment" unrivaled by any other North American metropolis, it quickly picked up the nickname "Sin City." The city continued its reign well into the 1940s and 1950s, even attracting popular burlesque performers like Lili St-Cyr to the town.

Despite the fact that the city is no longer a mecca for jazz clubs, or gambling, it still retains that "Sin City" vibe thanks in part to a number of after-hours clubs, live venues that double as someone's living room, and the various downtown strip clubs. If you look close enough you might still find some of that Sin City yet.

is one of the best places to grab a drink in the Latin Quarter, and not only because they give you 18 different brews to choose from. With a huge cross-section of patrons that includes university students and office workers, L'Amère has a convivial atmosphere that can sometimes be hard to find. Almost labyrinthian in design, there are multiple levels throughout the bar, and the stairs are seemingly endless. There's usually one corner or another available for you to tuck yourself into. They also have a selection of tapas-style food, though some of it can be pricey.

(BAR BAROUF
4171 rue St-Denis, 514/844-0119
HOURS: Daily 3 P.M.-3 A.M.
COST: No cover
Map 5

This large, open bar will likely remind you of the windowed bistros of Paris. With marble-topped tables, bistro chairs, and reddish lighting, it has a distinct Rive Gauche vibe, compacted by the fact that finding a seat here can sometimes be a task. The gold-plated bar and beer taps give the place an added sheen, and though you can get your usual Québécois beers, like Boreal, Barouf also offers more continental choices—order a Pastis and be transported to France.

BARFLY
4062 blvd. St-Laurent, 514/284-6665,
www.myspace.com/barflymtl
HOURS: Mon.-Sun. 4 P.M.-3 A.M.
COST: No cover; $5-15 shows
Map 5

A tiny hole-in-the-wall on the Main, this dive bar is known for its bluegrass nights and its dingy interior. Cheap beer, a pool table, and live shows throughout the week sum up the bar's appeal. During hockey season Canadiens games can be watched on their LCD screen, an anomaly compared to the rest of the bar. High stools, a small bar, and a large round table constitute the seating arrangements. What it lacks in size, however, it makes up for in realness.

BAR PLAN B
327 ave. du Mont-Royal E., 514/845-6060,
www.barplanb.ca
HOURS: Daily 3 P.M.-3 A.M.
COST: No cover
Map 5

Set in the heart of the Plateau, this modern bar, frequented by young professionals and local residents, has the feel of being at a friend's place. Leather banquette seating, club chairs, and a sizable outdoor terrace all lend themselves to a comfortable, casual atmosphere. With a number of snacks on the menu, including mixed nuts, smoked trout, and goat's cheese, it's a perfect place for a pre-dinner aperitif.

LE BAR SOLEIL
Hilton Montréal Bonaventure, 900 rue de la Gauchetière W., 514/878-2332, www.hilton.com
HOURS: May-Oct. daily 11:30 A.M.-11 P.M.
COST: No cover
Map 2

Tucked away on the roof of the Hilton hotel, surrounded by concrete, this is an urban oasis thanks to a flourishing garden that offers a welcome break from the hubbub of city life. With the speakers pumping a mix of lounge and African-Cuban rhythms, reasonably priced cocktails and local beers (they also have 5 à 7 specials) will have you relaxed in no time. The small pool is an added bonus and attracts a welcome mix of sophisticated tourists and locals. Service here is also low-key, making you feel even further away from the city.

BIFTEK
3702 blvd. St-Laurent, 514/844-5211
HOURS: Daily 3 P.M.-3 A.M.
COST: No cover
Map 5

A perennial favorite, this dive bar is usually full to capacity with university students and people in their 20s and 30s. Beer is the drink of choice and usually comes in a pitcher, but shooters with appetizing names like "Windex" are also a hit with patrons. Bare bones "decor" includes a pool table and a jukebox. Popcorn, usually stale though somehow still delicious, is unceremoniously placed

NIGHTLIFE

on the table along with your beer. Musical preference tends toward loud, and the bar is cash only.

◖ BILY KUN

354 ave. du Mont-Royal, 514/845-5392, www.bilykun.com
HOURS: Daily 3 P.M.–3 A.M.
COST: No cover
Map 5

Meaning "white horse" in Czech, Bily Kun is named after a bar of the same name found by friends Fabien Lacaille and Bruce Hackenbeck during a trip to the Czech Republic. Charmed by the bar's quiet but cool ambience, and the rumor that Goethe used to come there to grab a beer at the end of a hard day, the friends returned to Montréal determined to create something similar.

Mounted ostrich heads and tiles reminiscent of an old public pool make this one of the most distinctive bars in the city. Intimate tables and a chic but unpretentious crowd make this place a must.

BRASSERIE CHEZ BAPTISTE

1045 ave. du Mont-Royal E., 514/522-1384,
www.chezbaptiste.com
HOURS: Daily 2 P.M.–3 A.M.
COST: No cover
Map 5

This no-nonsense Mont-Royal bar is a great place to stop in with friends and catch up over a pitcher of beer. In summertime it moves outside, like a few bars along this strip, taking over a section of the street with a makeshift terrace. Popular among young Québécois, and even some known musicians, it can often get rowdy, especially around the foosball table. The vibe is super relaxed and friendly, so this is a good place to break out some French, like *"merci,"* or *"deux bieres,"* (two beers). Happy hour here, known as a 5 à 7 in Québec, lasts 2–9 P.M.

BRUTOPIA

1215 rue Crescent, 514/393-9277, www.brutopia.net
HOURS: Mon.–Sun. 3 P.M.–3 A.M., Fri. noon–3 A.M.
COST: No cover
Map 2

This brewpub is one of the most well known and well liked in the city. Though brand-name beers are available, the microbrew selection consists of classic beers all year, including an IPA and a Raspberry Blonde, while seasonal brews include the Chocolate Stout, the Maple Rousse, and the Scotch Ale. It takes up three floors (with three outdoor terraces) of an old stone building on Crescent, and the vibe can definitely steer toward student at times. Happy hours are extended here from opening till 8 P.M. daily, and they regularly host open mic nights and smaller, local bands.

LE CHEVAL BLANC

809 rue Ontario E., 514/522-0211,
www.lechevalblanc.ca
HOURS: Mon.–Sat. 3 P.M.–3 A.M., Sun. 3 P.M.–2 A.M.
COST: No cover
Map 4

One of the city's last great working-class taverns, Le Cheval Blanc (The White Horse) is unlike any other bar in Montréal. It's a long-time family-run business located in a turn-of-the-20th-century building; the green Formica on the walls, bar, and table tops is the main aspect of the decor, with the establishment simply decorated with counter stools and black bistro chairs. In 1986 it became the first brewpub in the city, and its white beer Cheval Blanc is famous throughout the province. Everyone comes here, from young artists to old regulars, and staff are friendly. It's mainly a Francophone hangout, and you'd be hard-pressed to find a less pretentious bar in Montréal.

LE CONFESSIONAL

431 rue McGill, 514/656-1350,
www.confessional.ca
HOURS: Tues.–Wed. 9 P.M.–3 A.M., Thurs.–Sat.
5 P.M.–3 A.M.
COST: No cover
Map 1

This inviting neighborhood bar has more swank than you'd expect from its unassuming front door. With a richly decorated interior enhanced by soft lighting, this bar has the cosy feel of an old-time pub. Hosting a number of

© MARCO CAMPANOZZI

Le Cheval Blanc is the oldest microbrewery in the city.

diverse events, everything from stand-up comedy to live performances, rock nights to R&B, Le Confessional has something to offer everyone and the crowd reflects that. Depending on the night's event, the place might be packed with old-school hiphop fans or young professionals winding down after work.

(DIEU DU CIEL
29 ave. Laurier W., 514/490-9555,
www.dieuduciel.com
HOURS: Daily 3 P.M.-3 A.M.
COST: No cover
Map 6

This microbrewery and brasserie is one of the best places in the city to experience real Québécois beer. Full of dark wood, tiny round tables, heavy velvet curtains, and a view of the beer vats themselves, Dieu du Ciel evokes a relaxed, friendly atmosphere, especially in winter when the windows are fogged by the heat from indoors. Beer menus change often, but usually include at least 15 choices, some of which are seasonal. Try the Péché Mortal (Mortal Sin), an imperial coffee stout, in the winter.

(DOMINION SQUARE TAVERN
1243 rue Metcalfe, 514/564-5056,
www.tavernedominion.com
HOURS: Mon.-Fri. 11:30 A.M.-midnight,
Sat. 5 P.M.-midnight
COST: No cover
Map 2

Built in 1926, Dominion is one of Montréal's oldest taverns. Recently renovated by new owners Alex Baldwin (of Baldwin Barmacie) and Alexander Wolosianski (of Whisky Café), it is now an old-timey chic gastro-pub. Serving fare like pigs knuckles, ploughman's lunches, and pan-seared salmon, it's the bar part of the equation that's really getting noticed, attracting everyone from Canadiens fans to moviegoers and more than a few hipsters. Tastefully decorated with a good amount of historic grit, it's a great place to grab a cocktail.

GOTHA
1641 rue Amherst, 514/525-1270
HOURS: Sun.-Thurs. 4 P.M.-1 A.M., Fri.-Sat. 4 P.M.-3 A.M.
COST: No cover
Map 4

This cozy bar in the Village has a bit of a mid-'60s

vibe with its round-backed chairs, banquette seating, and geometric pillows. Just because it is in the Village, however, doesn't mean the clientele comes exclusively from the LGBT community; patrons of all orientations can be found here.

Music on the stereo tends toward lounge, with bartenders and regulars setting the play list. Later in the week on Thursday and Friday evenings, the bar's piano serves as the center of jazz night.

HELM
273 rue Bernard W., 514/276-0473, www.helm-mtl.ca
HOURS: Mon.-Tues. and Sun. 4 P.M.-1 A.M., Wed.-Sat. 3 P.M.-3 A.M.
COST: No cover
Map 6

Though sleeker than other brewpubs in the city, with its wooden chairs and tables and bright orange upholstery, Helm's focus is still on the beer, with a classic and new rock edge. It's a popular place most nights of the week, and in the summer patrons of all ages often sit on the bar's street-level window ledge swigging a beer. Beer prices change depending on size and time of day, so if you want a real bargain get there early and grab a bite off the bar menu. Seven micro-beers feature on the menu, alongside wines and spirits and even a few regular domestic brews.

HURLEY'S IRISH PUB
1225 rue Crescent, 514/861-4111, www.hurleysirishpub.com
HOURS: Daily 11 A.M.-3 A.M.
COST: No cover
Map 2

There's no shortage of Irish pubs in Montréal—okay, make that the world—but there is something to be said of an Irish pub that actually feels Irish, and few come as close to the real thing. A few steps down into Hurley's and you're surrounded by stone walls and low ceilings, with the bar taking center stage. Classic low stools and tables take up the main room, but try to nab a place on one of the comfy club chairs near the fireplace. Traditional Irish music—and that includes U2—plays just about every night of the week.

NYKS
1250 rue de Bleury, 514/866-1786, www.nyks.ca
HOURS: Mon.-Fri. 11:30 A.M.-3 A.M.
COST: No cover
Map 3

Just south of Ste-Catherine, surrounded by a number of big, flashy venues, you'll find Nyks, an unpretentious, rustic haven in which to kick back and have a drink. With live music, mostly jazz, playing throughout the week, it's a nice alternative to the crowded and bars in the rest of the downtown core. If you get hungry choose from their light bistro or pub fare; either one should fill you up nicely.

LE SAINT-SULPICE
1680 rue St-Denis, 514/844-9458, www.lesaintsulpice.ca
HOURS: Winter daily noon-3 A.M., summer daily 11 A.M.-3 A.M.
COST: No cover
Map 4

Once the home of a Victorian banker, the immense Saint-Sulpice first opened its doors as a bar in 1980. Occupying four floors of the 19th-century house, it has 10 bars in the summer and seven in the winter, all of which has to be seen to be believed. Each floor has its own style; there's the library, the cabaret, the cave and annex, with the basement and top floors both doubling as dance floors. Outside, a massive outdoor terrace attracts patrons throughout the summer, and even features a babbling fountain and its own back alley entrance. Unlike most Montréal bars, this place asks for I.D., so don't forget to bring some, regardless of age.

SPARROW
5322 blvd. St-Laurent, 514/690-3964
HOURS: Mon.-Fri. 5 P.M.-3 A.M., Sat.-Sun. 6 P.M.-3 A.M.
COST: No cover
Map 6

The bird motif wallpaper, church pews, and fireplace/DJ booth make Sparrow one of the Mile End's coziest bars. This bar has an Old World pub atmosphere that is popular with neighborhood locals and those looking for a hang out where the music isn't too loud. If you find yourself here around dinnertime, grab a burger, beef cheeks in red wine sauce, or the po' boy sandwich.

After the dinner rush, Sparrow transforms into one of the busiest bars in the neighborhood, with standing room only on weekends.

(LE STE-ÉLISABETH
1412 Ste-Élisabeth, 514/286-4302, www.ste-elisabeth.com
HOURS: Mon.-Fri. 4 P.M.-3 A.M., Sat.-Sun. 6 P.M.-3 A.M.
COST: No cover
Map 3

A building that was built in the 1930s, Le Ste-Élisabeth's nondescript exterior hides a magnificent beer garden. Lush and green in the summer and surrounded by tall, ivy-covered walls, it's always hard to find a seat there. Inside, there's an old tavern atmosphere with club chairs, sofas, and striped wood floors. Even in the winter this place gets packed, and you'll sometimes find yourself yelling over the music, which ranges from top 40 hits to Québécois rock. If you can't find a seat in the garden there's a second-floor glassed-in terrace overlooking the outdoor one.

LA TERRASSE MAGNÉTIC
Hôtel de la Montagne, 1430 rue de la Montagne, 514/281-5349, www.hoteldelamontagne.com
HOURS: May-Oct. Thurs.-Sat. 4 P.M.-2 A.M.
COST: No cover
Map 2

Located on the top floor of the downtown Hôtel de la Montagne, La Terrasse Magnétic draws locals and tourists alike with their rooftop pool and bar. Men and women in their 20s and 30s flock here to work on their tans and bask in that laid-back summertime vibe that comes with being next to water. Service is always with a smile, and the drinks are much more affordable than at other top-of-the-city bars.

LE TERRASSE SUITE 701
Place d'Armes Hôtel and Suites, 701 Côte de la Place d'Armes, 514/904-1201, www.aixcuisine.com
HOURS: May-Oct. Mon.-Wed. and Sun. 11 A.M.-midnight, Thurs.-Sat. 11 A.M.-3 A.M.
COST: No cover
Map 1

This swank cocktail bar on the roof of Place d'Armes Hôtel and Suites couldn't give you

better views of the city's skyline. A DJ pumps tunes throughout the day, everything from top 40 to bossa nova, for the mostly local clientele who slip on their best dancing shoes for an evening of open-air dancing. Service is attentive and efficient, and your drink requests are answered by a mixologist. The mood is ambient and adult with an understated sophistication. If the weather turns, you can take refuge in the adjoining indoor lounge.

LES TROIS BRASSEURS
1658 rue St-Denis, 514/845-1660, www.les3brasseurs.ca
HOURS: Mon.-Wed. and Sun. 11:30 A.M.-midnight, Thurs.-Sat. 11:30 A.M.-2 A.M.
COST: No cover
Map 4

Located in the heart of the Quartier Latin, branches of this local microbrewery can be found throughout the city (in Vieux-Montréal at 105 St-Paul E., 514/788-6100, and downtown at 732 Ste-Catherine W., 514/788-6333), but this is the only location with a rooftop terrace. It's open year-round—don't worry, it is heated in winter—and popular with university students and office workers off the clock. The vibe is always lively and relaxed, and the service is like that too, with servers happy to bring you another pitcher and freshly chilled beer mugs. The interior isn't much—wooden tables, beer vats—but the view of St-Denis at night is perfect.

VERSES SKY
Hôtel Nelligan, 100 rue St-Paul W., 514/788-4000, www.versesrestaurant.com
HOURS: May-Oct. daily 11 A.M.-11 P.M.
COST: No cover
Map 1

During the summer months, this rooftop terrace in Hotel Nelligan is one of the top places to see and be seen. Populated with fashionable 20-something ladies, young professionals still in their business suits and, later in the evening, older Mafioso-types, this place appeals to high-rollers. It's located on the roof of a boutique hotel, so drinks are on the pricier

NIGHTLIFE

NIGHTLIFE

THE HEIGHT OF COCKTAIL HOUR: ROOFTOP BARS

Montréal is in winter's clutches for what feels like eight months of the year, so when the thermometer finally shows a positive number, everyone is out drinking in the sunshine.

- **Le Bar Soleil:** Take an all-inclusive break at this rooftop pool, bar, and garden with great views of the city beyond.

- **Narcisse Bistro:** Doubling as a wine bar, this rooftop terrace gives you a great view of the Old Port as you sip your Muscadet.

- **La Terrasse Magnétic:** Guests and locals alike flock to this rooftop pool and bar. Take the elevator all the way up to join the party.

- **La Terrasse Suite 701:** Looking out on to Notre-Dame Basilica and Place d'Armes you can enjoy your port, while contemplating the great architecture.

- **Les Trois Brasseurs:** This popular local microbrewery chain has the best patio of any bar in the Latin Quarter.

- **Verses Sky:** Rivaling the view from Narcisse is Verses. It's open 11 A.M.-11 P.M., you can sip your cocktail at just about any time of day.

© VERSES RESTAURANT

Verses Sky

side ($10 for a cocktail), but you can't beat the 200-degree view of the city that includes the Aldred Building, Habitat 67, and Notre-Dame Basilica.

VICES ET VERSA
6631 blvd. St-Laurent, 514/272-2498,
www.vicesetversa.com
HOURS: Sun.-Mon. 1 P.M.-1 A.M., Tues.-Sat. 1 P.M.-3 A.M.
COST: No cover
Map 6

This neighborhood brewpub, situated on the cusp of Mile End and Petite Italy, has a definite laid-back atmosphere, though things often get rowdy later in the night. The high tin ceilings give the impression that the bar is bigger than it actually is, with its built-in wooden banquettes and long, narrow terrace. Thirty-three beers are always on tap from microbreweries from around the province, including Vices et Versa's own IPA and Cream Ale. Selections change regularly, however, so if you loved the Framboise (raspberry) last time, they might not have it this time.

Dance Clubs

BAINS DOUCHES
390 rue St-Jacques W., 514/845-3056,
www.bainsdouches.ca
HOURS: Thurs.-Sat. 10 P.M.-3 A.M.
COST: $15-40
Map 1

Revelers can sip their Louis XIII Cognac ($6,000 a bottle) in the VIP section of this electronic mecca and keep an eye on the crowd below. Reputed to be one of the best clubs in the city—Paris Hilton even made a cameo—it boasts a cutting-edge sound system, three glass bars, leather furniture imported from Italy, and enough staff to ensure your glass is never empty. Already a popular nightspot, things get especially packed on Thursdays when the club celebrates ladies night, when women are treated to drink specials.

BLUE DOG MOTEL
3958 blvd. St-Laurent, 514/845-4258
HOURS: Mon.-Sun. 9:30 P.M.-3 A.M.
COST: No cover
Map 5

The Blue Dog is co-owned by DJ duo Team Canada, known for mix tapes that mash hiphop, rock, and electro. The internationally known duo took over the decks, bar, and venue of a once-flagging hiphop club and have brought it back with a vengeance. The single room is usually filled to capacity with skateboarders, hiphoppers, and kids dying to dance all week long. Sunday is a sad excuse to stay home. If you're unsure where you're headed just look for the sky-blue facade, which stands out against other stores and bars on the Main.

CIRCUS
917 rue Ste-Catherine E., 514/844-3626,
www.circusafterhours.com
HOURS: Thurs. and Sun. 2-8 A.M., Fri. 2-10 A.M.,
Sat. 2-11 A.M.
COST: $20
Map 4

Three different rooms catering to three different sounds make up the biggest after-hours club in Montréal. Living up to its name, the club features circus performers wandering around the crowd as they dance well into the morning. DJs on the decks spin mainly house, dark house, hiphop, tribal, and R&B, though celebrity DJs often bring their own sounds to the decks. Dress code here is less formal than most clubs in the city, but since the majority of the clientele have already been out all night, dress as though you have too. This place is popular, so lineups sometimes go around the block.

CLUB 1234
1234 rue de la Montagne, 514/395-1111,
www.1234montreal.com
HOURS: Fri.-Sun. 10 P.M.-3 A.M.
COST: $15
Map 2

This club gets a lot of flack for having a younger—sometimes under 21—crowd, but it often plays host to some of the hottest young DJs and electronic groups, and the surroundings are simply amazing. Originally built in 1859 as a personal residence (and now supposedly haunted), the enormous and, it has to be said, flashy building consists of a huge domed entrance with circular staircases carved out of white marble. The dome theme continues in the main room, as do the marble touches. The dress code here isn't too strict; women can get away with flats, and men, dressier jeans, but make sure to freshen up before you go.

KOROVA
3908 blvd. St-Laurent, 514/904-6444
HOURS: Mon.-Sun. 10 P.M.-3 A.M.
COST: No cover
Map 5

On the second floor of a building on the Main, Korova's wall-to-wall windows look out over the traffic and night crawlers on the street below. Catering to a rock crowd, but including many a dancier pop tune, it has a definite relaxed vibe amped up with the addition of a pool table and vintage Pac-Man console.

NIGHTLIFE

Dancing is not required here but it is encouraged. Many students and locals frequent the place for a midweek beer and dance-off.

NEWTOWN

1476 rue Crescent, 514/284-6555, www.lenewtown.com
HOURS: Mon.-Thurs. and Sun. 11:30 A.M.-1 A.M., Fri.-Sat. 11:30 A.M.-3 A.M.
COST: $15
Map 2

Opened by race-car driver Jacques Villeneuve (Newtown is a direct translation of his surname), this club and restaurant occupies three floors of an impressive corner lot in the heart of the downtown club district. A mix of old and new on the outside, the interior is huge, with a minimal gray and white decor and purplish lighting. Catering to the 25 and up crowd, this is a classy joint with good food, stylish patrons, and a range of music from electro house to hiphop and top 40.

LE SALON DAOMÉ

141 ave. du Mont-Royal E., 514/982-7070,
www.lesalondaome.com
HOURS: Tues.-Sun. 10 P.M.-3 A.M.
COST: $5
Map 5

Dedicated to electronic music, this dance club and lounge has a more opulent feel than most clubs, with plush seating and sparse surroundings. Set in a loft, the electronic music featured here is more varied and off-the-beaten-track than what you'll find elsewhere in the city. Patrons here are usually die-hard electronic fans seeking out the latest music in the scene.

STEREO

858 rue Ste-Catherine E., 514/286-0325,
www.stereo-nightclub.com
HOURS: Fri.-Sat. 11 P.M.-late
COST: $40
Map 4

This world-renowned after-hours club may have hit a couple of road bumps in the past few years—a fire and subsequent closure in 2008 and another in 2009—but it is now back up and running at top speed. Still one of the best places in the world to party late into the night and early morning, it is known for playing house music and attracting some of the world's top DJs. Though Stereo Bar opens at 11 P.M., the after-hours club doesn't open its doors till after 1 A.M., often later. With the renovations came a new DJ booth, swankier furnishings, and a couple of big screens for visuals.

TOKYO BAR

3709 blvd. St-Laurent, 514/842-6838, www.tokyobar.com
HOURS: Wed.-Sun. 10 P.M.-3 A.M.
COST: $5
Map 5

This popular bar, full of young patrons, has different rooms decorated in wildly different ways, from futuristic all white to gold and glitzy; there's even an outdoor terrace on which you can dance the night away, come rain or shine. On Thursday, Friday, and Saturday nights you might find a lineup outside, but they are usually accommodating and it shouldn't take long to get in. No matter the day of the week, the music here—top 40, '80s, hiphop—is usually better than what you'll find on other dance clubs on the Main; at the very least it offers you choice.

C WUNDERBAR

901 Square Victoria, 514/395-3100,
www.wunderbarmmontreal.com
HOURS: Tues.-Sat. 10 P.M.-3 A.M.
COST: No cover
Map 1

Rumor has it that when this bar first opened they bribed local hipsters with free drinks to populate the place. Whether the rumor's true or not, it remains one of the top bars in the city and a great place to cut a rug. With a roster that includes some of the city's top DJs playing everything from top-40 mash-ups to old school slow-jams, the dance floor is always packed. The clientele is decidedly diverse—everyone from college kids to high rollers—and keeping to the Montréal ethos, everyone is impeccably turned out, with women in up-to-the-minute fashions with a downtown edge and the men looking chic but casual.

Gay and Lesbian

CABARET CHEZ MADO

1115 rue Ste-Catherine E., 514/525-7566,
www.mado.qc.ca
HOURS: Mon.-Sun. 3 P.M.-3 A.M.
COST: $10
Map 4

The grande dame of Montréal drag, Mado Lamothe is the proprietor and star attraction of this cabaret showcase. Performances always include silliness, dancing, music, and a little improv. Showcasing some of the best drag acts from across the city and internationally, Mado's always attracts a diverse crowd. The setup, isn't particularly flashy, with a small(ish) stage, regular bar seating, and lots of black lights. Each performance is followed by a night of dancing, so come ready to bust a move. Mado herself takes to the stage every Tuesday.

◖ CLUB DATE

1218 rue Ste-Catherine E., 514/521-1242
HOURS: Daily 3 P.M.-3 A.M.
COST: No cover
Map 4

If the name didn't already attract you, the nightly karaoke battles should. Situated in the heart of the Village, this place is known for the intense level of commitment shown by die-hard karaoke fans of every walk of life.

Seat yourself at the bar or at one of the more intimate tables near the front window, which opens onto the sidewalk in the summer. Musical selections are vast and range from Led Zeppelin to Celine Dion. This place is all about the audience though, so if you're shy about your singing sit back and enjoy the show. Cash only.

CLUB UNITY

1171 rue Ste-Catherine E., 514/523-2777,
www.clubunitymontreal.com
HOURS: Wed.-Sat. 10 A.M.-3 A.M.
COST: $7, free before 11 P.M.
Map 4

Featuring three floors, a VIP lounge, and a roof-top terrace, Club Unity is one of the bigger clubs

Le Drugstore is one of the largest bars in the Village.

© PRODUCTIONS DE L'ILE JEAN-MARC AYRAL

in the Village. The casual atmosphere, epitomized by the lounge with its long benches and friendly environment, extends to the dress code as well. Music played here tends toward house, top 40, and hiphop with local and international DJs taking over the decks nightly. It also plays host to special events, including drag shows, karaoke nights, and even the occasional dance troupe.

LE DRUGSTORE

1366 rue Ste-Catherine E., 514/524-1960
HOURS: Daily 10 A.M.-3 A.M.
COST: No cover
Map 4

One of the largest gay bars in the world, this six-floor complex has rooftop terraces, karaoke, pool tables, and dance floors. Decor is decidedly casual with lots of neon signs, brightly colored walls (in honor of the gay flag), and an American diner feel with jukeboxes, a popcorn machine, and old movie cameras hung about the place.

Once a predominantly a lesbian bar, it now welcomes all clients, though there are "girls nights" throughout the week. The relaxed atmosphere and packed bars on the weekend attract those looking for a place to gab under the stars and cut a rug to the rock, pop, and disco tunes.

PARKING

1296 rue Amherst, 514/282-1199, www.parkingbar.com

HOURS: Thurs.-Sun. 10 P.M.-3 A.M.

COST: $5-15, free before 11 P.M.

Map 4

Quite possibly the most popular gay bar in the city, Parking has three distinct rooms: the Nightclub, the Urban Room, and the Terrace. On weekends the Nightclub is invaded by hip young gays, straights, bisexuals, transsexuals etc. partying to the sounds of house, electro, and hiphop or a special blend provided by the guest DJ. A former car garage, the interior is huge and open with high ceilings and a steel, industrial-style dance floor. If the dancing gets too much, head out to the terrace for a bit of fresh air.

SKY PUB CLUB

1474 rue Ste-Catherine E., 514/529-6969, www.complexesky.com

HOURS: Daily noon-3 A.M.

COST: Free first floor, $4 second-fourth floors

Map 4

This absolutely massive complex—a bit of a trend in the Village—has a ground floor pub (open for dinner 4–9 P.M.), a male strip club, a dinner and drag cabaret, a hiphop room, a huge disco, and even an outdoor terrace—with a pool.

Though it caters to a mostly gay male clientele, with this kind of choice, it is hard to keep everyone a away. In fact, it has girls only nights for lesbians, and it is a popular place for straight women looking for a place to party without the bad pickup lines.

Live Music

CAFÉ CAMPUS & PETIT CAMPUS

57 rue Prince Arthur E., 514/844-1010, www.cafecampus.com

HOURS: Tues.-Sat. 8:30 P.M.-3 A.M., Sun. 8 P.M.-3 A.M.

COST: $5-15; dance nights are often free before 10 P.M. or 11 P.M.

Map 5

Once a bar frequented by students of the Université de Montréal in the 1970s, Café Campus has become one of the most frequented venues in the city. The clientele still draws from the student sector, but it is no longer as closely associated with the university; instead university kids from all over the city come here for their dance and DJ nights or to check out an indie rock show. Divided into two venues, both Petit Campus and Café Campus are busy most days of the week, though entrance to one won't get you into the other.

CAFÉ CHAOS

2031 rue St-Denis, 514/844-1301, www.cafechaos.qc.ca

HOURS: Mon.-Fri. 3 P.M.-3 A.M., Sat.-Sun. 5 P.M.-3 A.M.

COST: $5-15

Map 4

The best punk bar in the city, since opening

its doors in 1995 Café Chaos has become a Quartier Latin staple. Fostering young talent from around the province and abroad, it hosts some of the wildest hard-core and punk bands currently touring. When the club is not blasting costumers with live music, DJs take over the decks for nights during the week, including Metal Wednesdays. Run as a co-op, it also has a small kitchen where you can get a bite to go with you locally brewed beer, both at affordable prices.

CASA DEL POPOLO

4873 blvd. St-Laurent, 514/284-3804, www.casadelpopolo.com

HOURS: Daily noon-3 A.M.

COST: No cover; $5-20 shows

Map 5

Started by a member of uber-cool ensemble Godspeed You! Black Emperor, this venue hosts both obscure and more well-known bands. It's a vegetarian café during the day, and later in the evening it transforms into a bar. True to its roots on the Main, it has authentic tin ceilings, mixed-matched furniture, and a lot of old, dark wood. Casa del Popolo recently

© SACHA JACKSON

Audience members are a part of the performances at Les Deux Pierrots.

expanded its second room, used exclusively for shows and DJ nights. No matter when you go there is always something happening, from doo-wop nights to rock, live bands to dance parties. During the summer head out back to the bustling terrace.

LES DEUX PIERROTS

104 rue St-Paul E., 514/861-1270, www.lespierrots.com
HOURS: Fri.-Sat. 8:30 P.M.-3 A.M., Sun. 11:30 A.M.-midnight
COST: $5
Map 1

If you're looking for a truly Québécois experience head to Les Deux Pierrots on a Friday or Saturday night. Since opening its doors in 1974, it has become one of the most well-known *boîtes à chansons* in Montréal. First springing up in the mid-1950s, *boîtes à chansons* combine well-known and home-grown songs with live entertainment in a bar setting, a phenomenon that is specific to Québec. Featuring some of the best singers (*chansonniers*) and entertainers in the province, the atmosphere is rowdy, in the

best way, with audience members often joining in with the antics on stage. Les Deux Pierrots has since expanded to include Le Pierrot just next door, and also has an outdoor terrace in the summer and a year-round sports bar. Don't expect a classy show bar however; like the performers themselves this place is down to earth.

DIVAN ORANGE

4234 blvd. St-Laurent, 514/840-9090, www.divanorange.org
HOURS: Tues.-Sun. 4 P.M.-3 A.M.
COST: No cover; $5-20 shows
Map 5

There's something about this bar that gives a particularly homey feel. It could be the regular kitchen range behind the bar and the fact that snacks include a homemade pizza, but it goes beyond that. Effortlessly bilingual, it attracts patrons from both sides of the language debate and has become, despite its small stage, one of a few places to hear bands as diverse the folksy Fleet Foxes and local punk band Grand Trine.

L'ESCOGRIFFE

4467 rue St-Denis, 514/842-7244,
www.lescobar.com

HOURS: Daily 8 P.M.–3 A.M.

COST: No cover; $5-20 shows

Map 5

This intimate, stone-walled basement bar is one of the best places to see emerging bands, which is what makes it so popular with the *branchée* Francophone crowd. Though it has a decidedly rock edge, playing mostly garage rock, '50s, '60s, and punk from the '70s and '80s, they also showcase jazz, indie rock, and electro bands. But they all come from underground scenes. Even the occasional dance night focuses on lesser-known tunes. If you're passing by during the day, grab a drink and sit on either one of their two terraces.

LES FOUFOUNES ELECTRIQUES

87 rue Ste-Catherine E., 514/844-5539,
www.foufounes.qc.ca

HOURS: Daily 4 P.M.–3 A.M.

COST: No cover; $5-20 shows

Map 3

Lovingly called Foufs by locals, the full name means Electric Ass. It opened in 1983 with the aim of showcasing different types of art—a large metal spider still hangs over the entrance. What started as an artists' hangout has turned into a club and bar and Montréal's answer to CBGB in the '90s, with bands like Nirvana, L7, and The Misfits taking the stage. It's still one of the best places to catch bands play and drink a cold beer, but it's also become a popular dance spot attracting young and old rockers and punks (and some wannabes) to the dance floor.

KATACOMBS

1222 blvd. St-Laurent, 514/861-6151,
www.myspace.com/katacombs

HOURS: Mon.-Thurs. 7 P.M.–3 A.M., Fri.-Sat. 8 P.M.–3 A.M., Sun. 8 P.M.–1 A.M.

COST: $5-15

Map 3

This punk club has been going for years, though it only recently moved into its black,

cubist digs on St-Laurent and Ontario. Catering to mainly punk, hard-core, and metal crowds, bands from all three genres as well as industrial DJs are usually found on stage here. The club sometimes branches out into one-off events like dress-up disco night. The venue has also hosted comedians and other non–G.G. Allin–type performers.

IL MOTORE

179 rue Jean-Talon W., 514/284-0122,
www.ilmotore.ca

HOURS: Daily 9 P.M.–3 A.M.

COST: No cover; $5-20 shows

Map 6

With Casa del Popolo and La Sala Rossa, Il Motore completes the holy trinity of cool Montréal venues. A collaboration between the owners of Casa and Sala and local promoters/record label Blue Skies Turn Black, it brings some of the most interesting, emerging international bands to the city and a frequently sold-out crowd. As such, it is usually full of young and not-so-young hipsters, checking out Europe's hottest new export. The atmosphere is understated cool, with dark red walls and a fully stocked bar about the extent of decoration. Seats are at a premium, though you might find a handful at the bar, so come prepared to stand. Depending on how booked they are, the weekly schedule varies, so check before coming.

O PATRO VYS

356 ave. du Mont-Royal E., 514/845-3855,
www.bilykun.com

HOURS: Tues.-Sun. 8 P.M.–3 A.M.

COST: $5-25

Map 5

Just upstairs from the ostrich heads at Bily Kun is O Patro Vys, their live-venue counterpart. Showcasing more jazz and minimal-electro than punk bands, some of the cool elegance of the downstairs bar continues upstairs, making it a more adult venue than some. An interested and interesting crowd can usually be found, and the atmosphere is always super relaxed.

PUB ST-PAUL

124 rue St-Paul E., 514/874-0485,
www.pubstpaul.com

HOURS: Daily 11 A.M.-3 A.M.

COST: $5

Map 1

Ideally located in a building that was established in 1875 and overlooking the Old Port, this rock bar is one of the few live venues in Old Montréal. The decor may be decidedly no-frills, but the pub grub is some of the most authentic in the area. Go for the chicken wings; they can be hard to find in Montréal. Spread out over two floors, Pub St-Paul offers live music—everything from hard rock to top 40—every Thursday through Saturday from some of Montréal and Québec's best bands.

UPSTAIRS JAZZ BAR AND GRILL

1254 rue Mackay, 514/931-6808, www.upstairsjazz.com

HOURS: Mon.-Thurs. and Sun. 11:30 A.M.-1 A.M., Fri.-Sat. 11:30 A.M.-2 A.M.

COST: $5-25

Map 2

This is the best jazz bar in the city, so plan to spend the night in a cozy, inviting atmosphere full of friendly, jazz-loving regulars. The Upstairs sign is cleverly turned upside-down since it's actually a few steps down, not up, to get in. With a heavy rotation of both Canadian and international jazz artists you're not likely to hear the same musician twice. Cover prices vary from $5–25, though most nights it won?t cost you more than $5 to hear some of the best musicians in the city. Though they serve food, the real reason to come here is for the music.

Lounges

ALTITUDE 737

1 Place Ville-Marie, Fl. PH2, #4340, 514/397-0737, www.altitude737.com

HOURS: Summer Thurs.-Sat. 10 P.M.-3 A.M., winter Fri.-Sat. 10 P.M.-3 A.M.

COST: $15

Map 2

Shining out over the city like a roving Bat-Signal, Altitude 737's spotlight is one of the most recognizable sights in the night sky. Situated on the top of Place Ville-Marie, the first skyscraper in downtown Montréal, Altitude 737 attracts a diverse clientele to its three-floor nightclub and lounge with a rooftop terrace in the summer that looks out over the entire city. Each floor here features different styles of music from house to top 40.

BALDWIN BARMACIE

115 ave. Laurier W., 514/276-4282, www.baldwinbarmacie.com

HOURS: Mon.-Sat. 5 P.M.-3 A.M., Sun. 7 P.M.-3 A.M.

COST: No cover

Map 6

Cutting-edge electro and indie rock are usually on the sound system at this retro-futuristic bar. Opened by two brothers whose father used to run a pharmacy on the same spot, the name is a clever nod to the family legacy, but it also serves as theme throughout the cocktail menu, which includes the "Pharmacien" drink. It's a popular spot for locals earlier in the week—stop by for an early evening cocktail to catch the vibe—but by the weekend, it is taken over by young professionals and trust-fund kids with a taste for dancing.

BLIZZARTS

3956 blvd. St-Laurent, 514/843-4860

HOURS: Mon.-Sat. 9:30 P.M.-3 A.M.

COST: No cover

Map 5

One of the first places in the city to exclusively play electro-techno, Blizzarts now plays various kinds of music all week long. Large, rounded banquettes give the space a retro-futurist feel. Art exhibitions are often held here, and the vernissages can go late into the night. A casual place for dancing, there's a small dance floor at the front that usually gets crowded. The attitude and crowd here are generally laid-back, and you're welcome to come dancing in your sneakers, or your winter boots for that matter, whatever suits.

BUONANOTTE
3518 blvd. St-Laurent, 514/848-0644,
www.buonanotte.com
HOURS: Mon.-Wed. noon-midnight, Thurs.-Fri. noon-1 A.M., Sat. 4 P.M.-3 A.M., Sun. 4 P.M.-midnight
COST: Cover varies; bottle reservation required
Map 5

Market-fresh Italian cuisine is on the menu at this restaurant turned nightclub, known to draw a celebrity crowd—a wall is dedicated to plates signed by hot Hollywood actors. The dress code is particularly stylish; don't expect to get in here unless you're wearing heels (if you're a woman) or a suit jacket (if you're a man). The super-modern interior consists of fuchsia sofas and sleek, wooden seating. Dinner is served late into the night, so expect to finish off your Italian meal next to a crowd dancing on tables.

GLOBE
3455 blvd. St-Laurent, 514/284-3823,
www.restaurantglobe.com
HOURS: Mon.-Wed. 6-11 P.M.
COST: Cover varies; bottle reservation required
Map 5

Owned by the people behind Buonanotte, this restaurant and nightclub is less about the food than the waitresses that serve and then party with the patrons all night long. Though the food is decent, the real reason people come is for the late-night parties that rival those across the street at Buonanotte. If you're looking for a one-stop evening, then look no further than Globe. Though be forewarned; with its loud techno and expense account clients this place can get a little cheesy.

GO-GO LOUNGE
3682 blvd. St-Laurent, 514/286-0882
HOURS: Daily 5 P.M.-3 A.M.
COST: $20
Map 5

This psychedelic '60s-themed bar does a nice job of staying on the good side of cheesy, with pop art themed walls, hand-shaped chairs, and lots of red lights. Known for their cocktails,

this is a great place to knock back a martini based on your astrological sign. The dance floor is small and tends to get packed, so come early to avoid the crowds.

JELLO MARTINI LOUNGE
151 rue Ontario E., 514/285-2009,
www.jellomartinilounge.com
HOURS: Tues.-Sun. 9 P.M.-3 A.M.
COST: $8
Map 3

Newly revamped and refurbished, this place retains its retro-chic with its signature lava lamps, multicolored stools and '60s-inspired tunes. As the name suggests, Jello is all about the martini, and there are over 50 varieties (and counting) to choose from here, making it the city's top bar for those who like it shaken or stirred. Live music pleases the crowd on most nights but keeps with the swinging vibe with classic soul.

TERRASSES BONSECOURS
Quays of the Old Port, 514/288-9407,
www.terrassesbonsecours.com
HOURS: May-Sept. daily 3 P.M.-3 A.M.
COST: $5-25
Map 1

Just past the Cirque de Soleil tent, surrounded by water, you'll find the four floors of Terrasses Bonsecours. A great place to rent ice skates and warm up with a hot chocolate in the winter, it transforms into a jumping open-air hotspot come summer. Avoid the cover (and crowds) and get there early to enjoy a cocktail and watch the sunset behind the city from one of the best vantage points. By midnight the place is packed with the bridge and tunnel crowd (local slang for suburbanites); stay and bump 'n' grind to the techno and R&B along with them—or head for a late-night stroll along the waterfront.

TIME SUPPER CLUB
997 rue St-Jacques W., 514/392-9292,
www.timesupperclub.com
HOURS: Tues.-Sat. 8 P.M.-3 A.M.
COST: $20
Map 2

Time Supper Club is typically a place to see and

be seen—this is where Timbaland partied after his concert. The crowd is impeccably groomed: heels and pin-straight hair for the ladies, cufflinks and cologne for the men. The decor matches the clientele and is chic but opulent with big white divans. It serves as both a restaurant and a club, and reservations are often available late into the night; think dinner at 10:30 P.M. and dancing by midnight. A catwalk runs through the restaurant and turns into a makeshift dance floor as the night wears on. Drinks can be pricey, and bottle service is almost a must.

LE VELVET
420 rue St-Gabriel, 514/878-9782
HOURS: Tues.-Sun. 10 P.M.-3 A.M.
COST: Free-$15
Map 1

Step down into this cavernous, candle-lit bar and you'll find yourself surrounded by stone walls and low ceilings, the foundations of a 17th-century basement. Despite the mysterious setting, Velvet is all about contemporary beats and a mix of electro, pop, and disco tunes keep the crowd moving. Velvet specializes in vodka; the drinks are affordable and the atmosphere is a far cry from the black light glitz of other Old Montréal clubs.

VINYL LOUNGE
2109 rue de Bleury, 514/312-5809,
www.vinyllounge.ca
HOURS: Tues.-Sun. 8 P.M.-3 A.M.
COST: No cover
Map 3

Taking up the ground floor of a former townhouse, Vinyl Lounge is low-lit and welcoming. Full of old antique couches, Victorian-style tables, and fringed light fixtures, it has a casual, relaxed atmosphere. The crowd here tends toward later 20s and early 30s, so it can be a nice break from clubs that attract a younger crowd. With an extensive martini list and a full bar, the place is usually filled to capacity—both inside and out.

Wine Bars

BU
5245 blvd. St-Laurent, 514/276-0249,
www.bu-mtl.com
HOURS: Daily 5 P.M.-1 A.M.
COST: No cover
Map 6

The first wine bar to open in the city, in 2003, Bu has become a neighborhood staple. Looking out on the Main, the huge storefront windows display guests as they sit in old cafeteria-style chairs, sipping their wine and munching on the tasting menu. Dim lighting and ambient sounds give it a laid-back atmosphere that attracts young professionals. Weekly, 25 wines are offered by the glass, alongside simple antipastis like olives, ceviche, and bruschetta. If eating in the minimal, contemporary dining room isn't to your liking, you can take your wine and dinner to go.

BUVETTE CHEZ SIMONE
4869 ave. du Parc, 514/750-6577,
www.buvettechezsimone.com
HOURS: Tues.-Sun. 4 P.M.-3 A.M.
COST: No cover
Map 5

On the border of Mile End and the Plateau is Chez Simone, a cozy wine bar that offers a great selection of local charcuterie. Traditionally, *buvette* means a place to grab a drink and a light snack while you wait for your train, and though Chez Simone is nowhere near the station, the bare tabletops, low lighting, and terrace give it a similar ambience. Relaxed elegance nicely describes the feel of the place, which attracts younger, sophisticated patrons (think upwardly mobile 20–30-year-olds) with its affordable wines and charcuterie plates adorned with peach halves.

NIGHTLIFE

NARCISSE BAR À VIN

L'Auberge de Vieux-Port, 97 rue de la Commune E.,
514/392-1649, www.narcissebistro.com

HOURS: Daily 5 P.M.–close

COST: No cover

Map 1

This wine bar in L'Auberge de Vieux-Port attracts both tourists and locals to its cozy and sophisticated stone surroundings with rich velvet accents and low lighting. Over 100 wines are featured on the menu, kept in a glass wine cellar that is the focal point of the room. Thirty are offered by the glass. A new selection is highlighted every month, often to reflect the season. Servers here are wine connoisseurs and are willing and eager to impart their knowledge. In the summer the rooftop terrace offers great views of the Old Port.

© PULLMAN

Pullman's extensive wine list features 300 wines.

PULLMAN

3424 ave. du Parc, 514/288-7779,
www.pullman-mtl.com

HOURS: Daily 4:30 P.M.–1 A.M.

COST: No cover

Map 5

The huge, crystal chandelier is likely the first thing you'll notice about this wine bar, visible through the massive front window. Situated on a bizarre strip of avenue du Parc, it faces a grocery store and is next to a Quality Inn. But Pullman is a gem in the rough. The high ceilings of this former carpet store make for a dramatic interior, full of chic, minimal furniture and stark walls. Three hundred wines are featured on the extensive wine list, 50 of which are available by the glass. Patrons here are an especially chic breed, but in a laid-back unpretentious way.

WHISKY CAFÉ

5800 blvd. St-Laurent, 514/278-2644,
www.whiskycafe.com

HOURS: Mon.–Fri. 5 P.M.–3 A.M., Sat. 6 P.M.–3 A.M.,
Sun. 7 P.M.–3 A.M.

COST: No cover

Map 6

With over 150 scotch whiskeys on their menu, the Whisky Café is a favorite of cigar and whiskey aficionados. The opulent surroundings, full of leather club chairs and rich wood, give off a cozy, masculine atmosphere, and are complemented by the adjoining cigar lounge, one of the last places in the city where you're allowed to smoke indoors. Though they serve food it is more a tasting menu than a full meal. This place is all about whiskey, and they even have designated drivers to make sure you arrive home safely.

ARTS AND LEISURE

Montréal has a thriving arts scene that attracts some of the country's and the world's biggest artists both in the visual and performing arts. The city is full of smaller commercial galleries representing both established and emerging artists well worth a look. Fans of French theater can enjoy some of the best this side of Paris, but not everyone has the keenest ear for French. Though not as big, Montréal's English theater offers diverse plays and performances by both established and independent production companies. No matter your mother tongue, the circus delights without words and there are a number of unconventional circuses in the city, from Cirque du Soleil to TOHU.

Galleries can be found throughout the city. From Old Montréal to Little Italy, these independent galleries show work from both local and international artists and offer an abundance of different styles and genres. Many hold vernissages (art openings) with complimentary drinks on Thursday evenings, making it a great time for a gallery crawl. Museums tend to be concentrated in the downtown core, with some dotted throughout Vieux-Montréal and the Plateau. Large or small, many of these offer free or half-price entry at least once during the week, though days vary so check with the specific museum for days and times.

Biking is a huge part of city life, and you'll see cyclists battling against the elements even in the middle of winter. The city's bike share scheme, Bixi, has helped to make cycling even more popular, not just for recreation but as an alternative to public transport. As such Montréal has 600 kilometers of paths in total that crisscross through the city as designated bike lanes. Look

© MUSÉE D'ART CONTEMPORAIN DE MONTRÉAL

HIGHLIGHTS

LOOK FOR **(C** TO FIND RECOMMENDED
ARTS AND ACTIVITIES.

(C Most Moving Museum: The Montréal Holocaust Memorial Museum provides testimonials of nearly 500 Holocaust survivors and thousands of personal artifacts (page 133).

(C Best Art Complex: Get all your art viewing out of the way at the **Belgo Building.** Once a warehouse it has since turned into a hive of artistic activity and now has five floors of independent galleries to check out (page 135).

(C Best Gallery: Dedicated to the contemporary arts, **DHC/ART** is one of the most sophisticated galleries in the city, featuring work by contemporary arts stars like Jenny Holzer and Sophie Calle (page 136).

(C Best Theater: Segal Centre for the Performing Arts offers some of the best new plays in the city. Architecture buffs will also get a kick out of the Mies van der Rohe–designed complex (page 139).

(C Best Dance Performance: With both classical and contemporary pieces, **Les Grands Ballets Canadiens de Montréal** brings classical dance into the 21st century (page 139).

(C Best Arts Festival: The festival Montréal en Lumière features 10 days of indoor and outdoor cultural events and performances, which include an all-night party when galleries, museums, and more stay open until dawn (page 144).

(C Best Festival for Film Buffs: With an emphasis on auteurs, the **Festival du Nouveau Cinéma** is one of the biggest in the world. Directors like Wim Wenders and Atom Egoyan are regular contributors (page 149).

(C Best New Music Festival: Pop Montréal is one of the most anticipated festivals of the year, with five days of the hottest new music and music legends (page 149).

(C Best Way to See the City: Rent a bike from **Ça roule Montréal** and explore the city on two wheels (page 150).

(C Best Sporting Event: The **Montréal Canadiens** have won the most Stanley Cups of any team in the National Hockey League. Montréalers are extremely devoted to the team, and the fan spirit at any of their games is palpable (page 157).

© SEGAL CENTRE

lobby at the Segal Centre for the Performing Arts

ARTS AND LEISURE

for the painted bikes on the asphalt or follow your fellow cyclists to find your way.

Montréalers enjoy a good celebration, which might explain why the city has so many festivals. No matter when you're visiting, be it the middle of summer or the middle of winter, you're bound to be confronted by a festival or two featuring the best in music, art, and cinema. And though it might have a major cultural side, Montréal is also big on the outdoors and spectator sports. There's little the city loves more than a good hockey game, whether it's a quick game of shinny on an outdoor rink or cheering on the Canadiens at the Bell Centre. Winter might sometimes feel like it lasts forever, but the city's many green spaces are bustling the year through with runners, cyclists, cross-country skiers, and skaters.

The Arts

MUSEUMS
CENTRE DES SCIENCES DE MONTRÉAL AND IMAX TELUS THEATRE
King Edward Pier, 514/496-4724,
www.montrealsciencecentre.com
HOURS: Daily 10 A.M.–5 P.M.
COST: $12 adult, $9 child, $11 senior and teen
Map 1

Taking up an entire quay-side warehouse in the Old Port, the Centre des Sciences de Montréal (Montréal Science Center) aims to woo 9- to 14-year-olds with interactive exhibitions focusing on the environment and technology. Permanent exhibits include Science 26, which invites you to learn about scientific concepts through trial and error, and Mission Gaia, which presents you with some of the worst environmental disasters of the 20th century and asks you for solutions. The IMAX and temporary exhibits draw the biggest crowds, so if

ARTS AND LEISURE

A former public bath, Éco Musée du Fier Monde is now a museum dedicated to the city's industrial and working-class history.

MONTRÉAL WRITERS

The 20th century saw a number of literary stars from many of the city's communities debut with unimaginable success. The most prominent of those is poet and musician **Leonard Cohen.** Born in Westmount, a well-to-do and predominantly English neighborhood, Cohen went on to study at McGill University before publishing his first book of poetry, *Let Us Compare Mythologies,* in 1956. In 1964 he published the novel *The Favourite Game,* a semi-autobiographical book about a boy growing up in Montréal. Tracing Cohen's adolescence from primary through high school and university, you'll find many recognizable places and streets that in some cases remain unchanged.

Another Jewish-Canadian writer who became known for his semi-autobiographical tales of Montréal is **Mordecai Richler.** Where Cohen grew up on the affluent side of the city, Richler was born on rue St-Urbain, a working-class, mostly Jewish neighborhood in the Mile End. One of his most well-known novels, *The Apprenticeship of Duddy Kravitz,* revolves around the neighborhood, and you can still visit many of the places mentioned in the book – and in some cases shown in the movie (starring Richard Dreyfuss) – today, including the timeless St-Viateur Bagel.

Life in the French community of the Plateau is vividly brought to life in the work of novelist and playwright **Michel Tremblay,** the preeminent Québécois writer of his time and famous for his 1965 play *Les Belles-Sœurs.* Tremblay's creations perfectly evoke life in the working-class neighborhood in the 1950s and '60s, right down to his use of *joual,* colloquial speech.

Born in Winnipeg, Manitoba, to a French-Canadian family, **Gabrielle Roy** eventually settled in Montréal, where she published her novel *Bonheur d'Occasion* in 1945 to rave reviews and a prestigious prize. Published in English two years later as *The Tin Flute,* it tells the story of a young woman during World War II, struggling with poverty and ignorance in the working-class neighborhood of St-Henri. Even today it remains one of the few novels to accurately describe the struggles of the neighborhood and its inhabitants.

you're looking to catch either, get your tickets in advance.

CENTRE D'HISTOIRE DE MONTRÉAL

335 Place d'Youville, 514/872-3207, www.ville.montreal.qc.ca/chm
HOURS: Tues.-Sun. 10 A.M.-5 P.M.
COST: $6 adult, $4 children, $4 student, $5 senior
Map 1

This converted firehouse, which served as the central fire station 1904–1908, now holds the Centre d'Histoire de Montréal (the Montréal Historical Center) and its three stories of civic history. Dating as far back as the first contact with the indigenous people in 1535 and extending to the cultural boom of the 1960s and '70s, the permanent collection looks at five important eras in the city's history through archival footage, interactive exhibits, and reconstructions. The museum also offers guided walking tours throughout the year focusing on different aspects or areas of the city.

ÉCO MUSÉE DU FIER MONDE

2050 rue Amherst, 514/528-8444, www.ecomusee.qc.ca
HOURS: Wed. 11 A.M.-8 P.M., Thurs.-Fri. 9:30 A.M.-5 P.M., Sat.-Sun. 10:30 A.M.-5 P.M.
COST: $6 adult, $4 student, senior, and child
Map 4

Housed in a former public bath, the Éco Musée du Fier Monde is dedicated to the city's industrial and working-class history. Though the exhibit is fairly straightforward, it is worth the price of admission alone to see the refurbished public bath, a historic building in itself and part of the area's history. The now empty pool is one of the first things you notice about the space, which was built in 1924 for the area's working-class residents, who didn't have access to showers or bathtubs. It was later used for recreation and remained popular and in full use into the 1970s.

MAISON SAINT-GABRIEL
2146 Place Dublin, 514/935-8136,
www.maisonsaint-gabriel.qc.ca
HOURS: Jan. 19-June 19 and Sept. 7-Dec. 19 Tues.-Sun.
1-5 P.M., June 20-Sept. 5 Tues.-Sun. 11 A.M.-6 P.M.
COST: $8 adult, $6 senior, $4 student, $2 child
Map 7

Situated in Pointe-Saint-Charles, a working-class neighborhood west of Old Montréal, the grounds that are now Maison Saint-Gabriel were given to Marguerite Bourgeoys in 1668. Bourgeoys used the land to start a farm and built the house to accommodate the *filles du roi*, young French women who came to Canada in the early days of the settlement.

Interpreters recreate the everyday tasks of the 17th and 18th centuries, and in the summer artisans recreate traditional trades on the museum's grounds. This is one of the more worthwhile interpretive museums and well worth the trip, especially if you have your own transportation. Tours are offered.

◖ MONTRÉAL HOLOCAUST MEMORIAL MUSEUM
5151 chemin de la Côte-Ste-Catherine, 514/345-2605,
www.mhmc.ca
HOURS: Mon.-Tues. and Thurs. 10 A.M.-5 P.M.,
Wed. 10 A.M.-9 P.M., Fri. and Sun. 10 A.M.-4 P.M.
COST: $8 adult, $5 student, senior, and child
Map 7

With over 7,000 documents, photographs, and objects in its collection, the Holocaust Museum reconstructs the life of Jewish communities before, during, and after World War II, exploring the rise of Nazism, life in the ghettos, and the diaspora of the communities after the war. The museum was founded in 1979 by Holocaust survivors, and the history of Montréal's Jewish community is explored here as well, in the testimonials and life stories of those who eventually chose Montréal as their home.

Found off of the beaten path in the residential area of Côte-des-Neiges, it was the first major museum dedicated to the Holocaust in the country, and it will take visitors a couple of hours or more to browse the museum and take in the multimedia displays. The personal artifacts (which include everything from suitcases and postcards to stars of David and identity cards) and moving testimonials of nearly 500 survivors make for a profound experience.

MONTRÉAL PLANETARIUM
1000 rue St-Jacques W., 514/872-4530,
www2.ville.montreal.qc.ca/planetarium
HOURS: Jan. 19-June 18 and Sept. 7-Dec. 17
Tues.-Thurs. 1-5 P.M., Fri. 1-5 P.M. and 6:45-9:30 P.M.,
Sat.-Sun. 9:30 A.M.-5 P.M. and 6:45-9:30 P.M.;
June 19-Sept. 6 Tues.-Thurs. 9:30 A.M.-5 P.M.,
Fri. 9:30 A.M.-4:30 P.M. and 7-9:30 P.M., Sat.-Sun.
12:30-4:30 P.M. and 7-9:30 P.M.
COST: $8 adult, $6 student and senior, $4 child
Map 2

Opened in advance of Expo 67 in the spring of 1966, the Montréal Planetarium was the first in the country and is still the largest, with almost 400 seats available. Offering shows in both English and French, it produces a number of different shows a year and has special themed shows for holidays like Halloween and Christmas. It is a great place to bring the kids. Designed to resemble Saturn, the enormous dome features faint rings, and the interior has an astronomical theme.

LE MUSÉE CHÂTEAU DUFRESNE
4040 rue Sherbrooke E., 514/259-9201,
www.chateaudufresne.com
HOURS: Wed.-Sun. 10 A.M.-5 P.M., tours 1:30 P.M. and
3:30 P.M.
COST: $7 adult, $3.50 child, $6 student and senior
Map 7

Not far from the modern organic architecture of the Olympic Stadium is the Musée Château Dufresne, the complete antithesis to its surroundings with its classic Beaux Arts style. Designed by Parisian architect Jules Renard in 1915, the museum was originally two houses owned by brothers Marius and Oscar Dufresne, who were wealthy entrepreneurs.

The interior of the house remains virtually untouched right down to murals and ceiling paintings by Guido Nincheri, best-known for his ecclesiastical works. Tours of the grand mansion are given twice daily and are free with admission.

MUSÉE DES HOSPITALIÈRES DE L'HÔTEL DIEU

201 ave. des Pins W., 514/849-2919, www.museedeshospitalieres.qc.ca
HOURS: Mid-June-mid-Oct. Tues.-Fri. 10 A.M.-5 P.M., Sat.-Sun. 1-5 P.M.; mid-Oct.-mid-Dec. and Mar.-mid-June Wed.-Sun. 1-5 P.M.; Jan.-Feb. reservations required
COST: $6 adult, $5 student and senior, child free
Map 5

Tucked inside the stone walls of l'Hôtel-Dieu de Montréal, the Musée des Hospitalières de l'Hôtel Dieu looks at the history of the hospital and its medical practices.

Visitors are greeted by a 17th-century staircase before learning about early treatments and practices administered by the nurses, as well as the history of national health care and the hospital.

If you are visiting during the summer months take a detour into the garden. The museum is closed from mid-December to mid-January, and reservations are required in January and February.

REDPATH MUSEUM OF NATURAL HISTORY

859 rue Sherbrooke W., 514/393-4086 ext. 00549, www.mcgill.ca/redpath
HOURS: Mon.-Fri. 9 A.M.-5 P.M., Sun. noon-5 P.M.
COST: $5 adult, $2 student and child
Map 2

Full of dinosaur bones, mummies, African masks, stuffed animals, and even a Victorian medical teaching auditorium, the Redpath Museum is for anyone who loves old stuff. Completed in 1882, it is the oldest museum in Canada and is found on the campus of McGill University. It's known for its ethnological displays and dedication to natural history—it has extinct animals like the passenger pigeon and the dodo bird—and the Victorian display cases and dark wood are reminiscent of the British Museum in London. Indoor shoes are recommended for winter, and no flash photography is allowed in the museum.

SIR GEORGE-ÉTIENNE CARTIER NATIONAL HISTORIC SITE OF CANADA

458 rue Notre-Dame E., 514/283-2282, www.pc.gc.ca/cartier
HOURS: April 27-June 20 and Sept. 6-Dec. 24 Wed.-Sun. 10 A.M.-noon and 1-5 P.M., June 21-Sept. 5 daily 10 A.M.-5:30 P.M.
COST: $3.90 adult, $1.90 child, $3.40 senior
Map 1

One of the founders of the confederation, George-Étienne Cartier originally practiced law before being elected co-prime minister of the province of Canada alongside John A. MacDonald in 1858 (nine years before the confederation). Home to the Cartier family 1848–1872, this historic site is the only Victorian house open to the public in Montréal. Tour guides in period dress show you through the house, which has been restored to match the customs of the bourgeoisie of 1860.

GALLERIES
ARTICULE

262 ave. Fairmount W., 514/842-9686, www.articule.org
HOURS: Wed.-Thurs. noon-6 P.M., Fri. noon-9 P.M., Sat.-Sun. noon-5 P.M.
COST: Free
Map 6

This artist-run center, which recently celebrated its 25th anniversary, often showcases the work of local Montréal artists, though it also offers residencies for international artists. Situated in the heart of the Mile End, it takes up the street level storefront of a grand old townhouse, but the bright-green facade sets it apart from the otherwise quiet street. Exhibits here range from video and performance art to installations—one artist filled the entire floor with sand. They close for a month during the summer but always have a window installation for passersby.

BATTAT CONTEMPORARY

7245 rue Alexandra #100, 514/750-9566, www.battatcontemporary.com
HOURS: Tues.-Fri. noon-6 P.M., Sat. noon-5 P.M.
COST: Free
Map 6

Though "contemporary" is in its name, Battat

is one of a few places outside a museum where you can occasionally see older works from the owner's collection. Occupying the second floor of an old warehouse in an up-and-coming part of the city, the collection includes the work of masters like Gustave Courbet and Francisco de Goya. The single-room format allows for an intimate viewing of the work, which also includes exhibitions by established and emerging Canadian and international artists.

C BELGO BUILDING

372 rue Ste-Catherine W.
HOURS: Hours vary
COST: Free
Map 3

Once an old industrial building, the Belgo has been given a new life, thanks to the various art galleries, dance studios, and cultural organizations that have opened here. What started as a haven for struggling artists in the 1980s and '90s is today an artistic hub with five floors housing over 30 art galleries—the real draw of the place. Some of the city's most respected galleries make their home here, like **Galerie René Blouin** (Ste. 501, 514/393-9969, www.galeriereneblouin.com) and **Galerie Push Vernissages** (Ste. 425, 514/544-9079, www.galeriepush.com).

CANADIAN GUILD OF CRAFTS

1460-B rue Sherbrooke W., 514/849-6091, www.canadianguildofcrafts.com
HOURS: Tues.-Fri. 10 A.M.-6 P.M., Sat. 10 A.M.-5 P.M.
COST: Free
Map 2

Founded in 1906, with the aim to preserve and promote Inuit and First Nations art, the Canadian Guild of Crafts has one of the most important permanent collections of aboriginal art in Canada. Prints, tapestries, and sculpture make up the majority of the collection, along with fine ceramic and glass work and handmade jewelry. Temporary exhibits by Canadian artists are displayed throughout the year in the gallery.

LA CENTRALE GALERIE POWERHOUSE

4296 blvd. St-Laurent, 514/871-0268, www.lacentrale.org
HOURS: Wed. noon-6 P.M., Thurs.-Fri. noon-9 P.M., Sat.-Sun. noon-5 P.M.
COST: Free
Map 5

Located on a bustling strip of St-Laurent, the floor-to-ceiling windows and kooky, eye-catching window displays effortlessly draw the attention of passersby to La Centrale Galerie Powerhouse. Opened in 1973, La Centrale is an artist-run center that focuses on the work of contemporary female artists and aims to expand on the history of feminist art practices. The works displayed here are often witty and humorous, as well as thought-provoking.

DARLING FOUNDRY

745 Ottawa, 514/392-1554, www.fonderiedarling.org
HOURS: Wed.-Sun. noon-7 P.M., Thurs. noon-9 P.M.
COST: $3, free on Thurs.
Map 1

Known for its ambitious installations and unusual surroundings—much of the foundry remains unchanged—the Darling Foundry is both an exhibition space and artists' residence, situated in what was once the industrial heartland of the city. Part of the gallery's aim was to help rejuvenate the area, something it has accomplished with addition of the Cluny Art Bar. Exhibiting the work of both Canadian and international contemporary artists, the Foundry approaches the work on a big scale and often holds outdoor and sight-specific exhibits.

DAZIBAO

335 blvd. de Maisonneuve E., 514/844-3250, www.dazibao-photo.org
HOURS: Tues.-Sat. noon-5 P.M.
COST: Free
Map 4

Focusing on contemporary photography and its related art forms, Dazibao is one of the few galleries in the city to exhibit solely photographic works. Established in 1980, part of Dazibao's mandate is to create discussion around the work, which they do by publishing essays and large-format art books, and organizing talks and dinners that surround a certain exhibit or theme. The space itself is in the same building as the Cinémathèque Québécoise, which gives it an overall multimedia feel.

◖ DHC/ART

451 rue St-Jean, 514/286-6626, www.dhc-art.org
HOURS: Wed.-Fri. noon-7 P.M., Sat.-Sun. 11 A.M.-6 P.M.
COST: Free
Map 1

Since opening in fall 2007, the DHC/ART Foundation for Contemporary Art has exhibited the work of some of the world's biggest contemporary artists, including Jenny Holzer, Sophie Calle, and Marc Quinn. Setting up shop in a converted, historic building, the gallery's ultramodern interior nicely brings the surroundings into the 21st century. In keeping with their dedication to dynamic programming, public art education classes and workshops are available. And their opening parties are, hands-down, some of the best in the city.

GALERIE ORANGE

81 rue St-Paul E., 514/396-6670,
www.galerieorange.com
HOURS: Tues.-Fri. 10 A.M.-6 P.M., Sat.-Sun. 11 A.M.-5 P.M.
COST: Free
Map 1

Established in 2003, Galerie Orange is one of the few galleries in the city to exclusively represent Québec-based artists. Though not all of them were born here, Orange takes pride in representing emerging and established artists who've chosen to make Montréal or the province of Québec their home. A few steps up and set on a stretch of Old Montréal that's busy with restaurants and boutiques, it's easy to overlook. Keep your eyes peeled for the small black-and-white sign with orange lettering.

GALERIE PANGÉE

40 St-Paul W., 514/845-3368, www.galeriepangee.com
HOURS: Daily 10 A.M.-7 P.M.
COST: Free
Map 1

There's no shortage of commercial galleries on Saint-Paul, but if you're interested in contemporary art and photography then Pangée should not be missed. The simple one-room space allows for some arresting ceiling-to-floor installations, and the intimate setting means a high concentration of work is usually on view. Named after Pangea, the supercontinent from which all of the current continents were made, part of the gallery's mandate is to introduce established and up-and-coming European artists.

GALERIE SIMON BLAIS

5420 blvd. St-Laurent, 514/849-1165,
www.simonblais.com
HOURS: Tues.-Wed. and Fri. 10 A.M.-6 P.M., Thurs. 10 A.M.-8 P.M., Sat. 10 A.M.-5 P.M.
COST: Free
Map 6

Initially founded to exhibit abstract works and those done on paper, Simon Blais is now recognized as one of the most diverse galleries in the city, representing both established international artists like Betty Godwin as well as known Québécois artists like Claude Tousignant and Guido Molinari. Given the wide range of work exhibited, shows can be hit-or-miss. The Guest Artist series, which invites emerging artists to exhibit in the two-story space, is usually more rewarding.

GALERIE YVES LAROCHE

6355 blvd. St-Laurent, 514/393-1999,
www.yveslaroche.com
HOURS: Tues.-Wed. 10 A.M.-6 P.M., Thurs.-Fri. 10 A.M.-8 P.M., Sat. 10 A.M.-5 P.M.
COST: Free
Map 6

This avant-garde gallery exhibits work that is influenced by subcultures, like graffiti, tattooing, comics, and cartoons, and art movements like pop-art and surrealism (think of Dali's melting clocks but with melting Mickey Mouses). Cutting edge and provocative, the work is often both dark and darkly funny. Opened in 1991, the gallery recently moved from its old historic digs in Old Montréal to a modern space in Little Italy, the perfect backdrop for the dynamic pieces on show.

PARISIAN LAUNDRY

3550 rue St-Antoine W., 514/989-1056,
www.parisianlaundry.com
HOURS: Tues.–Sat. noon–5 P.M.
COST: Free
Map 2

Spacious, with floor-to-ceiling windows, exposed wood beams, and a cavernous exhibition space referred to as the "Bunker," Parisian Laundry is a massive space dedicated to contemporary art. Though focused on Canadian artists—they represent some of the best up-and-comers in the country, like Kim Dorland and Rick Leong—they are also monumental in bringing top international artists to Montréal, like Kalup Linzy and Alex Da Corte. The sheer size of the gallery allows for a unique use of space, reserving the "Bunker" for sight-specific installations.

THEATER

AGORA DE LA DANSE

840 rue Cherrier E., 514/525-7575,
www.agoradeladance.com
COST: $15–30 depending on the show
Map 5

With over a hundred performances a year, Agora de la Danse is the place to see contemporary dance in Montréal. Started in the 1980s, it continues to present interesting works from both local and international choreographers and is the only venue in all of Canada dedicated to the presentation and creation of contemporary dance. The building itself is impressive, with its Beaux Arts facade and grand staircase at the entrance.

CENTAUR THEATRE

453 rue St-Francis-Xavier, box office 514/288-3161,
www.centaurtheatre.com
COST: $43.50 adult, $37.50 senior, $32.50 under 30,
$25 student
Map 1

Founded in 1969, the Centaur Theatre is Montréal's preeminent English-language theater company. Located in the Old Stock Exchange, which was built in 1903 by American architect George B. Post, the theater went through two major reconstructions in 1974 and 1996. As one of only a handful of English-language theater companies, Centaur's mandate is to present the plays of Montréal and Canadian playwrights. The company also consistently produces English-language

THEATER EN FRANÇAIS

Montréal has some of the best French theater this side of Paris; here is a list of some of the city's top theaters.

- **Espace Go** is committed to showing plays by women playwrights. It remains true to its roots, when it opened as Théâtre Expérimental des Femmes in the 1980s (4890 blvd. St-Laurent, 514/845-4890, www.espacego.com).

- **Espace Libre,** dedicated to experimental theater, is considered one of the best theater companies in the city (3081 rue Ontario E., 514/521-4191, www.espacelibre.qc.ca).

- **Théâtre d'Aujourd'hui,** founded in 1968, is focused on showing new work from Québé-cois playwrights (3900 rue St-Denis, 514/282-3900, www.theatredaujourdhui.qc.ca).

- **Théâtre de Quat'Sous** is a great venue to catch up-and-coming talent. The new building is as modern and daring as the company itself (100 ave. des Pins E., 514/845-7277, www.quatsous.com).

- **Théâtre du Nouveau Monde** stages traditional and modern classics and is better known as TMN (84 rue Ste-Catherine W., 514/866-8668, www.tnm.qc.ca).

- **Théâtre du Rideau Vert** is the oldest professional theater company in Québec, and it has a faithful fan base (4664 rue St-Denis, 514/844-1793, www.rideauvert.qc.ca).

ARTS AND LEISURE

© SACHA JACKSON

Housed in the old stock exchange building, the Centaur Theatre is one of the city's best English-language theaters.

productions of French-language plays by such noted Québécois playwrights as Michel Tremblay.

GESÙ CENTRE DE CRÉATIVITÉ

1202 rue de Bleury, 514/861-4378, www.legesu.com
COST: $10-50
Map 3

Adjacent to the Église du Gesù (Jesus in Italian), one of the oldest baroque churches in Montréal, Gesù Centre de Créativité's mission is to bring together the arts and spirituality. But don't let that lead you to expect only religious performances: Contemporary dance, visual arts, and musical performances including traditional African and Native American music take place here throughout the week. The unique surroundings, because it is after all connected to the church, give it a cozy ambience.

MAI

3680 rue Jeanne-Mance, 514/982-1812,
www.m-a-i.qc.ca
HOURS: Box office Tues.-Sat. 3-6 P.M.
COST: $10-35
Map 5

Promoting multidisciplinary and multicultural contemporary artists, the MAI (Montréal, Arts Interculturels) is the only venue in the city to focus on work by artists who have diverse origins and inspirations—meaning you could catch a traditional Thai dance performance one night and a psychedelic Middle Eastern post-rock band the next. The modern surroundings make it a nice place to have a drink or a coffee while you wander from the gallery into the theater to catch a play by a young, emerging playwright.

MAINLINE THEATER

3997 blvd. St-Laurent, 514/849-3378,
www.mainlinetheatre.ca
COST: $15-30
Map 5

The MainLine was originally established to produce the Montréal Fringe Festival, an event it continues to support. Nowadays, however, it is a theater company known for presenting more cutting-edge English theater, like a *Desperate Housewives*–tinged *Hedda Gabler,* a half-naked musical about Dionysus, or a play about stripping in the 1990s. It's directly above a grocery store on the Main; the surroundings might not be inspired but the plays always are.

◖ SEGAL CENTRE FOR THE PERFORMING ARTS

5170 chemin de la Côte-Ste-Catherine, 514/739-2301, www.segalcentre.org

COST: $25-50

Map 7

With a focus on creating a nurturing environment for developing performers and playwrights, the Mies van der Rohe–designed Segal Centre has a number of different stages and programs that make it one of the most exciting places to see English theater in the city. Independent companies use the Segal Stage as a place to refine and perform, while bigger productions are found on the larger stage. They also host a yearly Yiddish Theater Festival, with performers from all over the world.

THÉÂTRE STE-CATHERINE

264 rue Ste-Catherine E., 514/284-3939, www.theatrestecatherine.com

COST: $7-20

Map 3

This cozy, independently run theater is a great place to catch various, usually more experimental, acts. Emerging Montréal-based playwrights often stage new work here, but you could also find yourself chuckling along with a stand-up comedian—though you may not recognize the name on the marquee. Improv nights happen here regularly, with a stellar lineup of local talent that invites audience members to get in on the action every Sunday.

BALLET, OPERA, AND THE SYMPHONY

◖ LES GRANDS BALLETS CANADIENS DE MONTRÉAL

175 rue Ste-Catherine W., 514/849-0269, www.grandsballets.com

COST: $50-150

Map 3

Founded in 1957 by young choreographer and dancer Ludmilla Chiriaeff, Les Grands Ballets continues to be the only ballet company in the city and one of the most boundary-pushing in North America. Presenting both classical and more contemporary works, which have

included *Tommy,* Les Grands remains vibrant and is currently headed by artistic director Grandimir Pankov.

OPÉRA DE MONTRÉAL

175 rue Ste-Catherine W., 514/985-2222, www.operademontreal.com

COST: $30-110

Map 3

In the years since its foundation in 1980, the Opéra de Montréal has presented 91 operas, including *La Boheme, Werther,* and two world premieres. In a city full of bilingual arts, the opera is the one of the few places the two languages come together. Set to open in mid-2011 is a brand-new auditorium specifically designed with opera acoustics in mind. It presents a handful of operas a year, so there's always something new to catch. Young opera fans take note; there are often specials for 18- to 30-year-olds.

L'ORCHESTRA SYMPHONIQUE DE MONTRÉAL

175 rue Ste-Catherine W., 514/842-3402, www.osm.ca

COST: $30-165

Map 3

Currently led by world-renowned conductor Kent Nagano, the Montréal Symphony Orchestra was founded by Wilfrid Pelletier in 1935 and continues to be the leading company of classical music in the province and is one of the biggest and most respected in Canada. Their new specialized hall, which was inaugurated at the Place des Arts in spring 2011, ensures the sound is impeccable. Those 34 and under should check out their website for deals on tickets.

CIRCUS

CIRQUE DU SOLEIL

Quai Jacques-Cartier, 800/450-1480, www.cirquedusoleil.com

COST: $50-260

Map 1

The now infamous blue-and-yellow-striped Grand Chapiteau (Big Top) stands out among the rest of the more somber-colored buildings of the Vieux-Port. Started in the town of

Baie-Saint-Paul by stilt-walker Guy Laliberté, Cirque's first big gig was in 1984, in celebration of Jacques Cartier's discovery of Québec, and now they have reached near world domination with shows on almost every continent and a permanent show house in Las Vegas. This is the only Cirque du Soleil venue in Montréal and the premiere spot to see their latest productions.

CIRQUE ÉLOIZE

Clock Tower Quay, 514/596-3838, www.cirque-eloize.com
COST: $30-50
Map 1

Following in the footsteps of fellow Québec-founded circus Cirque du Soleil, Cirque Éloize also boasts a big top in the Vieux-Port and a world-wide audience (nearly 4,000 performances in 30 countries). Founded in 1993 by Jeannot Painchaud, Daniel Cyr, and Julie Hamelin, the performance group combines circus arts with music, dance, and theater. Éloize, which is an Acadian word referring to the heat and lightning before a storm, breaks away from the traditional circus mold and pushes the boundaries of the art with a youthful flair.

TOHU

2345 rue Jarry E., 514/376-8648, www.tohu.ca
COST: $25-50
Map 7

Montréal is a city full of circuses, but the TOHU is a little bit different. Founded in 2004 by En Piste, the National Circus School, and Cirque du Soleil, TOHU is one of the largest training grounds for performers of the circus arts in the world. Shows here might lack the pomp and circumstance (and the awesome costumes) of Cirque du Soleil, but you'll be hard-pressed to find performers who are more dedicated and astounding in their art.

CONCERT VENUES

L'ASTRAL

306 rue Ste-Catherine W., 514/288-8882,
www.salleastral.com
COST: $15-50
Map 3

Newly opened in the brand-new Quartier des Spectacles, L'Astral is situated in the building that now houses the International Jazz Festival. It's fitting then that L'Astral is mainly a jazz venue, with performances from international musicians throughout the week. The venue has a club atmosphere, with tables and chairs set up on the floor around the room for a more intimate setting.

CABARET JUSTE POUR RIRE

2101 blvd. St-Laurent, 514/845-2322
COST: $15-30
Map 3

Otherwise known as Cabaret Just for Laughs—yes, like the comedy festival—this two-floor venue is a popular place to catch well-known out-of-town bands. It has an 800-person capacity, and bands like Modest Mouse and The Walkmen have played here. True to its name the venue has a cabaret feel, with a second-floor balcony adorned with dark red and gold molding running along the venue's outer edges, adding an intimate vibe.

CLUB SODA

1225 blvd. St-Laurent, 514/286-1010, www.clubsoda.ca
COST: $15-30
Map 3

Around since the 1980s and similar in feel to Cabaret Just for Laughs but a little bigger and a little farther south, Club Soda hosts well-known international bands whose music you'd likely recognize on the radio. A second-floor balcony, flashier with accents of neon blue and LCD screens, accommodates more patrons, and bars on both levels ensure the beer keeps flowing.

JACQUES-CARTIER PIER

Jacques-Cartier Quay, 514/496-7678,
www.quaysoftheoldport.com
COST: $15-40
Map 1

It's standing room only at this outdoor auditorium. Situated at the end of the pier (just behind the Cirque du Soleil tent), it looks out over the St-Lawrence and offers an open perspective on the performers. The partially walled-in structure

© PARTENARIAT DU QUARTIER DES SPECTACLES

Club Soda

is also equipped with a balcony for better viewing and, despite its size, has the feel of a cozier, neighborhood venue. It hosts outdoor events and concerts throughout the year, and it is here that Igloofest takes place each January.

MÉTROPOLIS
59 rue Ste-Catherine E., 514/844-3500,
www.metropolismontreal.ca
COST: $25-50
Map 3

This is the biggest venue in the city other than the Centre Bell, and tickets to shows here usually sell out fast, but if a band is playing here, they've most likely made it to the top of their game. The large venue still manages to ooze a little charm with balconies and richly hued walls. Bars line the walls and TVs are in place around the venue for those whose view of the stage is obscured by a tall person.

LE NATIONAL
1220 rue Ste-Catherine E., 514/845-2014,
www.lenational.ca
COST: $20-35
Map 4

On the cusp of the Village and the Quartier Latin, Le National is a great old venue on an unassuming strip. With an austere blink-and-you-miss-it marquee, the names usually shown here range from popular French and English indie rock bands to acid jazz. Audience members lucky enough to get up to the balcony are welcome to a seat, while the rest of the venue is standing room only.

L'OLYMPIA
1004 rue Ste-Catherine E., 514/845-3524,
www.olympiademontreal.com
COST: $25-50
Map 4

Built in 1925, the Olympia theater remains one of the most majestic in the city. Once the place to go for "cinematic theater," it is now a great place to catch a band or dance the night away at a foam party—seriously. The main theater still has seats on both the main floor and balcony, a rarity in the city.

RIALTO THEATRE
5723 ave. du Parc, 514/272-3899
COST: $15-50
Map 6

Designed after the Palais Garnier in Paris, the Rialto Theatre is one of the most gorgeous venues in the city. Opened as a movie theater in 1924, its dark red and gold interior and near vertical balcony seating set it apart from any other theater in Montréal. Relegated to yearly showings of *The Rocky Horror Picture Show,* it has recently been given a new lease on life and is back to being a full-time venue.

LA SALA ROSSA
4848 blvd. St-Laurent, 514/284-0122,
www.casadelpopolo.com
COST: $15-50
Map 5

Sitting atop super-cool Spanish restaurant La Sala Rosa is super-cool venue La Sala Rossa (see the difference? two S's). Locals often grab a bite downstairs before heading upstairs to catch an indie rock band. The open space is nothing fancy, with chairs that might have been used at your bar mitzvah stacked in the corner. Though

© KATIE DUTTON

Opened in 1924, the Rialto Theatre is one of the most gorgeous concert venues in the city.

mainly a live music venue, it also hosts dance nights, film screenings, and weddings.

SAT

1195 blvd. St-Laurent, 514/844-2033,
www.sat.qc.ca
COST: $15-40
Map 3

Founded in 1996, SAT is dedicated to the research, creation, production, education, and conservation of digital culture. La Société des Arts Technologiques, or the Society for Arts and Technology, is one of most interesting and diverse venues in Montréal, hosting everything from fashion shows to electronic music nights and holiday craft fairs. The sparsely decorated, simple modular seating is forever shifting places. The open-concept space in the newly named Quartier des Spectacles has floor-to-ceiling windows that let passersby in on the action. If it's innovative, new, and cutting edge, it's happening here.

THEATRE OUTREMONT

1245 ave. Bernard W., 514/495-9944,
www.theatreoutremont.ca
COST: $25-70
Map 6

This art deco theater opened in 1929, and its music hall was subsequently filled with the voices that defined their eras. Renovated to include a cinema in the 1970s, it soon became a popular repertory cinema. Today it continues to be a venue for live music and also shows the occasional movie. Performances here are more of an adult, sit-down affair.

LA TULIPE

4530 ave. Papineau, 514/529-5000, www.lenational.ca
COST: $10-35
Map 5

La Tulipe has one of the most interesting histories of any theater in the city. Built in 1913, it was a traditional and movie theater until the early 1960s, when it became a popular place to see burlesque and stand-up comedy. Today, it has returned to its roots as a music hall, with popular bands playing here from all over the world. If you've had a long day, snag a seat in the balcony, sit back, and enjoy the show.

CINEMA

AMC

2313 rue Ste-Catherine W., 514/904-1250,
www.amctheatres.com/Forum22
COST: $13.50 adult, $8 child under 12, $11 senior
Map 2

It may be part of an international chain, but Montréal's AMC cinema is different for one reason and one reason only: the Canadiens. The theater took up residence in the Forum, the hockey team's former beloved rink. The Canadiens logo can still be seen at center ice and a few authentic stands still remain. The architecture may be a little underwhelming but its overall grandeur won't be.

CINEMA BANQUE SCOTIA

977 rue Ste-Catherine W., 514/842-5828,
www.paramountmontreal.com
COST: $12.50 adult, $10 child and senior
Map 2

A three-floor movie complex in the heart of downtown, this is your typical North American movie theater playing the latest Hollywood releases and little else. Lines can be brutal, especially for highly anticipated films, so buy your tickets early. Tuesdays are the cheapest night to catch a flick, a bargain under $10.

CINEMA DU PARC

3575 ave. du Parc, 514/281-1900,
www.cinemaduparc.com

COST: $11 adult, $8 senior and student

Map 5

Found in the basement of an out-of-place shopping complex, Cinema du Parc is the best repertory theater in Montréal. Playing everything from well-known American directors like Jim Jarmusch and Woody Allen to lesser known international directors like Fatih Akin, the best in international contemporary cinema is always on view here. Films are subtitled in both English and French; if it is an international title, double-check the language before heading off to the showing.

CINEMA L'AMOUR

4015 blvd. St-Laurent, 514/849-2727,
www.cinemalamour.com

COST: $10

Map 5

Montréal's foremost adults-only cinema started off as a theater hall/movie house in 1914, called Le Globe. Located at the time in the heart of Montréal's Jewish community, it was here in the 1920s and '30s that locals would flock to catch the latest Yiddish films. After a stint as a regular movie house (1930–1960s), it turned exclusively to adult films in the late-1960s and hasn't looked back since. The interior, however, remains virtually unchanged and is as opulent and, oddly, as beautiful as in its heyday.

CINÉMATHÈQUE QUÉBÉCOISE

335 blvd. de Maisonneuve E., 514/842-9763,
www.cinematheque.qc.ca

COST: $7 adult, $4 child, $6 senior

Map 4

Dedicated to preserving cinema, the Cinémathèque Québécoise is the place to catch celluloid classics, hard-to-find international titles, or Kenneth Anger's experimental gems. The schedule often includes a month dedicated to a single director or type of cinema. The modern architecture of the space adds to the overall ambience of the theater and puts you in mind of Paris's very own Cinémathèque. A must for film lovers.

© PARTENARIAT DU QUARTIER DES SPECTACLES

ARTS AND LEISURE

Catch celluloid classics at Cinémathèque Québécoise.

Festivals and Events

WINTER
FESTIVAL VOIX D'AMÉRIQUES
Various locations, www.fva.ca
COST: Free-$25
Map 5

The most important spoken word festival in Canada, Voix d'Amériques attracts spoken word and performance artists from all over the world. Founded in 2002 and rooted in literature and the written word, the eight-day event, which takes place in either February or March depending on the year, continues to evolve and change as a reflection of the art form. Performers have included spoken word pioneer John Giorno and the world-renowned poet and singer Baby Dee. A bilingual festival, it also hosts events with performers who express themselves in other languages, including Spanish, Creole, and aboriginal languages.

FÊTE DES NEIGES
Parc Jean-Drapeau, www.parcjeandrapeau.com
COST: Free
Map 7

The biggest winter festival in Montréal, La Fête des Neiges takes place in Parc Jean-Drapeau during three consecutive weekends between January and February. It's a great festival for the kids; make sure the whole family is bundled up for a day full of winter activities, including tubing, ice fishing, curling, hockey, and ice sculpture. It's hosted by Boule de Neige (a.k.a. Snowball), and furry suits, face paint, kid-friendly tunes, and hot chocolate are on the agenda.

IGLOOFEST
Jacques-Cartier Pier, www.igloofest.ca
COST: From $10
Map 1

At its base, electronic music festival Igloofest is a large outdoor winter rave full of trippy beats, mesmerizing visuals, an enormous igloo, and audience members dancing round in snowsuits. It takes over Jacques-Cartier Pier for three weekends at the end of January—it takes a lot of dancing to get rid of the chill that blows in off the St-Lawrence. DJs pack their mittens and touques and come from all corners of the world to keep revelers moving.

◖ MONTRÉAL EN LUMIÈRE
Various locations, www.montrealenlumiere.com
COST: Free

This 10-day cultural celebration of food, arts, and music takes place in mid- to late-February all over the city and is hands down the most anticipated of winter festivals if only because of the closing-night festivities. The whole Highlights Festival culminates in Nuit Blanche, an all-night party where people take to the streets and trek from live shows to free museum exhibits well into the wee hours of the morning, refueling with flasks of hot chocolate and stronger stuff as they go.

RENCONTRES INTERNATIONALES DU DOCUMENTAIRE MONTRÉAL
Various locations, 514/499-3676, www.ridm.qc.ca
COST: $10 per film adult, $8 senior and student, $85 pass
Map 3

Dedicated to documentary films, this 10-day festival, which takes place in mid- to late-November, was founded in 1998 by filmmakers who wanted to create a new platform for perspectives in the discipline. It now features the work of international and local documentary filmmakers with the aim of presenting the films in their original languages. Alongside the films the festival includes a number of panel discussions, workshops, and master classes.

RENDEZ-VOUS DU CINÉMA QUÉBÉCOIS
Various locations, 514/526-9635, www.rvcq.qc.ca
COST: $9 per film

Québécois cinema is celebrated annually in mid- to late-February during the Rendez-vous du Cinéma Québécois, which screens films made in the last 12 months. This 10-day festival is fascinating for those who are and aren't familiar with Québécois movies. The range on view here is spectacular, everything from mediocre comedies to astounding documentaries full of emotion and surprise. Though the festival's name is in French, selections are not limited to the French language; this is really dedicated to any and all films made in Quebec, so there are English and First Nations selections as well.

SPRING
BLUE METROPOLIS LITERARY FESTIVAL
777 ave. University, 514/790-1245, www.bluemetropolis.org
COST: Free-$30
`Map 1`

Internationally renowned authors converge on Montréal in late April to early May to take part in the world's first multilingual literary festival. Writers of fiction, nonfiction, poetry, and journalism come to be a part of the panel discussions, interviews, question and answer periods, book signings and launches, and of course to read their work to a captive audience. Unique in its vision, each year's event has a specific theme, with the discussions and authors invited tying into that theme. Previous years have included James Frey, Yann Martel, Margaret Atwood, and A. L. Kennedy.

ELEKTRA
Various locations, www.elektramontreal.ca
COST: $12-20

This cutting-edge digital arts festival which takes place in early May offers some of the most unusual experiences you're likely to come across at a festival. Internationally renowned and drawing artists from such diverse nations as Japan and Mexico, the exhibits here range from sound and light installations to live performances and interactive exhibits. The latest technologies and futuristic designs, like clothing with GPS tracking, are incorporated into almost every work, and there is an emphasis on new digital media, though the artists themselves come from varied backgrounds—everything from contemporary dance to musical composition.

FESTIVAL TRANSAMÉRIQUES
Various locations, 514/842-0704, www.fta.qc.ca
COST: $25-60

Contemporary dance and theater are the sole focus of this festival, which runs late May–mid-June. Though sharing the stage with theater, this is the most important contemporary dance festival in the city, and the works on view here are usually standouts. Drawing talents from across Canada and the world, there is often an aspect of audience participation in some of the works—a public dance performance, for example, or a play that invites the audience to join the cast, if only for a fleeting moment.

MUTEK
Various locations, www.mutek.org
COST: $10-35

Celebrating digital creativity and electronic music, Mutek is generally a sweaty four days of dancing and chilling out to the latest electronic sounds, while magical worlds are created on a screen behind a stage. Usually taking place in early June, it is presented by Mutek, a not-for-profit organization leading the way in digital sounds and visual arts. It draws talent from emerging and established international scenes and is a great festival for anyone drawn to the digital age and all that comes with it.

SUONI PER Il POPOLO
Various locations, 514/282-0122, ext. 222, www.suoniperilpopolo.org
COST: $10-35, $225 festival pass

As the name suggests, this festival, which takes place throughout the month of June, is organized by the same people behind café/bar/venue Casa del Popolo and is aimed at underground and experimental music. Started in 2001, the festival has since grown and is now one of the foremost festivals of experimental music of all kinds. If weird and wonderful is your thing, Suoni per II Popolo is the place for you. Past editions have seen the likes of Jay Reatard, The Microphones, Vic Chesnut, and Jandek.

ARTS AND LEISURE

© MUTEK

The Mutek festival celebrates digital creativity and electronic music.

SUMMER

CÉLÉBRATIONS DE LA FIERTÉ
Various locations, www.fiertemontrealpride.com
COST: Free-$35
Célébrations LGBTA Montréal took over organization of the gay and lesbian pride parade from Divers/Cité in 2007. Since taking over they have expanded these celebrations to include not only the Gay Pride Parade but also a community day and five days worth of gay pride activities, including outdoor concerts and dance parties, drag races, and performances by interdisciplinary artists in early August.

DIVERS/CITÉ
Various locations, 514/285-4011, www.diverscite.org
COST: Free-$25
This is a week-long celebration of gay pride in late July, and though it's not the only queer celebration in the city, Divers/Cité is the biggest, with free outdoor performances and art

shows happening throughout the week. The mission of this festival is to focus on the art and culture of the LGBT community, and as such the performances on view here range from modern dance to jazz, funk, and world music. It's recognized throughout the world, and members of the LGBT community flock to the city during this event.

FANTASIA FILM FESTIVAL
Various locations, www.fantasiafestival.com
COST: $8 per film
Running throughout the entire month of July, Fantasia is North America's premiere genre film festival. From the obscure to the grotesque, the Japanese to the Korean, it offers a wide range of films from all over the globe. Established in 1996, it has since grown to become the place where distributors come to scope out the best of the weird and the strange. Popular with movie-goers, it has become a destination festival for die-hard genre fans.

LGBT festival Divers/Cité.

FESTIVAL INTERNATIONAL DE JAZZ

Various locations, 514/840-3618,
www.montrealjazzfest.com
COST: Free–$120

One of the most recognizable festivals in the world, the Montréal International Jazz Festival attracts thousands of tourists to the city each summer, running from the end of June to early July. Some of the biggest names in music have played here, including Tony Bennett, B. B. King, and Norah Jones. The 11-day festival offers nonstop music with big international acts playing for free in the middle of a shut-down rue Ste-Catherine. The outdoor atmosphere and huge crowds make it one of the most exciting festivals in the city.

FESTIVAL INTERNATIONAL NUITS D'AFRIQUE

Various locations, 514/499-9215,
www.festivalnuitsdafrique.com
COST: $10–35

Fans of African music will rejoice at the Festival International Nuits D'Afrique, which focuses on music with African roots. From Ethiopian jazz to Algerian *raï* and even sounds from Latin America, this festival has it all. Established in 1987, it has become the springboard for African music in North America and has helped introduce many international groups to Canadian audiences. Happening throughout July and August with free shows at Place Émilie-Gamelin it is the city's premiere world music festival.

FESTIVAL MONDIAL DE LA BIÈRE

Various locations, 514/722-9640,
www.festivalmondialdelabiere.qc.ca
COST: Free entry, tasting $1–5

Canada's largest beer festival, the Festival Mondiale de la Bière, takes place every June with local and international microbreweries sharing the stage with giants like Molson and Stella Artois. Brewers from all over the world converge, allowing visitors to taste hundreds of different types of beers. Entrance is free, but a full pint will set you back about $8. Tasting coupons are also available for a dollar a pop.

FESTIVAL ST-AMBROISE FRINGE DE MONTRÉAL

Various locations, 514/849-3378,
www.montrealfringe.ca
COST: $10–25, $250 unlimited Fringe Pass

Though not as big as the Edinburgh Fringe, Montréal's comes close with over 55,000 catching a show at the week-long festival. Running in early June, the festival takes over venues around the city with local and international Fringe performances that are randomly picked by lottery; if your play makes it to the stage, it is all about luck. Though the program is released a few days early, the best way to see if there's anything that tickles your fancy is to stop by the Fringe for All a few days before opening to see snippets from upcoming shows.

LA FÊTE DES ENFANTS DE MONTRÉAL

Parc Jean-Drapeau, www.parcjeandrapeau.com
COST: Free
Map 7

This free children's festival takes place in Parc Jean-Drapeau for an entire weekend during

ARTS AND LEISURE

the month of August. Kids 12 and under can participate in 100 different activities, including creative and sports workshops, singing, dancing, games, and live music shows. Characters in costume entertain the kids as you walk around and take in the sights; they also have a specialty area for those with infants, offering changing tables, bottle warming, and stroller parking.

LES FRANCOFOLIES DE MONTRÉAL
Various locations, 514/876-8989, wwwfrancofolies.com
COST: Free–$120
This massive street festival in celebration of Francophone music takes over the downtown core every June. A whole strip of rue Ste-Catherine is blocked off to make way for the throngs of fans who come out in force to check out emerging and established Francophone bands and musicians. Not all concerts are free, however; bigger names play to a more contained crowd in venues across the city. It's a great way to check out the latest in Québécois music.

JUST FOR LAUGHS
Various locations, 514/845-4000,
www.hahaha.com
COST: $15–120
What started as a two-day Francophone comedy event, Juste pour Rire, has since grown into one of the biggest comedy festivals in the world. During the month of July streets all over downtown are closed off to make room for the street performers who perform throughout the city. Each year a number of established comedians, including Bill Cosby, Louis C.K., Jerry Seinfeld, and Flight of the Conchords, bring their own brand of stand-up to the city. The recently launched Zoofest, also part of Just for Laughs, has a younger take on funny and features more obscure, sometimes funnier acts.

OSHEAGA ARTS AND MUSIC FESTIVAL
Parc Jean-Drapeau, www.osheaga.com
COST: $75 per day, $135 weekend
Map 7
This two-day rock festival is one of the biggest in Montréal, taking place off-island in the

Osheaga Arts and Music Festival

picturesque Parc Jean-Drapeau. Thousands of people of all ages and creeds spend the weekend checking out lesser-known bands like Robyn and Radio Radio and big-name bands like Arcade Fire, Coldplay, and Jack Johnson. Local art collectives set up installations in a designated area of the site and you can often check out the work as it is in process. Among leafy-green forests, it is a great way to spend the last weekend of July.

FALL
FESTIVAL DU MONDE ARABE
Various locations, 514/747-0000,
www.festivalarabe.com
COST: $15-50
Established in 2000, the Festival du Monde Arabe, which takes place in late October to mid-November, aims to develop a dialogue between Arab and western cultures in the city. Featuring everything from dance to visual arts and music to movies, it attempts to present every aspect of the culture. Since many Arab cultures were once colonized by the French, many of the events are in French, though English events also exist; check the website for details.

◖ FESTIVAL DU NOUVEAU CINÉMA
Various locations, 514/282-0004,
www.nouveaucinema.ca
COST: $10 per film, $8 per film senior and student, $125 pass, $100 pass senior and student
Founded in 1971, the Festival du Nouveau Cinéma is an independent film festival dedicated to showing independent films from the world over. Taking place over 10 days in October, it has become a huge draw for cinemaphiles and is viewed as one of the most prestigious festivals for films of this kind. It is even a qualifying festival for the Academy Awards in the category of short film. Directors such as Kenneth Anger, Wim Wenders, and Atom Egoyan have attended the festival.

IMAGE+NATION
Various locations, www.image-nation.org
COST: $11.50 per film, $8 senior and student
Held at the end of October, Image+Nation is the preeminent gay and lesbian film festival in the city. With international titles and 11 days of screenings, and thanks to the collapse of independent film distribution, it has become one of the most important festivals of its kind. Titles by and for the LGBT community are on view here, though the films include animation and shorts.

MONTRÉAL WORLD FILM FESTIVAL
Various locations, 514/848-3883,
www.ffm-montreal.org
COST: $10 per film
With the aim of supporting cultural diversity in cinema, the Montréal World Film Festival supports many emerging filmmakers. The public festival invites viewers to be the jury, and audience members participate in the process by voting for films in various categories—like the Oscars but without Hollywood. That's not to say bigger name directors don't show here; they do, but they rarely come from Hollywood. During the late August festival, free viewings of films are offered out under the stars in front of Place des Arts.

◖ POP MONTRÉAL
Various locations, 514/842-1919,
www.popmontreal.com
COST: $10-35, $80 Pop Pass
This annual five-day festival (late September–early October) featuring Francophone, Canadian, and international pop musicians is one of the most highly anticipated festivals of the year, especially among fans of indie music. Emerging and underground artists might outnumber other bands on the schedule, but industry pioneers include Burt Bacharach, Naomi Shelton, and Os Mutantes. Though primarily a music festival it has grown to include shoot-offs like Puces Pop, Art Pop, Film Pop, Fashion Pop, and Kids Pop.

ARTS AND LEISURE

Recreation

BIKE RENTALS, TOURS, AND PATHS

🌑 ÇA ROULE MONTRÉAL

27 rue de la Commune E., 514/866-0633,
www.caroulemontreal.com
HOURS: Daily 9 A.M.-8 P.M.
COST: $25 day rental, $22-49 tours
Map 1

Just in front of the Vieux-Port, Ça roule Montréal provides a great option for hourly or daily bike rentals. If you want to explore the city's waterfront, biking is the most accessible and fastest way to do it. Different types of bikes are on offer so you're able to pick a ride that you're comfortable with. They also provide bikes for children, and tandems if you want to ride as a couple. They also offer tours of different lengths to various destinations and attractions around the city. Using the Vieux-Port as a starting point there's no better way to see the city.

LACHINE CANAL BIKE PATH

Btwn. Vieux-Port and chemin du Musée in Lachine
Map 1

Running along the base of the Vieux-Port and continuing west, the Lachine Canal bike path is one of the longest in the city. Following the river for 15 kilometers, riders get a view of the city skyline and can take in the old warehouses of what was once a bustling port. Open for cycling from April to when the snow flies, in winter it becomes a great path for cross-country skiing. One of the most popular paths in the city, it can get crowded, especially on summer weekends. Those who feel inspired to ride farther can connect with a number of adjoining paths and check their route on maps along the way. It's also a popular path for in-line skaters and walkers.

MY BICYCLETTE

2985 St-Patrick, 514/998-6252, www.mybicyclette.com
HOURS: Mon.-Fri. 10 A.M.-7 P.M., Sat.-Sun. 9 A.M.-8 P.M.
COST: $30 adult bike day rental, $25 child bike day rental
Map 7

Located on the Lachine Canal, near the Atwater Market, My Bicyclette offers hourly and daily rates for adult and children's bikes. One of the best locations in the city for bike riding, the canal is 15 kilometers long and runs from the Old Port to Lake St-Louise in the west. All bike rentals come with a helmet and a map of the city. Bike tours are offered between June and October, and My Bicyclette also helps organize specialty rides

HANG 10 IN MINUS-10: RIVER SURFING

Montréal may be surrounded by water, but anyone who's visited the city would be hard-pressed to think of it as surf heaven – there are no beachfront properties, no surf-shacks, no sun-bleached beach babes. But in recent years the sport has exploded, and it's now one of the fastest growing recreations in the city.

It works like this: Montréal is on the St-Lawrence River, and part of that river includes the Lachine Rapids, which create large standing waves. It is on these waves that surfing has become popular. In contrast to regular surfing, the standing wave doesn't really move, the surfer does.

Between May and October two surf schools can teach you how to carve like a pro. **Imagine Surfboards** (01320 Charlevoix, 514/504-5522, www.imaginesurfboards.com/eng/class.html) and **Kayak Sans Frontiéres** (7770 blvd. La-salle, Lachine, 514/595-7873, www.ksf.ca) both offer two-day courses as well as board and equipment rental. If you're simply curious and want to check out the scene before you sign up to ride the rapids, **Surf Montréal** (www.surfmtl.com) is a great resource on the sport and offers regular updates and suggestions for those looking for a taste of the coast 1,300 kilometers west of it.

BIXI-ING THE CITY

In the early summer of 2009, the city of Montréal launched the Bixi, a public bicycle sharing system with 3,000 bikes and 300 stations located around the city. Although Bixis are already established in cities like Paris and Barcelona, Montréal was one of the first to adopt the program in North America – and with great success. By the end of the summer of 2009, the Bixi network had grown to include 5,000 bikes and 400 stations. Montréal is a bike-friendly city to begin with, and the Bixi has extended the city's love of bikes to those in Montréal for a short stay. Available from April to November it is both an ideal way to see the city and one of the fastest ways to get around.

Getting in on the Bixi action is simple; subscriptions can be purchased at any Bixi station (or online at www.bixi.com), located on street corners in just about every neighborhood of the city. Swipe your credit card to get a number code, then type that number code into the bike of your choice to unlock it, and voilà! – you're ready to ride. When you get to your destination, push the Bixi into an empty slot and check for the red light to make sure it is locked in.

The idea behind the Bixi is really to get you from point A to point B, not to keep riding the same bike for the whole day. If you take the Bixi for a long morning ride along the Lachine Canal, don't be surprised when the bill comes for $50. Bixis are ideal for short rides and the payment scheme promotes that. A single-day subscription will cost you $5, but that's just to unlock the bike; trips that last longer than 30 minutes incur a charge of $1.50 to $6 for each subsequent 30-minute period. If you see yourself using them a lot, opt for the $28 per month plan available through the website, which is worth it even if you're just visiting for a week.

If this is your first time using a Bixi, take it for a spin before you head out on the road; they're nearly indestructible, so the movement is stiffer than a regular bike. And if you think you're going to do a lot of biking it's a good idea to bring a helmet. Montréal has specialized bike lanes, but when you're unfamiliar with a city, and the sometimes oblivious drivers, it is better to be safe than sorry.

© TOURISME MONTRÉAL

one of the many Bixi stations around the city

ARTS AND LEISURE

CRUISE TO QUÉBEC: SAILING UP THE ST-LAWRENCE

One of the most inspired ways to travel between Montréal and Québec City is by boat cruise. Sure, it's not the most cost- or time-effective (a single trip lasts about eight hours), but it is one of the most romantic. And the views of the St-Lawrence and the villages that dot its banks easily beat out those of the highway.

When it comes to choosing a company or cruise there are a few different options. **The CTMA Group** (www.ctma.ca) offers a week-long trip from Montréal with stops in other regions of the province, like Gaspé and the Îles-de-la-Madeleine, before a day in Québec City. **Croisières AML** (www.croisieresaml.com), meanwhile, offers great options for simple day-long cruises with early-morning Montréal departures that get you to Québec in time for dinner.

All companies offer a variety of cruise times and types – everything from a brunch cruise and a bus ride back to Montréal to a night in Québec with a cruise back the following day – allowing flexibility in your travels. The trips, however, do not take place every day, so make sure to plan well in advance and check the websites for exact dates and schedules.

and customized tours exclusively for groups; call or email ahead of time to secure a spot for both.

BOAT TOURS
LE BATEAU-MOUCHE
Jacques-Cartier Quay, 514/849-9952, www.bateau-mouche.ca
HOURS: Mid-May-mid-Oct. daily 11 A.M., 2:30 P.M., and 4 P.M.
COST: $23 adult, $21 senior and student, $11 child, child under 5 free
Map 1

Departing from the Old Port, Le Bateau-Mouche takes you on a boat tour of the Old Port and the surrounding islands, including sites such as the Biosphère, La Ronde Amusement Park, and Habitat 67. Sixty-minute tours depart three times daily, with a 90-minute cruise departing once a day around noon. Evening dinner cruises are also available, as are specialty cruises during popular events like the jazz festival.

SAUTE MOUTONS
Quai d'Horloge, 514/284-9607, www.sautemoutons.com
HOURS: May-Oct. daily 10 A.M.-6 P.M.
COST: Jet boating $65 adult, $55 adolescent (13-18), $45 child (6-12); speed boating $25 adult, $20 adolescent (13-18), $18 child (6-12)
Map 1

Thrill seekers take note: This is the wettest and wildest of boat tours on offer in Montréal. This hour-long tour takes you from the heart of the Old Port out onto the St-Lawrence River and the Lachine Rapids for an unparalleled experience on the water. An integral part of the city's history—the rapids are part of the reason explorers stopped in Montréal—the tours offer a unique view of the city and are guaranteed to get you wet.

CROSS-COUNTRY SKIING
JARDIN BOTANIQUE AND PARC MAISONNEUVE
4101 and 4601 rue Sherbrooke E.
HOURS: Jardin Botanique Tues.-Sun. 9 A.M.-5 P.M., Parc Maisonneuve daily 6 A.M.-11 P.M.
COST: Free
Map 7

When the flowers are no longer in bloom the Montréal botanical gardens become an urban winter wonderland. Situated out by the Olympic Stadium, the Jardin Botanique and the adjacent Parc Maisonneuve are some of the most picturesque places to cross-country ski. The mostly flat terrain includes 20 kilometers of trails that weave through both the park and the gardens and offer great views of the Biodôme and stadium. But you are required to bring your own gear.

GUIDED CITY TOURS

A great way to discover the city is through a mix of social and historical contexts. **L'Autre Montréal** (3680 Jeanne-Mance #331, 514/521-7802, ext. 226, www.autremontreal.com, $17 adult) offers guided tours with a focus on history, architecture, urban planning, and sociology and gives you a great vision of the city's unique culture and community. Some of the more interesting tours include a tour of Montréal's back alleys and a look at the various immigrant communities. Tours of smaller neighborhoods not included in this book are also available and a great way to see places off the beaten path.

Les Fantômes du Vieux-Montréal (469 rue St-François-Xavier, 514/844-4021, www.fantommontreal.com, May–Oct., $22 adult, $19 student, $13 child) is not for the easily scared. On this ghost tour of Old Montréal, guides in period costume tell you all about the hangings, sorcery, tortures, and spooky sightings that make up the city's past. They also have specialized tours come Halloween.

Guidatour (360 rue St-François-Xavier, 514/844-4021, www.guidatour.qc.ca, May–Oct., $18 adult, $16 student, $9 child) runs walking tours of Old Montréal, offering amusing anecdotes and snippets of history as you wander the cobblestone streets. Guides are bilingual and tours depart from the gift shop at Basilique de Notre-Dame.

Héritage Montréal (100 rue Sherbrooke E., 514/286-2662, www.heritagemontreal.qc.ca, May–Oct. Sat.-Sun., cost varies) is a nonprofit organization that takes visitors on various tours that explore the architectural, social, or historical evolution of the city's neighborhoods. Departure points vary depending on the week and the tour, and reservations are recommended.

PARC DU MONT-ROYAL
Beaver Lake Pavilion, Parc du Mont-Royal, 514/872-6559
HOURS: Daily 6 A.M.-11 P.M.
COST: Free
Map 7

Ideally located in the center of the city, Mont Royal Park transforms into one of the best places in the city to cross-country ski when the snow falls. Twenty-two kilometers worth of trails are easily accessible by public transport and offer both flat and inclined terrain, making it is a perfect choice for beginners and old pros alike. Skis are available for rent from the **Beaver Lake Pavilion** (Sun.–Thurs. 9 A.M.–8:30 P.M., Fri.–Sat. 9 A.M.–9:30 P.M.), but those with their own equipment are invited to simply enjoy the trails.

LE YETI
5190 blvd. St-Laurent, 514/271-0773, www.leyeti.ca
HOURS: Mon.-Wed. 10 A.M.-6 P.M., Thurs.-Fri. 10 A.M.-9 P.M., Sat. 9:30 A.M.-5 P.M., Sun. noon-5 P.M.
Map 6

Located in the Mile End, close to the Plateau and not far from Mont-Royal, Le Yeti rents cross-country ski equipment at reasonable daily and week-long rates. During a heavy snowfall it's not uncommon for Montréalers to cross-country ski around the city; for those visiting in winter, it is a great way to see the city. Snowshoes are also available.

GOLF
CLUB DE GOLF SAINTE-ROSE
1400 blvd. Mattawa, Laval, 450/628-6072, www.golfste-rose.com
HOURS: May-Nov. daily dawn-10 P.M.
COST: $55 for 18 holes
Map 7

North out of the city in the suburb of Laval is the Sainte-Rose Golf Club. Located on the Rivière des Mille-Îles and inaugurated in 1996, it was designed by course architect John Watson, one of the most renowned architects in the province. This 18-hole par-70 course has a rustic feel to it, with weather-worn pines lining the fairway and natural ponds along the course. Deceptively challenging, it's 6,400 yards in length and includes three par-5 holes.

DORVAL MUNICIPAL GOLF CLUB
1455 Cardinal, Dorval, 514/631-4711, golfmunidorval.com
HOURS: May–Nov. daily dawn–10 P.M.
COST: $26 for 18 holes
Map 7

This semi-private course about a 20-minute drive outside of the city is a convenient course if not the most spectacular. Opened in 1960, and located near the airport, it was created from leftover holes of Elmridge Golf Club, which had been used for to make room for housing developments. Bordered by subdivisions and the airport tarmac, it's a popular place for a nine-hole game, or for those just getting the hang of golf. Nonmembers may only tee off at specific times; call or check the site for details.

MEADOWBROOK GOLF CLUB
8370 rue Côte Saint-Luc, 514/488-6612, www.clubdegolfmeadowbrook.com
HOURS: May–Nov. daily dawn–10 P.M.
COST: $34 for 18 holes
Map 7

Located in the west-end borough of Côte-Saint-Luc, this 18-hole course got its start as part of the Canadian Pacific Recreation Club of Montréal in the early 20th century. Opened as a course in 1949, it's now tucked behind houses and railway tracks, though the tree-lined fairways and occasional babbling brook do a nice job of transporting players off the island. Although not the most challenging of courses, it's convenient to get to and offers a bit of an oasis without leaving the city.

HEALTH CLUBS
CLUB LACITÉ
3575 ave. du Parc, 514/288-8221, www.clublacite.net
HOURS: Mon.–Fri. 6:30 A.M.–10:30 P.M., Sat.–Sun. 8 A.M.–10 P.M.
COST: $12 day pass
Map 5

Workout among buff university students at this gym situated in the McGill ghetto. The affordable day pass, which drops to an even more respectable $5 after 7 P.M., gets you into

their weight room and cardiovascular center and gives you access to their tennis and squash courts (reservations required). The club even has a year-round outdoor pool, great for laps in the winter and for being seen sipping a cocktail at the swim-up bar in the summer.

MANSFIELD ATHLETIC CLUB
1230 rue Mansfield, 514/390-1230, www.clubmansfield.ca
HOURS: Mon.–Fri. 6 A.M.–10:45 P.M., Sat.–Sun. 7:15 A.M.–7:45 P.M.
COST: $22.50 day pass
Map 2

Housed in a former theater in downtown, the Mansfield Athletic Club is unlike any other gym in Montréal. Open at the crack of dawn (and hours before in the winter months) it is perfect for early-risers and offers top-of-the-line equipment; it even has its very own health clinic. Though day passes are available there is a limit to how many you can buy; those in the city for a while should talk with membership about other possible options.

YMCA
1440 rue Stanley, 514/849-8393, www.yquebec.org
HOURS: Mon.–Fri. 5:30 A.M.–11 P.M., Sat. 8 A.M.–6 P.M., Sun. 8 A.M.–5 P.M.
COST: $17 day pass
Map 2

Opened in 1851, the Montréal Downtown Y was the first YMCA to open in North America. Situated in downtown, the recently renovated building has a modern new interior that rivals that of any private gym. They offer a range of classes, everything from yoga to hiphop dance, spinning to tai chi, and have numerous facilities, including a weight room, squash courts, an indoor pool, and an indoor track. Just about everything you need for a varied and satisfying workout.

HORSE-DRAWN CARRIAGE RIDES
CALÈCHES
Place d'Armes and Place Jacques-Cartier
HOURS: Daily 8 A.M.–11 P.M.
COST: $45 for 30 min., $75 for 60 min.
Map 1

These horse-drawn carriage rides are a popular

way to see the city, and are commonly seen around Vieux-Montréal's two busiest squares. A tour will take you along the area's historic streets and point out buildings, areas of interest, and give you a bit of the city history while they're at it. Though the summer is the obvious season for a carriage ride, the horses and their drivers work all year-long, and winter rides come equipped with a heavy (sometimes fur) blanket. Take a thermos of hot chocolate for the ride during the winter.

ICE-SKATING
LE ATRIUM 1000
1000 rue de la Gauchetière, 514/395-0555, www.le1000.com
HOURS: June-Sept. Mon.-Fri. 11:30 A.M.-6 P.M., Sat. noon-9 P.M., Sun. noon-6 P.M.; Oct.-May Mon. 11:30 A.M.-6 P.M., Tues.-Fri. 11 A.M.-9 P.M., Sat.-Sun. noon-9 P.M.
COST: $6.50 adult, $5.50 senior and student, $4.50 child
Map 2

Open year-round, this indoor skating rink located in the atrium of a large office tower is a great place to bring the family or enjoy a little winter sport in the middle of a heat-wave. Special times are reserved for younger skaters and their parents, so if you are traveling with the kids make sure to check the site for days and times. They even offer skating lessons for adults and kids alike.

BEAVER LAKE
Beaver Lake Pavilion, Parc du Mont-Royal, 514/843-8949
HOURS: Dec.-Mar. Sun.-Thurs. 9 A.M.-9 P.M., Fri.-Sat. 10 A.M.-9 P.M.
COST: Free
Map 7

The donut-shaped rink isn't the biggest or the most diverse in Montréal, but Mont-Royal provides a beautiful backdrop and makes it one of the most popular outdoor rinks in the city. This place can get packed on weekends—head there at night for a calmer atmosphere. Rental equipment is available from the pavilion, which also offers storage lockers as well as a café and

a cafeteria. Hours and dates vary depending on weather conditions, so check before heading out.

BONSECOURS BASIN
Bonsecours Basin, 800/971-7678
HOURS: Mon.-Wed. 10 A.M.-9 P.M., Thurs.-Sun. 10 A.M.-9 P.M.
COST: $6 adult, senior, and student, $4 child; $8 skate rental, $6 helmet rental
Map 1

During the winter months (about mid-December to mid-March), head south from rue de la Commune in the Vieux-Port toward Bonsecours Basin. Depending on the weather, skaters are either lucky enough to skate free on the larger open-water basin—it's approximately 1.5 times the size of a regular rink—or are restricted to a smaller pond. Either way, it's a great family (or date) activity on a lovely cold and crisp day.

PARC JEANNE-MANCE
Ave. du Parc and the corner of Duluth
HOURS: Dec.-Mar. daily 10 A.M.-10 P.M.
COST: Free
Map 5

Reserved for those with their own equipment, this seasonal rink is put up by the city each winter and is one of the more sought-after in Montréal, especially by those wanting to pay game of shinny (ice hockey). The rink has a real Canadian feel to it. Directly across the street from Mont-Royal Park it is easily accessible by bus and doesn't get as busy as the more popular Beaver Lake.

PARC LAFONTAINE
3933 ave. du Parc-Lafontaine, 514/872-2644
HOURS: Dec.-Mar. Mon.-Fri. 11 A.M.-10 P.M., Sat.-Sun. 10 A.M.-10 P.M.
COST: Free
Map 5

The most idyllic place to go for a skate in the city, Parc Lafontaine's large pond offers a huge rink on which to meander and practice your camel spins and backwards technique. Hockey enthusiasts can usually be found shooting the

© TOURISME MONTRÉAL

Parc Lafontaine

puck off in their own corner, and beginners are able to find their own spot of ice on which to get their balance. Skate and equipment rental is available on-site at a minimal cost, but those with their own skate for free.

KAYAKING
H2O ADVENTURES
2985B St-Patrick, 514/842-1306, www.h2oadventures.com
HOURS: June-Sept. daily 9 A.M.-9 P.M., Sept.-close Mon.-Fri. noon-8 P.M., Sat.-Sun. 9 A.M.-8 P.M.
COST: Kayak rental $15/hour; kayak lessons $39 Mon.-Fri., $45 Sat.-Sun.
Map 7

Located along the bank of the Lachine Canal, H2O Adventures rents sea kayaks, pedal boats (*pedalos* in Montréal parlance), and electric boats. They also offer two-hour lessons in sea kayaking and have over 32 kinds of kayaks to choose from, including single and tandem (two-person) kayaks. Rentals are available on a first-come, first-served basis and are limited to two-hour time slots. It is a popular place come the summer so reservations are recommended.

SPECTATOR SPORTS
Football
LES ALOUETTES DE MONTRÉAL
Molson Stadium, 475 ave. des Pins W., 514/871-2266, www.montrealalouettes.com
COST: $15-50
Map 5

The team was originally founded in 1872, playing a hybrid of English rugby and football, but a game against Harvard University in 1874 changed the rules and created Canadian football. The team was rechristened the Montréal Alouettes in 1946 and has had a sometimes-troublesome history that includes name changes and a brief move to Baltimore. Back in Montréal since 1996, the team has since gone on to win two Grey Cups (the Canadian Football League's equivalent of the Super Bowl). There is a serious lack of professional sports teams in Montréal, at least compared to the enthusiasm harbored by fans, so the Alouettes are popular and the screams of the crowd can be heard far across the Plateau.

CATCH HABS FEVER: THE MONTRÉAL CANADIENS

A fast way to make friends in this town is to strike up a conversation about the city's beloved hockey team, the Montréal Canadiens. One of the oldest and most storied franchises, in not only hockey but in all North American sports, the Canadians are one of the original six teams to make up the National Hockey League and have been around since 1909. Also known as the Habs (short for *habitant*, a term used to describe early French settlers), the Canadiens hold the record for the most Stanley Cups: The team has won the title a record 24 times, though the Cup has been elusive since last being hoisted here in 1993.

During the season (September to April) you can't go wrong to take in the atmosphere in most of the bars in town, which will be showing the game. Water cooler talk, newspapers, and entire radio stations are dedicated solely to discussing last night's game and dissecting coaching strategies. Passionate is an understatement when describing Hab fans, who are known to voice their opinions about anything Hab related. Sit down next to one for a game and you'll see for yourself.

The team plays out of the centrally located Centre Bell, and tickets are a hot commodity. Having sold out the previous six seasons, tickets can most easily be bought from scalpers around the arena or on sites such as Craigslist. Seeing a game live, you'll find out why this city lives and dies with this team; the atmosphere is infectious and insane, and even the most lax of supporters will be olèing with the rest of them by the end of the third period.

Hockey
◀ MONTRÉAL CANADIENS

Centre Bell, 1250 rue de la Gauchetière W.,
877/668-8269, http://canadiens/nhl.com
COST: $40-240
Map 2

One of the original six teams to play in the National Hockey League, the Canadiens have won the Stanley Cup 24 times. To say that the city supports the "Habs" is an understatement; Montréalers of all stripes and creeds are devoted to the team. Despite the fact that they haven't won the cup since 1993, games routinely sell out, though scalpers can be found "buying" tickets around the entrance on game days. If you can wait long enough you might be able to get a half-price ticket after the game has started.

Car Racing
CANADIAN GRAND PRIX

Circuit Gilles Villeneuve, Parc Jean-Drapeau,
514/350-0000, www.grandprixmontreal.com
COST: $50-150
Map 7

A yearly event since 1961, the Canadian Grand Prix is part of the Formula One World Championship and takes place on the Gilles Villeneuve circuit off island on Île Notre-Dame near Parc Jean-Drapeau. Drivers cover the 2.7-mile-long circuit 70 times before crossing the finish line. A popular event—it is one of the most-watched sporting events in the world—visitors from all over flock to the city and the three-day event has a number of street parties and events in its honor.

Soccer
MONTRÉAL IMPACT

Saputo Stadium, 3200 rue Viau, 514/328-3668,
www.montrealimpact.com
COST: $10-40
Map 7

We may not have a player as internationally recognizable as David Beckham or Mia Hamm, but the Montréal Impact still bring in the crowds. In a city full of citizens with strong ties to their family heritage (Italian, Greek, Portuguese) it is no surprise that soccer pulls at their heartstrings, and a subculture around the club has even started to emerge. Founded in 1992, the Impact currently

ARTS AND LEISURE

play in the second division of the United States Soccer Association but will be moving to Major League Soccer (MLS) in 2012.

Tennis
ROGERS CUP
Uniprix Stadium, Parc Jarry, 514/273-1234, www.rogerscup.com
COST: $10-200
`Map 7`

Otherwise known as the Canadian Masters, and formerly called the Canadian Open, the Rogers Cup is the country's preeminent tennis tournament and annually hosts the world's top players. Established in 1881, the weeklong competition is the third longest-running tennis tournament in the world after Wimbledon and the U.S. Open. Montréal splits the duty with Toronto, and the cities annually take turns hosting the men's and women's championships.

Roller Derby
MONTRÉAL ROLLER DERBY LEAGUE
Various locations, www.mtlrollerderby.com
COST: $10
This league was founded in 2006. Over the

last few years roller derby has made a comeback in cities all across North America, and Montréal is no exception. Consisting of three home teams—The Contrabanditas, Les Filles du Roi, and La Racaille—and two traveling teams, the league always sees a lot of action. The season runs May–October, and during that time unused ice rinks around the city fill with fans cheering on their favorite players. The matches attract so many people the lineups are often down the block.

SWIMMING
JEAN-DRAPEAU AQUATIC COMPLEX
Parc Jean-Drapeau, Île Sainte-Hélène, 514/872-7368
HOURS: Mid-June-late Aug. daily 10 A.M.-8 P.M.
COST: $5 adult, $4 senior, $3 child
`Map 7`

Three pools, including a lane pool, diving pool, and recreational pool, let you cool off from the heat of the summer surrounded by the greenery of the park. Open throughout the summer the off-island location gives it an edge over the competition, and it's less frequented throughout the week than those in the heart of the city.

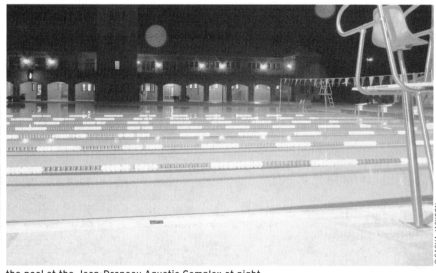

the pool at the Jean-Drapeau Aquatic Complex at night

OLYMPIC POOL

4141 ave. Pierre-De Coubertin, 514/252-4622,
www.rio.gouv.qc.ca

HOURS: Mon.-Fri. 6:30 A.M.-8:55 P.M., Sat.-Sun.
9 A.M.-4:25 P.M.

COST: $5.50 adult, $4.65 senior and student, $4.10
child

Map 7

With seven different types of pools—a competition pool, a training pool, water polo pool, diving pool, underwater diving pool, warm-up pool, and wading pool for kids—the Olympic swimming center is without doubt the largest and most varied of its kind in the city. Open for daily open swims it is a must for those looking for the thrill of swimming Olympic waters; doing a few laps of the backstroke is the best way to admire the architecture. It's sometimes closed for competitions, rentals, or for holidays, so call ahead.

SIR WILFRED-LAURIER POOL

5200 rue Brebeuf, 514/872-4050

HOURS: Mid-June-late-Aug. daily 10:30 A.M.-8 P.M.

COST: Free Mon.-Fri.; $4 adult, $2 senior, $1 child (18
and under) Sat.-Sun.

Map 5

This local pool situated in one of the prettiest parks on the Plateau recently underwent a well-deserved renovation and now boasts an enlarged lounging area and a brand-new wading pool for the kiddies. A popular spot for locals of all ages, it gets crowded here on weekends, but weekday and evening swims are the best.

YOGA

MOKSHA YOGA

3863 blvd. St-Laurent, 514/288-3863,
www.mokshayogamontreal.com

HOURS: Mon.-Fri. 7 A.M.-9:30 P.M., Sat.-Sun.
8 A.M.-8:30 P.M.

COST: $5 community classes

Map 5

This hot yoga studio on the Main is a great place to stop in and get a serious workout. Classes are available throughout the week, but the community classes are the best for beginners or those just looking to drop in. For a small fee, the public is welcome to drop into these community classes, which are taught by new teachers and cater to all yoga levels. Participants are asked to bring a bath towel, a bottle of water, and a yoga mat; everything except for the bottled water is available for rent on-site. Check the schedule for correct dates and times.

PASSPORT TO PRANA

www.passporttoprana.com

COST: $30

A unique concept in every way, Passport to Prana gives you access to 30 yoga studios all over the city and allows you 10 months to use it up. The only catch is that you can only use the card at each yoga studio once. The idea behind the card is to allow people the opportunity to try out different studios and find one that best suits them. For those traveling or in the city for an extended amount of time this is a great way to get in your yoga practice.

ARTS AND LEISURE

160

SHOPS

Montréal style is unlike anything else in Canada, and the boutiques found around the city reflect that. Back in the early 20th century it was the chicest place on the continent, thanks to its position as the hub of travel. Passengers traveling to and from Europe would disembark here, bringing the latest fashions from the continent with them before traveling on to places like New York and Toronto. Montréal remains at a crossroads style-wise, with both European and North American tendencies, all of which have been shaped by the cold winters. Anyone who's visited when the snow is piled high knows that winter fashion here is particularly idiosyncratic, one that can be summed up by puffy parkas and fur-trimmed boots.

Even before the words sustainability and eco-friendly became part of everyday parlance,

there was a tradition of artisan products and a dedication to made-in-Québec goods. Though many of the garment factories have closed, the city's flourishing design scene remains dedicated to producing products within the province. All over the city there are home decor and clothing boutiques dedicated to selling exactly that. Just as Montréal is a hotbed for artists it's also a hotbed for up-and-coming designers, and stores throughout the city carry their work, or you might come across the designer's own eponymous boutique.

The city's main shopping district is concentrated in the downtown core along, and underneath, rue Ste-Catherine. It's here that you'll find Montréal's shopping malls, department stores, popular chain stores, electronics shops, and the legendary Underground City that lets

© DRAWN & QUARTERLY

HIGHLIGHTS

LOOK FOR TO FIND RECOMMENDED SHOPS.

Best Hat Store: Henri Henri has barely changed since it opened in 1932. It remains a dapper hat store with selections for men and women for all types of weather (page 162).

Best Kitsch: Kitsch 'n' Swell is a great place to find a unique gift or that perfect kitschy item you've been wanting for your home (page 164).

Best Bookstore: Small but mighty, the physical store of independent comic publishers **Drawn & Quarterly** stocks both new and classic literature, a fine selection of comics and graphic novels, and even has a reading corner and kid-friendly shelves for the tykes (page 169).

Best Music Store: Although the albums at **Primitive Records** are fastidiously categorized and organized, you could still dig here for ages, where the sheer scope of vinyl is almost unreal (page 170).

Most Inspired Children's Store: The wooden toys at **La Grande Ourse** will capture the imagination of kids of all ages (page 171).

Best Men's Boutique: The classic minimalism of Philippe Dubuc's designs and the rock walls of his eponymous boutique, **Dubuc,** make this store a must-visit shopping destination (page 174).

Best Québécois Fashion: Marie Saint Pierre is one of Montréal's best-known and most-respected fashion designers. Her flagship boutique, **Marie Saint Pierre,** provides a glimpse into the world of Québécois fashion (page 177).

Best Kitchen Supplies: Find your dream kitchen decor items, chic utensils, and elegant bakeware at **Les Touilleurs** (page 183).

Best Gift for a Sweet Tooth: Valrhona chocolate is the base for all the artisanal goodies made at **Les Chocolats de Chloé,** which includes chocolate-dipped marshmallows and homemade drinking chocolate (page 184).

Quintessential Québec designer Marie Saint Pierre's boutique is all about the modern woman.

you explore the entire shopping mecca without stepping outside. If you want a bit of chic, head for upscale rue Sherbrooke with its high-end fashion boutiques and department stores. Still downtown, the grand buildings and wide boulevard will make you feel as though you're somewhere else entirely. Of course, there are other streets and districts in which to window shop, each with its own district flavor. In fact, no matter where you are in Montréal, chances are you'll find a cute little neighborhood store to pop in to.

Accessories and Jewelry

You can usually spot a Montréaler by the modern, uncluttered leather bag they're toting around. Synonymous with the city's style are simple leather goods. Of course, if their bags are simple, don't expect the rest of the outfit to be; if they're not rocking a whole bunch of exclusive bling, Montréalers are likely wearing something handmade from a local jeweler.

BIRKS

1240 Square Philips, 514/397-2511,
www.birks.com
HOURS: Mon.-Wed. 10 A.M.-6 P.M., Thurs.-Fri.
10 A.M.-9 P.M., Sat. 9:30 A.M.-5 P.M., Sun. noon-5 P.M.
Map 3

It may not have a movie with its name in the title, or an iconic heart-shaped pendant, but Birks is Canada's answer to Tiffany's—even their boxes are a particular shade of blue. Founded in 1879, this store opened on rue Ste-Catherine in 1894. It's here that you'll find men picking out an engagement ring, women trying on the pair of sapphire earrings to wear to the opera or family members picking out a keepsake for the newborn. The interior remains virtually unchanged, except for an update or two, so it's worth popping in for a look at the turn-of-the-20th-century accents.

BLEU COMME LE CIEL

2000 rue Peel, 514/847-1128,
www.bleucommeleciel.com
HOURS: Mon.-Wed. 10 A.M.-6 P.M., Thurs.-Fri.
10 A.M.-9 P.M., Sat. 10 A.M.-5 P.M., Sun. noon-5 P.M.
Map 2

This is the place to pick up costume jewelry in the city, though from the window display, you'd never know these rocks are fake. And that's just how owner Marie-Hélène Chartray likes it, mixing real stones with Swarovski crystals and silver or other metals for one-of-a-kind pieces. Women of all ages and bank accounts, and men looking for the prefect gift, come here to find that needed piece of affordable bling.

Taking the Côte d'Azur vibe even further, the boutique itself mimics the coastal region, with soft, sandy-colored floors and blue walls; even the display cases act as shells, showing off their treasured finds.

🌙 HENRI HENRI

189 rue Ste-Catherine E., 514/288-0109,
www.henrihenri.ca
HOURS: Mon.-Thurs. 10 A.M.-6 P.M., Fri. 10 A.M.-9 P.M.,
Sat.-Sun. 10 A.M.-5 P.M.
Map 3

To those who say "I don't suit hats," Henri Henri's answer is that a person who doesn't suit hats, simply doesn't have a head. And after nearly 80 years in business, they know their stuff. Founded by Honorius Henri and Jean-Maurice Lefebvre in 1932, the store remains devoted to hats, and they've got all kinds of 'em, from a classic Panama to a fedora, from a Stetson to a Basque beret.

Part of this store's charm is its appearance, from the virtually unchanged window displays and 1930s-style awning to the all-wood interior, with hats tucked away in cubbies. Attracting old-time hat lovers and young men and women looking to be different, the service is genuine and thorough. Just try leaving without something new on your head.

M0851

3526 blvd. St-Laurent, 514/849-9759,
www.m0851.com
HOURS: Mon.-Wed. 10 A.M.-6 P.M., Thurs.-Fri.
10 A.M.-7 P.M., Sat. 10 A.M.-5 P.M., Sun. noon-5 P.M.
Map 5

The minimalist leather creations from this Montréal-based brand may have leaked into international territory—they have stores in New York, Paris, and Antwerp—but they remain a strong part of the city's design scene and their creations continue to be made in Montréal. Known for its bags (once you've seen one, you'll notice their style anywhere), this boutique also sells other leather goods, including outerwear. The open-concept store on the Main with wooden shelves and unfinished floors is always welcoming.

OZ BIJOUX

3933 rue St-Denis, 514/845-9568,
www.ozbijoux.com
HOURS: Mon.-Wed. 11 A.M.-6 P.M., Thurs.-Fri.
11 A.M.-9 P.M., Sat.-Sun. 10 A.M.-5 P.M.
Map 5

Working mostly in sterling silver, jeweler Monic Dahan creates unique handmade pieces that are both capricious and stunning. It's a few steps down into this St-Denis boutique, whose plain white walls are filled with glass display cases on all four walls and a huge semicircle display case in the middle, showing off the intricateness of the work, which features natural stones like onyx, turquoise, and quartz crystals. Staff are knowledgeable, and two large cats are often found sprawled on the counter, warming themselves under the fluorescent spotlights.

Antiques and Kitsch

Montréal has a torrid love affair with antiques and kitsch, one that's led to an overabundance of these types of stores. There are so many, from bizarre back-room family-run affairs to huge, engrossing warehouses full of a lot of junk and a few treasures. Montréalers love it all though, so don't be surprised if you find a deer-footed table in even the classiest of houses.

CITÉ DÉCO

1761 rue Amherst, 514/528-0659,
www.citedecomeubles.com
HOURS: Tues.-Fri. 11 A.M.-6 P.M., Sat. 11 A.M.-5 P.M., Sun.
noon-5 P.M.
Map 4

Cité Déco features an exquisitely curated collection of furniture with a focus on pieces from the 1930s to the 1960s. Squeezed between other charming antique stores on rue Amherst, Cité Déco may not be the biggest store on the block but it does have some of the best finds, like Danish-designed teak dinning room sets, reupholstered Rococo chairs, art deco mirrors, and earthenware vases.

COULEURS

3901 rue St-Denis, 514/282-4141,
www.couleurs.qc.ca
HOURS: Mon.-Wed. noon-6 P.M., Thurs.-Fri.
noon-9 P.M., Sat. 11 A.M.-5 P.M., Sun. noon-5 P.M.
Map 5

This store's modern aesthetic might trick you into thinking you've walked into the wrong place. Tucked away on busy St-Denis, a simple sign in their trademark sea-foam green (okay, so that may tip you off) leads you down a few stairs into this little piece of mid-20th-century heaven. Calling itself both a store and a gallery, Couleurs brings the already "modern" furniture into the 21st century with new upholstery and contemporary styling, letting you see the timeless style in a set of cornflower blue stoneware mugs, without associating it with the teachers lounge.

L'ECUYER ANTIQUES

1896 rue Notre-Dame W., 514/932-8461
HOURS: Tues.-Sat. 11 A.M.-5 P.M.
Map 2

Old traveling trunks and luggage are elegantly stacked along the walls of this beautifully decorated store, with black-and-white photos hanging on the walls. You feel as though you've just entered the corridor of a family about to go on vacation. Set designers are in love with this place, as are those with a thing for classic nostalgia pieces. The fashion-conscious will immediately have their eye on the antique Louis Vuitton or the full snakeskin set with hardly a nick on it. Owner André also has a lovely collection of walking sticks, as well as the occasional picnic set for those who want to eat alfresco in style.

GRAND CENTRAL

2448 rue Notre-Dame W., 514/935-1467, www.grandcentralinc.ca
HOURS: Mon.-Fri. 9:30 A.M.-5:30 P.M., Sat. 11 A.M.-5 P.M.
Map 2

The ceiling here is dripping in chandeliers. Owners Wayne and Gordon Downs have an eye for those from the 18th and 19th centuries, and at the right time at day—dusk, for example—the view from outside is stunning, giving it a romantic and old-timey feel. Though lighting is their specialty—beyond chandeliers they have a range of floor lamps, desk lamps, table lamps…the list goes on—they also have the furniture to match your early-20th-century hurricane lamp.

KITSCH 'N' SWELL

3968 blvd. St-Laurent, 514/845-6789, www.kitschnswell.ca
HOURS: Mon.-Wed. noon-6 P.M., Thurs.-Fri. noon-9 P.M., Sat. 11 A.M.-5 P.M., Sun. noon-5 P.M.
Map 5

Step inside this fantasyland of kitsch and you're surrounded by leopard-print walls, fringed light fixtures, and hook-rugs of flamenco dancers. This place is so stuffed that you could easily lose yourself for a good hour or two. Dedicated to kitsch from the 1940s up to the '70s this store is unlike anything you've seen before. Once you've pulled yourself away from the hypnotizing leopard-print, however, there's a ton of great, unique items that could easily work in your home, like a teak side table or set of themed highball glasses.

MONASTIRAKI

5478 blvd. St-Laurent, 514/278-4879, www.monastiraki.blogspot.com
HOURS: Mon.-Wed. noon-6 P.M., Thurs.-Fri. noon-8 P.M., Sat.-Sun. noon-5 P.M.
Map 6

It's hard to classify just what Monastiraki is. Part gallery, part antique shop, comics shop, and all kitsch, it's unlike any store you've been in. Owned by local artist, cartoonist, and all-round nice guy Billy Maveras, who knows the merchandise inside and out, it has undergone a complete revamp in the last couple of years, one that has cleared the floor space enough for you to enter without knocking into something. The antiques and collectibles, like back issues of *The New Yorker* and *Gourmet*, are still all there, only now they're just a little bit organized.

ORIENTAL TREASURES

1849 rue Notre-Dame W., 514/759-0998, www.orientaltreasures.org
HOURS: Tues.-Sat. 11 A.M.-5 P.M.
Map 2

Much of the stock here comes from shipwrecks. You read correctly, shipwrecks. Sure, it's a bit of a bizarre concept since Montréal is just about as far away as you can get from the Asian coastline, but Oriental Treasures were granted exclusive retail rights in Canada for shipwrecked artifacts. Collectors searching for a missing piece can be found here and the staff are more like archaeology professors. Many of these artifacts are from shipwrecks found off the coasts of Malaysia, Thailand and Vietnam and all come with a certificate of authenticity. If you weren't already convinced you should at least check out this place, pieces here have been featured in *National Geographic* so you know it's legit.

RETRO-VILLE

2652 rue Notre-Dame W., 514/939-2007
HOURS: Tues.-Sat. 11 A.M.-5 P.M.
Map 2

Montréal's original nostalgia store—it was formerly called Nostalgia-Ville—and arguably "the only place to visit in Montréal," at least according to the unflagging owner, this store appeals to the collector in all of us. Around for over 30 years, it's stocked with everything from vintage toys to antique cookie tins, Charles and Di commemorative tea cups, old street signs, and seltzer bottles. It's less antique-y than a lot of the stores on the strip—there is something here that will trigger childhood memories for everyone. Those with an appetite for kitsch and schmaltz would do well to stop in.

SECONDE CHANCE
1691 rue Amherst, 514/523-3019,
www.secondechance-retro.com
HOURS: Tues.-Sat. 11 A.M.-5 P.M.
Map 4

Dwindling vintage stock has caused prices to rise in the last few years, but Second Chance keeps things budget-friendly with their kitschy but well-selected finds. Design students are frequent shoppers here looking for inspiration or to sift through the awesome selection of Expo '67 memorabilia that includes everything from drinking glasses to travel bags.

SPOUTNIK BOUTIQUE
2120 rue Amherst, 514/525-8478,
www.boutiquespoutnik.com
HOURS: Tues.-Wed. and Sat. noon-5 P.M., Thurs.-Fri. noon-6 P.M.
Map 4

With lime-green walls and a packed floor-space, Spoutnik stands out among its Amherst brethren. The store offers everything from

lamps adorned with mosaics, bizarre geometric wall-hangings, and clustered bubble light-fixtures that would make even Lady Gaga jealous. There's a definite 1960s and '70s feel to the goods, lots of stainless-steel lamps and Formica kitchen tables, but you?ll also find more classic goods like elegant teak desks and simple chandeliers. Prices here vary greatly but you're often able to find something that fits your budget.

STYLE LABO
122 rue Bernard W., 514/658-9910,
www.stylelabo-deco.com
HOURS: Tues.-Sat. 10:30 A.M.-6 P.M.,
Sun. 11:30 A.M.-5 P.M.
Map 6

Style junkies beware; this new addition to the scene strikes a distinct balance between the old and the modern, the high-end and the low-end. When it's warm enough, a number of goodies are out on the sidewalk to tempt you, so passing by can leave you with a mid-20th-century school desk and an $80 hole in your wallet. Industrial pieces like galvanized steel desks and wall-mounted clocks from decommissioned factories are displayed next to a row of Pantone mugs in 25 different shades. They also sell old jewelry overstock and brightly patterned pillows to play off ultra-modern Design House lamps. Office supply fetishists can rejoice—tables are cluttered with vintage in-and-out trays, pencil sharpeners, and even manual desk calendars.

Arts and Crafts

A few hobbies are lucky enough to have their very own specialized stores, but most arts and craft supplies can easily be found at a big art store. What it lacks in charm it makes up for in choice.

DESERRE
334 rue Ste-Catherine E., 514/842-3021
HOURS: Mon.-Wed. 9:30 A.M.-6 P.M., Thurs.-Fri. 9:30 A.M.-9 P.M., Sat.-Sun. 10 A.M.-5 P.M.

Map 4

Started by Omer DeSerre in 1908, this was a hardware store and a department store before it was influenced by the École des Arts des Apliques (now a part of UQÀM) in the 1950s and started to carry a range of art materials. Still near the original location at Ste-Catherine and St-Denis, it's still popular with art students and hobbyists and is now a national chain. This is one of the largest in the city (other locations

GET CRAFTY: MONTRÉAL'S CRAFT OBSESSION

Little brings Montréalers together more than a craft fair. Held throughout the year, with an abundance of them around the holidays, these fairs take all shapes and sizes with vendors traveling from all over to attend.

The biggest show of all attracting, international vendors, is **Le Salon des Mètiers d'Art** (www.metiers-d-art.qc.ca/smaq, December, free), which takes over Place Bonaventure come winter. One of the biggest exhibition halls in the city, it houses the over 400 professional exhibitors and the 200,000 people who come to take it all in. Running throughout the entire month of December, it encompasses traditional and artisan crafts, such as blown-glass jewelry, felted winter accessories, and handmade bed linens. There's even a section dedicated to gastronomy.

After Mètiers, **Souk at SAT** (www.souk.sat.qc.ca) is one of the most popular pre-Christmas craft fairs. Attracting a diverse clientele of hipsters and suburban moms, this show always strikes a perfect balance of vendors with the emphasis on local producers. Greeting cards and ceramics are on sale here, as is the work of a number of emerging designers. The only trick with this fair is walking away with gifts for anyone but yourself. A word to the wise; this place gets packed, so if you want to browse without heating up, check your winter coat before you shop.

Held during the weeklong music festival Pop Montreal, **Puces Pop** (www.popmontreal.com/puces) attracts a hipster crowd of shoppers and sellers with young crafters coming from all over Canada and the United States to participate. It's usually held in a church basement, and there's a definite nostalgic feel to the whole event, but the work on sale here is top-notch and includes everything from cupcakes to screen prints, from natural beauty products to toys. A pre-Christmas edition is usually held mid-December with a third event in the spring.

Organized by a group of local designers, the **Smart Design Mart** (www.smartdesignmart.com) runs a few times a year and aims to put local designers of housewares, clothing, and jewelry as well as artists in the spotlight. Vendors here are less about traditional crafts and more about a platform for new talent.

are at 1500 McGill College and 1515 rue Ste-Catherine W.). It has two floors of art and craft supplies and is the perfect place to pick up everything from needlepoint kits to acrylic paints and frames.

EFFILOCHÉ

6252 rue St-Hubert, 514/276-2547, www.effiloche.com **HOURS:** Tues.-Wed. 11 A.M.-7 P.M., Thurs.-Fri. 11 A.M.-9 P.M., Sat. 10 A.M.-5 P.M., Sun. noon-5 P.M.

Map 6

This knitting and sewing lounge—the name means unraveled in English—has been around for the better part of five years and has the lived-in feeling of your grandma's kitchen. The bare, wooden floors, cubbies full of wools in an appetizing range of colors and textures, and big, comfy antique couches in the middle for kitting and chatting give the whole space a welcoming atmosphere. There's even a sewing room set up with machines in the back, and drawers full of punchy, quirky fabrics and trimming.

LOZEAU

6229 rue St-Hubert, 514/274-6577, www.lozeau.com **HOURS:** Mon.-Wed. 8 A.M.-6 P.M., Thurs.-Fri. 8 A.M.-9 P.M., Sat.-Sun. 9 A.M.-5 P.M.

Map 6

This family-owned and -operated business goes back to 1927, when it was started by founder Leo Laurent Lozeau as a wedding photography and film processing business. Since then it has become a retail outlet of any- and everything related to photography; whether you've got a problem with your old SLR or are looking for a reliable digital point-and-click, they've got you covered. The big, modern interior with good lighting and subtly red walls is a good backdrop for all the digital wares. The bilingual workers here really know their stuff, and if you're looking to rent out equipment for a specific project, they can help with that too.

AU PAPIER JAPONAIS
24 ave. Fairmount W., 514/276-6863,
www.aupapierjaponais.com
HOURS: Mon.-Sat. 10 A.M.-6 P.M., Sun. noon-4 P.M.
Map 6

A seriously beautiful store, with soft lighting and reels of *washi* hanging off the wall, Au Papier Japonais—or the Japanese paper store, as locals call it—carries over 500 different kinds of Japanese paper. It is not, however, the only type they stock; they also have paper from Nepal, India, Mexico, and Montréal, as well as journals, photo albums, and even kimonos for you to wear around at home. One of the store's biggest draws, however, is its courses,

which cover everything from simple bookbinding and box making to Japanese gift-wrapping and paper quilting.

A LA TRICOTEUSE
779 rue Rachel E., 514/527-2451
HOURS: Wed.-Fri. 10:30 A.M.-6 P.M., Sat.
10:30 A.M.-5 P.M.
Map 5

This charming corner store is minimally decorated with pops of color from the wool exploding out of the white, square cubbies that line the walls. Catering to the more mature knitter, wool here tends to be on the more expensive side, but the quality is always top-notch—though don't expect to find anything too psychedelic. They also offer a range of patterns, needles, and other tools for the trade and will help you work out a problem, or get started if you're new to the pastime.

Bath and Beauty

For the amount of beauty products that are made and conceived close to Montréal, you'd expect more independent boutiques to pop up. For the moment, however, we have to contend with a slim but excellent selection.

LISE WATIER INSTITUT
392 ave. Laurier W., 514/270-9296,
www.institutlisewatier.com
HOURS: Mon. 8:30 A.M.-5 P.M., Tues.-Wed. 8 A.M.-6 P.M.,
Thurs.-Fri. 8 A.M.-9 P.M., Sat. 7:30 A.M.-5 P.M., Sun.
10 A.M.-5 P.M.
Map 6

One of the biggest names in Canadian beauty, Lise Watier's Institut offers everything from massages and facials to pedicures and blowouts. Starting in 1972, Watier first made waves as a makeup artist, and her eponymous line of cosmetics is available at this modern, silvery, almost space-age Outremont store. A veritable beauty maven, her fragrance Neiges has been a bestseller in the province since it debuted in 1993. Ladies who lunch pop in for a quick

pedicure, and younger women stop by for a touch-up before heading out. If you're looking for a day of pampering they have a number of packages available at various price points. They also offer special treatments for men and can teach you how to do your own make-up in a simple one- or two-hour lesson ($45–100).

MURALE
1 Place Ville-Marie, 514/875-1593,
www.murale.ca
HOURS: Mon.-Wed. 9 A.M.-7 P.M., Thurs.-Fri.
9 A.M.-9 P.M., Sat. 9 A.M.-5 P.M.
Map 2

The Canadian answer to Sephora—well, at least it's trying—Murale is a one-stop beauty store with internationally recognized brands and emerging beauty labels. The first Murale to open in Canada, this one can be found on the ground level of Place Ville-Marie. Uber-sleek and futuristic looking, the entirely white store has a high-gloss shine to it and the vibe is super modern. Taking a more holistic approach, alongside

SHOPS

beauty and fragrance experts there is a pharmacist on hand and a dermatological skin-care center offering facials and other services. Those interested in checking-out lesser-known brands like Gosh and Dr. Hauschka should stop in here.

SAVON POPULAIRE
273 St-Zotique E., 514/270-0539,
www.savonpopulaire.ca
HOURS: Mon.-Wed. 10 A.M.-6 P.M., Thurs.-Fri.
10 A.M.-8 P.M., Sat. 10 A.M.-5 P.M., Sun. 11 A.M.-5 P.M.
Map 6
A wide array of organic, sustainable soaps line

the walls at this small, charming store in Little Italy. Made of all natural ingredients, these vegetable-based soaps first got their start as Christmas gifts in owner Alysia Melnychuk's kitchen. Melnychuk's business has since expanded beyond just soaps to include exfoliating scrubs, body butter, lip balms, and even shampoo. Fragranced with essential oils like lemon ginger, mint, anise, lavender, and chamomile, the smell in the store is inviting, not overpowering. Melnychuk also offers soap-making workshops and courses on skin care and essential oils.

Books and Music

There are a ton of great record stores in Montréal, most of them carrying a spectrum of musical styles from acid jazz to prog-rock and classic albums by Québécoise singers like Celine Dion and Isabelle Boulay and everything in between. Fans of vinyl will find new and old albums to pad out their collection, and most of these houses of vinyl also carry a range of CDs both new and used.

Though the majority of bookstores in the city are French there are a couple of independent English-language bookstores, though the majority of them are large chains. If you're looking for a hard-to-find title the city's used bookstores are your best bet.

ATOM HEART
34-B rue Sherbrooke E., 514/843-8484,
www.atomheart.ca
HOURS: Mon.-Wed. 11 A.M.-7 P.M., Thurs.-Fri.
11 A.M.-9 P.M., Sat. 11 A.M.-5 P.M., Sun. noon-5 P.M.
Map 4
With a large selection of rock and electronic albums, a dedication to vinyl, and the latest underground releases, Atom Heart could easily be branded a music-snob's paradise—and that's the way they like it. Long and narrow and completely white, the minimal interior puts the attention on the music. A regular stop for UQÀM students and Francophone cool kids, this is a great place to check out albums by local groups or get

introduced to some ultra-cool Francophone artists. Staff might be a bit cold at first, but drop a few band names and they'll soon warm up.

BEATNICK MUSIC
3770 rue St-Denis, 514/842-0664,
www.beatnickmusic.com
HOURS: Mon.-Wed. 11 A.M.-7 P.M., Thurs.-Fri.
11 A.M.-9 P.M., Sat.-Sun. 11 A.M.-6 P.M.
Map 5
Die-hard record collectors and vinyl fanatics come from far and wide to check out the selection at Beatnick. Heck, they've even got their own online store, but nothing beats heading into this cavern of sound and listening to a rare Northern Soul album on their turntables. Everything here revolves around the album, from the walls full of vinyl to the fastidiously organized shelves. The staff's knowledge is encyclopedic and their tastes individual. Of course, they also carry a number of CDs and the latest albums, usually on vinyl, by well-known contemporary bands.

CHEAP THRILLS
2044 rue Metcalfe, 514/844-8988,
www.cheapthrills.ca
HOURS: Mon.-Wed. and Sat. 11 A.M.-6 P.M., Thurs.-Fri.
11 A.M.-9 P.M., Sun. noon-5 P.M.
Map 2
Established in 1971, Cheap Thrills harmoniously

brings books and music together in this second-floor mecca. Specializing in jazz, avant-garde, experimental, and blues albums they also stock the latest rock and indie rock albums on vinyl and CD. No matter what you're looking for they likely have it, since their stock of used and new vinyl and CDs is over 10,000.

Being a stone's throw from McGill University, this is an ideal place to pick up a lightly used *Norton Anthology* or annotated version of *To the Lighthouse*. The selection of used books here is so vast it almost reaches the ceiling, so don't be afraid to use the ladder provided.

◖ DRAWN & QUARTERLY
211 rue Bernard W., 514/279-2224,
www.drawnandquarterly.com
HOURS: Mon.-Tues. 11:30 A.M.-6 P.M., Wed.-Sat.
11 A.M.-9 P.M., Sun. 11 A.M.-7 P.M.
Map 6

Possibly one of the best bookstores on the continent—seriously—Drawn & Quarterly is the physical extension of the art and graphic novel publishing house of the same name. Located in a turn-of-the-20th-century building, it has an old-store feel with tables full of books, low and accessible wooden shelves, and exposed bricks, making the whole place cozy. It's filled with locals just passing by, and the staff couldn't be sweeter. Carrying graphic novels and comics, gorgeous art books, literature, and kids' books (they have their own kid-size corner), this place offers everything a bibliophile could ask for. It's also a popular spot for book launches for local and bigger-name authors like Adrian Tomine, William Gibson, and Seth.

LIBRISSIME
1448 rue Sherbrooke W., 514/841-0122,
www.librissime.com
HOURS: Mon.-Fri. 11 A.M.-6 P.M., Sat. 11 A.M.-5 P.M., Sun.
noon-5 P.M.
Map 2

A book lover's dream, this store will make you feel as though you've fallen down the rabbit hole and ended up in your own kind of literary wonderland. They specialize in exceptional books on just about any subject you can think of, with

some of the most rare and beautiful books on the market. It's not all $5,000 art books, however; they also sell more affordable gifts like greeting cards, destination guides, and notebooks. A must for art and photography book lovers, it's also the perfect place to grab a gift for your favorite reader. Librissime's interior is impeccably designed, and they'll even help you design and build your own customized library.

MEDIAPHILE
1901 rue Ste-Catherine W., 514/939-3676
HOURS: Mon.-Sat. 8 A.M.-11 P.M., Sun. 10:30 A.M.-11 P.M.
Map 2

This independently owned newsstand sells a number of international daily and weekend papers and offers a wide selection of magazines in just about every language you can think of. This is a cute little place that has a homey feel; they even have wrapping paper, greeting cards, and trinkets for a last-minute gift that you can send right away because there is also a post office in the back. If you need an emergency loan while you're in town they're even a part of Western Union. Wait, there's more—cigars. This store has a huge selection of pipes, cigars, fancy cigarettes, and all the paraphernalia that goes with them, including beautiful, and pricey, humidors. Locals come to get the dailies and browse the tabloids, and tourists pop in for a Cuban.

MULTIMAGS
3552 blvd. St-Laurent, 514/287-7355
HOURS: Mon.-Wed. 8 A.M.-10 P.M., Thurs.-Sat.
8 A.M.-11 P.M., Sun. 9 A.M.-10 P.M.
Map 5

This city-wide chain has eight stores around Montréal where locals come to get their morning papers and peruse the selection of international magazines. Other central stores are located at 825 ave. Mont-Royal E. (514/523-3158) and 370 ave. Laurier W. (514/272-9954). They also carry stationery, including Moleskin notebooks, greeting cards, art books from publishers like Taschen and Phiadon, as well as of novelty items. Though the choice is generally the same at each store, it sometimes varies; ask the knowledgeable staff if you're looking for something specific.

PARAGRAPHE

2220 ave. McGill College, 514/845-5811,
www.paragraphbooks.com

HOURS: Mon.-Fri. 8 A.M.-9 P.M., Sat.-Sun. 9 A.M.-9 P.M.

Map 2

A long-time independent bookstore, Paragraphe was bought out by Quécécois company Archambault in the mid-aughts. Somehow, though, it's managed to retain its charm and the feel of a neighborhood bookstore. Kitty-corner to McGill University and on the northern tip of downtown, it always has a good selection of fiction and nonfiction to browse. A long-time favorite with authors— Yann Martel in particular drops in when he's in town—it hosts a number of readings and book launches throughout the year.

PAUL'S BOUTIQUE

112 ave. du Mont-Royal E., 514/284-7773

HOURS: Mon.-Wed. and Sat. 11 A.M.-6 P.M., Thurs.-Fri. 11 A.M.-9 P.M., Sun. noon-5 P.M.

Map 5

Started with just 100 vinyls and 20 CDs in 2001, Paul's Boutique has since grown to 20,000 vinyls and has taken over the two floors of a sagging, shabby house on Mont-Royal filled to the rafters with every kind of music available. Named for the store's owner, not the iconic Beastie Boys album—though the band has visited—the interior is chaotic, with fake sharks and disco balls hanging from the ceiling and the walls painted bubble-gum pink. From the albums of a prepubescent Celine Dion to Hawkwind's entire back catalogue, vinyl fiends are sure to find something here. Staff can be grumpy so don't expect the warmest welcome, but don't take it personally either.

PHONOPOLIS

207 ave. Bernard, 514/270-4442,
www.phonelopie.blogspot.com

HOURS: Tues.-Sun. noon-7 P.M.

Map 6

If the storefront of this record store on one of the Mile End's coolest strips looks vaguely familiar, that's because its monthly window displays mimic the covers of new releases. Don't be surprised if you brush past a member of Plants and Animals on your way in. Carrying new and used vinyl and CDs, they have a great collection of indie rock, obscure bands and labels, and vintage finds—unsurprisingly it's popular with local hipsters. The interior isn't much to speak of, just albums lined up on the walls. The atmosphere is detached and cool with some Springsteen or new sensation playing on the stereo.

◖ PRIMITIVE RECORDS

3830 rue St-Denis, 514/845-6017

HOURS: Mon.-Wed. 11 A.M.-6 P.M., Thurs.-Fri. 11 A.M.-9 P.M., Sat. 11 A.M.-6:30 P.M., Sun. noon-6 P.M.

Map 5

There are literally too many records in this shop. From 78s to 45s and 33s, this is by far the most comprehensive—and well-organized— collection in the city. Local DJs come here to stock up and so do the vinyl-curious, but it doesn't matter what kind of music you're into, if there's a style of music that exists, they've got a record of it, or more likely 10 records of it. Though used vinyl takes up the majority of the space, there's also a ton of new vinyl, new and used CDs, as well as books, zines, and magazines.

S.W. WELCH

225 rue St-Viateur W., 514/848-9558,
www.welchbooks.com

HOURS: Mon.-Sun. 11 A.M.-7 P.M.

Map 6

In business since 1984, second-hand bookstore S.W. Welch was a longtime staple on the Main before relocating to the Mile End in 2007. Locals spend hours browsing the shelves or pop in to take a look at the New Titles table. The topics range from transportation to science fiction, sexuality to Canadiana, though they also have a large selection of poetry, fiction, and children's books. The walls are lined with bookshelves, and they often have a display outside. Many titles come from people in the neighborhood, and it's not unlikely to find a brand-new title on the shelves.

THE WORD

469 rue Milton, 514/845-5640

HOURS: Mon.-Wed. 10 A.M.-6 P.M., Thurs.-Fri.
10 A.M.-9 P.M., Sat. 11 A.M.-6 P.M.

Map 3

In the heart of the McGill ghetto, this tiny lopsided house was once a Chinese laundry. In 1973, Adrian King-Edwards and his wife started an underground bookstore out of their apartment living room, and when the laundry went up for rent, they moved the shop next door. It specializes in secondhand academic books, so literature lovers will swoon at the shop's selection, which includes titles by local authors, and the old world feel of the interior. This is the kind of place where you could, and should, spend hours browsing the shelves.

Children's Stores

In case you missed the memo from the Québec government, the province is currently experiencing a baby boom. After winter hibernation it feels as though more and more infants arrive with the thaw each spring. Hopefully, that will translate to more kid-specific stores, because at the moment, there are only a few great ones. Since Montréal is a bilingual city, not all children's toys are in English, so double-check the label before buying that present for your nephew.

BOUTIQUE CITROUILLE

206 ave. Laurier W., 514/948-0555,
www.boutiquecitrouille.com

HOURS: Mon.-Wed. 10 A.M.-6 P.M., Thurs.-Fri.
10 A.M.-8 P.M., Sat. 10 A.M.-5 P.M., Sun. noon-5 P.M.

Map 6

Started by a couple of Parisian parents, Boutique Citrouille is chockablock with wooden toys. In fact this midsize store is so full of toys that it's a miracle that any parent can pull their child out of here—and vice versa. Anyone eco-conscious or even just with a weakness for old-fashioned toys will immediately fall for this place. But just because the toys here are wooden doesn't mean they're any less modern; you can still get helicopters, tea sets, kites (not wooden), cranes, and of course plush stuffed animals.

BUMMIS

4302 blvd. St-Laurent, 514/289-9415,
www.boutiquebummis.com

HOURS: Mon.-Wed. 10 A.M.-6 P.M., Thurs.-Fri.
10 A.M.-8 P.M., Sat. 10 A.M.-5 P.M., Sun. noon-5 P.M.

Map 5

All expecting and new mothers in Montréal love Bummis. Started as a cloth diaper business in the 1980s it has since expanded into a specialized boutique for mums and their newborns. Walls are still stacked with cloth diapers, but they now carry a multitude of items like breastfeeding bras, pumps, changing table pads, booties, books on mothering, natural skin-care products, and mini-sleepers—many things are made in-house. The space has a warm feeling with exposed brick and two big comfy couches.

◀ LA GRANDE OURSE

263 ave. Duluth E., 514/847-1207

HOURS: Tues.-Wed. noon-6 P.M., Thurs.-Fri.
noon-9 P.M., Sat.-Sun. noon-5 P.M.

Map 5

Unlike at any other children's store in the city, practically all the toys sold in La Grande Ourse are made of wood and crafted by local artisans. The store's aim is to inspire children to use their imagination during play, so most of the toys have simple gestures and expressions. Plainly decorated with white walls, the small store's shelves are filled instead with toys. There are pull-along toys and rocking horses for toddlers and kitchen sets, sailboats, and doll houses for older children. Despite the nondescript decor the store is full of wonder and excitement, and staff are willing to answer parents' questions or play with the little ones. But parents aren't the sole customers—those looking for unique gifts are regulars.

OINK OINK

1343 ave. Greene, Westmount, 514/939/2634, www.oinkoink.com
HOURS: Mon.-Sat. 9:30 A.M.-6 P.M., Sun. noon-5 P.M.
Map 7

There's something about the selection of toys and games at this store that makes you think it wasn't made for kids at all but for the adults that accompany them. Painted bright green with a rainbow-stripped awning the exterior is an anomaly in this somber neighborhood. The bright color continues inside, matching the store's atmosphere of exuberance and fun. Just as silly and kid-like as the clients, the staff like to have a good time and know their products inside out.

Clothing and Shoes

From locally made to high-end fashion, Montréal clothing stores have it all, sometimes simultaneously. In smaller, independently owned boutiques there's a trend toward emerging local and international talent with an emphasis on exclusivity, so if you see it at one store, you might not be able to find it elsewhere. There's also a push to appeal to both men and women, so many boutiques are unisex and more often than not they'll also carry a range of footwear and accessories or even fragrances to ensure you leave with a total look. Montréal's love affair with classic pieces means you'll come across vintage in the unlikeliest of stores.

ABE & MARY'S

4175 rue Jean-Talon W., 514/448-6223, www.abeandmarys.com
HOURS: Mon.-Fri. 10 A.M.-6 P.M., Sat. 10 A.M.-5 P.M., Sun. noon-5 P.M.
Map 7

On the outer edge of the city, just two Métro stops from the end of the line, you'll find Abe & Mary's. Often described as "a bit of L.A. in Montréal," the massive 7,000-square-foot store is full of high-end goods and surrounded by car dealerships. They stock enough jeans to fill an entire wall, and enough chic designer goods to occupy a second floor. Designer pieces might not fit everyone's budget, but luckily they also carry novelty items and beauty products. If it all gets a bit overwhelming, have a seat at the in-house café and regroup with a cupcake and a coffee.

BELLE ET REBELLE

6321 rue St-Hubert, 514/315-4903, www.belleetrebelle.ca
HOURS: Mon.-Wed. 10 A.M.-6 P.M., Thurs.-Fri. 10 A.M.-9 P.M., Sat. 10 A.M.-5 P.M., Sun. 11 A.M.-5 P.M.
Map 6

Those wanting a picture of the current state of Québécois design, or those looking for ethical and organic clothing, will get a good picture of it here. Committed to Québécois design, this boutique carries the work of over 60 young designers, all of whom work and live in the province. Though the ambience is nonexistent the helpful staff and range of products give the store some depth. Clothing, bags, jewelry, and even shoes are available here, the majority of which are made in Montréal. Ranging from casual, ethical T-shirts by Oom to the simple, classic dresses of Birds of North America and the repurposed leather purses of Cokluch, every type and style is represented.

BILLIE

1012 ave. Laurier W., 514/270-5415, www.billieboutique.com
HOURS: Mon.-Wed. noon-6 P.M., Thurs.-Fri. noon-8 P.M., Sat.-Sun. 11 A.M.-5 P.M.
Map 6

No matter the time of day the ceiling-to-floor glass storefront of this boutique gives you a full view of the lovely girly finds inside. Elegant but youthful, the decor consists of a number of small, cabin-style cubbies, a long dresser topped with perfectly selected accessories, and a luxurious satin-walled changing room that makes you feel as though you've just stepped into a Chanel purse. Pieces here are from a number of designers, everything from J Brand to Orla Kiely, but the look is distinctly soft and feminine, with occasional edgier pieces.

BODYBAG BY JUDE
17 rue Bernard W., 514/274-5242,
www.bodybagbyjude.com
HOURS: Mon.-Wed. 11 A.M.-6 P.M., Thurs.-Fri.
11 A.M.-8 P.M., Sat. 11 A.M.-5 P.M., Sun. noon-5 P.M.
Map 6

Working out of her atelier in the back room of her eponymous boutique, which is light and airy in all white and large floor-to-ceiling windows, designer Judith Desjardins creates both her Bodybag and j.u.d.e. labels. A regular at Montréal Fashion Week, Desjardins first came to international prominence in 2002 when Nicole Kidman wore one of her dresses on David Letterman. At the time punky and streetwise, Bodybag has since evolved into a line of well-tailored classics with a bit of an edge that appeal to young, streetwise women. Though the selection is concise, the easy-to-wear pieces tie in with any wardrobe.

BROWNS
1191 rue Ste-Catherine W., 514/987-1206,
www.brownsshoes.com
HOURS: Mon.-Fri. 10 A.M.-9 P.M., Sat. 10 A.M.-5 P.M.,
Sun. noon-5 P.M.
Map 2

It may have grown into a national chain with over 40 stores, but the history of Browns starts right here in Montréal. The first Canadian retailer to import European marks like Salvatore Ferragamo, Charles Jourdan, and Bruno Magli, it continues to carry some of the world's top shoe designers as well as their very own Browns and trendier B2 labels. In the heart of downtown the atmosphere of the store is akin to a crowded disco, with the staff dressed to impress and the music pumping. They offer a range of men's and women's styles and have a second-floor mezzanine reserved for designer labels.

LA CANADIENNE
273 ave. Laurier W., 514/270-8008,
www.lacanadienneshoes.com
HOURS: Mon.-Wed. 10 A.M.-6 P.M., Thurs.-Fri.
10 A.M.-9 P.M., Sat. 10 A.M.-5 P.M., Sun. 11 A.M.-5 P.M.
Map 6

When the weather is nice, Montréalers do their best to ignore the fact that winter is coming, but when the first frost arrives, stylish ladies get themselves to La Canadienne. Producing boots that are on-trend, comfortable, waterproof, and, most importantly, warm, for nearly 50 years, this flagship store on Laurier is big and glossy with lots of windows and a sleek gray interior. It may be the go-to brand for stylish and functional winter boots, but they also carry a range of sandals, heels, coats, and bags, all made with the same attention to detail and practicality.

CLUSIER HABILLEUR
432 rue McGill, 514/842-1717, www.clusier.com
HOURS: Mon.-Wed. 10 A.M.-7 P.M., Thurs.-Fri.
10 A.M.-8 P.M., Sat. 10 A.M.-5:30 P.M.
Map 1

More than just a store, this menswear boutique in Old Montréal offers made-to-measure pieces that range from suits and tuxes to jeans, dress shirts, and even cashmere coats. Since they offer bespoke services the staff here know their stuff and can guess your neck size just by looking. Sip a coffee in their espresso lounge as you wait for them to get your size in a pair of multicolored Lacoste topsiders. Alongside well-known marks the store has its own in-house Clusier line. Though it's found in Old Montréal, the boutique is distinctly modern with occasional brickwork accenting the white walls.

LES CRÉATEURS
1444 rue Sherbrooke W., 514/284-2102,
www.lescreateurs.ca
HOURS: Mon.-Wed. 10:30 A.M.-6 P.M., Thurs.-Fri.
10:30 A.M.-9 P.M., Sat. 10:30 A.M.-5 P.M., Sun. noon-5 P.M.
Map 2

For a bit of Japanese or Belgian minimalism head to Maria Balla's Les Créateurs, a mainstay since its debut in 1983. Balla's (well-heeled) clients know what they want, and those wants include runway pieces from designers like Yohji Yamamoto, Junya Watanabe, and Ann Demeulemeester. Pieces here are always edgy with a hint of futurism. Located in a historic Beaux Arts townhouse on classy rue Sherbrooke, the store's ambience is as dramatic as the pieces it carries. Among the younger, lesser-known designers that fit into Balla's no-nonsense aesthetic are Haider Ackermann and Rick Owens—both of whose outerwear adds automatic drama.

DEUXIÈME PEAU

4457 rue St-Denis, 514/842-0811,
www.deuxiemepeau.com
HOURS: Mon.-Wed. 10:30 A.M.-6 P.M., Thurs.-Fri. 10:30 A.M.-9 P.M., Sat. 10:30 A.M.-5 P.M., Sun. noon-5 P.M.
Map 5

The decoration in this small, bottom-floor boutique, which specializes in swimwear and lingerie, is minimal, letting the prettiness of the garments stand out. Supporting women of all shapes and sizes, they carry bras in sizes AA to G from European brands like Princess Tam-Tam, Simon Pérèle, Aubade, and Chantal Thomas. Swimwear comes in a range of different sizes and includes pieces from Seafolly and Sunfair. Though they will happily measure you to determine proper bra size, owner Zoé Mitsakis's keen eye (along with a little bit of prodding) is better than any tape measure.

◖ DUBUC

4451 rue St-Denis, 514/282-1424, www.dubucstyle.com
HOURS: Mon.-Wed. and Sat. 11 A.M.-6 P.M., Thurs. 11 A.M.-7 P.M., Fri. 11 A.M.-9 P.M., Sun. noon-5 P.M.
Map 5

Philippe Dubuc, known for his menswear designs, was the first Canadian designer to be asked to present at Paris Fashion Week. Dubuc's eponymous St-Denis boutique is, like most of his collections, almost entirely black and slate gray, with rough stone taking up the bottom half of the walls. Could you get more masculine? The boutique takes up an entire row house, with a floor for menswear, a floor for accessories, and one for his atelier (but that's off-limits to the public). His pieces are precise and impeccably cut and tailored.

DUO

24 and 30 rue Prince-Arthur W., 514/848-0880, www.boutiqueduo.com
HOURS: Mon.-Wed. and Sat. 10 A.M.-7 P.M., Thurs.-Fri. 10 A.M.-9 P.M., Sun. noon-7 P.M.
Map 5

One of the top men's boutiques in the city, Duo first opened its doors in 2003 and became so successful it has since expanded to take over the shop next door. The sleek modern interior is distinctly masculine and is the perfect backdrop for the exclusive lines the store carries. Labels available here are more upscale than what you'll find at most boutiques and include Dior Homme, Raf Simons, Y3, and Moncler. Alongside suits and clothes for the every day they carry a range of watches, fragrances, and footwear.

ENVERS

4935 rue Sherbrooke W., Westmount, 514/935-7117, www.yvesjeanlacasse.com
HOURS: Mon.-Wed. 10 A.M.-6 P.M., Thurs.-Fri. 10 A.M.-9 P.M., Sat. 10 A.M.-5 P.M.
Map 7

Adored for his bespoke tailoring and three-quarter-length coats for men, local designer Yves Jean Lacasse's work always involves an ethnic, romantic, or historical twist. The Lacasse man is not afraid of color, and clientele vary from flamboyant artists to conservative businessmen with an eye for tailoring. The ambience of the boutique is definitely creative but masculine as Lacasse mixes subtle hues like gray and black with rich pops of color. The boutique also carries accessories and swimwear. Though best known for menswear, the boutique also carries a range of pieces from his womenswear line, which focuses on the same elements.

ESPACE PEPIN

350 rue St-Paul W., 514/287-5005, www.espacepepin.com
HOURS: Mon.-Wed. 10 A.M.-6 P.M., Thurs. 10 A.M.-8 P.M., Sat. 10 A.M.-6 P.M., Sun. noon-6 P.M.
Map 1

Owner and artist Lysanne Pepin has created a unique space where her artwork serves as a backdrop to a carefully selected array of clothing,

Boutique Espace Pepin carries everything from jewelry to artwork.

© ESPACE PEPIN

jewelry, accessories, and lingerie. Created by local and international designers, the pieces are affordable and have a classic, relaxed appeal. White walls and shabby-chic decor invite you into the open-concept boutique that's as welcoming as a friend's apartment.

LES ÉTOFFES

5253 blvd. St-Laurent, 514/544-5500,
www.lesetoffes.com
HOURS: Tues.-Wed. and Sat.-Sun. noon-6 P.M.,
Thurs.-Fri. noon-8 P.M.
Map 6

Started by a chic young couple, this new boutique on the Main carries a range of mens- and womenswear from contemporary, hard-to-find labels like Australia's Lover and Montréal's own Naked and Famous Jeans. There's a modern aesthetic to the store but it also has a welcoming warmth, thanks to the rich, dark-blue wall and wooden fixtures. There's a real sense of timelessness in the pieces on sale here.

LA GAILLARDE

4019 rue Notre-Dame W., 514/989-5134,
www.lagaillarde.blogspot.com
HOURS: Tues.-Wed. 11 A.M.-6 P.M., Thurs.-Fri.
11 A.M.-9 P.M., Sat.-Sun. 11 A.M.-5 P.M.
Map 7

Opened in 2000, La Gaillarde (which means "strapping young woman" in English) was one of the first boutiques in the city dedicated to ecological fashion. Over a decade later it is still unparalleled in its commitment, with a selection of recycled and repurposed accessories and clothes for both men and women. One step into this modern, newly renovated store with sleek black floors, immaculate white walls, and antique lights and you'll be hooked. The clothes here are inventive and contemporary; nothing about them screams "eco." To ensure you leave with a bit of their ethics, organic and free trade coffee, tea, and chocolate sit enticingly at the cash for one last impulse buy.

HARRICANA

3000 rue Ste-Antoine W., 514/287-6517,
www.harricana.qc.ca

HOURS: Mon.-Fri. 10 A.M.-6 P.M., Sat.-Sun. 10 A.M.-5 P.M.

Map 2

Designer Mariouche Gagné first started working with fur as a struggling fashion student. Having entered a competition with the Fur Council of Canada she'd used her mother's old coat to create a piece and her business was born. Working with recycled fur she transforms pieces into hats, mittens, a chic *gilet,* or a new coat entirely. The store space is modern and clean, and though it's slightly below street level huge windows let in lots of light. If you have a fur coat you'd like restyled, take it with you: Gagné will transform it into something else entirely and ship it back to you.

JOHN FLUEVOG

3857 rue St-Denis, 514/509-1627, www.fluevog.com

HOURS: Mon.-Wed. 10 A.M.-6 P.M., Thurs.-Fri.
10 A.M.-9 P.M., Sat. 10 A.M.-5 P.M., Sun. noon-5 P.M.

Map 5

The chance to buy a warehouse full of early-20th-century shoes gave designer Fluevog his start, and his style has become unmistakable. Women's shoes often sport a rounded toe and an exaggerated spoon heel (wider at the top and bottom but narrower in the middle), while his colorful men's brogues and desert boots are some of his best, remaining classic but with a modern touch. The design and ambience of this store, however, are fairly unremarkable, with beige throughout and shoes displayed on walls and on a low circular table at the front; the footwear is the main focus. Clients and staff are always a little bit kooky, bold enough to wear something out of the box.

KANUK

485 rue Rachel E., 514/527-4494, www.kanuk.com

HOURS: Mon.-Wed. 9 A.M.-6 P.M., Thurs.-Fri.
9 A.M.-9 P.M., Sat. 10 A.M.-5 P.M., Sun. noon-5 P.M.

Map 5

Designed and made in Québec, Kanuk was established in 1974, by a few outdoor enthusiasts who realized the only way to get a winter coat warm enough for the province's climate was to make it themselves. Specializing in outerwear, this Plateau store is brightly lit and spacious with floor and wall space dedicated to coats, accessories, and other outerwear. With 35 models to choose from in a range of colors, a parka from this place may be pricey—they start around $500—but it will last you a lifetime. Staff are more than happy to help you figure out the type and fit that will work for you and know the products inside and out.

LOLA & EMILY

3475 blvd. St-Laurent, 514/288-7598,
www.lolaandemily.com

HOURS: Mon.-Wed. 11 A.M.-6 P.M., Thurs.-Fri.
10 A.M.-7 P.M., Sat. 10 A.M.-5 P.M., Sun. noon-5 P.M.

Map 5

Because of the white-washed floors, vintage furnishings, and feminine touches—candles here and there, fresh flowers on the counter—walking into Lola & Emily's has the feel of walking into your good friend's cozy but chic apartment. Young and romantic best describes the look of the majority of pieces found here—if you're looking for a soft, flirty dress to wear to your best friend's wedding this a good place to start. Lines change with the seasons, but core brands include Filippa K, Free People, and Designers Remix. The furniture used for display is also available for purchase, so you may walk in looking for a simple shoe and walk out with a four-poster bed.

LUSTRE

4068 blvd. St-Laurent, 514/288-7661,
www.lustreboutique.blogspot.com

HOURS: Mon.-Wed. noon-7 P.M., Thurs.-Fri. noon-9 P.M.,
Sat. noon-6 P.M., Sun. noon-5 P.M.

Map 5

Owner and designer Yasmine Wasfy creates both the Lustre line and her own eponymous label, which can be found in this independent boutique full of one-of-a-kind pieces. Designs are fresh and young—think a great, well-tailored shift with a cutout back or an on-trend black-lace blouse. Popular with women in their 20s and early 30s with a DIY aesthetic, the store's various decorations, art, and accessories have a definite vintage feel. Whimsical scarves and bags can be found next to locally made jewelry and hats. Service is sweet and friendly, and Wasfy herself can sometimes be found doling out tailoring advice or picking out the perfect accessory.

LYLA

400 ave. Laurier W., 514/271-0763, www.lyla.ca
HOURS: Mon.-Wed. 10 A.M.-6 P.M., Thurs.-Fri. 10 A.M.-9 P.M., Sat. 10 A.M.-5 P.M.
Map 6

This two-floor boutique on quietly chic Laurier is the go-to place for top-quality lingerie and swimwear. It was started by sisters Sophie and Esther Paquette in 1983, and the staff here are knowledgeable and especially dedicated to find the suit or bra that best fits your form. The store's atmosphere is reserved but elegant and European lingerie from Princess Tam Tam, Eres, and Andres Sarda hangs tantalizingly along the wall. The bathing suits have a bit more spunk, with fun pieces by Jean-Paul Gaultier and punchier, Pucci-inspired looks from New York–based Milly. They also carry a number of evening wear pieces and beach accessories so that even lounging next to the pool your look is pulled together.

◖ MARIE SAINT PIERRE

2081 rue de la Montagne, 514/281-5547, www.mariesaintpierre.com
HOURS: Mon.-Wed. and Sat. 10 A.M.-6 P.M., Thurs.-Fri. 10 A.M.-8 P.M., Sun. noon-6 P.M.
Map 2

Marie Saint Pierre is a leading figure in Canadian fashion, and her creations are available in high-end boutiques from New York to Paris. But this boutique on the ritzy de la Montagne is her only flagship store in her native city. Working with a mostly neutral palette, Saint Pierre focuses instead on texture, volume, and shape, and the results are stunningly modern. The boutique itself has a strong masculine feel with its concrete floors and smoke-like murals, though the soft lighting helps give it is a feminine touch. Those wanting a more personal

shopping experience can request an evening of private shopping.

MICHEL BRISSON

384 rue St-Paul W., 514/285-1012, www.michelbrisson.com
HOURS: Mon.-Sat. 11 A.M.-6 P.M., Sun. noon-6 P.M.
Map 1

Wanting to recreate the feel of an old haberdasher where men could shop in a relaxed atmosphere, Michel Brisson created his eponymous menswear boutique with the help of architects Saucier + Perrotte. The classic storefront in Vieux-Montréal (there's a second boutique in Outremont: 1012 ave. Laurier W., 514/270-1012, www.michelbrisson.com) is the perfect hint of the masculine minimalism of the interior—for added drama, one room retains its original wood paneling. Sharp touches of steel and the heavy use of black nicely mimic the aesthetic of the contemporary brands the store carries, like Dries Van Noten, Rick Owens, and Acne.

Michel Brisson

© MICHEL BRISSON

SHOPS

MONA MOORE
1446 rue Sherbrooke W., 514/842-0662,
www.monamoore.com
HOURS: Mon.-Fri. 10 A.M.-6 P.M., Sat. 10 A.M.-5 P.M.
Map 2

Women who love shoes peer wide-eyed into this deliciously elegant shoe store, minimally decorated with only a few, well-chosen feminine touches: sorbet-hued baroque furniture, soft-pink walls, and a simple mirror, leaned gracefully against the wall. The shoes here, mostly off the runway, take center stage and are effortlessly placed along the wall. This may not be the most affordable of stores—prices are usually in the $1,000 range, but even if you're not looking to buy, just entering into the store allows you to indulge in a little fashion-world fantasy. And of course, it helps that staff are just as sweet and welcoming as can be.

OLD GOLD
256 ave. du Mont-Royal E., 514/509-1675,
www.oldgoldboutique.com
HOURS: Sun.-Mon. noon-6 P.M., Tues.-Wed. and Sat. noon-7 P.M., Thurs.-Fri. noon-9 P.M.
Map 5

Jonah Leslie started his career selling clothes he'd bought in Southeast Asia out of box at a St-Laurent street sale. Now he's the owner of this exquisitely curated boutique, which carries classic but hip footwear and comfortably cool and surprisingly affordable street wear for both guys and girls. Leslie still spends months out of the year traveling Asia and combing its streets for the best new goods. The store is tiny, with the feel of a street-wise Victorian sitting room—antique display cases, dark wood, black walls. The vibe is young, laid-back, and irreverent.

REBORN
231 rue St-Paul W., 514/499-8549, www.reborn.ws
HOURS: Mon.-Wed. and Sat. 11 A.M.-6 P.M., Thurs. 11 A.M.-8 P.M., Sun. noon-6 P.M.
Map 1

Carrying some of the most cutting-edge designers, Reborn seems almost to echo the physical shape the fashion world so adores, with a long, skinny space that never seems to

get overpopulated. Owner and buyer Brigitte Chartrand's keen eye and discerning taste mean the choices from designers like Natalia Brilli, Gareth Pugh, Preen, and Rad Hourani are ever changing and ever challenging. Often dressed in all black, staff can seem intimidating, but get them talking you'll soon realize how well they know their stuff and how to make you look your best. Though some pieces can be pricey they carry mid-priced goods as well and have great sales.

RIEN À CACHER
4141 rue St-Denis, 514/907-6187, www.rienacacher.com
HOURS: Mon.-Wed. 10 A.M.-7 P.M., Thurs.-Fri. 11 A.M.-9 P.M., Sat. 10 A.M.-5 P.M., Sun. noon-5 P.M.
Map 5

In English this store's name translates to "nothing to hide," a fitting title for a store that sells only ethical clothing. The selection here isn't huge, and the decor doesn't get past beige walls. They carry tees, skirts, and pants in jersey material, and they do have a pretty cute kids' section as well as varied accessories, like brightly patterned baby slings. Staff are friendly and eager to help, even if you're just browsing, and they also carry a range of Veja sneakers, the cool, young ethical label launched in Paris and Tokyo in 2005. Their clean design is reminiscent of '70s sneakers and lets you be ethical and in style.

SCANDALE
3639 blvd. St-Laurent, 514/842-4707,
www.boutiquescandale.ca
HOURS: Mon.-Wed. and Sat. 11 A.M.-6 P.M., Thurs. 11 A.M.-7 P.M., Fri. 11 A.M.-9 P.M., Sun. noon-5 P.M.
Map 5

One look at the whimsical storefront and window displays of this boutique on the Main and you know Scandale is no ordinary store. A St-Laurent staple since the early '80s, the store is dedicated to the unique vision of designer Georges Lévesque, whose idiosyncratic creations oscillate between the supremely elegant and the supremely…Lévesque. He's a fan of mixing patterns (tartan is a favorite) and styles, and much of this is reflected in the store's surroundings.

Cluttered with dresses and displays, the store gives off a dark and brooding yet somehow joyful vibe. Staff are helpful and often have clear ideas of what will suit you best, before you've even had a chance to contemplate.

U&I

3650 blvd. St-Laurent, 514/844-8788,
www.boutiqueuandi.com
HOURS: Mon.-Wed. 11 A.M.-7 P.M., Thurs.-Fri.
11 A.M.-9 P.M., Sat. 10 A.M.-7 P.M., Sun. noon-6 P.M.
Map 5

When owner and buyer Eric Toledando opened U&I at the tail end of the '90s, he wanted to focus on the conceptual side of modern style. Now considered one of the best unisex boutiques in the city, it has made a name for itself carrying upscale, typically hard-to-find or emerging designers. The modern, open-concept design of the store is welcoming and the racks are perfectly balanced—not too much, not too little—making it an inviting place to browse. Selections from labels like See by Chloé, Vivienne Westwood,

Opening Ceremony, 3.1 Philip Lim, and Comme des Garçons are all found here, as are denim brands Acne and Paper Denim, shoes by Chie Mihara, and bags by Denis Gagnon.

UNICORN

5135 blvd. St-Laurent, 514/544-2828,
www.boutiqueunicorn.com
HOURS: Mon.-Wed. noon-6 P.M., Thurs.-Fri.
noon-8 P.M., Sat.-Sun. 11 A.M.-5 P.M.
Map 6

It can be hard to find a name that works in both French and English, so when boutique owners Mélanie Robillard and Amélie Thellen finally stumbled on Unicorn the name stuck. Since opening in 2008, it has become a hit with fashionable ladies from both cultures. Full of modern classics, the store recently expanded to include a room dedicated to shoes and accessories. The boutique, which is effortlessly decorated with a damask-covered couch and other repurposed and black-lacquered finds, is devoted to local and Canadian designers.

Department Stores

LA BAIE

585 rue Ste-Catherine W., 514/281-4422,
www.thebay.com
HOURS: Mon.-Wed. 10 A.M.-7 P.M., Thurs.-Fri.
10 A.M.-9 P.M., Sat. 9 A.M.-6 P.M., Sun. 10 A.M.-6 P.M.
Map 3

A Canadian institution, La Baie was first founded in 1670 as the Hudson's Bay Company and controlled much of the fur trade throughout North America. By the early 20th century it had morphed into one of the biggest chain department stores in Canada. Housed in a grand redbrick building that was constructed in 1891, the Bay's seven floors offer everything from kids' shoes to perfumes, housewares to electronics. Fans of Canadiana will do well by picking up an iconic Hudson's Bay blanket, a simple off-white blanket striped with the company's colors: green, red, yellow, and blue.

HOLT RENFREW

1300 rue Sherbrooke W., 514/842-5111,
www.holtrenfrew.com
HOURS: Mon.-Wed. 10 A.M.-6 P.M., Thurs.-Fri.
10 A.M.-9 P.M., Sat. 9:30 A.M.-5 P.M.,
Sun. noon-5 P.M.
Map 2

This luxury department store, which is not for every size bank account, is housed in an illustrious art deco building. It has all the top-name designer brands from around the world. Established as a furrier in 1849 in Québec City, the Montréal store opened in 1910 and continues to be one of the few places you can find the labels Marni, Dries Van Noten, and Balenciaga. This is also the only store in Montréal to exclusively carry the designs for Denis Gagnon, one of Montréal's best designers. The Holt Renfrew Café on the ground level is a chic

SHOPS

place to grab a light lunch or catch up with a friend over coffee.

LA MAISON OGILVY

1307 rue Ste-Catherine W., 514/842-7711, www.ogilvycanada.com

HOURS: Mon.-Wed. 10 A.M.-6 P.M., Thurs.-Fri. 10 A.M.-9 P.M., Sat. 9 A.M.-5 P.M., Sun. noon-5 P.M.

Map 2

Established in 1866 by Montréal linen merchant James A. Ogilvy, Ogilvy's is a timeless Montréal institution, and its tartan bags and boxes are ubiquitous throughout the city. The only high-end department store of its kind, it carries exclusive labels like Louis Vuitton and Burberry, and those who shop here have the pocketbooks to afford it. Completed in 1912, the building itself is impressive, with a large circular staircase at the main entrance. On the fifth floor is Tudor Hall, the city's first music hall.

LA MAISON SIMONS

977 rue Ste-Catherine W., 514/282-1840, www.simons.ca

HOURS: Mon.-Wed. 10 A.M.-6 P.M., Thurs.-Fri. 10 A.M.-9 P.M., Sat. 9:30 A.M.-5 P.M., Sun. noon-5 P.M.

Map 2

Started as a dry goods store in Québec City in 1840, over the years Simons has become the quintessential Québécois department store, particularly popular among Francophones. Though the Montréal location only opened in 1999, its European-flavored products and design give it a different feel than other North American department stores and make it a shopper's staple. More compact than most, it carries everything from affordable and fashionable knitwear and accessories to lingerie and housewares. For men, there is a large suit section, and the store also carries a number of designers, like Vivienne Westwood and Dolce and Gabbana.

Gift and Home

Things for the home can pretty much be divided into two categories: things that come from Europe and things that are made right in our own backyard. Montréal's French heritage has led to a bit of an obsession with European (read, often French) imports. Many of the stores for the home carry products from abroad, things to give you that *je ne sais quoi* once you've plunked them down on your shelf at home. On the other hand there's a big push for sustainable and eco-friendly products, which are designed and produced in the province. All the good stores, however, offer both.

ARTHUR QUENTIN

3960 rue St-Denis, 514/843-7513, www.arthurquentin.com

HOURS: Mon.-Wed. 10 A.M.-6 P.M., Thurs.-Fri. 10 A.M.-9 P.M., Sat. 9 A.M.-5 P.M., Sun. noon-5 P.M.

Map 5

Couples in the know come here to pick out their wedding registry. The selection here is classic yet unconventional, with many of the

products imported from France. Divided into three distinct mini-stores—a British-style haberdashery, cookware, and tableware—these mini-boutiques help you keep your focus as you browse everything from leather bags to red-checkered canister sets and fine bone china. All three rooms are modest in size and pretty much filled to capacity, so each space demands a bit of concentration. Can't find the tea towels? They're hung up inconspicuously next to the doorframe.

BEIGE

2475 rue Notre-Dame W., 514/989-8585, www.beigestyle.com

HOURS: Mon.-Wed. 10 A.M.-6 P.M., Thurs.-Fri. 10 A.M.-7 P.M., Sat. 10 A.M.-4 P.M.

Map 2

One of a few stores along Notre-Dame West that sell new pieces, Beige has just about everything you need to set up house: lighting, mirrors, bedding, kitchen tables, four-poster beds, and a lounge chair to put next to the pool. The store appeals to a wide range of customers, from 20-year-olds just starting out to empty-nesters, and prices here are just as varied, from $25 for a big fat candle to hundreds for a custom reupholstery. It's great for picking up a gift or something new for your home. The staff here are also interior designers and can help you with tough decisions.

CHEZ FARFELU
843 and 838 ave. du Mont-Royal E., 514/528-6251
HOURS: Mon.-Wed. 10 A.M.-6 P.M., Thurs.-Fri.
10 A.M.-9 P.M., Sat. 10 A.M.-5 P.M., Sun. 11 A.M.-5 P.M.
Map 5

This place, admittedly, is a little crazy. Best described as a five-and-dime on steroids, it has a definite nostalgic feel with its rows of lollipops and candy machines, and notebooks and coffee mugs emblazoned with 1960s comic-strip heroes. They also stock of bunch of jewelry and novelty items like blow-up chairs shaped like frogs. Over half the merchandise seems to be neon. A good portion of the store is dedicated to gift-wrapping your finds. Across the street at number 838, you'll find slightly tamer gifts for the kitchen and bathroom, including peel-and-stick decals for tiles and motif beach towels.

CO
5235 blvd. St-Laurent, 514/277-3131,
www.galerie-co.com
HOURS: Tues.-Thurs. and 10 A.M.-6 P.M.,
Fri. 10 A.M.-7 P.M., Sun. noon-5 P.M.
Map 6

With an eye to the ecological, this boutique on the Main specializes in art and design pieces that are sustainable. Owner Sarah Richardson has a great eye, and the pieces here are sharply modern while remaining green. Pieces include cardboard bookcases and shelving, as well as organic cotton pillows printed with a picture of a penguin or a gorilla that could just as easily be dragged around by a toddler as sit coyly on your couch. The range of products displayed on simple white shelves throughout the Zen-like store is impressive, from pencil cases and political potato mashers to coffee tables and hanging light fixtures, so prices range accordingly from $20 to hundreds.

INTERVERSION
4273 blvd. St-Laurent, 514/284-2103,
www.interversion.com
HOURS: Mon.-Wed. 10 A.M.-6 P.M., Thurs. 10 A.M.-9 P.M.,
Fri. 10 A.M.-7 P.M., Sat. 10:30 A.M.-5 P.M., Sun. noon-5 P.M.
Map 5

It doesn't get any more local than the Québec-designed and -made furniture at Interversion. The pieces here are made from local materials and often in a limited series or as one-of-a-kind pieces that blur the lines between furniture design and functional art. This huge showroom is set up to mimic real rooms, giving it a welcoming homey atmosphere that makes you want to sink into an oversized wooden rocker. Helpful and friendly floor staff are also designers and will gladly answer any and all of your questions.

JAMAIS ASSEZ
5155 blvd. St-Laurent, 514/509-3709,
www.jamaisassez.com
HOURS: Tues.-Thurs. 11 A.M.-6 P.M., Fri. 11 A.M.-8 P.M.,
Sat. 11 A.M.-5 P.M.
Map 6

Practical and modern are two traits you'll find belong to most of the goods in this bright, open and modern St-Laurent store. But there is also a fair amount of whimsy in what they stock—a yellow bookcase custom-made for your collection of *National Geographic* magazines, a rocking horse in the shape of a dodo bird, a wine rack with a spot for glasses, a spiral umbrella rack, or a designer kitty litterbox. Much of the stock is made in Montréal or Québec, and the staff are very knowledgeable about where their products are from.

NOTA BENE
3416 ave du Parc, 514/485-6587,
www.nota-bene.ca
HOURS: Mon.-Fri. 11 A.M.-7 P.M., Sat. 11 A.M.-5 P.M.
Map 5

The classic storefront windows of this chic stationery shop are always filled with covetable items like a classic, oversize Stendig calendar or notebooks in a rainbow of colors from Mark's Tokyo Edge. A stationery-lover's dream, this

© TOURISME MONTREEAL

chic stationary shop Nota Bene

place carries notepads, agendas, pens, paper, and everything in between, from the top-quality international companies all over the world, including Lamy pencils, Atoma notebooks, Faber Castell, and graph-paper notebooks from Sweden's elusive Whitelines. A mezzanine level at the back of the store serves as an art gallery with work by local artists featured regularly.

QUINCAILLERIE DANTE

6851 rue St-Dominique, 514/271-2057
HOURS: Mon.-Wed. 9 A.M.-6 P.M., Thurs.-Fri.
9 A.M.-9 P.M., Sat. 9 A.M.-5 P.M., Sun. 11 A.M.-5 P.M.
Map 6

The word *quincaillerie* means "hardware," but don't run into this corner shop expecting to find the shelves full of nuts and bolts and the walls adorned with 50 different kinds of hammers. Established in 1956, Quincaillerie Dante was the first Italian-owned and -operated hardware store in the city, and it's still run by the same friendly family. They are on a first-name basis with most of their clients. Though they carry a few crucial tools, they also have an assortment

of kitchenware, like pots, pans, delicate china, stove-top espresso makers—and then there are the rifles. It's a bit jarring to be browsing the *Tintin* mugs next to a display case of hunting knives, but that's the kind of juxtaposition that's made this place such an important neighborhood store—it has everything.

3 FEMMES ET 1 COUSSIN

783 rue Gilford, 514/987-6807, www.3f1c.ca
HOURS: Mon.-Wed. 10 A.M.-6 P.M., Thurs.-Fri.
10 A.M.-7 P.M., Sat. 10 A.M.-5 P.M.
Map 5

Specializing in tableware, 3 Femmes et 1 Coussin offers a number of dinnerware lines, many of which are imported directly from Europe. The dishes on sale here are almost exclusively white and their shapes are always slightly out of the ordinary. To show off the white china the walls are beautifully covered in bright damask prints, and the simple layout ensures the china stays unbroken. In contrast to the stark dishes, the glassware here is bright and colorful with a number of tumblers,

© PIERRE-LUC DUFOUR

Pick up everything from espresso makers to hunting knives at Quincaillerie Dante.

champagne flutes, and wine glasses available in sparkling primary colors. It's the go-to place for locals and small restaurants. It also offers unique gift ideas.

◖ LES TOUILLEURS

152 ave. Laurier W., 514/278-0008,
www.lestouilleurs.com
HOURS: Mon.-Wed. 10 A.M.-6 P.M., Thurs.-Fri.
10 A.M.-7 P.M., Sat. 10 A.M.-5 P.M., Sun. 11 A.M.-5 P.M.
Map 6

Styled to look like a cross between an art gallery and a dream kitchen, the wares at Les Touilleurs are displayed along white walls, stacked on butcher-block tables, and neatly put away in perfect cubbies. From cookware to tableware, small kitchen appliances like old-fashioned scales to scoops for your coffee canister, this store has the chicest stuff for your kitchen. Owners François Longré and Sylvain Côté also offer cooking workshops, and most of the staff are self-proclaimed foodies, so not only will they tell you which pot to cook pot roast in, they'll also give you insider tips on their favorite restaurants.

ZONE

4246 rue St-Denis, 514/845-3530,
www.zonemaison.com
HOURS: Mon.-Wed. 10 A.M.-6 P.M., Thurs.-Fri.
10 A.M.-7 P.M., Sat. 10 A.M.-5:30 P.M., Sun. 10 A.M.-5 P.M.
Map 5

Montréalers with a taste for affordable design are lucky; when they want to add a little pizzazz to their homes they don't have to schlep all the way out to Ikea to do it. Instead they can hit up this small local chain—there are only four stores province-wide—for everything from fridge magnets to Bodum coffee makers and shower curtains to loveseats and everything in between. Urban and young, this two-floor store is airy, all-white, the largest in the city, and offers the best selection of the store's modern design pieces.

ZONE ORANGE

410 rue St-Pierre, 514/510-5809,
www.galeriezoneorange.com
HOURS: Mon.-Fri. 10 A.M.-6 P.M., Sat. noon-6 P.M.
Map 1

Art gallery, store, and café, Zone Orange is a tiny jack of all trades just off of the busy, bigger rue St-Paul. As soon as you step into this small boutique, you're surrounded by 100 percent Québec-made goods. It's dedicated to local producers and to supporting the local arts, and every product they carry (with the exception of the coffee) comes from the province. They're displayed in white cubbies and on long white shelves, and an espresso machine takes center stage next to the till. The laid-back and inviting the staff know the products and producers well and can answer most questions about who made the product you're holding and how. Handmade paper puppets, silver jewelry, and recycled-leather bags are just some the goods you can browse as you sip a latte and check out the latest exhibition in the back room.

Gourmet Treats

Food. Montréal is known for it. There's a ton of different types of food stores all over the city, but even your regular grocery store will have more than a few surprisingly gourmet products on the shelves. You don't have to look far in this city to find something to please even the pickiest of eaters.

LE CANARD LIBÉRÉ

4396 blvd. St-Laurent, 514/286-1286, www.canardsdulacbrome.com
HOURS: Mon.-Wed. 10 A.M.–6 P.M., Thurs.-Fri. 10 A.M.–8 P.M., Sat. 10 A.M.–5 P.M., Sun. 11 A.M.–5 P.M.
Map 5

If you like the idea of local food, check out Le Canard Libéré ("the liberated duck" in English), exclusively dedicated to duck products produced in nearby Lac Brome. Sausages, pâtés, duck fat, smoked duck, dried duck, duck pasta, even duck wings seasoned with garlic and honey are available in this sparse, open boutique with a huge counter and refrigerated display cases showing off the assorted products. If all the duck is making you hungry, have a seat at one of the few tables and dig into the duck of the day.

◖ LES CHOCOLATS DE CHLOÉ

546 ave. Duluth E., 514/849-5550, www.leschocolatsdechloe.com
HOURS: Tues.-Wed. 10 A.M.–6 P.M., Thurs.-Fri. 10 A.M.–8 P.M., Sat. 11 A.M.–4 P.M., Sun. 11 A.M.–5 P.M.
Map 5

Chloé Germain-Fredette is the artisanal chocolatier behind this quaint and slightly quirky chocolate shop in the Plateau. This all-wood interior is modern, with chocolate-filled shelves lining one wall and freshly made chocolate in a case on the other. The products are made in-house using Valrhona chocolate as a base and infusing it with unlikely flavors, including fig and balsamic vinegar, raspberry, hibiscus, cardamom, saffron, pastis, lemon, and even basil. With over 30 different flavors, whose availability changes depending on the season, the best-seller is still Fleur de Sel. Those with a sweet-tooth and 98 percent of kids can't get enough of this stuff. In winter stop in for a rich and thick cup of home-made drinking chocolate with or without marshmallows.

FROMAGERIE HAMEL

220 rue Jean-Talon E., 514/272-1167, www.fromageriehamel.com
HOURS: Mon.-Wed. and Sat. 8 A.M.–6 P.M., Thurs. 8 A.M.–8 P.M., Fri. 8 A.M.–9 P.M., Sun. 8:30 A.M.–5:30 P.M.
Map 6

If you love cheese, you'll love Fromagerie Hamel. Established in 1961, it continues to be one of the most well-stocked cheese stores in the city. Locals come here to stock up on weekly specials and have a taste at the sample counter, while tourists pop in for a light meal at the on-site café. A huge, U-shaped display case featuring wheels of cheese from all over the world takes up the majority of the store, with workers behind the counter busily cutting cheese and serving the clients. They also sell things to pair with your cheese, like meat, crackers, spreads, and freshly baked bread.

GENEVIEVE GADBOIS

162 rue St-Viateur W., 514/394-1000, www.chocolatsgg.com
HOURS: Mon.-Wed. 10 A.M.–6 P.M., Thurs.-Fri. 10 A.M.–9 P.M., Sat.-Sun. 10 A.M.–5 P.M.
Map 6

Chocolatier Genevieve Gadbois's tiny boutique with its steel, walk-up counter is reminiscent of an ice cream shop. Stepping up to the window, you make your selection from a precise menu that includes chocolates from places like Madagascar, Cuba, and Tanzania, and from flavors like chai, extra-virgin olive oil, and maple syrup. Your order comes to you perfectly packaged in a neat little box and ready to eat. Locals pop in for a warming hot chocolate or rich ice cream in summer.

GOURMET LAURIER

1042 ave. Laurier, 514/274-5601,
www.gourmetlaurier.ca
HOURS: Mon.-Wed. 9 A.M.-7 P.M., Thurs.-Fri.
9 A.M.-9 P.M., Sat. 9 A.M.-6 P.M., Sun. noon-5:30 P.M.
Map 6

Calling itself the "Queen mother of fine foods in Montréal," Gourmet Laurier offers an exclusive range of products from both inside and outside of the province. The decor and layout of this specialty grocery store look like most, but their shelves and in-house coffee, delicatessen and cheese counters filled with local products like foie gras and Québec Brie tell a different story. Some well-to-do ladies do all their shopping here, but most locals pop by to get specialty products like French comfort food, including Pépito cookies, Gallettes St-Michel, Banania drink mix, and Mousline mashed potatoes.

LA GUILDE CULINAIRE

6381 blvd. St-Laurent, 514/750-6050,
www.laguildeculinaire.com
HOURS: Tues. and Sun. noon-5 P.M., Wed. and Sat.
10 A.M.-5 P.M., Thurs.-Fri. 10 A.M.-8 P.M.
Map 6

One of the most exciting places to open up in recent years, La Guilde Culinaire is both a kitchen store and a cooking school. It's a few steps up into this store, which proudly displays its Nespresso machine in the window—chances are you'll be offered a complimentary coffee before the door behind you even shuts. Modern and uncluttered, the all-white store has top-of-the-line cookware and the sleekest kitchen utensils you've ever seen. Fine groceries, such as olive oil from La Belle Excuse or a box of Christophe Morel's macaroons, are also available and momentarily distract you from the beautiful kitchen set up in the back room, where they teach classes.

MILANO

6862 blvd. St-Laurent, 514/273-8558
HOURS: Mon.-Wed. 8 A.M.-6 P.M., Thurs.-Fri.
8 A.M.-9 P.M., Sat.-Sun. 8 A.M.-5 P.M.
Map 6

Around for over 50 years, Milano is an Italian supermarket in the middle of Little Italy, making it *the* place to get things like olive oil, balsamic vinegar and Christmastime panettones. Always bustling with locals yelling at each other in Italian and patrons shouting back and forth with workers, the setup here is different than pretty much any grocery store you've been in before. Instead of aisles, it's set up with little islands around the store overflowing with packages of imported Italian coffee, 10 different kinds of arborio rice, and jars of roasted vegetables. They also have a mean selection of cheeses at great prices and a range of stove-top espresso makers.

AUX PLAISIRS DU BACCHUS

1225 ave. Bernard W., 514/273-3104,
www.auxplaisirsdubacchus.com
HOURS: Mon.-Wed. 10 A.M.-6 P.M., Thurs.-Fri.
10 A.M.-8 P.M., Sat. 10 A.M.-5 P.M., Sun. noon-5 P.M.
Map 6

Devoted to Roman god Bacchus's drink of choice, this charming store in Outremont has anything you could ever want to do with wine. Corkscrews of any size, shape, and dimension, as well as wine buckets, cabinets, decanters, and glasses—even those designed specifically for tasting—are all displayed here. The staff are real wine aficionados and they take every aspect of the drink seriously; they will even help you design and build your very own wine cellar to meet both your needs and your budget.

SABOR LATINO

4387 blvd. St-Laurent, 514/848-1078,
www.saborlatino.ca
HOURS: Mon.-Wed. 8 A.M.-6 P.M., Thurs.-Fri.
8 A.M.-9 P.M., Sat.-Sun. 8 A.M.-5 P.M.
Map 5

When the owners realized that just as many people, whether locals or tourists with an eye for food, were popping in to get a quick bite to eat as were coming to get their groceries, they renovated this place to make the hot food the centerpiece. Now there's a cute dining area with simple chairs and table that lets you eat your *churro* in-house. Specializing in South American foods, they carry at least 2,500 Latin American products, everything from hot sauces, beans, and corn meal to Arepa. Stop in to pick out your favorite South American salsa and get Peruvian, Colombian, or Salvadoran tamales while you're at it.

LA VIEILLE EUROPE

3855 blvd. St-Laurent, 514/842-5773
HOURS: Mon.-Wed. and Sat. 7:30 A.M.-6 P.M., Thurs.-Fri. 7:30 A.M.-9 P.M., Sun. 9 A.M.-5 P.M.
Map 5

The intoxicating smell of cheese and coffee hits you as soon as you walk into this veritable institution on the Main. With over 300 cheeses and 30 different types of coffee for patrons to choose from it's no wonder this is the go-to place for Montréal chefs and foodies looking for that particular ingredient. It specializes in products from France, Germany, Eastern Europe, Scandinavia, and England, so you can pick up pickled herring, sauerkraut, camembert, and black currant jam all at the same place, and it attracts a number of expats or passing tourists led by their nose. They also have a selection of sandwiches available from the deli counter—you can't go wrong with the Polish sausage—perfect for a quick lunch.

Shopping Districts and Centers

BOULEVARD SAINT-LAURENT

Blvd. St-Laurent btwn. rue Sherbrooke and rue St-Viateur
Map 5

A number of independent, mainly fashion boutiques are concentrated here starting at the corner of St-Laurent and Sherbrooke and moving steadily north. Historically an immigrant neighborhood and the dividing line between the western (English) and eastern (French) sides of the city, there is a real mix of influences in the stores here, so you can pick up everything from a $400 pair of shoes to a vegetable steamer to an authentic lava lamp. When day turns to night, St-Laurent is a major hotspot, with late-night falafel and pizza joints often found next to high-end boutiques. As you head farther north on the strip, the boutiques change from clothing to housewares and furniture. Between Rachel and Mont-Royal there's a large concentration of Québec-designed and -made furniture stores.

LES COURS MONT ROYAL

1445 rue Peel, www.lcmr.ca
HOURS: Mon.-Wed. 10 A.M.-6 P.M., Thurs.-Fri. 10 A.M.-9 P.M., Sat.-Sun. 10 A.M.-5 P.M.
Map 2

The crème-de-la-crème of brands can be found in this upscale shopping center. The province's sole Club Monaco is situated here, as are DKNY and Harry Rosen, Canada's top men's store. It's a former hotel, and the original ceiling mosaic and dazzling chandelier can still be seen, adding a certain amount of elegance to the main hall. Independent boutiques carrying local and well-known international brands can be found here, as well as one of the city's top spas and salons. It connects to the Métro system and other shopping centers through the Underground City. Opening times vary depending on the boutique.

EATON CENTER

705 rue Ste-Catherine W., 514/288-3710, www.centreeatondemontreal.com
HOURS: Mon.-Fri. 10 A.M.-9 P.M., Sat. 10 A.M.-5 P.M., Sun. 11 A.M.-5 P.M.
Map 2

Four floors of shops, kiosks, restaurants, and exhibition spaces make up Montréal's Eaton Center. It is here that you'll find North American staples like the Gap, Levi's, Old Navy, and Aldo. The largest shopping mall in downtown Montréal, it boasts 175 boutiques, services, and restaurants.

RUE NOTRE-DAME WEST

Rue Notre-Dame W. btwn. Atwater and Guy, www.qam.ca
Map 2

In the southwest part of the city, east of Marché

Atwater, you'll find rue Notre-Dame West. Once an important route for the fur trade, it experienced an economic boom at the end of the 19th century, and homes, offices, banks, and even a library went up along the street. By the 1950s, however, it was virtually deserted and in bad decline. It wasn't until the mid-'70s that independent antiques dealers started opening shops on the strip between Guy and Atwater streets, making it the street with the highest concentration of antiques stores in the city. You can find everything here, from vintage finds to quirky trinkets to relics from the sea and 18th-century chandeliers. Known as the "Quartiers des Antiquaires," it even has its own website (www.qam.ca), with a helpful map. Stores along this strip keep their own hours, so your best bet is to head there on a Saturday afternoon.

RUE SAINT-DENIS

Rue St-Denis btwn. blvd. de Maisonneuve and ave.Laurier

Map 4

The vibe of the stores on St-Denis, the major Francophone shopping district, is distinctly different from that on St-Laurent even though they consist of similar elements—independent boutiques and a mishmash of restaurants and furniture stores. Because this is the French side of the city, it is no surprise that cafés and restaurants, most of them with their own sidewalk terraces, are more plentiful here—the perfect cure for mid-browsing fatigue. Major Québécois designer Philippe Dubuc's eponymous boutique is situated here, as are a number of high-end designer home stores. Québécois chains like Bedo, Le Château, Jacob, and Zone are here, as are outposts for the Gap, Mexx, Lululemon, and Urban Outfitter—though, sorry guys, it's women only—making it the perfect antidote to downtown.

RUE SAINTE-CATHERINE

Rue Ste-Catherine W. btwn. rue Bishop and rue de Bleury

Map 2

This is the main commercial shopping district for the city. Starting at rue Bishop in the west, stores run the length of the street till about Bleury, where it becomes the new Quartier des Spectacles. All the big-name brand stores are concentrated here, including Apple, Nine West, Urban Outfitters, H&M, Banana Republic, and Zara. It is also along this strip that you'll find a number of shopping centers and department stores. Below ground, the majority of the Underground City is found; the various malls and department stores are all connected through walkways and shopping malls and you can walk about a third of the Ste-Catherine strip below street level.

Spas

Sure, you can go to spas anywhere in the world, but Montréal offers a number of different types of spas, in various locations on—and slightly off—the island. If you've yet to experience the hammam, a traditional Turkish bath, this is where to take the plunge, giving you a bit of the Orient in the middle of North America.

ESPACE NOMAD

4650 blvd. St-Laurent, 514/842-7279, www.espacenomad.ca

HOURS: Mon. 10 A.M.-6 P.M., Tues.-Sat. 10 A.M.-10 P.M., Sun. 11 A.M.-9 P.M.

Map 5

Offering massage and organic body treatments, Espace Nomad is one of only a few green spas in the city. It's situated on the Main in the heart of the Plateau, and the atmosphere is relaxed but the surroundings are distinctly more modern and design-oriented than some places, with vibrantly colored walls contrasting with earth-tone furniture. Organic treatments include body wraps and scrubs, and they also offer private yoga classes. Prices start at $75 for an hour-long massage and organic treatments.

SCANDINAVE LES BAINS VIEUX-MONTRÉAL

71 rue de la Commune W., 514/288-2009,
www.scandinave.com

HOURS: Mon.-Fri. 7 A.M.-9 P.M., Sat.-Sun. 10 A.M.-9 P.M.

Map 1

Taking over a large 19th-century building directly across from the Vieux-Port, the Scandinave Les Bains focuses its attention on hydrotherapy, relaxation, and massages. Modeled after traditional Scandinavian spas, the surroundings are as natural as possible, with stone walls, wood floors, and an earthy color scheme. Even the baths are a calming slate-gray. Massages, which start at $128 for 60 minutes and include access to the baths, are from the Nordic mold and include deep tissue ($138), Swedish exfoliation ($208), and hot stone massages ($198).

STROM SPA NORDIQUE

1001 blvd. de la Forêt, Île-des-Sœurs, 514/761-2772,
www.stromspa.com

HOURS: Daily 10 A.M.-10 P.M.

Map 7

For a mini-getaway without actually going too far outside of the city, you can't get any better than this. Trickier to get to than some places, it's worth the hassle. Situated on Nuns Island, this Scandinavian spa is all clean, slate-gray lines in bucolic surroundings. The thermal baths are restorative and look out over a large pond and forest. Seven kinds of massages are offered ($79 for 60 minutes), including Thai, Swedish, and hot stone therapy, and an additional $34 will get you a thermal experience. A brand-new spa, it's distinctly modern with professional, helpful staff.

STUDIO BEAUTÉ DU MONDE

1455 rue Drummond, Ste. 2B, 514/841-1210,
www.studiobeautedumonde.com

HOURS: Tues.-Sat. 10 A.M.-7 P.M., Sun.-Mon. 10 A.M.-6 P.M.

Map 2

If there's one beauty treatment in Montréal that you'll be hard-pressed to find outside of the city, it is the hammam spa. This spa is bright and open with Middle Eastern touches like rich, striped pillows and low wood furniture. The traditional Turkish bath for both men and women offers two steam rooms and a hot room. Traditional treatment, which starts at $89, involves black soap exfoliation, *rassoul* body wrap, and oil application to rehydrate your skin. Though the hammam is shared by both men and women, men are only allowed on Saturdays. Other treatments include Oriental honey waxing and facials.

Thrift Stores and Vintage Boutiques

THE ANNEX

56 rue St-Viateur W., 514/271-2129,
www.general54.blogspot.com

HOURS: Mon.-Wed. and Sat.-Sun. noon-6 P.M., Thurs.-Fri. noon-7 P.M.

Map 6

From boots to jackets, wide belts from the 1980s and more than few plaid shirts for men, The Annex is the newest vintage store to open in the Mile End. Run by the same ladies who take care of neighboring General 54, it draws a number of hipsters and thrift lovers of any age. Filled with finds like old chests of drawers, wooden rocking chairs, and old luggage, the store has a homey, nostalgic feel. Sales associates here are pretty hands off, but if you're looking for an honest opinion, they'll be happy to dish it out. Music here is usually indie rock, though CBC talk radio often sets the mood.

ARTERIE

176 rue Bernard W., 514/273-3933,
www.arterieboutique.blogspot.com

HOURS: Tues.-Fri. noon-6 P.M., Sat.-Sun. 11 A.M.-5 P.M.

Map 6

Located in an old Victorian building, Arterie has classic deep storefront windows that feature some of the best displays in the neighborhood—think dressmaker forms in vintage garb next to a tray of cocktails. They sell a bit of everything, including vintage martini shakers, handmade cards, and vegan shoes, but the focus is on vintage pieces and work from emerging designers for both men and women. Large and open with wood floors and high ceilings with beautiful moldings, the store is welcoming and laid-back, and salespeople are always friendly.

ERA VINTAGE
1800 rue Notre-Dame W., 514/543-8750
HOURS: Mon.-Wed. and Sat. 11 A.M.-5 P.M., Thurs. 11:30 A.M.-9 P.M., Fri. 11 A.M.-6 P.M.
Map 2

This is one of the best vintage stores in the city. Owner Élaine Léveillée lovingly color-coordinates her merchandise—including many designer pieces from labels like Lanvin, Gucci, and YSL—making it all the more beautiful when seen through the floor-to-ceiling windows. The natural light gives it a bright, open feel that is added to by the white walls and simple displays. Chic, modern, and elegant is the feel it gives off, and the customers often fall into that category. Nothing here looks old or secondhand, just cared for. Staff will approach you in a similar manner—helpful when you need them to be but otherwise as enthralled by their surroundings as you are.

EVA B
2013 blvd. St-Laurent, 514/849-8246,
www.eva-b.ca
HOURS: Mon.-Sat. 10 A.M.-10 P.M., Sun. noon-8 P.M.
Map 3

Quirky and chaotic, this huge secondhand store feels like it goes on for miles, with entire sections dedicated to menswear, leather jackets, cowboy boots, dresses, hats, and even a costume trunk full of gloves. A favorite with students and those who love the thrill of searching for a good deal, the atmosphere here is laid-back and yet intense, thanks to the sheer volume of stuff to dig through. The store itself has definitely seen better days, but the creaky floor boards and exposed brick still have their own charm. Staff here leave you to your own devices, though they'll happily serve you a coffee from the on-site café.

FOLLES ALLIÉES
365 ave. du Mont-Royal, 514/834-4904
HOURS: Mon.-Wed. 11 A.M.-6 P.M., Thurs.-Fri. 11 A.M.-9 P.M., Sat. 11 A.M.-6 P.M., Sun. noon-5 P.M.
Map 5

Men and women can both leave this cave of vintage well turned out in everything from medieval costumes to 1930s evening wear. Jam-packed with secondhand finds, the racks, display cases, shelves, and even the floor are stuffed with goods, making for a chaotic, vintage mess. Giving off the vibe of a hoarder's closet (moth balls included), this small, narrow store is always full of eccentrics, both behind and in front of the till, who are not afraid to indulge their inner Don Draper, Daisy Buchanan, or Holly Golightly.

FOUNDERIE
6596 blvd. St-Laurent, 514/507-7755
HOURS: Wed.-Fri. noon-9 P.M., Sat.-Sun. noon-6 P.M.
Map 6

Located on the border of Petite Italie, this vintage store carries a number of designer finds—Ferragamo boots, Gucci purses, Diane von Furstenberg scarves—as well as new and repurposed furniture and home accessories by up-and-coming designers. The floor-to-ceiling windows allow for lots of light while a brocade couch, vintage mirrors, and hardware-style fittings give the store a nostalgic yet practical edge. Appealing to young men and women with a thing for vintage, the modern furniture also attracts design fans looking for affordable yet modern pieces. The vibe here is current and fresh and the staff are friendly and helpful.

FRIPERIE ST-LAURENT
3976 blvd. St-Laurent, 514/842-3893
HOURS: Mon.-Wed. 11 A.M.-6 P.M., Thurs.-Fri. 11 A.M.-9 P.M., Sat. 11 A.M.-5 P.M., Sun. noon-5 P.M.
Map 5

Arbiters of vintage style should make a stop at this friperie on the Main. Elegant yet quirky window displays are sure to entice you into the well-laid out store full of cubbies and glass shelves on which accessories like clutch bags and shoes are artfully displayed. A vintage soundtrack with jazz and '60s pop fills the nostalgic

FRIPERIES (SECONDHAND CLOTHIERS)

Montréal is full of skilled *friperie* shoppers. Whether it's a fruitful search-and-destroy mission at the local Salvation Army or a more refined browse through the well-organized racks at a local vintage boutique, Montréalers are keen to find treasure. *Friperies* (French for "secondhand") are all over the city, and each has its own interpretation of what secondhand means. Many boutiques deal exclusively with authentic pieces, so you won't find your mid-'90s floral-patterned jeans there, while other *friperies* sell goods on consignment or receive donations from people in the neighborhood.

Head up to the Mile End to scope out a holy trinity of *friperies*, all within a block of each other. **Local 23, The Annex,** and **General 54** are run by Jen Glasgow and Genevieve Heisteck and offer some of the best vintage shopping in the city. Local 23 and the Annex deal exclusively in secondhand: from boots to fur hats, blouses to belts, and big old '80s earrings (they also have a large selection of menswear). General 54 was the first of the three stores to open, and its concept is a little different, though they do carry some secondhand pieces, like their enviable collection of leather boots, most of their stock is now dedicated to local designers. Jen Glasgow's eponymous label is available, as are the handmade leather bags of Broundoor and the PinPals' needle-pointed earrings, pendants, and hair bows.

West of Local 23, you'll find **Arterie,** a *friperie* and boutique dedicated to local, emerging designers. This big space was one of the first places to provide a platform for emerging Montréal designers, and though many of them have gone on to bigger and better things, like complexgeometries and Valerie Dumaine, most have remained loyal to their early supporter. You'll find various authentically vintage pieces for both men and women at the back of the store. They also carry kitschy pieces for the home and a range of shoes for vegetarians.

Head north on St-Laurent and you'll come across **Founderie,** one of the new vintage boutiques that specialize in rare designer finds. If you're not sold on vintage but are interested in modern furniture this store also carries the work of local up-and-coming industrial designers.

Connoisseurs of vintage will get a kick out of **Friperie St-Laurent.** Always one for elegant window displays full of hatboxes and trench coats,

atmosphere. Staff practice what they preach and are usually decked out in rare vintage finds and will help you find some gems as well. Carrying some of the best secondhand men's selections in the city, it's great place to pick up a leather jacket or a silk tie from the 1940s.

GENERAL 54

54 rue St-Viateur W., 514/271-2129,
www.general54.blogspot.com
HOURS: Mon.-Wed. and Sat.-Sun. noon–6 P.M.,
Thurs.-Fri. noon–7 P.M.
Map 6

The first of Jen Glasgow and Genevieve Heisteck's secondhand stores to open is now dedicated to the local designers. Finds include everything from jewelry to coats and dresses, though you can still find vintage pieces like shoes and accessories. Artfully curated antique furniture doubles as display cases for handmade leather goods, while jewelry pieces are often pinned on the wall and you'll find silk-screened pillowcases coming out of old hatboxes. The atmosphere is low-key, with talk radio or oldies in the background, and the staff are always ready to offer a hand or opinion.

LOCAL 23

23 rue Bernard W., 514/270-9333,
www.general54.blogspot.com
HOURS: Mon.-Wed. and Sat.-Sun. noon–6 P.M.,
Thurs.-Fri. noon–7 P.M.
Map 6

The latest boots and shoes line the windowsill of this secondhand floor, and the huge, seasonal selection lines the walls. It's divided by item (menswear, skirts, dresses, blouses), and you'll find a number of scores here, including

Friperie St-Laurent deals in vintage finds from the 1940-1970s. It's a great place to look for a fur stole or a leather jacket; the men's selection here usually outweighs the women's, though they do have a great collection of accessories. Pieces here are timeless, so you're likely to find a gem.

Gems can also be found at **Maskarad**, especially if you're looking for an evening dress. There is a touch of old-time boudoir to this boutique, which is enhanced by their selection of vintage slips, the occasional feather boa, and big, bold costume jewelry. Not all of the stock is vintage, however; mixed in with the authentic are a few new pieces but always cut and styled to match the aesthetic of a bygone era.

If you want your vintage straight up, **Folles Alliées** has a selection of evening and casual wear for both men and women. Vintage tuxes hang casually on the frame of the changing room in this cave of vintage delights. Looks here are distinctly "Mad Men," with full, calf-length dresses for women and casual short-sleeve button-downs for men. Some of the best finds in the store are in the display case at the cash register. Costume jewelry, vintage frames, and evening bags beg for a closer look.

It's all about the hunt at **Eva B.** This sprawling boutique on the lower Main has been among the top go-to places for vintage for the past decade. Racks of leather and jean jackets are flanked by rows of vintage cowboy boots. Selection and prices here run the gamut, but if you're willing to dig there's a trunk or two full of goodies to sort through. If all that hunting makes you thirsty, and it should, they've also got a small café at the front.

If you like the look of vintage but don't like the idea of scrounging through seamlessly unending racks of the stuff to find it, then head down to **Era Vintage.** Tucked among the antiques stores on Notre-Dame West, this bright boutique is a refreshing change, with the clothes organized by color, giving the place the look of a candy store, especially during the summer when the bright pinks and turquoise pop out at you. Owner Élaine Léveillée has an excellent eye for both pieces and merchandising; nothing in this store looks, or smells for that matter, vintage. Every garment is dry cleaned and pressed before being hung on the rack. Details are everything here – there's even an on-site seamstress who can alter a piece so that it fits just right.

vintage fur hats or berets come winter. An old record player has been transformed into a jewelry display case, and luggage adds a bit of old-time flavor. It's staffed by a number of vintage-savvy young women who'll help you dig though the latest finds, while their well-thought-out getups add to the ultra-cool vibe.

MASKARAD
103 ave. du Mont-Royal, 514/844-7676
HOURS: Sun.-Wed. 11 A.M.-6 P.M., Thurs.-Fri. 11 A.M.-9 P.M., Sat. 10 A.M.-6 P.M.
Map 5

Stepping in here is like delving into a closet full of your grandmother's unmentionables. Maskarad carries vintage dresses and slips as well as crystal studded accessories, and everything here will make you feel like a lady. Decked out with heavy velvet curtains, gilded mirrors with jewelry casually hung on their edges, and old wardrobes full of crinoline and lace, it has a definite feminine vibe. Shoppers here are looking for something special, out-of-the-ordinary, or long for the days of real glamour. Staff are nostalgic for the bygone era as well, and though the store carries new pieces as well they're all about helping you find that perfect unique piece.

HOTELS

Montréal has accommodations for any size budget. But depending on the time of year, you might find you're paying for more than what you're getting. There's no disputing that Old Montréal is the ideal location, as there's nothing quite like walking out of your hotel and into the ancient cobblestone streets. However, it's one of the more expensive areas in the city, so a night or two in this quarter might not fit every budget. Its numerous boutique hotels, stylish modern accommodations, and a few intimate inns offer a number of choices.

The majority of international chain hotels, like Holiday Inn, Marriott, etc., are concentrated on rue Sherbrooke between University and avenue du Parc, but there are lots of other options, including smaller inns, hostels, and independent hotels, usually found in the eastern or western end of the downtown core, that will give visitors a more distinctive experience.

Being a student hub, the Quartier Latin is full of budget options and the rowdier, party-on-your-doorstep crowd that usually comes with them. Still, larger hotels and smaller intimate boutique-style inns can be found here, and all are within walking distance to downtown and the Plateau, making it a great choice for those who want to see the city by foot, bike, or Métro.

When choosing, don't forget location. Old Montréal might be pretty, but if you're coming to enjoy the city's nightlife in the middle of January, come expecting to cab it back to your hotel nightly. If you want to be able to roll out of bed and into the party, a hotel closer to the spots you want to hit might be wiser.

HIGHLIGHTS

LOOK FOR █ TO FIND RECOMMENDED HOTELS.

█ **Best-Kept Secret:** The huge rooms, aerodynamic furniture, and minimalist design of **Hôtel Gault,** tucked away in a quiet corner of Old Montréal, make it perfect if you're looking for your own private paradise in the city (page 195).

█ **Best Design:** One of the first boutique hotels in the city, **Hôtel St-Paul** has bold interiors that remain cutting edge, and the location is unbeatable (page 196).

█ **Best Boutique Hotel:** Modern design and a youthful attitude meet classic Old Montréal architecture at **Le Petit Hôtel** (page 196).

█ **Most Romantic Hotel: Pierre du Calvet**'s opulent Louis IX-inspired decor and charming Old Montréal setting make it perfect for a couple's weekend away (page 196).

█ **Most Historical Room:** Yoko Ono and John Lennon holed up in room 1742 of the **Fairmont Queen Elizabeth** during their famous 1969 peace protest. Request the same suite and make your own history (page 197).

█ **Most Likely to Make You Extend Your Stay:** Designed with the comfort of guests in mind, **Hôtel le Germain** makes you feel like you're entering your own private loft. The hotel also boasts a 24-hour gym, a four-star restaurant, and panoramic views of the city (page 199).

█ **Best Classic Hotel:** In the heart of Montréal's swanky rue Sherbrooke, the **Ritz-Carlton** is as opulent as ever, with its top-hatted doorman, a sharply dressed staff, and afternoon tea that is guaranteed to transport you to a different era (page 200).

█ **Best Contemporary Hotel:** Ideally located on the edge of the Plateau Mont-Royal

Hôtel St-Paul's lobby

© HÔTEL ST-PAUL

and downtown, the **Opus Montréal** has a sleek, modern design and stunning Gaudi-like Art Nouveau architecture that will make you feel like you're stepping into a luxury European hotel (page 201).

█ **Best Neighborhood Inn:** Take yourself out of the downtown and in among the locals at **Auberge de la Fontaine.** Located in the heart of Plateau Mont-Royal, it looks out onto one of the nicest parks in the city (page 203).

█ **Best Service:** With more than 30 years as the training ground for those entering the hotel business, **L'Hôtel de l'Institut** raises the bar on hospitality (page 203).

HOTELS

PRICE KEY

$ Less than CAN$150 per night

$$ CAN$150-250 per night

$$$ More than CAN$250 per night

Some of the best rates can be found in the suburbs or close to Montréal's airport, but though public transit is (generally) fast and efficient, there's little reason to stay so far outside of the city center. Those booking online would be wise to double-check the address before hitting the confirmation button.

The farther north of rue Sherbrooke you go, the harder it is to find accommodations. Though a few hotels are available in the Plateau, residential areas like the Mile End and Little Italy have very few options, most of which are independently run bed-and-breakfasts or rental apartments—accommodations that don't suit everyone's taste but can be ideal if you're planning on visiting for an extended amount of time.

Hostels can be found throughout the city and are a great option for those traveling on a budget. Though dorms are popular with student travelers, a number of the hostels offer private rooms and cater to more mature travelers.

CHOOSING A HOTEL

Because it's a large North American city, Montréal hotels have all the usual amenities travelers are used to, like air-conditioning in the summer and standard double beds. Some, however, follow a more European model and offer a single queen-sized bed for double occupancy. Breakfast is usually, but not always, included. And those expecting a daily buffet may be disappointed with some hotels offering a simple continental breakfast with fresh pastries, coffee, and juice instead. If breakfast at the hotel is going to put you back more than $10 per person, chances are you can find a more palatable and affordable option not far from your accommodation.

Though most hotel websites can be trusted to give authentic photos, it is always a good idea to check visitor review sites like www.virtualtourist.com for feedback before booking. Tired-looking decor might have been recently updated, or a five-star hotel might no longer be up to standards.

Parking in the city can be a hassle, and expensive, so double-check to make sure your hotel offers parking or at the very least a reasonably close alternative. Street parking is usually safe, but watch out for unusual parking rules—like having to move the car for an hour each day—and finding a spot close to the hotel isn't always easy.

Vieux-Montréal   Map 1

AUBERGE DU VIEUX-PORT **$$$**
97 rue de la Commune, 514/876-0081,
www.aubergeduvieuxport.com

Overlooking the waterfront, this boutique *auberge* (inn) offers a number of rooms, as well as self-sufficient lofts and apartments (often walk-ups) that are a short distance away from the main building. It's decorated with rustic touches—exposed ceiling beams, wrought-iron balconies—so the feel is more homey than modern, like visiting a friend's summer home. The in-house restaurant, Narcisse, boasts both a rooftop terrace (with a panoramic view of the

river) and a downstairs bistro, complete with remnants of the city's original fortifications.

L'HÔTEL CHAMPS-DE-MARS **$$**
756 rue Berri, 514/844-0767,
www.hotelchampsdemars.com

On the eastern border of Vieux-Montréal, this establishment has a long history as a hotel. Built in 1889, it first opened its doors as Hôtel le Relais, and its street-level tavern soon became a popular meeting place for sailors and port workers alike. Though it's anything but fancy it has a family-run feel and is an affordable option for those who want the experience of staying in the historic center. It also offers a filling American-style breakfast, not always the easiest to find.

◖ HÔTEL GAULT ❸❸❸

449 rue Ste-Helene, 514/904-1616, www.hotelgault.com

A 19th-century textile store in Old Montréal was converted into Hotel Gault, one of the most scenic and serene boutique hotels in the city. The 30 spacious rooms (300–1,000 square feet each) come complete with movable ergonomic workstations and heated slate bathroom floors, essential for Montréal winters. The hotel is also pet-friendly, and guests are welcome to bring along their treasured feline or canine companion. Though luxury is everywhere you step in the Gault, it's understated: From the reproduction midcentury modern furniture to the bar that greets you at reception, nothing about the place is ostentatious.

HÔTEL LE ST-JAMES ❸❸❸

355 rue St-Jacques, 514/841-3111, www.hotellestjames.com

Madonna, Victoria Beckham—this is where the celebrities stay when they come to Montréal. Decorated with lovingly preserved antiques, four-poster beds, and marble accented bathrooms, the St-James has gone to great lengths to create a luxurious, European atmosphere. Located on the cusp of Vieux-Montréal and the modern Quartier International, this former merchants bank still has many of its defining features, including John Hammond's 1930 murals, which are an ode to hydroelectric energy, and the idiosyncratic window treatments that grace each of the building's eight floors. If you are looking for a unique spa experience, theirs is located in the bank's former vault.

L'HÔTEL MONTREAL ❸❸

262 rue St-Jacques, 514/985-0019, www.lhotelmontreal.com

Situated on what was once "Canadian Wall Street," this Second Empire–style building, erected in 1870, was originally the Montréal City and District Savings Bank. It also housed the law office of Jean Drapeau, who would later

© SACHA JACKSON

HOTELS

Tucked away on a quiet sidestreet Hôtel Gault is a well-kept secret.

become the city's mayor. The hotel has a focus on art; works by Warhol, Litchenstein, and Christo are on view throughout the premises, and each room is uniquely decorated, mixing modern decor with the existing architectural elements, such as the ceiling friezes. They also offer indoor parking—a perk, especially if you're visiting in winter.

HÔTEL NELLIGAN ❸❸❸

106 rue St-Paul W., 514/788-2040, www.hotelnelligan.com

Occupying two buildings that date back to the 1830s, the hotel features an indoor Mediterranean-style atrium and has a more traditional approach than some of the other boutique hotels in the area. The dark-wood furniture and earthy palette give every one of their 120 rooms a sophisticated gravitas. Judging from the modest facade, you'll be surprised to find their rooftop terrace offers some of the best views (and cocktails) the city has to offer.

◖ HÔTEL ST-PAUL ⑤⑤⑤

355 rue McGill, 514/380-2222, www.hotelstpaul.com

As you enter the sleek lobby of this Beaux Arts building you'll notice the large marble fireplace, which seems to appear almost out of nowhere. Opening in 2001, the St-Paul was one of the first converted buildings in the area and led the way for further reconstruction and rejuvenation. Designed by Ana Borrallo, the warm, monochromatic and minimalist decor, accented with leather, suede, and fur (a nod to Québec's past and the freezing winters) makes it one of the first "design" hotels in the city. It also offers services like valet parking and babysitting that you'd expect from a luxury hotel. Even if you're not staying, pop into Vauvert, the hotel's restaurant, for a drink and a peek at the gorgeous interior.

◖ LE PETIT HÔTEL ⑤⑤

168 rue St-Paul W., 514/940-0360,
www.petithotelmontreal.com

The simply named Le Petit Hôtel takes a relaxed approach to the boutique hotel concept. Recently opened on rue St-Paul West, it has a hipper, younger atmosphere with a café on the first floor that turns into a bar in the evening (or the afternoon, if you need it) as well as a mini-spa offering massages. Rooms come in small, medium, large, or extra large, and inside, they are sleek and modern—white duvets, splashes of color, iPod-docking systems—with traditional touches like exposed brick walls and cathedral ceilings.

◖ PIERRE DU CALVET ⑤⑤⑤

405 rue Bonsecours, 514/282-1725,
www.pierreducalvet.ca

Just in front of Chapelle Notre-Dame-de-Bon-Secours, this ancestral mansion was built in 1725 and maintains its old-world charm thanks to the sumptuous decor—there is something Louis XIV about the bedrooms—and the use of family heirlooms and antique furniture. Named for Pierre du Calvet, who immigrated to Canada in 1758, it's one of the oldest buildings in Montréal to offer accommodation. An outdoor terrace and fireside library with exposed

© SACHA JACKSON

Classic meets contemporary at Le Petit Hôtel.

beams are nice additions, as is the inclusion of the coat of arms of the Trottiers (who rejuvenated the premises and still run the hotel), featuring the motto My House Is Your House.

PLACE D'ARMES HÔTEL AND SUITES ⑤⑤⑤

55 rue St-Jacques W., 514/842-1887,
www.hotelplacedarmes.com

Mixing elements from the 1880 structure with contemporary design, the hotel, which was the first of its kind to open in Vieux-Montréal, offers a fine balance of classic and modern—brick walls and industrial lighting-fixtures meet colonial furniture—giving it a cozy, yet luxurious atmosphere. Looking out onto Place d'Armes and the Notre-Dame Basilica, Aix Cuisine du Terroir restaurant's rooftop terrace offers stunning views. The hotel also has an in-house hammam spa, and take advantage of the complimentary cheese and wine during afternoon cocktail hour in La Terrasse Suite 701.

© SACHA JACKSON

Pierre du Calvet

W HOTEL $$$

901 Square Victoria, 514/395-3100,
www.whotels.com

Already established in the U.S., this high-fashion world-class hotel muscled its way into Vieux-Montréal in 2004 with its ultra-modern and sleek design. Part of the Quartier International, the '60s-modernist architecture of the converted Banque du Canada building gives the hotel a sort of timeless edge and allows it to blend in seamlessly with the existing structures. Though some aspects of the place might make your eyes roll—the Wow Suites, the Whatever/Whenever button, the glass-walled shower—there is no denying this is one of the city's most enviably hip addresses.

Centre-Ville   Map 2

CHÂTEAU VERSAILLES $$

1659 rue Sherbrooke W., 514/933-3611,
www.chateauversaillesmontreal.com

An intimate hotel in a grand old house on the western end of downtown, Château Versailles is a great option if you're looking for a cozy but lavish atmosphere. Each room and suite is uniquely decorated, giving the hotel the feel of an old manor house. The decor itself falls somewhere between contemporary and classic, with big, heavy furniture, modern art, and opulent touches like gilded mirrors. A babysitting service is available.

FAIRMONT QUEEN ELIZABETH $$$

900 blvd. René-Lévesque W., 514/861-3511,
www.fairmont.com/queenelizabeth

One of the most famous hotels in the city, the Fairmont Queen Elizabeth has been the temporary home of Queen Elizabeth II, Nelson Mandela, and Mikhail Gorbachev. And it was here in 1969 that Yoko Ono and John Lennon staged their infamous "Bed-In" in suite 1746 and wrote and recorded *Give Peace a Chance*. Opened in 1958, this world-class luxury hotel is an imposing structure and has over

© FAIRMONT HOTELS & RESORTS

John Lennon and Yoko Ono's historic "Bed-In" took place in this suite at the Fairmont Queen Elizabeth.

1,000 rooms, 100 of which are suites. A classic Montréal hotel, it is directly connected to the train station and is accessible through the Underground City.

L'HÔTEL DE LA MONTAGNE $$

1430 rue de la Montagne, 514/288-5656, www.hoteldelamontagne.com

Once a place to be and be seen, L'Hôtel de la Montagne may have lost a bit of its cachet, but this centrally located hotel in the middle of everything is still unique, full of various kinds of nightlife. A flamboyant, Beaux Arts fountain greets you in the lobby, as does the gilded decor of the ground-floor café Les Beaux Jeudis. The rooms are more modern with flatscreen TVs and clean design. The 20th floor boasts a rooftop pool and bar with a great view of the city.

L'HÔTEL DU FORT $$

1390 rue du Fort, 514/938-8333, www.hoteldufort.com

In the western part of downtown, close to the Center for Canadian Architecture and the old Forum, this independent hotel offers standard rooms at reasonable rates. Situated on a busy side street, with access to the highway, it's a good option for those who want easy access in and out of the city. The staff are friendly, bilingual, and often helpful. The rooms themselves are standard hotel fare, clean and neat, and some afford views over the city. It also has an underground parking lot.

L'HÔTEL ESPRESSO $

1005 rue Guy, 514/938-4611, www.hotelespresso.ca

This former Days Inn in the heart of downtown, within walking distance to Vieux-Montréal and close to the Métro, has been renovated and given a boutique hotel touch. Warm earth tones are found throughout the hotel from the lobby to the rooms, which have a comfortable but sleek and modern feel with parquet floors and crisp white duvets. Not all the rooms have been renovated, however, so some are terribly outdated and have seen better days. Amenities include a 24-hour gym, sauna, reasonably priced on-site massage facilities, and an outdoor pool in summer.

HOSTELS

If you're looking for alternatives to the swanky boutique hotels of Old Montréal and the recognizable hotel chains of downtown, there are a number of great hostels or bed-and-breakfasts in the city, located in various quarters. You'll find accommodations to suit all kinds of travelers, from simple dorm-style rooms to private rooms.

Those looking to stay in Old Montréal but without the hefty price tag should look no further than **Auberge Alternative de Vieux-Montréal** (358 rue St-Pierre, 514/282-8069, www.auberge-alternative.qc.ca, $25 dorm room, $75 private room). This converted warehouse still retains the arched windows and high ceilings of its 1875 construction. Decorated with an eclectic collection of found or made objects (the dorm's bunk beds, for example), the hostel's dorms and private rooms are brightly colored, enlivening the old stone walls. Conveniently located in the western part of Vieux-Montréal, close to rue McGill, it's easily accessible by Métro and within walking distance to downtown. One caveat: It's three floors up to the reception area, so be prepared to lug your bags.

Visitors looking to be close to the downtown action should check out **L'Auberge Apéro** (1425 Mackay, 514/316-1052, www.aubergeapero.com, $21-24 dorm room), an affordable, popular alternative to less-than-favorable cheaper hotels. Clean and minimally decorated, it is relatively small, with only 18 beds available in an old building built in the 1880s. It boasts an outdoor terrace as well as knowledgeable and bilingual staff.

The center of activity for Francophone students, the Latin Quarter has a number of hostels, though if you're well out of university, choose carefully; the area and the hostels themselves can get rowdy. Location-wise it is perfect, a stone's throw from the Plateau and close to downtown. All the choices here have a truly French vibe.

Offering private rooms and small apartments, **Auberge de Jeunesse Alexandrie** (1750 rue Amherst, 514/522-9420, www.alexandrie-montreal.com, $22 dorm room, $70-90 private room) in the Latin Quarter is in the center of the action and a good choice for those traveling in small groups. Same goes for **Hostel Montréal Central** (1586 rue St-Hubert, 514/843-5739, www.hostelmontrealcentral.com, $27 dorm room, $40-90 private room), though it has more of a student vibe with an outdoor terrace and in-house restaurant and bars.

For a more residential location, the Plateau is perfect, but be warned – once you get used to the laid-back pace and tree-lined streets you might not want to venture downtown. Close to Parc Lafontaine in the eastern Plateau, **La Gîte du Parc Lafontaine** (1250 rue Sherbrooke E., 514/522-3910, www.hostelmontreal.com, $28 dorm room, $65-80 private room) offers private rooms or dormitory beds in a classic-style townhouse.

L'HÔTEL LE CRYSTAL ❸❸

1100 rue de la Montagne, 877/861-5550, www.hotellecrystal.com

Newly opened in the heart of downtown, and looking out over the Centre Bell, this gleaming glass tower boasts 131 spacious suites with free Wi-Fi and flat-screen TVs. Contemporary in design, the furnishings are modern and monochromatic. There is also a pool and spa on the premises. Since it's situated kitty-corner to the Centre Bell, members of the Canadiens are sometimes residents here, so don't be surprised if you bump into one of them in the elevator or hot tub.

⬛ HÔTEL LE GERMAIN ❸❸❸

2050 rue Mansfield, 514/849-2050, www.germainmontreal.com

Once an office building, this austere concrete structure—certainly a product of the 1970s—was renovated in 1999 to become Hôtel le Germain. Totally redesigned to give their clients the feel of entering their own private loft, the boutique hotel's decoration is all dark wood, earth tones, and glass. With a full gym, spa, and restaurant, all of which are staffed by experienced practitioners in their fields, their facilities are considered some of the best in the city. Panoramic views of Montréal only add to the hotel's charm.

LOEWS VOGUE HOTEL $$$

1425 rue de la Montagne, 514/285-5555, www.loewshotel.com

A classic Montréal hotel, Loews can be found in the heart of the city close to shopping and nightlife. Modeled after rue Sherbrooke "Golden Square Mile," which was popular in the early 20th century, Loews is more opulently decorated than a number of hotels in the city, with dark cherrywood, richly hued fabrics, furniture in the Late Empire style and marble in the bathrooms. On the smaller side, this boutique hotel has 126 rooms and 16 suites, so don't be surprised if staff know your name by the end of the trip. Those traveling with children, however, might find the atmosphere too reserved.

MARRIOTT CHÂTEAU CHAMPLAIN $$

1 Place du Canada Place, 514/878-9000, www.montrealchateauchamplain.com

With 38 floors, the Château Champlain is the tallest hotel in the city and one of the most interesting architecturally. Designed by Roger D'Astous and Jean-Paul Pothier, it was completed in time for Expo 67. It was set apart by its arched windows, which won it the unfortunate nickname "the cheese grater." Now owned by Marriott, the lobby features a golden ceiling made up of numerous domes. Similar opulent touches can be found throughout the hotel. Located on the outer edge of downtown, it is a short walk to Old Montréal and looms over the Cathedrale Marie-Reine-du-Monde.

LE PETIT PRINCE $$

1384 ave. Overdale, 514/938-2277, www.montrealbandb.com

This small, four-bedroom bed-and-breakfast located a quiet secluded street just south of the downtown core is a nice break for those

wanting to be close to the action. It's located in a Victorian townhouse that was built in 1876, and the wood floors, stone work, and impeccably designed rooms give it a unique and welcoming charm. It's steps away from the Métro and within walking distance to Old Montréal. Breakfast is made to order and in summer you can enjoy it on their quiet outdoor terrace.

◖ RITZ-CARLTON $$$

1228 rue Sherbrooke W., 514/842-4212, www.ritzcarltonmontreal.com

Opened in 1912, on posh rue Sherbrooke, the Ritz-Carlton is still "La Grande Dame" of Montréal hotels, as it's the only Canadian hotel of its era still in existence. Started by five investors who wanted to capitalize on the city's carriage trade, this luxury hotel still has a wrought-iron awning and top-hatted doormen that greet guests on the rich, blue carpet. The imposing Beaux Arts building is still as elegant as when it first opened. Still the top choice for those who can afford it, it underwent a huge renovation in 2010 to ensure the interior is as stunning as the exterior. In homage to a past era, condos are still for rent on the top floors.

SOFITEL MONTRÉAL $$$

1155 rue Sherbrooke W., 514/285-9000, www.sofitel.com

Set in the historical Golden Square Mile, close to McGill University and the Musée des Beaux-Arts, it may be part of a chain but French-owned Sofitel is one of the sleekest and most stylish hotels in the downtown core. Tall and lean with huge windows, its ultra-modern design continues inside with a minimalist decor, stained-glass windows in the lobby, and contemporary art throughout. This is a European chain, so room sizes are slightly smaller than their North American counterparts, and the per room Internet charge is a bit of a letdown. The hotel of choice with European travelers, it's also pet friendly.

Centre-Ville Est   Map 3

HOLIDAY INN SELECT $

99 ave. Viger W., 514/878-9888,
www.yul-downtown.hiselect.com

There's a lot of European flavor in Montréal hotels but this place is a little different. Located in Chinatown on the edge of Vieux-Montréal, it has an Asian theme. As the rooftop pagodas indicate, the Far East aesthetic runs throughout, with a water garden and more pagodas and paper lanterns in the foyer. The rooms are standard, with queen-sized beds, TVs, and windows onto Vieux-Montréal or Chinatown. Kitty-corner to the Métro, but right next to a highway, it's within walking distance to downtown and the Vieux-Port, and visitors can take advantage of their indoor pool, gym, and spa services.

OPUS MONTRÉAL $$

10 rue Sherbrooke W., 514/843-6000,
www.opushotel.com/montreal

A great mix of old and new, Opus Montréal has some of the most stunning architecture in the city. Located on the corner of St-Laurent and Sherbrooke it is the perfect distance between downtown and the Plateau. Originally built in 1914 by Joseph-Arthur Godin, the Art Nouveau–style building was the first poured-concrete structure in North America. Incorporating the existing structure into the new design, Opus balances sleek design and decor with old world charm. The friendly and bilingual staff are always helpful and the in-house bar, Succo Lounge, has a great outdoor terrace and is a popular hangout.

HOTELS

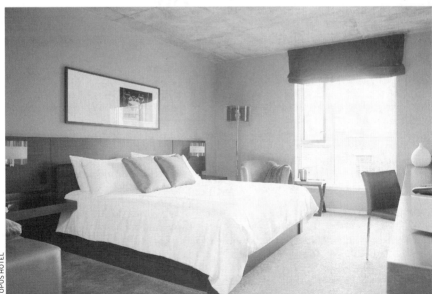

© OPUS HOTEL

Color adds warmth to the sleek and modern rooms at Opus Montréal.

Quartier Latin and the Village   Map 4

CELEBRITIES LOVELY HOTEL ⑤
1095 rue St-Denis, 514/849-9688,
www.celebritieshotelmontreal.com

The name might sound a little silly, but Celebrities Lovely Hotel is just that, a lovely, movie-themed hotel in the Latin Quarter. Situated in an old Victorian mansion built in 1897, the house has been renovated to turn it into a small boutique hotel. Taking inspiration from *Breakfast at Tiffany's*, shots of Audrey Hepburn adorn almost all the rooms and give it its glamorous atmosphere. Portraits of Holly Golightly and a pink and white color scheme make it more the spot for a girls' weekend than a romantic getaway.

L'HÔTEL GOUVERNEUR PLACE DUPUIS ⑤⑤
1415 rue St-Hubert, 514/842-4881,
www.gouverneur.com

This moderately priced hotel isn't anything spectacular, but because it's situated in the Latin Quarter, close to the Village, Old Montréal, Berri-UQÀM Métro station, and within walking distance to the Plateau and downtown, it's a great option for those looking for affordable accommodations. Though the rooms are showing a bit of wear and tear, they are large, comfortable, and a great choice for families. The 18-floor high-rise also affords great views of the city and the St-Lawrence, and an indoor pool and gym sweeten the pot.

L'HÔTEL LORD BERRI ⑤⑤
1199 rue Berri, 514/845-9236, www.lordberri.com

Located in the Latin Quarter, just steps away from the Berri-UQÀM Métro station and Old Montréal, L'Hôtel Lord Berri is a nonsmoking hotel with 154 rooms and features like free Wi-Fi and parking nearby. Currently under renovation, not all the rooms or bathrooms have been updated, so some rooms might be more tired and out of date than others; either way, you can expect a clean hotel with friendly and helpful staff and a great location.

L'HÔTEL MANOIR DES ALPES ⑤⑤
1245 rue St-Andre, 514/845-9803,
www.hotelmanoirdesalpes.qc.ca

This small, Swiss-style hotel in the center of the Latin Quarter takes its cues from European inns and offers a simple lodging in a cosy atmosphere. The hotel has been around for more than 30 years, and the staff are knowledgeable and helpful with a great handle on the city. Close to the Métro and within walking distance to Old Montréal, Chinatown, downtown, and the Plateau, the hotel has just about everything, except for the feel of a big hotel. With complimentary continental breakfast, free Wi-Fi, and free parking there's little more to ask for.

L'HÔTEL ST-DENIS ⑤
1254 rue St-Denis, 514/849-4526, www.hotel-st-denis.com

Built in the 1920s, L'Hôtel St-Denis is in the center of the action, not far from downtown and only a block away from the Berri-UQÀM Métro station. The rooms themselves, which are your standard hotel fare, can seem a bit out of date, while others have recently undergone a renovation. Some guests might find the rooms to be noisy in the summer due to the air conditioners. Parking is available just around the corner and Wi-Fi is free for guests. Breakfast isn't included at the hotel, but since it's next to a number of cafès and restaurants, finding a good meal is hardly a problem.

LA LOGGIA ⑤
1637 rue Amherst, 514/524-2493, www.laloggia.ca

Located on Amherst in the center of the Village, this charming bed-and-breakfast serves up both art and breakfast. Situated in a three-story early-20th-century townhouse, the five rooms are all uniquely decorated with antique chairs, modern art, and personal touches here and there like vibrant cushions or Persian rugs, all of which gives it a homey vibe. Close to the Plateau and Berri Métro station, they offer packages that include private yoga classes, personal trainer sessions, or a course in sculpture. Breakfast is made with local, fair-trade, and organic ingredients and is served on the terrace in summer.

SIR MONTCALM ⑤⑤

1453 rue Montcalm, 514/522-7747, www.sirmontcalm.com

This ultra-chic bed-and-breakfast in the Village—think matte black walls, sleek white linens, and ambient lighting—may cater to the LGBT community, but anyone with an eye for design will be instantly smitten. It's a perfect blend of comfortable yet polished. Perks include a day pass to the local gym, access to the gorgeous patio in summer, and a filling four-course breakfast. Close to Vieux-Montréal and the Métro, the only drawback is that although the rooms come with adjoining bathrooms, the only thing separating the bed from the bath is a heavy curtain.

Plateau Mont-Royal   Map 5

ANNE MA SŒUR ANNE ⑤

4119 rue St-Denis, 514/281-3187,
www.annemasoeuranne.com

Situated in the middle of the Plateau close to Parc Lafontaine and the restaurant-filled avenue Duluth, this hotel studio is a good option for those traveling on a budget or those looking to stay in the heart of the action. No-frills rooms are comfortable enough, and most come equipped with Murphy beds that you can fold into the wall when not in use. Since it's directly above a jazz club, the noise, especially on weekends, will keep some up at night. The small rooms also come equipped with a micro kitchen for some simple self-catering.

◖ AUBERGE DE LA FONTAINE ⑤

1301 rue Rachel E., 514/597-0166,
www.aubergedelafontaine.com

This turn-of-the-20th-century townhouse looks out onto Parc Lafontaine, one of the most pleasant spots in the city. Three floors of rooms offer an intimate place to stay in a residential, mainly Francophone area. Though parking can be a bit of a hassle—the hotel only has three spots, the rest is on the street—it is situated on a bike path and is perfect for anyone wanting to bike the city. A buffet breakfast and free Wi-Fi are available, and guests also have access to the kitchen after hours, where they can help themselves to tea, coffee, and various snacks.

GINGERBREAD MANOR ⑤

3445 ave. Laval, 514/597-2804,
www.gingerbreadmanor.com

Just off of Carré St-Louis between St-Denis and St-Laurent and located in a Victorian three-story townhouse built in 1885, this charming bed-and-breakfast is a different way to see the city. With large bay windows, original molding (it's named after the period's "gingerbread" ornamental details), and an attached carriage house it harkens back to a bygone golden age. All five rooms are fitted with either a king or queen bed, have hardwood floors, and are uniquely furnished. Only one, however, has a private bath. A hot breakfast includes croissants and fruit salad, and they also have bikes available to rent.

◖ L'HÔTEL DE L'INSTITUT ⑤⑤

3535 rue St-Denis, 514/282-5120,
www.ithq.qc.ca

As this is the training ground for future hotel staff, you're unlikely to find better service in the city. A recent renovation has modernized this 35-year-old hotel to rival the sleek design of just about any hotel in Montréal. With only 42 rooms, it is relatively small, but each room has its own balcony affording views of the city. Ideally located in the Plateau, it is within walking distance to downtown and is directly above a Sherbrooke Métro station. The sole drawback is the slightly overpriced parking, which isn't always available.

HOTELS

PENSIONE POPOLO $

4871 blvd. St-Laurent, 514/284-0122,
www.casadelpopolo.com

Those behind cafè and venue Casa del Popolo have opened a small, European-inspired pensione above the cafè (look for the red door). Ideally located on the border of the Plateau and Mile End, it's perfect for the self-sufficient traveler looking for a no-frills bed. Bathrooms and kitchen are shared, but the cozy rooms and the location above one of the city's hottest bars is worth it. Guests also get free passes to see bands playing during their stay, and the location alone, near tons of affordable restaurants and within walking distance to the city's coolest addresses, sweetens the deal.

LE PLUMARD $

4432 rue de Lanaudière, 514/526-7660,
www.leplumard.com

This tiny three-room bed-and-breakfast in the Plateau is a total 360 from most travel experiences in the city. Offering visitors a taste of what it's like to live like a real Montréaler, this traditional townhouse walk-up is ideally located, close to Parc Lafontaine and the bustling avenue Mont-Royal. They even have bikes for visitors to borrow, ideal for a true summertime experience. Rooms are minimally decorated but have nice bursts of color for that laid-back Plateau vibe, and two have their own private balconies. Breakfast is quite French with a number of sweet things, crêpes, French toast, and hot chocolate on the menu.

EXCURSIONS FROM MONTRÉAL

One of the greatest things about Montréal is its proximity to nature. Montréalers are always heading out of the city for some antiquing, apple picking, and cycling in the Cantons de l'Est (Eastern Townships in English) or leaving the office en route to some of the best skiing in the world and a cozy chalet weekend in the Laurentides (the Laurentians).

Depending on which way you leave the island—to the mountains in the north, or the valleys in the south—you're headed for some diverse geography. To the southeast you'll find the lowlands, lakes, and rolling hills populated with a number of wineries and towns, each with their own—often British-influenced—style. Located 80 kilometers from Montréal and bordering on New Hampshire and Vermont, certain parts of the Eastern Townships can seem almost indistinguishable from some of their American counterparts. The covered bridges, Victorian gingerbread houses, and antiques stores give it a certain Anglophone touch you don't always see elsewhere in the province.

This was a predominantly English area until the 1970s, and English and French are spoken so fluently here it can be hard to figure out the native from non-native speakers. On your way out of the city, drivers will pass three unique Monteregian hills. Mont St-Hilaire, Rougemont, and Yamaska explode out of the otherwise flat lands; these mini-mountains created by what many think may have been intrusions of long extinct volcanoes are now accessible ski stations in the winter.

Leave Montréal to the north and you'll soon be in the thick, dense boreal forests and driving

© TOURISME DE LAURENTIDES

HIGHLIGHTS

LOOK FOR ◖ TO FIND RECOMMENDED
SIGHTS, ACTIVITIES, DINING, AND LODGING.

◖ **Most Exhilarating Views:** Nothing beats the panoramic views from the top of **Mont-Tremblant Resort.** It's the highest mountain in the region, surrounded by hills, lakes, and rivers, so you're guaranteed a scenic ride even as you slalom down the slopes (page 209).

◖ **Most Multicultural Cottage Country:** Jewish, Francophone, and English populations pioneered the summer existence of **Sainte-Agathe-des-Monts,** and to this day all three cultures can be seen in the town, making it the most culturally diverse in the region (page 213).

◖ **Best Rock Climbing:** Experienced and inexperienced climbers alike come to **Dufresne Regional Park,** the site of the best rock climbing in Québec, as well as some delicately preserved ecology (page 214).

◖ **Best Place to See the Leaves in Fall:** There's no better way to see the seasons change than riding or walking along the **Parc Linéaire le P'tit Train du Nord,** which is 230 kilometers long and cuts through the Laurentians (page 214).

◖ **Best Kid-Friendly Sight:** Over 1,000 animals call the **Granby Zoo** home. With unique attractions like Hippo River, it's a great day out for the kids (page 217).

◖ **Best Children's Museum:** Interactive exhibits at the **Museum of Science and Nature** beautifully mix history and art (page 217).

◖ **Best Summer Stage:** Located in the picturesque town of Knowlton, **Theatre Lac Brome** is one of the most respected English summer stages in the province, with performances of classic and contemporary plays (page 219).

◖ **Best Place to Tune Up Your Gregorian Chant:** Located on the banks of Lake Memphremagog, **Abbaye St-Benoît-du-**

© ERICLEFRANCAIS/WWW.123RF.COM

The ski slopes at the Mont-Tremblant Resort are some of the highest in the region.

Lac is home to 50 monks who produce some of the tastiest cheese and gourmet goods in the region. A bonus: They'll also let you pray with them and join in a little Gregorian chant three times a day (page 220).

◖ **Most Likely to Give You Vertigo:** One of the longest pedestrian suspension bridges in the world can be found at the **Parc de la Gorge-de-Coaticook.** The bridge sits 50 meters above the gorge (page 220).

◖ **Most Unexpected Way to Explore the Region:** Few people associate Québec with wine, so following **La Route des Vins** to the many wineries in the region will give you a totally different perspective on the region and its geography (page 221).

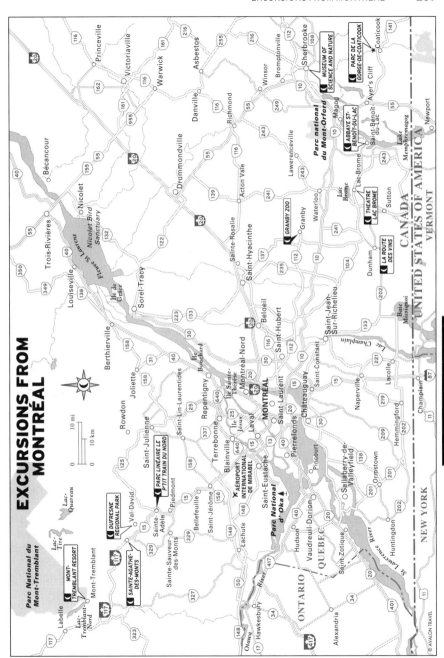

EXCURSIONS FROM MONTRÉAL

through the foothills of the Laurentian mountains, first colonized in the mid-1800s. It was a priest, Antoine Labelle, who first saw the area's great potential and pushed to exploit it. Saddened by the number of French Canadians moving south of the border for work, he convinced mills and logging companies and their works to move north into the mountains. The opening of the northern railway Petit Train du Nord in the late 1800s also pushed development.

Today this region remains particularly close to the hearts of many Montréalers, and it has become a popular place to retire. Amid the woods and the lakes and mountains are a number of cottage towns and, of course, some of the best ski slopes in the country.

PLANNING YOUR TIME

All of these excursions, to the south and the north, can be made from Montréal in a day by car, though those who have the time should think about staying a night or two in the region for more exploring. The Laurentians in particular offer a number of different types of escapes, and you could spend weeks hiking the various trails, canoeing some of the area's bigger lakes, and camping out in a different area each night.

The Cantons de l'Est, meanwhile, are great for a day out of town or a romantic getaway; it all depends on what you're looking for. Camping is popular here as well, but the quaint inns and many towns to explore allow for a more relaxed visit, and because it's barely a 90-minute drive from the city, it's ideal for those on short stay.

Weekends are always busiest no matter the time of year or whether you're heading north or to the southeast. If you're flexible in your travel times, avoid the crowds and opt for midweek break, then head back to the city for the weekend. Between December and March 15 snow tires are the law for any vehicle registered in the province, so if you're driving a rental you'll be covered. But if you've got your own set of wheels, then sticking to major (read, plowed) roads and avoiding dirt tracks is the safest bet. Many of the roads, especially those that lead to out-of-the-way privately owned chalets and cottages, rely on local residents to shovel and plow them.

Mont-Tremblant

With its lakes, streams, mountains, and untamed wilderness, Mont-Tremblant is one of the most popular destinations in the Laurentians. A 90-minute drive from Montréal, it boasts a national park and an internationally renowned resort that attracts tourists year-round.

Autumn is an ideal time to head up to the mountains and catch the tremendous colors of the leaves as they turn. The mixed Laurentian forest with its boreal and big woods species is one of the most diverse in the world, and its beauty is undeniable.

This is considered the premier ski and snowboarding region in Eastern Canada, and during winter (December–March in particular) sport enthusiasts, and those just wanting to kick back in an Icelandic sweater with a drink next to a roaring fire, flock to the region. Though the biggest draw is the resort itself, where you can spend an entire vacation and never get board, it's also worth visiting the region's many heritage buildings and churches, all of which can be discovered in the old towns.

Though it's possible to do Mont-Tremblant in a day, provided you rise early and stay late, to get the most out of the region requires at least a one-night stay, especially if you plan on doing outdoor activities.

SIGHTS AND RECREATION
Mont-Blanc

Just over an hour's drive from Montréal is Mont-Blanc (1006 Route 117, St-Faustin-Lac-Carré, 800/567-6715, www.skimontblanc.com, late Nov.–mid-Apr. daily 8:30 A.M.–3:30 P.M., $40 adult), the second-highest mountain in the Laurentians. Boasting 41 trails including five expert trails it also has a major ski school and is one of the more affordable hills in the region, perfect for beginners or pros. There's also an on-site spa, the perfect answer to a day on the slopes.

Mont-Tremblant National Park

Smack dab in the middle of the Laurentian mountains, Mont-Tremblant National Park (819/688-2281, www.sepaq.com/pq/mot) is the biggest and oldest of the province's national parks. Measuring 1,500 square kilometers it boasts six rivers, 400 lakes and streams, and 40 diverse animal species, including the wolf and moose. The park is so vast, it is accessible from three different entrances: St-Donat, St-Côme, and de la Diable.

Mont-Tremblant, which literally means "trembling mountain," is a popular holiday spot year-round; kayaks and canoes traverse the rivers and streams while pedal-boats and rowboats share the lakes with fishers and swimmers. Over 150 kilometers of hiking trails are available as well as 59 kilometers of mountain biking tracks. These turn into cross-country skiing and snowshoeing trails in the winter. Unique to the park is the Via Ferrata du Diable, a mix of hiking and climbing that takes you through part of the park not accessible otherwise.

If there's one northern pastime you have to indulge in, it's dogsledding. Not far from the park's Diable entrance is **Nordic Adventure Dog Sledding** (Place St-Bernard, 819/681-4848, www.tremblantactivities.com, $132). Offering the ultimate in Jack London fantasies, the guides here will teach you how a powerful team of eight harnessed huskies is steered and stopped before you hop on the sled to experience the ride firsthand. The two-hour ride winds up mountains, across frozen lakes, and through thick forest with a quick stop for hot chocolate to warm you up.

C Mont-Tremblant Resort

Just next door to the national park is Mont-Tremblant Resort (1000 Chemin des Voyageurs, Mont-Tremblant, 888/738-1777, www.tremblant.ca, late Nov.–mid-Apr. daily 8:30 A.M.–3:30 P.M., $75 adult), the premier ski resort in Eastern Canada and one of the best-known spots in the region. The first lodge and ski lift opened here in 1939, and no one has looked back since. The view from the mountain remains just as stunning now as then, and you can see the whole countryside from atop the 95 runs and numerous lifts. Acres of ramps, rails, and jumps are also available. Come for the day or stay over in one of the resort's brightly colored Disney-fied versions of a mountain town. In summer activities like biking and hiking take over the hills.

Ville de Mont-Tremblant

The actual village from which everything else got its name, the town of Mont-Tremblant (877/425-2434, www.villedemont-tremblant.qc.ca) is a nice change of pace from the hustle and bustle of the resort. Established in the late 1800s, Mont-Tremblant was one of many new villages founded by Father Antoine Labelle, who encouraged city folk to colonize the country. Since the late 1930s it has become a popular village, and the stores and restaurants reflect that. Take a stroll down the main strip, or pop into the **Maison des Arts et de la Culture Saint-Faustin** (1171 rue de la Pisciculture, 819/688-2676, www.maisondesarts.ca, Wed.–Sun. 11 A.M.–5 P.M.) to see the latest in the region's arts. Those visiting in the summer can get a taste of local life at **Le Marché d'Été de Mont-Tremblant village** (1875 chemin du Village, July–Sept. Sat. 9:30 A.M.–1 P.M.), the seasonal local market. And no matter when you're there stop by **La Cave à Bières** (856 Rue de St-Jovite, 819/681-7447), peruse the 200-plus beers they have in-store, and pick up a few hard-to-find microbrews.

RESTAURANTS

There are tons of restaurants in and around Mont-Tremblant Resort, but there are also plenty of independently run places worth checking out—many of them located in old converted houses—only a 10- to 15-minute drive away. If you head into downtown Mont-Tremblant stop at **Couleur Café** (415 rue Léonard, 819/681-0723, www.couleurcafe.ca, Tues.–Fri. 8 A.M.–6 P.M., Sat. 10 A.M.–5 P.M., $6–8) for a coffee, where the java is fair-trade and roasted on-site.

Not far away, ◖ **Seb l'Artisan Culinaire** (444 rue St-Georges, 819/429-6991, www.resto-seb.com, Wed.–Mon. 6 P.M., table d'hôte $45) is modern yet romantic. This converted old house is the setting for dishes made with fresh local ingredients like smoked organic duck breast and bison steak. The food is hearty but delicate and the wine list full of soon-to-be favorites.

Those lusting after some Québec seafood should head to **Le Cheval de Jade** (688 rue de St-Jovite, 819/425-5233, www.chevaldejade.com, Tues.–Sat. 5:30–9:30 P.M., $25–35) with delicacies like oysters and scallops and black cod on the menu. Situated in a house that was built in 1925, there's an elegant, relaxed vibe to the restaurant Though known for seafood Le Cheval de Jade also offers a unique specialty, duckling *à la Rouennaise,* a French dish in which the duck carcass is squeezed in a "duck press" that extracts the juices. A hard-to-find delicacy, even in France, it?s a must for any hard-core food fanatic. Call ahead to make a reservation for the dish, which serves two for $95.

There's no better place to dig into traditional, hearty Québécois grub than in the backcountry, surrounded by woods and mountains. Southeast of the ski hills is **La Cabane à Sucre Millette** (1357 rue St-Faustin, Saint-Faustin-Lac-Carré, 877/688-2101, www.tremblant-sugarshack.com, Mar.–Apr. Tues.–Sat. 11:30 A.M.–8 P.M., Sun. 10 A.M.–7 P.M.), a traditional Québec sugar shack, complete with log cabin and servers in checkered shirts and traditional *ceinture fléchée* (arrowed belts). A menu that's as long as your arm offers dishes like "scrunchies," eggs and sausages in maple syrup, baked beans, and maple taffy; it's sure to put you in a the best kind of food coma. If visiting in the off-season call ahead.

HOTELS

When it comes to hotels in Mont-Tremblant the obvious choice is the **Fairmont Mont-Tremblant** (3045 chemin de la Chapelle, 866/540-4415, www.fairmont.com/tremblant, $250–525), with its luxurious rooms, great views, and the convenience of skiing down the mountain and right up to your hotel. The spa and restaurant with a roaring winter fire are icing on the cake.

Built in 1942 by Joe and Mary Ryan, the founders of the Mont-Tremblant Resort, it is no surprise that ◖ **Château Beauvallon** (6385 Montée Ryan, 888/681-6611, www.chateaubeauvallon.com, $174 and up) is equally as luxurious as the Fairmont but off the well-beaten path. Offering 70 different suites, Beauvallon has a secluded feel with views of Lake Tremblant.

Many of the best places to stay are small inns a few minutes away from the mountain. Looking out over Lac Mercier, the **Auberge la Porte Rouge** (1874 chemin du Village, 819/425-3505, www.aubergelaporterouge.com, $184–234) looks and feels more like a friend's cottage than a midsize inn. In a nice surprise the rates include a gourmet dinner and hearty breakfast.

If bed-and-breakfasts are more your thing, the **Crystal Inn** (100 Joseph Thibault, 819/681-7775, www.crystal-inn.com, $120 and up) offers an intimate and unique experience. Each of the four suites is decorated according to the healing powers of different crystals—agate, amethyst, sun stone—and each room has its own fireplace and is decorated with hand-painted murals. Breakfast and a session at the in-house nature spa are also included.

INFORMATION AND SERVICES

Covering all aspects of the area, including the resort and the old Mont-Tremblant village, **Tourisme Mont-Tremblant** (www.tourismemonttremblant.com, 877/605-4746) has all the information you need to get your bearings in the area. Local maps and even package deals are accessible on-site, and it also has links to the chamber of commerce and detailed information on getting to and from the area. Once there the **Tourist Information Bureau** (5080

Montée Ryan, daily 9 A.M.–5 P.M.) will be able to help you with anything else.

GETTING THERE
By Air
Boutique airline **Porter** (888/619-8622, www.flyporter.com) offers direct flights to Mont-Tremblant International Airport from major U.S. and Canadian hubs, including Boston, Chicago Midway, New York Newark, Toronto Island Airport, and Ottawa. There's even a flight from Montréal that will take all of 25 minutes in the air. Many of these flights are only offered December–March. Shuttles are available from the airport to the resort and town.

All international and national flights to Montréal arrive at **Pierre Trudeau International Airport** (www.admtl.com) in Dorval. A shuttle bus service offered by **Skyport** (800/471-1155, www.skyportinternational.com, $68 one-way) departs Trudeau for Mont-Tremblant four times a day in winter and twice a day in summer.

By Bus
A coach is available daily from Montréal's main bus terminal, **Gare d'Autocars** (505 blvd. de Maisonneuve E., 514 842-2281, www.stationcentrale.com). The trip with **Galland** (514/333-9555, www.autobusgalland.com, $61 round-trip) takes about 2.5 hours and will deposit you at a gas station/convenience store about 10 minutes from the resort.

By Car
Driving from Montréal to Mont-Tremblant couldn't be simpler. Take Highway 40 West to Highway 15 North and drive straight for about 90 minutes. After Sainte-Agathe the 15 becomes Route 117 North; continue till you get to Mont-Tremblant.

GETTING AROUND
The easiest way to get around Mont-Tremblant is by car. If you don't have your own there is a **Performance Laurentides Budget** (1345 Route 117, 888/357-3157, www.budget.ca) rental agency in the center of town. Public buses are available for a cost of $2 per ride; the schedule and routes can be found on the chamber of commerce's website (www.ccdemonttremblant.com).

Lower Laurentians

Even closer to the city, about an hour or so drive from downtown, there are different areas to be explored that are perfect for an entire day, or even just an afternoon. Still part of the Laurentians, the geography overall is slightly flatter, and though a few ski hills can still be found, you won't find bigger mountains than those in the north. Instead the Lower Laurentians are populated with towns and villages and summer homes laid out along the shores of freshwater lakes. Forests and low mountains still define the area, but it's the lakes and villages that set it apart.

Many of the places could be visited individually in a day, or if you get an early start or stay out late, some places that are closer together, like Sainte-Agathe-des-Monts and Val-David, are doable in a single day. If you want to take advantage of the area but only have a day to spare, pick a single town and spend the day exploring by foot. Returning to the city along smaller roads is also a great way to feel like you're getting the most out of your day.

SIGHTS AND RECREATION
Oka
Northwest of the city just off the island is **Oka National Park** (2020 chemin Oka, 450/479-8365, www.sepaq.com/pq/oka, $8/adult). Easily accessible, it offers outdoor recreation year-round. June–September locals flock to the beaches on the shores of Lac des Deux-Montagnes for a swim or to try their hand at windsurfing, one of the lake's popular sports.

© TOURISME DE LAURENTIDES

the village of Saint-Sauveur in the winter

Another one of the park's biggest draws is the wetlands, where marshes mingle with the boreal forest. Explore them by walking the Grande Baie trail, or canoeing through the Rivière des Serpents. In 1742 the Sulpicians defined their presence in this area when they built the Way of the Cross. Revisit the stone structures and chapels by walking the 4.5-kilometer Calvaire d'Oka path. In winter the park offers 47 kilometers of cross-country skiing trails and 16 kilometers of snowshoeing. Throughout summer the park is accessible by Route 644 in the east and Highway 640 in the west, with the latter closed during winter.

The **Marina d'Oka** (257 rue des Anges, 450/479-8323, www.marinadoka.com, mid-May–mid-Oct.) is one of the more picturesque marinas in the area. Located on Lac des Deux-Montagnes, accessed by downtown Oka, a small shop sells boating accessories and decorative items as well as seafaring wear, while the small lakeside bistro is great place to grab a bite and look out over the water.

Saint-Sauveur

Head north out of the city and in less than an hour you'll hit Saint-Sauveur. Incorporated in 1855, the village and the surrounding ski hills have since become a weekend destination. There's still a feel of an old downtown main street with many of the stores situated in converted houses. Though they've since been turned into restaurants and stores, many of them are dedicated to sports gear and winter wear with a few dedicated to antiques.

Those looking to nab a bargain are likely to find it at the city's many outlet stores. Nike, Diesel, Guess, La Senza, and Reebok can all be found at **Les Factoreries** (100 Guindon, 800/363-0332, www.factoreries. com, Mon.–Wed. 10 A.M.–6 P.M., Thurs.–Fri. 10 A.M.–9 P.M., Sat.–Sun. 10 A.M.–5 P.M.).

The town also plays host to yearly celebration of music and dance. Around since the early 1990s, the **Festival des Arts de Saint-Sauveur** (www.fass.ca, late July–early Aug.) has everything from contemporary to hiphop dance and traditional music from around the world. Many of the events are for free.

Also in summer, **Parc Aquatique du Mont St-Sauveur** (350 ave. St-Denis, 450/227-4671, www.mssi.ca, $33 adult, $27 youth, $15

PICK YOUR OWN: APPLE ORCHARDS

Vergers or apple orchards flourish in Québec, and from September to late October the Eastern Townships are full of different varieties of apples ready to be picked. The perfect afternoon outing, especially if you're with the kids, apple-picking offers a great escape form the city as well as a closer look at the leaves in all their autumn glory. Orchards can be found throughout the Townships, but here are a few that are just a short drive from Montréal. Though most orchards are open throughout the week in high season, call ahead if you're unsure of times, since opening hours are often dependent on weather conditions.

• **Cidrerie et Verger Léo Boutin:** A-710 Rang de la Montagne, Mont St-Grégoire, 450/346-3326, www.vergerboutin.com, daily 8 A.M.-4 P.M.

• **Vergers et Cidrerie Denis Charbonneau:** 575 Rang de la Montagne, Mont St-Grégoire, 450/347-9184, www.vergersdc.qc.ca, Sept.-Oct. daily 9 A.M.-4 P.M., Oct.-Sept. Sat.-Sun. 9 A.M.-4 P.M.

• **Verger du Flanc Nord:** 835 chemin Rouillard, Mont St-Hilaire, 450/464-7432, www.vergerduflancnord.com, mid-Aug.-mid-Oct., daily 8 A.M.-7 P.M.

• **Verger du Flâneur:** 1161 La Petite Caroline, Rougemont, 450/469-0505, Sept.-Oct. daily 9 A.M.-5 P.M.

• **Verger du Pavillon de la Pomme:** 1130 Sir Wilfrid Laurier, Mont St-Hilaire, 450/464-2654, www.pavillondelapomme.com, daily 9 A.M.-6 P.M.

child) is one of the area's biggest attractions. One of Canada's largest water parks, it features rafting, a wave pool, a tidal-wave river, and slides.

Thanks to a few hard-working snow machines, **Mont-Saint-Sauveur** (350 rue St-Denis, 450/277-4671, www.montsaintsauveur.com, Dec.–late Apr., $50) has one of the longest winter seasons in the country with hills and snowboard runs open well into April and sometimes even May. The hills also have nighttime lighting for after-work runs, and the latest attraction is a year-round alpine roller coaster.

Sainte-Agathe-des-Monts

Continue further north on Route 117 and you'll reach the quaint town of Sainte-Agathe-des-Monts (www.ville.sainte-agathe-des-monts.qc.ca). Situated on Lac des Sables, it's one of the most popular cottage towns in the region. Established in 1849, by the 1860s it was a thriving, mostly Francophone community that eventually grew to include many Anglophone residents. Today, it's one of the most diverse towns in the region, with a large population of English-speaking and Jewish

summer residents originally drawn here in the early part of the 20th century not only for the town's proximity to Montréal but also for the good, clean mountain air (part of Mordecai Richler's *The Apprenticeship of Duddy Kravitz* was even set here). For a fair number of years one of the town's main draws was its benefits for the ill and convalescing and those suffering from tuberculosis. The Laurentian and Mount Sinai Sanatoriums were both located here, and you can see their influences reflected in the architecture of old homes equipped with large covered balconies and solariums.

At the end of the main street (rue Principale)—lined with the original Catholic church and restaurants and boutiques that have been refurbished to capture their original glory—you'll find the Lac des Sables and the **Croisières Alouette** (866/326-3656, www.croisierealouette.com, late May–late Oct., $14). A staple in the area since the 1940s, these 50-minute cruises give you a bit of context by pointing out historical sights, celebrity homes, and features of the landscapes. They're especially nice in fall when the leaves are multicolored.

EXCURSIONS

Val-David

Few towns in this region have the same hippie commune vibe as Val-David, one that is slowly but surely changing into a younger and slightly more accessible boho vibe. Nestled in the Laurentians this former mill town has become known for the amateur artists that have worked and lived here. Because of the large number of artists who make Val-David (www.valdavid.com) their home, the town offers self-guided tours that point out public art works and take you to a number of artist studios. Since the town is highly concentrated it's fairly easy to get around, with many of the sites next door to each other. The **Centre d'Exposition de Val-David** (2495 rue de l'Église, 819/322-7474, www.culture.valdavid.qc.ca, summer daily 11 A.M.–5 P.M., winter Wed.–Sun. 10 A.M.–5 P.M.) holds regular exhibits by local and regional artists with exhibitions changing regularly.

Those interested in the history of the town's architecture can guide themselves around the various historic buildings, including **Magasin Général Alexis-Guindon** (2475 rue de l'Église),

a general store built in 1919 that remains virtually unchanged, and **Moulin Georgine-du-Perré** (1267 rue de la Sapinière), a private residence that was built to resemble an old French mill—stone work, circular roof, and all.

Dufresne Regional Park

For the best climbing on the country's East Coast head to Dufresne Regional Park (1165 chemin du Condor, 888/322-7030, www.parcregionaldufresne.com). The site of the first ever rock climbing competition in Québec, the park now has over 500 routes, including walls for those just beginning to learn and walls that'll challenge those who've been doing it for a lifetime. Dedicated to preserving the local ecosystem—it was created largely by locals—it is also a great place to bird-watch, check out the native plants, hike through in the summer, and cross-country ski in the winter.

Parc Linéaire le P'tit Train du Nord

After drawing people to the region in the mid-

Parc Linéaire le P'tit Train du Nord

© TOURISME DE LAURENTIDES

1800s, Antoine Labelle's second feat was the construction of a railway that carried visitors and holiday makers from the outer reaches of the city all the way into the northern Laurentians. Built between 1891 and 1901, it was this advancement that allowed the area to grow. Made obsolete 100 years later by highways and cars, the old railway is now the Parc Linéaire le P'tit Train du Nord (800/561-6673, www.laurentians.com/parclineaire), a 230-kilometer-long recreational trail running from Saint-Jérôme to Mont-Laurier.

Providing a north–south crossing, it's most used by cyclists in the summer, many of whom spend days exploring the region. If cycling's not your bag, inline skating and hiking are also permitted on the trail and will still let you see the beauty of the area and the stunning vistas the trail offers. In winter snowmobiling is allowed between Labelle and Mont-Laurier, and cross-country skiing is possible between Saint-Jérôme and Val-David. All along the trail the old railway stations have been converted into cafés, repair shops, and information centers. There are campsites along the way, and the park will help you arrange baggage transport.

Village du Père Nöel
The spirit of Christmas, and Santa himself, can be found throughout the year at Village du Père Nöel (987 Morin, 819/322-2146, www.noel.qc.ca, June–Sept. daily 10 A.M.–6 P.M., Dec.–Jan. daily 11 A.M.–5 P.M., $12.50 both adult and child). This outdoor children's play park offers a ton of activities for kids age two and up. A tree house, electrical train, goat run, zip line, and slides are open no matter the weather, and kids will get a kick out of winter skating and Santa's house, where they can meet the man himself.

RESTAURANTS
Before heading out for a morning of apple picking in Oka, dig into breakfast at the orchard's restaurant. **O'Verger Gourmand** (4354 chemin Oka, Oka, 450/472-2463, www.vergerduparc640.populus.org, Fri.–Sun. 7:30 A.M.–1:30 P.M., $17) serves weekend brunch using fresh, seasonal ingredients. Brightly decorated with lots of light, it's a perfect place for families with kids.

Orange & Pamplemousse (120 rue Principale, Saint-Sauveur, 450/227-4330, www.orangepamplemousse.com, Wed.–Thurs. and Sun. 8 A.M.–9 P.M., Fri.–Sat. 8 A.M.–10 P.M., closed daily 3–5 P.M., $20) in Saint-Sauveur is a young and modern bistro with an outdoor patio in summer. They serve breakfast staples like eggs Benedict and crêpes and dynamic dinner fare like veal with maple syrup and cranberries and lamb with walnuts and honey, all at reasonable prices.

For more classic bistro fare there's **La Bohème** (251 rue Principale, Saint-Sauveur, 450/227-6644, www.restoboheme.com, daily 5–10 P.M., $20), a dark, cozy neighborhood staple with a bar that's often busy. The dishes here include mussels and fries and New York steak.

In Val-David you can smell the deliciousness of the freshly baked bread at **La Vagabonde** (1262 chemin de la Rivière, Val-David, 819/322-3953, www.boulangerielavagabonde.com, daily 8 A.M.–6 P.M., $10) from around the block. Organic homemade breads (chocolate and cranberry loaf, sourdough rye) and pastries (croissants, *chocolatines*) are the specialties here, but they also offer great sandwiches and soups, and whip up a mean latte.

The minimal design of **Les Zèbres** (2301 rue de l'Église, Val-David, 819/322-3196, www.restaurantleszebres.com, Thurs.–Sun. 5 P.M.–close, $30) means it is essentially a glass-walled cabin that looks both totally out of place and totally at home in this natural setting. The menu of market-fresh food changes regularly, so heading to the restaurant for a specific dish is besides the point; instead it's all about the modern design and vibrant ambience. It is often packed so call ahead to reserve.

HOTELS
When it comes to spending the night in **Oka National Park** (2020 chemin Oka, 450/479-8365, www.sepaq.com/pq/oka) the only accommodation choice you have is your tent

or theirs. That being said, the park does offer rental Huttopia tents ($109 per night), which are large enough for a family of four and have a kitchen, two bunk areas, and even wood floors—perfect if you're not in the mood for roughing it. You can reserve tents through the park's website.

In the middle of Saint-Sauveur valley and overlooking the ski hill is **Hotel St-Sauveur** (500 chemin des Frênes, 450/227-1800, www.hotelstsauveur.ca, $99–300), a modern hotel that mixes cozy, antique-style furnishings and minimal design. It's a great option especially if you're traveling in a group. Each unit has a fireplace and balcony, and a kitchen where you can whip up your own breakfasts.

Reminiscent of an old ski chalet—peaked roofs, stone walls in the foyer—the **Manoir Saint-Sauveur** (246 chemin du Lac Millette, Saint-Sauveur, 800/361-0505, www.manoir-saint-sauveur.com, $169–350) is located in the middle of the village with views overlooking the slopes. Those staying in summer can hang out at the outdoor pools or play a round of tennis before heading off for an afternoon hike. Luxuriously decorated rooms are all fitted with an espresso machine, Wi-Fi, and views of the surrounding hills.

Staying true to the area's roots, **Auberge du Lac des Sables** (230 rue St-Venant, Sainte-Agathe-des-Monts, 800/567-8329, www.aubergedulac.com, $169–300), with its back on to the forest and view of the lake, is the personification of good, clean mountain air. Though the interior is nothing spectacular, it has a cozy, cottage feel that is perfectly at home in the surroundings.

The Laurentians have been a vacation destination since vacations became a thing, so why not stay at the most storied of hotels? **Hôtel la Sapinière** (1244 chemin La Sapinière, Val-David, 800/567-6635, www.sapiniere.com, $166–250) in Val-David was built in 1936 by Mayor Léonidas Dufresne to advance tourism in the region. It remains the quintessential Laurentian hotel. The charming country-style hotel has a cottage feel with antique-style furniture, stone walls, exposed ceiling beams, and

fireplaces in many of the rooms. As in the early days the emphasis here is on the cuisine, which you can experience while looking out over the lake.

INFORMATION AND SERVICES

Each town has its own tourist center with all the information you need for the town and surrounding area. **Oka National Park's Discovery and Information Center** (450/479-8365, www.sepaq.com/pq/oka, mid-May–mid-Oct., daily 8 A.M.–5 P.M.) is located just inside the Route 644 entrance. There's also the easily accessible **Oka National Park's Le Littoral Visitors Centre** (450/479-8365, www.sepaq.com/pq/oka, daily 8 A.M.–5 P.M., open year-round), which has a ski shop, waxing room, first aid services, and a restaurant.

Saint-Sauveur's Tourist Office (605 chemin des Frênes, 450/227-3417, daily 9 A.M.–5 P.M.) covers all aspects of the region, including the slopes. **Sainte-Agathe-des-Monts's Tourist Office** (24 rue St-Paul, 888/326-0457, www.sainte-agathe.org, summer daily 9 A.M.–6 P.M., winter daily 9 A.M.–5 P.M.) is open year-round.

In Val-David, road maps, brochures, and souvenirs are all available at **Val-David Tourist Office** (2525 de l'Église, 888/322-7030, ext. 235, mid-May–mid-Oct. and mid-Dec.–mid-Mar. 9 A.M.–5 P.M.).

GETTING THERE AND AROUND
By Bus

All of the Laurentians can be reached by **Galland** (514/333-9555, www.autobusgalland.com) coach lines, which are available daily from Montréal's main bus terminal, **Gare d'Autocars** (505 blvd. de Maisonneuve E., 514/842-2281, www.stationcentrale.com). To Oka the trip takes about 45 minutes and costs $22 round-trip. The same coach that takes you to Mont-Tremblant will also take you to Saint-Sauveur in about 90 minutes ($38 round-trip), Sainte-Agathe-des-Monts in two hours and ten minutes ($47 round-trip), and Val-David in two and a half hours ($47 round-trip).

By Car

Driving is by far the easiest way to there and get around, especially if you want to see more than one village or are taking equipment like ski gear. From Montréal take Highway 40 West to Highway 15 North and watch out for the signposts. All of the towns are easily accessible off of Highway 15 (which eventually becomes Route 117 North). To get to Oka, take Highway 15 to Highway 13, then head west on Highway 640.

Cantons de l'Est

Southeast of the city you'll find the low, rolling hills, flatlands, and picturesque towns of the Cantons de l'Est (Eastern Townships). Traditionally the home of the Abenaki Amerindians, the Eastern Townships were later colonized by the United Empire Loyalists, who sided with the British during the American Revolution. Though many of the town's roots started with the Loyalists, it wasn't until the turn of the 19th century that immigration from the United States exploded, especially by wealthy folk looking for a place to build their dream summer home. This distinct patrimony is what sets the Eastern Townships apart from the rest of the province, and it can still be seen today in the architecture, the culture, and the language.

Interesting towns and villages can be found throughout the region. Since many of them are also close to one another, you can easily visit one or two in a day. Depending on what sights you're attracted to, an afternoon or day in the region is enough time to get the overall feel of the place. If you want to do a bit more serious exploring it's better to spend at least one night in one of the many towns, and a weekend is ideal for those interested in cycling around the region or exploring the area's many wineries.

SIGHTS
Granby

One of the bigger towns on the Eastern Townships map, Granby (www.ville.granby.qc.ca) has a lovely old main street (called rue Principale) down which you can stroll browsing the shops and cafés and seeing some of the area's older architecture. Built on the textile, lumber, and dairy businesses it is one of the more commercial towns, but the main attraction is the Granby Zoo.

◖ GRANBY ZOO

The Granby Zoo (1050 blvd. David-Bouchard, 877/472-6299, www.zoogranby.ca, late June–Aug. daily 10 A.M.–7 P.M., Sept.–Oct. Sat.–Sun. 10 A.M.–5 P.M., $33 adult, $22 child) is home to over 1,000 animals. Watch the hippopotamus swimming underwater in the Hippo River, feed the sharks, see the gorillas in their very own valley, and get to know the kangaroos as they hop around.

Sherbrooke

The largest city in the Eastern Townships and the region's commercial center, Sherbrooke (www.ville.sherbrooke.qc.ca) has a downtown core filled with shops and restaurants. First settled by Loyalists in 1793, it was originally an English-speaking town, but today the majority of the city's 200,000 residents are Francophones. It also has a large student population and is the home of two universities, the Francophone Université de Sherbrooke and the Anglophone Bishops University, which became part of the city in 2002 when Lennoxville merged with Sherbrooke.

◖ MUSEUM OF SCIENCE AND NATURE

Some of the best sights in the city are the many museums. Kids (and parents) get a chance to learn about southern Québec's natural surroundings at the Museum of Science and Nature (225 rue Frontenac, 819/564-3200, www.naturesciences.qc.ca, early Sept.–mid-June Wed.–Sun. 10 A.M.–5 P.M., mid-June–early Sept. daily 10 A.M.–5 P.M., $7.50 adult,

EXCURSIONS

ORFORD EXPRESS

Russia may have the Trans-Siberian Railway, but the Eastern Townships have the Orford Express (720 rue Minto, Marché de la Gare, 866/575-8081, www.orfordexpress.com, May–late Oct. Wed.–Sun., $66–100). Mixing a little sightseeing with a gourmet meal the train takes you through the countryside of the Eastern Townships from Sherbrooke, through Magog, to Eastman, and back.

The train ride offers views of the region that you might not get otherwise. The train consists of three restaurant-coach cars; each one is decorated to recall the good old days of rail travel with white tablecloths, soft lighting, and sumptuous curtains on the windows of the main car. The latest edition to the trains is the lounge car, with panoramic windows that give you an unobstructed view of the landscape.

Three different journeys are available: a weekend brunch, a late-afternoon lunch (Le P'tit Plaisir Gourmand), and a dinner meal (Le Souper à Brunante), all served as three-course meals. They include dishes like chef's quiche, duck confit, veal carpaccio, guinea fowl, and puff pastry with snails and mushrooms.

For those interested in the view but not so interested in the meal, they offer specially priced "l'Escapade" tickets at the station depending on availability.

$5 child), where interactive exhibits teach kids about everything from the river ecology to renewable energy.

MUSÉE DES BEAUX ARTS DE SHERBROOKE

Situated in the old Eastern Township Bank, the Musée des Beaux Arts de Sherbrooke (241 rue Dufferin, 819/821-2115, www.mbas.qc.ca, summer Tues.–Sun. 10 A.M.–5 P.M., winter Tues.–Sun. noon–5 P.M., $7.50 adult) has a diverse collection of works dating from the 19th right up to the 21st century from both Canadian and Québécois artists.

LA SOCIÉTÉ D'HISTOIRE DE SHERBROOKE

Discover the history of the town and the people who created it through the permanent exhibits at La Société d'Histoire de Sherbrooke (275 rue Dufferin, 819/821-5406, www.histoiresherbrooke.com, early Sept.–mid-June Tues.–Fri. 9 a.m.–5 p.m., Sat.–Sun. 1–5 p.m., mid-June–early Sept. Tues.–Fri. 9 a.m.–5 p.m., Sat.–Sun. 10 a.m.–5 p.m., $4). The center also offers a number of tours, including a self-guided one of the downtown streets ($4 with iPod and map) and a tour of the Frontenac Power Station ($4).

RÉSEAU RIVERAIN

Explore the area's riverside with a stroll (or ride) along the Réseau Riverain. This bike and walking path runs alongside the Magog River for 18 kilometers. Starting at Blanchford Park it takes you through the Magog River Gorge and has panels all along the pathway pointing out interesting points or historical facts.

LION D'OR

Beer fans should pop in to the Lion d'Or (2 rue de College, Lennoxville, 819/562-4589, www.lionlennoxville.com) for a well-pulled pint of Lion's Pride, the pub's flagship dark brown brew. It opened in 1973, and they started brewing their own in 1986, making the Lion d'Or the oldest microbrewery in Québec. Call ahead for a guided tour and an "après-tour" tasting.

Lac Brome

Surrounding the lake of the same name, the town of Lac Brome is made up of seven smaller villages. One of the more popular tourist destinations is the village of **Knowlton,** whose downtown core is full of restaurants, boutiques, antiques dealers, and cafés, which set in restored Victorian buildings.

The town is also known for the Lac Brome duck. Reared in the area, the duck is found on menus throughout the region and is celebrated with the yearly **Duck Festival** (www.canardenfete.com), which takes place in the month of September. Visitors are given the chance to taste the world-renowned duck and enjoy concerts and the farmers market, and watch a winner waddle its way to victory at the duck race.

BROME COUNTY HISTORICAL MUSEUM

Stop into the Brome County Historical Museum (130 chemin Lakeside, 450/243-6782, daily mid-May–mid-Sept., $5 adult, $3 senior/student, $2.50 child) in the center of town to check various artifacts connected to the area's past, including a rare World War I Fokker plane.

◖ THEATRE LAC BROME

During the summer months, Theatre Lac Brome (9 Mont-Echo, Knowlton, 450/242-2270, www.theatrelacbrome.ca) becomes one of the best summer stages in the province, presenting a number of works in English, from classics like *Pygmalion* and *Our Town* to pieces

by Canadian playwrights and a number of its own commissioned works. They also have other events, including musical performances happening throughout the year.

North Hatley

Sitting on the northern shore of Lake Massawippi, North Hatley is one of the most beautiful towns in the region. A popular summer resort, it first attracted aristocrats, savvy businessmen, and other rich, mostly American tourists in mid-1800s. The town's popularity grew even more with the opening of the railway in the 1880s and it became a haven for many American playboys during Prohibition. Today, much of that history remains in the architecture, with many of the grand old homes converted into hotels and bed-and-breakfasts.

Though the year-round population here is under 1,000, it is home to a few antiques shops, artist studios, folk art shops, and a few galleries, including **Galerie Jeannine Blais** (102 rue Main, 819/842-2784, www.galeriejeannineblais.com, Nov.–mid-June

EXCURSIONS

© STEPHANE LEMIRE

the quaint town of North Hatley in autumn

© PAUL LARAMEE

Abbaye St-Benoît-du-Lac is known for its cheeses.

Thurs.–Mon. 10 A.M.–5 P.M., mid-June–Oct. daily 10 A.M.–5 P.M.), devoted entirely to art naïf.

English plays take over the summer stage at **Théâtre Piggery** (215 chemin Simard, 819/842-2431, www.piggery.com), and musical acts can be seen all year. In summer cool off on the shores of the lake with a dip or a day out boating. North Hatley is quiet town, and there isn't much in the way of sights, but that hasn't stopped it from being one of the most sought-after places in the region; those thinking of visiting and staying should book well in advance.

Abbaye St-Benoît-du-Lac

Founded in 1912, overlooking Lake Memphremagog, Abbaye St-Benoît-du-Lac (819/843-4080, www.st-benoit-du-lac.com, church daily 5 A.M.–8:30 P.M., shop Mon.–Sat. 9–10:45 A.M. and 11:50 A.M.–4 P.M.) is home to more than 50 monks who continue to work and live here. Designed by Dom Bellot, the abbey is known throughout the province for

the monks' cheeses—they make 10 different types including Blue Ermite and Fontina—jams, cider, and other goods that are made on the premises. Those looking for a quiet place for contemplation can stay at their men's hostel, and there's also a women's hostel in a nearby nunnery. The public are invited to join the monks in daily prayer and Gregorian chant (daily 7:30 A.M., 11 A.M., and 5 P.M.).

Coaticook

In the southernmost part of the Eastern Townships, bordering on the U.S., is the town of Coaticook. Though the town is full of quaint buildings there are few sights here; instead, people come for the scenic surroundings.

PARC DE LA GORGE-DE-COATICOOK

Parc de la Gorge-de-Coaticook (135 rue Michaud, 888/524-6743, www.gorgedecoaticook.qc.ca, summer daily 9 A.M.–5 P.M., winter Mon.–Fri. 11 A.M.–5 P.M., Sat.–Sun. 9 A.M.–5 P.M.) is best known for its magnificent suspension bridge, one of the longest pedestrian suspension bridges in the world. It sits 50 meters above the gorge. There is more to this park than the breathtaking views (though admittedly they are the main attraction)—hiking and mountain biking trails are available throughout the summer, as is horseback riding, with horses and gear available for rent by the hour. In winter the main attractions are snowshoeing and sledding. Stay at one on the park's campsites, or rent one of their on-site cabins.

◀ La Route des Vins

Not far from the American border, in the Brome-Missisquoi lowlands you'll find over 120 kilometers of wineries. Inaugurated in 2003, La Route des Vins (888/811-4928, www.laroutedesvins.ca) takes you through the valleys and bends of a picturesque region with a winery at almost every corner. Seventeen wineries can be found on this route, and maps can be picked up at the region's tourist centers. All of the wineries are open June–October with some of them open throughout the year.

Québec's specialty is ice wine, a dessert wine that is semi-sweet and produced from grapes that have been frozen on the vine. **Vignoble Chapelle Ste-Agnès** (2565 chemin Scenic, Sutton, 450/583-0303, www.vindeglace.com, June–Oct. Wed. and Sun. 1:30 P.M., reservations required otherwise, $25 tasting tour) has a monastic feel with its Romanesque stone chapel and vaulted stone cellars.

Domaine Pinnacle (150 chemin Richford, Frelighsburg, 450/298-1226, www.domainepinnacle.com, May–Dec. daily 10 A.M.–5 P.M., Jan.–Apr. Sat.–Sun. 10 A.M.–5 P.M.) produces one of the best-known ice wines in the region in the shadow of Mount Pinnacle. The winery's 1859 farmhouse is an inviting place for a tasting.

A unique selection of wines is available to taste at **Val Caudalies** (4921 rue Principale, Durham, 450/295-2333, www.valcaudalies.com, mid-May–Nov. Wed.–Sun. 10 A.M.–6 P.M., Dec. Sat.–Sun. 10 A.M.–6 P.M., Jan.–May reservation only), where they make everything from rosé to ice cider, cider liqueur, and Vidal semi-dry white wine. Visitors are

invited to pick apples and grapes in their vineyards and orchards.

The only producer of chardonnay in Québec is **Vignoble Les Pervenches** (150 chemin Boulais, 450/293-8311, www.lespervenches.com, June–Oct. Wed.–Sun. 10 A.M.–4 P.M., free, self-guided tours). It's also one of the few organic wineries in the region. Along with chardonnay they produce two varieties of red using traditional methods.

Producing dry whites, rosés, and reds, **Domaine Vitis** (1095 chemin Nord, Bromont, 450/263-4988, www.domainevitis.com, May–Dec. Wed.–Sun. 10 A.M.–5 P.M., tours 10 A.M., noon, 2 P.M., and 4 P.M., $10–20) is one of the largest wineries in the region, offering tours throughout the day. Don't pass up a tasting of their Glace Noire, a dark, fruity ice wine that is unlike the others in the area.

RESTAURANTS

If one microbrewery in Sherbrooke isn't enough for you, check out hip **Siboire** (80 du Dépôt, Sherbrooke, 819/565-3636, www.siboire.ca, daily noon–to close, $20), located in the downtown core. The high ceilings and open floor plan make it a welcoming place to grab a pint. Four permanent beers and two seasonals are made on the premises. You can also enjoy them on the sidewalk *terrasse*. For a sweet treat head over to **Savoroso** (720 rue Minto, Sherbrooke, 819/346-2206, www.savoroso.com, winter daily 10 A.M.–6 P.M., summer daily 10 A.M.–10 P.M., $10) in the train station market. A popular place for gelato in the summer, it also serves up coffees, pastries, sandwiches, and salads, making it perfect for a light lunch.

In Knowlton pick up some fresh, homemade bread at **Panissimo** (291-A rue Knowlton, Knowlton, 450/242-2412, daily 8 A.M.–5 P.M., $10), where they specialize in traditional French baguettes and aromatic focaccia. Gourmands and cheese fiends will love **Brie et Cie** (291-C rue Knowlton, Knowlton, 450/242-2996, www.brieetcie.com, Mon.–Sun. 10 A.M.–5 P.M., $10 lunch, $25 dinner), a small café and bistro that has a wide selection of international and local cheeses as well as specialty foods. Go for breakfast or try their Québec cheese plate. They also serve a select number of dishes on Saturday night; call ahead to reserve.

As the saying goes, when in Brome...you have to try Lac Brome duck, and there's no better place to taste it than at Knowlton's **Le Relais** (286 chemin Knowlton, Knowlton, 450/242-6886, www.aubergeknowlton.ca/relais, daily 11 A.M.–10 P.M., $25). Located in Auberge Knowlton, it has an entire menu dedicated to the local delicacy, as well as a number of standard dishes.

North Hatley's **Pilsen** (55 rue Main, North Hatley, 819/842-2971, www.pilsen.ca, Mon.–Sat. noon–11 P.M.) is one of the livelier restaurants in the area. Located on the water, this pub and restaurant serves classic pub grub like bangers and mash as well as finer selections like grilled salmon and ribs. Get a taste of local ingredients and cooking at the upscale **Plaisir Gourmand** (2225 Rte. 143, North Hatley, 819/838.1061, www.plaisirgourmand.com, Oct.–June Thurs.–Sun. 6:30 P.M., June–Oct. Wed.–Sun. 6:30 P.M.); go for gold with the seven-course tasting menu or opt for à la carte selections like braised lamb and roast boar.

Coaticook is well known for its cheeses, and **Fromagerie La Station** (440 chemin de Hatley, Compton, 819/835-5301, www.fromagerielastation.com, June–Nov. daily 10 A.M.–5 P.M., Dec.–May Thurs.–Sun. 10 A.M.–5 P.M.) specializes in raw organic milk cheese and gives tours of their workshop and farm. Try the freshest goat cheese you'll ever taste at **Domaine de Courval** (825 chemin de Courval, Waterville, 819/837-0062, Wed.–Mon. 11 A.M.–5:30 P.M.). This artisanal *fromagerie* has five different flavors of rich but delicate cheese as well as two aged varieties and a triple cream. A map of all the local *fromageries* is available at the tourist office.

Anyone who grew up in Québec likely has a soft spot for **Coaticook Ice Cream** (1000 rue Child, Coaticook, 800/846-7224, www.laiteriedecoaticook.com, Oct.–Mar. Mon.–Sat. 8 A.M.–6 P.M., Apr.–May Mon.–Wed. 8 A.M.–6 P.M., Thurs.–Sat. 8 A.M.–9 P.M., Sun.

11 A.M.–6 P.M., June–Sept. Mon.–Sat. 8 A.M.–10 P.M., Sun. 11 A.M.–10 P.M.). Established in 1940, the small business has grown to become one of the biggest in the region, but they still make it the way they used to, with real cream. Their *bar laitier*, or ice cream bar, is open all year around and has all the latest flavors on hand for you to choose from as well as other products for you to check out, like their Capricook goat cheese and Québec cheddar.

RECREATION
Bicycling
Spanning 4,000 kilometers and linking all parts of the province, **La Route Verte** (800/567-8356, www.routeverte.com) is the ultimate cyclist's dream. Initiated in the late 1990s, most of the major cycling trails in Québec, like those that travel alongside the St-Lawrence River or head deep into the Laurentians, are part of this linking route. The proximity of the towns in the Eastern Townships and the area's lower-lying lands, however, make it an ideal spot to use the Route Verte, even for the most occasional of bikers. Bring your own ride with you or rent one for the day from rental outlets in Lac Brome, Sherbrooke, Orford, and Granby.

Skiing
Ski hills can be found not too far from the city, great for hitting the runs after work or for a day-long outing. Not too far from the town of Magog is **Mont-Orford** (4380 chemin du Parc, 866/673-31, www.orford.com, Dec.–Apr. Mon.–Fri. 8 A.M.–4:30 P.M., Sat.–Sun. 9:30 A.M.–4:30 P.M., $47 day pass), one of the best skiing spots in the province. With the fourth highest summit in Québec, it consists of three mountains (Orford, Giroux, and Alfred Desrochers) and 61 trails.

Rising over the western shores of Lake Memphremagog, **Owl's Head** (40 chemin du Mont Owl's Head, 800/363-3342, www.owlshead.com, Dec.–Apr. daily 8:30 A.M.–4 P.M., $42 day pass) offers 45 trails of varying difficulty with the majority in the intermediate range and is about an hour and 20 minutes outside of Montréal.

Even closer to the city, about a 45-minute drive away, is **Ski Bromont** (150 Champlain, 866/276-6668, www.skibromont.com, Dec.–Apr. Mon.–Thurs. and Sun. 8:30 A.M.–10 P.M., Fri.–Sat. 8:30 A.M.–10:30 P.M., $49 day pass). Taking over Mont Brome, Mont Spruce, and Pic du Chevreuil, it is the largest illuminated alpine ski resort in North America, making it ideal for night runs. In the summer (June–Sept.) the same hills are home to an extensive water park.

Opened in 1960, **Ski Mount Sutton** (671 Maple C.P. 1850, 866/538-2545, www.montsutton.com, Dec.–Apr. Mon.–Fri. 9 A.M.–4 P.M., Sat.–Sun. 8:30 A.M.–4 P.M., $60 day pass) was started by a family who wanted to pursue their favorite pastime. Nowadays it's one of the most popular ski resorts in the area, a little over an hour's drive from the city, it has 54 trails and offers ski packages for weekday visits.

HOTELS

A century-old house makes sleeping in Sherbrooke a welcoming experience at **Le Marquis de Montcalm** (797 rue Générale-Montcalm, Sherbrooke, 819/823-7773, www.marquisdemontcalm.com, $104–135). The five rooms at this bed-and-breakfast are charmingly decorated with antiques and personal touches like the hand-painted mural in the Place de Voges room.

Built in 1849, **Auberge Knowlton** (286 chemin Knowlton, Knowlton, 450/242-6886, www.aubergeknowlton.ca, $125–167) has been fully renovated but still holds much of that old-world charm, with hardwood floors and country pine furniture. Looking out on Lac Brome, it's also got one of the best views in the village. Breakfast isn't always included.

Auberge du Joli Vent (667 chemin Bondville, Lac Brome, 866/525-4272, www.aubergedujolivent, $125–145) is a great little bed-and-breakfast with charming, brightly colored rooms and a fine-dining restaurant on-site. Surrounded by nature, they even have a large outdoor pool great for kids.

North Hatley's reputation as a place for vacationing aristocrats is safe with **Auberge**

La Raveaudière (11 chemin Hatley, North Hatley, 819/842-2554, www.laraveaudiere.com, $130–175), an elegant guest house in an old Victorian home. Along with seven guest rooms it has two acres of gardens, a comfortable living room, a large, open patio, and it backs onto the local golf course.

Located just outside of North Hatley on Lake Massawippi is **Manoir Hovey** (575 chemin Hovey, North Hatley, 800/661-2421, www.manoirhovey.com, $250–820), one of the more charming inns in the region. Modeled after George Washington's Mount Vernon home it was built at the turn of the 20th century and has 40 comfortably luxurious rooms, a pool, two beaches, touring bikes, an exercise room, and complimentary haute-cuisine dinners and breakfasts.

North of Coaticook is **Le Bocage** (200 Moe's River Rd., Compton, 819/835-5653, www.lebocage.qc.ca, $90–490), a charming Victorian home that's been converted into a welcoming four-room bed-and-breakfast. Handmade quilts lie atop pine bed frames, giving the place a country farm feel. Breakfast is served in a cozy, stone-walled dining room or outside on the terrace.

INFORMATION AND SERVICES

Coming from Montréal, stop off at the **Regional Tourist Office** (Autoroute 10, exit 68, 800/355-5755, www.easterntownships.org, June–Sept. Mon.–Fri. 8 A.M.–10 P.M., Wed. till 10 P.M., Sat.–Sun. 9 A.M.–5 P.M., Sept.–June Mon.–Fri. 8:30 A.M.–4:30 P.M.), the first center in the Eastern Townships region. Though some towns have their own tourist centers, larger centers can be found in **Granby** (111 rue Denison E., Place de la Gare, Granby, 800/567-7273, daily 9 A.M.–5 P.M.), **Sherbrooke** (785 rue King W., 800/561-8331, www.tourismsherbrooke.com, mid-Aug.–mid-June. Mon.–Sat. 9 A.M.–5 P.M., Sun. 9 A.M.–3 P.M., mid-June–mid-Aug. daily 9 A.M.–7 P.M.) and **Coaticook** (13 rue Michaud, 866/665-6669, www.tourismecoaticook.qc.ca, mid-Aug.–mid-June Mon.–Fri. 8 A.M.–10 P.M., Wed. till 10 P.M., Sat.–Sun. 9 A.M.–5 P.M., mid-June–mid-Aug. Mon.–Fri. 8:30 A.M.–4:30 P.M.).

EXCURSIONS

BORDER CROSSING: STANSTEAD, QUÉBEC

Stanstead is one of those rare places that is actually located on a border – the division line between the United States and Canada literally cuts right through the town.

Settled in 1790s by the Taplin family, who came north from New England looking for affordable land, Stanstead and its counterpart, Derby Line, Vermont, have always had a long and intertwined history. On Canusa Street the border cuts right down the middle, so the homes on the south side are in America and those on the north side are in Canada, with the American and Canadian Customs situated at the west end of the street. The stone building now facing Customs was once a post office; cut in two by the border, for a while it was the only international post office in the world, with two different counters: one serving Vermont and the other serving Québec.

One of the town's greatest attractions is the **Haskell Free Library and Opera House** or **La Bibliotheque Gratuite de Haskell** (93 Caswell Ave., Derby Line, VT, and 1 rue Church, Stanstead, QC, 819/876-2471, www.haskellopera.org, Tues.-Wed. and Fri.-Sat. 10 A.M.-5 P.M.,

Thurs. 10 A.M.-9 P.M.). A gift of Martha Stewart Haskell in memory of her late husband, who was a prominent merchant, the cultural center was deliberately built across the border in order to give residents of both sides equal access to culture and the arts.

The library is located on the first floor and the music hall on the second, with the original notion that one would pay for the other. Opened in 1904 it is unlike anywhere else; where else you can watch a performance where one-half of the audience and the performers on stage are in another country entirely?

Though the border might be one of the more interesting things about the town, it's not the only thing. It's called the Capital of Granite, and many of Montréal's most famous buildings, including Sun Life, were made with granite from the nearby quarry. And like many towns in this region it is unbelievably picturesque with a number of historical homes and scenic surroundings. The only difference here is, when you go for a stroll in the town, you need your passport.

GETTING THERE AND AROUND
By Bus
A coach is available daily from Montréal's main bus terminal, Gare d'Autocars (505 de Maisonneuve E., 514 842-2281, www.stationcentrale.com). **Galland** (514/333-9555, www.autobusgalland.com) takes travelers to most major spots in the Eastern Townships, including to Sherbrooke's main bus station (two hours and five minutes, $65 round-trip), Knowlton's Depanneur Rouge (483 rue Knowlton, two hours and ten minutes, $43 round-trip), to Magog (90 minutes, $56 round-trip).

Smaller towns, including Sutton, Cowansville, Farnham, and Knowlton, can be reached by **Veolia Transport** (877/348-5599, www.destinationknowlton.com), which departs from Montréal's main bus terminal twice on weekdays and three times a day on weekends (including

Friday). The trip to Knowlton takes two and a half hours and costs $36 round-trip.

By Car
The simplest way to travel to the Eastern Townships and around them is by car. Head out of Montréal by the Champlain Bridge, then head for Autoroute 10 East. The roads are clearly marked with signs for the Cantons de l'Est, but they can sometimes come up quickly, so keep your eyes peeled. Once on Autoroute 10 all the towns are easily accessible; it's just a matter of watching for the right exits.

Once you've arrived, getting from one town to the next is just as simple. Many of the small, country roads are signposted, ensuring you get from Lac Brome to North Hatley by the quickest way possible. Depending where you are, however, you might have to get back on Autoroute 10 to reach your next destination.

QUÉBEC CITY

SIGHTS

The only fortified city left in North America, Québec City is like no other place on the continent. Constructed on the top of Cap Diamant, a cliff that looks out over the St-Lawrence River, the city is defined by its natural hills and cliffs, though from afar it's not always easy to notice. It's the cradle of Canadian society, where in 1608 the first settlers arrived. Led by Samuel de Champlain, they built the first habitation on the site that's now called Place Royale. It was under French rule until 1759, when it fell to the British at the Battle of the Plains of Abraham, but this political feat did not alter the existing French-Canadian culture and way of life. Despite 100 years of British rule and the eventual founding of the Canadian Dominion, the city's roots to the early settlers remain remarkably intact. It's this lineage and incredible architectural heritage that give it its own unique, albeit European, feel.

Quebéc City is divided into two main areas, Haute-Ville (Upper Town) and Basse-Ville (Lower Town). They are easy to differentiate thanks to their geography. Upper Town constitutes the area on the top of the cliff, while Lower Town constitutes everything below it. It's in Upper Town that you'll find Les Fortifications, the walled defenses that encircle Old Québec's Upper Town and many of the biggest sights, including Château Frontenac and La Citadelle.

Directly below, between the cliff and the river, is Vieux-Québec's Basse-Ville (Old Québec's Lower Town). The oldest area in Canada, this is where the first settlement was established, near Place Royale, and where

HIGHLIGHTS

LOOK FOR ◖ TO FIND RECOMMENDED SIGHTS.

◖ **Most Iconic Sight:** The most photographed hotel in the world, **Château Frontenac,** has become an indelible image of Québec City (page 229).

◖ **Best Views:** Stroll along the top of **Les Fortifications** for the most stunning views of the city both within and outside of the historic walls (page 231).

◖ **Best Crash History Course:** Running nightly throughout the summer, **Le Moulin à Images** is a multimedia projection of the city's history onto an old grain silo (page 236).

◖ **Best Museum:** Dedicated to the history of Québec, **Musée de la Civilisation** offers an in depth look at Québécois culture and beyond (page 237).

◖ **Most Historic Sight:** The site of the first settlement in Québec, **Place Royale** is the birthplace of both the French-Canadian nation and Canada itself (page 237).

◖ **Most Picturesque Neighborhood:** Once home to Irish immigrants and dock workers, **Quartier du Petit-Champlain** has been revived and rejuvenated by a co-op of artists (page 238).

◖ **Most Unusual City Street:** Rue Sous-le-Cap is a charming three-meter-wide street that runs along the cliff-face, lined with tiny old cottages (page 239).

◖ **Best Collection of Québécois Art:** With a 19th-century prison incorporated into its design, the **Musée National des Beaux-Arts du Québec** beautifully mixes history and art (page 242).

◖ **Most Patriotic Site:** The **Plains of Abraham and Battlefield Park** is the site of the historic 1759 battle between the French and British, an event that changed the course of North American history (page 243).

◖ **Most Historical City Street:** Learn about the city's history in the older buildings that line **rue Saint-Jean** as you wander down what is now one of the busiest commercial streets in the city (page 245).

© SACHA JACKSON

Completed in the early 20th century, the Château Frontenac is one of the most recognizable buildings in Canada.

SIGHTS

SKY HIGH: ÉDIFICE PRICE

Completed in 1931, Édifice Price is the only skyscraper in Vieux-Québec. Built as the headquarters for Price Brothers Limited, one of the biggest printing companies in Québec at the time, it was designed by Montréal firm Ross and Macdonald. Despite heavy criticism from the public, the government ignored accusations that it wasn't protecting Québec's historic area – two historic houses were demolished to make way for the new building – and gave the company a building permit anyhow.

Completed within a year, the art deco building is reminiscent of the Empire State Building in New York, though much smaller. The design uses setbacks to gradually taper the building's width. Unlike the Empire State Building, however, the roof is classical in design, with a château-style steepled copper roof that blends well with its surroundings. The interior includes bas-reliefs that depict the origins of the Price company, which would be forced into bankruptcy during the Depression.

Since 2001, the 16th and 17th floors have become to the official residence of the premier of Québec, and the two-floor apartment includes a 14-guest dining room, two bedrooms, and offices. Decorated to reflect the province's history, it boasts maple hardwood floors, traditional Québec style furnishings, and paintings by local artists.

historic areas like the Vieux-Port (Old Port) and the Quartier du Petit-Champlain are situated. Getting from the lower to the upper part of the city isn't complicated, provided the winding, hilly streets aren't a sheet of ice. Taking the Escalier Frontenac (Frontenac Stairs) is the easiest, but the funicular and the brand-new Ecobuses offer some good alternatives.

Though separated by a cliff, Vieux-Québec is quite small and dense, so it's easy to cover by foot. In fact the best way to get around the city, in winter or summer, is by walking. Expect to get quite a workout, though, thanks to the hilly geography. No matter where you are in the city, if you want to get down or up, there are likely stairs involved, or at the very least, a city bus. Due to the density of the city, even peripheral areas like the Plains (just outside of the walls in Upper Town) and Saint-Roch (the city's coolest post code, located in Lower Town) are only a 15-minute walk from Vieux-Québec.

Of course, Québec is a vastly different city in winter than it is in summer. Those on a trip in the middle of January can expect a completely different landscape than the one found in summer. Many sites close during the winter or have truncated hours. What constitutes the different seasons, however, is a complicated matter. A good general rule of thumb is the following: Summer hours usually run from June 24, Saint-Jean-Baptiste day and the province's national holiday, to Labor Day, the first Monday in September. Winter hours, meanwhile, could start as early as Labor Day or Canadian Thanksgiving (the second Monday of October) and run till May or June. Many of these dates fluctuate according to the weather, so make sure to double-check hours if there's a particular sight you want to visit.

With so many interesting historical sites just about everywhere you turn in Québec City—even a stroll down Faubourg Saint-Jean Baptiste is a lesson in the city's evolution—there's no time for a dull moment.

Vieux-Québec's Upper Town   Map 8

BASILIQUE-CATHÉDRALE NOTRE-DAME-DE-QUÉBEC

16 rue de Buade, 418/692-2533,
www.patrimonie-religieux.com
HOURS: Nov.-Apr. Mon.-Fri. 7:30 A.M.-4 P.M.,
Sat. 7:30 A.M.-6 P.M., Sun. 8:30 A.M.-6 P.M.; May-Nov.
Mon.-Fri. 7:30 A.M.-5 P.M., Sat. 7:30 A.M.-6 P.M.,
Sun. 8:30 A.M.-6 P.M.
COST: Free

It was on this site, high above the St-Lawrence River, that explorer Samuel de Champlain built Québec's first church in 1647. Thirty years later in 1664, the Basilique-Cathédrale Notre-Dame-de-Québec became the first parish church in North America. It was given the title of cathedral 10 years later, when the diocese of Québec was established with the arrival of Monsignor de Laval, the first bishop of New France.

Destroyed by fire during the English conquest in 1759, it was entirely reconstructed a few years later, only to be remodeled again in 1843, by Thomas Baillairgé. Inspired by Sainte-Geneviève in Paris, Baillairgé, whose father François designed the church's interior, gave it today's neoclassical facade. That too had to be reconstructed when the church was once again ravaged by fire—one set by arsonists who used the fire to steal priceless paintings—in 1922. During this rebuilding period, however, they tried to stay as true as possible to the original building, working off of François Baillairgé's original 18th-century drawings for the interior. Despite the fact that it has been rebuilt a number of times, the bell tower and portions of the walls are from the original structure.

Long and narrow, the interior is a soft buttery yellow with a high arched ceiling, lined with windows and intricate moldings. A stunning gold-plated baldaquin stands at the altar, and other items include paintings of the Virgin Mary that date back to the French regime, the bishop's original throne, and a chancel lamp that was a gift of Louis XIV.

Between 1654 and 1898 over 900 people were buried in the crypt below the church, including

© SACHA JACKSON

Basilique-Cathédrale Notre-Dame-de-Québec stands on the site of the first chapel in Québec.

20 bishops and four governors. It's also rumored that Samuel de Champlain himself is buried nearby; archaeologists have been searching for the grave for over 50 years. Hour-long guided tours of the crypt and basilica are available but must be reserved in advance, so call ahead.

◖ CHÂTEAU FRONTENAC

1 rue des Carrières, 866/840-8402,
www.fairmont.com/frontenac
HOURS: Tours May-Oct. daily 10 A.M.-6 P.M. every hour on the hour, Oct.-Apr. Sat.-Sun. noon-5 P.M. every hour on the hour
COST: Tours $8.50 adult, $7.75 senior, $6 child

Proudly holding the title of "most photographed hotel in the world," Château Frontenac is without a doubt one of the most stunning buildings in Québec. It's not every day that a hotel garners so much attention, but the fortress-like architecture and its location on the top of the Cap Diamant, a bluff overlooking the St-Lawrence, give it an especially majestic feel.

SIGHTS

Built in 1893, it is part of a chain of "château style" hotels that were constructed across the country by the Canadian Pacific Railway. One of the North American ports before the long trip across the Atlantic, Québec's hotel was designed to rival any European counterpart and grab the attention of travelers both leaving and arriving in the country. Designed by New York architect Bruce Price, it has a distinct mix of architectural styles. Price drew from both the Middle Ages and Renaissance for the history of the two founding cultures and used elements like the turrets found on Scottish castles and the bastion towers of French châteaus.

Named after Louis de Buade de Frontenac, who was governor of New France twice between 1672 and 1698, the hotel sits on the site of what was once Château St-Louis, the official residence of the governor of New France and later home of the British governors, built in 1648. The ruins of the many incarnations of the residence lie just in front of the hotel.

It has been the temporary residence of everyone from Queen Elizabeth II to Charles Lindburgh as well as the site of Alfred Hitchcock's *I Confess,* but the hotel's proudest moment took place in 1943. It was the site of the Quebec Conference of World War II, where U.S. president Franklin D. Roosevelt, British prime minister Winston Churchill, and Canadian prime minister William Lyon Mackenzie King discussed the eventual invasion of France.

Hour-long tours are available throughout the year by guides in 19th-century costume who tell the hotel's history in detail and will take you through the grand ballrooms, up the back staircases, and occasionally let you have a peek at one of the rooms.

LA CITADELLE

1 Côte de la Citadelle, 418/694-2815,
www.lacitadelle.qc.ca
HOURS: Bilingual tours Apr. daily 10 A.M.-4 P.M.,
May-Sept. daily 9 A.M.-5 P.M., Oct. daily 10 A.M.-3 P.M.,
Nov.-Mar. daily at 1:30 P.M.
COST: $10 adult, $9 student and senior, $5.50 child, 7 and under free
The largest British fortress in North America,

La Citadelle is also the largest defense on the continent to have never seen battle. Covering 2.3 square kilometers and perched on the edge of the cape at the highest point in the city, overlooking the St-Lawrence, this strategically placed defense is an imposing figure, standing out along the rolling plains and the copper roofs of Vieux-Québec.

Built under the direction of British officer Lieutenant-Colonel Elias Walker Durnford, the design is entirely French. Modeled in the style of military engineer Vauban, it is shaped like a four-pointed star and as such has no blind spots. Construction on the Citadelle started in 1820, took 30 years to complete, and incorporated two existing buildings from the French regime, the oldest of which is a battery dating back to 1750. The winding gate that is used as entrance into the Citadelle is also the only real gate remaining from the French regime, and is reminiscent of what all gates into the city were once like.

Though it never saw any action, the Citadelle continues to be the official residence of the Royal 22e Régiment, the only Francophone infantry regiment in the Canadian Forces Regular Force. The low stone barracks are a mix of English and French influences with symmetric casement windows and doors and pitched tin roofs. Two small museums held in a former battery and former military jail are dedicated to the regiment's distinguished military history. Starting with the early days and Québec's most important battles, the exhibits continue up to the modern day with the regiment's tour in Bosnia and other United Nations missions included. One exhibit is dedicated to the war heroes of the 22e Régiment who fought in the World War I and II, summarizing their duties, showing personal artifacts, and in one case showing a spy's various identity cards.

As early as the 1860s there was talk of tearing down the Citadelle, but then Governor General Lord Dufferin refused, instead pointing to the fortifications' historical importance. Since that time his residence has become the official residence of the governor general of Canada. It is here too that Georges Vanier, the first French-Canadian governor general and a war hero, is laid to rest in a battery turned chapel.

Since it is still an active military residence, the only way to get inside the Citadelle is to take a tour. Both the regiment and city get equal tour time, and though there's a lot to see, the most interesting aspects, such as the barracks and doors that lead inside the walls, are off-limits.

◖ LES FORTIFICATIONS

2 rue d'Auteuil, 418/648-7016

HOURS: Interpretation Centre May–Sept. daily 10 A.M.–6 P.M.; tours June 1-24 daily 2 P.M., June 24–Sept. 6 daily 10 A.M. and 2 P.M., Sept. 7–Oct. 11 2 P.M.

COST: Interpretation Centre $4 adult, $3.50 senior, $2 youth; tours $9.80 adult, $7.30 senior, $4.90 child

Québec is the only fortified city in North America, and its walls encircle the entirety of Upper Town, covering 4.6 kilometers. The Fortifications offer some of the most stunning views of the city and are a great place to hang out in the summer and have a picnic or take a break from sightseeing. As you walk along the walls, every angle of the city can be explored, from the defenses of the Citadelle to the lookouts over the river. Lined with cannons and grass-covered in spots, the stone walls of the Fortifications frame the city in a way that transports visitors back to the days when they were a practical defense against attacks.

Built in a classic urban style, the Fortifications are characterized by the geometry of flanking and the adaptation of the walls to the city's topography, which sees the walls grow in height and depth at different parts. Though Québec was a bustling city by 1700, its defense system was inadequate, and the city was a maze of temporary and permanent structures. It wasn't until the fall of Louisbourg, a fort in Cape Breton, in 1745, that serious consideration was given to the state of the Fortifications. It was Governor Beauharnois who, following Chaussegros de Léry's designs, authorized a new enceinte that permanently closed the city to the open countryside.

In the late 19th century citizens complained about the impracticality of the gates, complaining that they stopped circulation and calling them a nuisance—the gates would close at curfew, and up until the British troops left the ramparts were for military and pedestrian use only. Though Lord Dufferin, then governor general of Canada, understood their complaints, he also saw the historical importance of the fortifications—during the summer-long siege of Québec, it was these walls that kept the citizens from British invasion—and instead suggested the gates be dismantled and then rebuilt to make them wider.

The Interpretation Centre of the Fortifications of Québec is located by the St-Louis Gate, beneath the city's ramparts. It offers information about the history of city's defenses as well as exhibits and guided tours, which depart from Terrasse Dufferin Terrace.

MUSÉE DE L'AMÉRIQUE FRANÇAISE

2 Côte de la Fabrique, 418/692-2843, www.mcq.org

HOURS: Early Sept.-mid-June Tues.-Sun. 10 A.M.-5 P.M., mid-June-early Sept. daily 9:30 A.M.-5 P.M.

COST: $8 adult, $7 senior, $5.50 student, $2 child, free for children under 12

Entering the modernized foyer of the museum you're almost not prepared for the historic chapel that you enter shortly after. Full of green marble pillars, beautiful stained-glasses windows, golden busts of important members of Québec's history, and a 1753 organ, the most alluring part of this exhibit is the baroque music that is played throughout the day.

After a bit of maze-like wandering—through the chapel, into an elevator, and across an outdoor walkway—you arrive at the building that houses the Musée de l'Amérique Française, an old building that once belonged to the Séminaire de Québec. The first exhibit on the ground floor looks at the history of the seminary itself, with artifacts like old keys, chalices, and furniture that once belonged to the seminary.

Moving on to the museum's permanent collection, visitors get a well-rounded view of the history and trajectory of the Francophone population, not just in Canada but within the whole of the continent. It retraces the roots of Francophone explorers and guides who helped explore the United States and found American cities like Detroit, Pittsburgh, Buffalo, and St. Louis. The design of the exhibit is modern and easy to navigate, even in high season when there are more crowds. For the most part, however, it's rarely overcrowded and visitors can wander the exhibits at their leisure.

MUSÉE DES URSULINES

12 rue Donnacona, 418/694-0694, www.museedesursulines.com

HOURS: May-Sept. Tues.-Sat. 10 A.M.-noon and 1-5 P.M., Sun. 1-5 P.M., Oct.-Nov. and Feb.-Apr. Tues.-Sun. 1-5 P.M.

COST: $6 adult, $5 student and senior, $4 child

Founded in 1639 by Marie de l'Incarnation, an Ursuline nun, and Madame Marie-Madeline de Chauvigny de la Peltrie, a rich widow, the Couvent des Ursulines is the oldest school in North America dedicated to the teaching of women. Girls still study at this institution, which now boasts a museum and a chapel, alongside the schoolrooms and courtyard playgrounds.

The first Ursuline nuns landed in Québec on August 1, 1639, and soon started teaching, though at the time the French-Canadian population was so small, the majority of their students were Amerindian girls. Just outside of the convent's walls is the Musée des Ursulines de Québec, which tells the story of these pioneer women who were both teachers and students. Newly reopened and renovated, the new permanent collection, The Young Ladies' Academy, allows visitors into the heart of the boarding school and the daily lives of the nuns and pupils that passed through the convent's halls. Artifacts from the time of the French regime are also on view, including teaching materials, personal objects, and sacred artwork.

When French governor Montcalm died after the Battle of the Plains of Abraham, he was buried in the convent chapel by night so as not to arouse suspicion. For a long time his skull was part of the museum's permanent collection, to the delight of visiting schoolchildren.

Despite the simple, austere pews found in the small Ursuline chapel, it has some of the most beautiful sculpted wood in Québec. They were created by master craftsman Pierre-Noël Levasseur between 1723 and 1739, and it was the Ursulines themselves who gilded the carvings, which now adorn the nave of the chapel. The tomb of founder Marie de l'Incarnation can also be found here. The chapel is open to the public from May to October, and entry is free.

PARC DE L'ARTILLERIE

2 rue d'Auteuil, 418/648-7016, www.pc.gc.ca

HOURS: Early May-early Sept. daily 10 A.M.-6 P.M., early Sept.-Oct. daily 10 A.M.-5 P.M.

COST: $4 adult, $3.50 senior, $2 child

The position of the Parc de l'Artillerie, looking out over the west of the city and across the St-Charles River, has made it a strategic military site since the late 17th century. Four vastly different buildings trace the city's history from the French regime right up to the 1940s. Of the four buildings that make up the site, the Dauphine Redoubt is the most striking, with massive white supports that plunge down the side of a hill. Built in 1712 and finally completed in 1748, it was army barracks both before and after the British conquest and eventually became the home of the superintendent. During the summer, characters in period costume bring the barracks to life with demonstrations and tours through the rooms, which have been decorated to reflect various periods in the building's evolution.

Kitty-corner to the Redoubt is the interpretation center, a former foundry used to make arsenal for the Canadian military, from the Boer War up to World War I and II, and even the Korean War. The site now holds a 200-year-old scale model of Québec. Constructed 1806-1808, by draftsman Jean-Baptiste Duberger and John By, a military engineer, it was sent to England in 1810 to convince the British government that the city needed new fortifications. Alongside uncovered ruins, there are artifacts that were found on and around the site, including toothbrushes, children's toys, and belt buckles.

PARC DU CAVALIER-DU-MOULIN

At the end of rue Mont-Carmel

HOURS: Daily 24 hours

COST: Free

This tiny little park tucked away at the end of a quiet residential street is one of the city's best-kept secrets. Passing through the park's wrought-iron gates, visitors enter onto Mont-Carmel, the spot of an old windmill (*moulin* in French). Originally a military outpost, the small 1,500-square-meter park was one of the few defenses constructed by the French military in the 17th century. This small defensive outpost was then named "cavalier," a nod to its solitary position. In 1663, the windmill was erected here and included in the military fortification. By 1700, with the building of the first surrounding walls, *le cavalier du moulin* was no longer needed.

Nowadays the park acts as a window onto history, allowing visitors to imagine a city that once had nothing but fields beyond this hillock. It's adorned with a cannon to remind people of its past life as a military defense; the cannon juts out over the hill, directed at the houses and winding streets beyond.

PLACE D'ARMES

Btwn. rue du Trésor and rue du Fort

The history of Place d'Armes is the history of Québec. Once situated behind Château St-Louis, which was at the time also a fort, it was in this public square, safely behind the defenses, that the military would perform their various parades and military inspections. When construction of the Citadelle was undertaken in 1820, however, the military moved and the regular parades went with it, moving instead to the Parc de l'Esplanade in front of the fortress and running alongside the city walls.

Though it lost its military importance, the square continued to be a popular meeting place, and in 1915 a monument was erected to the notion of faith. Dedicated to the Récollets, the first religious community to live in New France, the monument today stands in the shadow of the Château Frontenac at the center of a bustling square surrounding by busy restaurants and cafés.

SÉMINAIRE DE QUÉBEC

1 rue des Remparts, 418/692-3981,

www.seminairedequebec.org

Established in 1663 by Monsignor François de Laval, the first bishop of New France, to train young men for the priesthood, this seminary was expanded five years later to include the Petit Séminaire, which, in a push to Gallicize the indigenous population, accepted both Indian and French students to study at the Collège des Jésuites. It continued to be the training ground of future priests right up until the conquest, when its connection to the priesthood was somewhat lost. The studies instead began to focus on the liberal arts, and the school began accepting students who didn't want to become priests. By 1852 the college part of the Séminaire de Québec became the University of Laval.

© SACHA JACKSON

SIGHTS

The grand Séminaire de Québec is one of the oldest structures in the city and is still home to those studying to be a priest.

Laid out according to 17th-century principles, the *séminare* has various wings, all of which center around interior courtyards (you can enter one through the Musée l'Amérique Français). Though the time periods vary there is a continuity in the architecture, with stone masonry covered with stucco, casement windows, steep roofs with dormers, and raised firewalls evident in all of the buildings. The bursar's wing in particular is interesting. Designed from 1678 to 1681 and restored in 1866 after a fire, its vaulted kitchen is still intact, along with the chapel of Monsignor Briand, who was bishop of Québec 1766–1784.

Today, it remains both a school and seminary, with Laval's school of architecture located on the site and priests who continue to live here and dedicate their lives to the church.

TERRASSE DUFFERIN
At rue des Carrières and Place d'Armes

Along the front of Château Frontenac, looking out over the St-Lawrence and across to Lévis, is the wide boardwalk of Terrasse Dufferin. Created in 1879 by the governor general of Canada, Lord Dufferin, the 671-meter-long promenade was designed by Charles Baillairgé, the same designer behind the kiosks and street lamps that line the boardwalk.

It was during his summer stay at the Citadelle, now at the opposite end of the promenade, that Lord Dufferin conceived of the idea to build the boardwalk, a place for residents and visitors to take their daily stroll. The use of wooden planks gives the whole thing an air of summer, even in the middle of winter. Though he left his post in 1879, Dufferin himself inaugurated the project and put down the first stone.

Beneath the *terrasse* lie the ruins of the former St-Louis Fort and Château, which was destroyed by fire in 1834. Visitors are able to visit the excavation site thanks to a new interpretation center, cleverly hidden by the boardwalk. Only a few steps down and you're face-to-face with the foundations of the original building and some of the artifacts they uncovered there.

During the winter a huge slide is built at the Citadelle end of the *terrasse* and children of all ages line up to take a super-fast ride down *les glissades* overlooking the frozen river.

Vieux-Québec's Lower Town   Map 9

ÉGLISE NOTRE-DAME-DES-VICTOIRES
Place Royale, 32 rue Sous-le-Fort, 418/692-1650, www.patrimoine-religieux.com
HOURS: Mon.-Sun. 9 A.M.-5 P.M.; tours May-Oct., reservations required in the off-season
COST: Free

The oldest stone church in Québec, Église Notre-Dame-des-Victoires was built on Place Royale in 1688, on the site of l'Abitation, Québec's first building. In the basement of the church you can still see one of the building's walls, and archaeological digs have uncovered one of the building's turrets in the church's facade. The king's storehouse also stood on this site, and it was this particular location that attracted François de Laval, the bishop of New France. For years Laval requested a chapel be built on the site of the king's storehouse, an extension of Upper Town's Notre-Dame-de-Québec church, but it was his successor, Monsignor de Saint Vallier, who would see the work completed in 1723.

Designed by Claude Baillif the church was originally named l'Enfant Jesus, but it's name was changed twice. In 1690 the British admiral Phipps was defeated by Governor Frontenac, and the church was renamed Notre-Dame-de-la-Victoire. In 1711, the city was again saved when the fleet of Admiral Walker, on its way to attack Québec, was shipwrecked in the St. Lawrence. This time the name change was easy; they made it plural. Despite two failed attempts, the British would eventually destroy the church in 1759 during the siege of Québec.

BRIDGE OVER TROUBLED WATER: LE PONT DE QUÉBEC

The longest cantilever bridge in the world, the Pont de Québec is also the easternmost bridge to cross the St-Lawrence River. Measuring 987 meters long, 29 meters wide, and 104 meters high, it has three highway lanes, one rail line, and one pedestrian walkway and connects Québec City in the north with Lévis in the south.

Before the bridge was completed, after two disasters, the only way to get from one side of the St-Lawrence to the other was by ferry. Politicians and government officials were looking into building a bridge as early as 1852, but it wasn't until the turn of the century that construction got underway, headed by the Phoenix Bridge Company out of Pennsylvania.

In the summer or 1907, with three years of work nearing completion, the bridge collapsed, killing 75 workers, the majority of which were Mohawk steelworkers from the Kahnawake reserve near Montréal. Though engineer Norman McClure had noticed abnormalities in the foundation structure his eventual call to halt production never made it to Québec. That same afternoon the southern arm and central section collapsed into the river in 15 seconds.

After a Royal Commission of Inquiry, construction started on a second bridge. This time construction was headed by three engineers: Canadian H. E. Vautelet, Maurice Fitzmaurice from Britain (who worked on the construction of the Forth Bridge in Scotland), and Chicago's Ralph Modjeski. With the bridge nearing completion the central span was raised into position on September 11, 1916, only to crash into the river, killing 13 workers. Because it was in the midst of World War I rumors quickly spread that it was German sabotage. It soon became clear, however, that it was another unfortunate accident.

Reconstruction started almost immediately after the collapse and the project was granted special permission to use steel, which was in high demand because of the war effort. After nearly 20 years of construction, the bridge opened for rail traffic on December 3, 1919. Today it is still one of the most impressive engineering feats in North America. Though it's not visible from downtown Québec City, those traveling to and from Québec City by Autoroute Duplessis or heading for a stroll beside the river in Parc de la Plage Jacques-Cartier will get a stunning view of the bridge in all its glory.

The subsequent reconstructions were meticulous and took place 1762–1766 under the eye of Jean Baillairgé.

The interior itself is rather austere, with a few pews and a tiny, circular staircase leading up to the organ. Designed by students of Thomas Baillairgé, it was constructed 1854–1857 and features several paintings from the 17th, 18th, and 19th centuries. The oldest part of the church is the tabernacle; originally found in the Sainte-Geneviève Chapel it dates from 1724. Unique to Québec, the frescos on either side of the main altar retrace the history of the church and city, and were done by local painter and decorator Jean-M. Tardivel. The most striking church accent, however, is the single ex-voto, a model of a vessel that arrived in 1664 transporting the Carignan Regiment

and the Marquis de Tracy, which hangs suspended over the pews.

LA FRESQUE DES QUÉBÉCOIS
Place Royale

Reaching nearly three stories tall and at 420 meters high La Fresque des Québécois is the largest and most historical trompe l'œil in the city. Unveiled in 1999, it took 12 artists to complete the immense mural that cleverly shows the city's history and its important figures. Sixteen important Québécois are featured in the painting, including historical figures like Jacques Cartier, Samuel de Champlain, and Lord Dufferin as well as cultural icons like singer/songwriter Félix Leclerc and politician Louis-Joseph Papineau. Also shown in the mural are typical Québécois buildings

© SACHA JACKSON

The easiest way to get from Upper Town to Lower Town is via the Funiculaire du Vieux-Québec, which also affords great views of the river.

through whose windows the important figures peek. One of the gates figures prominently, as do the famous L'Escalier du Casse-Cou and the province's four seasons.

A popular tourist sight (it's fun to try and slip yourself in among the historical figures), it kicked off a trompe l'œil craze around the city, and many buildings are now covered in historically clever murals.

FUNICULAIRE DU VIEUX-QUÉBEC
16 rue du Petit-Champlain, 418/692-1132,
www.funiculaire-quebec.com
HOURS: Early Sept.-mid-June 20 daily 7:30 A.M.-11 P.M., June 20-early Sept. daily 7:30 A.M.-midnight
COST: $2
The only funicular of its kind in North America, the Funiculaire du Vieux-Québec was built in 1879 and designed by William Griffith. Wood-covered and steam-powered, it operated six months a year as an alternative to horse and buggy, transporting passengers and merchandise from Lower Town to Upper

Town. The arrival of electrical power in 1907 meant it could work year-round, which it did until 1945, when the wooden structure caught fire and was subsequently rebuilt with metal shelters. It lets passengers off and on at Terrasse Dufferin.

Transportation is still its main function, though today, it transports more tourists than merchandise since it allows incomparable views of Lower Town, the port, and Lévis, across the water.

The entrance of the funicular is situated in a historical house, built in 1683 by Québec architect Baillif, that once belonged to one of the country's first explorers, Louis Jolliet. Jolliet, along with Father Jacques Marquette, was the first to explore and map the Mississippi River. Jolliet lived here until his death in 1700.

◖ LE MOULIN À IMAGES
Vieux-Port, www2.quebecregion.com/Moulin
HOURS: Mid-June-early Sept. Tues.-Sat.
COST: Free
The brainchild of creative genius Robert Lepage and his company Ex Machina, Le Moulin à Images is a breathtaking multidisciplinary projection of the history of Québec City. Originally made for the city's 400th anniversary, the 50-minute-long projection will be shown each summer until 2013. Using the Bunge grain silo, which is 600 meters wide by 30 meters high, as an oversized screen the film is projected onto the silos to create an experience unlike any other. Because the silos are curved it gives the entire film a sense of movement and vitality that it wouldn't have otherwise.

The Image Mill transports viewers through four centuries of the city's history through four transportation-inspired movements. The opening Waterways section recounts the city's discovery and exploration, Roadbuilding focuses on development, Rail Expansion on industrialization, and Air Travel on airplanes and communication. Don't let the ho-hum titles fool you, however; this is a thrilling film that includes upheavals, controversies, and the best of the city's times.

Since the work is so huge, it can be seen from

CROSSING THE ST-LAWRENCE: QUÉBEC-LÉVIS FERRY

One of the best views of the city is from across the river in the city of Lévis. Get there by hopping on the Québec-Lévis Ferry located right on the port (10 rue des Traversiers, 877/787-7483, www.traversiers.gouv.qc.ca, $3 adult, $2 child, $7 car). The views of the city are stunning, especially at night, and the 10-minute trip on the commuter ferry will give you a new appreciation for the city's geography. The ferry runs all year long several times an hour 6 A.M.-2:30 A.M. (hourly from 6 P.M. onwards). July-August a bus tour to Lévis is also available and includes such sights as Fort No. 1, which was built by the British as a defense between 1865 and 1872.

just about anywhere in the city, but the best places to hear and see the spectacle are along the wharves between the Old Port Market and rue Dalhousie, though standing along the rue de Remparts, overlooking the wharves below, isn't bad either. Times and dates change for the projections from summer to summer so check the website before you head out.

🎫 MUSÉE DE LA CIVILISATION

85 rue Dalhousie, 418/643-2158, www.mcq.org
HOURS: Mid-June-early Sept. daily 9:30 A.M.-6:30 P.M., early Sept.-mid-June Tues.-Sun. 10 A.M.-5 P.M.
COST: $12 adult, $11 senior, $9 student, $4 child, 11 and under free; Nov.-May free on Tuesday

In the heart of the port district, not far from the shores of the St-Lawrence and surrounded by historical buildings, the modern facade of the Museum of Civilization strikes out against its surroundings. Designed by Moshe Safdie, the architect behind Montréal's Habitat 67, the front of the museum is built into an incline, tucking the museum away and adding a touch of nature, with a glass roof and greenery sprouting from along the sides. Inaugurated in 1988, the museum is dedicated to the history, present, and future of Québec civilization, as well as that of cultures from around the world.

Inside the harmony with the surroundings continues with a large open lobby, full of glass and light. The three-story building accommodates 10 exhibits simultaneously, three of which are permanent exhibits rooted in the region's history. Le Temps des Québécois is an overview of the history of this nation within a nation, from the first explorers to Expo 67. It's a fun exhibition with bits of pop culture—like videos of iconic TV presenters and shows from the '80s and '90s—placed within context next to religious iconography, old tramway signs, sabers, and World War II ration boxes. Presented in conjunction with the National Film Board of Canada (the NFB), historic films, political speeches, and important cultural events are shown on film here.

With a focus on the province as a whole, Territoires looks at the various regions of the province and the problems the areas, and their inhabitants, face. Not an overly optimistic exhibit, but a real one, it examines issues like suburban sprawl and the Amerindians' lost connection to the land, and tries to provide solutions. The breathtaking photos and videos of the regions give visitors a good overview of the expansive province.

Those wanting to learn more about Québec's First Nations will enjoy Encounter with the First Nations, which looks at the 11 different tribes that inhabit the province and includes videos, artifacts—a birch canoe, a tepee, Inuit sculpture—as well as a look at the history and migration patterns of the particular tribes.

🎫 PLACE ROYALE

27 rue Notre-Dame, 418/646-3167, www.mcq.org
HOURS: Mid-June-early Sept. daily 9:30 A.M.-5 P.M., early Sept.-mid-June Tues.-Sun. 10 A.M.-5 P.M.
COST: $7 adult, $6 senior, $5 student, $2 child, 12 and under free; Nov.-May free on Tuesday

For all intents and purposes this is the birthplace of Canada—or more specifically the

SIGHTS

birthplace of the French-Canadian civilization. It was here that Samuel de Champlain, founder of Québec, built l'Abitation, the first establishment in Québec, and though the structure itself is long gone, slate stones mark where the building once stood. As early as 1623, the square started to take on a life of its own alongside the settlement's second habitation. A military parade ground, marketplace, and the surrounding houses burnt to the ground during a fire that destroyed Lower Town in 1682. It got its name in 1686 when Intendant Jean Bochart de Champigny erected a bust of King Louis XIV in its center. As in all towns in France it was the custom to have a square dedicated to royalty, but unlike in France, there was nothing ceremonious about the square or its surroundings; in fact the merchants complained that the bust took up valuable space, and so it was removed and placed at the intendant's house.

Damaged during the Seven Years' War, it was gradually rebuilt, and by the 19th century the square was part of an urban complex that included warehouses, two markets, and a number of businesses. Up until the early 20th century many of the buildings went through major transformations; floors were added, roofs were flattened, storefront windows were built on the ground floor, and it wasn't until an economic downturn in the 1960s forced the city to reconsider its purpose that the area was restored.

After restoring a few buildings (the Chevalier hotel, the Maison Fornel, and the Notre-Dame-des-Victoires church), the government decided it wanted to recreate the ambience of the early 17th century and went about completely renovating the buildings to closely resemble how they would have looked during the French regime. Following the detailed plans of the original structures, they were rebuilt using Norman construction with firewalls, stone, spirits to hold up the walls, and ladders on the roofs.

Set on the same square is the Place Royale Interpretation Center. Opened in 1999, it's in the former home of merchant François Hazeur as well as part of the Smith home next door. Exhibits here include a scale model of the original settlement, which would've been situated just outside the modern glass doors. Built against Côte-de-la-Montagne—the steep road established by Samuel de Champlain in 1623—it also houses a public staircase that links the Lower Town with the street above.

◖ QUARTIER DU PETIT-CHAMPLAIN
Btwn. rue du Petit-Champlain and Place Royale

The charming restaurants, quaint boutiques, and tourist-packed cobblestone streets of this picturesque neighborhood often belie its rich and interesting history. The oldest street in the city, rue du Petit-Champlain in the 17th century was little more than a dirt path down which residents would walk to get their water. Over the next 200 years, the street would grow to become an bustling area full of houses and businesses of many working-class families and men who worked in the port.

In the mid-1800s, the area saw an influx of immigrants. The Irish Potato Famine saw the Irish fleeing the country in boatloads and consequently arriving in Québec, one of the first ports of call. Many of these immigrants stayed, settling on la rue du Cul-de-Sac and la Petit rue Champlain, calling it instead Little Champlain Street. In time, the Francophones adopted the name as well, turning it into rue Petit-Champlain. This was a poor, working class neighborhood, and the reconstruction of the nearby Place Royale in the 1970s forced a change in Petit-Champlain as well. The low rent meant that many artists had moved into the area, and it was the artists who rejuvenated it, financing renovations themselves and doing much of their own work. Since none of the buildings were entirely destroyed, a walk through this quarter gives visitors a view of the city's architecture through the ages, with buildings from different eras lovingly preserved.

At one end of rue Petit-Champlain you'll find L'Escalier du Casse-Cou, or the Breakneck Stairs, a narrow and steep set of steps that are one way to get from Upper Town to Lower Town. First built in 1660, the steps are squished between two buildings and can get icy in winter. The unusual name is rumored to come from American soldiers during their attempted

© SACHA JACKSON

The hidden rue Sous-le-Cap is completely charming and unique.

invasion. At the other end of the street, you'll find La Fresque de Petit Champlain, which represents the life and history of the area, including the 1759 siege and the fires that came with it.

◖ RUE SOUS-LE-CAP

Behind rue du Sault-au-Matelot btwn. rue de la Barricade and rue St-Paul

La rue Sous-le-Cap, which means "street beneath the cape," is unlike any other street in the city and totally enchanting. Wedged between the cliff face and the backs of the houses that face rue St-Paul, at the beginning of the 19th century it was the only road that pedestrians could use to get from their homes in this section of Lower Town to the Côte du Palais, a winding street that would take them to Upper Town. What today are the backs of houses fronting on rue St-Paul used to be front entrances of homes along the waterfront, and during high tide the roadway would be submerged under water.

The narrow street, which measures three meters across, was also at one time the city's red-light district, with a number of brothels operating on the street. Characterized by the stairs and walkways that cover almost all of the street, it's here that you'll find tiny, slightly crooked houses and some of the best private patios in the city.

VIEUX-PORT DE QUÉBEC

100 Quai St-André, 418/648-3300

HOURS: May-Aug. daily 10 A.M.–5 P.M., Sept.-Oct. daily noon-4 P.M.

At the base of Cap Diamant where the waters of the St-Lawrence and St-Charles Rivers converge, the Vieux-Port de Québec (Old Port) is steeped in history. Lined with buildings that are both old and new, it maintains a connection to the past while looking to the future. The basins that once accommodated large cargo and passenger ships are now marinas docked with pleasure cruisers and sailboats, though the old locks of Louise Basin are still in use.

During its heyday in the 19th century, it was one of the world's five biggest ports, a hub of activity with commerce and transatlantic voyages. It was and still is a major contributor to the economic development of the region. Ships from here deal in commercial trade with over 60 countries, and the city is a popular cruise destination. On the very outskirts of Petit-Champlain, one of the areas that border the Vieux-Port, are some of the city's oldest defenses. Low walls, cannons, and a moat are the only remnants of what was once part of the Lower Town's fortifications. The 400th anniversary has seen the waterfront rejuvenated with a long bike path that follows the water's edge and takes riders right in to the Old Port. It's here along the quays and among the docked boats that people stop for an ice cream or a cold drink in the summer and to look back at the city that stands, perfectly lit, on the hill. The newly built Vieux-Port Interpretation Centre presents exhibitions related to the timber trade and shipbuilding, and characters in period costumes evoke a sense of history as they tell old-time tales. Guided walking tours of the port are also available.

SIGHTS

Parliament Hill and the Plains   Map 10

FONTAINE DE TOURNY
Ave. Honoré Mercier btwn. La Grande-Allée and blvd.
René-Levesque

Fontaine de Tourny was a gift from La Maison Simons to Québec City for its 400th anniversary. It came to its place in front of the Parliament by a circuitous route. Created in France in 1854, it won an award at the Universal Exposition in Paris the following year before being installed in 1857, in the heart of Bordeaux in the Allées de Tourny. By 1960, however, the city no longer wanted the fountain, which was in a state of near disrepair. It was dismantled and stored in the Château Larivière near Bordeaux before finally being sold to a Parisian antiques dealer at the beginning of the 21st century.

During a trip to Paris in 2003, Peter Simons, president of Simons department store, discovered it in a flea market and had it shipped to Québec for restoration. Measuring seven meters high and four meters wide, it's adorned with 43 jets and decorated with statues by sculptor Mathurin Moreau, of one man and three women symbolizing water, which matches well with the history of the port city. Five other statues were made from the same mold and can be found in cities across Europe, including Geneva in Switzerland and Porto in Portugal.

LA GRANDE-ALLÉE
Btwn. Fontaine de Tourny and rue de l'Amérique Française

Dubbed the "Champs d'Elysées of Québec," La Grande-Allée is one of the larger boulevards in the city and is the city's nightlife hotspot. It's lined with grand Victorian mansions, and the homes have been converted into cafés, restaurants, and the nightclubs. Once lined with terraced houses, it was the chi-chi neighborhood of the Québec, but many of those homes

---

CONFESSION: QUÉBEC CITY'S LOVE AFFAIR WITH CHURCHES

If you weren't convinced about the Catholic Church's involvement in the development of New France, you will be after a trip to Québec City. There are so many churches in the city a single trip alone couldn't cover them all. Most are free and open to the public for both prayer and sightseeing. Here are a few to get you on your way.

- **Chalmers-Wesley United Church:** Another neo-Gothic Protestant church, this one was completed in 1853 and was designed by architect John Wells. Its steeple is the tallest inside the walls of Old Québec at 164 feet above the sidewalk (78 rue Ste-Ursule).

- **Chapelle Historique Bon Pasteur:** Designed by Charles Baillairgé in 1868, the slanting roof hides an ornate baroque-style interior (1080 rue de la Chevrotière).

- **Église Saint-Dominique:** Run by Dominican

monks, this church and former monastery boasts a stunning wood-beamed ceiling reminiscent of medieval architecture (175 Grande-Allée).

- **Holy Trinity Anglican Cathedral:** Inspired by St-Martin's in the Fields in London, this was the first Anglican cathedral to be built outside of the British Isles (31 rue des Jardins).

- **Sanctuaire Notre-Dame-du-Sacré-Cœur:** Tucked back from the road, this slender, neo-Gothic church was built in 1901 by François-Xavier Berlinguet and is renowned for its stained-glass windows and marble plaques that line the walls (71 rue Ste-Ursule).

- **St. Andrew's Presbyterian Church:** This congregation had its start among the Scottish Fraser Highlanders that were part of Wolfe's Army in 1759 (106 rue Ste-Anne).

© SACHA JACKSON

Fontaine de Tourny

were torn down to make way for the Hôtel du Parlement, found on the south end of the *allée,* just in front of the St-Louis Gate.

It is the Grande-Allée that separates the rest of the city from the Plains of Abraham, which run along its back. The architecture of the strip's buildings is still stunning, with much of the stonework dating from the late 19th century.

HÔTEL DU PARLEMENT

1045 rue des Parliamentaires, 866/337-8837, www.assnat.qc.ca

HOURS: First Tues. of Sept.-June 23 Mon.-Fri. 9 A.M.-4:30 P.M.; June 24-first Mon. of Sept. Mon.-Fri. 9 A.M.-4:30 P.M., Sat.-Sun. 10 A.M.-4:30 P.M.

COST: Free

The Parliament Building, house of the National Assembly of Québec, is one of the most impressive buildings in the national capital. Located on one of the highest spots of Upper Town, just outside the city walls, the quadrilateral building was constructed between 1877 and 1886 by the French architect Eugène-Étienne

Taché. Inspired by the Louvre in Paris, the style of building, Second Empire neo-French Renaissance, is unique in North America. The front of the building also features a pantheon representing the province's rich history.

Incensed by the Durham Report, in which the British Lord said that the French-Canadians could not be civilized because they had no history, Taché included 15 statues of important figures in the province's history, to show that they did indeed have a strong past. Figures include Samuel de Champlain, Louis de Buade de Frontenac, James Wolfe, the Marquis de Montcalm, and, at the very top, an indigenous family. As the province's political life continues to grow, so does the number of statues; there are now 22 in front of the Parliament Building.

Since it is still a functioning government office, the only way to see the interior of the building is to take a free guided tour. At 30 minutes long, they provide a great opportunity to appreciate the unique architecture of the building, as well as gain insight into Québec's history and political scene. Make sure to have a photo I.D. with you, however, otherwise you won't pass the security check. In the summer outdoor tours are also given to discover the surrounding gardens, which highlight the many trees and flowers of Québec and also give an overview of the many sculptures. All tours leave from the visitors center.

MANÈGE MILITAIRE

805 ave. Wilfrid-Laurier

This iconic piece of Canadiana was destroyed by fire in 2008, and though 90 percent of the museum's artifacts were saved, only the shell of the historic drill hall remains.

Built in 1887, between the Plains of Abraham and the Grande-Allée, the Manège Militaire is home to the Voltigeurs de Québec, a primary reserve regiment founded in 1862. It was designed by Eugène-Étienne Taché, who also designed the Parliament Building, and the architectural style is inspired by the French chateaus of the 14th and 15th centuries, with circular turrets, pointy roofs, and high dormer windows. This particular style, extremely

SIGHTS

© SACHA JACKSON

Situated on the Plains of Abraham, the Musée National des Beaux-Arts du Québec is a great place to see Québécois masters.

unique in North America, would be recreated by countless other important structures in the country. It is one of the most recognized of Canadian military buildings in the world.

◖ MUSÉE NATIONAL DES BEAUX-ARTS DU QUÉBEC

Parc des Champs-de-Bataille, 418/644-6460, www.mnba.qc.ca

HOURS: Tues.-Sun. 10 A.M.-5 P.M., Wed. until 9 P.M.

COST: $15 adult, $12 senior, $7 student, $4 child, 12 and under free

Located in the middle of the Plains of Abraham, Musée National des Beaux-Arts du Québec holds the largest existing collection of Québec art, with works dating from the 17th century onward. The major focus here is on fine art, and the exhibits rarely revolve around the work of contemporary artists, though plans for a new addition are hoping to change that.

It consists of three distinct structures: the Gérard-Morisset Building, the Charles-Baillairgé building, and the Grand Hall. Each has its own atmosphere and the work exhibited therein

reflects that. Inaugurated in 1933, Gérard-Morisset is classical in style. It was designed by architect Wilfrid Lacroix and built in a neo-Italian Renaissance style. The first of the buildings to hold the museum's collection, it's full of white marble, wide Victorian steps, sculpted ceilings, and columns and it's here that you'll find permanent collections dedicated to Québécois artists like Emile Bourdos and others.

Much less conventional is the Charles-Baillairgé building, a former prison. It was incorporated into the museum in 1991 but retains a number of cells, which visitors are invited to explore. Opened in 1867, the prison was modeled after the Auburn Penitentiary in New York state and was all about rehabilitation through isolation. Overpopulated from the beginning, it sheltered not only criminals but the poor and needy. Despite its old-fashioned design it housed inmates until 1970.

The Grand Hall joins these two structures with its pyramid-like glass facade, which adds light and airiness to the entire structure. A monument directly out front of the museum commemorates the place where General James Wolfe was shot and killed.

OBSERVATOIRE DE LA CAPITALE

1037 rue de la Chevrotière, 418/644-9841, www.observatoirecapitale.org

HOURS: Feb.–Canadian Thanksgiving daily 10 A.M.–5 P.M.

COST: $5 adult, $4 student and senior, 12 and under free

It might not look like much on the outside, but on the 31st floor of the building is one of the best views of the city. Perfect for a general overview of Québec, at 221 meters high the *observatoire* is the highest spot in the Québec and offers 360-degree views of the city and its environs.

As you look out over the city at various vantage points, important buildings and monuments are pointed out and explained on the easy-to-read plaques that adorn the windows. Sights like the far-off Québec bridge are easily seen, along with the Laurentian mountains and the St-Lawrence River. Alongside points of interest the Observatoire de la Capitale also gives you information on the province and its history, such as the destruction of Chinatown, which took place to make way for highways to the suburbs. Temporary exhibits, including photographs of local sights, are also on view.

PLAINS OF ABRAHAM AND BATTLEFIELD PARK

Discovery Pavillon, 835 ave. Wilfrid-Laurier, 418/649-6157, www.theplainsofabraham.ca

HOURS: Daily 10 A.M.–5 P.M.

COST: $10 adult, $8 senior and student, 12 and under free

It was here on the Plains of Abraham on September 13, 1759, that the French fell to the British, forever changing the course of North American history. After Champlain's arrival in 1608, there were skirmishes on and off with the British, who at the time were fighting for control of the North American colonies against the French, but it wasn't until 1759 that the real battle took place.

Led by General James Wolfe, the British army advanced up the St-Lawrence in the spring of 1759, setting up camp north of Québec. During that summer they laid a near constant siege on the city, destroying houses and monuments but not breaking French general Montcalm's reserve. For all intents and purposes life continued within the walls of the city amid the bombardments and fires. The siege lasted three long months. With winter approaching, Wolfe discovered the Canadians were awaiting a shipment of supplies from France to arrive on September 13. The supplies never arrived, but Wolfe continued with his plan regardless, maneuvering his men through the hard-to-navigate narrows in rowboats and mounting the cliff by way of a dried-up creek. By the time the Canadians arrived on the battlefield the British army was already in formation. It was all over in 15 minutes. Wolfe was shot and killed on the spot, but Montcalm was only wounded; he was rushed back inside the city walls, where he was taken to a friend's house and died the following day. Five days later Québec capitulated.

The peculiar name Plains of Abraham can be traced as far back as 1635, when the Scot Abraham Martin, a pilot of the St-Lawrence and a friend of Samuel de Champlain, was given 12 acres of land in the area and an additional 20 acres 10 years after. Today there is little trace of the battle on the rolling green hills of the plains that border the cliff above the river. The grandiose stone building set back from the Plains houses the interpretation center, which offers a multimedia exhibit of its history, from the battle to its popularity with prostitutes in the 19th century and as a choice spot for duels, hangings, and the Stanley Cup playoffs. The park itself was part of the 300th anniversary celebrations and was designed by Frederick Todd. Many of the cannons that line the park were gifts from other nations to remind people that this was once a battlefield.

TOURS MARTELLOS

Parc des Champs-de-Bataille, 418/648-5371, www.ccbn-nbc.gc.ca

HOURS: Mid-June-early Sept. daily 10 A.M.-5 P.M.

COST: $14 adult, $8 senior and student, 12 and under free (included with entrance into Plains of Abraham's Odyssey tour)

In 1807 the United States Congress closed

U.S. ports to all exports and restricted imports from Britain, because of British and French interference with U.S. merchant ships during the Napoleonic Wars. Dubbed the American-Anglo crisis, it prompted Sir James Craig, then governor in chief of Canada, to increase the city's fortifications. Built between 1808 and 1812, four Martello towers were constructed around Québec as defenses and were positioned at various points outside of the city walls, mostly along the Plains of Abraham.

Round in shape, with limited openings, the west sides of the towers were built stronger than the east sides, based on the idea that if an attack were to happen, it would likely come from the west. In the event that the Martellos were under siege from the east, the eastern wall could easily be battered down and the men able to escape and continue fighting.

The smooth sandstone was cut in such a way that the constructions are perfectly rounded. Each Martello has a single door, placed at 4.5 meters above ground, 2.5 times the height of men at that time. It was originally reached by a ladder.

They became obsolete in the 1860s but continue to stand as monuments of and windows onto the city's past. Martello Tower 1, located on the Plains of Abraham, hosts an exhibition come summer (mid-June–early Sept.) inviting visitors to discover the military history and examine the lives of the soldiers who occupied the towers. Martello Tower 2, located not far from the Plains on the corner of Taché and Wilfrid-Laurier, invites you to drink beer in 19th-century style while you discuss the appropriate punishment for a British solider with the locals. These are hosted daily July–Aug. and on weekends from late August to early September. Those under 18 must be accompanied by an adult.

Saint-Jean-Baptiste and Saint-Roch   Map 11

ÉGLISE SAINT-JEAN-BAPTISTE
400 rue St-Jean, 418/525-7188,
www.saintjeanbaptiste.org
HOURS: Mon.-Sat. noon-4 P.M., Sun. 11 A.M.–4 P.M.;
tours daily
COST: Free

Built in 1882, this parish church is one of the most stunning in Québec City. Situated outside of the walls in Saint-Jean-Baptiste, a neighborhood that at the time was home to blue-collar workers of both French-Canadian and Irish origin, it's now surrounded by shops, restaurants, and residential homes.

A fire destroyed the previous church and much of the neighborhood in 1881, and the job of rebuilding the church was passed on to Joseph-Ferdinand Peachy. Of mixed Québécois (his mother) and Irish (his father) descent, Peachy was an ideal choice for an architect in this region. First learning the craft under Thomas Baillairgé, he started his own architecture firm in 1866. Inspired by both a church built in the 12th century and Église-de-la-Sainte-Trinité in Paris (which was built a mere 10 years earlier), Église Saint-Jean-Baptiste is a combination of very distinct styles; neo-Renaissance, neo-Roman, and Second Empire.

Though the facade is unmistakably Second Empire, and almost a direct copy of the Sainte-Trinité, the interior styles are subtler. The gallery features semicircles under the windows as well as triptychs in the arcade, both neo-Roman elements. Neo-Renaissance, meanwhile, can be seen in the use of blue pastel for the roof and in the placement of the window.

The church finally opened to the public in 1884, but it wasn't until 1896 that the church would be completely finished. Staying close to its parish roots, much of the financing for the church came from the public, and many of the church's embellishments, from the pews to the baldaquin, were made in Québec City, by members of the parish. Only three elements came from outside of the province: the Italian ceramic floor tiles, the paintings of the stations of the cross, and the three types of white marble that are used throughout, on the pillars and for the statues. Even the organ was built by local Napoléon Déry in 1885, though it was reconstructed by the Casavant brothers in 1921.

JARDIN SAINT-ROCH

Btwn. Côte d'Abraham and blvd. Charest at rue du Parvis and rue de la Couronne
HOURS: Daily 24 hours
COST: Free

Once an empty dirt lot, the Jardin Saint-Roch has become a symbol for the ongoing revitalization of the Saint-Roch (pronounced "ROCK") area in the city's Lower Town. Inaugurated in 1992, it was one of the first places to get a much-needed facelift. With the opening of park, the centerpiece of which is a waterfall featuring local stone, other businesses came to the area, taking up residence in old warehouses and factories and transforming them into workable, creative environments.

Displayed in the park are busts of René Richard, Alfred Pellan, and Horatio Walker, three important Québécois painters. Though their styles differed wildly, they represent the diversity and the richness of art and culture in Québec. The park is now surrounded by gaming companies, art studios, galleries, and theaters.

◖ RUE SAINT-JEAN

Rue St-Jean btwn. Autoroute Dufferin and ave. Salaberry
This section of rue St-Jean, part of the area known as Faubourg Saint-Jean-Baptiste, is a continuation of the St-Jean found within the city's historic walls. And though these two sides of the street—within and without the walls—are linked by a shared past, their appearance and history are markedly different. The word *faubourg* refers to "outskirts" in English, and during the early days of the city when its gates were opened in the morning and closed in the evening, that's exactly what Faubourg Saint-Jean Baptiste was, an outskirt with no services or protection available from the city center once the gates were locked.

In beginning of the 18th century craftsmen built their workshops and homes along the inside walls of the fortifications. In 1745, however, the defenses were expanded, forcing many to move. This construction pushed them outside of the walls and they quickly established themselves and took their trades to the *faubourg,* bringing commerce to the area for the first time. In 1845, however, the first of two fires would decimate the area. Two churches, three schools, and 1,300 homes were burned to the ground during the 1845 fire, which subsequently led to the widening of the street. This and other fire prevention measures, such as restrictions on the layout of foyers in homes, were soon put into practice. In 1881 the area was hit with a second fire, and in just seven hours the church went up in flames and 5,000 were left without homes. This time the architectural restrictions were more drastic and wood was banned in construction.

These two disasters and the resulting architectural restrictions, coupled with a meshing of cultures that came later (the working-class Protestants and Catholics), have created the vibrant street today. The *faubourg* remains a vital part of day-to-day life as one of the busiest commercial streets in a busy residential neighborhood. As you wander along the street, the city's history is mapped out before you in the various architectural styles and businesses telling the story of each important epoque.

RUE SAINT-JOSEPH

Rue St-Joseph btwn. rue St-Dominique to rue Caron
From the end of the 19th-century until the 1960s, this was one of the most important commercial streets in the city. Akin to Fifth Avenue in New York, it was the chi-chi shopping district, the home of upscale shops and historic department stores. The construction of large shopping centers on the outskirts of town in the 1950s and '60s, however, drew consumers out of the downtown core. Soon the stores left too, moving to new digs in the suburban malls, leaving the stores boarded up and the street run-down.

With hopes of luring business and shoppers back to the street, the city decided to turn it into the closest thing they could to a mall. In

NEW QUÉBEC: UP-AND-COMING LIMOILOU

Like its neighbor Saint-Roch, Limoilou is fast becoming one of the coolest neighborhoods in the city. Full of cozy bars and cafés, artist boutiques, kid-friendly restaurants, and some of the best food shops in Québec City, it's an ideal place to spend the day wandering and scouring for antiques.

Situated across the St-Charles River, it is one of the oldest boroughs in the city. The first thoroughfare, now called 1e avenue (1st Avenue) was built in 1665. Entirely rural up until the end of the 19th century, its proximity to downtown and placement alongside the river allows for an exceptional view of the city. It's a predominantly residential neighborhood, and the majority of shops and cafés are found in Vieux-Limoilou, easily reached by crossing the rue du Pont in Saint-Roch. Inspired by the grid system used in New York, the streets and avenues are numbered. The majority of cafés and shops are concentrated on 3e avenue, a continuation of rue du Pont, once you've crossed the St-Charles River. Cafés and neighborhood shops are on 1e avenue, while 2e avenue is perfect for taking in the old Victorian architecture and apartment blocks with spiral staircases, reminiscent of those in Montréal's Plateau.

Open and bright with a modern, minimalist decor **Le Fun en Bouche** (1073 3e ave., 418/524-7272, www.lefunenbouche.com, Tues. 9 A.M.-2 P.M., Wed.-Sun. 8 A.M.-2 P.M., $10) is a neighborhood bistro in the heart of Vieux-Limoilou. Head there for the daily brunch and try one of the eggs Benedict or French toast. The lunch selections include bagel with smoked trout and blueberry port spread, and smoked chicken, leek, and parmesan quiche. If you're in the mood for something to warm you up, **Soupe et Cie** (522, 3e ave., 418/948-8996, www.soupecie.com, daily 11 A.M.-9 P.M., $15) has hearty soups and open-faced sandwiches on the menu. Closer to the bridge but still in the center of the community, this long restaurant with brick walls, old chandeliers, and tons of bright cushions is a cozy place to grab a bite. Despite its chic decor it's kid-friendly — in fact kids rule here and their exuberance and chit-chat make up most of the ambience.

Just down the block is **Hosaka-Ya** (491 3e ave., 418/529-9993, Tues.-Fri. 11:30 A.M.-2 P.M. and 4:30-9 P.M., Sat.-Sun. 4:30-9 P.M., $6), a

1974 they covered the majority of the street with a Plexiglas arcade. Instead of drawing business, however, the new scheme attracted the marginalized and disenfranchised—the arcade was ideal shelter against the elements. Except for department store Laliberté and the Brunet pharmacy next door, who resisted the original exodus, most businesses consisted of cheap cafés and diners and five-and-dime stores.

It was Mayor Jean-Paul L'Allier, who governed for four terms, who would eventually bring business back to the area and the street. His first gamble was convincing Université Laval to move its art school from its campus on the fringes of the city to an old, unoccupied corset factory. The gamble paid off, and slowly but surely other businesses, drawn by incentives, returned to the strip. Sections of the Plexiglas eyesore, however, remained. It was finally fully removed for the city's 400th anniversary in 2008, but there are still sections along this diverse and interesting street where you can see where the arcade roof once sat.

ST-MATTHEW CHURCH AND CEMETERY

755 rue St-Jean, 418/641-6798,
www.bibliothequesdequebec.qc.ca

HOURS: Mon.-Tues. and Thurs. noon-5:30 P.M., Wed. noon-8 P.M., Fri. 10 A.M.-5:30 P.M., Sat.-Sun. 1-5 P.M.

COST: Free

Distinctly English with its slender steeple and neo-Gothic stonework, reminiscent of medieval English parish churches, St-Matthew Church and Cemetery stands out in an otherwise French-influenced Faubourg St-Jean Baptiste. The first cemetery in the city to exclusively bury Protestants, it encircled the church and was in use from 1772 to 1860. It is relaxed Japanese restaurant inspired by the traditional *izakaya*. The menu is more well-rounded than most, offering classic dishes like *gyoza* and udon noodles as well as seasonal sushi dishes. If you're looking for a drink, stop into **Le Bal du Lézard** (1049 ave. 3e, 418/529-3829, www.lebaldulezard.com, daily 2 P.M.-3 A.M.), a friendly little neighborhood bar that's been a staple here since 1985. It has a laid-back feel and features a foosball table and nice sidewalk *terrasse* come summer.

Decked out in red and green tablecloths and multicolored streamers adorning on the walls, **Restaurant la Salsa** (1063 3e ave., 418/522-0032, Tues.-Sat. 11:30 A.M.-10 P.M., $15) is one of the most authentic Mexican restaurants in the city. The interior might border on kitsch, but their *pupusas*, enchiladas, and tamales are nothing but classic. Cheese lovers should make a stop at **Yannick Fromagerie** (901 3e ave., 418/614-2002, www.yannickfromagerie.ca), which specializes in specialty cheese from Québec, while a fresh baguette from **La Fournée Bio** (1296 ave. 3e, 418/522-4441, Mon.-Wed. 7 A.M.-6:30 P.M., Thurs.-Fri. 7 A.M.-7 P.M., Sat.-Sun. 7 A.M.-5:30 P.M., $10) acts as the perfect accompaniment. Open for over 14 years, La Fournée Bio is an artisanal organic bakery that makes everything from croissants to sourdough and even serves a good cup of coffee.

For a bit of antiquing head into **Le Retour du Passé** (500 1e ave., 418/524-8885, www.leretourdupasse.net, Mon.-Sat. 9 A.M.-5 P.M., Sun. 9 A.M.-4 P.M.), an antiques store that deals in old electronics like radios, clocks, and record players, as well as the usual mishmash of stuff. New boutique **L'Usine** (986 3e ave., 418/614-8408, Tues.-Wed. 11 A.M.-4 P.M., Thurs.-Sat. 11 A.M.-5 P.M.) specializes in jewelry, accessories, bags, and clothes made by local designers with an eye to sustainability. If you want to see something truly different check out designer **Sylvain Primeau**'s workshop and boutique (519 3e ave., 418/524-0101, www.sylvainprimo.com, Tues.-Fri. 11 A.M.-5 P.M., Sat. 10 A.M.-4 P.M.), where he creates corsets and baroque-style fashions with a modern twist (think tutus). For more street-friendly wear, **La Boutique du Skate** (412 3e ave., 418/781-2030, Tues.-Fri. and Sun. noon-5 P.M., Sat. 10 A.M.-4 P.M.) has a selection of skateboarding shoes as well as a huge selection of boards – perfect if you're traveling with your teen.

the burial place of many of the earliest English settlers in Canada and is the oldest cemetery in Québec City.

The church was originally the city gravedigger's house. It was only in 1822 with the arrival of French-speaking Protestant immigrants from the Channel Isles that services started to be held in French. By 1827, the services had become so popular, with a French service in the morning and an English one in the evening that the house was modified into a chapel. Destroyed by the great fire of 1845, it was rebuilt into today's incarnation by John Cliff. The interior, which now houses a public library, maintains its late-19th-century architecture with its exposed beams, rounded moldings at the top of the arcades, and delicate embellishments in the stonework.

Today it is a public library, and visitors can stroll among the bookshelves and the admire the preserved interior, which has remained virtually untouched.

SIGHTS

Greater Québec City   Map 12

AQUARIUM DU QUÉBEC
1675 ave. des Hôtels, Sainte-Foy, 866/659-5264,
www.sepaq.com/aquarium
HOURS: June-early Sept. daily 10 A.M.-5 P.M., early
Sept.-May daily 10 A.M.-4 P.M.
COST: $17 adult, $15.50 senior, $8.50 child (3-17)

Staying true to its roots, this aquarium specializes in boreal and arctic wildlife, though over 10,000 animals call this place their home. It's divided into eight areas, both indoor and outdoor, and the main attraction is the Awesome Ocean, a glass tunnel through a massive seawater tank that allows visitors to get up close and personal with the marine life. Species from Québec wetlands and the St-Lawrence River are also here, along with polar bears, harp seals, and walruses from both coasts in the Arctic display. The newest addition is a tropical exhibition space showcasing jellyfish, stingrays, seahorses, and other southern species.

First opened in 1956 as a marine biology laboratory and research center it soon attracted visitors eager to see the species that occupied the two aquariums. Continuing its slow growth over the next 40 years the sight was given a major renovation in 2002 that saw it expand with outdoor gardens and seal and polar bear viewing pools. Located just outside of the city in Sainte-Foy, this is a great attraction for families and has drawn over eight million visitors.

In summertime kids can cool off in the adjoining water park or clamber their way through the Abre-en-Abre pathway adventure.

RESTAURANTS

There's no shortage of choice when it comes to dining in Québec City, with the most restaurants per capita in the country. The challenge here isn't finding a decent place to eat, it's deciding which ones you have time for. The number of noteworthy, award-winning chefs and restaurants in Québec, well respected for its gastronomy, can be both tiring and exhilarating. Whether serving up a simple breakfast or an intricate haute-cuisine meal, chefs tend toward *terroir,* cooking that uses local produce and ingredients. In this region of the province those ingredients include wild game, such as elk, red deer, and bison, and seafood like scallops and cod.

Whereas the trend in Montréal tends toward market-fresh cuisine cooked by up-and-coming chefs in a boisterous atmosphere, the trend in Québec is more traditional, with a focus on details and inventive preparation, though a few young, breakout stars can be found, mostly in the Saint-Roch section of town. Even the decor of some of the city's best restaurants can feel a little staid and reserved—few, if any, of the city's restaurants turn into night clubs once the tables have been cleared. The ones that do, however, can be found on the Grande-Allée, just outside the old walls.

Since so many of the restaurants offer top-quality ingredients and service the price tag can also be high, though it's often worth it. One way to circumvent the costs without sacrificing the experience is to order the table d'hôte, which gives you the option of a three-course meal, usually appetizer, main, and dessert, for a set price. Another option is to go

© L'ECHAUDEE

HIGHLIGHTS

LOOK FOR **(** TO FIND RECOMMENDED RESTAURANTS.

(**Best Views:** Le Café de la Terrasse in Château Frontenac is in a picturesque setting looking out over the St-Lawrence (page 254).

(**Best Late-Night Eats:** Credited with popularizing *poutine*, **Chez Ashton** is Québec's preeminent fast-food joint and the ideal spot to refuel after a night on the town (page 257).

(**Best Tasting Menu:** One of the best haute cuisine restaurants in the city, **Restaurant L'Initiale** features tasting menus with local food in a down-to-earth, modern interior (page 258).

(**Most Authentic Québécois Grub:** Established in 1975, **Buffet de l'Antiquaire** serves heaping portions of traditional cuisine and some great breakfasts in a tiny '50s-style diner (page 260).

(**Best Upscale Bistro:** Situated on a tiny street in the Vieux-Port, **L'Échaudé** has both an elegant and relaxed atmosphere with classic bistro dishes (page 260).

(**Best Homestyle-Meets-Haute Cuisine Meal:** **Panache**'s exposed wood beams, stone walls, and original wood flooring create the perfect setting for trying a revamped shepherd's pie (page 260).

(**Best Café:** **Brûlerie St-Roch** is packed for a reason; the lattes here are the best and the ambience is effortlessly cool (page 265).

(**Most Authentic Crêpes:** Run by an expat from Brittany, **Crêperie le Billig** serves up the best crêpes in the city, which are even more delicious when you down them with cider (page 266).

(**Best Restaurant/Bar/Café:** Le Cercle is your one-stop-shop for a night out on the town (page 267).

(**Most Bang for Your Buck:** Eat among savvy locals at **Le Clocher Penché,** where the bistro fare is made with fresh, regional ingredients and the bill is always a pleasant surprise (page 267).

© SACHA JACKSON

The line-up starts early at Brûlerie St-Roch.

PRICE KEY

⑤ Entrées less than CAN$10

⑤⑤ Entrées CAN$10-20

⑤⑤⑤ Entrées more than CAN$20

to one of the more expensive restaurants for lunch. Following the French tradition, restaurants here serve lunch well into the afternoon (service ends around 2 P.M.), often with a specific lunchtime menu. Also in the French tradition is the city's love affair with cafés and bakeries, and in these categories it easily trumps Montréal.

Barely a street goes by that doesn't feature a cute, independent café or two, most of which serve delectable pastries, light lunches, and choice coffee. Though you can always get your coffee to go, it's rare to see resident Québeckers striding along with their lattes; in fact there are only two Starbucks shops in the city, and other chain coffee shops are just as rare. Bakeries too can be found in every neighborhood, each offering its own take on freshly baked bread and pastries.

There are a few things, however, that the Québec culinary scene is lacking: vegetarian and ethnic restaurants. Though many restaurants offer a vegetarian option, many do not, and doing research ahead of time is sure to save some frustration. Vegetarians who eat fish have abundant choices, but vegans will be sorely disappointed. When it comes to ethnic eats in Québec, Asian is the most popular, and there good Chinese and Vietnamese restaurants available. Japanese is little harder to find, but the restaurants that do exist have excellent sushi thanks to the abundance of fresh fish.

The city is no stranger to tourists, and menus in Québec are often written in English. Even when they're not, there's no reason to be shy; servers here are happy to translate for you. A lot of fuss can be made about the dangers of falling into a "tourist trap" when you're visiting a city like Québec, but the reality is, most restaurants, regardless of the number of tourists at their tables, are adept at making some seriously good meals. Whether you're enjoying a tasting menu by one of the top chefs or eating meat pie by candlelight in a laid-back bistro, you'll always find a lively and welcoming atmosphere, the city's most charming and infectious trait.

Vieux-Québec's Upper Town   Map 8

ASIAN
APSARA ⑤⑤⑤
71 rue d'Auteuil, 418/694-0232,
www.restaurantapsara.com
HOURS: Mon.-Fri. 11:30 A.M.-2 P.M. and 5:30-10:30 P.M., Sat.-Sun. 5:30-10:30 P.M.
If you're fed up with bistro fare and all this "Europe in North America" business head over to Apsara for some traditional Asian cooking. The decor here doesn't stray far from typical dining rooms, with its white tablecloths and wicker chairs, but a sense of the Far East is evoked in the golden statues, Thai artwork, and traditional masks featured throughout the restaurant. The ambience is quiet and calm with

traditional music playing in the background and impeccable service. Apsara specializes in Cambodian, Thai, and Vietnamese cuisine, and with five or six mains available from each region, deciding on a single dish can be tough. Those facing a bout of indecision should go for the Apsara Plate, featuring dishes from each country, including Khemara beef from Cambodia and Vietnamese shrimp d'Anam.

CHEZ SOI LA CHINE ⑤⑤⑤
27 rue Ste-Angèle, 418/523-8858
HOURS: Tues.-Fri. noon-2 P.M. and 5:30-10 P.M., Sat.-Sun. 5:30-10 P.M.
The sign at the entrance reads Authentic

Chinese Food, a simple but bold statement in a city that isn't overflowing with ethnic food choices. It's located on the down slope of a hilly street, and the sidewalk cuts in front of the door at nearly a 45-degree angle. Inside, the yellow paper lanterns and traditional Chinese music are just about the only Asian touches in this otherwise sparse restaurant. Despite its austerity, it's one of the best Asian restaurants in the city, serving up traditional Chinese fare that is both filling and tasty. It's popular with young locals and the city's Asian community, and specialties like duck with Chinese mushrooms, crispy chicken, and perfectly steamed pork dumplings keep customers coming back. There is, however, one ingredient this place is missing: alcohol. It's bring your own, so don't forget to bring a bottle of wine or beer with you to dinner.

CAFÉS AND CHEAP EATS
CAFÉ-BOULANGERIE PAILLARD ❺
1097 rue St-Jean, 418/692-1221,
www.paillard.ca
HOURS: June-Aug. daily 7:30 A.M.-11 P.M.; Sept.-June Sun.-Thurs. 7:30 A.M.-6 P.M., Fri.-Sat. 7:30 A.M.-7 P.M.

Modern and open, the long communal tables of this pastry shop, bakery, and *sandwicherie* are cafeteria-like in style, but the tall ceilings and lots of light make it feel effortlessly spacious. In traditional New York style you must line up to order, be it a fresh Paillard salad with walnuts, blue cheese, and pears or a frothy cappuccino and almond croissant. Their known for their macaroons, those sweet, one-bite-and-you're done cookies; they come in a rainbow of colors and flavors and rival any that you'd find in the tiny back lanes of Paris.

A QUICK GUIDE TO QUÉBÉCOIS FOOD

Over the past 400 years or so Québec has developed its own cuisine; some foods are variations on old French recipes and some are creations that are uniquely their own. In the early days of the colony much of Québec society relied on hunting and fishing for sustenance, and wild game is still a big part of cooking in the region. Here's a quick guide to some of the more common but obscure foods you may come across in the region.

• **Caribou:** This is one of the more popular meats, and you'll find it on menus across the city. It's an especially popular ingredient in meat pies.

• **Caribou (the drink):** During the city's world-famous annual Winter Carnival this stuff is available in all the SAQs (liquor stores). This mixture of port, vodka, black-currant liqueur, and maple syrup might be tough to get down but it will keep you warm and give you enough courage to tackle *les glissades* – the enormous toboggan run on Terrasse Dufferin.

• **Cheese Curds:** This is the special cheese they put on top of *poutine*, but it is also eaten on its own as a snack and can be found at most corner stores. Made from fresh cheddar, it has a rubbery texture and squeaks when it's chewed.

• **Cheval:** Though it's not as common a meat here as in Belgium, you can still find horse on menus across the city, mostly likely listed as *bavette du cheval*, horse steak. Similar to beef in consistency it is both sweeter and more tender.

• **Cretons:** If you order a traditional Québécois breakfast, there's a good chance you'll find a serving of this on your plate. A salty pork product, it's made by boiling the pork in milk with onions and spices until its consistency is halfway between a spread and a pâté. Best eaten on toast.

• **Foie Gras:** Made from duck and goose liver (the name literally means "fatty liver"), this typical French dish has turned into an industry in Québec. Locally produced foie gras is now a staple in most bistros and restaurants serving haute cuisine.

CHEZ TEMPOREL ❸

25 rue Couillard, 418/694-1813

HOURS: Daily 7 A.M.–1 A.M.

Established in 1974, this two-story café on rue Couillard, a quaint and winding side street, has become an institution. A favorite with students and artists, it is frequented by locals who come here to grab a quiet coffee or light lunch, and offers a nice alternative in the otherwise touristy and busy part of Old Québec. It's simply decorated with wood tables, brick walls, and work by local artists on the wall, and the food follows suit with homemade croissants, muffins, soups, salads, and quiches.

LE PETIT COIN LATIN ❸❸

8½ rue Ste-Ursule, 418/692-2022

HOURS: Mon.–Fri. 8 A.M.–11 P.M., Sat.–Sun. 7:30 A.M.–11 P.M.

Just inside the city walls on a steep side street you'll find Le Petit Coin Latin, one of the oldest cafés in Québec. Stone walls, a fireplace, and burgundy banquettes give it an intimate, homey atmosphere. Like its surroundings the food here is unpretentious and includes Québécois classics like *tourtière au caribou* (caribou pie) and *tarte au sucre* (sugar pie). It's a popular place for breakfast and brunch, especially in the summer when the garden terrace is open out back, and their plentiful omelets and *pain doré* will leave you stuffed. In winter order the hearty and warming *raclette*.

CRÊPERIES

CASSE-CRÊPE BRETON ❸

1136 rue St-Jean, 418/692-0438, www.cassecrepebreton.com

HOURS: Daily 7 A.M.–10 P.M.

No matter the time of day, the line at this

- **Galvaude:** A variation on *poutine*, in this dish chicken and peas are added to the fries, gravy, and cheese for a more "rounded" meal.

- **Grand-père dans le Sirop:** A popular dessert during the Great Depression, this is essentially a sweet dumpling made by boiling batter in sugar water, then serving it doused with maple syrup. Translated it means "Grandpa in the syrup."

- **Guedille:** Found mostly in *casse-croûtes* (snack shacks) *guedilles* are hot dog buns stuffed with lettuce, mayonnaise, and just about anything else, including egg, chicken, and fries. Commonly found outside of the cities, it's one version of Québec's take on fast food.

- **Oreilles de Crisse:** Translated this means "Christ's ears." Made from fried salted pork, they've been a snack since the time of Nouvelle France. Variations on this can be found in upscale restaurants across the province, especially those that specialize in *terroir* cooking.

- **Poutine:** Fries, gravy, cheese curds — this is the unofficial national dish of Québec. Though *poutine* has recently been embraced by food lovers everywhere it was invented in this region and remains close to their hearts.

- **Ragoût de Pattes de Cochon:** This stew made with pig's feet is part of the *réveillon,* or Christmas meal. A variation on this includes *ragoût de boulettes*, which means meatballs, though likely made with pork and not beef.

- **Tourtière:** Otherwise known as meat pie, this is likely the most common of all the dishes as well as the oldest. Records show it first being made in Québec as early as 1611. It's usually made with beef or pork, but different regions in the province have different versions. In Montréal it's a shallow pie filled with ground pork, while in the Lac-Saint-Jean region, north of Québec City, the pie is deeper and made with wild game like moose, caribou, elk, and hare. It's called *cipaille* in most restaurants.

bustling crêperie on St-Jean is usually out the door. Luckily, it moves pretty fast and customers are soon seated in the banquettes that line the restaurant's walls or at the bar with a full view of the action. Open since 1983, it can sometimes feel like an upper-class fast-food joint, in the swiftness of service and the way they churn out the crêpes. Choose from a list of suggestions—egg, bacon, mozzarella—or build your own with fillings like berries, chocolate, asparagus, and swiss cheese. Not the best crêperie in the city, it's a good choice for a quick and inexpensive meal.

FRENCH
LE CAFÉ BUADE $$

31 rue de Buade, 418/692-3909
HOURS: May-Sept. daily 7 A.M.-11 P.M., Oct.-Apr. daily 7 A.M.-9 P.M.

Established in 1919, Café Buade is the oldest restaurant in the city. Not far from Château Frontenac and facing the Notre-Dame-de-Québec Cathedral, it's a popular place with both tourists and long-time regulars. Serving basic family restaurant fare like pasta, pizza, and prime rib, it may not be the best meal you'll eat in the city but it won't break the bank either. If you do find yourself intrigued by the homey and warm atmosphere, opt for a classic club sandwich or one of their generous breakfasts, available daily till noon.

LE CAFÉ DE LA TERRASSE $$$

1 rue des Carrières, 418/691-3763,
www.fairmont.com/frontenac
HOURS: Daily 7 A.M.-2 P.M. and 5:30-10 P.M.

Situated in Château Frontenac with stunning views of the St-Lawrence, Le Café de la Terrasse is luxury without the price tag. Overseen by Jean Soulard, executive chef at Le Champlain, the café's haute-cuisine sibling, the menu varies according to season and tends toward regional gastronomy. The wine list too stays close to home and features many Canadian selections. The restaurant runs along the facade of the hotel, with picture windows onto the river, and the soft green decor reminiscent of a summer house is welcoming

© SACHA JACKSON

The oldest restaurant in Québec City, Le Café Buade, opened in 1919.

and sumptuous. Mains include classics like beef Wellington and lamb with marinated herbs, and buffets are often theme-based, like the lavish brunch buffet. Backpackers and mature travelers alike come here to grab a pre-dinner or post-skiing cocktail, especially in winter when the city of Lévis is lit up across the water.

LE CHAMPLAIN ❸❸❸
1 rue des Carrières, 418/266-3905,
www.fairmont.com/frontenac
HOURS: Daily 6-10 P.M., Sun. 10 A.M., 1 P.M.
Chef Jean Soulard brings French cuisine with creative flourishes to this storied restaurant. Dedicated to fresh, local ingredients, Soulard's menu changes with the seasons but diners can count on staples like pea soup, rack of lamb, and trout Chablis. Located in the historic Château Frontenac, it has gorgeous views of the river and boasts a glass-roofed sun lounge. With patterned carpets, luxurious chandeliers, and rich wood paneling, the decor is traditionally elegant. Adding to the classic ambience a harpist performs throughout the weekend dinner service. In a century-old tradition, afternoon tea is served Thursday–Saturday June–October. Reservations and smart casual attire are a must.

LA CRÉMAILLÈRE ❸❸❸
73 rue Ste-Anne, 418/692-2216,
www.cremaillere.qc.ca
HOURS: Mon.-Fri. 11:30 A.M.-2:30 P.M., daily 5-10 P.M.
Just in front of City Hall, you'll find award-winning restaurant La Crémaillère. Situated in a historic Victorian townhouse, the rooms of the restaurant have been diligently restored to show the intricate moldings and woodwork of a bygone era. The rich, patterned upholstery contrasts nicely with the white walls, giving the setting a bit of a modern kick. Taking inspiration from both French and Italian traditions, dishes are classic in presentation and flavor. House specialties include roasted rack of lamb, milk-fed veal, and lobster in champagne sauce. The atmosphere is elegant and romantic, making it perfect for a date night.

LES FRÈRES DE LA CÔTE ❸❸
1190 rue St-Jean, 418/592-5445
HOURS: Mon.-Fri. 11:30 A.M.-10 P.M.,
Sat.-Sun. 10 A.M.-10 P.M.
A cheerful and festive ambience oozes from this restaurant full of bon vivants. Located on one of the busiest corners in Old Québec, the casual dining room, decorated with checkered tablecloths and banquette seating, can be a bit cramped at times, with neighboring diners squished in beside each other. This, however, is all part of the lively ambience, which in summer extends to a tiny sidewalk *terrasse*.

Cuisine here runs the gamut from *bavette de cheval* (horse flank) and osso bucco to thin-crust pizzas and mussels with fries.

LE PAIN BÉNI ❸❸❸
24 rue Ste-Anne, 418/694-9485,
www.aubergeplacedarmes.com
HOURS: May.-Sept. daily 11:30 A.M.-10:30 P.M.; Oct.-Apr. Mon.-Fri. 11:30 A.M.-2 P.M., Tues.-Sat. 5:30-10 P.M.
Le Pain Béni is all about mixing influences. Located in the 200-year-old Auberge Place d'Armes, the dining room's stone walls are juxtaposed against the ultramodern design of bright orange chairs and simple table settings, creating a fresh and modern take on fine dining. On the menu you'll find dishes inspired by both French and Italian traditions, including lamb ravioli, beef tartare, goose leg confit, and parsnip gnocchi. With popular music on the sound system creating a laid-back ambience, there are few places that mix fine cuisine and contemporary atmosphere so well.

LE PATRIARCHE ❸❸❸
17 rue St-Stanislas, 418/629-5488,
www.lepatriarche.com
HOURS: July-Aug. daily 5:30-10 P.M., Sept.-June Wed.-Sun. 5:30-10 P.M., Thurs.-Fri. 11:30 A.M.-2 P.M.
Situated in a converted heritage home that was built in 1827, Le Patriarche retains the feeling of an old house, giving it an especially warm and romantic atmosphere and making it a choice spot for couples. It specializes in *gastronomie du terroir,* and the service here is unique; each course is served as a trio of dishes, sort of

like a choose-your-own tasting menu. An order of Québec lamb, for example, comes as mini-servings of roasted lamb rack, pan-fried lamb loin, and braised lamb tongue. Since Patriarche emphasizes *terroir* cooking, wild game features on the menu, but they also have one of the better vegetarian selections, offering three mini-dishes that change daily.

LE SAINT-AMOUR $$$
48 rue Ste-Ursule, 418/694-0667,
www.saint-amour.com
HOURS: Mon.-Fri. 11:30 A.M.-2 P.M., daily Tues.-Sat.
6-10:30 P.M.

Le Saint-Amour is one of the most renowned restaurants in Québec. Chef Jean-Luc Boulay has won all the honors, the most recent of which was a visit by Sir Paul McCartney. After his historic concert for the city's 400th anniversary it was here that the former Beatle and noted vegetarian brought his band. The French-inspired dishes are creative, though, sadly, not vegetarian friendly. Try the foie gras served with brioche, sturgeon caviar from New Brunswick, or the red deer seared and served with mushrooms. Art Nouveau touches can be found throughout the restaurant, framing the mirrors and illuminating the bar with a beautiful stained-glass mosaic. Watch the kitchen magic happen through the open kitchen design and sip a glass of red from their exquisite wine list, reputed to be one of the best in the country.

ITALIAN
CONTI CAFFE $$$
32 rue St-Louis, 418/692-4191,
www.conticaffe.com
HOURS: Daily 11:30 A.M.-11 P.M.

The resolutely modern decor of this Italian-style restaurant is a breath of fresh air compared to many restaurants in Old Québec that stick to a staid, traditional look. The little brother of Le Continental, from which it took its name, Conti Caffè has an atmosphere that is younger, more relaxed, and more fun than that of its older counterpart. It serves Italian dishes like veal parmigiana and spaghetti carbonara,

and specialties include lamb chops, filet mignon, and pan-fried sea scallops. Of course, the classic brick and stone walls still add an air of charm and romance, but the rich blue walls and contemporary furnishing are a vibrant touch.

LE CONTINENTAL $$$
26 rue St-Louis, 418/694-9995,
www.restaurantlecontinental.com
HOURS: Mon.-Fri. noon-3 P.M. and 6-11 P.M.,
Sat.-Sun. 6-9 P.M.

Waiters in white dinner jackets prepare mains tableside, making Le Continental the pinnacle of fine dining. Set in an elegant Victorian house, Le Continental is a traditional, rather formal restaurant known for impeccable service and unmatched cuisine. Blending Italian and French traditions, the restaurant is known for its flambé dishes, which include shrimp with whiskey, orange duckling, and flambé sirloin. Other classic dishes include braised veal sweetbreads and steamed snow crabs. Though there is no formal dress code, this is the time to break out your dinner jacket and dress shoes.

IL TEATRO $$
972 rue St-Jean, 418/694-9996,
www.lecapitole.com/en/restaurant.php
HOURS: Daily 7 A.M.-2 A.M.

With one of the most eye-catching terraces in the city—with overflowing flower pots and a view of St-Jean Gate—Il Teatro is a no-brainer when it comes to dining alfresco and is popular with theater-goers and tourists alike. It's located in the magnificent Capitole de Québec theater (hence the name), and the interior is modern and welcoming with brick walls, simple decoration, and huge windows that look on to Place d'Youville. Chef Serge Gagné, despite his not-too-Italian name, has been cooking some of the best Italian food in the city for the past 18 years. The risotto al mascarpone and scaloppini del capo are some of the best dishes, and the tuna steak with pepper is perfect for fish lovers. Cap the night off with a cappuccino, a slice of panforte, and a stroll around the city's walls.

LATE-NIGHT EATS
◖ CHEZ ASHTON ⑤
54 Côte du Palais, 418/692-3055,
www.chez-ashton.com
HOURS: Sun.-Wed. 11 A.M.-2 A.M., Thurs. 11 A.M.-4 A.M.,
Fri.-Sat. 11 A.M.-4:30 A.M.

Founded in 1969 by Ashton Leblond, Chez Ashton is fast-food *à la québécoise.* Sure you can get your burgers and fries here but what Ashton prides itself on is its *poutine.* It's the single culinary achievement of the region (origins remain obscure and hotly debated), and Mr. Leblond helped popularize the combination of French fries, cheese curds, and brown gravy that has since gone on to conquer the rest of the province. Add shredded turkey and green peas onto the rest and you have a *galvaude,* a popular selection here. The decor is typical of fast-food chains—neon lights, vinyl banquettes, and a lineup of starving late-night revelers. You can find many Chez Ashton locations in the city, including one in Saint-Roch (830 blvd. Charest, 418/648-0891) and one near the Parliament (640 Grande-Allée, 418/522-3449).

QUÉBÉCOIS
AUX ANCIENS CANADIENS ⑤⑤⑤
34 rue St-Louis, 418/692-1627,
www.auxancienscanadiens.qc.ca
HOURS: Daily noon-9:30 P.M.

Located in the oldest house in the city (built in 1675), Les Anciens Canadiens is firmly planted in Québécois tradition. With its white-washed walls, red roof, and miniature stature, it's not hard to fall under its charm. It's a huge tourist destination. Servers are dressed in slightly unconvincing old-timey costumes, and the food on the menu is traditional Québécois—that is to say plentiful and heavy. Despite the kitschy costumes and themed dining rooms, the food is excellent. If you want to discover everything about traditional regional cooking, try the Trapper's Treat (meat pie with a pheasant and bison casserole) or the Québec Tasting Platter (meat pie with meatball and pig's knuckle ragout and baked beans). As for dessert—well, you'd better like maple syrup.

Vieux Québec's Lower Town   Map 9

CAFÉS AND CHEAP EATS
LES CAFÉS DU SOLEIL ⑤
143 rue St-Paul, 418/692-1147
HOURS: Winter Mon.-Fri. 7 A.M.-5:30 P.M., Sat. 8:30 A.M.-5:30 P.M., Sun. 10 A.M.-5:30 P.M.; summer Mon.-Wed. 7 A.M.-7 P.M., Thurs.-Fri. 7 A.M.-10 P.M., Sat.-Sun. 8:30 A.M.-10 P.M.

Over 40 kinds of coffee, some from as far as India and Japan, line the walls of this Vieux-Port café. Dedicated to the art of coffee and coffee making, this popular neighborhood café full of locals and browsing tourists was originally a store selling espresso makers and other coffee accessories and making a little *allongée* on the side. It only became a full-fledged café when they decided to make sandwiches and snacks for the customers who were spending more and more time hanging out and sampling their coffee. A small but lively place, it's usually packed with regulars. Besides coffee they also

offer sandwiches, salads, soups, and pastries as well as a selection of teas.

CRÊPERIES
CAFÉ BISTRO DU CAP ⑤⑤
67 rue du Sault-au-Matelot, 418/692-1326
HOURS: Tues.-Sun. 11:30 A.M.-2:30 P.M. and 5:30-9:30 P.M.

On a narrow cobblestone street backing onto the sheer cliff face, Café Bistro du Cap is in a gem of a spot. With a small *terrasse* out front and a modest, no-frills interior, the entire atmosphere is unpretentious and intimate. This is a small operation run by a couple; he mans the kitchen while she runs the front of house, so selection here isn't huge and is often determined by the availability. Praised by both locals and tourists their menu includes items like pan-fried salmon, lamb shank, and chowder. They are especially known for their crêpes. Savory or sweet, they are some of the best in the city, and perfect for a midafternoon snack.

FRENCH
CAFÉ DU MONDE $$$
84 Dalhousie, 418/692-4448, www.lecafedumonde.com
HOURS: Mon.-Fri. 11:30 A.M.-11 P.M., Sat. 9 A.M.-11 P.M.

Café du Monde is in the Vieux-Port on a quay that juts out into the river. Aiming to bring a little Rive-Gauche (Left Bank) to Québec, the interior is precisely decorated with black and white checkered tiles, walls of wine, and even black-apron-clad servers (who have tempered their accents in some cases) to really give diners that Parisian feel. Though the atmosphere isn't entirely convincing—since when is the Rive-Gauche surrounded by grain silos and shipping relics?—the food is, with mains like mussels, salmon tartare, and rabbit hindquarter transporting you across the Atlantic in no time.

LE COCHON DINGUE $$
46 blvd. Champlain, 418/694-0303,
www.cochondingue.com
HOURS: Mon.-Fri. 7 A.M.-11 P.M., Sat.-Sun. 8 A.M.-11 P.M.

Started in 1979, French bistro Le Cochon Dingue (The Crazy Pig) has become one of the most popular restaurants in the city. Famous for mussels, steak frites, and pork filet mignon, they also serve breakfast and lunch, with daily specials. Though they've since opened other outlets, including one near rue Cartier (46 blvd. René-Lévesque, 418/523-2013), the original establishment is still the most charming, with brick walls, sharp white tablecloths, and bistro chairs. It's both elegant and relaxed. In summer their sidewalk *terrasse* takes up almost the entire street, with Le Petit Cochon Dingue at number 24, serving coffees and sweets.

LAPIN SAUTÉ $$$
52 rue du Petit-Champlain, 418/692-5325,
www.lapinsaute.com
HOURS: Mon.-Fri. 11 A.M.-10 P.M., Sat.-Sun. 9 A.M.-10 P.M.

Run by the same people who own Le Cochon Dingue, the Lapin Sauté (Jumping Rabbit) is more laid-back and romantic than its bustling

Lapin Sauté's sidewalk *terrasse*
© SACHA JACKSON

neighbor. Located in a turn-of-the-20th-century home, the small dining room—it seats 32—has a rustic feel with a low, wood ceiling and a stone fireplace. The food here is rustic as well, specializing in country-style cuisine. Their specialty is rabbit, served in a pie, a cassoulet, or roasted with maple and raspberry sauce. They also have a refined kids' menu that includes grilled salmon and caesar salad.

◖ RESTAURANT L'INITIALE $$$
54 rue St-Pierre, 418/694-1818,
www.restaurantinitiale.com
HOURS: Tues.-Fri. 11:30 A.M.-2 P.M. and 6-9 P.M.,
Sat. 6-9 P.M.

One of the most renowned restaurants in the city, this is a must for those who enjoy haute cuisine. It is frequented by foodies from the world over. There is no set menu but various tasting menus that change with the seasons and the local products available. Known for his innovative dishes, head chef Yvan Lebrun marries unlikely flavors, such suckling pig with squash and crispy sweetbreads with mustard kidneys.

© SACHA JACKSON

Le 48 St-Paul is a great place for outdoor dining.

Housed in a century-old building, the interior of L'Initiale is distinctly modern with a sleek comfortable design. The entire restaurant follows a beige and cream color scheme and this subtly works in achieving a rich atmosphere.

INTERNATIONAL
LE 48 ST-PAUL ⑤⑤
48 rue St-Paul, 418/694-4448, www.le48.ca
HOURS: Mon.-Fri. 7 A.M.-11 P.M., Sat.-Sun. 8 A.M.-11 P.M.
Located in an old stone warehouse in the heart of the Vieux-Port, Le 48 St-Paul couldn't be in a better location. In summer the large *terrasse* with chic black umbrellas and overflowing flowerpots is one of the most enviable places in the city. Encompassing *cuisine monde* (world cuisine), the dishes run the gamut from pizza to burgers, cassoulet to pad thai, making it the choice of groups and families with picky eaters. The interior has a bit of "world" flair as well with brightly colored fabrics accenting the chic leather seats and international music playing on the stereo.

ITALIAN
LA PIZZ ⑤⑤
299 rue St-Paul, 418/692-5005, www.la-pizz.com
HOURS: Mid-Oct.-late May Mon.-Wed. 11:30 A.M.-2 P.M., Thurs.-Fri. 11:30 A.M.-10:30 P.M.; late May-mid-Oct. daily noon-10:30 P.M.
The delicious thin and crispy crust may be the trademark of this pizza joint, but the secret of their success is their ingredients. Fresh vegetables from the Marché du Vieux-Port and imported French cheese are mixed to produce unique flavor combinations, like tomato, bacon, egg, and Emmenthal or tomato, crème fraiche, leeks, scallops, and Emmenthal. The restaurant on St-Paul, which has a homey feel with bistro chairs and warm red walls, has been so successful they recently opened another place right on Place Royale (3A Place Royale, 418/692-3003), making it a default tourist destination. So you can now eat your Frenchified 'za on the oldest spot in Canada.

PIZZA MAG ⑤⑤
363 rue St-Paul, 418/692-1910, www.pizzamag.com
HOURS: Mon.-Fri. 11 A.M.-midnight, Sat.-Sun. 2 P.M.-midnight
Serving up delicious pizza since 1984, Pizza Mag has 30 pizzas to choose from, including European and Mediterranean classics as well as more original pies like the Parmentière, with potatoes and sausage; the Smoked Meat Supreme, with, uh, smoked meat; and la Prétentieuse (pretentious), with smoked salmon, goat cheese, and caviar. The dining room is not the best in town—with basic tables and chairs it has little ambience and it can be hot and packed—but the pizza is worth it. It's the best pizza in town according to locals. When it's warm grab one of the few tables outside on rue St-Paul or get them to bring the deliciousness to you. They deliver daily 5 P.M.–midnight.

QUÉBÉCOIS
BRYND SMOKED MEAT ⑤⑤
369 rue St-Paul, 418/692-4693, www.brynd.com
HOURS: Sun.-Tues. 11 A.M.-9 P.M., Wed.-Thurs. 11 A.M.-10 P.M., Fri.-Sat. 11 A.M.-11 P.M.
Located on the former spot of the famous

RESTAURANTS

Thomas Dunn Pub, Brynd specializes in smoked meat sandwiches, a well-known Montréal specialty. This Québec variation, a smoked meat sandwich on rye served with "class" (the "class" seems to apply solely to the fact that you can choose between fries or salad and you don't have to wait in line for an hour to order) is one of the best in the city. The decor is minimally chic with mirrors lining the walls and the wooden banquettes filled with local office workers and hungry tourists. The waiters in all black duds are especially cool and congenial.

◖ BUFFET DE L'ANTIQUAIRE ❸❸
95 rue St-Paul, 418/692-2661
HOURS: Daily 6 A.M.–11 P.M.

Set among the chi-chi bistros and idyllic antiques stores of rue St-Paul, the Buffet de l'Antiquaire is a no-frills diner. Established in 1975, it serves up breakfasts and traditional Québécois grub like *ragoût de boulettes* (meatballs, potatoes, and gravy), *pâté à la viande* (meat pie), and *cipaille* (game meat pie). Usually the busiest place on the block, it's adored by locals and tourists alike for its old-time charm—diner stools, vinyl banquettes, and line cooks in full-view. The all-day-long breakfast is served in heaping amounts and with their unforgettable homemade jam. In summer tables and chairs are set up on the sidewalk outside for a makeshift patio.

◖ L'ÉCHAUDÉ ❸❸❸
73 rue du Sault-au-Matelot, 418/692-1299, www.echaude.com
HOURS: Mon.–Sat. 11:30 A.M.–2 P.M. and 5–10 P.M., Sun. 10:30 A.M.–2:30 P.M. and 5–10 P.M.

With a stainless-steel bar and tables covered with butcher paper, the vibe at this Vieux-Port bistro strikes the perfect balance of relaxed elegance. Classic bistro dishes like steak tartare, veal liver and duck confit are on the menu here but they also offer *marché* (market fresh) selections that diverge from the standard fare to include mains like quail kebab, grilled mackerel, and pasta with duck gizzards. No matter what you order it is always fresh, and the value excellent, especially if you opt for a table d'hôte.

Pair your meal with a wine from a choice of over 300 stocked in the cellar, many of them available by the glass.

LAURIE RAPHAËL ❸❸❸
117 rue Dalhousie, 418/692-4555, www.laurieraphael.com
HOURS: Tues.–Fri. 11:30 A.M.–2 P.M. and 6:30–10 P.M., Sat. 6:30–10 P.M.

At Laurie Raphaël it's all about infusing the flavors and aromas of the region into the cuisine. Dishes include foie gras terrine, duck supreme, pressed octopus, arctic char, lychee pudding, and pistachio sponge cake. Those on a budget should try the "Chef! Chef!," a three-course meal ($26 at lunch, $60 at dinner) improvised by head chef Daniel Vézina. The interior is luxurious and inviting thanks to the subtle color palette, with tones of grays and sand; floor-to-ceiling windows open onto the dining room, but gauzy, sheer curtains afford the perfect balance of privacy and light. Reservations are a must.

◖ PANACHE ❸❸❸
10 rue St-Antoine, 418/692-1022, www.restaurantpanache.com
HOURS: Mon.–Tues. 6:30–10:30 A.M. and 6–10 P.M.; Wed.–Fri. 6:30–10:30 A.M., noon–2 P.M., and 6–10 P.M.; Sat.–Sun. 7–11 A.M. and 6–10 P.M.

Situated in the Auberge St-Antoine, this former 19th-century warehouse has been transformed into one of the most inviting dining rooms in the city, with exposed wood beams, stone walls, and original wood flooring. A wrought-iron staircase leads to a second dining level, with tables tucked away under the eaves for an intimate and romantic setting. Inspired by the home cooking of the generations of Québécois before him, chef François Blais takes a dish like your grandmother's shepherd's pie or roasted guinea hen and turns it into something fresh (and miniature). Because it uses local produce the menu changes regularly. Reservations recommended.

SSS ❸❸
71 rue St-Paul, 418/692-1991, www.restaurantsss.com
HOURS: Daily 11:30 A.M.–2 P.M. and 5 P.M.–midnight

The latest endeavor from the people who

brought you Toast!, SSS (Simple, Snack, Sympathique) is newly opened and more relaxed and hipper (not counting the name) than its progenitor. Drawing a young, fashionable crowd, it has two different rooms—a small bar lounge with high tables, red accents, and lips on the wallpaper—and an adult dining room with stone walls, black-lacquered floors, and crisp white tablecloths. The main menu is French-influenced and heavy on the meat with dishes like ribs, New York cut steak, and pasta with duck confit. The relaxed atmosphere along with a late-night kitchen cooking up snacks like grilled chicken curry, gourmet hot dogs, and burgers makes it a great choice for an evening cocktail or late dinner.

TOAST! ❸❸❸

17 rue du Sault-au-Matelot, 418/692-1334, www.restauranttoast.com

HOURS: Mon.-Fri. 11:30 A.M.-2 P.M. and 6-10:30 P.M., Sat. 6-10:30 P.M., Sun. 10:30 A.M.-10 P.M.

Located in the heart of the Vieux-Port in the Priori hotel, Toast! offers modern cuisine in a picturesque setting. The atmosphere here is hip, with ambient red lighting illuminating the 200-year-old stone walls. Using French and Italian influences, dishes include vegetarian risotto with stuffed zucchini, salmon with smoked sour cream, and red deer bacon. For dessert they offer a selection of cheeses, including a Québec cheese plate, *croque monsieur,* and a sheep's milk plate with figs and rye bread. In the summer a large terrace is open out back, drawing everyone from young families to passing tourists and young professionals.

SEAFOOD
CAFÉ RIVIERA ❸❸

155 rue Abraham-Martin, 418/694-4449, www.riviera-quebec.com

HOURS: May-Sept. Mon.-Fri. 9 A.M.-10 P.M., Sat.-Sun. 8 A.M.-10 P.M.

Located next to the Silo de la Bunge, this is the hangout for wannabe sailors and those who actually own boats docked in the marina. Even if you left your Breton shirt and Top Siders at home, a trip to Café Riviera is worth it for the outstanding view of the city alone. It's owned by the same guy as Poisson d'Avril, Captain Bernier, and there are definite similarities—blue-checkered tablecloths, lanterns hanging from the ceiling, boat miniatures. Dishes here range from classic (fries and pasta) to haute snacks (shrimp *poutine,* lobster sandwiches) and sophisticated meals (filet mignon). Open throughout the summer.

MARIE-CLARISSE ❸❸❸

12 rue du Petit-Champlain, 418/692-0857, www.marieclarisse.qc.ca

HOURS: Winter daily 6-10 P.M., summer daily 11:30 A.M.-2:30 P.M. and 6-10 P.M.

There are only 12 tables, each set with a blue tablecloth and yellow flowers, in this cozy, romantic restaurant that occupies the ground floor of a 340-year-old house. Situated at the bottom of L'Escalier du Casse-Cou, the stone walls, wooden floors, and blazing fire in wintertime only add to the warm atmosphere. One of the top restaurants in the city for fish and seafood, it also offers fine meat dishes like chestnut and maple duck breast and calf's sweetbread. The menu changes daily according to the fresh fish available, but the specialty remains the *marmite de poisson sauce rouille* (fish soup with bouillabaisse).

POISSON D'AVRIL ❸❸❸

115 quai St-André, 418/692-1010, www.poissondavril.net

HOURS: Daily 5 P.M. onward

"Poisson d'Avril" is what you say when you play a trick on someone for April Fools Day, but this restaurant is no joke! With a large choice of mussels, fresh fish, oysters, and squid, it promises to serve the best seafood in the city. The house specialty is Provençal bouillabaisse with calamari, scallops, shrimp, mussels, fish, and rouille, but if fish is not your thing they also have grilled chicken and filet mignon. It's in front of the marina and old port, and the interior features low ceilings, thick wooden beams, and long tables. It's the closest thing there is to dining on a boat. The atmosphere is lively and familiar.

Parliament Hill and the Plains   Map 10

CAFÉS

BÜGEL FABRIQUE DES BAGELS $$

164 rue Crémazie W., 418/523-7666

HOURS: Mon.-Wed. and Sat. 7 A.M.-7 P.M., Thurs.-Fri. 7 A.M.-9 P.M., Sun. 7 A.M.-6 P.M.

Bügel Fabrique des Bagels makes the best Montréal-style bagels in Québec City—wood fired and smothered in sesame seeds. The small neighborhood staple is decorated with old church pews, and lively patrons give it a homey, comfy atmosphere. In the summer the tiny outdoor patio is the perfect place to chow down one on one of their breakfast bagels, like *le poussin,* a bagel with an egg (served daily until two), or dig in to one of their sandwich creations with smoked chicken and curried mayonnaise. Vegetarian meals are served, as well as soups, salads, and desserts.

LE FASTOCHE $

1191 ave. Cartier (Halles du Petit-Quartier), 418/948-3773, www.sandwicheriefastoche.com

HOURS: Mon.-Fri. 9 A.M.-7 P.M., Sat. 9 A.M.-6 P.M.

This great *sandwicherie,* located in the Halles du Petit-Quartier on the upscale rue Cartier, has been turning sandwich making into an art since 2008. This take-away counter caters to workers on lunch or locals needing a quick bite. Creative sandwiches with a unique blend of ingredients include the baguette with duck, port, and blueberries and the prosciutto with two pestos. If you're looking for something more substantial try the *boîte-à-lunch,* which comes with salad, dessert, and a drink. Close to the Plains of Abraham, it's a great place to pick up a last-minute picnic.

DESSERTS

GLACIER ABERDEEN $

90 rue Aberdeen, 418/648-6366

HOURS: Mid-Apr.-mid-Sept. daily 10 A.M.-midnight

This ice cream shop, tucked into a nook behind rue Cartier, is one of the best in the city, and locals flock here from all over the city just for a scoop. It has just a slim, long hallway and a walk-up window, so customers savor their treats on the sunny terrace. Across the street, a statue by a local artist also attracts some ice cream eaters. Sundaes, sorbets, frozen yogurts, and milkshakes are all made here, but the place is especially known for its soft-serve coated with Belgian chocolate and a trickle of maple syrup.

FRENCH AND QUÉBÉCOIS

L'ASTRAL $$$

1225 Cours du Général-de-Montcalm, 418/780-3602, www.lastral.ca

HOURS: Mon.-Sat. 11:45 A.M.-11 P.M., Sun. 10 A.M.-11 P.M.

Québec City's only revolving restaurant, L'Astral is on the 29th floor of the Concorde Hotel on the Grande-Allée. Those who dine here have a variety of choices when it comes to dinner menus: à la carte, a tasting menu, buffets, and seasonal table d'hôtes are available year-round. Breakfast and lunch menus offer similar choices. Whatever you order, however, will likely be second to the view. The restaurant rotates a full 360 degrees every hour and a half, so diners get a magnificent view of the city and its environs. Dining here is always a dressy affair, not too fancy, but don't show up in shorts and sneakers.

CAFÉ KRIEGHOFF $$

1091 ave. Cartier, 418/522-3711

HOURS: Mon.-Fri. 7 A.M.-10 P.M., Sat. 8 A.M.-11 P.M., Sun. 8 A.M.-9 P.M.

No matter the time of day this place is always packed with both locals and tourists. Named after a famous early-Canadian painter who lived in the area, Café Krieghoff serves everything from your basic breakfast (eggs, toast, potatoes) to bistro-style dinners (quiche lorraine, grilled salmon). Neither the food nor the coffee is out of this world, and beyond the hustle and bustle ambience is lacking, but the prime real estate (on the popular rue Cartier close to the Plains of Abraham and Fine Arts Museum) and the large front and back terraces keep customers coming back.

GRAFFITI ❸❸❸
1191 ave. Cartier, 418/529-4949
HOURS: Mon.-Thurs. 11:30 A.M.-2:30 P.M. and 5-10 P.M.,
Fri. 11:30 A.M.-2:30 P.M. and 5-11 P.M., Sat. 5-11 P.M., Sun.
9:30 A.M.-3 P.M. and 5-11 P.M.

This chic and modern restaurant—exposed brick, soft lighting, modern furnishings—serves dishes influenced by both Italian and French traditions. Chef Robert Saulnier is known for his personal touch, which includes creations like veal sweetbread in pastry with candied apples, and roast rack of lamb with sun-dried tomato risotto. Located in the food emporium Les Halles des Cartier it's popular with neighborhood locals and especially young couples and groups of friends in their late 20s, early 30s. On Sunday they serve a decadent brunch; pop in for the poached eggs and blintzes.

RESTAURANT DU MUSÉE DES BEAUX-ARTS ❸❸❸
Parc des Champs-de-Bataille, 418/644-6780,
www.mnba.qc.ca
HOURS: Daily 10 A.M.-5 P.M., Wed. until 8:45 P.M.

One of the first things you notice when you enter the Musée des Beaux-Arts is the restaurant, located just off the entrance hall. The clink of glasses and plates and wafting aromas immediately grab your attention (especially if you're hungry). Featuring regional cuisine and local, organic produce, mains include pork breast, halibut, and stuffed portobello mushrooms. The atmosphere inside is fairly subdued with sparsely designed chairs and simple white tablecloths. During the summer, however, the *terrasse* out back has a stunning view of both the St-Lawrence and the Plains. It's a perfect spot for lunch, and dinner is served once a week, on Wednesday nights when the museum is open late.

INTERNATIONAL
LE COSMOS ❸❸❸
575 La Grande-Allée E., 418/640-0606,
www.lecosmos.com
HOURS: Mon.-Thurs. 7 A.M.-midnight, Fri. 7 A.M.-1 A.M.,
Sat. 8 A.M.-1 A.M., Sun. 8 A.M.-midnight

Right next to the Voo Doo Grill, Le Cosmos shares the same fusion spirit and exotic decor. Dishes here are international, from General Tao chicken to burgers and pastas. It's a trendy and hip restaurant. The decor has organic influences with a sort of *Space Odyssey: 2001* vibe and is a bold mix of neon tree-like columns, illuminated pictures of forests, and an aquarium that runs the length of the floor. The contemporary furniture is '60s-inspired. Bordering on kitsch, somehow it all seems to work. They have great selection of cocktails and a big *terrasse* on Grande-Allée on which to knock one back.

VOO DOO GRILL ❸❸❸
575 La Grande-Allée E., 418/647-2000,
www.voodoogrill.com
HOURS: Mon.-Fri. 11 A.M.-midnight, Sat.-Sun.
5 P.M.-midnight

Part of a big complex that houses the famous Maurice nightclub, the Voo Doo Grill serves international food that, despite the name, tends toward Asian and fusion. As if that weren't confusing enough the decor, once Africa-inspired with roaming drum circles, has recently been replaced by an art deco look, full of cast iron, fur, and gilded mirrors. Specialties of the house, however, haven't changed, so you can still get the same filet mignon, tandoori shrimp, and snow-crab cakes, all of which are better than what you'd expect. They also have a great selection of wine, over 200. Customers, from traveling businesspeople to 20-something students, come for dinner and stay to burn off the calories on the Maurice and Charlotte dance floors afterwards, where the door fee is waived with proof you ate at Voo Doo.

ITALIAN
CASA CALZONE ❸❸
637 La Grande-Allée E., 418/522-3000,
www.casacalzone.com
HOURS: Winter Mon.-Sat. 11:30 A.M.-2 P.M. and
5:30-10 P.M., summer daily 11:30 A.M.-11 P.M.

If you're looking for Québec City's Little Italy look no further than Casa Calzone. The red-checkered tablecloths, postcards of

Italy on the wall, Italian music, and bottles of chianti subtly let you know you've arrived. Pastas and homemade pizzas are always good, but the real standouts here are their famous calzones. The proud owner often makes the rounds of the tables just to make sure what you've ordered has sent you to food heaven. Don't forget to please him as much as he pleased you and leave your comments on the wall provided.

MILANO PIZZA $$

194 rue Crémazie W., 418/529-2919
HOURS: Mon.-Thurs. 11 A.M.-1 A.M., Sat.-Sun.
11 A.M.-midnight

This pizza joint's reputation as one of the best in Québec City has been cemented over the last 40 years, thanks to the neighborhood regulars who drop in a least once a week. Though it's not gourmet (black olives are the fanciest topping), it's always fresh and delicious, and the unpretentious attitude keeps bringing people back. It's just off avenue Cartier, and for late-night cravings it's the perfect place, especially during the summer when they often close after 1 A.M.

MOMENTO $$$

1144 ave. Cartier, 418/647-1313,
www.bistromomento.com
HOURS: Mon.-Thurs. 11 A.M.-1 A.M., Sat.-Sun.
11 A.M.-midnight

Situated on a corner lot, the front of Momento is all big picture windows overlooking avenue Cartier. Since opening in 2004, its reputation has been building as one of the more authentically Italian restaurants in the city—so don't expect any checkered tablecloths here. Soberly decorated with crisp white tablecloths and rich red walls, everything here is in good taste. The restaurant attracts couples on romantic dates and locals craving a grown-up meal Classic Italian dishes include goat cheese and *bocconcini* pizza, hearty manicotti, and osso bucco or veal scallopini in a butter-lemon sauce. Their wine list includes many Italian selections, categorized by region.

JAPANESE
KIMONO $$$

1034 ave. Cartier, 418/648-8821, www.kimonosushibar.com
HOURS: Mon.-Fri. 11:30 A.M.-2:30 P.M. and 5-11 P.M., Sat.
5-11:30 P.M., Sun. 5-10:30 P.M.

Primarily a sushi bar, Kimono also has hard-to-find traditional Japanese food on the menu, like chicken *yakitori,* udon noodles, and pork *gyoza.* Also in the Japanese tradition, smaller, more intimate rooms are available just off of the main dining room. The modern decor, with white banquettes, bar stools, and walls, can be a bit much at times when everything is lit in a neon blue hue, but the servers here are welcoming, and the sushi is above average in presentation and taste.

MÉTROPOLITAN EDDIE SUSHI BAR $$$

1188 ave. Cartier, 418/649-1096, www.eddiesushi.com
HOURS: Mon.-Fri. 4:30-10:30 P.M., Sat. 5-11:30 P.M.,
Sun. 5-10:30 P.M.

This restaurant's name might be lost in translation, but they got everything else right at this authentic Japanese restaurant on Cartier. The large, open dining room is painted white with dark wood accents in the door and window frames. The rest of the decor is kept simple with the tables and chairs almost precisely matched to the existing wood, evoking a particularly Zen ambience. Though you can still order your California and kamikazi rolls here the emphasis is on traditional Japanese sashimi and sushi with *unagi, tobiko,* and scallops featuring on the menu.

TEA
SEBZ THÉS AND LOUNGE $

67 blvd. René-Lévesque E., 418/523-0808, www.sebz.ca
HOURS: Mon.-Sat. 10 A.M.-9 P.M., Sun. 10 A.M.-6 P.M.

On the busy and less than picturesque boulevard René-Lévesque, the interior of this teahouse makes up for the exterior. The vibe here is more relaxed than British afternoon tea, and the friendly atmosphere makes it popular with local residents and students alike. More than 150 teas from China, Japan, India, and Africa are available here. Detox Tuesdays are popular with regulars, as are the infusion blends, which they roast and blend on the spot.

Saint-Jean-Baptiste and Saint-Roch   Map 11

BAKERIES

LA BOÎTE À PAIN $

289 rue St-Joseph E., 418/647-3666

HOURS: Mon.-Fri. 6:30 A.M.-8 P.M., Sat.-Sun. 6:30 A.M.-5:30 P.M.

This artisanal bakery has freshly baked bread all day long and the smell lures in just about anyone who passes by. The pastries are also awesome, from the croissants to the *pains aux chocolates* to the brioche. They also serve sandwiches—try the tomato, mozzarella, and basil—delicious soups spiced with curry, and great salads. Though the interior is nothing fancy it does have a few non-descript chairs and tables where locals and weary tourists recharge with a coffee and a treat.

LE PAIN GRÜEL $

375 rue St-Jean, 418/522-7246

HOURS: Tues.-Fri. 6 A.M.-6:30 P.M., Sat. 6 A.M.-5 P.M.

This self-proclaimed *"boulangerie creative"* makes its breads and pastries by hand and with some of the healthiest ingredients. All breads are made using sourdough, but a variety of flours and ingredients are added according to the season. The result: multi-grain bread, cheese bread, bread with nuts. They even have a bread with chocolate and dried pears. The ambience is all business, with a simple counter and not much else. This is a take-away place, so you can feel French and eat your baguette as you stroll the street.

CAFÉS

BRÛLERIE ST-ROCH $

375 rue St-Joseph E., 418/529-1559, www.brulerie-st-roch.com

HOURS: Sun.-Wed. 6:30 A.M.-11 P.M., Thurs.-Sat. 6:30 A.M.-midnight

This is one of the best cafés in the city, and the lineup starts early in the mornings when regulars pop in to get their usual before heading off to work. Ideally located on a corner lot, it has two walls of picture windows with bars and seats along both that are usually occupied. If it's not too packed try to grab a seat on the tiny second-floor mezzanine that looks out over the action.

Front and center when you enter is the gleaming Nuova Simonelli (the espresso machine), backed by a wall of coffee beans ready to be ground. The lattes here are outstanding—it's all in the foam—and the sandwiches and pastries are mouthwatering. There is a second location on rue St-Jean (881 rue St-Jean, 418/614-3359).

CAFÉ BABYLONE $

181 rue St-Vallier E., 418/523-0700, www.cafebabylone.com

HOURS: Mon.-Fri. 10 A.M.-10 P.M., Sat. 9 A.M.-10 P.M., Sun. 9 A.M.-3 P.M.

With different events happening here almost every night of the week, Café Babylone is a great place to take in a different kind of show. Local musicians hit the tiny stage to try out new material, and Tuesday nights you can stop by to hear everything from slam poetry to storytelling. Most of these events are pay-what-you-can. During daylight hours it's a cozy café serving Turkish specialties as well as sandwiches, salads, and even breakfasts. The atmosphere is laid-back and so is the decor; most of the furniture has been salvaged from secondhand shops.

LIBRAIRIE ST-JEAN-BAPTISTE $

565 rue St-Jean, 581/999-0951, www.librairiesjb.com

HOURS: Daily 11 A.M.-9 P.M.

A bookshop and café in one, Librairie St-Jean-Baptiste is one of the latest additions to the street. Situated in a building that dates from the early 1900s, the bookstore, dealing in mostly used books, has quickly become a meeting point for local artists and students. There's also a small café, where you're invited to while away the afternoon in this inviting and relaxed atmosphere. Snacks, including sandwiches, soup, and grilled cheese, are also available.

NEKTAR $

235 rue St-Joseph E., 418/977-9236, www.lenektar.com

HOURS: Mon.-Wed. 7 A.M.-11 P.M., Thurs.-Fri. 7 A.M.-midnight, Sat. 8:30 A.M.-midnight, Sun. 9:30 A.M.-9 P.M.

At Nektar, coffee is an art. Baristas here are

experts and will explain the ins-and-outs of a good cup of joe to you, all in a thinly veiled attempt to lure you into tasting their *"grands crus,"* the latest vintage of coffee. If they succeed in getting you to taste the Nektar, you'll have a hard time going back to your Starbucks Breakfast Blend. Despite their devotion to java, they also have pastries, crêpes, and pizzas on hand in the off-chance you might want something solid. The interior is a bit of a letdown; chocolate brown walls give the place a cozy feel in winter, but in warmer months it all seems a bit too dark. Still, you can always get your coffee to go.

PAIN ET PASSION ❸
85 rue St-Vallier E., 418/525-7887,
www.painetpassion.com
HOURS: Mon.-Fri. 7 A.M.-7 P.M., Sat.-Sun. 9 A.M.-5:30 P.M.
Located in what used to be a cookie factory, this Mediterranean grocery store offers pretty much everything. Alongside various kinds of homemade bread, you'll find deli, pastry, and cheese counters. They've also got hot meals, salads, pastas, and good coffee. Locals come here for special ingredients or for a quick and easy take-away dinner. Grab a seat at one of the few tables and eat among the old artifacts, imported European products, and old factory decor and lounge in the laid-back, almost soothing atmosphere. They also offer nice breakfasts on weekends 10 A.M.–2 P.M.

CRÊPERIES
◖ CRÊPERIE LE BILLIG ❸
526 rue St-Jean, 418/524-8341
HOURS: Tues.-Sat. 11 A.M.-9 P.M., Sun. 11 A.M.-3 P.M.
This is the most authentic crêperie in Québec City—some even say it's better than the ones found in France. It was founded by a true Breton, and authentic *galettes* made of organic buckwheat flour and sweet crêpes made of sarrazin are both available. First-timers should try the classic crêpe suzette, flambéed with Grand Marnier. Sweet or savory, don't forget to wash your crêpe down with a cider. The lively and boisterous ambience is palpable since the place is always full of locals packed into the seven

tables or taking up the one or two outside tables in the summer. Reservations are a must.

DESSERTS
TUTTO GELATO ❸
716 rue St-Jean, 418/522-0896, www.tuttogelato.ca
HOURS: Late Apr.-early Oct. daily 10:30 A.M.-8 P.M. or midnight depending on the weather
This 100 percent authentic Italian *gelateria* comes from the heart of a 100 percent authentic Italian. When owner Giacomo Donati moved to Canada he brought with him gelato recipes and lots of them. All the gelato here is homemade, and with over 100 recipes there's always a different flavor to try, including matcha, saffron cream, ginger, sea-salt caramel, and all the classics. Modern and sleek, this slim take-away counter also has cakes, biscuits, coffees, and even homemade soy milk ice cream.

FRENCH
AU BONNET D'ÂNE ❸❸
298 rue St-Jean, 418/647-3031
HOURS: Mon.-Fri. 11 A.M.-10 P.M., Sat.-Sun. 8 A.M.-10 P.M.
Situated in what was once the local general store, this café and restaurant is a local favorite. It's not hard to imagine a shopkeeper behind the dark, heavy bar, or think of the long bay windows, now comfortable banquettes, as filled with stuff for sale. The relaxed, sometimes boisterous atmosphere is laid-back and inviting. Old artifacts line the shelves, the menu is written on the mirror behind the bar, and old photos hang on the walls. Burgers are some of the best, along with their steak frites and their weekend brunch, always hearty but refined. A small *terrasse* on the side is a great spot in the summer.

LES BOSSUS ❸❸
620 rue St-Joseph E., 418/522-5501, www.lesbossus.com
HOURS: Daily 11 A.M.-10 P.M., Sat.-Sun. 9 A.M.-10 P.M.
This is a classic French bistro, from its checkered-tile floor to the waiters in long black aprons to the menu that lists everything from breakfast to dessert. Simply decorated, the narrow restaurant has a long bar on the right, an entire wall with banquette seats on the left, and

© SACHA JACKSON

French bistro Les Bossus in Saint-Roch

black-lacquered chairs and tables in the middle. All this might look very elegant but everything here stays simple and relaxed. Not convinced? Bossus in English means "The Hunchbacks." The diners here are diverse—businessmen and -women, locals, and tourists. They come to eat bistro classics like tartare, *boudin noir,* duck confit, and filet mignon. Les Bossus also serves an excellent breakfast.

LE CERCLE $$$

228 rue St-Joseph E., 418/948-8648, www.le-cercle.ca
HOURS: Tues.-Fri. 11:30 A.M.-3 A.M., Sat. 10 A.M.-3 A.M.
Defying all conventions, Le Cercle is a restaurant, a bar, a café, and a venue and is the go-to place for the young and hip. With its concrete floors, light wood interior, and floor-to-ceiling windows, it is one of the city's coolest restaurants. Serving both tapas-style munchies (try the grilled sardines and rabbit shoulders—seriously) and mains (smoked salmon tartare and veal smoked ribs) it's also one of the more popular brunch places in town. It may not be surprising to learn that they serve up some of the most sought-after cocktails (at brunch you can order an entire carafe of mimosas), but one surprising twist about Le Cercle is the wine cellar. It blends in so well, you barely even notice the $1,600 bottles of Château Pètrus stacked up against the wall.

LE CLOCHER PENCHÉ $$$

203 rue St-Joseph E., 418/640-0597,
www.clocherpenche.ca
HOURS: Tues.-Fri. 11:30 A.M.-2 P.M. and 5-10 P.M., Sat. 9 A.M.-2 P.M. and 5-10 P.M., Sun. 9 A.M.-2 P.M.
If you ask Québec City residents what their favorite restaurant is, or at least which one gives you the best bang for your buck, they'll tell you Le Clocher Penché. It's set in an old bank, and the washrooms are where the big safe used to be. The ever-changing menu includes dishes like roasted snails, scallops with spaghetti squash, and black pudding with apple chutney. They use all local, fresh products. It's called Clocher Penché (Leaning Belfry) because the church next door has a slanted bell tower. Large windows open on to the street in summertime

and give the dining room lots of light no matter the time of year. The light wood chairs and tables give the whole atmosphere a delightful airiness. Reservations recommended.

LE MOINE ÉCHANSON ⑤⑤⑤
585 rue St-Jean, 418/524-7832,
www.lemoineechanson.com
HOURS: Tues.-Fri. 11:30 A.M.-2 P.M., Sun.-Wed. 5-10 P.M., Thurs. 5-11 P.M.

First the translation—*échanson* means "cupbearer," an officer whose duty was to serve the drinks at a royal table. *Moine* means "monk." The concept at this *bistro à vin* is to discover a new wine region of France every time you visit. The menu, using Québécois and French products, varies according to season and climate. For example, you'll be in Savoy and Alsace in winter, the Mediterranean in the summer (including Greece, Portugal, Spain), and Québec in fall.

It's small and cozy with wood tables, a chalkboard menu, and lots of natural light; the ambience here transports you to France without crossing the Atlantic. In summer prime tables are available outside, to let you appreciate the vibe of Faubourg Saint-Jean-Baptiste. A favorite with couples or friends on dates, it can get packed, so reservations are recommended.

PAPILLES ET POÊLON ⑤
190 rue St-Vallier W., 418/524-3594,
www.papillesetpoelon.com
HOURS: Mon.-Fri. 8 A.M.-8 P.M., Sat. 10 A.M.-6 P.M.

Located in a nice little place on St-Vallier since 2006, Papilles et Poêlon (which means "taste buds and casserole") is all about healthy food: fresh ingredients, no preservatives or artificial flavors. Painted a deep red with simple light-wood chairs and tables, it's a great place for a cheap lunch and draws office workers and other locals with two hot meals cooked daily and four kinds of sandwiches, all made with a fresh baguette, naturally. Creative salads, soups in winter, and tasty desserts are all prepared with care and passion by owners Véronique and Philippe.

VERSA ⑤⑤⑤
432 rue du Parvis, 418/523-9995,
www.versarestaurant.com
HOURS: Mon. 11:30 A.M.-2 P.M., Tues.-Fri. 11:30 A.M. onward, Sat. 5 P.M. onward

One of the first restaurants to open in the revitalized Saint-Roch neighborhood, this oyster bar headed by young chef Christian Veilleux is the only one of its kind in the city. It looks just as much like a club as a fine dining establishment. The centerpiece of the dining room is a long communal table illuminated by a modern disco ball. The atmosphere is hip and young. Aside from the oysters, mains include seared sweetbreads and baby-back ribs. In summertime the floor-to-ceiling window slides open and revelers mingle on the tiny, cobblestone street.

GREEK
LA TAVERNA ⑤⑤
821 rue Scott, 418/977-9933, www.restolataverna.com
HOURS: Tues.-Fri. 11:30 A.M.-1:30 P.M. and 5 P.M.-midnight, Sat.-Sun. 5 P.M.-midnight

Recently opened across from the Église Saint-Jean-Baptiste, La Taverna is seen as a blessing of sorts, saving the city from the mediocre Greek franchises you find elsewhere in the province. Simply decorated with a rustic feel, the dining room features white stucco walls (just the top half) and blue-and-white checked tablecloths. It serves authentic Greek with a home-cooked feel; the grilled calamari is a no-brainer and the same goes for the *pikila,* an appetizer of all the cold *mezzes* on one plate. Greek wines and aperitifs help get the meal started, while the delicious, hot baklava closes the night on a high-note. More than anything this family-run restaurant is memorable for its impeccable service, good prices, and quality.

JAPANESE
YUZU SUSHI BAR ⑤⑤⑤
438 rue du Parvis, 418/521-7253, www.yuzu.ca
HOURS: Mon.-Fri. 11:30 A.M.-2:30 P.M., Mon.-Wed. 5-10 P.M., Thurs.-Fri. 5-11 P.M., Sat. 5-11 P.M.

This sushi bar is named after a small Japanese citrus fruit whose delicate grapefruit-meets-mandarin flavor is often found in fusion cooking. There could be no better symbol for what Yuzu does: blend traditional Japanese with North American flavors. The interior of this modern sushi bar is just peachy, with the color on the walls, the plush upholstery of the chairs, and even the pink hues of the wooden tabletops. It's frequented by young, chic professionals. Dishes like tempura, beef sashimi, and dragon rolls are all available here, but where Yuzu differs is with its specialties and tasting menus, which mix flavors like bluefin tuna with pesto and salmon tartare with quinoa salad.

MIDDLE EASTERN
LE CARTHAGE ❸❸❸
399 rue St-Jean, 418/529-0576
HOURS: Tues.-Fri. 11 A.M.-2 P.M. and 5-11 P.M., Sat.-Mon. 5-10 P.M.

Named after the ancient African city, Le Carthage serves fine Tunisian cuisine. The atmosphere here is laid-back and the surroundings majestic; the slightly curved ceiling and intricate moldings give the whole room an exotic feel. Seating here is North African as well, and low chairs and tables adorned with colorful plush cushions invite you to take your shoes off and relax. Bring your own wine to accompany dishes like tahini, royal couscous, or *merguez* and quail brochettes. On weekends enjoy traditional music and belly-dancing as you sit back and finish your meal with some sticky baklava.

LE SULTAN ❸
467 rue St-Jean, 418/525-9449
HOURS: Mon.-Thurs. 11:30 A.M.-11 P.M., Fri. noon-midnight, Sat.-Sun. noon-11 P.M.

Decorated with hookahs and gilded tea pots, Le Sultan looks like something out of *Arabian Nights*. It's super casual; you can get takeout or eat in one of their brightly decorated rooms. It's the perfect place for a Moroccan mint tea. Their simple food is fresh, healthy, and delicious, and their *shish taouk "gigot d'agneau"* is not to be missed. A salon at the back is welcoming; you leave your shoes at the door and let yourself sink into the cushions. Cash only.

QUÉBÉCOIS
CHEZ VICTOR ❸❸
145 rue St-Jean, 418/529-7702, www.chezvictorburger.com/st-jean
HOURS: Sun.-Wed. 11 A.M.-9 P.M., Thurs.-Sat. 11 A.M.-10 P.M.

The ambition of this self-proclaimed burger gourmet is to make a hamburger a "piece of art." And so far, everybody in Québec—artist or not—would agree they make the best burgers in town. The salmon burger, duck burger, and wild boar burger are interesting takes on the old standard. Vegetarians get choices as well, a rarity in Québec, with tofu, nut and spinach, and cereal burgers available. The success led them to open new restaurants, including one in the Vieux-Port (300 rue St-Paul, 418/781-2511), but the one on St-Jean remains the best and definitely worth the walk, with its stone walls, low ceiling, and casual atmosphere.

JOE SMOKED MEAT ❸
275 rue St-Vallier E., 418/523-4545
HOURS: Mon.-Wed. 11 A.M.-9 P.M., Thurs.-Fri. 11 A.M.-10 P.M., Sat. noon-10 P.M.

The menu, printed on the paper placemats, details other stuff like pizza, subs, or pasta, but the reason you're here is for a pound of beef. Really, no one should look past the dressed smoked meat combo, which includes a smoked meat sandwich, chips, coleslaw, and pickles. The interior here is quainter than you'd expect for a temple to the gods of beef; the ruffled curtains, soft red walls, and '70s-style cane chairs give it a definite feminine touch. Appealing to hungry workers and neighborhood locals, the vibe is distinctly down-to-earth and unpretentious.

TAVERNE STEAKHOUSE LE TONNEAU ❸❸
732 rue St-Joseph E., 418/525-9337
HOURS: Daily 11 A.M.-3 A.M.

Opened in 1939, Taverne le Tonneau, one of the oldest restaurants in the city, has witnessed a lot of history. Rumor has it that the first separatist powwows were held here, when St-Joseph was still slightly unsavory. Most recently it's witnessed the cleanup of the area, and though it's been cleaned up itself, it has managed to retain its unique personality and clientele. The Formica tables and refrigerators in imitation wood, paired with the long bar, give it the air of an urban saloon. The regulars are still here but they're surrounded by a younger, hipper generation. Smoked meat, liver, *poutine,* and blood pudding are popular, as are new additions like beef and salmon tartare. If you manage to eat the hulking 72-ounce sirloin steak in less than an hour, the boss picks up the tab. You have been warned.

TEA

CAMELLIA SINENSIS $

624 rue St-Joseph E., 418/525-0247,
www.camellia-sinensis.com

HOURS: Mon.-Wed. and Sat. 10 A.M.-6 P.M., Thurs.-Fri. 10 A.M.-8 P.M., Sun. 10 A.M.-5 P.M.

Québec City deserves its own branch of this great Montréal-based teahouse and it's no surprise to find it here, on St-Joseph. Tea tasters travel the world to find the best and rarest of teas. More than 180 fresh teas are kept in store, and they come from as far way as Japan, India, China, and Taiwan. This small store is set up like an old sweet shop with a counter, and the soft green walls are filled with silver tea tins. The shelves in heavy dark wood give it a feel of gravitas. Tea being a serious business for them, the owners organize a number of tea-centered activities, including tastings, workshops, and even classes on traditional tea ceremonies.

VIETNAMESE

LA PETITE BOÎTE VIETNAMIENNE $$

281 rue de la Couronne, 418/204-6323,
www.chefle.com

HOURS: Tues.-Fri. 11 A.M.-10 P.M., Sat. 4-10 P.M.

The brainchild of young chef Thi Cam Nhung Lê, La Petite Boîte Vietnamienne brings together western and eastern influences. Vietnamese classics, like *phô,* the national soup, alternate with Québécois dishes that Nhung Lê then revisits, like duck breast with Hanoi spices and mussels in Vietnamese spices. It's a must among local adventurous eaters and those wanting a change from bistro fare. The tiny dining room is simply decorated with rich red walls and paper lanterns; seats are also available at the bar, where you can watch the chef at work and sip a mojito, her own drink of choice.

NIGHTLIFE

Québec City might have more historic sights but Montréal has it trumped when it comes to nightlife. Though the rejuvenation of the Saint-Roch neighborhood has led to new hipster venues and interesting bars, La Grande-Allée remains the epicenter of the city's nightlife, with dance clubs and bars chockablock along the strip. The late-night scene, however, still lacks a certain amount of diversity. Sure, you can always catch a band or find a place to dance the night away, but the selection is limited compared to most major North American cities. Nightlife here tends to stick to the neighborhood bar, and it is in these small establishments that you'll find the city's true ambience.

One facet of Québec's nightlife that you won't find much of in Montréal, however, is *chansonniers* (singer/songwriters). These folk singers perform in *boîtes à chansons* ("music boxes"). These venues, deeply entrenched in Québécois identity, give singers and songwriters a platform to sing about their heritage and experience and were first popular shortly after World War II. Famous *chansonniers* have included Félix Leclerc and Raymond Lévesque, who helped popularize this new form of folk music in the 1950s. It's still popular today, and there are venues in the city dedicated solely to supporting emerging songwriters, who sing both old classics and new material. Those looking for a uniquely Québécois experience should make time to check out one of these performances, even if the lyrics might remain something of a mystery.

Montréalers love to antagonize Quebeckers

© SOCIÉTÉ CIGARE

HIGHLIGHTS

LOOK FOR TO FIND RECOMMENDED NIGHTLIFE.

 Best Microbrew: La Barberie is socially and environmentally conscious, so you can down your tasting selection of eight beers guilt free (page 273).

 Best Place to Find Your Sea Legs: With 50 different cocktails and an interior that makes you feel like you're drinking in the captain's cabin, **Bar Ste-Angèle** will soon have you swaying with the ship (page 273).

 Best Place to Skip the Meal: Pitchers of beer are served in watering cans at **La Cuisine,** which cooks up full-on dance parties that rage on well into the night (page 274).

 Best Terrace: The ho-hum facade of local haunt **Le Sacrilège** hides a cozy stone-walled garden terrace that stays open until the snow flies (page 276).

 Most Authentic Québécois Tavern: Taverne Jos Dion is one of the oldest bars in the city. Head here for the live accordion music and stay for the cheap beer (page 277).

 Best Dance Club: The sheer size of the dance floor and variety of music at **Le Maurice** will keep you dancing all night long (page 278).

 Best Drag Show: Gay bar and nightclub **Le Drague** is nothing but unadulterated fun, and the dance floor is always packed with people letting loose (page 279).

 Most Incomprehensible Good Time: You might not understand the lyrics to the songs sung at **Le Pape-Georges,** but the energy at this *boîte à chansons* is infectious (page 280).

 Best Game Selection: Head downstairs to the Game Bar at **Le Boudoir** for some old-school Pac-Man and new-school sounds (page 281).

 Best (and Only) Place to Smoke Indoors: With its walk-in humidor and selection of over 200 cigars, **Société Cigare** lets smokers enjoy their stogies in dignified surroundings (page 281).

© MAURICE NIGHT CLUB

This huge nightlife complex on La Grande-Allée houses Le Maurice and Société Cigare, among other top nightlife venues.

by calling it a "town," rather than a city, and though it can feel small at times, that isn't always a bad thing. When the city comes alive at night, it's in the numerous bars and taverns in neighborhoods all over the city. Even in the deepest of winter the bars are packed with men and women downing pints from local breweries. Many of the bars also feature regular live music that ranges from jazz trios to local rock acts, and if you feel like dancing, chances are you aren't alone. Quebeckers are always up for a good time, so it doesn't take much to get the city's population out of their seats, even if there's no actual dance floor.

Those in the mood for neon lights, thumping bass, and big crowds should head to La Grande-Allée, the city's biggest boulevard, which is full of historical buildings that have been converted into bars and dance clubs. The legal drinking age is 18 throughout the province, so many teens can be found reveling in their newfound freedom here. If you're looking to dance but want something more *branchée* (trendy) head over to Le Drague, the city's gay club, for some guaranteed fun. Though smaller than the clubs found in Montréal it still offers a variety of events and a good time without discrimination.

When looking for a place to pop in for a nightcap or hear some local music, don't be afraid to wander along quiet side streets or go beyond the old city walls—it's in these places that you'll find the most authentic ambience and the most affordable beer.

NIGHTLIFE

Bars

◖ LA BARBERIE
310 rue St-Roch, 418/522-4373, www.labarberie.com
HOURS: Daily noon–1 A.M.
COST: No cover
Map 11

This artisanal microbrewery started out as a small co-op in 1996 and now exports its beer to bars throughout the province. Situated in the heart of Saint-Roch, the brewery and bar—technically their tasting salon—are right next door to each other so you know exactly where your pint is coming from. The owners, who are passionate about their beer but also dedicated and involved in the local community, made just about every inch of the bar and the rustic interior—wood tables, lots of light—couldn't be more welcoming. First time visitors should try the tasting carousel featuring eight different draft beers. And if the weather is nice, drink them out on the sidewalk *terrasse*.

◖ BAR STE-ANGÈLE
26 rue Ste-Angèle, 418/692-2171
HOURS: Daily 8 P.M.–3 A.M.
COST: No cover
Map 8

Cocktails here come in a rainbow of colors and

a brightly colored cocktail at Bar Ste-Angèle

© SACHA JACKSON

LOCAL BREWS

When you order a beer in Québec, there's a decent chance the beer you're ordering hasn't traveled more than 300 kilometers – the distance between Québec City and Montréal. Even brands that after a while start to feel as commonplace as Labatt and Budweiser have come from some local, Québec-owned and -run brewery. There's a proud history of beer in the province, and the more time you spend in bars the more you notice it.

Beer has been a part of Québécois culture for as long as the Québécois culture has existed. When the first colonists arrived in Québec City from France at the beginning of the 17th century they brought with them the tradition of brewing and were soon replicating century-old production techniques in the new world. In Québec though, they replaced hops with spruce, which made the particularly tangy spruce beer. An integral part of their diet, beer was full of important vitamins and nutrients that helped the colonists fend off scurvy. By the late 1640s, the Jesuit priests, headed by brother Ambroise, were brewing their own for themselves and the community.

People carried on brewing their own throughout the colony, and it wasn't until 1671 that Intendant Jean Talon opened the Brasserie du Roi, the first brewery in Québec City. Made entirely of Québec products, it was shipped as far away as the Caribbean and Europe. After that, home brewing started to die out in the French regime for one reason or another and only starts to resurface again in the late 1700s with the arrival of British rule. With the Brits came true life-long brewers who were making beer here as early as 1791.

It's this mix of British and French (as well as some Belgian) brewing techniques that makes Québec beer so unique. Each micro- and independent brewery has its own distinct flavors and blends that can be traced back to brewing practices from one tradition or another. Some well-known local breweries include: La Barbarie, Microbrasserie de l'Ile d'Orléans, and Inox.

---

a multitude of flavors, including Red Devil, Blue Angel, and Kamikaze. With 50 choices to choose from, which you can get by the pitcher, they all start to become tempting after a while. They also have an extensive selection of imported beers and scotch. The bar is designed to resemble the cabin of a ship; there's a lot of heavy woodwork, tiny windows, and mini tables. Small and often packed, it's the perfect retreat when it's super cold or rainy out. Live jazz plays Thursday, Friday, and Saturday nights.

LE CHANTAUTEUIL
1001 rue St-Jean, 418/692-2030
HOURS: Daily noon-3 A.M.
COST: No cover
Map 8

Founded by Québécois singer Gilles Vigneault in 1968, this is one of the nicest places to have a drink—be it a cocktail or coffee—in Upper Town. Once the heart of the city's cultural life, it

has since lost its predominance, but you still see popular writers and artists popping in for their regular drink. No longer a *boîte à chanson,* it has become instead a meeting point for locals, artists, students, and curious tourists. The interior is all stone walls and checkered-board floors, giving it a cool, easy ambience. In the summer there is a nice *terrasse* on the sidewalk right by gate St-Jean.

LA CUISINE
205 rue St-Vallier E., 418/523-3387
HOURS: Mon.-Thurs. 11 A.M.-1 A.M., Fri. 11 A.M.-3 A.M., Sat. 2 P.M.-3 A.M., Sun. 2 P.M.-1 A.M.
COST: No cover
Map 11

Started in 2006, this brightly decorated spot with a retro feel is a daytime restaurant and nighttime hotspot. The restaurant formula goes like this: five meals per night (changing every week), all at the same price and all home-cooked. Québécois classics like *pâté chinois* and lasagna are staples on the menu, which is all made to reproduce the comfort food of your mom's kitchen. Truth be told, however, most people who go to La Cuisine (The Kitchen) have likely never eaten there, despite the name. It's a place to drink and dance the night away, especially among *branchée* 20- and 30-somethings. Music here tends toward popular indie hits, good '80s hits (we're talking Blondie, Elvis Costello, the Jesus and Mary Chain) and a few top 40 tunes.

FOU-BAR

525 rue St-Jean, 418/522-1987,
www.foubar.ca
HOURS: Daily 3 P.M.-3 A.M.
COST: No cover
Map 11

Open since 1984, Fou-Bar is a veritable institution in the Faubourg Saint-Jean-Baptiste area, hosting everything from art exhibitions and vernissages to comedy nights, musical improv events and concerts. People of all ages meet up there. Many musicians have regular nights here and the beer on tap is almost all from local breweries. Like all bars worth their weight, it also has a foosball table at the back.

L'INOX

655 La Grande-Allée E., 418/692-2877, www.inox.qc.ca
HOURS: April-Oct. daily noon-3 A.M., Nov.-Mar. daily 3 P.M.-3 A.M.
COST: No cover
Map 10

Founded in 1987, L'Inox is the beer institution of Québec. Formerly located in the Vieux-Port, it recently moved up to nightlife mecca of the Grande-Allée. Its new interior is modern with high ceilings and basic bar seating. In respect to the forefathers of New France, L'Inox tries to hold up the long tradition of brewing and drinking beer, which has existed in Québec since the early days of the colony. The big vats are visible at the back of the bar and patrons are more than welcome to go downstairs for a more personal visit. Come and savor a Viking or a Trouble-Fête (with coriander and citrus flavors), brewed on the spot, and enjoy it with one of their famous European hot dogs.

LE JULES ET JIM

1060 ave. Cartier, 418/524-9570
HOURS: Daily 3 P.M.-3 A.M.
COST: No cover
Map 10

Just like the famous François Truffaut film from which it took its name, this little *bar de quartier* has become a classic. Since it's a popular neighborhood bar the clients here are mostly locals, and there's no better place to soak up the city's authentic atmosphere. Clearly stuck on the notion of French classics, music here tends toward Edith Piaf, Jacques Brel, Georges Brassens, and the like. The low wooden tables and deep red velvet banquettes give it an added old-world charm.

MO

810 blvd. Charest E., 418/266-0221,
www.moresto.ca
HOURS: Sun.-Tues. 11:30 A.M.-midnight, Wed.-Sat. 11:30 A.M.-1 A.M.
COST: No cover
Map 11

In Japan sushi bars have built-in taps that spout hot water; at Mo's in the hip Saint-Roch region the built-in taps spout beer. This new breed of urban tavern mixes a minimalist design esthetic—cream leather couches, geometric light fixtures—with classic cheap beers and attracts hip young professionals and beer lovers. Local Québec brew Belle Gueule is available from the taps, and Mo stays true to its tavern roots and offers big 325-milliliter bottles of Tremblay and Labatt 50, a particularly Québec phenomenon. A large sidewalk *terrasse* is an inviting place in the summer, though sadly, no table taps here.

LA NINKASI

811 rue St-Jean, 418/529-8538,
www.ninkasi.ca
HOURS: Mon.-Fri. 2 P.M.-3 A.M., Sat.-Sun. noon-3 A.M.
COST: No cover
Map 11

This two-floor bar in the middle of the action on St-Jean has a nice terrace out back with a view of the St-Matthew cemetery next door.

NIGHTLIFE

A popular student hangout, with a boisterous vibrant atmosphere, it's dedicated to promoting Québec music and local beer, making it one of the best spots to catch emerging bands in the city. DJs take over the sound system on Thursdays and Fridays, so stop by if you're in the mood for a dance or two. With big-screen TVs, foosball, and pool tables it's also a great place to watch hockey or any other big-time sports game.

L'ONCLE ANTOINE
29 rue St-Pierre, 418/694-9176
HOURS: Winter daily 11 A.M.-3 A.M., summer daily 10 A.M.-3 A.M.
COST: No cover
Map 9

Right next to Place Royale, L'Oncle Antoine is one of the coolest looking bars in the city. Located in the cellar of one of the oldest buildings in the city, it dates back to 1754, and the vaulted brick ceilings and walls make you feel like you're hanging out in an old bunker. In wintertime, a raging fireplace gives a unique ambience and keeps things cozy. Fifty different beers are on tap, including local specialties like Fin-du-Monde, and bar snacks like hot dogs and nachos are also available.

L'OSTRADAMUS
29 rue Couillard, 418/694-9560
HOURS: Daily 4:30 P.M.-3 A.M.
COST: No cover
Map 8

It's not every day that a popular student bar is found in a historic building. Designed by Eugène-Étienne Taché and built in 1890, L'Ostradamus takes up two floors of this impressive Victorian structure, which is hidden on the twisty-turny rue Couillard. The all-wood interior gives it a warm though distinctly bar-like feel. The young and hip have been flocking here for the cheap drinks and fun atmosphere since it opened in 1973. The top floor is a show lounge dedicated to showcasing new music, stand-up comedy, and other events while the vibe on the first floor is more relaxed, perfect for beer with friends.

LE PUB DE L'UNIVERSITÉ LAVAL
1312 Pavillon Alphonse-Desjardins, Cité Universitaire, Sainte-Foy, 418/656-7075, www.cadeul.ulaval.ca/pub
HOURS: Mon.-Fri. 11 A.M.-2 A.M., Sat. 5 P.M.-2 A.M.
COST: No cover
Map 12

If you're a student looking for a place to party, hop the bus out to Université Laval to find your kindred spirits. Barely 15 minutes by bus, Le Pub de l'Université Laval is the campus hotspot. Located in the Pavillon Alphonse-Desjardins, it has the usual student bar vibe, nondescript tables and chairs, and TVs mounted on the walls. What it lacks in ambience, however, it makes up for in cheap beer. Drink specials are available throughout the week, including weekends, when the entire bar turns into one gigantic dance floor.

LE SACRILÈGE
447 rue St-Jean, 418/649-1985, www.lesacrilege.net
HOURS: Daily noon-3 A.M.
COST: No cover
Map 11

This popular bar on St-Jean draws a range of clients, from *fonctionnaires* (civil servants) and drunkards in the afternoon to university students at night. Everybody mixes here for the famous 5 à 7—Québec's version of happy hour. They have a good choice of microbrewery beers on tap. Thanks to stone walls, long, almost pew-like seats, and small round tables, the entire atmosphere is welcoming and unpretentious. Out back you'll find one of the biggest and best terraces in the city. Music here tends toward rock and indie music with particular DJs taking over the decks and switching things up.

LES SALONS D'EDGAR
263 rue St-Vallier E., 418/523-7811
HOURS: Wed.-Sun. 4:30 P.M.-2 A.M., closed July-Aug.
COST: No cover
Map 11

Part billiard room, part bistro, part tango club, Les Salons d'Edgar wears a number of different hats. Once a theater, it has since been converted into one of the most diverse bars in the city, though it's still the hangout of choice for established Québécois actors and up-and-coming stars. Located in the front of house, the bistro is fairly typical with heavy velvet curtains adorning the windows and candlelight on each table. In the second room, however, it's a whole different story. The electric blue walls of the billiard room are in striking contrast to the resto, but somehow it works. The five pool tables are never free for long, so make sure to grab a drink while you wait your turn. On Sundays, from 6 P.M. onward, it turns into a tango club for amateurs and old pros alike.

SCANNER

291 rue St-Vallier E., 418/523-1916, www.scannerbistro.com
HOURS: Mon.-Sat. 11 A.M.-3 A.M., Sun. 3 P.M.-3 A.M.
COST: No cover
Map 11

This punk-edged alternative bar is quiet in the afternoon but gets wilder at night when the garage-rockers, punks, indie-kids, and rockabillies come to hang out. It's a no-nonsense bar with screens projecting videos and artwork, loud music on the stereo, arcade games, pool tables, and two different kinds of foosball—European and North American. They have some of the best-priced microbrewery beer in the city and typical Québécois snack foods like nachos and hot dogs to go with it. Bands play here most weekends—think metal, punk, country—so check the site. They also have free Wi-Fi, if you're looking for an afternoon beer but still need to get some work done.

TAVERNE BELLEY

249 rue St-Paul, 418/692-4595
HOURS: Daily 8 A.M.-midnight
COST: No cover
Map 9

Located in a hotel of the same name, Taverne Belley looks out over the marina and the farmers market. In the summer the outdoor *terrasse* attracts everyone from office workers to cyclists looking for a refreshing drink and a rest. Opened in 1933, it also has a popular *pétanque* court just in front of the terrasse, to which players flock daily in the summertime. True to its name the Belley is really all about the beer, and there are a number of imported and local microbrews

available. There's also a large selection of wines and port to sip next to the fireplace as you take in the warm wintertime ambience.

TAVERNE JOS DION

65 rue St-Joseph W., 418/525-0710
HOURS: Mon.-Sat., 8 A.M.-3 A.M., Fri. 11 A.M.-3 A.M., Sat. 2 P.M.-3 A.M., Sun. 2 P.M.-1 A.M.
COST: No cover
Map 11

Set in the heart of the working-class district of Saint-Sauveur, Taverne Jos Dion stands as a testament to taverns of a bygone era. Opened in 1933, it is the oldest tavern in Québec and, according to some, in North America. In fact women have only been allowed since 1986, when the government forced their hand, telling them to either accept women or close. Wanting to be democratic they put it to a vote and *les habitués* (the regulars) voted to keep the bar open, and subsequently let the ladies in. It remains, however, decidedly masculine and is a good place to watch sports games as well as drink your weight in beer, which is ridiculously cheap. Live accordion music is featured on Thursdays and Fridays to give it an even more authentic touch.

LE TEMPS PARTIEL

698 rue d'Aiguillon, 418/522-1001, www.letempspartiel.com
HOURS: Daily noon-3 A.M.
COST: No cover
Map 11

Run as a co-op, this is Québec City's alternative bar, as the website says: *une place différente pour des gens différents* (a different place for different people). In a past life it was known as the Fourmi Atomique, a mythic place located in Old Québec whose walls collapsed in 2001. The bar relocated to the current location while waiting for a reconstruction that never came, hence the name Temps Partiel—it was supposed to be temporary. In many ways the big square room with artwork occasionally on the wall still looks temporary, but the music (punk, indie, and electro), cheap beer, and alternative events like video projections, concerts, DJs, and exhibitions keep customers coming back. They also have free pool on weekends.

Dance Clubs

LE CHARLOTTE ULTRA LOUNGE

575 La Grande-Allée, 418/647-2000,
www.mauricenightclub.com
HOURS: Sun.-Tues. 9 P.M.-3 A.M., Wed.-Sat. 8 P.M.-3 A.M.
COST: $5 cover
Map 10

This club is in what used to be the attic of this grand old house, which is now a nightlife complex. It's named after former premier Maurice Duplessis's secretary, Charlotte, with whom he is suspected of having an affair—in this very attic! Québec political scandal aside, the ambience here tends toward chill, compared to the dance floor action in the main bar. Retro and pop nights are popular here. Appealing to a mid-20s to late-30s crowd, the interior is refined and rich with padded walls, velvet couches, and fur throws.

LE DAGOBERT

600 La Grande-Allée E., 418/522-0393, www.dagobert.ca
HOURS: Daily 9 P.M.-3 A.M.
COST: No cover
Map 10

Set in a huge castle-like house on the Grande-Allée, the "Dag" as it's known has been an institution for more than 30 years. Inside there are two distinct sounds; the first floor has a rock vibe with regular live shows by cover bands, while the second floor is a full-blown club with a huge dance floor, neon lights, and a mezzanine running along its edges. It's here that you'll catch sets by some of the world's best DJs. The crowd here is younger than what you'll find at Maurice, however, with many of them barely over drinking age. During the summer a line forms quickly for entrance onto the *terrasse,* so get there early to avoid it.

☾ LE MAURICE

575 La Grande-Allée E., 418/647-2000,
www.mauricenightclub.com
HOURS: Sun.-Wed. 8 P.M.-3 A.M., Thurs. 11 P.M.-3 A.M., Fri. 8:30 P.M.-3 A.M., Sat. 10 P.M.-3 A.M.
COST: $5 cover Wed.-Sat.
Map 10

Le Maurice is housed in the former headquarters of the Union Nationale, a conservative political party headed by Maurice Duplessis (hence the name), which governed the province throughout

sleek and cool Le Charlotte Ultra Lounge

the 1940 and '50s. The epicenter of a good 70 percent of the city's entire nightlife, this complex includes Le Charlotte Ultra Lounge, Voo Doo Grill, and Société Cigare. The complex's main attraction remains Le Maurice, with its immense dance floor and eclectic music, everything from electro to salsa and rock to R&B. It is a good place to lose yourself in the beat. Come winter don't miss the famous Iceothèque, the ice disco that takes up the entire front *terrasse*.

L'OZONE LAURIER
2810 blvd. Laurier, Sainte-Foy, 418/652-2020,
www.ozonehotelbar.com
HOURS: Daily 7 P.M.–3 A.M.
COST: $5–20 cover
Map 12

Outside of the city center, close to the malls of Sainte-Foy and the campus of Université Laval, is L'Ozone. Situated in a hotel of the same name, this lounge and dance club has become a popular place thanks to a number of cool after parties—this is where the Black Eyed Peas came after their performance at Festival d'Été, and French rap group TTC has also made an appearance. Appealing to university students and 20-something Sainte-Foy residents, the vibe is youthful and energetic. The decor is minimalist chic, with stone walls, low leather couches, and neon lights. With hiphop, house, top 40, and hits from the '80s and '90s on rotation, the two dance floors are always bumping when the party finally gets underway around 10 at night. A second Ozone can be found on the Grande-Allée (270 Grande-Allée E., 481/529-7932, www.ozonehotelbar.com), but it is more of a bar than a club.

Gay and Lesbian

BAR LE ST-MATTHEW
889 Côte Ste-Geneviève, 418/524-5000
HOURS: Daily 11 A.M.–3 P.M.
COST: No cover
Map 11

Two former gay bars, Taverne 321 and the 889, have come together to create the Bar le St-Matthew, a small, welcoming bar in Upper Town. Located on a small side street, the gay-friendly bar is popular with both gay and straight locals who pop in for affordable drinks. The atmosphere is laidback with simple decor, pool tables, and a friendly staff. During the summer the *terrasse* is open for cocktails alfresco.

◖ LE DRAGUE
815 rue St-Augustin, 418/649-7212,
www.ledrague.com
HOURS: Daily 10 A.M.–3 A.M.
COST: No cover
Map 11

Le Drague takes up most of the real estate on this small cobblestone street that constitutes the city's Village Gai. It's divided into four different sections, and each area of the club has

Everyone comes out to party at LGBT hot spot Le Drague.

NIGHTLIFE

NIGHTLIFE

its own vibe, from the quiet bar Verrière to the dance floor intensity of the main room, from the men-only vibe of Zone3 to the Cabaret with almost nightly performances. The events calendar is packed here and includes weekly

drag acts, karaoke, quiz games, and country dancing. Most people, though—gays, straights, lesbians, and transsexuals—come to dance like a fool to the house and top 40 hits that blare out over the crowded dance floor.

Live Music

BOÎTES À CHANSONS
◖ LE PAPE-GEORGES

8 rue du Cul-de-Sac, 418/692-1320, www.papegeorges.com
HOURS: Summer daily noon-3 A.M.; winter Mon.-Wed.
4 P.M.-3 A.M., Thurs.-Sun. noon-3 A.M.
COST: No cover
Map 9

It's easy to miss Le Pape-Georges, one of the best and only *boîte à chansons* bars in Vieux-Québec's Lower Town; it's hidden down a little back lane, off the popular rue Petit-Champlain. Though it calls itself a wine bar, the crowds don't come here for the selection of wine, ports, and microbrewery beers alone. They come instead for the ambience of this welcoming bar,

Le Pape-Georges is one of the best-known *boîtes à chansons* in the province.

located in a historical house built in 1790. The patrons gather around small tables and huddle up against the stone walls to hear the songs of *chansonniers* (folk singers) and jazz bands. While you listen, snack on some Québec cheese and charcuterie, or a pot-au-feu in the winter.

LES VOÛTES NAPOLÉON

680 La Grande-Allée E., 418/640-9388
HOURS: Daily 8 P.M.-3 A.M.
COST: No cover
Map 10

With its stone arches and low ceiling this *boîte à chansons* has a cozy, albeit cave-like feel. Located in the basement of what used to be Restaurant Bonaparte (and is now the Savini), it's a great place to listen to some traditional Québécois music. The stage here is so tiny, there's little room for a backup band for the singers who pass through here, so instead they're backed by a modest-sized sound system. It's busy from the moment it opens to the moment it closes, so don't be surprised if the crowd ends up singing louder than the musician. Shows usually start around 10 P.M.

LES YEUX BLEUS

1117½ rue St-Jean, 418/694-9118,
www.barlesyeuxbleus.com
HOURS: Daily 8 P.M.-3 A.M.
COST: No cover
Map 8

If you want to experience the peculiarly Québécois institution of *boîtes à chansons,* this is the place to do it. It was in these small filled-to-capacity rooms that emerging Québécois singers first got their start in the 1950s, and the tradition continues to this day, especially at Les Yeux Bleus (The Blue Eyes), the most popular

© SACHA JACKSON

venue for *chansonniers* in the city. Situated at the end of a courtyard off of St-Jean, the room here gets packed early with audiences of all ages. Even if you don't understand a word of what the musician three feet from your table is singing, you'll witness the magical effect it has on the audience.

JAZZ BARS
LE CHARLES BAILLAIRGÉ JAZZ BAR
57 rue Ste-Anne, 418/692-2480,
www.hotelclarendon.com
HOURS: Daily 7-10:30 P.M.
COST: No cover
Map 8

Situated in the Hotel Clarendon, the Charles Baillairgé Jazz Bar continues the 30-year tradition originally started here by L'Emprise. Found on the street level of the hotel, the large, open-concept bar with low lights, bucket chairs, and a small stage makes for an intimate atmosphere. With jazz groups playing almost every night, the stage has hosted such legendary names as Diana Krall and John Zorn and continues to be a showcase for Québec's emerging and established jazz musicians.

LE LARGO
643 rue St-Joseph E., 418/529-3111,
www.largorestoclub.com
HOURS: Daily noon-1 A.M.
COST: Free-$20 cover
Map 11

Serving Mediterranean-inspired dishes, this Saint-Roch restaurant turns into a jazz club later in the night. Long and narrow, with floor-to-ceiling picture windows that open out onto the street in the summer, the interior is exuberantly decorated with plush, bright-red banquettes, blond-wood floors, and lots of light from exquisite chandeliers. Live jazz is played here almost every night of the week, with bigger-named musicians taking the Thursday through Saturday evening time slot. Many of the musicians here are local, but well-known bands are also known to pass through. You don't have to eat here to enjoy the music; those solely interested in the performance should pass by around 10 P.M.

Lounges

☾ LE BOUDOIR
441 rue du Parvis, 418/524-2777,
www.boudoirlounge.com
HOURS: Mon.-Fri. noon-3 A.M., Sat.-Sun. 4 P.M.-3 A.M.
COST: Free-$20 cover
Map 11

This two-floor lounge in the heart of Saint-Roch has multiple personalities, each attracting a diverse clientele. Upstairs it's a restaurant by day and a lounge by night; most people skip the meals, however, and come solely for the ambience. Windows roll open in the summer onto the tiny rue du Parvis, giving the dark bar a bit of ambient lighting when the sun sets. Mixing the feel of a gentleman's club with 1960s futurism, the decor is distinctly modern and perfectly suited to the clientele of young professionals. Downstairs it's a different story. Called the Game Bar, it features '80s arcade games like Pac-Man and Donkey Kong as well as foosball and darts. Wii and Playstation 3 can also be found, hooked up to a screen on the dance floor. Drawing a younger, hipper crowd, nights here include iPod battles and DJ sets by international DJs as well as popular musicians.

☾ SOCIÉTÉ CIGARE
575 La Grande-Allée E., 418/647-2000
HOURS: Daily 1 P.M.-3 A.M.
COST: No cover
Map 10

If you're nostalgic for the days when you used to be able to light up as you sipped your vintage cognac, then Société Cigare is sure to put a smile on your face. The only place in Québec City where you're allowed to smoke indoors, Société Cigare is part of the huge nightlife complex on Grande-Allée that includes Le Maurice and Voo Doo Grill. Customers can choose from a selection of over 200 brands of cigars, including Cuban Cohibas and Dominican Ashtons, from the Société's walk-in humidor. The soft lighting, all-wood bar, and leather club chairs give the bar a distinctly masculine feel. Smokers can choose from a range of scotch, port, and cognac to go with their cigars, and those with their own stogies are free to cut and light them here, as long as they get a drink to go with them.

SONAR

1147 ave. Cartier, 418/640-7333
HOURS: Winter Sun.-Wed. 5-11 P.M., Thurs.-Sat.
5 P.M.-3 A.M.; summer Sun.-Wed. 11:30 A.M.-11 P.M.,
Thurs.-Sat. 11:30 A.M.-3 A.M.
COST: Free-$20 cover
Map 10

A tapas bar and nightclub, Sonar is sleek and sophisticated, with low, white leather couches, ambient lighting, silent images projected on a large screen, and the occasional disco ball. It's a popular hangout for singles and friends in their 20s and 30s, and the party starts early with after-work drinks and tapas at the 5 à 7. As the night progresses so does the music, and by the end of the night you can expect to be dancing your heart out to classic house beats. Internationally renowned DJs play sets here

regularly, and the decks have seen the likes of Gui Boratto. Arrive early on weekends—this place gets packed quickly.

ST-LAURENT BAR AND LOUNGE

1 rue des Carrières, 418/266-3919,
www.fairmont.com/frontenac
HOURS: Daily 11:30 A.M.-1:30 A.M.
COST: No cover
Map 8

Like its sibling establishments Le Champlain and Café de la Terrasse, Château Frontenac's Bar St-Laurent affords the same great views of the St-Lawrence River. Unlike its siblings, however, this is the only establishment that is exclusively a bar (though light meals are available from the restaurants). The circular, rich wood bar is the centerpiece of the St-Laurent, with massive picture frame windows that look out onto the *terrasse* and river beyond. The seating is placed around the bar, and old wingback-style chairs are the standard. Evening or afternoon, the cocktail reigns supreme, with a number of classics on the menu like whiskey sours, gin fizz, and Tom Collins, as well as a list of martinis like the Winston Churchill or F. D. Roosevelt, all named after illustrious guests. Dress code is smart casual. Men in sleeveless shirts will be turned away.

Pubs

PUB GALWAY

1112 ave. Cartier, 418/522-5282,
www.pubgalway.com
HOURS: Daily 10 A.M.-3 A.M.
COST: No cover
Map 10

This charming Irish pub in what was traditionally the English-speaking part of town is a little slice of Ireland, full of wood paneling, stained-glass windows, and smaller tables and chairs. It's not hard to imagine yourself in a country pub some 3,000 miles away. With a selection of 15 different whiskeys and over 20 different kinds of (mostly imported) beer,

they also serve up pub classics like Irish *poutine* (it involves whiskey), fish and chips, and Irish stew with Guinness. Staff here know the regulars by name but still give unknowns the same warm welcome.

PUB LE TURF

1179 ave. Cartier, 418/522-9955, www.turfpub.com
HOURS: Mon.-Fri. 11:30 A.M.-3 A.M., Sat.-Sun.
3 P.M.-3 A.M.
COST: No cover
Map 10

Though the sign says pub, this place has the vibe of an American sports bar. Big-screen TVs and hockey memorabilia are scattered throughout this modern but classic bar. A lively place, especially during weekday happy hours, this is an ideal spot to catch the game. The crowd here tends to be younger, with most clients in their 20s or 30s. Shunning pub fare for more standard American food, they serve pizza, burgers, chicken, New York–style steaks, and the ever-so-elusive chicken wings.

PUB ST-ALEXANDRE
1087 rue St-Jean, 418/594-0015,
www.pubstalexandre.com
HOURS: Daily 11 A.M.-3 A.M.
COST: No cover
Map 8

If you like beer, then you'll love Pub St-Alexandre. It's the English pub of Québec City, with mahogany paneling, big mirrors, and an "olde British pub" facade to prove it. Pub St-Alexandre has been there for more than 20 years and offers the largest selection of beer in the province. More than 250 beers are available here, mostly from Ireland, Britain, Germany, and Belgium. They also carry a selection of 40 single malts. It's a hangout that attracts both locals and tourists. If you find yourself confounded by choice, the servers here are all beer experts.

PUB ST-PATRICK
1200 rue St-Jean, 418/694-0618
HOURS: Daily 11:30 A.M.-3 A.M.
COST: No cover
Map 8

Pub St-Patrick is hard to miss, with its ideal location and large, usually packed *terrasse* full of students, tourists, and professionals still in their suits after work. Inside this bustling pub is some of the most fascinating architecture. The building dates back to 1749, and several of the rooms are made completely of stone and feature vaulted ceilings. Once used as barracks during the French regime, they are now some of the coziest places to sip a pint of Guinness. Imported beer is a specialty here and you'll find Harp, Kilkenny, and Smithwick's on tap, as well as an outstanding scotch selection.

NIGHTLIFE

ARTS AND LEISURE

Nowhere is the spirit of Québec culture more evident than in its arts. Though the province counts for just over 24 percent of the entire Canadian population, the cultural community is diverse and thriving. Québec City is the center for Francophone arts in the country, and the latest in theater and performing arts can be found here as well as a strong visual arts community. There is an emphasis on homegrown talent, and though you'll often find European influences and artists, the Québec artist is championed. And why not? The culture here is so rich and uniquely their own, it needn't depend on outside sources.

Since Québec is a predominantly Francophone city, English productions are rarely mounted, and it's in music, visual art, and dance that the language barriers come tumbling down. And with many of the most cutting-edge producers creating and exhibiting in cultural hotspot Méduse, you barely have to leave the building to catch it all. Though contemporary visual art can be a bit harder to find, traditional artwork is abundant here, including the work of First Nations artists.

Surrounded by nature, Québec also has a strong connection to the outdoors, no matter if the ground is buried under four feet of snow. Cross-country skiing and snowshoeing are easily accessible in the city come winter. What better way to see the historical sights than skiing from one place to the next? There's also no shortage of outdoor skating rinks, many of which are made out of frozen rivers and ponds. Ice-skating is an idyllic and truly Canadian pastime. The city is on one of the largest waterways in North America, so boating is a popular sport, and in summer

HIGHLIGHTS

LOOK FOR (TO FIND RECOMMENDED ARTS AND ACTIVITIES.

(**Best Contemporary Gallery:** Made up of 10 different galleries, **Méduse** is the city's one-stop art complex for emerging talent (page 289).

(**Best Art Complex:** Home of the opera, the orchestra, the ballet, and theater company Théâtre du Trident, **Grand Théatre de Québec** is the center of all things high culture in Québec City (page 290).

(**Best Winter Party:** Following a long-held tradition of beating away the winter blahs by getting together and cutting loose, **Carnaval de Québec** is two weeks of the most fun you've ever had in chilly weather (page 293).

(**Best Art Festival:** Held every two years, **Manif d'Art** is filled with the most delightful, puzzling, and invigorating work from the province's best new talent (page 294).

(**Best Free Performance:** Where else in the world can you see Cirque du Soleil for free? *Les Chemins Invisibles* is a breathtaking masterpiece that takes place under a highway (page 294).

(**Best Music Festival:** Eleven days of pure, unadulterated music takes over the city every July for the **Festival d'Été de Québec** (page 295).

(**Best Place to Have a Picnic:** Once the grounds of the governor general's residence, **Parc du Bois-de-Coulonge**'s groomed gardens and amazing views of the St-Lawrence are still worthy of royalty (page 300).

(**Best Bike Path:** Running alongside the St-Lawrence River and through Cap Blanc and various parks, **Corridor du Littoral** is a great path for exercise and to see some of the lesser-known parts of the city (page 301).

(**Best Winter Sledding:** At 250 meters high the **Glissades de la Terrasse Dufferin** is the biggest (and only) winter slide in Québec City; speeding from the top down to the *terrasse* at speeds of up to 70 kilometers per hour has been a tradition since 1884 (page 304).

© CHANTAL GAGNON

Promenade Samuel Champlain, part of the Corridor du Littoral the St-Lawrence is dotted with white sails and even the occasional sea kayak. Though it's one of the hilliest cities in Canada, it's also home to two of the longest bike paths in the country, running alongside the river; a trip down the Promenade Champlain is like a mini-break from the city. And of course, come winter it's one of the best ski trails.

The Arts

The center for Francophone arts and culture in the province, this is the place to catch the newest Québécois play, musician, dancer, writer, or art star. Even if you don't speak French, art has the ability to cross language barriers, and hanging out in a room full of Québécois will give you a whole new perspective and appreciation for this idiosyncratic part of North America.

MUSEUMS

MAISON CHEVALIER

50 rue du Marché Champlain, 418/646-3167, www.mcq.org
HOURS: Tues.-Sat. 10 A.M.-5 P.M.
COST: Free
Map 9

Built by trader and ship owner Jean-Baptiste Chevalier in 1752, the Maison Chevalier incorporates other buildings that date back to 1675 and 1695. A great example of early New France architecture, the house features firewalls, high chimneys, and vaulted cellars. Ravaged by fire, the house was rebuilt in 1762 and was run as an inn throughout the 19th century. Inside you'll find exposed wood beams, wide wooden floorboards, and stone fireplaces. The permanent exhibit A Sense of the Past focuses on life in the 18th and 19th centuries, and English guidebooks are available at the front desk. One weird fact: The facade, which looks out on the St-Lawrence River, was originally the back of the house.

MAISON HENRY-STUART

82 Grande-Allée W., 418/647-4347, www.cmsq.qc.ca/mhs
HOURS: Tours mid-June-early Sept. daily on the hour 11 A.M.-4 P.M.
COST: $7 adult, $2.50 child 6-12
Map 10

Take afternoon tea and cake in this charmingly authentic 19th-century cottage. Built in 1849 for Mrs. William Henry, the wife of a rich wood merchant, the house today is found on one of the biggest boulevards in the city, but inside it has retained its elegant and rich decor. Tours of the garden and house give visitors an idea of what life was like for well-to-do English families in Québec at the turn of the 20th century, and tea time is part of the hour-long tour.

MORRIN CENTRE

44 Chaussée des Écossais, 418/694-9147, www.morrin.org
HOURS: Tues. noon-9 P.M., Wed.-Fri. and Sun. noon-4 P.M., Sat. 10 A.M.-4 P.M.; tours June-Sept. Mon.-Sat. 11 A.M. and 3 P.M., Sun. 1:30 P.M.
COST: Tours $6 adult, $4 child 10 and under
Map 8

Military barracks, city jail, and an English college make up the past lives of this cultural center dedicated to preserving and sharing the history of Anglophone culture in Québec. Built during the French regime in 1712, the original structure was used to house French troops and eventually prisoners of war. The current neoclassical structure was built in 1808 and was the first jail in Canada based on the ideas of prison reformer John Howard. Converted in 1868, it became the first English college in the city. Today visitors can see remnants of these histories as they tour the Victorian library and head down to the old jail cells.

MUSÉE BON PASTEUR

14 rue Couillard, 418/694-0243, www.museebonpasteur.com
HOURS: Tues.-Sun. 1-5 P.M.
COST: $3 adult, $2 senior, $2 student, free for children 12 and under
Map 8

This congregation of nuns, the Good Shepherd

Sisters of Québec, was established by a mother of three, Marie Fitzbach, in 1856. Started as a women's shelter it soon became a place of refuge for marginalized women and abandoned children in the 19th and 20th centuries. Housed in a structure that was built in 1878, the museum takes up three floors. Exhibits look at the past and future of the congregation, with many personal artifacts of the founders and their predecessors as well as a trip through the trials and tribulations facing Québec women throughout the congregation's history.

MUSÉE DU FORT
10 rue Ste-Anne, 418/692-2175, www.museedufort.com
HOURS: Feb.-Mar. and Nov. daily 11 A.M.-4 P.M., Apr.-Oct. daily 10 A.M.-5 P.M., Dec.-Jan. closed
COST: $8 adult, $6 senior, $5 student
Map 8

Situated in the shadow of the Château Frontenac, the Musée du Fort, located in a historic house, features a 30-minute multimedia show that recreates the six sieges of Québec City and the Battle of the Plains of Abraham. Other highlights include a model of the city as it was in 1759 at the time of British conquest, as well as a small exhibit of weapons, uniforms, and military badges.

MUSÉE NAVAL DE QUÉBEC
170 rue Dalhousie, 418/694-5387, www.museenavaldequebec.com
HOURS: July-Aug. Tues.-Fri. and Sun. 10 A.M.-noon and 1-4 P.M., Sept.-June Tues.-Fri. 1-4 P.M.
COST: Free (donations accepted)
Map 9

This small museum in the Vieux-Port is dedicated to the city's naval history. The new permanent exhibit Meanders looks at the major historic events that have taken place on the river, from the first Amerindian settlements to the numerous invasion attempts by the British to the German U-boat attacks that happened in her waters.

Personal stories add a human face to the history, and objects includes bows and arrows, 18th-century muskets, and a model of the hull of a World War II warship. It also hosts various traveling exhibitions.

QUÉBEC EXPERIENCE
8 rue du Trésor, 418/694-4000, www.quebecexperience.com
HOURS: Mid-May-mid-Oct. daily 10 A.M.-10 P.M., mid-Oct.-mid-May daily 10 A.M.-5 P.M.
COST: $7.50 adult, $5 senior and student, children under 6 free
Map 8

As the name suggests this exhibit invites you to experience the history of Québec City—but in 3D. Admittedly, the technology is in need of an update, and what was once state-of-the-art now feels like a throwback to the late-'80s. Still, if you're into a bit of kitsch (which is a must in Québec), this show presents all the major events, from the falling bridge to rifle crossfire, and real falling water.

GALLERIES
ATELIER GUY LÉVESQUE
79 rue du Sault-au-Matelot, 418/694-1298, www.guylevesque.com
HOURS: Mon.-Sat. 10 A.M.-5 P.M.
COST: Free
Map 9

Self-taught artist Guy Lévesque takes inspiration from traditional theater like Commedia dell'Arte, Japanese nô theater, and the Venice Carnival to create his leather masks. Using a mold technique that dates back to Middle Ages, the masks consistently take on a personality of their own. Entering his gallery and workshop, visitors are able to see the work in process, and it gives them a better understanding of how his vision comes together. Though masks are his specialty, he also creates sculpture and chairs, mostly out of metal and leather.

CENTRE MATERIA
395 blvd. Charest E., 418/524-0354, www.centremateria.com
HOURS: Wed. and Fri.-Sun. noon-5 P.M., Thurs. noon-8 P.M.
COST: Free
Map 11

This artist-run center is dedicated to the field of fine crafts. With an aim to broaden the public's familiarity with and recognition of this art

OPEN-AIR GALLERY RUE DU TRÉSOR

Back in the 1960s, a group of art students looking for a place to show their work got together and started hanging their pieces on the walls of a narrow alleyway not far from Château Frontenac.

Called Rue du Trésor (Treasure Street, www.ruedutresor.qc.ca), it is one of the oldest streets in the city and has been around for three centuries. At the time of the French regime it was along this street that the colonists would pass in order to reach the Royal Treasury, where they paid their taxes. After the British conquest the street was no longer so important and instead served its purpose as a service alley.

In fact, when the students started using it as an open-air art gallery, it was little more than a shortcut. Today, 36 different artists exhibit their work, and some of those original students are still here, selling their picturesque watercolors of Québec City scenes or abstract etchings of something completely indefinable. What started out as a ballsy venture has turned into a popular spot for emerging and established artists to show off and sell their work. Locals and tourists alike come here looking for a little piece of the city to take home with them.

© LUC-ANTOINE COUTURIER

form, they host a number of openings and exhibits by diverse artists, everything from glasswork to textiles. Both emerging and established artists exhibit here, but unlike conventional galleries, Materia doesn't represent the individual artists. Located in a bright, open space on the busy boulevard Charest, the space has an industrial feel with white walls and exposed pipes and ceiling beams.

GALERIE D'ART BROUSSEAU AND BROUSSEAU

35 rue St-Louis, 418/694-1828, www.sculpture.artinuit.ca
HOURS: Daily 9:30 A.M.–5:30 P.M.
COST: Free
Map 8

Founder Raymond Brousseau first started collecting Inuit art in 1956 after receiving a sculpture

as a present. In 1974 he opened his first gallery, and it has since become one of the most respected commercial galleries dealing in Inuit art. The large, open space with carpeted floors is a blend between store and gallery, but the aim here is to display the works in the best light possible. Works from four specific regions (Kitikmeot, Kivalliq, Nunavik, and Baffin) are available, each with their own style and materials. Staff here are all expertly qualified in specific fields.

GALERIE MADELEINE LACERTE

1 Côte Dinan, 418/692-1566, www.galerielacerte.com
HOURS: Mon.-Wed. 9 A.M.–5 P.M., Thurs.-Fri. 9 A.M.–6 P.M., Sat.-Sun. noon-6 P.M.
COST: Free
Map 9

Housed in an old car garage on a corner lot in

the Vieux-Port, Galerie Madeleine Lacerte is one of the most prominent contemporary art galleries in Québec City. It was founded by Madeleine Lacerte in 1986, and her son Louis Lacerte is now gallery director. It's dedicated to supporting Québec and Canadian artists on both national and international levels. The artists they represent are all based in Canada. Exhibits here range from painting and photography to installation and conceptual pieces and feature both established and emerging artists. They continue to be on the forefront of contemporary art.

GALERIES D'ART BEAUCHAMP AND BEAUCHAMP

10 rue du Sault-au-Matelot, 877/694-2244, www.galeriebeauchamp.com

HOURS: Daily 9:30 A.M.–6 P.M.

COST: Free

`Map 9`

Six commercial galleries make up this large collection of exhibition spaces located in the Vieux-Port. All in close proximity, often right next door or back to back, each gallery has its own mandate, allowing for a huge variation in the types and the prices of work. Each gallery has its own layout; many have so many pieces on the walls you can barely see the wall at all. The galleries represent over 140 artists, and the focus is on working with local artists. Both classical and contemporary works are on view here as well as photography. The vibe of each gallery is defined by the work, and visitors can browse the galleries depending on interest. Though typical closing time is six o'clock, they often stay open much later in summer.

GALERIE TZARA

375 rue St-Paul, 418/692-0330, www.galerietzara.com

HOURS: Wed.–Sun. noon–5 P.M.

COST: Free

`Map 9`

Former lawyer Hélène Pélissier was inspired to open a contemporary art gallery by the people she met in a plastics arts class. Named after Tristan Tzara, the father of the Dada movement, this gallery's aim is to give emerging

artists a place to exhibit, initiating a dialogue with the public. Housed in a long, narrow modern space the gallery hosts 11 or 12 exhibitions a year, in a variety of disciplines. Though the majority of the artists they represent are up-and-coming, there is also a strong relationship with established artists. It's open and spacious, and the low ceilings and concrete floors give it a distinctly modern vibe. Locals who are regulars here tend to be cooler and more open-minded than what you'd find at other commercial galleries.

LE LIEU

345 rue du Pont, 418/529-9680, www.inter-lelieu.org

HOURS: Daily 1–5 P.M.

COST: Free

`Map 11`

Situated in Saint-Roch, this artist-run center was established in 1982, and focuses on multidisciplinary arts. The floor-to-ceiling windows of the sparse space look out on to the street—perfect for catching the attention of passersby. Le Lieu works with artists both at home and abroad, and the contemporary work shown here focuses on practices like installation, performance, and audio and visual art. It's often quite conceptual. It's rare that you'll see a painting hanging on these walls. They also host Rencontre Internationale d'Art Performance (RAIP), a yearly international festival dedicated to performance art.

MÉDUSE

541 rue St-Vallier E., 418/640-9218, www.meduse.org

HOURS: Wed.–Sun. noon–5 P.M.

COST: Free

`Map 11`

Established in 1995, Méduse is an arts complex filled with galleries, studios, and offices dedicated to arts and culture. Made up of linked buildings, some of them modern, others refurbished historical structures, it's the home of 10 different businesses, from a radio station to art galleries. L'œil de Poisson, which exhibits contemporary works, and VU, the only gallery in the city dedicated to contemporary photography, are always worth checking out. Dance company

La Rotonde often performs in the center's *salle multi*. This hub has become integral to all forms of the city's contemporary arts scene, and if you want to check out a specific space, check the times before you leave since they often vary.

MORGAN BRIDGE

367 rue du Pont, 418/529-1682,
www.morganbridge.blogspot.com
HOURS: Wed. and Fri. noon–6 P.M., Thurs. noon–7 P.M.,
Sat.–Sun. noon–5 P.M.
COST: Free
Map 11

Morgan Bridge takes the idea of what we perceive an art gallery to be and turns it on its head. With a strong connection to graffiti and skateboard culture—spray paint is sold in the gallery, along with zines, and many of the artworks are created on skate decks—the work is subversive, exciting, and out of the ordinary. It's not all street art though; throughout the space you'll find art naïf and work that toes the line between graphic and street art. In short, this is where you'll find the work of emerging underground artists in Québec.

THEATER
LA CASERNE DALHOUSIE

103 rue Dalhousie, 418/692-5323, www.exmachina.qc.ca
COST: Varies
Map 9

This center for the multidisciplinary arts was established by Robert Lepage and his creative collaborators—actors, writers, set designers, technicians, opera singers, puppeteers—in 1997. The ultramodern venue looks almost mechanical, with visible pipes, scaffolding, and stairs. It's used primarily as a workspace for the company, called Ex Machina, to try out and create new performances. They occasionally hold public events to show off new works.

GRAND THÉÂTRE DE QUÉBEC

269 blvd. René-Lévesque E., 877/643-8131,
www.grandtheatre.qc.ca
COST: $20-120
Map 10

The largest arts complex in Québec City, the Grand Théatre was built to commemorate the country's centennial in 1967. Designed by Montréal-based architect Victor Prus, the large concrete structure finally opened in 1971. Home to the Québec Symphony Orchestra, l'Opéra de Québec, and the Théâtre du Trident, it's here that most large-scale performances happen, whether it's a dance piece by the Ballet du Québec, a rock extravaganza like Jason Bonham's Led Zeppelin Experience, or a concert by Québec indie rock kings Karkwa.

THÉÂTRE LA BORDÉE

315 rue St-Joseph E., 418/694-9721, www.bordee.qc.ca
COST: $32 adult, $26 senior, $22 under 30
Map 11

Established in 1976 by a group of young actors directly out of theater school, this independent theater company situated in Saint-Roch mounts four productions a year. Walking the line between classical and experimental, their aim is to produce excellent theater that is also accessible to a large public. They focus on plays from Québec, but there is also a variety in their programs, and past seasons have included productions of Shakespeare's *Richard III,* Dumas' *Le Reine Margot,* and *The Pillowman* by Irish playwright Martin McDonagh. Consisting of two presentation halls, an Italian-style theater that seats 350 and one that seats 60, the settings are decidedly intimate. All productions are in French.

CONCERT VENUES
L'AGORA DU VIEUX-PORT

84 rue Dalhousie, 418/691-7211,
www.agoraportdequebec.ca
COST: Free-$100
Map 9

Looking out on to the St-Lawrence River, this outdoor theater couldn't be better located. Built down into the ground, the sunken stage and raised seating give it the air of a natural amphitheater. With seating for just over 4,000 (22 reserved for wheelchairs) it is one of the largest venues in the city, and its location near the Champlain bike path means an audience of passersby. It's open throughout the summer

© SACHA JACKSON

Le Capitole

season from June to September, and shows here include everything from rock concerts to comedy shows and have included performers like Green Day and Bill Cosby. Events are cancelled when it rains.

LE CAPITOLE

972 rue St-Jean, 800/261-9903, www.lecapitole.com
COST: $30-120
Map 8

Opened in 1903, this playhouse retains many of the architectural charms that made it so illustrious back then: a sweeping marble staircase, gold trimmings, and balustrades. Originally the place to see the biggest music hall and vaudeville acts, Le Capitole is mainly a venue for movie screenings and concerts. Tributes to bands like Emerson, Lake, and Palmer and Supertramp are popular, as are classic French singers like Charles Aznavour. It's here that you'll also catch long-running performances like the *Elvis Story* and *Ring of Fire* (the Johnny Cash musical), often shown with English subtitles.

IMPÉRIAL DE QUÉBEC

252 rue St-Joseph E., 418/523-2227,
www.imperialdequebec.com
COST: $15-50
Map 11

This theater and concert hall in Saint-Roch has a long history. Originally the site of the neighborhood's cemetery, this was a factory before becoming a theater with a second-floor art gallery in 1912. Rebuilt under new ownership in 1917, in the style that was popular at the time—a flat, square marquee, and the Imperial's sign illuminated and protruding from the center of the building—it's this facade that still exists and is one of the few theaters in Québec that recall the golden age of silent films. Inside the old-time charm remains, with balustrades adorned with winged cherubs and moldings framing the stage. It's a midsize venue; bands like Gwar and Broken Social Scene have hit the stage along with cabaret acts and the occasional movie screening.

PALAIS MONTCALM

995 Place d'Youville, 877/641-6040,
www.palaismontcalm.ca

COST: $20-60

`Map 8`

Built in 1932, this art deco building just outside of the walls was originally a public pool before being converted into a concert hall. After undergoing major reconstruction in 2007, Palais Montcalm has emerged as one of the main centers for artistic life in the city. Seating close to 1,000, this is the home stage of chamber orchestra Les Violons du Roy (the King's Violins) as well as the site of many jazz, classical, and world music concerts.

Along with the large auditorium it also has a multipurpose café/theater and café/bar.

LE THÉÂTRE DU PETIT CHAMPLAIN

68 rue du Petit-Champlain, 418/692-2631,
www.theatrepetitchamplain.com

COST: Free-$25

`Map 9`

Situated in the pretty Quartier du Petit-Champlain, this small venue was built in the mid 19th century and was originally used as a theater, but since 1994 it's become a mecca for emerging and established artists. It consists of two smaller stages: La Salle Ulric Breton, which seats 140, and the Mezzanine, which seats 90. The shows are always intimate. The exposed brick walls and balcony seating give both rooms a cozy, cavern-like atmosphere. Many popular, and cool, French-language performers play here as well as the occasional English-language band. They also host shows by the Québec Gospel Choir come the holidays (it's a lot rockier than it sounds) as well as comedy acts.

CINEMA

CINÉMA CARTIER

1019 ave. Cartier, 418/522-1011, www.cinemacartier.com

COST: $9 adult

`Map 10`

This repertory cinema, located above a pharmacy, might bring you back to your adolescence if you grew up watching unlikely films in unlikely places. It's devoted to screening original films that have never before been screened in Québec City, and the emphasis here is on classics, modern-day masterpieces, and of course, independent features. With 117 seats, it's intimate with out being uncomfortable. English films here screened with French subtitles but no matter the language, this place is for film buffs.

LE CLAP

2360 chemin Ste-Foy, 418/653-2470, www.clap.qc.ca

COST: $10 adult, $7 senior and student, $6 child

`Map 12`

If you can get past the unfortunate name, the Clap is a great repertory cinema that plays films that don't always get wide distribution in the province. It plays English movies with French subtitles. Fans of international and art house cinema will enjoy their selection of festival hits from fests like Cannes, TIFF, and Festival Nouveau Cinéma. With none of the bells and whistles you find at bigger name cinemas, the smaller auditoriums and intimate setting aren't for everyone.

Festivals and Events

There's no helping Québec—it's simply a province that wants people to get together and have a good time. If you had to spend six months locked up indoors, you'd want to get out and celebrate too, which is why one of the biggest festivals of the year is held during the coldest months. Of course, when the warm weather finally arrives they throw it a big party too.

WINTER
☾ CARNAVAL DE QUÉBEC
Various locations, 418/626-3716, www.carnaval.qc.ca
COST: Varies

The most iconic of all the festivals in the province, Carnaval de Québec, has its roots in the early days of New France, when everyone got together in the weeks leading up to Lent to drink and let loose. Following tradition the festival is held between the end of January and early February. The first big

Carnaval took place in 1894 as a way of combating the winter blahs, and it's in this spirit that the festival has taken place every winter since 1955. Lead by Bonhomme, a life-size snowman with a floppy red hat and a *ceinture fléchée* (a traditional Québécois belt), the festival is all about fun in the outdoors. From parades to dog-sled races, tobogganing to ice canoeing, ice skating to outdoor dance parties and snow sculpture competitions, there's always something going on. It's also the only festival to give adults full rights to wander the town in snowsuits without shame while sipping on something to keep them warm. An added bonus? Most events are free.

MOIS MULTI
Various locations, 418/524-7553, www.moismulti.org
COST: Varies

This international festival, founded in 2000,

© CLAUDEL HUOT

Québec City's winter mascot, Bonhomme, in front of the Ice Castle during Carnaval de Québec focuses on multidisciplinary and electronic arts. Artists from such diverse countries as Russia, Australia, and Mexico have exhibited here, bringing with them their various light and sound installations and multimedia performances that explore topics like synesthesia, sound-architecture, and light chaos. Throughout the month-long festival in February, visitors are invited to witness these man-made realms, making it more than just an event; it becomes an experience.

RED BULL CRASHED ICE
Various locations, 877/643-8131, www.redbullcrashedice.ca
If you find walking the icy streets of Québec City tough, imaging skating down them. That's the challenge with the yearly Red Bull Crashed Ice, which takes place in March. Competitors from all over the world kitted out in full hockey gear take to the ice track laid out throughout the steep winding streets of Old Québec and attempt to skate their way to the bottom. Fans are free to line the 550-meter track and watch as both the men's and women's heats go by like a flash in this mashup between downhill skiing, hockey, and boardercross.

SPRING
CARREFOUR INTERNATIONAL DE THÉÂTRE DE QUÉBEC
Various locations, 418/692-3131, www.carrefourtheatre.qc.ca
COST: Varies
The city's preeminent theater festival, Carrefour International de Théâtre de Québec, presents innovative theater work from Canada and beyond. Though established playwrights often present here, there's an eye on emerging playwrights and artists as well. Held from the end of May to early June, all the productions presented are premieres in the province—they do not accept pieces that have already been mounted in Québec. Since it is an international festival there are often a few English or bilingual selections.

FESTIVAL DE LA GASTRONOMIE DE QUÉBEC
Expo Cité, 418/683-4150, www.crq.ca
COST: $12 adult
Map 12
For gourmands interested in seeing and tasting the latest in cuisine, the Gastronomy Festival brings out the best in new merchandise. Over three days in mid-April, 200 exhibitors invite the public to taste their wares, from wineries to microbreweries, pastries to cheese, with over 60 percent of the products coming from Québec. Visitors are welcome to browse the aisles pick up some cooking tips and indulge in all kinds of different food. Restaurants from around the city are also there, cooking up new or classic dishes. A word of warning: With fees for entering, parking, and the occasional bite, it can add up to be an expensive day.

◖ MANIF D'ART
Various locations, 418/524-1917, www.manifdart.org
COST: Varies
Simply put this is the Québec City biennial, held in May and June. Every even year the city and the world's established and up-and-coming artists present their works at what is the biggest contemporary art festival in Québec City. Events outside of the exhibitions are held as well, including colloquiums and forums, and satellite activities with other disciplines such as live performances and shows. A nominal fee allows visitors to see all the exhibitions and gives them access to guided tours, theme-related events, and creative workshops.

SUMMER
◖ LES CHEMINS INVISIBLES
L'Îlot Fleurie, www.cirquedusoleil.com
HOURS: Mid-June–early Sept. Tues.-Sun.
COST: Free
Map 11
Running five days a week all summer long, this free, hour-long Cirque du Soleil show takes place amid the columns and supports of the highway underpass. Created in collaboration with Robert Lepage, *Les Chemins Invisibles* (Invisible Paths) tells the story of three tribes

ROBERT LEPAGE

When you catch a show like *Les Chemins Invisibles* or the Moulin à Images, you're looking, at least in part, at the imagination of Robert Lepage.

A playwright, actor, film and stage director, Robert Lepage was born and grew up in Québec City, and though his works have been performed the world over, it's Québec that continues to be his creative base. Working with his creative team, Ex Machina, out of an old revamped fire station now known as La Caserne Dalhousie, Lepage has created internationally renowned works like *Lipsynch* and *Kà*, Cirque du Soleil's permanent show at the MGM Grand in Los Angeles. In Québec, across Canada, and in cultural communities around the world his name is synonymous with larger-than-life spectacles that continually raise the bar.

from different cultures who meet and share their experiences. Like many Cirque productions, it features several aerial acts swinging beneath the concrete slabs, as well as acrobats and special effects. It's located between Lower Town and Saint-Roch, and the lineup to get in starts early, about two hours before the show is scheduled to start. Standing-room only tickets are available before the show for a nominal fee. Shows start around sundown, between 8:30 and 9:30 depending on the dates.

EXPO QUÉBEC

Expo Cité, 250 blvd. Wilfrid-Hamel, 888/866-3976, www.expoquebec.com
COST: $25 adult, $20 senior, $12 child
Map 12

The largest agricultural fair in Eastern Canada was founded in 1911 and has been celebrating with a public exhibition every August since. The 10-day event is aimed at families with attractions like candy, inflatable castles, mini-rollercoasters, educational exhibits on science and organic food production, and concerts for

kids and adults alike. The real draw here, however, is the animals; with close to 2,000 animals on view kids and adults have a chance to learn more about horses, ponies, cattle, sheep, goats, alpacas, and a host of other, smaller animals.

FESTIVAL DES JOURNÉES D'AFRIQUE, DANSES ET RYTHMES DU MONDE

Various locations, 418/640-4213, www.festivaljourneedafrique.com
COST: Varies

Celebrating African dance and music, this two-week festival (late July–early Aug.) sees artists from all over the world performing a diverse range of African-roots music. Everything is represented here, from soukous from the Congo to Trinidadian calypso, South African Afrobeat, and roots reggae from Québec. Dance troupes, drumming, and dance workshops are also part of the fest. Prices vary depending on venue with some events for free.

◖ FESTIVAL D'ÉTÉ DE QUÉBEC

Various locations, 888/992-5200, www.infofestival.com
COST: $50 adult pass

One of the biggest events in the entire calendar year, Festival d'Été de Québec (Québec Summer Festival) is essentially one 11-day-long concert. With literally hundreds of shows—some of them for free—happening during the beginning of July, this event gives the city the attitude of a nonstop party. Started in 1968, the focus was mainly on Francophone and world artists, but since 2000 the festival has presented some of the most interesting international acts in the world, including Ethiopiques, Andrew Bird, Caribou, Black Eyed Peas, and a number of emerging talents. The biggest outdoor shows take place on the Plains of Abraham and in the past have featured musicians like Iron Maiden, Arcade Fire, and Paul McCartney.

FÊTE ARC-EN-CIEL DE QUÉBEC

Various locations, 418/809-3383, www.glbtquebec.org
COST: $12 adult

Taking place in early September, usually over Labor Day weekend, Fête Arc-en-Ciel de

© XAVIER DACHEZ

Les Fêtes de la Nouvelle-France

Québec (Rainbow Celebration) is Québec's gay pride celebration. Each year the three-day event is based on a different theme, usually one that can be loosely interpreted and allow for some great street decorations. Though the center of the celebrations is the gay pride parade, they include a number of free performances, concerts, and conferences that look at important topics like homophobia in high schools.

FÊTE NATIONALE ST-JEAN BAPTISTE

Plains of Abraham, 418/640-0799, www.snqc.qc.ca
COST: Free
Map 10

This is the province of Québec's national holiday, which takes place on June 24. In this context "nation" refers to the nation of Québec and as such it is not celebrated elsewhere in Canada. Though Saint-Jean-Baptiste Day has been celebrated in Québec since the first settlers, it took a patriotic turn in 1834 after Ludger Duvernay, who would later found the Saint-Jean-Baptiste Society, was inspired by St-Patrick's Day celebrations in Montréal. In celebration of the province's national holiday the people of Québec usually spend the afternoon with an aperitif before heading out to the free concert on the Plains of Abraham in the evening, featuring famous Québécois performers and stars.

LES FÊTES DE LA NOUVELLE-FRANCE

Various locations, 866/391-3383,
www.nouvellefrance.qc.ca
COST: $12 adult, free under 12

For four days in August, the public is invited to step back in time to the days of Nouvelle France, or Québec as it was during the French regime. Bringing to life over a dozen sites in the Vieux-Québec's Lower Town, each year is centered around a theme in order to give viewers a fuller picture of what life was like in New France. Past events have included the baptism of an Amerindian and a public blessing of women's pregnant bellies. Visitors are encouraged to dress up in period costumes, which are available to buy or rent. Good family fun.

LE GRAND RIRE
Various locations, 877/441-7473, www.grandrire.com
COST: $20 and up, free under 12
The Québec City equivalent of Just for Laughs, Le Grand Rire (the Big Laugh) caters to a Francophone audience. Occasionally, however, they have some big-name English acts like Bill Cosby on the bill. It runs throughout the month of June and into early July, and with over 70 shows on the schedule there are often a few offered in English. Shows take place at indoor and outdoor venues all over the city.

QUÉBEC CITY INTERNATIONAL FESTIVAL OF MILITARY BANDS
Various locations, 888/693-5757, www.fimmq.com
COST: Varies
For five days at the end of August, military bands and a few dancers from all over the world take to the stage and streets. Bands from all over Canada, Germany, France, Italy, and America regularly participate, including surprising acts like the New York City Police Department's Jazz Band. Locals line the Grande-Allée during the opening parade then head to the main stage near the Manège Militaire to catch a free show. Most events are free, but some shows require tickets, including the grand finale Tattoo.

FALL
ENVOL ET MACADAM
Various locations, 418/522-1611, www.envoletmacadam.com
COST: Varies
This festival of alternative music was founded in 1996, with the aim of both nurturing up-and-coming talent and bringing established artists to the city who wouldn't necessarily play here otherwise. Taking place in September, the festival has three main outdoor stages in the downtown core and takes over a number of indoor venues during the fest. Though "alternative" isn't as defining a moniker as it was in the 1990s, bands here are still outside of the mainstream, and have included acts like Bloc Party and Metric as well as punk, hardcore, and metal bands like Mastadon, Pennywise, and Bad Religion.

FESTIVAL ANTENNE-A
Various locations, www.antenne-a.com
COST: Varies
Music, books, art, film, theater; it's all here at this arts-focused festival that brings together emerging artists from all disciplines from late September to early October. Though the schedule is often heavy with bands and DJs from Québec, Canada, and the world, there is a focus on acts that go beyond just the musical aspects and delve into the realms of visual art and technology.

The festival also presents a number of group talks and conferences in both English and French around various themes, including emerging culture.

FESTIVAL DE JAZZ DE QUÉBEC
Various locations, www.jazzaquebec.ca
COST: Varies
For real jazz buffs only; you won't find any top 40 artists here. The target audiences for this fest, running from the end of September to early October, are jazz aficionados. Montréal's International Jazz Festival might be known for huge, big-name performers like Stevie Wonder and Lionel Ritchie, but here you'll find entire sets dedicated to greats like Charles Mingus and John Coltrane. Local jazz musicians also take to the stage, including younger avant-garde artists.

FESTIVAL DES MUSIQUES SACRÉES DE QUÉBEC
Église Saint-Roch, 590 rue St-Jean, 866/525-9777, www.festivalmusiquesacree.ca
COST: Varies
Map 11
The Québec Festival of Sacred Music is just that, a three-week-long October festival filled with compositions inspired by spirituality. Taking place at the Église Saint-Roch where they are the proud owners of a (partly) Casavantes organ, programs here include standards like Brahms's and Verdi's requiems, as well as occasional dance performances, gospel concerts, and compositions from lesser-known sources like sacred songs from Anatolia.

ARTS AND LEISURE

JOURNÉES DE LA CULTURE
Various locations, 866/734-4441,
www.journeesdelaculture.qc.ca
COST: Free

This province-wide celebration opens a number of cultural and artistic hubs to the public by inviting visitors into architecture offices, design studios and local theaters for a behind-the-scenes look. Also called "Days of Culture," this free, three-day event runs at the end of September, with cities offering complimentary shuttle services to various sites and events, so there's no excuse to miss out. Various workshops and kid-specific events make it an adventure for the whole family.

PARADE DES JOUETS
Various locations, 418/780-3006,
www.paradesdesjouets.ca
COST: Free

Held annually at the end of November, this children's parade has a long history. Started at the end of World War II by fireman Marcel Bourassa, firemen of the city worked together to repair old toys and make new ones for the less-fortunate children in the city. The tradition continues today, and since 2004, 900 underprivileged children are the recipients of new and refurbished toys each year. This parade is run in celebration of that event and includes floats and marching bands.

Recreation

There's no fighting nature. Québec City was blessed with huge green spaces, a waterfront, and a cliff face perfect for scaling. Sometimes a trip to the local store can feel like a hike. This is a city that embraces its proximity to nature, and those who live here bring urbanized elements of the outdoors to the city center with biking, walking, and even snowshoeing come winter.

PARKS
DOMAINE MAIZERETS
1248 ave. de la Verendrye, 418/660-7357,
www.domainemaizerets.com
COST: Free
Map 12

Situated just across the St-Charles River, Domaine Maizerets is both a public park and a historic site. Bought by the church in 1705, the land served as a farm and some of the church's old buildings are still standing. Tours of the beautifully landscaped gardens and arboretum are available, and concerts are often held on the park grounds. Two bike trails, Corridor des Cheminots and Corridor du Littoral, cut through the park, and in the winter it's a popular place for skating, cross-country skiing, snowshoeing, and tobogganing.

PARC CARTIER-BRÉBEUF
175 rue l'Espinay, 888/773-8888
COST: Free
Map 12

South of Saint-Roch, this national historic site commemorates both the winter of 1535, when Jacques Cartier and his shipmates spent the season near the Iroquoian village of Stadacona, and the site of the Jesuit missionaries' first home in Québec. To honor its past, commemorative monuments are set up around the park, which is divided into east and west by a small river. With 6.8 hectares, it's a popular place for outdoor sport and a bike path cuts through most of it. An interpretation center is open on-site from early May to early September, offering guided tours and various family activities.

PARC DE LA PLAGE JACQUES-CARTIER
3636 chemin de la Plage Jacques-Cartier, Ste-Foy, 418/641-6300
COST: Free
Map 12

Located outside of the city, just on the other side of the Québec Bridge, this waterfront park is open from May to October and gives

A TOUR OF ONE'S OWN: QUÉBEC CITY'S BEST WALKING TOURS

There's more than one way to see the city, but the best way to see it is on foot. Here are a few fun, kookier ways to get to know the town.

If you like to be spooked, **Ghost Tours of Québec** (418/692-9770, www.ghosttoursofquebec.com) is for you. Reservations are recommended for these nighttime tours that whisk participants down darkened streets while talking about the city's 400-year-old history and all the ghosts and hauntings that go with it. Guides will even take visitors into one of the most haunted buildings in the city, though taking a pass and staying outside is totally okay. Learn about the previous job experience needed to qualify you for the job of executioner in the 1600s, or how the murder of an American in Québec could be the source of an unexplained haunting.

Equally exciting but slightly less grim, **La Compagnie des Six Associés** (418/692-3033, www.sixassocies.com) offers a handful of walking tours, all with a different theme. They often involve a stop at a bar. Lust and Drunkenness is one such tour; it will take you past and into some of the forgotten brothels and taverns of the 19th century and give you an idea of how both the rich and the poor spent their free time and money. Things get a little darker with their Crime and Punishments tour, which lets visitors follow the wife of a French torturer through the streets by lantern-light as they learn about the various crimes, the criminals, and inevitably their punishment.

If you love the history but hate the gore (well, some of it anyway), **Les Tours Voir Québec** (866/694-2001, www.toursvoirquebec.com) hits up all the important sights on their Grand Tour. The architecture, the events the history – it's all here along with a few lesser-known sights. If you're not quite full yet, take a second helping and try their Food Tour, which looks at the influence of British, French, and Amerindian cooking in the kitchen. Of course, a taste of local wine, beer, chocolate, cheeses, pastries, and crêpes will only give you a better idea of exactly how this whole mix has come together.

Fed up with walking? **Tours Ludovica** (418/655-5836, www.toursludovica.com) will do the work while you sit back and relax. Guides ride around on bikes while visitors sit back and enjoy the scenery, in a sort of mash-up between a rickshaw and horse-drawn carriage. Going off map, Tours Ludovica offers tours of lesser-known areas like Saint-Roch, Saint-Sauveur, and Limoilou. A ride out to Saint-Sauveur lets visitors take in the historical architecture of a neighborhood that – had Samuel de Champlain's plans gone through – would have become a large city called Ludovica. It's here that you'll find many old seminaries and other church buildings as well as the Hôpital Général de Québec, the city's original hospital and the oldest building in the city. Up-and-coming Limoilou can also be explored by pedicab; let the guide lead you through the history of this emerging neighborhood before hoping out to grab a coffee at one of the sidewalk cafés.

If you'd rather be the person riding the pedicab than sitting in it, **Quebec Jogging Tours** (418/255-0602, www.quebecjoggingtours.com) could be for you. The multi-tasker's ideal tour, it enables you to get both your sightseeing and your daily workout out of the way. And this is indeed a workout, whether you opt for the tour of Upper and Lower Town; Plains of Abraham and Saint-Jean-Baptiste; or of the St-Charles River, Saint-Roch, and Limoilou, you'll be running 6 kilometers, just the right amount to get you good and hungry for your next meal.

© JEAN-PAUL HUARD, SÉPAQ

canoeing on one of the many lakes at Parc de la Plage Jacques-Cartier

visitors direct access to the St-Lawrence River. The winding paths and roads that take you to the shore, coupled with the boulders and pebbles that line the beach, make you feel as though you're somewhere else entirely. Since swimming is prohibited, boating is the summer's most popular sport, along with the 2.5 kilometers of hiking trails.

◖ PARC DU BOIS-DE-COULONGE

1215 Grande-Allée W., 800/442-0773
COST: Free
Map 12

The former home of the governor-general of United Canada, Spencer Wood was bought by the Québec government in 1870 and was home to the province's lieutenant-governors until 1966. Though a fire destroyed the main residence the splendid gardens remain, including a park that runs along the St-Lawrence, offering great views of the city. The park is a favorite for picnicking, self-guided tours, and its 3 kilometers of hiking trails. There's also a children's playground and sledding in winter.

PARC LINÉAIRE DE LA RIVIÈRE ST-CHARLES

332 rue Domagaya, 418/691-4710,
www.societerivierestcharles.qc.ca
COST: Free
Map 12

Starting at the Vieux-Port and running on for a total of 32 kilometers, this park runs along the banks of the St-Charles River covering both urban and natural environments. Open year long, it has 4 kilometers of bike and rollerblade paths, ice skating, snowshoeing, and 10 kilometers of cross-country skiing in winter. An interpretation center lies at the middle of the park.

PARC VICTORIA

Rue Robert-Rumilly, 418/641 6654
COST: Free
Map 12

Situated at the southern tip of Saint-Roch on the banks of the St-Charles River, Parc Victoria has been one of the few green spaces in the area since 1897. Almost completely surrounded by water, the small park was named after Britain's Queen Victoria. It provides excellent views of the river and it's here that you'll catch a baseball game by Les Capitales de Québec.

AMUSEMENT PARK
MEGA PARC DES GALERIES DE LA CAPITALE

5401 blvd. des Galeries, 418/627-5800, www.mega-parc.com
HOURS: Sept.-mid-June Mon.-Wed. noon-5 P.M., Thurs.-Fri. noon-9 P.M., Sat. 9:30 A.M.-5 P.M., Sun. 11 A.M.-5 P.M.; mid-June-Aug. Mon.-Wed. 10 A.M.-5 P.M., Thurs.-Fri. 10 A.M.-9 P.M., Sat. 9:30 A.M.-5 P.M., Sun. 11 A.M.-5 P.M.
Map 12

A child's paradise, this amusement park in the middle of a mall is designed for toddlers through tweens. Twenty different rides are waiting for kids to take them for a whirl, from physical fun like the Magic Castle's ball pit, slides, and rope games and the Baby Jungle's plush obstacle course to more traditional fairway staples like mini-bumper cars, a miniature train, a merry-go-round, Ferris wheel, and a rollercoaster. For kids wanting a bit more sport there's also a climbing wall, an ice rink and mini-putt. Each ride requires a varying number of tokens, anywhere from two to six, with each token costing 50 cents.

BICYCLING
Bike Paths
CORRIDOR DES CHEMINOTS

Just north of Estuaire de la Riviere Saint-Charles to Haute Saint-Charles, 418/641-6412, www.bikely.com/maps/bike-path/Corridor-des-Cheminots-Route-Verte
COST: Free
Map 12

Intersecting with the Corridor du Littoral just outside Saint-Roch, the Corridor des Cheminots is 22 kilometers long and takes riders from the city to Haute Saint-Charles in the north. Since it passes through various area, including the St-Charles River and Wendake Village, riders can view a diverse landscape. Open to cyclists, walkers, runners, and in-line skaters it becomes a popular place for cross-country skiing and snowshoeing in the winter.

(CORRIDOR DU LITTORAL

Saint-Augustin-de-Desmaures to Chute Montmorency, 418/641-6290, www.ville.quebec.qc.ca
COST: Free
Map 9

This 48-kilometer bike path stretches all the way from Saint-Augustin-de-Desmaures west of Québec City way to Chute Montmorency to the east. Running alongside the St-Lawrence, the path includes the Promenade Samuel Champlain; redone for the city's 400th anniversary in 2008, this section of the path is located below the Plains of Abraham and includes various parks and rest stops. It takes you along Cap Blanc, a charming working-class area built directly against the cliff.

Though it's mainly a path for cyclists, runners, walkers, inline skaters, and those in wheelchairs are free to use the path for both recreation and mobility. Open throughout the year, in wintertime it becomes an ideal place to snowshoe and cross-country ski.

Bike Rentals and Tours
CYCLO SERVICES

289 rue St-Paul, 418/692-4052, www.cycloservices.net
HOURS: Daily 9 A.M.-9 P.M.; tours May-Oct. 9 A.M.-9 P.M.
COST: $14-27 per hour depending on bike type
Map 9

Offering both rentals and tours, Cyclo Services has different types of bikes on offer, including hybrids, road bikes, tandem, and children's bikes. All rentals come with a helmet, lock, and a map. Located across the street from the Corridor du Littoral, it couldn't be easier to jump on your bike and go. Five bike tours are available throughout the summer season; some, like the one through Lower Town and the Vieux-Port, stay closer to home, while others, like Huron-Wendake, take you further afield. Prices vary and times change often so call or email ahead. For those with their own wheels an on-site mechanic is available seven days a week.

ARTS AND LEISURE

ÉCOLOCYCLO

Marché du Vieux-Port, 160 Quai St-André,
418/692-2517, www.ecolocyclo.net
HOURS: May–Oct. daily 9 A.M.–6 P.M.
COST: $17–45 per hour depending on bike type
Map 9

Located at the Marché du Vieux-Port, Écolocyclo is perfectly situated on the Corridor du Littoral, the longest bike path in the city. The majority of their rental fleet bikes are mountain and city bike hybrids, with at least 21 speeds, perfect for those steep Québec streets. They also offer electric bikes to help give your pedaling a bit of a push, as well as tandems, trail-a-bikes for children, and recumbent bikes for those who want to give laid-back riding a try. Though they don't offer tours, they will give you suggested routes to try, and all off their bikes are available for rentals of up to three days, at reasonable prices—perfect for getting around.

BOAT CRUISES

CROISIÈRE AML

Chouinard Quay, 10 rue Dalhousie, 866/856-6668,
www.croisereaml.com
Map 9

Cruises are available on the *Louis Jolliet,* a restaurant boat that can take you as far north as the Charlevoix region. Divided into day and night cruises, options include the Brunch Cruise with activities for kids, a tour of Île d'Orléans, a Fireworks Cruise, and a Five-Course Dinner Cruise, just to name a few. The captain's lounge, three dining rooms, and terraces are on board as well as a gift shop and a bistro. Entertainment is part of every cruise and guide Louis Jolliet—an early Canadian explorer—will reveal all the area's secrets. An orchestra plays in the evenings and later a dance floor gets the party going.

CROISIÈRE DUFOUR

57 rue Ste-Anne, 800/463-5250, www.dufour.ca
HOURS: May–Oct. daily 1:30 P.M., mid-July–mid-Aug.
daily 1:30 P.M. and 3:30 P.M.
COST: $64 adult, $59 senior and student, $29 child,
children under 6 free for 90-minute cruise
Map 8

This company offers two different cruises in and around Québec. La Touristique is a 90-minute historical tour that will take visitors from the Vieux-Port along the coast of the Île d'Orléans and Montmorency Falls and allows for waterfront views of Château Frontenac and Cap Diamant. The Image Mill cruise allows you to take in Le Moulin à Images multimedia event from the water; with panoramic windows and three terraces it gives you a different take on the spectacle. They also offer longer cruises into the Charlevoix region to see the whales and the fjords.

CROISIÈRES COUDRIER

Bassin Louise, Pier 19, 180 rue Dalhousie,
888/600-5554, www.croisierescoudrier.qc.ca
HOURS: May–mid-Oct. Sat.–Sun. 1:30 P.M., July–Aug.
daily 3:30 P.M.
COST: $32 adult, $30 senior and student, $15 child,
children under 5 free for 90-minute cruise
Map 9

Departing from the Vieux-Port, Croisières Coudrier offers some unique and interesting tours. Mixing sightseeing with a little bit of learning, many of the cruises are also educational. Learn about Québec's own Ellis Island, Grosse-Île, a quarantine station between 1832 and 1937 and the home of Irish immigrants; passengers will have a chance to visit the island. Or experience the charms of Isle-aux-Grues by bike and taste their well-known cheese. Apple-picking and five-course dinner cruises are also available, as is a sightseeing tour, which lets you see the city from the river.

CLIMBING

LE CHAMPLAIN AND LE PYLÔNE

Near Pont de Québec
Map 12

For experienced climbers only, this natural climbing wall can be accessed from rue Champlain. Located just outside of the city, near the Pont de Québec, are two cliffs perfect for climbing. This outdoor climbing area is a popular place with local climbers and caters to both learners and intermediate climbers. Le Pylône is the beginner area with 5.8 routes, while Le Champlain, 30 feet high by 200 feet long with lots of overhanging routes, is great for experts. Known as the "School of Rock," it's a great place to practice, especially since the rock face is made up of difficult gritstone.

ROC GYMS

2350 ave. du Colisée, 418/647-4422, www.rocgyms.com
HOURS: Mon.-Sat. 10 A.M.-10 P.M., Sun. 10 A.M.-6 P.M.
COST: $18 day rental with equipment
Map 12

Opened in 1993, Roc Gyms is a climbing school that offers indoor climbing lessons. Over 75 climbing lines are available in the main room, while two bouldering rooms are also available on-site, as are a number of indoor aerial courses. Those that are already experienced climbers can sign up for courses in outdoor and ice climbing. Located in Limoilou, it's easily accessible from downtown and Vieux-Port.

GOLF
Full Course
LA TEMPÊTE

51 rue des Trois Manoirs, Lévis, 418/832-8111, www.golflatempete.com
HOURS: May-Nov. daily dawn-10 P.M.
COST: $95-155 for 18 holes
Map 12

Situated across the water in the city of Lévis, La Tempête is one of the top courses in the metropolitan area (of course, the green fees reflect this). Newly opened it hosted the World Skins tournament in 2009 and has been called the first 18-hole golf course of international caliber in the area. Designed by golf architect Darrell J. Huxham, the 7,203-yard course is topped with a luxurious clubhouse and high-class restaurant.

Miniature Golf
GOLF TOURISTIQUE DE QUÉBEC

Parc-de-l'Artillerie, 2 rue D'Auteuil, 418/977-2453, www.golftouristique.com
HOURS: June-Sept. daily 10 A.M.-5 P.M.
COST: $15 adult, $13 senior, $13.50 youth, children under 8 free
Map 8

Sign in at the clubhouse to receive your specialized club and ball before hitting the Upper

Town links. A way of combining history with golf, this nine-hole course (rumor has it, it's a par 4) has you teeing off at various points around the city's fortifications (which are for the most part covered in grass), through its historic back streets, and even up along the walls of the Citadelle. A round takes approximately two hours and the course is open come rain or shine.

ICE-SKATING
PARC DU MUSÉE

Parc des Champs-de-Bataille
HOURS: Late Oct.-mid-Mar. daily 11 A.M.-6 P.M.
COST: Free
Map 10

This outdoor skating rink, directly in front of the Musée des Beaux-Arts and right on the Plains of Abraham, is a great place to bring the kids. Easily accessible and popular with locals it was completely renovated in 2011. Skaters here should bring their own skates and equipment, since there are no rental facilities on the premises.

PATINOIRE DE LA PLACE D'YOUVILLE

995 Place d'Youville, 418/641-6256
HOURS: Late Oct.-mid-Mar. Mon.-Thurs. noon-10 P.M., Fri.-Sat. 10 A.M.-10 P.M.
COST: Free
Map 8

Located directly in front of the Palais de Montcalm, this outdoor skating rink is a veritable winter wonderland once the snow has settled. A great place to bring the kids, it is frequented by tourists and locals alike who want to go for a skate in the shadow of the old city walls. Skate rental and sharpening are available during opening hours, as is a warm change room fitted out with lockers, but visitors have to bring their own padlock.

POINTE-AUX-LIÈVRES

5 rue de la Pointe-aux-Lièvres, 418/641-6345
HOURS: Late Oct.-mid-Mar. daily 24 hours
COST: Free
Map 12

When the St-Charles River, which separates

Saint-Roch from Limoilou, freezes over it becomes a natural skating rink, measuring 1.5 kilometers long. It's here that you'll find people playing pickup hockey and families teaching the youngest members how to skate. If you want a real Canadian experience, there's nothing like plopping your bum on a cold park bench to lace up your skates. Of course, a warm changing room and heated pavilion with hot chocolate and skate rental are also available.

SKIING, SNOWBOARDING, AND SNOWSHOEING

PARC DES PLAINES D'ABRAHAM

Discovery Pavilion, 835 rue Wilfrid-Laurier (equipment rental), 418/648-2586, www.ccbn-nbc.gc.ca
HOURS: Late Dec.-mid-Mar. daily 8:30 A.M.-4 P.M.
COST: Free
Map 10

Come winter, this historical sight becomes an outdoor sport paradise. From beginner to pro the 12.6 kilometers of cross-county trails and 3.8-kilometer (round-trip) trails for snowshoers, there's no better place to experience the winter right in the city's own backyard. Four classic trails, made up of one easy trail and three intermediate are open. Those without their own equipment—boots, poles, skis, and snowshoes—can rent them from the Discovery Pavilion. A waxing room and two heated rest areas are available around the plains, and they also offer cross-country ski lessons.

SWIMMING AND WADING POOLS

PARC DE L'ESPLANADE

Parc des Plaines d'Abraham, 418/523-5695
HOURS: Mid-June–mid-Aug. daily 11 A.M.-4 P.M.
COST: Free
Map 8

This children's wading pool is in the heart of Vieux-Québec's Upper Town. Situated in the shadow of the Fortifications this wading pool is simple with hardly any bells and whistles; still, it's the perfect place to let the kids cool off and let off some steam in the middle of the day. A children's playground can be found just a little further along.

PISCINE PARC DU MUSÉE

Parc des Champs-de-Bataille
HOURS: Mid-June–mid-Aug. daily noon-7 P.M.
COST: Free
Map 10

Located on the Plains of Abraham this public pool and wading pool were scheduled to be completely renovated in 2011, giving them a brand-new look. Conveniently located right on the Grande-Allée, it's easily accessible from all points of the city. A haven for locals this is a great place to bring the kids, especially to let them go a little wild after an afternoon at the museum.

WATER SPORTS

BAIE DE BEAUPORT

418/266-0722, www.baiedebeauport.com
HOURS: Mid-June–mid-Aug. daily 10 A.M.-9 P.M.
Map 12

A five-minute drive from downtown Québec City is a world of boating fun. Though swimming in the river is forbidden, a ton of boating and beach activities make you feel like you're on the coast. Canoe, kayak, sailboard, dinghy, and catamaran rentals are offered at various rates and lengths, and those looking to learn how to sail can sign up for classes. Beach soccer and volleyball courts are free for all to use and the large children's park keeps the kids busy.

WINTER SLEDDING

(GLISSADES DE LA TERRASSE DUFFERIN

Terrasse Dufferin, at rue des Carrières and Place d'Armes, 418/829-9898
HOURS: Mid-Dec.-mid-Mar. daily 11 A.M.-11 P.M.
COST: $2 pp per ride
Map 8

This entertainment of sliding down a steep 250-meter run at speeds of up to 70 kilometers per hour has been around since 1884. The Glissades de la Terrasse Dufferin (*les glissades*) are a Québec tradition. In front of the Château Frontenac, with great views of the St-Lawrence, families line up in full winter regalia to ride a toboggan down to the base of the wooden structure. Up to four people can ride down on a single toboggan, though you're also allowed to try it solo and in pairs. A mini-sugar shack full of refreshments is available on the spot. Lineups can be long, especially on weekends, so be prepared to wait.

GYMS AND HEALTH CLUBS
PLANÈTE FITNESS GYM
400 blvd. Jean-Lesage, 418/523-0284, www.planetefitnessgym.qc.ca
HOURS: Daily 24 hours
Map 9

This 24-hour gym is open seven days a week and offers à la carte memberships that allow up to 10 visits. Longer memberships are available for three months up to a year. Along with a weight and cardio room they also offer a number of classes, including crossfit, spinning, and toning, many of which start as early as seven in the morning.

YOGA
ASHTANGA YOGA QUÉBEC
Centre Culture et Environnement Frédéric Back, 870 ave. de Salaberry, 418/682-0654, www.ashtangaquebec.com
HOURS: Mon.-Sat., hours vary depending on season
COST: $15 per class for nonmembers
Map 10

A number of different types and levels of classes are available at this Ashtanga yoga studio located in a local community center. Guided classes are available for levels one through three, that is to say from beginners to intermediate and regular practitioners. Courses run here throughout the day, seven days a week, typically starting at 6:30 A.M. and ending at 7:30 P.M. Those already comfortable with their yoga, just looking for a place to practice, are welcome to drop in; there are free practice times available throughout the week.

SPECTATOR SPORTS
Baseball
LES CAPITALES DE QUÉBEC
Stade Municipal, Parc Victoria, 418/521-2255, www.capitalesdequebec.com
Map 12

Members of the Can-Am Baseball League,

Les Capitales are one of the most successful teams in the league. Making the playoffs almost every year since they entered the league in 1999, they garnered leagues titles in 2006, 2009, and 2010.

They play at the Stade Municipal, which seats approximately 5,000 and is located in Parc Victoria. The stadium opened in 1938 and has a long history within local baseball legend. This rich history and the affordable tickets ($10, $15 box seats) give you the feeling that you're still in touch with what sport used to be and should be.

Basketball
LES KEBS DE QUÉBEC
PEPS de l'Université Laval, 2300 rue de la Terrasse, 418/656-7377, www.kebsdequebec.com
Map 12

Formerly called the Kebekwa de Québec, this basketball team is now called the Kebs. The team got their weird name after a public survey showed that 70 percent approved of the name. (Weirdly enough, 70 percent of the grassroots Québécois population polled is also proindependence.) After playing for a couple of years in the American Basketball Association they now play in Premier Basketball League. The season runs January–March, tickets are around $15, and they play in the arena at Laval University.

Football
LE ROUGE ET OR
PEPS de l'Université Laval, 2300 rue de la Terrasse, 418/656-7377, www.rougeetor.ulaval.ca
Map 12

This university football team has amassed a strong following in a city craving more spectator sports. Le Rouge et Or (the Red and the Gold, which are the school colors) won the Vanier Cup, the highest distinction for a Canadian university football team, four times in six years (2003, 2004, 2006, and 2008). The also hold the record for the longest winning streak in Canadian Interuniversity Sport football with 19 consecutive wins. If you happen to be visiting in the fall, a trip to Sainte-Foy to

ARTS AND LEISURE

see a game is worth it; the bleachers are always packed and the energy is palpable.

Université Laval's outdoor stadium can hold up to 10,000 spectators but fit double that in 2005 with standing room only. Their loyal fan base has also mastered the art of tailgating, getting to the stadium parking lot early on game day mornings.

Hockey
REMPARTS DE QUÉBEC

Colisée Pepsi, 250 blvd. Wilfrid-Hamel, 418/525-1212, www.remparts.qc.ca
Map 12

Ever since they won the Memorial Cup (the Canadian Junior Championships) in 2006, the Remparts, Québec's Major Junior Hockey team, have become the hottest show in town. And things will probably stay that way so long as this crazy-about-hockey city doesn't have an NHL team. Their home rink is the Colisée Pepsi, the former home of les Nordiques (RIP), which moved in Colorado in 1995.

They're coached by former goalie Patrick Roy, considered one of the best goalies in the history of the game. Roy, who ranks with Celine Dion as far as Québec hero hierarchy goes, brings a colorful edge to the team. Famous Remparts alumni include legendary player Guy Lafleur, ex-Nordiques Michel Goulet, left-winger Simon Gagné, center Mike Ribeiro, and right-winger Alexander Radulov.

SHOPS

Québec has a long history with commerce. As the site of the first settlement in New France, its entire founding was based on trade with the Amerindians, and as the colony grew, trade became vital to its survival. Its genetic makeup as a commercial city is still apparent, and over the centuries it has created some of Canada's most recognized stores and brands.

In fact many of those same stores exist today, with their long history intact. Holt Renfrew, La Maison Simons, and J.A. Moisan (the oldest grocery store in North America) are businesses that first bloomed in Québec and whose rich past can still be seen when you enter their establishments.

With all that history, however, it's important to have something new, and the revival of rue St-Joseph in Saint-Roch has been one of the most important developments of the past few years. The area was abandoned by businesses who opted for the malls of the late 1950s, but new customers and retailers are now emerging in the area. Filled with young, modern stores and independent boutiques, it has given the city a much-needed boost of cool. Rue St-Jean, outside of the walls, is experiencing a similar rejuvenation, with youthful stores popping up, many with an eye on local products and design.

Unlike most major Canadian cities, when it comes to the downtown core, Québec sticks to its roots. Though you might find H&M, Gap, and Zara taking up residence in prominent downtown buildings all over the world, here they are relegated to the malls, about a 15-minute drive away. Though name-brand chains can be found, mostly in Upper Town, they are few and far between. Instead the historic houses and beautiful Beaux Arts buildings are small independent boutiques or established Québec businesses.

© SACHA JACKSON

HIGHLIGHTS

LOOK FOR TO FIND RECOMMENDED SHOPS.

(Best Store for Romantic Gifts: Pont Briand Joallier has a number of beautiful, handcrafted pieces perfect for that special someone (page 309).

(Best Artisanal Crafts: Carrying the work of over 125 local artisans, **Boutique des Métiers d'Art** is a perfect one-stop-shop for everything from jewelry to salad bowls (page 311).

(Best Toy Store: Parents can let kids run wild and kids can let parents do the same at toy emporium **Benjo** (page 315).

(Best Hat Store: Bibi et Compagnie has approximately 3,000 men's and women's hats for all kinds of weather and in all kinds of styles (page 316).

(Best Interior Design: Located in a former bank, women's boutique **Esther P**'s open-concept interior and high-concept design bring an edge to shopping for the latest trends (page 317).

(Best Selection of Local Designers: Dedicated to local designers, **Jupon Pressé** exclusively carries lines from some of the province's most exciting emerging designers and does it with some fun in a bright, eclectic boutique (page 318).

(Best Pedicure and a New Pair of Heels: Sleek high-end shoe store **Tohu Bohu** makes sure your feet look as good as the designer heels you just bought (page 320).

(Unique Gifts: Connoisseur of kitsch, Mr. Blouin carries everything from old milk jugs to vintage magazines at the cabin-esque **Magasin Général P.L. Blouin** (page 323).

(Best Gourmet Goodies: Find artisanal cheese from all over the province at **L'Artisan et Son Pays** (page 325).

(Best Outdoor Gear: If you're headed for an outdoor adventure, **Mountain Equipment Co-op** has everything from bike gear to arctic sleeping bags to get you ready (page 328).

Bright and inviting, Jupon Pressé carries a number of up-and-coming Québec designers.

© JUPON PRESSÉ

There is no denying that many of the stores that line the streets of Vieux-Québec's Upper and Lower Town cater to tourists. Though many of them strive to have their own personality, a lot easily blend into one another. The stores included in this chapter, however, all offer something a bit different and veer off down what is hopefully a slightly lesser-worn path.

In high-tourist season during the summer, boutiques in Upper and Lower Town stay open as late as they want, some even as late as midnight, if the crowds are still out. By contrast, in winter stores often close early, or for months at a time, depending on the nature of their business. If there's a store you particularly want to visit but you're unsure about their hours, it's always best to call ahead, especially in the off season.

Accessories and Jewelry

There are independent jewelry stores throughout Québec City. Rue Petit-Champlain has a good mix of high-end and more artsy offerings. In fact, these are the two main kinds of jewelry stores found all over the city: super kitsch costume jewelry and high-end designer pieces. One thing that remains the same in upscale or costume jewelry is that it's all handcrafted.

MADEMOISELLE B
541 rue St-Joseph E., 418/522-0455
HOURS: Mon.-Wed. 10 A.M.-5:30 P.M., Thurs.-Fri. 10 A.M.-9 P.M., Sat. 10 A.M.-5 P.M., Sun. 11 A.M.-5 P.M.
Map 11

This narrow storefront would be easy to miss if it weren't for the floor-to-ceiling windows and old-fashioned sign that pops out over the door. Situated in a newer building in the Saint-Roch neighborhood, Mademoiselle B has an old-world charm with dark chocolate parquet floors, soft pink walls, and plush velvet display shelves. In keeping with the romantic interior the costume jewelry here is very girly, with collections coming from France, and the south of Italy, and of course, Québec.

PONT BRIAND JOALLIER
48 rue du Petit-Champlain, 418/977-5800, www.pontbriand.net
HOURS: Winter daily 10 A.M.-5:30 P.M., summer Mon.-Sat. 10 A.M.-9 P.M., Sun. 10 A.M.-6 P.M.
Map 9

Open for over 40 years, this high-end jeweler located in a historic stone house in Petit-Champlain

is one of the city's best. The super-sleek interior with white display cases built into the walls gives it an added bit of glamour. The pieces here, many of which are made by Québec artisans, are exquisitely crafted with a wide range of styles and materials available, from rough-hued gold rings set with brilliant turquoise from the exclusive Louis Perrier collection to refined platinum engagement rings with a simple butterfly setting.

ROSE BOUTON
387 rue St-Jean, 418/614-9507, www.boutiquerose.blogspot.com
HOURS: Tues.-Wed. 11 A.M.-5 P.M., Thurs.-Fri. 11 A.M.-9 P.M., Sat.-Sun. 11 A.M.-5 P.M.
Map 11

A lot of time could be spent in this kitschy store filled with overwhelming amounts of jewelry and accessories and vibrantly decorated with bubble-gum pink walls, bright florals, pink fun fur, and circle motif wallpaper: Find fabric-covered earrings, hand-drawn pins, long-fringe pendants and earrings, bracelets and necklaces made with buttons, the store's namesake *bouton*. A fun and vibrant store, it also carries seasonal accessories like bags, scarves, and hats.

ZIMMERMANN
46 Côte de la Fabrique, 418/692-2672, www.zimmermann-quebec.com
HOURS: Mon.-Wed. and Sat. 9:30 A.M.-5:30 P.M., Thurs.-Fri. 9:30 A.M.-9 P.M.
Map 8

Having studied jewelry design and gemology in

SHOPS

Paris, Michel Zimmermann returned to Québec in the late 1970s to open his very own jewelers. Zimmermann's has since become one of the most respected jewelers in the business, known for unique handcrafted gems. Working exclusively with 925/1000 silver and 18-carat gold or platinum, the pieces are all meticulously handcrafted without the use of any cast. Styles vary from simple, leaf-shaped earrings to detailed wedding bands and teardrop birthstone pendants.

Antiques

If you're on the hunt for antiques look no further than the narrow cobblestone rue St-Paul, where just about every other store is dedicated to antiques. If you're looking for something specific, however, it's best to pop into them all. Just about every single store is stocked full of everything from antique bedposts to silverware.

ANTIQUITÉS BOLDUC
89 rue St-Paul, 418/694-9558,
www.lesantiquitesbolduc.com
HOURS: Mon.-Fri. 9:30 A.M.-5 P.M., Sat. 10:30 A.M.-5 P.M.,
Sun. 11 A.M.-5 P.M.
Map 9

Owned and staffed by a young helpful and friendly couple, Stéphanie and Frédéric Bolduc, this small antique store situated in an old stone house is bright, uncluttered and artfully laid out with furniture, chandeliers, and just about anything else. Clocks and sconces line the walls while tables, cabinets, and dressers are topped with children's toys, rotary telephones, firefighters' helmets, china tableware, steak knives, and vanity sets. Price here vary depending on the item.

BOUTIQUE AUX MÉMOIRES ANTIQUITÉS
105 rue St-Paul, 418/692-218
HOURS: Mon.-Sat. 9:30 A.M.-5 P.M.
Map 9

A staple on the strip since the 1970s, Boutique aux Mémoires Antiquités is filled with treasures like Victorian furniture, oil lamps, old office desks, glittery chandeliers, and other curiosities. The low tin ceilings add even more charm to the crowded space in a historic building. The owner has a keen eye for finery, so fans of Tiffany lamps, fine silverware, and dinner china should keep their eyes peeled here. Though most of the stuff will look like it could come from anywhere, just about all of the finds here are directly from Québec's past.

MAISON DAMBOURGÈS
155 rue St-Paul, 418/692-1115,
www.antiquitesdambourges.com
HOURS: Mon. and Thurs.-Fri. 11 A.M.-5 P.M., Sat.-Sun. 11 A.M.-4 P.M.
Map 9

Named after a French shopkeeper who was also the head colonel of the militia in 1790, Maison Dambourgès is one of the larger stores on the street. Specializing in 19th-century pine country furniture from Québec and folk art, the store is perfectly curated. The large store is spacious compared to others on the strip and has a country feel. Just about everything here looks like it was fished out of an abandoned farm house in the country, and the owners have an impeccable eye for everything from stoneware jugs and weathervanes to old pine hutches with peeling paint and armoires built for the sole purpose of cooling pies.

Arts and Crafts

Though Québec doesn't have crafts in the traditional sense, there is a certain aesthetic found in the various artisanal works. A mix of materials is one element, as is an unexpected juxtaposition of colors and shapes. Inuit art, though not exclusive to the province, can also be found in a number of arts and craft shops, since northern Québec is home to many native and Inuit tribes.

BOUTIQUE CANADEAU

1124 rue St-Jean, 418/692-4850, www.canadeau.com
HOURS: Summer daily 10 A.M.-7 P.M., winter daily 10 A.M.-6 P.M.
Map 8

Situated in the heart of Vieux-Québec's Upper Town, this small boutique located in a historic building offers high-end pieces from artists in the region. Stone and ivory carvings, both Inuit and local, are some of the more sought-after pieces, as are intricately carved chess pieces. It's a popular tourist shop, and handmade hunting knives are among the less conventional items, as are woven and knitted goods like the handmade sweaters reminiscent of the kind Bill Cosby made famous in the '80s.

◖ BOUTIQUE DES MÉTIERS D'ART

29 Place Royale, 418/694-0267,
www.metiers-d-art.qc.ca
HOURS: June 24-late-Aug. daily 9:30 A.M.-9:30 P.M.;
Sept.-Dec. Sat.-Wed. 9 A.M.-6 P.M., Thurs.-Fri.
9:30 A.M.-9 P.M.; Jan.-late-Apr. daily 9:30 A.M.-6 P.M.;
May-June 24 Sat.-Wed. 9 A.M.-6 P.M., Thurs.-Fri.
9:30 A.M.-9 P.M.
Map 9

Devoted to the work of Québécois artisans, the Boutique des Métiers d'Art showcases the work of over 125 craftsmen and -women, all members of the Québec Craft Council. Situated on the famous Place Royale, it couldn't be better located, with huge, floor-to-ceiling windows and shelves and display cases lining the stone walls. Everything is well plotted out. Goods here are divided by materials and include wood, ceramic, metals, and glass, though other materials can be found in the work throughout the shop. Whether it is simple wood kitchen utensils you're looking for, a tin candelabra, or a unique silver pendant, you'll find it here.

GALERIE D'ART LES TROIS COLOMBES

46 rue St-Louis, 418/694-1114
HOURS: Mon.-Wed. 9:30 A.M.-7 P.M., Thurs.-Sun.
9:30 A.M.-9 P.M.
Map 8

Situated in a beautiful historic house complete with a red-peaked roof and white-washed facade, Galerie d'Art les Trois Colombes is one of the most picturesque of arts and craft stores. Filled with selections from both Québécois and Canadian arts and crafts, it also carries works by Inuits and Amerindians, including thick-wool parkas trimmed with fur and moccasins and mukluks in both child and adult sizes. Authentic snowshoes, soapstone sculptures, and weavings occupy the downstairs, while upstairs visitors will find handmade hats, rag dolls, and sweaters.

KETTO

951 ave. Cartier, 418/522-3337,
www.kettodesign.com
HOURS: Mon.-Wed. and Sat.-Sun. 10 A.M.-5 P.M.,
Thurs.-Fri. 10 A.M.-9 P.M.
Map 10

Located in a skinny corner house decorated with deep blue trim, lots of flower pots, and their unmistakable yellow sign, Ketto has an aesthetic all its own. In the late 1990s, Onge was working at a ceramic store when the pieces with her cutesy, big-headed, stick-limbed characters painted on them started flying off the shelves. Today, Ketto carries hand-painted ceramics, jewelry, clothing, glassware, and stationery all with Onge's signature style. The interior can be a bit chaotic but everything is perfectly laid out, with a simple wood cabinet taking up almost an entire wall and full of cups and saucers.

SHOPS

LAMBERT & CO.

1 rue des Carrières, 418/694-2151, www.lambertco.ca
HOURS: Mon.-Fri. 10 A.M.-7 P.M., Sat.-Sun.
9:30 A.M.-6:30 P.M.
Map 8

This teeny-tiny store, approximately two meters wide, in the interior courtyard of Château Frontenac is a splendid gem. The emphasis here is on quality not quantity, and their finely made, striped wool socks, black-and-red checkered blankets, and fur-trimmed hats have become a recognized brand in this region. Alongside the cozy woolen goods they also sell a few natural beauty products, like moisturizer, body wash, and shampoo, for both people and their pets.

PAULINE PELLETIER

38 rue du Petit-Champlain, 418/692-4871,
www.paulinepelletier.com
HOURS: Oct.-May Mon.-Wed. 9:30 A.M.-5:30 P.M.,
Thurs.-Fri. 9:30 A.M.-9 P.M., Sat.-Sun. 9 A.M.-5 P.M.;
June-Sept. daily 9 A.M.-9 P.M.
Map 9

Pauline Pelletier's ceramic and porcelain artwork is both unconventional yet modern. Using unusual shapes as a base, a square teapot for example, the ceramic is then smoke-fired to create the final effect, giving it a marbled finish. The unusual pieces of art, popular with tourists and locals alike, include vases, tea sets, and serving platters. The colors are unconventional—navy blue, red, and jade, many with a touch of rich gold adorning the edges. The boutique, open since 1983, also carries the work of other Québec artisans and jewelers, giving it a more dynamic atmosphere and added quirkiness.

POINT D'EXCLAMATION

762 rue St-Jean, 418/525-8053
HOURS: Sat.-Wed. 10 A.M.-6 P.M., Thurs.-Fri.
10 A.M.-9 P.M.
Map 11

Founded by Diane Bergeron of Euphory Design in 2004, Point d'Exclamation was at the forefront of the movement to champion Québec-based designers. Nowadays the entire neighborhood is full of shops dedicated to locally produced and designed goods (Jupon Pressé, Code Vert, Rose Bouton), but it was Bergeron and her eye for local artisanal work that got the ball rolling. The boutique carries the work of 30–40 local designers at any one time, and the goods range from jewelry to accessories and clothes. The all-white interior is a bit too bright at times but puts the focus on the work while their constantly changing storefront window is a always a feast for the eyes.

SOIERIE HUO

91 rue du Petit-Champlain, 418/692-5920,
www.soieriehuo.com
HOURS: Summer daily 9:30 A.M.-8 P.M., winter daily
9:30 A.M.-5 P.M.
Map 9

This unique shop is run by artist Dominique Huot, who has been creating her one-of-a-kind silk products since the late 1970s. A descendant of Québécois artist Charles Huot, Dominique uses natural silk and wool fibers to create her scarves and men's ties. The designs on many of the scarves are spontaneous, though she continually recreates certain themes, including abstracts, florals, and maple leafs. The shop itself is quite small with the scarves predominantly displayed throughout.

Bath and Beauty

Though you'll likely stumble across quite a few local natural beauty products in boutiques around the city, individual stores are hard to come by. Many women simply pick up their cosmetics in the dedicated section at their local pharmacy or department store; unlike in Europe or the United States, stores dedicated solely to beauty and body products are still in their infancy phase.

CANDEUR

1187 rue St-Jean, 418/694-1731, www.candeur.com
HOURS: Fall and spring Mon.-Fri. 10 A.M.-6 P.M., Sat. 10 A.M.-9 P.M., Sun. 10 A.M.-5 P.M.; summer daily 10 A.M.-9 P.M.; winter daily 10 A.M.-5 P.M.
Map 8

The storefront of this natural soap shop has the old-school look of the a 1950s, with a slightly slanted window, its name painted in cursive, and products displayed like a goodies in cake shop. Inside things are a little more sparse with the products arranged on tables around the room, though their color, shape, and smell still manage to give off a bakery air. Everything here is

naturally made with the content list for all to see. Soaps for special skin conditions like eczema and rosacea are available, as are moisturizing shops, body scrubs, and other natural body products, including shampoo, lotion, and lip balm.

COSMÉTIQUES BLOOMI

507 rue St-Joseph E., 418/529-7470
HOURS: Mon.-Wed. 9:30 A.M.-5:30 P.M., Thurs.-Fri. 9:30 A.M.-9 P.M., Sat. 9:30 A.M.-5 P.M., Sun. 11 A.M.-5 P.M.
Map 11

This sleek and modern cosmetics store is reminiscent of international chain Sephora. Products are beautifully arranged on white high-gloss lacquered shelves and the whole interior is given an added bit of warmth thanks to the exposed brick walls. It carries high-end make-up lines, a large range of perfumes, and just about any color of polish you could want. Pop in to get a manicure or pedicure, your makeup done for a special occasion, or just to get some tips from the beauticians, who are always ready to give you some pointers and a bit of a touchup.

Books and Music

Unlike in Montréal, English books are hard to come by in Québec City. Although most hotels carry a few national and international English-language papers, finding anything more than a best-seller can be tough. Magazines, however, are much easier to find, and both European and North American versions are readily available.

If you're looking for a new disc or want to pick up some vintage Félix Leclerc after an inspiring night at a *boîte à chansons,* head along rue St-Jean, where you'll find both new and used vinyls and CDs. The implosion of the record industry has been tough on Québec's independent music stores but a few gems remain.

ARCHAMBAULT

1095 rue St-Jean, 418/694-2088, www.archambault.ca
HOURS: Jan.-May Sun.-Wed. 9:30 A.M.-6 P.M., Thurs.-Sat. 9:30 A.M.-9:30 P.M.; June-Dec. daily 9:30 A.M.-9:30 P.M.
Map 8

One of the biggest music stores in the province, Archambault has 15 stores throughout Québec, and sells everything from CDs and DVDs to books, magazines, newspapers, video games, and musical instruments. Deep red walls are the backdrop for this location's selection of small instruments and musical accessories. It was founded in 1896 by Edmond Archambault, who wanted to open a sheet music store; he teamed up with piano man and musical instrument specialist J.A. Hurteau to create the first Archambault retail outlet. Locals pop in here to pick up a new release or get strings for their guitar.

CD MÉLOMANE
248 rue St-Jean, 418/525-1020, www.cdmelomaneinc.supersites.ca
HOURS: Mon.-Wed. and Sat. 10 A.M.-5 P.M., Thurs.-Fri. 10 A.M.-9 P.M., Sun. noon-5 P.M.
Map 11

Established in 1996, this is the best record store in the city. Totally unpretentious, the staff here simply know their stuff, with certain clerks knowing the store's entire stock almost by heart. New and used CDs are available here, as are racks upon racks of vinyl, which take up the majority of the space. Brick arches divide the store. They'll happily transfer your cherished 33s, 45s, and 78s onto CD.

LIBRAIRIE PANTOUTE
1100 rue St-Jean, 418/694-9748, www.librairiepantoute.com
HOURS: Mon.-Sat. 10 A.M.-10 P.M., Sun. noon-10 P.M.
Map 8

Founded in 1972 by a bunch of counterculture kids, Librarie Pantoute (its name means "not at all" in Québécois lingo), this is one of the most important independent bookstores in the province. Situated in the heart of Upper Town this location has high ceilings and walls full of bookshelves. They carry popular English titles, mostly best-sellers like John Grisham and Ken Follett, although they usually have a title or two by still popular but slightly lesser-known authors. No matter what you're looking for the well-informed staff, usually bilingual, will be able to help.

LA MAISON ANGLAISE
Place de la Cité, 164-2600 blvd. Laurier, 418/654-9523, www.lamaisonanglaise.com
HOURS: Mon.-Wed. 9:30 A.M.-5:30 P.M., Thurs.-Fri. 9:30 A.M.-9 P.M., Sat. 9:30 A.M.-5 P.M., Sun. 11:30 A.M.-5 P.M.
Map 12

The only bookstore dedicated to English books in Québec City is in Place de la Cité, one of the megamalls on the outskirts of town. Staff here know their English-language stuff and are always ready to help. The selection is, unsurprisingly, unbeatable, from *New York Times* best-sellers to literary fiction, humor, philosophy, travel, and kids books. It might not be as big as your local Barnes & Noble but it does have the most comprehensive collection of English books in the city and the atmosphere is quiet and calm—like it should be.

MAISON DE LA PRESSE INTERNATIONALE
1050 rue St-Jean, 418/694-1511
HOURS: Mon.-Sat. 7 A.M.-11 P.M., Sun. 8 A.M.-11 P.M.
Map 8

If it is published on a daily, weekly, or monthly basis, they likely have it here. From periodicals to newspapers to magazines and specialized reviews in a number of languages—English, Spanish, Russian, German, Arabic, etc.— this is your best bet for finding your favorite daily. *Le Monde, le Figaro,* the *New York Times,* the *Wall Street Journal* and the *International Herald Tribune* can all be found here. If you want something with a bit more meat, they also have books including paperbacks, usually bestsellers, in English. Also set up partially as a gift shop, it sells postcards and trinkets and also offers money exchange.

PREMIÈRE ISSUE
27A rue d'Auteuil, 418/692-3985
HOURS: Mon.-Fri. 10 A.M.-7 P.M., Sat. 10 A.M.-5 P.M., Sun. 11 A.M.-5 P.M.
Map 8

Die-hard comic fans will want to make Première Issue a definite stop on their map. Sitting at a 45-degree angle in Vieux-Québec's Upper Town directly across from Les Fortifications, this comic book paradise is filled with back issues of DC and Marvel comics, as well as cult classics like *The Watchman.* Local fans can be found browsing and reading or having an intense discussion about *Tintin* with staff. The atmosphere is laid-back with a bit of whimsy. Though they also carry comics from Québec and France, known as *bande dessinée,* the focus here is on classic English-language comics.

SILLONS LE DISQUAIRE

1149 ave. Cartier, 800/287-7455, www.sillons.com
HOURS: Mon.-Fri. 10 A.M.-9 P.M., Sat. 10 A.M.-5 P.M., Sun. 11 A.M.-5 P.M.

Map 10

This is one of the best independent music stores in the province, open since 1984; what they lack in floor space they make up for in the huge choice. It's close to the Plains of Abraham. The staff here are highly knowledgeable and can advise you on everything from Ye-Ye pop to the latest Québec rock sensation. The selection is contemporary with 15,000 to 20,000 CDs available in-store. Listening booths are set up around the store.

Children's Stores

Though Québec City is full of children, and the province has experienced a baby boom in the last few years, children's clothing stores remain few and far between in the downtown core—unless you count novelty tees. Two toy stores are brick and mortar versions of the magical world of a child's imagination.

BENJO

550 blvd. Charest E., 418/640-0001, www.benjo.ca
HOURS: Mon.-Wed. 10 A.M.-5:30 P.M., Thurs.-Fri. 10 A.M.-9 P.M., Sat.-Sun. 9:30 A.M.-5 P.M.

Map 11

You could spend all day at this 25,000-square-foot store, and that's exactly the point. It's filled with educational toys, accessories for infants, model trains, planes automobiles, party favors, candy, books, and a whole whack of costumes; if it's meant for children you'll likely find it here. Take the kids to lunch at the Benjo restaurant, or sign them up for a ceramic painting, jewelry, or paper-making workshop. Staff here are always helpful and delightfully off-kilter, as is mascot Benjo, a frog, whom the kids can meet on weekends (Sat.–Sun. 11:15 A.M.–3:15 P.M.).

BOUTIQUE L'ÉCHELLE

1039 rue St-Jean, 418/694-9133, www.boutiqueechelle.com
HOURS: Summer daily 10 A.M.-11 P.M., winter Mon.-Wed. 10:30 A.M.-5 P.M., Thurs.-Fri. 10:30 A.M.-9 P.M., Sat. 10 A.M.-5 P.M., Sun. noon-5 P.M.

Map 8

Established in 1966, this chaotic boutique just

Kids get VIP treatment at Benjo.

inside of the old walls carries old-time toys. Marionettes, matryoshka dolls, model cars, trains, and stuffed animals line the walls, alongside traditional Québécois wood toys like spoons for playing traditional songs and the *gigueux,* a wooden doll that is made to dance the jig on a platform. Board games for all ages and in both English and French are available here, as are party favors and balloons.

SHOPS

UNIVERS TOUTOU

Galeries de la Capitale, 5401 blvd. des Galeries,
418/623-5557, www.plushfactory.com
HOURS: Mon.-Wed. 9:30 A.M.-5:30 P.M., Thurs.-Fri.
9:30 A.M.-9 P.M., Sat. 9 A.M.-5 P.M., Sun. 10 A.M.-5 P.M.
Map 12

A special treat for kids of all ages, this store is located in one of the malls outside of the city. Over 20 different kinds of plush toys are available, from teddy bears to rabbits, moose, and pigs. Once the selection has been made the plush is then stuffed and given a passport with its date and place of birth printed inside. Staff are kid-friendly and excited about helping them pick a companion. Choices hang at kid level all around the brightly decorated store. Clothing like bathrobes and boxers and accessories like sunglasses and jewelry can then be added to give the new plush toy a bit of its own personal style.

Clothing and Shoes

Shoppers looking for well-known chains like Zara, H&M, and others should head to the malls because shopping in Québec City is all about independent, locally owned boutiques. There's an emphasis on local designers as well, and one way to measure a designer's success is if they have exclusive boutiques in both Montréal and Québec. A few hours browsing the shops here and you'll soon get a strong idea of what Québécois style is all about.

ATELIER LA POMME

47 rue Sous-le-fort, 418/692-2875
HOURS: Sept.-June Sat.-Wed. 10 A.M.-5 P.M., Thurs.-Fri.
10 A.M.-9 P.M.; July-Aug. daily 9 A.M.-9 P.M.
Map 9

This store located in the quaint Petit-Champlain district carries lines by Québécois designers, from young, lesser-known labels like Véronique Miljkovitch (whose bias-cut dresses and asymmetrical shapes have won her the adoration of fashion insiders) to the mixed-textile playfulness of Myco Anna. Situated in a historic building the interior is plain, featuring white walls with red trim. Carrying both men's and women's wear it's a popular tourist shop for watches, jewelry, leather bags, and seasonal products like fur coats and hats, all made in Québec.

◖ BIBI ET COMPAGNIE

42 rue Garneau, 418/649-0045
HOURS: Feb.-Oct. Mon.-Sat. 9 A.M.-7 P.M., Sun.
10 A.M.-6 P.M.; Nov.-Jan. Thurs.-Sun. noon-7 P.M.
Map 8

If you ask the owner of this headwear wonderland tucked down a quiet side street how she would describe her store, she will tell you, "I sell hats. That's it. Point final." And she's right. Men's hats, women's hats, they are all available here from panamas to fedoras, caps to cloches, and in an array of colors and sizes stacked up along the shelves or

© SACHA JACKSON

Check out Le Capitaine d'Abord for seafaring gear.

SHOPS

modeled by body-less mannequins. The service is hands off, unless customers show real interest, and the atmosphere quite sober, depending on the mood of the staff, who are mostly mature ladies who look lovely in hats.

BLANK
223 rue St-Joseph E., 418/977-6718,
www.portezblank.com
HOURS: Mon.-Wed. 10 A.M.-6 P.M., Thurs.-Fri.
10 A.M.-9 P.M., Sat. 10 A.M.-5 P.M., Sun. 11 A.M.-5 P.M.
Map 11

This T-shirt and casual wear company is dedicated to making quality clothes that are socially and environmentally responsible. Designed and produced in Québec, their T-shirts, yoga pants, baby clothes, and men's hoodies are always made with American cotton thread and water-based dyes. Even their trimmings are reused and turned into accessories like scarves and hats. The design of the store is pretty straightforward but it matches their design aesthetic and ethos.

BOUTIQUE LUCIA F.
422 rue Caron, 418/648-9785
HOURS: Wed.-Fri. 11 A.M.-6 P.M., Sat. 11 A.M.-5 P.M.
Map 11

Tucked down a quiet side street in Saint-Roch, Boutique Lucia F. is a vintage store carrying everything from old 45s to ladies' pumps. Owned by a young graduate of design, there is an easy feel to how the whole place has been put together; bags line the windowsills, hats are pegged on the exposed brick wall, and old mismatched sitting room chairs are placed throughout the store. Styles for men and women are carried, and the majority of prices are $10–20. And if you like that magazine rack currently holding scarves, well, you can likely buy that too.

LE CAPITAINE D'ABORD
59 and 63 rue du Petit-Champlain, 418/694-0694,
www.capitainedabord.com
HOURS: Sun.-Tues. 9 A.M.-6 P.M., Wed.-Sat. 9 A.M.-9 P.M.
Map 9

If you need a pea coat or a stripped Breton sweater this is a good place to start, whether you're a man or a woman. The goods here all have a nautical flair and put you in mind of the coast of Cape Cod even when it's mid-January outside. The bright blue walls, low ceilings, and high-gloss wood floors give the vague impression you're on a ship, but the thick knitted sweaters and heavy down jackets will put you in mind of the weather outside. They are exclusive carriers of yachting brands like Paul & Shark, Armor-Lux, and Meyer, and if you're sailing the St-Lawrence this is the only store you need.

CODE VERT
586B rue St-Jean, 418/524-4004,
www.codevert.ca
HOURS: Mon.-Tues. 10 A.M.-5:30 P.M., Wed.
10 A.M.-6 P.M., Thurs.-Fri. 10 A.M.-9 P.M., Sat. 10 A.M.-5 P.M.,
Sun. 11 A.M.-5 P.M.
Map 11

The ethos here is simple: sustainable, eco-friendly fashions that are made in Québec and fair-trade certified. The store carries 35 different eco-friendly lines, including several for men. The store itself has a no-frills feel with the clothes taking center stage. There's also an emphasis on products that are made of recycled or natural fibers.

◖ ESTHER P
873 rue St-Jean, 418/704-7774,
www.estherp.com
HOURS: Mon.-Wed. and Sat. 10 A.M.-6 P.M., Thurs.-Fri.
10 A.M.-9 P.M., Sun. 11 A.M.-5 P.M.
Map 11

Located in a former bank, women's boutique Esther P is one of the most stunningly designed stores on St-Jean. Carrying labels that are typically hard-to-find in Québec City—James Perse, French Connection, Ella Moss, Graham & Spencer—owner Esther Pichette's aim is to dress women not only their 20s but also their 40s, 50s, and 60s. Situated on two floors, the boutique has an open-concept feel with high ceilings that show off the original moldings, blonde-wood floors, punches of red, and lots of windows and glass to keep things modern.

FANAMANGA

383 rue du Pont, 418/614-5052, www.fanamanga.com

HOURS: Tues.-Wed. 10:30 A.M.-5:30 P.M., Thurs.
10:30 A.M.-10 P.M., Fri. 10:30 A.M.-11:30 P.M., Sat.
11 A.M.-11:30 P.M.

Map 11

Fans of manga and cosplay congregate at this store turned hangout that brings a touch of Tokyo to Québec. It's filled with Gothic Lolita outfits, cosplay accessories, manga, magazines, Japanese treats like Okonomiyaki chips, curry-flavored sweets, and any of number of trinkets, dolls, and ephemera associated with the culture. The stools at the bar are usually filled with fans in cosplay, sipping their bubble-tea and bobbing their heads to the Visual Kei videos playing on the TVs above. They also have a karaoke box you can rent by the hour that has songs in Japanese, English, Korean, Chinese, and Vietnamese.

FLIRT

525 rue St-Joseph E., 418/529-5221

HOURS: Mon.-Wed. 9:30 A.M.-5:30 P.M., Thurs.-Fri.
9:30 A.M.-9 P.M., Sat.-Sun. 10 A.M.-5 P.M.

Map 11

As the name suggests, this brightly colored boutique is all about clothes that bring out your inner flirt, specializing in lingerie for both men and women. The walls are lined with intimate apparel hanging tantalizingly in rows. The store prides itself not only on the many hard-to-find European brands they import, like Eva Racheline and Parah, but also on the fact that they carry hard-to-find sizes, including the line Empreinte, for the fuller-busted woman. Those looking for swimwear can pick from lines here like Cristina and Canadian company Shan. They also offer made-to-measure but you must make an appointment first.

FOURRURES RICHARD ROBITAILLE

329 rue St-Paul, 418/692-9699,
www.economusees.com/richard_robitaille_en.cfm

HOURS: Mon.-Sat. 9:30 A.M.-4 P.M.

Map 9

Established in 1894, Richard Robitaille is a family business passed down through four different generations. While visitors are invited to browse the luxurious fur coats and hats (worn just as much by men and women in this province), the real draw here is to see how the coats get made. Serge Richard repairs and makes fur coats from scratch and invites you to see the process, from the skins to the final product, at the store's Eco Musée. Richard will tell you about different hunting methods and species, and the evolution of fur in fashion, all while creating a brand-new look.

LA GODASSE

559 rue St-Joseph E., 418/614-9773,
www.lagodasse.ca

HOURS: Mon.-Wed. 10:30 A.M.-6 P.M., Thurs.-Fri.
10:30 A.M.-9 P.M., Sat. 10:30 A.M.-5 P.M., Sun. noon-5 P.M.

Map 11

All sneakers all the time. This store has all the latest styles from old-school high-top Reeboks to classic New Balance. The large, open store is divided into three sections for women, men, and kids. The latest hiphop and indie rock, both in French and English, is usually blasting from the speakers, and the staff are young but knowledgeable and can tell you just about anything you need to know about your kicks, including when the newest version will be out. It is not all fashion streetwear though, they also carry a range of shoes for hiking and climbing, from Merrell, Teva, and Gravis.

◖ JUPON PRESSÉ

790 rue St-Jean, 418/704-7114

HOURS: Mon.-Wed. 10 A.M.-6 P.M., Thurs.-Fri.
10 A.M.-9 P.M., Sat.-Sun. 10 A.M.-6 P.M.

Map 11

This inviting women's boutique on St-Jean is dedicated to emerging designers including from Québec City, Montréal, and beyond. Brightly decorated with purple walls, flashes of yellow, bright floral wallpaper, and an inflatable moose head, the layout here is especially clean with pieces from designers like Eve Gravel, Supayana, and Valérie Dumaine. Nicely hung and spaced, nothing looks to crowded. T-shirts are perfectly piled on Formica tables, while accessories are laid out deliciously on cake plates; jewelry is displayed like art, framed and hung on the wall, though always easily accessible. Along with things for you to wear, they also carry cute, kitschy finds for the home.

LOBO LAVIDA

511 rue St-Jean, 418/521-3397

HOURS: Summer Mon.-Wed. and Sat. 11 A.M.-7 P.M., Thurs.-Fri. 11 A.M.-9 P.M., Sun. noon-6 P.M.; winter Mon.-Wed. noon-5:30 P.M., Thurs.-Fri. 11 A.M.-8 P.M., Sat. 11 A.M.-5:30 P.M.

`Map 11`

Fans of vintage will get a kick out of this high-ceilinged store, filled to the gills with vintage and consignment pieces. From a pair of barely worn knee-high boots to hats from the 1930s and authentic RayBan Aviators this store has it all. Situated in what was once an old house, the entire first floor has been taken over with display cases full of costume jewelry and purses with clothes lining the walls and on carousels in the center of the room. Prices here are reasonable and those usually put off by second-hand goods should know that everything here has been cleaned, ironed, and hung according to color.

LA MAISON DARLINGTON

7 rue de Buade, 418/692-2268

HOURS: Mon.-Wed. 9:30 A.M.-6 P.M., Thurs.-Fri. 9:30 A.M.-7 P.M., Sat. 9:30 A.M.-5 P.M., Sun. 10 A.M.-5 P.M.

`Map 8`

One of the oldest boutiques in Québec, it's named after an English tailor who took over a business that sold military garments and turned it into a wool and cashmere boutique. The antique till and specialized wooden sweater shelves are reminders of times past and though the styles may have changed since he opened in 1872, the ethos remains the same and you'll find a range of accessories, toques, berets, mittens and scarves of only the highest-quality from brands such as Ballantyne, Johnston of Elgin and Tilley Endurables. Dapper gentlemen who still wear caps are fans, as are well-heeled older women who come for their cozy knits.

© PHILIPPE DUBUC

menswear boutique Philippe Dubuc, in the trendy Saint-Roch neighborhood

OCLAN

67½ rue du Petit-Champlain, 418/692-1214, www.oclan.net

HOURS: Sat.-Wed. 10 A.M.-6 P.M., Thurs.-Fri. 10 A.M.-9 P.M.

`Map 9`

This two-floor store on the tiny rue de-Petit-Champlain carries contemporary designer brands, including Martinique for men and Michael Kors for women. Entering the menswear section you'll find a fairly small floor space tastefully packed with the latest from GStar, J Lindeberg, and Energie among others. Down a camouflaged staircase you'll reach the women's floor (which you can also enter or exit from the larger rue Champlain), similar in size but much more stocked, with pieces from Velvet, In Wear, and Nougat among others.

PHILIPPE DUBUC

537 rue St-Joseph E., 418/614-5761, www.dubucstyle.com

HOURS: Tues.-Wed. 10:30 A.M.-5:30 P.M., Thurs.-Fri. 10:30 A.M.-9 P.M., Sat. 10:30 A.M.-5 P.M., Sun. noon-5 P.M.

`Map 11`

This newly opened boutique of Montréal-based

SHOPS

designer Philippe Dubuc couldn't be sleeker. The long, narrow store is like a mirrored corridor with all-white floors, ceilings, and walls giving it an extra modern kick. Distinctly masculine clothes are represented in the store, made all the more cool by its location in the Saint-Roch neighborhood. Though Dubuc is primarily a menswear designer, fashion-forward women shouldn't think twice about trying on a piece or two in this fabulous hall of mirrors.

SCHÜZ

748 rue St-Jean, 418/523-4560,
www.schuz.ca
HOURS: Mid-June-mid-Oct. Mon.-Sat. 10 A.M.-9 P.M., Sun. 11 A.M.-7 P.M.; mid-Oct. 9-mid-June Mon.-Wed. and Sat. 10 A.M.-6 P.M., Thurs.-Fri. 10 A.M.-9 P.M., Sun. 11 A.M.-5:30 P.M.
Map 11

Casual shoes for men and women can be found at this relaxed boutique on St-Jean. Steve Madden, Tsubo, and Chinese Laundry are available for women while men's brands include Asics, Onitsuka Tiger, and Camper for both sexes. Though there is definitely more of a choice for women, men looking for something unfussy, masculine, and modern, or just a new pair of everyday sneakers, are sure to find it here. The decor is minimal with the shoes displayed on the wall and the center of the room taken up with seating and seasonal displays. Winter boots are one of their specialties, so they always have a range of styles for both sexes come autumn.

TOHU BOHU

775 rue St-Joseph E., 418/522-1118, www.tohubohu.ca
HOURS: Mon.-Wed. 10 A.M.-5:30 P.M., Thurs.-Fri. 10 A.M.-9 P.M., Sat.-Sun. 10 A.M.-5 P.M.
Map 11

Though this store specializes in upscale footwear and carries lines like Emilio Pucci, Kate Spade, and Marc by Marc Jacobs, it's not just a shoe store—they also do pedicures. With a name that means "confusion" and "hubbub" you wouldn't necessarily expect the store's dynamic, streamlined design—plush gray banquettes, mixed with high-gloss red-and-black shelving and illuminated cubbies—which puts the emphasis on the shoes and bags. Come to browse or come just for a pedicure or manicure, which you can enjoy

© TOHU BOHU

Get a pedicure and a new pair of pumps at Tohu Bohu.

while you eat; their pedi-sushi deal allows you to chow down on dinner from Yuzu while you get your toes prepped for those new peep-toes.

URBAIN PRÊT-À-PORTER

996 ave. Cartier, 418/521-1571
HOURS: Mon.-Wed. 10 A.M.-6 P.M., Thurs.-Fri.
10 A.M.-9 P.M., Sat. 10 A.M.-5 P.M., Sun. 11 A.M.-5 P.M.
Map 10

This corner boutique in a well-heeled part of town carries fashion-forward brands aimed at women of various ages. The decor changes throughout, from the deep gray walls and designs that cater to more mature women, to adjoining white space that features younger brands like Miss Sixty and Nolita. The store also has its own shoe section, with seasonal footwear from the likes of Diesel and Ilse Jacobsen among others, as well as a wall dedicated to denim.

Department Stores

HOLT RENFREW

Place Ste-Foy, 2452 blvd. Laurier, 418/656-6783,
www.holtrenfrew.com
HOURS: Mon.-Wed. 9:30 A.M.-5:30 P.M., Thurs.-Fri.
9:30 A.M.-9 P.M., Sat. 9:30 A.M.-5 P.M., Sun. 11 A.M.-5 P.M.
Map 12

Originating on rue Buade in Vieux-Québec's Upper Town, this high-end department store is now the only branch of Holt Renfrew in Québec City. Opened at this location in 1965, it retains its elegance, with high ceilings, simple design, and the designer brands customers have come to expect. This location also offers fur services, which include everything from proper storing and cleaning to alterations and remodeling. Made to measure tailoring is available here as well.

LALIBERTÉ

595 rue St-Joseph E., 418/525-4851,
www.lalibertemode.com
HOURS: Mon.-Wed. 9:30 A.M.-5:30 P.M., Thurs.-Fri.
9:30 A.M.-9 P.M., Sat. 9:30 A.M.-5 P.M., Sun. noon-5 P.M.
Map 11

In May 1867, 24-year-old Jean-Baptiste Laliberté founded a modest fur shop that by the beginning of the 20th century was one of the best fur stores in North America. From its humble beginnings the store eventually grew to become an arresting five-floor department store with huge arched windows and a corner clock tower looking over St-Joseph. When many stores upped and moved to the new malls

© SACHA JACKSON

SHOPS

Laliberté is one of the oldest surviving department stores in Québec City.

outside of town, Laliberté was one of the few that stayed. Though the store has since been scaled back (the unused floors are now lofts), Laliberté continues to be a leader in furs. Bring your old furs to be remodeled here or browse their seasonal collections.

LA MAISON SIMONS
20 Côte de la Fabrique, 418/692-3630, www.simons.ca
HOURS: Winter Mon.-Wed. 9:30 A.M.-5:30 P.M.,
Thurs.-Fri. 9:30 A.M.-9 P.M., Sat. 9:30 A.M.-5 P.M., Sun.
noon-5 P.M.; summer Mon.-Sat. 9:30 A.M.-9 P.M., Sun.
noon-5 P.M.
Map 8

One of the city's most important businesses, La
Maison Simons was started in 1840 by 17-year-old
John Simons, who opened a dry goods store near
Porte St-Jean. Thirty years later, in 1870, the store
moved to a new location close to the basilica, and
here it has remained. Though opened in the late
19th century, it has a definite art deco feel, with
a beautiful, concave ceiling made of pearl glass.
Known for its trendy labels like Twik for women
and Le 31 for men, the products here are more
fashion forward than what you'd find at most department stores. Other locations can be found at
Place Ste-Foy (2450 blvd. Laurier) and Galeries de
la Capitale (5401 blvd. des Galeries), both of which
can be reached through the number above.

Gifts and Home

Since Québec is such a tourist draw many stores
could just as easily be classified as arts and crafts
as gift and home, especially those that boast artisanal products. The stores found here, however, have a definite gift feel to them, and they
are stores not usually frequented locals.

When it comes to home decor Québec
City residents are resourceful picking different pieces from here and there for an eclectic
style, and the home stores found in the city
reflect this; nothing is uniform.

Québec City spends at least six months out
of the year under snow, so that may explain
why there are two stores dedicated entirely to
Christmas decorations. Situated kitty-corner
to each other, snowy landscape or not, these
places are packed even in the summer.

BALTHAZAR
461 rue St-Joseph E., 418/524-1991
HOURS: Mon.-Wed. 10 A.M.-5:30 P.M., Thurs.-Fri.
10 A.M.-9 P.M., Sat. 10 A.M.-5 P.M., Sun. 11 A.M.-5 P.M.
Map 11

This two-floor home and design store in Saint-
Roch brings together modern furniture, trendy
kitchen utensils, and various objets d'art to
place around your home. Super sleek in design, the over-100-year-old building has been
meticulously redesigned so that the black slate
staircase to the second floor blends in seamlessly with the ground floor walls lined with
products like vases, espresso cups, and kitschy
alarm clocks. Filled with brands that come
from all over the world that are typically hard
to find in the city, the store also carries collections from Québécois design firms.

BOUTIQUE ARTISANS CANADA
30 Côte de la Fabrique, 418/692-2109,
www.artisanscanada.com
HOURS: Summer daily 9 A.M.-10 P.M., winter daily
10 A.M.-6 P.M.
Map 8

Open since World War II, this large, open boutique in Vieux-Québec's Upper Town has subsequently been run by three generations of the
Théberge family. It stocks jewelry, leather goods,
fur hats, plush toys, sweaters, T-shirts and outerwear. The majority of the lines are made and
designed in Québec. It's recommended by the
New York Times as a store to visit, and staff will
remind you of this designation. The back of the
store is dedicated to toy soldiers, and they have a
huge collection of figurines there, including the
French battling the English at Waterloo and on
the Plains of Abraham.

BOUTIQUE CLAUDE BERRY
6 Côte de la Fabrique, 418/692-2628, www.claudeberry.com
HOURS: Mid-Sept.-mid-May Mon.-Wed.
9:30 A.M.-6 P.M., Thurs.-Fri. 9:30 A.M.-9 P.M., Sat.-Sun.
10 A.M.-7 P.M.; mid-May-mid.-Sept. daily 9 A.M.-9 P.M.
Map 8

Open since 1981, Boutique Claude Berry

specializes in European earthenware. Situated just in front of the basilica, this is the only store in the city dedicated to this particular kind of ceramics. Walking in here can be a bit of a visual overload; patterned platters, teapots, cups and saucers, and tableware are set out before you, each item perfectly displayed so as to give visitors the optimal view of the pattern. At this family-run business service is hands off unless you get too close to the products. This is the only store in North America to carry Faience d'Art de Gien earthenware.

LA BOUTIQUE DE NOËL

47 rue de Buade, 418/692-2457, www.boutiquedenoel.ca
HOURS: Jan.-Apr. daily 10 A.M.-5 P.M., May-June and Oct. daily 9 A.M.-10 P.M., July-Aug. daily 8 A.M.-midnight, Sept. daily 9 A.M.-11 P.M., Nov.-Dec. daily 9 A.M.-9 P.M.
Map 8

No matter the time of year, it's always Christmas at La Boutique de Noël. In a three-story building whose facade is permanently decorated with fairy lights, the interior is painted a deep hunter green with red trim and high-flying angels. Christmas trees line the aisles fully decorated while the walls are hung with an almost inconceivable number of ornaments, from Disney characters to sophisticated icicles and everything in between. They also carry Nativity scenes, stockings, tinsel, and anything else you want to hang on your tree. If you're unsure of the number of days left until the big event, this place has a running countdown.

BOUTIQUE LE SACHEM

17 rue des Jardins, 418/692-3056
HOURS: Summer daily 9 A.M.-9 P.M., winter daily 10 A.M.-6 P.M.
Map 8

A silent statue of a native chief greets you at the entrance of this boutique, setting the tone for what's inside. This entire store is filled with Amerindian-inspired pieces, from moccasins to hunting knives, traditional woven blankets, and fur hats, even some à la Davy Crockett. One of the most serious gifts on display, however, has to be the stuffed wolf retailing for

a cool $4,000. If you can get past the overwhelming kitsch of the place there are some nice traditional crafts to be found.

MACHIN CHOUETTE

225 rue St-Paul, 418/525-9898,
www.machinchouette.com
HOURS: Mon.-Wed. and Sat. 10 A.M.-5 P.M., Thurs.-Fri. and 10 A.M.-6 P.M.
Map 9

This place takes things you love but seemingly have no real use for, like that first pressing of the Grateful Dead's "Anthem to the Sun," and turns them into something useful like a CD rack. The brainchild of Lise Maheu, this large, open boutique in the Vieux-Port has some great pieces, from the aforementioned vinyls-turned-CD racks. They also turn old butter boxes into ottomans and teapots into lights and carry various kinds of furniture, from old country pine tables to contemporary pieces that would look just as good in a loft as in a 19th-century townhouse.

◖ MAGASIN GÉNÉRAL P.L. BLOUIN

1196 rue St-Jean, 418/694-9345,
www.magasingeneralplblouin.com
HOURS: Nov.-Apr. Sun.-Wed. 9 A.M.-6 P.M., Thurs.-Sat. 9 A.M.-9:30 P.M.; May-Oct. daily 9 A.M.-10 P.M.
Map 8

Without a doubt one of the best stores in the city, Magasin Général P.L. Blouin is filled with novelty items and pieces of historic kitsch. Old Québec license plates line the walls, along with models of old cars. They stock everything here, from brand-new checkered hunters' caps to vintage magazines, old Coca-Cola paraphernalia, and magnetic Elvises. Owner Mr. Blouin is a connoisseur of kitsch, and people wanting to get rid of the 40 years worth of junk in the attic come to him first.

POT EN CIEL

27 rue du Petit-Champlain, 418/692-1743
HOURS: July-Aug. daily 9 A.M.-10 P.M., Sept.-June Sun.-Wed. 9 A.M.-6:30 P.M., Thurs.-Sat. 9 A.M.-9:30 P.M.
Map 9

This split-level store in Petit-Champlain carries

SHOPS

© CLAUDEL HUOT

Housewares and quirky ceramics can be found at Pot en Ciel.

ceramics and kitchenware. On the lower floor they carry an array of charming things for the home, including mugs with mustaches, checkered canisters, and artisanal pieces like carved owls and polar bears as well as a few gourmet products like dried pasta imported from Italy and loose-leaf teas from France. On the upper level it's all serious kitchen stuff like baking sheets, cookie cutters, and French brands like Emile Henry, as wall as a range of Bodum presses.

AU ROYAUME DU PÈRE NOËL

12 Côte de la Fabrique, 418/692-3022
HOURS: Daily 9:30 A.M.–5 P.M.
Map 8

Small and densely packed, Au Royaume du Père Noël is filled to the max with ornaments and accessories. Fully decorated Christmas trees line the aisles, making turning around virtually impossible. The store specializes in hard-to-find ornaments, usually from limited-edition collections, so if you've got something

specific in mind this is a good place to look. Though they've got everything you could possibly need to hang on your tree, they also carry some non-Christmas-specific gifts, including toys and trinkets.

ZONE

999 ave. Cartier, 418/522-7373, www.zonemaison.com
HOURS: Mon.–Wed. 9:30 A.M.–6 P.M., Thurs.–Fri. 9:30 A.M.–9 P.M., Sat. 9:30 A.M.–5:30 P.M., Sun. 10 A.M.–5 P.M.
Map 10

This modern living and design store carries an array of products, all chic, sleek, and sophisticated for your home. The all-white store is artfully decorated with stock arranged as you might arrange it in your own home. Recently expanded, the store now takes up not only the corner lot but the one next to it, with mirrors, chandeliers, table lamps, drinking glasses, tableware, shower curtains, jewelry boxes, cool wall clocks, and furniture from kitchen tables to small couches and chairs.

SHOPS

Gourmet Treats

There are so many places that could count for gourmet treats in Québec City, it's overwhelming. Even a trip into the corner *dép* will uncover microbrewery beers and gourmet, fresh, made-to-order sandwiches.

C L'ARTISAN ET SON PAYS
241 rue St-Joseph E., 418/522-6924
HOURS: Mon.-Wed. 11 A.M.-6 P.M., Thurs.-Fri.
10 A.M.-7 P.M., Sat. 10 A.M.-6 P.M., Sun. 11 A.M.-5 P.M.
Map 11

This small, rustic shop in Saint-Roch specializes in artisanal cheese from Québec. It opened in the summer of 2009, and part of the owner's aim is to remind people that there is a country outside of the city. L'Artisan et Son Pays offers cheese from around the province, with the list of cheeses changing seasonally. A display case the length of the store shows off the goods, which include local charcuterie. It's a must for anyone who loves *la fromage;* the variety of type and range of flavors will amaze. They also offer regular tastings, like their specialized *croque monsieur,* and carry other artisanal products like terrines and charcuterie.

CHAMPAGNE LE MAÎTRE CONFISEUR
783 rue St-Joseph E., 418/652-0708
HOURS: Mon.-Fri. 8 A.M.-9 P.M., Sat.-Sun. 10 A.M.-6 P.M.
Map 11

This chocolate and sweets shop has a few unique specialties. With only a few marble-topped tables to sit at, this fairly small store serves up some of the best marzipan treats in the city and also offers a range of fine sugar-free chocolate made in the European tradition in flavors that range from saffron to goat cheese with honey. Port glasses made of chocolate are the ultimate companion to the aged wine, as are their buttery French biscuits. The most unusual treat, though, is the cherry blossom—cherries soaked with champagne and cherry kirsch, covered in dark chocolate, and topped with a chocolate-dipped marshmallow. Totally decadent.

CHOCO-MUSÉE ERICO
634 rue St-Jean, 418/524-2122, www.chocomusee.com
HOURS: Mon.-Wed. and Sat. 10 A.M.-5:30 P.M.,
Thurs.-Fri. 10 A.M.-9 P.M., Sun. 11 A.M.-5:30 P.M.
Map 11

Established in 1987, this artisanal *chocolatier* is one of the most decadent stops in the city. Chocolate lines the walls in this quaint kitchen and boutique, with an array of seasonal treats (like nachos dipped in chocolate) on one side and displays of freshly made chocolates (with flavors like chestnut cream, rum, and allspice) on the other. Line up to get your gourmet hot chocolate, ice cream, or one of their many desserts—the brownies and chocolate cake here are said to be among the best in the province. The adjoining room is the Chocolate Museum, which gives you a history of the treat, lets you taste some wares, and allows you to watch the magic being made in the kitchen.

CONFISERIE C'EST SI BON
1111 rue St-Jean, 418/692-5022
HOURS: Summer daily 9 A.M.-9 P.M.; winter Mon.-Wed.
9 A.M.-5 P.M., Thurs.-Fri. 9 A.M.-9 P.M., Sat.-Sun.
9 A.M.-5:30 P.M.
Map 8

This picturesque shop has the feel of an old-time confiserie, or candy shop. The shelves are lined with containers full of candy, old-fashioned treats, novelty cups and saucers, magnets, and bowls, making it a great place to pick up a gift. Homemade chocolate, fudge, and hot chocolate are made on the premises and there's also an emphasis on local products like spices, teas, candies, and maple goodies. It's been open for over 20 years, and just about everything here is for sale, from the antique display case to the squares of maple sugar candy sitting temptingly at the cash register.

LES DÉLICES DE L'ÉRABLE
1044 rue St-Jean, 418/692-3245, www.mapledelights.com
HOURS: Fall and spring Mon.-Thurs. 7 A.M.-9 P.M., Fri.
7 A.M.-10 P.M., Sat. 9 A.M.-10 P.M., Sun. 10 A.M.-10 P.M.;
winter Mon.-Thurs. 7 A.M.-8 P.M., Fri. 7 A.M.-9 P.M.,
Sat. 9 A.M.-9 P.M., Sun. 10 A.M.-9 P.M.; summer

SHOPS

Mon.-Fri. 7 A.M.-midnight, Sat. 9 A.M.-midnight, Sun.
10 A.M.-midnight
Map 8

Everything here is drizzled with maple, from the blueberry gelato to the fleur du sel. Part store, part café, one side of this large, open store is dedicated to pastries, coffees, desserts, and gelatos, while the other is filled with rows of gourmet maple syrup, maple cookies, maple pork rub, coffees, teas—you get the idea. A small seating area at the back is a pleasant place to try a taste of their hot maple-flavor milk, but the real draws here are the gourmet products.

EPICERIE EUROPÉENNE

560 rue St-Jean, 418/529-4847,
www.epicerie-europeenne.com
HOURS: Mon.-Wed. 9 A.M.-6 P.M., Thurs.-Fri.
9 A.M.-9 P.M., Sat. 9 A.M.-5 P.M.
Map 11

This shop was founded in 1959 by two Italians, nostalgic for their homeland. The massive wooden shelves are stocked with imported products. Italian coffees, olive oils, pestos, and balsamic vinegars take center stage, while at the back you'll find a cheese and meat counter, where you can order a great panini—but hurry up they go fast. Along with the groceries they also sell imported kitchen accessories, coffee makers, crockery, and the famous French Laguiole knives. Stop in and try one of their specialties, an authentic *espresso ristretto*—the shortest coffee around.

LA FUDGERIE

16 rue du Cul-de-Sac, 418/692-3834, www.lafudgerie.com
HOURS: Mon.-Wed. 9:30 A.M.-5:30 P.M., Thurs.-Fri.
9:30 A.M.-9 P.M., Sat.-Sun. 9:30 A.M.-5 P.M.
Map 9

As the name suggests this place is a fudge fanatic's fantasy. Well established outside of the city, this cozy, old-timey store is the company's first in downtown Québec. The low ceilings, old wood floors, and exposed ceiling beams make you feel as though you're stepping into the past, a feeling added to by the workers in pristine white coats who circle the store with a platter offering tastes of their divine homemade

fudge. Nougat, gourmet hot chocolate, and candied pecans are also made here.

MADAME GIGI CONFISERIE

84 rue du Petit-Champlain, 418/694-2269
HOURS: Winter Mon.-Wed. 9 A.M.-5:30 P.M., Thurs.-Fri.
9 A.M.-9 P.M., Sat.-Sun. 9 A.M.-6 P.M.; summer daily
9 A.M.-11 P.M.
Map 9

This sweets shop in Petit-Champlain boasts one of the most dangerous sounding treats—chocolate pizza. With floor-to-ceiling windows and display cases prettily decorated with the day's chocolate special this place will easily break your resolve and lure you in to try their various goodies, including fudge, chocolate-dipped fruit kebabs, and Belgian chocolate. In summer they also have homemade ice cream, and their homemade jam is available year-round.

O PETITES DOUCEURS DU QUARTIER

51 rue du Petit-Champlain, 418/692-4870
HOURS: Apr.-Aug. Mon.-Sat. 9:30 A.M.-9 P.M.,
Sun. 9:30 A.M.-5 P.M.; Sept.-Oct. Mon.-Wed.
9:30 A.M.-5:30 P.M., Thurs.-Fri. 9:30 A.M.-9 P.M., Sat.-Sun.
9:30 A.M.-5 P.M.; Nov.-Mar. Sat.-Wed. 10 A.M.-5 P.M.,
Thurs.-Fri. 10 A.M.-9 P.M.
Map 9

Less exciting than some of the other gourmet stores, this bright, feminine shop—it's all creams and soft pinks—in Petit-Champlain carries old-fashioned sweets and local products. Creamy nougats, flavored oils, spices, fairtrade chocolate, sweets, teas, and spreads (such as Verger du Sureau's organic jams and jellies) are some of the goods available. They also carry non-foodie gifts like beauty products from Blue Lavender and small ceramics for the home.

LA PETITE CABANE À SUCRE DE QUÉBEC

94 rue du Petit-Champlain, 418/692-5875,
www.petitecabaneasucre.com
HOURS: Winter Sat.-Wed. 10 A.M.-5 P.M., Thurs.-Fri.
10 A.M.-9 P.M.; summer daily 9 A.M.-9 P.M.
Map 9

This little shop at the end of the rue du Petit-Champlain is all kitted out in wood paneling, both inside and out. Exclusively selling maple goods it is the downtown extension of a sugar shack outside of the city. "The little sugar shack" sells maple syrup, maple candy, ice cream, maple lollipops, nougat, butter and spreads, and a ton of other maple products.

Markets

It's not surprising that in a city so defined by its food, its best markets revolve around farmers and fresh produce. And though winters can be harsh the farmers markets keep going all year long. Unlike in other major North American cities, the flea market trend has yet to make the jump from country to city, so those looking for a bit of one-on-one time with vendors will have to be satisfied with the artisan summer market.

ARTISANS DE LA CATHÉDRALE
31 rue des Jardins, www.artisansdelacathedrale.com
HOURS: Mid-June-early Sept. daily 10:30 A.M.-10 P.M.
Map 8

This outdoor market runs throughout the summer on the grounds of the Holy Trinity Anglican Cathedral, in the shadow of Château Frontenac. The cozy, makeshift stalls erected here put you in direct contact with the artist or crafter who made the goods, making the shopping and browsing experience all the more memorable. The products here are completely unique and different than what you'll find in other artisan and gift shops. Vendors here sell everything from jewelry to sweaters to glass and woodwork.

LES HALLES DU PETIT QUARTIER
1191 ave. Cartier, 418/688-1635,
www.hallesdupetitquartier.com
HOURS: Mon.-Wed. and Sat. 7 A.M.-7 P.M., Thurs.-Fri. 7 A.M.-9 P.M., Sun. 7:30 A.M.-7 P.M.
Map 10

Less like a market than a mini-gourmet shopping center, Les Halles du petit Quartier is a brick and mortar building filled with great shops. It's popular with locals. An organic fruit and produce stand, a fishmonger, butcher, cheese shop, fresh pasta shop, a pastry, and a

J.A. MOISAN, THE OLDEST GROCERY STORE IN NORTH AMERICA

If you're tired of museums but still want a trip back in time head to J.A. Moisan (699 rue St-Jean, 418/522-0685, www.jamoisan.com, daily 9 A.M.-10 P.M.), the oldest grocery store in North America, established in 1871. The Victorian-era look of the store has been meticulously recreated. Every little detail has been accounted for, from the crisp white shirts of the serving staff to the large wooden framed display cases, to the tin roof, wooden shelves lined with goods, and the French music from the 1930s and '40s piping in over the speakers.

When it first opened, Moisan's aim was to offer the area's well-to-do clients gourmet foods, and that tradition continues today with items like charcuterie, imported foie gras, biscuits, chocolates, and even soaps, filling the walls of the two-room grocery store. What has changed, however, is the addition of a small café near the entrance, where locals come to grab a quick lunch or indulge in a fresh pastry and coffee. Built in the early 1800s it is one of the oldest buildings in Saint-Jean and was one of the few structures that wasn't destroyed by the great fire of 1881, which decimated the area. Though it retains a Victorian aesthetic it is still a functioning grocery store, with locals popping in to get their morning bread and fresh produce. It may look and feel like the oldest grocery store in North America but it is also very modern.

SHOPS

bakery shop all offer top-quality products. It also boasts not one, but two coffee shops where you can take a break with a cappuccino; get one to go as you carry on with your browsing.

LE MARCHÉ DU VIEUX PORT
160 quai St-André, 418/692-2517,
www.marchevieuxport.com
HOURS: Jan.-mid-Mar. Thurs.-Sun. 9:30 A.M.-5 P.M.; mid-Mar.-Sept. Mon.-Fri. 9 A.M.-6 P.M., Sat.-Sun. 9 A.M.-5 P.M.; Oct.-late Nov. daily 9 A.M.-5 P.M.; late Nov.-Dec. Sat.-Wed. 9 A.M.-5 P.M., Thurs.-Fri. 9 A.M.-9 P.M.
Map 9

Located right on the marina, this is the city's largest farmers market. A tradition that's been going on since 1841, the Marché du Vieux Port continues the practice of country farmers bringing their goods to city dwellers. Everything available here is locally grown and produced, and many of the products are organic. You'll find everything from fruits and vegetables to cheese, meats, and seafood to wine and beer. If seeing all that food makes you hungry there are a number of places to grab a sandwich or a light lunch. There's also a section dedicated to gifts and artisanal goods, including handmade jewelry, knitted scarves and socks, artwork, and leather goods.

Outdoor Gear

Québec is surrounded by some pretty rugged terrain and immense forests, so sports stores here deal mostly in equipment for the outdoors. Hiking, camping, fishing, and hunting are all popular pastimes in Québec, and the range of goods out there reflects that. Since an active outdoor life is part of the culture, sportswear is also weekend wear.

LATULIPPE
637 rue St-Vallier W., 418/529-0024,
www.latulippe.com
HOURS: Mon.-Tues. 8:30 A.M.-5:30 P.M., Wed.-Fri. 8:30 A.M.-9 P.M., Sat. 9 A.M.-5 P.M., Sun. 11 A.M.-5 P.M.
Map 12

With over 70 years of history, Latulippe is one of the highly regarded stores in the region when it comes to gear for hunting and fishing. What used to be just a tiny, family run store was recently renovated and is now a large, modern two-floor store with everything you need for an outdoor adventure—boots, bags, tents, waterproof outerwear, and accessories. They even have gear for snowmobiling and ammunition,

guns, and knives for hunting. And the staff are always full of advice and helpful tips, so just ask.

MOUNTAIN EQUIPMENT CO-OP
405 rue St-Joseph E., 418/522-8884, www.mec.ca
HOURS: Mon.-Wed. 10 A.M.-7 P.M., Thurs.-Fri. 10 A.M.-9 P.M., Sat. 9 A.M.-5 P.M., Sun. 10 A.M.-5 P.M.
Map 11

Better known as MEC, this co-op was started by couple of Canadian climbers in the '70s and now has almost three million people as registered members. You must sign up to become a member in order to make a purchase, but the five bucks good-for-life membership pays for itself by the time you get to the checkout. The open-concept store design give you lots of room to roam the goods, which include everything from cycling gear to hiking boots, tents to sleeping bags. Even rental equipment is available; there really isn't a better store dedicated to the outdoors (unless you want to hunt). Eco-friendly and pro-sustainability, clerks here are friendly, patient, and know their stuff.

Shopping Districts and Centers

GALERIES DE LA CAPITALE

5401 blvd. des Galeries, 418/627-5800,
www.galeriesdelacapitale.com

HOURS: Mon.-Wed. 9:30 A.M.-5:30 P.M., Thurs.-Fri.
9:30 A.M.-9 P.M., Sat. 9:30 A.M.-5 P.M., Sun. 10 A.M.-5 P.M.

Map 12

About a 20-minute drive from downtown Québec City, you'll come across Galeries de La Capitale, the biggest and most fascinating mall in all of the province. Opened in 1981, it was the brainchild of businessman Marcel Adams and was filled with Canadian department store heavyweights Eaton's, The Bay, Simons, and Woolco. Today, it has 280 stores, 35 restaurants, the biggest IMAX theater in Canada, and an indoor amusement park. Called Le Mega-Parc, it has 20 rides including a Ferris wheel, roller coasters, a skating rink, and smaller rides and games that will make kids go wild.

LAURIER QUÉBEC

2700 blvd. Laurier, 418/651-5000, www.laurierquebec.com

HOURS: Mon.-Wed. 10 A.M.-5:30 P.M., Thurs.-Fri.
10 A.M.-9 P.M., Sat. 9 A.M.-5 P.M., Sun. 10 A.M.-5 P.M.

Map 12

The biggest of the three malls, Laurier Québec, formerly called Place Laurier, is three levels high and boasts 350 stores. Opened in 1961 it is the largest mall in eastern Canada and one of the city's top tourist attractions. Well-known stores like Old Navy, H&M, The Bay, Nike, Aldo, and American Apparel are all situated here, as are specialized boutiques including Laine, which carries wool and other knitting materials, and Vision Rock, where you can get a tattoo while you pick up a KISS wall-clock and T-shirt from your favorite hard-rock band. Laurier Québec offers free shuttle service between Vieux-Québec and the mall as well as to the nearby Aquarium du Québec.

PLACE DE LA CITÉ

2600 blvd. Laurier, Sainte-Foy, 418/657-6920,
www.placedelacite.com

HOURS: Mon.-Wed. 9:30 A.M.-5:30 P.M., Thurs.-Fri.
9:30 A.M.-9 P.M., Sat. 9 A.M.-5 P.M., Sun. noon-5 P.M.

Map 12

Part of the large shopping complex on boulevard Laurier in Sainte-Foy, Place de la Cité stands out thanks to the 17-story office building that's attached to the mall's concourse. It's the home of 150 stores and restaurants, and you'll

© SACHA JACKSON

Quartier du Petit-Champlain

find independent boutiques including Simone Paris, which caters to sizes 6–18; Québécois label Myco Anna; and Corset Corsaire, carrying exclusive prêt-à-porter labels from Europe. La Maison Anglaise, the only bookstore dedicated to English books in the region, is located here, as are sports stores including O'Neill, Sport Select, and Québec brand Chlorophylle.

PLACE STE-FOY

2452 blvd. Laurier, 418/653-4184,
www.placestefoy.ca
HOURS: Mon.-Wed. 9:30 A.M.-5:30 P.M., Thurs.-Fri.
9:30 A.M.-9 P.M., Sat. 9 A.M.-5 P.M., Sun. 10 A.M.-5 P.M.
`Map 12`

One of the three shopping malls that make up the impressively large complex in the region close to Université Laval just outside of the city, Place Ste-Foy is also one of the oldest. Built in 1958 it is considered the best shopping center in Québec City for upscale boutiques and labels. Canada's preeminent luxury department store, Holt Renfrew, has been located here since 1965, and among the mall's 135 stores you'll find other top-of-the line brands like Birks, Swarovski, Lacoste, and BCBG Maxazria.

QUARTIER DU PETIT-CHAMPLAIN

Btwn. Place Royale and rue Petit-Champlain
`Map 9`

Full of artisanal shops, many of which double as the artist's workshop, Quartier du Petit-Champlain is the perfect place to support the local arts and pick up some unique gifts. It's run as a co-op, and there is a real neighborhood spirit and camaraderie here due in part to the fact that many of these stores have been here since its inception in the late-'80s. From silk scarves to leather goods, gourmet fudge and maple syrup to expensive handmade jewelry, it is all here.

RUE SAINT-JEAN

Btwn. rue Couillard and ave. Salaberry
`Map 11`

Whether inside or outside the walls, rue Saint-Jean is Québec City's main shopping street. In Vieux-Québec's Upper Town you'll find a string of well-known stores, including Québec chains, women's stores Jacob, San Francisco, Le Château, and internationally recognized brands like Crocs, American Apparel, and Foot Locker. It's also along this strip that you'll find magazine and bookstores selling English-language material. If you want to shop like the locals, check out the independent clothing boutiques and record stores in the Faubourg Saint-Jean-Baptiste, a continuation of the same street; you'll find interesting shops just beyond the fortifications.

RUE SAINT-JOSEPH

Btwn. rue St-Dominique and rue Caron
`Map 11`

The main shopping strip in the Saint-Roch neighborhood, this street has an illustrious past that has recently been revived. Once the Fifth Avenue of Québec City, it is now the city's coolest shopping district. You won't find many well-known chains here, except for the recently opened Urban Outfitters, the only store of its kind in the city. Independent lingerie boutiques can be found here as well as some great shoe stores, home stores, and other fashion-forward boutiques. The best children's store in the province, Benjo, is also located here, with a VIP entrance especially for the little ones.

RUE SAINT-PAUL

Btwn. rue St-Pierre and rue Rioux
`Map 9`

This narrow cobblestone street in the Vieux-Port is Québec City's antiques row. With the exception of a few cafés, bars, and restaurants, almost all of the stores here are filled with antiques. There is a real emphasis on classic antiques— that is to say, don't expect to walk in and find a midcentury modern gem (though it could happen). The pieces aren't often dated later than the 1940s, and even objects from that period can be hard to find. Instead the focus in many stores is on traditional Québécois antiques.

Spas

Most hotels in the city offer their own in-house spas; for those that don't there are a variety of spas that offer everything from quick therapeutic massages to day-long adventures in pampering.

INSPIRATIONS SPA

44 Côte du Palais, 800/463-6283,
www.manoir-victoria.com
HOURS: Daily 9 A.M.-9 P.M.
`Map 8`

Located inside the Hôtel Manoir Victoria, this full-service spa offers manicures ($52) and pedicures ($73) and signature treatments like Cocoon facials ($100), Jin Shin Do massage ($100), and maple body scrubs ($85). A 30-minute Swedish massage will set you back $65. It's frequented by hotel guests, but nonguests may also make a reservation here. Many of the treatments use products made with local, organic maple sugar, and a day-package to the spa also gives visitors access to the hotel's gym, sauna, and indoor pool, all of which have an early-20th-century, Turkish bath feel with mosaic tiles and arched columns around the pool.

IZBA SPA

36 blvd. René-Lévesque E., 418/522-4922,
www.izbaspa.qc.ca
HOURS: Mon.-Tues. 9 A.M.-7 P.M., Wed.-Fri. 9 A.M.-10 P.M., Sat.-Sun. 9 A.M.-5 P.M.
`Map 10`

This spa mixes traditional Russian Banya treatments (steam baths) with therapeutic massage. Banya treatments here involve a humid environment in which the person starts to perspire; soaked oak leaves are then warmed and used to stroke, brush, and tap the body before a honey rub is used to draw out toxins and soften the skin. Trained and certified staff will give you a 60-minute Izba massage that starts at $90, or a deluxe Izba with facial and seawater wrap goes for $175. The stone walls, low lighting, and vaulted ceilings give it an especially luxurious feel.

LA QUINTESSENS

656 rue St-Joseph E., 418/525-7270,
www.quintessens.ca
HOURS: Tues.-Fri. 10 A.M.-7 P.M., Sat. 10 A.M.-5 P.M., Mon. noon-5 P.M.
`Map 11`

This urban spa in Saint-Roch is great for a massage or a quick bit of pampering. The decor is relatively simple, with the rooms filled with massage tables and not much else. Though they offer treatments the focus is on massage, and five different kinds are available: Swedish, Californian, Amma (also known a Japanese massage), Thai-yoga massage, and massage with hot stones. Hour-long massages cost $65 and body-wraps including chocolate, algae, and sea salt are $75. They also offer half-hour lunchtime massages 11:30 A.M.–1:30 P.M. for $25 and 15-minute chair massages for $15.

SHOPS

HOTELS

Staying in Québec City can be expensive. Contrary to Montréal there is a lack of choice when it comes to affordable accommodations, and it can sometimes feel as though hotels are taking advantage of a lucrative situation. The majority of the time, however, this isn't the case and service, at both moderately priced and more expensive hotels, couldn't be better. Like restaurants, hotels don't lack numbers, and the highest concentration of hotels can be found in Vieux-Québec's Upper Town, where down just about every little street you'll find a couple of smaller inns. It's here as well that the Château Frontenac is located, standing sentinel on the cliff and casting a shadow on some lesser-known but equally good hotels. Because of its proximity to sights such as the Château and the Citadelle as well as a number of restaurants, Upper Town is the most sought-after area, but by extension it's also the most touristy.

If you're a fan of sleek, minimal boutique hotels opt for something in Vieux-Québec's Lower Town or Vieux-Port, once the center of the city's financial district. Old banks, office buildings, and warehouses have been converted into some of the most exciting new hotels. Though it's just as much a tourist attraction as Upper Town the area has a more relaxed vibe. And although you step out of your hotel into one of the oldest places in North America, it maintains a neighborhood feel that gives it a unique touch of authenticity.

One thing that stands out in Québec City's hotel landscape is the lack of major chains. The Delta and Hilton can be found in Upper Town on René-Lévesque just outside of the city

HIGHLIGHTS

LOOK FOR **((** TO FIND RECOMMENDED HOTELS.

((**Best Hostel:** One of the few hostels in the city center, **Auberge Internationale de Québec** is friendly, affordable, and couldn't be closer to the action (page 335).

((**Most Romantic Hotel:** Situated in two of the most beautiful buildings in the Vieux-Québec's Upper Town, **Auberge Place d'Armes's** 17th-century meets 21st-century decor makes it perfect for a getaway for two (page 335).

((**Most Luxurious Hotel:** The **Fairmont le Château Frontenac** is one of the most recognized hotels in the world. A stay here is nothing short of fantasy (page 335).

((**Most Distinctive Building:** A former marine warehouse, **Auberge Saint-Antoine's** high ceilings, exposed beams, and stone floors match perfectly with the minimal decor at these opulent digs (page 338).

((**Best Budget Hotel:** With only eight rooms but great views of the Vieux-Port, **Hôtel Belley** is affordable, ideally located, and welcoming (page 338).

((**Best Boutique Hotel:** The nine-floor **Hôtel le Germain-Dominion** is both chic and homey with an inviting atmosphere and great views of the St-Lawrence River and Lower Town (page 339).

((**Best Guest House:** Situated above the oldest grocery store in North America, **Auberge J.A. Moisan** is authentically Victorian without being stuffy (page 341).

((**Most Ecological Hotel:** Because it's committed to sustainability and fair trade, you can stay at **Auberge L'Autre Jardin** in good conscience (page 341).

((**Hippest Hotel:** The modern, sleek interior, stunning views, and location in the heart of Saint-Roch make **Hôtel Pur** the ultimate hip hotel (page 342).

((**Worth the Trip:** It might be outside of the city, but **Hôtel Sépia's** modern decor brings an urban edge to the suburban location (page 342).

© AUBERGE PLACE D'ARMES

Auberge Place d'Armes mixes contemporary with romantic.

PRICE KEY

$ Less than CAN$150 per night

$$ CAN$150-250 per night

$$$ More than CAN$250 per night

walls, but they are just about the only ones. Most chain hotels are located outside of the city center, close to a collection of shopping malls in Sainte-Foy on the aptly named Avenue des Hôtels. Most of these hotels offer competitive rates and daily shuttles to downtown in the summer. In winter this service doesn't necessarily apply, and though city buses are available they take much longer but aren't complicated. If you're traveling without a car it might be more practical to spring for something closer to downtown.

If you want to be close to the action but also want to experience a bit of the city's hipper, younger side check out hotels in the Saint-Roch and St-Jean Baptiste areas. Since they are not traditional tourist areas the rates here can be more competitive, and though you might not find yourself looking out onto the oldest square in North America, the history here is just as rich.

CHOOSING A HOTEL

When choosing a hotel in Québec City one of the first things to consider is mobility and how you travel. Charles Dickens famously called it the "Gibraltar of America," and that is still a fitting description. Though it's possible to spend your entire trip in either Upper Town (on the hill) or Lower Town (below the hill), it is unlikely, and even then you'll encounter inclines and hills no matter where you go. Québec isn't a large city by any stretch but if you're limited in mobility or by the length of your stay getting a hotel near the sights you most want to see makes sense. Upper and Lower Town are easily accessible by the funicular and Ecobuses, but if you like boutique hotels, for example, and only

have a night, plan it all in the Vieux-Port and spend the next morning doing the rounds in Upper Town. Driving to the sights, especially in summer and unless they are far way, will be much more hassle than it's worth.

The competitive prices of Sainte-Foy hotels might be tempting, but if you're arriving by train or bus at the main station, you'll end up crossing the entire city just to get there. Instead pick something more modest in the Vieux-Port or Saint-Roch neighborhoods that can be easily accessible when you arrive. Or make sure you get a ticket to the Sainte-Foy station instead.

As in Montréal, the majority of hotels have standard North American style rooms and amenities like air-conditioning and coffee in the room. But since many of the hotels are also in historic buildings, the rooms in Québec City are usually more European in size. If you've book a room in a quaint-looking Victorian house avoid disappointment and expect it to be smaller than usual. Since they are old homes it means some of them might not have elevators; it's worth inquiring about before you book, though most will have a bellhop for those purposes.

Breakfasts also come in European sizes or not at all. Many hotels don't include breakfast as part of the room, or if they do, they are continental with fresh pastries, breads, cheeses, and fruit. In some cases it's wisest to skip the hotel breakfast altogether and head to one of the city's many bistros for a filling first meal instead.

Packages offer different options for guests when they book and can include breakfast as part of the deal as well as things like tours, museum entrances, and bottles of champagne. Parking, even at bigger hotels, can be hard to come by, but most paid parking lots are safe and relatively affordable. If you're staying near the Plains you might be lucky enough to find free street parking amid the upscale homes. Even if they don't provide parking themselves, the hotels are usually more than willing to help you find a spot or at the very least give you various options.

Vieux-Québec's Upper Town   Map 8

🆇 AUBERGE INTERNATIONALE DE QUÉBEC 💲

19 rue Ste-Ursule, 418/694-0755,
www.aubergeinternationaledequebec.com

This hostel is a member of Hostelling International, and you won't find a more affordable place to stay in Vieux-Québec. Situated in what used to be a convent, this comfortable youth hostel has been providing sparse but spacious and spotless rooms for over 40 years. Along with dormitories—male, female, or mixed—they also offer private rooms available for 1–5 people, perfect if you're traveling with a group. Communal areas include a self-serve kitchen and a café bistro, a great place to relax and chat with fellow travelers. In summertime, you can enjoy breakfast in their charming little interior courtyard. The bilingual staff are warm and welcoming and offer number of different activities, from tours outside the city to organized pub crawls.

🆇 AUBERGE PLACE D'ARMES 💲💲

24 rue Ste-Anne, 418/694-9485,
www.aubergeplacedarmes.com

Spread throughout two buildings, one an old hotel and the other an old wax museum, Auberge Place d'Armes is one of the most beautiful hotels in the city, situated in the shadow of Fairmont le Château Frontenac. Although walls date back to the 17th century, there is nothing old about this hotel, just charming. The rooms are all decorated in a mix of modern meets antiques, the most lavish of which is, appropriately, The Marie Antoinette Suite. With its eggshell-blue walls, ornate gold moldings, and rich fabrics the room is kept light by the addition of pieces like a Plexiglas take on an baroque lamp and Philippe Stark–inspired Louis XIV chairs. Complimentary breakfast is served at Le Pain Béni, their on-site restaurant and one of the best in the city. Those traveling with pets can bring them here (for a small extra fee) but must request a specific room at time of booking.

LE CAPITOLE DE QUÉBEC 💲💲

972 rue St-Jean, 800/363-4040, www.lecapitole.com

Blink and you might miss the sliver of a sign marking this discreet hotel. Tucked into an old building near the St-Jean Gate that includes restaurant Il Teatro and Le Capitole theater—special packages for all three are available—this small four-floor hotel with 45 rooms is in a great location. The interior is distinctly contemporary with bright colors and modern takes on classic furniture shapes. Rooms, however, can be quite small, and though they all boast ensuite bathrooms, some tubs are located next to the bed. Romantic, but not necessarily practical.

CHEZ HUBERT 💲

66 rue Ste-Ursule, 418/692-0958,
www.chezhubert.com

This small three-room bed-and-breakfast is good option for those looking for the Upper Town experience without the cost. This grand old Victorian townhouse has chandeliers in every room, stained-glass windows and a beautiful curved staircase at the entrance. Tucked away on a quiet side street, owner Hubert is warm and amiable and offers guests a hearty buffet breakfast. Each of the rooms is decorated in soft hues, and one looks out one the Château while another has a balcony. All three rooms, however, share bathroom facilities.

🆇 FAIRMONT LE CHÂTEAU FRONTENAC 💲💲💲

1 rue des Carrières, 418/692-3861,
www.fairmont.com/frontenac

This is luxury at its finest. This historic hotel and landmark is one of the most sought-after temporary addresses in the city. Just entering the sumptuously decorated lobby you feel as though you've stepped into a Victorian salon, with its rich wood paneled walls and ceilings, wall sconces in the shape of candelabras, and antique chandelier hung above the grand staircase. The decor of the 618 rooms and suites follows suit with high ceilings, classic fabrics, and a room at the storied Fairmont le Château Frontenac

© FAIRMONT HOTELS

Victorian-style wood furnishings. Like most fine hotels it has all the amenities you'd expect: pool, spa, gym, and ballroom.

HÔTEL CAP DIAMANT $$

39 ave. Ste-Geneviève, 418/694-0313, www.hotelcapdiamant.com

Located in a historic building on a small and quiet street not far from the walls of the Citadelle, Hôtel Cap Diamant is a charming bed-and—breakfast. Each of the 12 rooms is furnished with rich antiques, giving it a European charm. It's run by Mme. Guillot and her daughter, and the staff here are warm, welcoming, and helpful. Guests are treated to a complimentary continental breakfast, which they're welcome to eat in the hidden backyard full of flowers in the summer. Though there's an elevator for luggage, guests will have to climb the stairs to their rooms, some of which are on the fourth floor.

HÔTEL CLARENDON $$

57 rue Ste-Anne, 418/692-2480, www.hotelclarendon.com

Built in 1858 and designed by Charles Baillairgé, this historic hotel is the oldest in Vieux-Québec. First a home, then offices, it became hotel in 1870 and has remained one since. Originally a four-story building, it underwent two additions in the 20th century, one to include two floors and the mansard roof and the other a six-floor art deco extension, making it particularly striking. It's across the street from City Hall and next door to Édifice Price. Upon entering the Clarendon you're immediately hit with the art deco feel—wood beams feature on the ceiling and large mirrors are placed throughout. The rooms themselves are rather modest with simple decor, though some feature gorgeous circular windows.

HÔTEL LE CHAMPLAIN $$

115 rue Ste-Anne, 418/694-0106, www.champlainhotel.com

Eclectically decorated with bright modern furniture and subtly bold wallpaper, Hôtel le Champlain is a welcoming boutique hotel. Surrounded by historic buildings the hotel is distinctly modern, though the hardwood floors and exposed brick walls add a bit of European charm to the 49 rooms. Ideally located on a quiet street, it is close to everything but avoids the noise and bustle of streets like St-Jean and St-Louis. Guests are treated to a complimentary breakfast as well as cappuccinos and espressos that are available throughout the day in the lobby.

HÔTEL LE CLOS SAINT-LOUIS ⑤⑤⑤

69 rue St-Louis, 418/694-1311, www.clossaintlouis.com

If you're an old-fashioned romantic Hôtel Le Clos St-Louis will make you swoon. Calling itself the "most romantic Victorian hotel in the city," it's fastidiously decorated with period antiques, including wardrobes, four-poster beds, and fainting couches. Its location close to the St-Louis gate makes sights both inside and outside the walls walkable. Catering to couples, this isn't a place for kids. They offer a variety of packages, including Engagement, Newlywed, and the Babymoon package, for expectant mothers.

HÔTEL MANOIR VICTORIA ⑤⑤

44 Côte du Palais, 418/692-1030, www.manoir-victoria.com

Though the building that now houses the Hôtel Manoir Victoria was built in 1904, the hotel's history dates back to the 1830s when Thomas Payne opened the city's most exclusive hotel across the street from its current location. Situated just off of St-Jean in Upper Town on a street that connects to Lower Town and the Saint-Roch area, Hôtel Manoir Victoria is sumptuously decorated with rich, embellished fabrics and classically comfortable furnishings. The rooms are modern but still traditional, and there's something home-like about both the superior rooms and more luxurious suites. The hotel enjoyed its heyday in the 1920s, and no place is this more evident than with the pool. With its Grecian columns and small black-and-white tiles it's like something out of The Great Gatsby.

HÔTEL STE-ANNE ⑤⑤

32 rue Ste-Anne, 418/694-1455, www.hotelste-anne.com

Chic and sophisticated is the best way to describe the feel of this 20-room hotel just across the square from Château Frontenac. Located on a busy cobblestone street, this historic building has been perfectly transformed into a sleek, boutique-style hotel. The stone walls, exposed ceiling beams, and Normanstyle windows are the prefect complement to the simple, clean lines of the furnishings and the ultramodern bathrooms—black slate tiles, glass shower doors. The rooms can be quite small, however, so keep size in mind if you're choosing between a superior room and a junior suite.

MANOIR SAINTE-GENEVIÈVE ⑤

13 ave. Ste-Geneviève, 418/694-1666, www.quebecweb.com/msg

The decor of this small nine-room hotel, in a historic house built in 1800, makes you feel like you've stepped into a time machine. Richly decorated with lived-in antiques, its mish-mash of patterned wallpaper, carpets, and upholstery sometimes gives the impression it hasn't been redecorated since the reign of Queen Victoria. The rooms run the gamut from drab but modern to a classic Victorian bedroom with chandeliers and luxurious velvet curtains. Staff are accommodating and gracious and it's located near the Terrasse Dufferin.

LA MARQUISE BASSANO ⑤

12 rue des Grisons, 418/692-0316, www.marquisedebassano.com

Located on a quiet street lined with historic homes in Vieux-Québec's Upper-Town, this charming bed-and-breakfast is steps away from Château Frontenac and Les Fortifications. It's run by a young, outgoing couple, and the five rooms of this gray-stone townhouse are uniquely decorated and priced, with touches like a full bookshelf, writing desk, and vintage typewriter in the "library room," a claw-footed bathtub, or antique pieces. Only two rooms have their own bathrooms, however; the other three must share. Breakfast is served in the cold European style with meats, hardboiled eggs, and various breads and pastries.

Vieux-Québec's Lower Town   Map 9

(AUBERGE SAINT-ANTOINE ⑤⑤⑤

8 rue St-Antoine, 418/692-2211, www.saint-antoine.com

Once a port-side warehouse, Auberge St-Antoine retained its high ceilings, exposed beams, and stone floors, all the things that make it one of the most inviting hotels in the city today. It was built on the archaeological site of Ilôt Hunt, an area full wharfs and warehouses at the peak of the Québec's port history, and artifacts that were found on this site have been incorporated in the hotel design. The rooms are sleek and modern with a touch of luxury—plush headboards with unique motifs and heated bathroom floors. Many also have balconies, terraces, or fireplaces, so request one when you book. Unique services include an archaeological tour, on-site cinema, and Wednesday drinks with the family of owners. One of the city's top restaurants, Panache, is also located here, in what was once the warehouse lobby.

AUBERGE SAINT-PIERRE ⑤⑤

79 rue St-Pierre, 418/694-7981, www.auberge.qc.ca

The first of the boutique hotels to open in Québec City, Auberge Saint-Pierre has a charm all its own. Instead of minimalist decor and sleek furniture, Saint-Pierre makes you feel as though you're staying with a close friend or family (but without the bickering). Brick walls are the backdrop for cozy wood furniture accented with bright, patterned duvets and comforters. Each room comes with its own coffee maker, iron, and umbrella—now that's thinking ahead. The feeling of home continues in the main area with a complimentary gourmet breakfast in the relaxed dining room and a library with a roaring fireplace, perfect for relaxing with a nightcap.

(HÔTEL BELLEY ⑤

249 rue St-Paul, 418/692-1694, www.quebecweb.com/hotelbelley

Looking out over the marina and farmers market, Hôtel Belley is just a close walk to sights in both Upper and Lower Town and is a stone's throw from the cool Saint-Roch area. This tiny eight-room hotel has a definite laid-back atmosphere perhaps helped in part by the historic tavern on the ground floor, which provides an

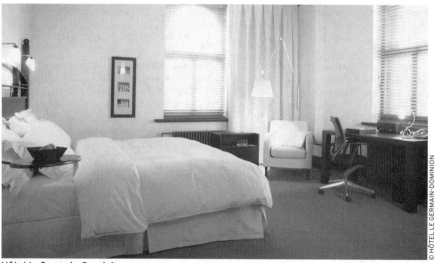

Hôtel le Germain-Dominion

© HÔTEL LE GERMAIN-DOMINION

CHILL OUT AT QUÉBEC CITY'S ICE HOTEL

Come winter the **Hôtel de Glace** (www.icehotel-canada.com) is one of the most magical places to lay your head. Started in 2001, it was the first ice hotel in North America and has since become one of the most extraordinary hotel experiences in the city. Open from January to March, and situated just outside of the city, the hotel takes roughly a month and a half and 60 workers to construct, with the ice built around a metal base that forms its foundations. Entirely redesigned and rebuilt every year, each incarnation is built around a different theme.

Though the design, theme, and architecture change the materials don't. The interior is always decked out with ice furniture, sculptures, and touches of fur and animal hide to soften and warm up the space. Everything here, except for the heated bathrooms in a separate building, is made of ice, from the glasses at the bar, to the bar itself, the lobby chairs, the serving plates, and of course, the beds. Made of blocks of ice the base of the bed is then layered with solid wood as well as a mattress, which is topped with an insulating bed sheet and pillow that are brought to your room just as you're getting ready for bed, along with an arctic sleeping bag. Though temperatures outside might dip to -25°C (13°F) the four-foot thick walls keep the room between -3°C and -5°C (27°F and 23°F) no matter the temperature outside.

A typical night at the Ice Hotel starts at three in the afternoon with a check in at the Four Points by Sheraton, the base for the ice hotel, and where guests eat a hot breakfast the following morning. A free shuttle takes guests out to the hotel, where they can spend the afternoon and evening drinking in the ice bar, trying out the gigantic ice slide, or warming up in the outdoor hot tubs before heading to their rooms later in the night. Some rooms and suites even come with an optional fireplace or both a fireplace and private spa, perfect for a romantic getaway. The hotel even has its very own ice chapel for midwinter marriages. A night at the hotel will typically cost $400 per person, which includes a hotel room at the Four Points Sheraton as well as breakfast at Le Dijon, among other perks. Early-bird specials are available starting in the fall with prices hovering around $225 per person.

If you're not convinced sleeping in -3 degree weather is for you but feel oddly compelled to try out the **Nordic slide** (and who could blame you), tours are available daily between 10:30 A.M. and 4:30 P.M.

---

excellent place to socialize and relax all year long. The rooms here are small and simply furnished but the views, especially at night, are lovely. Come summer, *terrasses* are open in both the front and back of the building, attracting locals and tourists alike.

🔲 HÔTEL LE GERMAIN-DOMINION ⑤⑤⑤

126 rue St-Pierre, 418/692-2222, www.germaindominion.com

With its grandiose neoclassical facade and modern, understated interior you'd never guess that this chic boutique hotel started off as a fish warehouse. Located in the former financial district this nine-floor hotel, the first of Le Germain's to open in North America, offers great views over both the St-Lawrence and Lower Town. The large, open lobby with big windows, comfy couches, and a laid-back atmosphere is immediately inviting. You'll want to spend all morning in the adjoining dining room, sinking back into your plush seat with a paper while you finish off breakfast. The rooms themselves are equally inviting, with big windows, simple, uncomplicated design, and a Nespresso machine making it the ultimate getaway.

HÔTEL LE PRIORI ⑤⑤

15 rue du Sault-au-Matelot, 418/692-3992, www.hotellepriori.com

At the base of Cap Diamant in the Vieux-Port on one of the oldest streets in North America, Hôtel le Priori occupies the space that once the home of architect Jean Baillairgé. In summer its white-washed facade is punctuated with color from hanging flowers and vines that crown the entrance and its surrounding windows. Inside a modern interior contrasts with the stone walls that date as far back as 1734. The hotel features 21 bedrooms and five suites. The emphasis is on minimalist chic but with a touch of art deco at this boutique hotel. Furniture in asymmetrical shapes and unusual colors like deep purple or bright red can be found in most rooms. Each suite, however, is uniquely decorated. Make sure to take advantage of the secluded outdoor *terrasse* or make reservations at the in-house restaurant Toast!

HÔTEL PORT-ROYAL $$

144 rue St-Pierre, 418/692-2777, www.leportroyal.com

This old storehouse with gray stone exterior in the center of the Vieux-Port has since been converted exclusively into suites. Offering three different types of suites (deluxe, superior, and executive), Hôtel Port-Royal provides a home away from home with each suite equipped with living room and kitchenette, a great option of you want to save costs by eating in. The decor throughout is simple and modern with blonde-wood floors, sandy-colored walls, and large floor-to-ceiling windows.

HÔTEL 71 $$$

71 rue St-Pierre, 418/692-1171, www.hotel71.ca

Located on a cobblestone street in what was once the city's financial district, Hôtel 71 is in a building that was once the National Bank's head office. The neoclassical facade of this boutique hotel is juxtaposed against the sleek, modern interior. Rooms are uncluttered, with earth-toned furniture with clean lines giving them an especially Zen feeling. The bathrooms too are relaxing, with gray slate tiles and geometric lines. Large windows in almost every room allow not only for natural light but also great views of the city and surrounding area. It's the choice of design lovers with a larger budget. Breakfast is served in a long, narrow, light-filled room with warm tones and comfy peach chairs in which to sink with your coffee.

Parliament Hill and the Plains   Map 10

HÔTEL CHÂTEAU LAURIER $$

1220 Place Georges-V W., 418/-522-8108, www.oldquebec.com/en/laurier

Set back from the Plains of Abraham and a two-minute walk to Vieux-Québec's Upper Town, Hôtel Château Laurier is ideally located. The newly renovated lobby is open and inviting with a blazing fire in the winter to greet you. Rooms here run the gamut from European-style rooms that are smaller than usual North American rooms and simply decorated to big, bright newly renovated rooms with updated modern furniture and more of a Zen quality. No matter your room type, all guests are welcome to try the indoor saltwater pool.

HÔTEL LOEWS LE CONCORDE $$$

1225 Cours du Général-de-Montcalm, 418/647-2222, www.loewshotels.com

In among the dignified Victorian mansions of the Grande-Allée, Hôtel Loews le Concorde, stands out as an ode to 1970s brutalist architecture. The 45-degree slanted roof at the entrance and the circular revolving restaurant that crowns the hotel are an interesting contrast to the surroundings. It overlooks the Plains of Abraham and is about a five-minute walk to Vieux-Québec; its location is one of the best things about this hotel. Boasting 26 floors, the interior is above what you'd expect in a large hotel, with bright, modern rooms decorated with flashes of color. Not all of the rooms have been renovated, however, so the room you're given might not resemble the pictures on the website. And beware of unseen charges; this place can sometimes have a panache for little add-ons.

Saint-Jean-Baptiste and Saint-Roch   Map 11

(AUBERGE J.A. MOISAN $$

699 rue St-Jean, 418/529-9764,
www.jamoisan.com/auberge

This four-bedroom guesthouse invites you to be a part of history by sleeping above the oldest grocery store in North America. Charmingly decorated with impeccable moldings, antique furniture, homemade quilts, and Laura Ashley prints, it gives just a taste of what it was like to be a successful businessman in the 19th century. The beautifully restored Victorian house also boasts a living room, library, solarium, and *terrasse,* all of which guests have access to. Just to take things that little bit further 4 o'clock tea is served.

(AUBERGE L'AUTRE JARDIN $$

365 blvd. Charest E., 418/523-1790,
www.autrejardin.com

If traveling gives you eco-anxiety, then staying at Auberge L'Autre Jardin will give you a clear conscience. This 28-room hotel is dedicated to sustainable and responsible tourism, with organic breakfasts made with fair-trade products and furnishings that come from sustainable sources. Owned by Carrefour Tiers-Monde, a Québec-base charity that raises awareness on issues in developing countries, the hotel is their money-making side of the business. The rooms are tastefully decorated and feel more like a friend's place, with classic but not swank bedding. They're decorated with art from Africa, Asia, and India. The hotel also has a fair-trade store selling coffee, jewelry, and different international art crafts and accessories.

AUBERGE LE VINCENT $$$

295 St-Vallier E., 418/523-5000,
www.aubergelevincent.com

The keyword here is "concierge." Every effort is put into making your stay here nothing less than fantastic and tailor made. From the made-to-order breakfasts to in-house movie rentals (there are over 100 to choose from at the front desk), the staff here evince old-school charm, taking

© SACHA JACKSON

Located between Upper Town and Lower Town, Auberge le Vincent has 10 well-appointed rooms.

care of dinner reservations, walking tours—you name it and they're on it. Of course they can handle it all because this is a small, 10-room hotel located in the trendy Saint-Roch area. It is impeccably designed. Each room is uniquely decorated, but all feature exposed brick walls, 400-thread-count sheets, and the most modern bathrooms, often separated by a crystal-clear glass window—with optional blind.

CHÂTEAU DES TOURELLES 💲💲

212 rue St-Jean, 418/346-9136,
www.chateaudestourelles.qc.ca

Just across the street from Château du Faubourg is this light and airy bed-and-breakfast, marked by a turret that stands out on this strip of St-Jean, which is lined with neighborhood bistros and small boutiques. Climb a flight of stairs up into this warm and welcoming place. Wood floors and exposed brick give the rooms a cozy and a little bit country feel, without being kitschy. A filling breakfast is served in the sunny dining room, and a roaring fire in the sitting room is great for guests in the winter, while the rooftop terrace offers views of (nearly) all of the sights in the city.

LE CHÂTEAU DU FAUBOURG 💲

429 rue St-Jean, 418/524-2902,
www.lechateaudufaubourg.com

Set back from the road on busy rue St-Jean is a huge Second Empire–style chateau. Built by the rich Imperial Tobacco family in the 1800s, it retains its original grandeur and is one of the city's most impressive bed-and-breakfasts. A gilded staircase and chandelier greet you as you enter and set the tone for the rooms, which give off the air of an old manor house with rich antique furnishings, sumptuous fabrics, and, in the case of one room, an entire library as headboard. Each room has its own individual bathroom. Breakfast is served in a grand library, and though the owners are lovely and charming, their 12 pet birds get on the nerves of some.

🏨 HÔTEL PUR 💲💲

395 rue de la Couronne, 418/647-2611,
www.hotelpur.com

This chic, boutique-style hotel in the heart of Saint-Roch, one of the city's up-and-coming neighborhoods, couldn't be cooler. Standing 18 floors tall it's the highest building in the area, so just about every room has a view from the floor-to-ceiling windows, looking out on to the city, the Laurentian mountains, or the newly refurbished Saint-Roch church. The sleek design and minimal color palette—gray, black, and white with bursts of orange—give it an uncluttered but still relaxed vibe. The slate-gray bathrooms give it an added touch of Zen, as do the Japanese-style baths and glass-door showers. Visitors can dine in the adjoining restaurant Table, which is equally as chic with long communal tables, comfy couches, and a menu that goes all day long.

Greater Québec City   Map 12

CHÂTEAU BONNE ENTENTE 💲💲

3400 chemin Ste-Foy, 418/653-5221,
www.chateaubonneentente.com

This large, sprawling hotel outside of the city offers an alternative to those who want the feel of a country getaway with the proximity to the downtown. Just about every room in this cottage-style hotel with mansard roofs and soft-yellow clapboard is distinctly decorated, from the hardwood floors and country fabrics of the "Cocooning" room to the carpeted, sleek but comfortable decor of the "Business" room. With an on-site spa, large outdoor pool and hot tub, and golf course, relaxation is never far away.

🏨 HÔTEL SÉPIA 💲💲

3135 chemin St-Louis, 418/653-4941,
www.hotelsepia.ca

Located outside of the city center close to other hotels, the city's largest shopping malls, and the aquarium, Hôtel Sépia is a bit of urbania in suburbia. With its sleek modern design—rain shower heads, Barcelona chairs, and refinished wood floors—this boutique-style hotel will make you feel like you're in the middle of downtown even when you're not. It's approximately a 15-minute drive to downtown, and the hotel offers free shuttle services during the summer months; those traveling without a car, however, might find it impractical come winter. This hotel might not give you a great view of the Vieux-Port but it will give you a great view of the famous Québec Bridge.

EXCURSIONS FROM QUÉBEC CITY

Montréal and Québec City might give you a clear picture of the province's urban population, but if you really want to get to know the province and see the culture and nature that have shaped it, you have to go north.

Referred to as the *régions* (literally the "regions"—see, learning French can be easy), it's in the forests and the jagged cliffs of the St-Lawrence that you get a real sense of the province and its rugged beauty. Barely a half-hour-drive from Québec you'll find yourself in the picturesque Côte-de-Beaupré, lined with quaint ancestral homes—most continue to be residential homes. Not every historical event took place in and around the city; in fact this area was where General Wolfe and his men camped before they laid siege to the city.

Once mostly farmland the area is now a large tourist destination thanks to the pilgrimages to the Basilique Sainte-Anne-de-Beaupré and Chute Montmorency. Across the water on the Île d'Orléans, however, things have stayed much the same as they have for hundreds of years. Île d'Orléans is full of vineyards and farms, and agri-tourism is a big part of the island; visitors should take full advantage by picking their own fruits and vegetables to take home.

Navigating the Côte-Nord (North Coast) couldn't be easier; two highways take you to the same destination, and it all depends on whether you want the scenic route, Route 362 or the faster route, Route 138. Truth be told even the faster route could be described as scenic; the high cliffs, rolling hills, and patches of tundra landscape as you head further north

HIGHLIGHTS

LOOK FOR **(** TO FIND RECOMMENDED SIGHTS, ACTIVITIES, DINING, AND LODGING.

(**Best Historic Road:** One of the oldest roads in North America, **Route de la Nouvelle France** is lined with ancestral homes dating back hundreds of years (page 347).

(**Best Waterfall Feature:** Taller than Niagara Falls and rushing down a rocky cliff, **Chute Montmorency** is an impressive sight, especially when you're on the suspension bridge over the falls with 360-degree breathtaking views (page 348).

(**Oldest Pilgrimage Site:** Built in honor of Sainte-Anne, the patron saint of shipwrecked sailors, the **Basilique Sainte-Anne-de-Beaupré** is one of the oldest pilgrimage sites in the world, and the interior is lined with crutches as a testament to its healing powers (page 348).

(**Best Place to Pick Your Own Fruits and Vegetables:** Île d'Orléans is an island in the middle of the St-Lawrence River. It has some of the oldest homes in the region and some of the best agriculture. Head to the island to pick your own fresh fruit and vegetables (page 349).

(**Best Place to Bring the Kids:** The **Village Vacances Valcartier** is a water park in summer and a wonderland in winter (page 353).

(**Most Artistic Town:** The birthplace of Cirque du Soleil, **Baie-Saint-Paul,** is full of galleries and folk art boutiques worth a visit (page 354).

(**Best Bike Excursion:** Only 11 kilometers long and three kilometers wide, the **Isle-aux-Coudres,** near Tadoussac, with old churches, windmills, and other rarities, should be discovered by bike (page 354).

(**Best Whale-Watching:** At the confluence of the Saguenay and St-Lawrence Rivers, the shores surrounding the historic town of

© YVES MARCOUX

Chute Montmorency on the Côte-de-Beaupré

Tadoussac have one of the most diverse ecosystems in the world. This is the annual meeting place for 10 species of whales, from humpbacks to belugas (page 355).

(**Best Hiking:** The gorges and fjords of **Parc National des Hautes-Gorges-de-la-Rivière-Malbaie,** along with its unique mix of tundra and taiga, make it one of the most breathtaking sites to hike in the region (page 357).

(**Best Skiing:** Overlooking the St-Lawrence River and cutting through the boreal forest, the views from the hills at **Le Massif** are just as stunning as the slopes themselves (page 357).

EXCURSIONS

EXCURSIONS FROM QUÉBEC CITY

Chicoutimi   170   372   Fjord du Saguenay

Lac
Kénogami   Laterrière   La Baie   Saint-Bruno   Lac
Otis   170   **Parc national
du Saguenay**

Saint-Félix-d'Otis   170

Lac à
la Carpe   Saguenay

Lac
Brébeuf

Lac
Ha! Ha!

Le Trou-de-la-Vieille

Lac aux
Écorces   381   ◖ PARC NATIONAL DES
HAUTES-GORGES-DE-LA-
RIVIÈRE-MALBAIE

175

Lac
Métascouac   Lac-
Pikauba   Lac des
Martres

Lac
Saint-Henri   Lac-
Fronsac   **Parc national des
Grands-Jardins**   138

Lac
Beauséjour   Lac
Jacques-
Cartier   To Saint-Siméon and
◖ TADOUSSAC

L-Étape   Lac-
Malbaie   Saint-Joseph-
de-la-Rive   362

◖ BAIE-SAINT-PAUL

Lac
Batiscan   **Parc

national

de la

Jacques-

Cartier**   Mare-du-
Sault   Lac-
des-
Neiges   Baie-Saint-Paul

◖ ISLE-
AUX-COUDRES

◖ LE MASSIF   ST. LAWRENCE RIVER

La Barrière-du-Maurice   Grande-Pointe

0   10 mi

0   10 km   175

Parc du Mont
Sainte-Anne   138   Île-aux-
Oies

Cape-Tourmente
National
Wildlife Area   Île-aux-
Grues   Lamartine

◖ VILLAGE VACANCES
VALCARTIER   ◖ BASILIQUE SAINTE-
ANNE-DE-BEAUPRÉ   Beaupré

Saint-Gabriel-de-Valcartier   ◖ ROUTE DE LA
NOUVELLE FRANCE   ◖ ÎLE D'ORLÉANS   Montmagny

◖ CHUTE
MONTMORENCY

Lac
Saint-Joseph   Beauport

Val-Bélair   Charlesbourg   Sainte-Pétronille   20

L'Acienne-Lorette   **QUÉBEC CITY**

40   Saint-Romuald

Neuville   Charny   Saint-Jean Chrisostome

To Montreal   Saint-Nicolas   Sainte-Claire

20   216   73

© AVALON TRAVEL

are hard to ignore. Baie-Saint-Paul seems to emerge like a mirage, its church steeple sparkling on the shores of a low valley flanked by stone cliffs and the St-Lawrence. More picturesque than most of the other towns, it's worth a wander.

North again, La Malbaie sneaks up on you from the corners of the twisting turning road, and though the sites aren't much, the landscape is lovely. Once you're this far north you might as well continue to the jewel of Charlevoix and cross the majestic Saguenay by ferry to Tadoussac. The massive cliffs that plunge into the river make for breathtaking scenery, and if you're lucky enough to catch a view of the diverse whale life that thrives in these waters, you'll understand the atypical beauty that defines the region and the province.

PLANNING YOUR TIME

Each of these excursions can be done by day or even an afternoon by car. If you have the time, it's always fun to stay a little bit longer, even overnight, in order to really get to know a place. Though Québec is a big province and you could literally drive for hours without hitting on any sights, all the excursions in this section are easily reached, the longest taking at most 2.5 hours from the city.

Most of the sights are accessible by national highways, though in some places these highways slim down to two lanes. If you're driving in winter the journey could take a little longer, especially if there are bad driving conditions. Snow tires are required by law December–March, so if you don't have them on your car avoid trips into the rocky and hilly Charlevoix, or rent a car with the right tires.

High season is May–October; those traveling north to Charlevoix later in the year should make sure to plan well ahead, or opt for a package deal at places like La Massif. Getting a hotel, dinner, and recreation in one deal, will allow you to see the beauty of the area without worrying about whether there'll be restaurants open or not.

Côte-de-Beaupré and Île d'Orléans

Minutes outside of Québec on Route 138, you'll reach the Côte-de-Beaupré. Located on the banks of the St-Lawrence River, this historical area boasts ancient ancestral homes and open farmland running along the Route de la Nouvelle France, one of the oldest roads in North America. As you pass along the 50 kilometers of roadways, you'll pass through a number of small towns, all of which are between the high cliffs of the Laurentians and the shores of the river.

From the Côte-de-Beaupré you can see the Île d'Orléans, an island in the stream of the St-Lawrence. Linking the two historical areas is the Île d'Orléans Bridge, which can be used by car, bike, or foot. The island itself has one main road, Chemin Royal, that circles the entire island. It's dotted with towns, but much of the island is devoted to local agriculture and can be visited year-round.

SIGHTS
C Route de la Nouvelle France

Leave Québec City heading northeast and you'll soon be on the Route de la Nouvelle France (www.routenouvelle-france.com), one of the oldest roads in North America. In 1626 Samuel de Champlain established a livestock farm on Cap Tourmente farther along the river, but it was Bishop Monsignor de Laval who originally traced the road, which brought provisions from the Côte-de-Beaupré to the city.

All along the 50-kilometer road are heritage homes, some dating as far back as the 1600s. Each is designed in its own particular style, indicative of early New France architecture. Though many of the homes are private residences the public can visit **Maison Vézina** (171 rue des Grenadiers, 418/822-3183, www.maisonvezina. ca, May–late-Aug. Tues.–Sat. 10 A.M.–4 P.M., Sept.–Apr. Tues.–Sat. noon–4 P.M.). Built in

© JEAN SYLVIAN

view of Chute Montmorency from Île d'Orléans

1720, it's now an interpretation enter and exhibition space. If you're looking to get in touch with your roots, **Centre de Généalogie** (277 rue du Couvent, 418/824-3079, www3.telebecinternet.com/archives.chateau-richer, summer daily 9 A.M.–4 P.M.) can help you with genealogical research, a popular Québécois pastime.

If you want a little history of the area the **Centre d'Interprétation de la Côte-de-Beaupré** (7976 ave. Royale, 418/824-3677, www.histoire-cotede-beaupre.org, May–Oct. daily 9:30 A.M.–4 P.M., Oct.–May Mon.–Fri. 9:30 A.M.–4:30 P.M., $6) has lots of documentation and exhibits and is housed in an old seminary.

As you travel the along the road, you'll notice cavern-like structures built directly into the hillsides; these are root cellars, some of which date back more than 300 years. Also along the route is the **Moulin du Petit Pré** (7007 ave. Royale, 418/824-7007, www.moulin-petitpre.com, mid-Apr.–mid-Oct. daily 9 A.M.–5 P.M.). Founded in 1695 it's the oldest operating flour mill in North America. Take a guided tour, then have lunch at the on-site café or get some bread for the road.

◖ Chute Montmorency

Carry on along the Route de la Nouvelle France and you'll soon reach Chute Montmorency (4300 blvd. Ste-Anne, 800/665-6527, www.sepaq.com/ct/pcm, $10) an 83-meter-high waterfall (even taller than Niagara Falls, as everyone will point out) that dominates the landscape between the cliffs of the Laurentians and the St-Lawrence. It's a stunning natural wonder in the middle of lush greenery, and visitors can discover the falls by foot. There's access at either side of the falls and a suspension bridge that allows you to cross along the top; it offers great views of Île d'Orleans and even looks onto Québec City. Open year-round, the falls can also be reached by cable car.

◖ Basilique Sainte-Anne-de-Beaupré

This is the oldest pilgrimage site in North America, and people have been coming to Basilique Sainte-Anne-de-Beaupré (10018 ave. Royale, 418/827-3781, www.shrinesainteanne.org, May daily 6 A.M.–7 P.M., June–late-Sept. 6 A.M.–9 P.M., Oct.–Apr. Mon.–Sat. 6 A.M.–6 P.M., Sun. 6 A.M.–5 P.M.)

Basilique Sainte-Anne-de-Beaupré has been a pilgrimage site since the late 1600s.

© YVES TESSIER, TESSIMA

Île d'Orléans

Located five kilometers from downtown Québec City, Île d'Orléans is an island in the middle of the St-Lawrence and one of the oldest parts of New France to be colonized. It measures 34 kilometers long and 8 kilometers wide. Explorer Jacques Cartier first called it Île de Bacchus, because of the amount of wild grapes found growing on the island. Today, it's home to a number of small villages, but agriculture is still a large part of life on the island.

The first parish was founded here in 1661, and a visit to **Maison Drouin** (4700 chemin Royal, 418/829-0330, mid-June–Aug. daily 10 A.M.–6 P.M., Aug.–late Sept. Sat.–Sun. 1–5 P.M., $4) will give you an idea of what the early houses looked like. Built in 1730 it has been preserved in its original state.

Manoir Mauvide-Genest (1451 chemin Royal, 418/829-2630, June–Aug. daily 10 A.M.–5 P.M., Sept.–Oct. Tues.–Sun. 10 A.M.–5 P.M.) offers a view of the seignorial home of the 18th century, with furniture, objects, and reenactments of daily life on view.

Agri-tourism is a big draw to the island; you can visit **Cassis Monna & Filles** (721 chemin Royal, 418/828-2525, www.cassismonna.com, May.–Nov. daily 10 A.M.–6 P.M.) and learn about how they make their black currant liqueur, or go for a tasting at **Vignoble de Sainte-Pétronille** (1A chemin du Bout-de-l'Ile, 418/828-4554, www.vignobleorleans.com, May.–Dec. daily 10 A.M.–5 P.M.) and try their reds and whites as you look at the Chute Montmorency. Visitors are also welcome to pick their own fruits and vegetables at local farms, including **Ferme la Rosacée** (165 chemin Royal, 418/828-9662, June–mid-Oct. daily 8:30 A.M.–6:30 P.M.), where you can pick everything from raspberries to seasonal vegetables and buy homemade products like jam, pickles, and ketchup.

RESTAURANTS

If you left Québec City early in the morning, stop in at **Patisserie Praline et Chocolat** (7874 ave. Royale, 418/978-0528, mid-June–early Sept. daily 8 A.M.–6 P.M., early Sept–mid-June Thurs.–Sun. 8 A.M.–6 P.M., $10) for some

since the 1660s. The first chapel was constructed on the site in 1658, as a place of worship for the area's new settlers and to house a statue of Sainte-Anne, Québec's patron saint. She's also the patron saint of shipwrecked sailors, and it was a group of Breton sailors caught in a storm that vowed to erect a chapel in Sainte-Anne's honor if they got safely back to land. While the chapel was being constructed, a man with rheumatism is said to have been cured after laying just three bricks, and a pilgrimage was born.

The first basilica was built in 1876 to accommodate the legions of pilgrims who visited the shrine. The structure that exists today, built in the shape of a Latin cross and featuring 214 stained-glass windows, was constructed in 1926 after the first church was destroyed by fire in 1922. One image that strikes you as you enter the church is the multitudes of the crutches, club shoes, and other pieces of ephemera that hang on the pillars, from those who have been cured. A small museum in the church's parking lot exhibits some of the church's treasures as well as donations made by pilgrims.

TRADITION MEETS CONTEMPORARY: WENDAKE RESERVE

Drive northwest out of Québec City and you'll soon come across Wendake, a First Nations reserve that is home to over 3,000 residents. The home of the Huron-Wendat tribe since 1697, this unique reserve offers both a historical and modern perspective on the tribe and its people. It's an active town, and many of the 19th-century buildings resemble those found back in the city – white-washed houses and clapboard churches – but look a little closer and you'll see something entirely different.

Shaped like an old Algonquin smoke house, the **Huron-Wendat Museum** (15 Place de la Rencontre, 418/847-2260, www.museehuronwendat.com, mid-June–Oct. daily 9 A.M.–4 P.M., Nov.–mid-June Wed.–Sun. 9 A.M.–4 P.M., $9 adult, $4 child) conserves and promotes the tribe's heritage. Territories, Memories, Knowledge, the permanent exhibit, takes visitors from the creation myth to the forming of the Huron-Wendat people and events that shaped the tribe right up till today. The museum also offers tours of the numerous heritage sites throughout the town, including Notre-Dame-de-Lorette Church, the Kabir Kouba waterfall, and Tsawenhohi House.

Those who want to experience the past firsthand can head over to **Onhoüa Chetek8e** (575 Chef Stanislas-Koska St., 418/842-4308, www.huron-wendat.qc.ca) a traditional Huron site, where a tour guide will take you through typical buildings and rituals of the Huron First Nations people. Visitors will get to meet the Clan Mother, enter a traditional long house, learn about meat preservation at the smokehouse and the drying tent, and also how to make canoes. Native games, traditional cooking, and dances are also part of the visit.

One of the latest additions to Wendake is the **Hôtel-Musée Premières Nations** (5 Place de la Rencontre, 866/551-9222, www.hotelpremieresnations.ca, $180-400), a beautiful hotel connected to the museum. Its 55 rooms seamlessly blend minimal contemporary design with natural accents, including tree trunks and stone. While you're there have dinner at **La Traite Restaurant,** which takes inspiration from traditional Huron cooking to create dishes like grilled bison and pan-seared seal.

To orient yourself when you get there, head to the **Wendake Tourism Center** (100 blvd. Bastien, Wendake, 418/847-1835, www.tourismewendake.ca, mid-June-mid. Oct. Mon.-Fri. 8:30 A.M.-4:30 P.M., Sat.-Sun. 9 A.M.-5 P.M.; mid-Oct.-mid-June Mon.-Fri. 8:30 A.M.-4:30 P.M.) for useful maps and other information.

mouthwatering pastries. They offer 10 different kinds of *viennoiseries* made fresh daily, as well as artisanal bread, jams, and other treats.

Whether you're looking for breakfast or dinner, **L'Aventure** (355 rue Dupont, 418/827-5748, www.laventure.ca, daily 11 A.M.–11 P.M., $30) in Beaupré has you covered with everything from grilled trout and filet mignon to eggs Benedict, all in a relaxed atmosphere. If you're in the mood for something less refined, **Casse Croute Chez Chantale** (17 rue de l'Église, 418/827-7005, daily 8:30 A.M.–7:30 P.M., $10) has over 100 different kinds of *poutine* on the menu, including the house specialty, *poutine* with goose.

On Île d'Orléans tuck into some traditional cuisine or take part in the *cabane à sucre* experience at **Le Relais des Pins** (3029 chemin Royal, 418/829-3455, www.lerelaisdespins.com, June–Sept. daily 11 A.M.–9 P.M., winter reservation only, $15). Open year-round, this delightful log cabin has lots of natural light and a modern take on decor.

If you've got a sweet tooth, **Chocolaterie de Île d'Orléans** (150 chemin du Bout de Île, 418/828-2250, www.chocolaterieorleans.com, $10) will satisfy with rich chocolate desserts, homemade ice cream, and delicious coffees.

Treat yourself to fine dining overlooking the St-Lawrence at **La Goéliche** (22 chemin de Quai, 418/828-2248, www.goeliche.ca, daily 8 A.M.–8:30 P.M., $40), where breakfast includes dishes like French toast with custard, and dinner has choices like rack of lamb and boneless ribeye with shallots.

RECREATION
Bird-Watching and Hiking
CAP-TOURMENTE
The site of a livestock farm established by Samuel de Champlain in the early 1600s, Cap-Tourmente (570 chemin du Cap-Tourmente, 418/827-4591, www.captourmente.com, mid-Apr.–Nov. daily 8:30 A.M.–5 P.M., Jan.–Mar. daily 9 A.M.–5 P.M., $6) became a farm headed by Monsignor de Laval in 1664. It was an active farm well into the 20th century, and some of the early buildings still remain. Today the area is mostly a nature reserve; it's a great place to bird-watch and learn about the greater snow goose and American bulrush marshes. Interpretive guides and 20 kilometers of hiking trails are available.

Golf
LE GRAND VALLON
One of the best courses in eastern Canada, Le Grand Vallon (100 rue Beau-Mont, Beaupré, 418/827-4561, www.legrandvallon.com, May–Nov. daily dawn–10 P.M., $42–90 for 18 holes), designed by Howard Watson, was once nicknamed the "minister's club" because of the number of high-level politicians that frequented the links. Along the 6,583-yard course there are four lakes and 42 white-sand bunkers, and the changing scenery moves from rolling tree-lined fairways to a large open plan at mid-course. Equipment rentals, driving range, and lessons are also available here and an electric cart and use of the practice range are included in the green fee.

Skiing, Snowboarding, and Snowshoeing
MONT-SAINTE-ANNE
The most popular ski station in the Québec City region, Mont-Saint-Anne (2000 blvd. Beau Pré, Beaupré, 888/827-4579 www.mont-sainte-anne.com, Mid-Nov.–mid-Apr. Mon.–Fri. 9 A.M.–9 P.M., Sat.–Sun. 8:30 A.M.–9 P.M., $64 adult, $54 senior, $51 youth, $34 child 7–12), offers both day and night skiing, with the highest elevation of night skiing in the country. Officially opened in 1966, the history here goes back to 1947, when the Canadian Championships where held on these slopes. About an hour's drive north of the city, 66 trails cover both the north and south face of the mountain. It also has popular cross-country and snowshoeing trails.

HOTELS
Cozy but modern, the 31 rooms at **Auberge la Camarine** (10947 blvd. Ste-Anne, 800/567-3939, www.camarine.com, $100–250) in the Côte-de-Beaupré are often fitted with a warming gas fire, perfect after a long day outdoors.

On Île d'Orléans grab a room with a view at **Auberge La Goéliche** (22 chemin de Quai, 418/828-2248, www.lagoeliche.ca, $104–144). Named after a small schooner, the white clapboard house has charm in spades; the views of the river and well-appointed rooms with country touches like handmade quilts make it an ideal choice.

Total country charm is the best way to describe ◖ **Auberge Le Canard Huppé** (2198 chemin Royal, 800/838-2292, www.canard-huppe.com, $150–250). The oversized wood furniture, pine paneling, and wood floors are welcoming, and the beautiful garden and seasonal regional cuisine on offer in the restaurant are icing on the cake.

INFORMATION AND SERVICES
Before you go to the area, read up on the Côte-de-Beaupré area at **www.cotedebeaupre.com,** which offers useful information on restaurants, hotels, grocery stores, and events. Once you're on the ground the **Côte-de-Beaupré Tourist Office** (3 rue de la Seigneurie, Château-Richer, 866/932-9082, Mon.–Sat. 9 A.M.–5 P.M., Sun. 10 A.M.–4 P.M.) can provide you with hands-on information.

The year-round **Île d'Orléans Tourist Office** (490 Côte du Pont, St-Pierre, 418/828-9411 or 866/941-9411, www.iledorleans.com, July–Aug. daily 8:30 A.M.–7:30 P.M., Sept.–June. daily 10 A.M.–5 P.M.) has a wealth of information and tips on hand.

GETTING THERE AND AROUND
By Bus

Old Québec Tours also known as **Tours Dupont** (800/267-8687, www.tourdupont. com, June–Oct. daily 9 A.M. & 1 P.M., Nov.–May daily 1 P.M., $50) offers different tours that essentially drop you off at the highlights along the Côte-de-Beaupré and pick you up later. They leave from three points throughout Québec City for your convenience, so check before you book.

Sainte-Anne-de-Beaupré can be reached by **Intercar** (320 Abraham Martin, 888/861-4592, www.intercar.qc.ca) coach, which leaves from Québec City's Gare du Palais bus terminal heading toward Baie Comeau three times a day Mon.–Sat. and once on Sunday. A return ticket costs $14 and the journey takes 25 minutes.

By Bike

Bike path **Corridor du Littoral** will take you right from Québec's Vieux-Port all the way the Chute Montmorency and even along the **Route de la Nouvelle France.** Once you've made it onto the Île d'Orléans, bikes are available to rent from **Écolocyclo** (517 Chemin Royal, 418/828-0370, www.ecolocyclo.net, May–mid-June Sat.–Sun. 9 A.M.–6 P.M., mid-June–Sept. daily 9 A.M.–6 P.M.). The Chemin Royal encircles the island and a great way to sightsee is by bike.

By Car

The simplest and quickest way to get around is to take Autoroute 440 east out of Québec City and watch for the signs; all of the sights are well pointed out with the exits that accompany them. To get to Île d'Orléans take the Pont Île d'Orléans to the island.

Lac-Saint-Charles and Vicinity

LAC-SAINT-CHARLES
Golf
ROYAL CHARLESBOURG

Approximately a 10-minute drive from downtown Québec City, Royal Charlesbourg (17280 chemin de la Grande-Ligne, 418/841-3000, www.royalcharlesbourg.com, May–Nov. daily dawn–10 P.M., $43–52 for 18 holes) is considered to be one of the most challenging courses in the region. This relatively new championship course is 7,000 yards in length and plays as a par 72. Designed by Philip Watson, the fairway is heavily lined with the trees and the entire course is set amid low, rolling hills. Alongside the 18-hole course they also have a driving range, pro shop, and restaurant.

LAC-BEAUPORT
Skiing, Snowboarding, and Snowshoeing
LE RELAIS

Open in 1936, this ski hill (1084 blvd. du Lac, Lac-Beauport, 418/849-1851, www.skirelais.com, Dec.–mid-Mar. Mon.–Thurs.

9 A.M.–9:30 P.M., Fri.–Sat. 8:30 A.M.–10 P.M., Sun. 8:30 A.M.–9:30 P.M., $36 adult, $29 student and senior, $20 youth, $9 child for a day pass) just outside of the city was the first of its kind in the region and changed the development landscape of the surrounding area. Well-established, Le Relais has 29 different kinds of trails, everything from family-friendly bunny hills to various black diamonds and even four double-black diamonds. Some wind in and out of the woods while others offer moguls and jumps. At the end of the day head back to the chalet for a restorative drink at the bar. They also offer babysitting, and lessons for all levels of skiers.

Golf
MONT TOURBILLON

This 18-hole course (55 Montée du Golf, Lac-Beauport, 418/849-4418, www.monttourbillon.com, May–Nov. daily dawn–10 P.M., $25–48 for 18 holes), a 15-minute highway drive away from Québec City, was opened in 1962. Designed by Howard Watson, one of the

PARC NATIONAL DE LA JACQUES-CARTIER

Less than a half-hour drive from downtown Québec City is Parc National de la Jacques-Cartier (700 blvd. Lebourgneuf, Stoneham, 418/848-3169 summer, 418/528-8787 winter, www.sepaq.com/pq/jac). Situated in a valley with the same name, this park boasts both calm waters and rapids. Home of a 26-kilometer-long river, this the perfect place to learn basic maneuvers. Those who haven't had the opportunity to learn how to canoe or kayak can do so here, they also have a number of mini-rafts, inflatable canoes, and inner tubes to rent for more relaxed water fun. Though the park is open year-round, equipment rental (canoe $14 per hour, kayak $13 per hour, dinghy $11 per hour) is only available mid-May-mid-October. There are also a number of bike trails here for those who want to do some off-roading.

country's foremost golf architects, the course is flanked by a mountain and the terrain is relatively hilly, making many of the holes par 4 and 5. Measuring 6,010 yards, the overall par of the course is 70. A popular place to hold tournaments and receptions, it also has a training green and offers golf lessons. In winter the course is used throughout the week for sledding and snowshoeing. Reservations required.

STONEHAM
Skiing
STONEHAM RESORT
Started by 20 amateur skiers in the beginning

of the 1960s, Stoneham (600 chemin du Hibou, Stoneham et Tewkesbury, 418/848-2411, www.ski-stoneham.com, Mid-Nov.–mid-Mar. Mon.–Wed. 9 A.M.–4 P.M., Thurs.–Fri. 9 A.M.–8 P.M., Sat. 8:30 A.M.–8 P.M., Sun. 8:30 A.M.–4 P.M., $52 adult, $44 senior, $39 teen, $24 youth for a day pass) opened with three ski trails and two ski lifts. A 20-minute drive from Québec City, the resort now boasts 32 trails with a vertical drop of 1,380 feet, with hills that are suitable for those seeking everything from extreme skiing to trails fit for learners. At night 16 trails remain open, covering 15.6 kilometers. One of Stoneham's newest attractions, however, has nothing to do with skiing; the Arctic Spa zone, with outdoor hot tubs, is the perfect end-of-the-day reward.

SAINT-GABRIEL-DE-VALCARTIER
Water Park
◖ VILLAGE VACANCES VALCARTIER
If the kids have been really, really good and you want to give them a treat, than the 20-minute drive to Village Vacances Valcartier (1860 blvd. Valcartier, Valcartier, 888/384-5524, www.valcartier.com, June–Sept. daily 10 A.M.–7 P.M., mid-Dec.–Mar. daily 10 A.M.–closing, $31.01 tall 4.33 ft and up, $24.81 small and senior) might just be perfect. Opened in 1963, this waterpark and winter playground is awesome outdoor fun, no matter the time of year. In the summer the kids can splash around on Game Island or test their nerves on the Daredevil Drop. Come winter the waterslides become part of a winter wonderland that has parents and kids of all ages clambering into a snow raft to go barreling down a snow-covered slide. An outdoor skating rink is also part of the winter fun, and in summer families can sign up for river rafting.

EXCURSIONS

Charlevoix

EXCURSIONS

Some of the most stunning views of the province can be found here. People come here to camp, hike, and to catch a glimpse of the whales.

Follow Route 138 north out of Québec City and you'll come across some of the most spectacular scenery you've ever seen. The impact of a meteorite 350 million years ago has shaped the face of the Charlevoix region and could be the cause of its mysterious seismic activity (rest assured—most temblors hit little more than 2.0 on the Richter scale).

One of the first vacation destinations in Canada thanks to a couple of enterprising Scottish soldiers, Charlevoix's landscape is distinct in its variety. At times pastoral and hilly, the region's high cliffs and breathtaking fjords are adorned with tundra, while nearby, steep sand dunes rise unexpectedly along the coastline. These manifold landscapes translate into an area rich in biodiversity, where moose and caribou thrive alongside an astounding range of sealife. Where else can you sit on a sandy beach waiting to catch a glimpse of a pod of white beluga whales?

SIGHTS
◖ Baie-Saint-Paul

One of the biggest towns in Charlevoix, Baie-Saint-Paul is known for its unique artist community, galleries, off-beat boutiques, and as the home of Cirque du Soleil. The home of roughly 7,000 full-time inhabitants, the downtown core is quaint, full of shops and cafés, and is a lovely place to spend the afternoon strolling the streets no matter the season. The **Musée d'Art Contemporain Baie-Saint-Paul** (23 rue Ambroise-Fafard, 418/435-3681, www.macbsp. com, summer Tues.–Sun. 11 A.M.–5 P.M., winter Tues.–Sun. noon–5 P.M., $6 adult) honors the area's artistic heritage with a collection and temporary exhibits dedicated to contemporary works. Founded in 1992, the museum is located in what was once an old cinema.

On the outskirts of town is **Le Moulin de la**

Rémy (235 Terrasse de la Rémy, 418/435-6579, www.moulindelaremy.com, summer Tues.–Sun. 10 A.M.–4 P.M., $5). Built in 1827, this is one of the few flour mills still active in Québec; tours and tastings are available throughout the summer and visitors are invited to explore the surrounding paths and countryside. Pick up a fresh loaf at the bakery, traditionally made with wheat grown in Charlevoix and ground on-site.

◖ Isle-aux-Coudres

Off the shores of Baie-Saint-Paul is Isle-aux-Coudres, one of the most picturesque islands in the St-Lawrence. Hop on the free ferry from St-Joseph-de-la-Rive just south of Baie-Saint-Paul and take the 15-minute ride out to the island. Named Isle-aux-Coudres after the hazelnuts that Jacques Cartier found here, the 11-kilometer-long and three-kilometer-wide island is easily discovered by bike. **Vélo-Coudres** (2926 chemin des Coudriers, 418/432-2118, www. charlevoix.qc.ca/velocoudres, May–June and Sept. daily 9 A.M.–5 P.M., July–Aug. 8 A.M.–sunset, $7/hour) has different models available, including tandem, kids' bikes, and even quadricycles with room for a family of four.

With a parish that dates back to 1741, **Église Saint-Louis de Isle-aux-Coudres** is one of the oldest religious sites on the island, built in 1885. It boasts hand-painted frescoes and impressive stone work. Also worth looking out for are a pair of windmills, built in 1825 and 1836. They are still used to grind wheat and buckwheat and are also open to visitors.

La Malbaie

Back on the mainland continue north on Route 362 till you arrive at La Malbaie, one of the oldest tourist spots in the region. Originally called Murray Bay, the area was first made popular by two Scottish officers who saw the potential in the area's beauty and made it the top resort choice from the 19th century right up until the 1950s. Learn all you need to know about the region at **Musée de Charlevoix** (10

EXCURSIONS

© SACHA JACKSON

the sand dunes in Tadoussac

chemin du Havre, 418/665-4411, www.mu-seedecharlevoix.qc.ca, June–mid-Oct. daily 9 A.M.–5 P.M., mid-Oct.–May Mon.–Fri. 10 A.M.–5 P.M., Sat.–Sun. 1–5 P.M., $7 adult/$5 senior). This charming little museum offers exhibitions about the region's culture and history including photographs of beluga whale-hunting, artifacts from Manoir Richelieu, and folk art from the 1930s and '40s.

In more recent times one of the biggest draws to the region has been the **Casino de Charlevoix** (183 ave. Richelieu, 800/665-2274, www.casino-de-charlevoix.com, Mon.–Thurs. and Sun. 11 A.M.–midnight, Fri.–Sat. 11 A.M.–3 A.M., free). Opened in 1994, it has cherrywood paneling, granite floors, and is a step up from most casinos. Visitors must be 18 years old or over to enter.

🄲 Tadoussac

A further half-hour drive north and you get to Tadoussac, meeting point of the Saguenay and St-Lawrence Rivers. A free ferry will take you the short trip across the water to the historic town, one of the oldest places in Québec. It was France's first trading post and was established in 1600. Today the area's main draw is the rich marine life that thrives here, thanks to the confluence of warm St-Lawrence saltwater and the freshwater of the Saguenay. The town itself is quite small but completely charming, the perfect place to stroll around. Visit **Chauvin Trading Post** (157 rue Bord De L'Eau, 418/235-4433, June–Oct. daily). This may just be a reconstruction, but it's still cool to visit a reasonable facsimile of the first trading post in Québec, and the exhibitions, though brief, are informative.

Between mid-May and mid-October tourists come from all over the world to see the whales that flock to the region; approximately 10 different species can be found every year, including humpback, finback, blue whales, and white belugas. The best places to catch a glimpse of these majestic creatures are the **Parc Marin du Saguenay-Saint-Laurent** (182 rue de l'Église, 888/773-8888, www.parc-marin.qc.ca) and **Parc du Saguenay** (91 rue

Notre-Dame, Rivière-Éternité, 800/665-6527, www.sepaq.com/pq/sag). Both of these national parks offer a number of different ways to see the whales, including boat excursions and sea kayaking. Interpretation centers are open along the trails and they both offer stunning views of the fjords and the rivers.

Independent companies offer up-close and personal whale tours, including **Croisières AML** (Baie du Tadoussac, 866/856-6668, www.croisieresaml.com, May–Sept., $64) and **Group Dufour** (329 Highway 138, Baie-Sainte-Catherine, 800/463-5250, www.dufour.ca, May–Sept., $64), both of which offer tours of varying lengths. Most of the tours take place on larger boats with food facilities and naturalists who'll walk you through the action; Zodiac tour lets you get even closer to the animals. Passengers are given lifejackets and waterproof overalls but will likely get wet anyhow, as you bump along the waves.

For the brave and experienced, kayak trips are also available through **Mer et Monde Ecotours** (866/637-6663, www.mer-et-monde.qc.ca, May–Sept., $43) whose three-hour-long tours start at the bay of Tadoussac, just past the lawn of the Hotel Tadoussac.

RESTAURANTS

Baie-Saint-Paul has the best range of restaurants in the region. Fans of a good microbrew shouldn't miss ⟨ **Le Saint-Pub** (2 rue Racine, 418/240-2332, www.saint-pub.com, late May–Oct. daily 11:30 A.M.–10 P.M., Nov.–late May daily 11:30 A.M.–8 P.M., $25). This pub and bistro keeps things local and serves seasonal mussels, fresh fish, Charlevoix sausage, and deer steaks. They also offer more regular pub-style dishes like nachos and fries.

Relaxed dining can be found at **Vice-Café** (1 rue Ste-Anne, 418/435-0006, daily 11:30 A.M.–onward, $20), situated directly in front of the church. Their specialties include grilled salmon and crêpes. Head there for dinner on Friday night and stay for the local musical entertainment.

On Isle-aux-Coudres many restaurants are located in hotels. **La Marinière** (1933 chemin des Coudriers, 418/438-2208, $25) is located in the interestingly named Hôtel Motel Les Voitures d'Eau (Hotel Motel for Water Vehicles) but offers a menu prepared exclusively with local products, including Charlevoix meats and seafood. The food is so fresh here, the menu changes daily.

In Tadoussac most of the restaurants are only open May–October, something to keep in mind if you're traveling north in winter. If you're visiting in summer there's a lot more choice but it isn't always varied. One of your best bets for a light breakfast, lunch, or dinner is **Café Bohême** (239 rue des Pionniers, 418/235-1180, May–Oct., $15). Serving different types of fair-trade coffee, they also have a selection of desserts (try the brownie) and other treats as well as a range of soups, sandwiches, and salads. On the second floor they also have a small book exchange library and you can pick up some gourmet Charlevoix products.

For something more upscale there is the **Restaurant le William** (165 rue Bord-de-l'Eau, 418/235-4421, www.hoteltadoussac.com, May–Oct., $70 tasting menu) in the Hotel Tadoussac, which offers a four-course tasting menu and views over the Bay of Tadoussac and the St-Lawrence.

RECREATION
Hiking
PARC NATIONAL DES GRANDS-JARDINS

Once you're in the area you might as well take advantage of the nature that's available to you. West of Baie-Saint-Paul is the Parc National des Grands-Jardins (800/665-6527, www.sepaq.com/pq/grj), open year-round. This gorgeous national park has some of the most interesting vegetation, with a mix of both taiga and tundra. The landscape is vaguely arctic, with thick layers of lichen and black spruce forest. Home to a large caribou population it has many activities available, including 34 kilometers of hiking trails in the summer as well as kayaking and canoeing. In winter visitors can use the 55 kilometers of cross-country ski trails and try their hand at ice fishing.

© JEAN SYLVIAN

Charlevoix's largest ski mountain, Le Massif, has some of the best views of the St-Lawrence.

EXCURSIONS

◖ PARC NATIONAL DES HAUTES-GORGES-DE-LA-RIVIÈRE-MALBAIE

Named after a series of valleys, Parc National des Hautes-Gorges-de-la-Rivière-Malbaie (800/665-6527, www.sepaq.com/pq/hgo, late May–Oct.) has steep sloping mountains that fall to meet Rivière Malbaie. With its unique mix of fauna Hautes-Gorges is one of the most beautiful spots in eastern Canada. Not far west from La Malbaie, it offers a huge amount of outdoor activities like boat cruises, rock climbing, cycling, and 33 kilometers of hiking. Swimming, canoeing, and kayaking can also be done here.

Skiing
◖ LE MASSIF

One of the best hills in the province, Le Massif (877/536-2774, www.lemassif.com, mid-Dec.–mid-Apr. daily 8:30 A.M.–4 P.M., $64 adult day pass) is the area's largest ski mountain. Many high-ranking skiers come to train here, but even if you're more comfortable on the bunny runs, the views alone are worth the fees. It's

on a cliff that looks out over the St-Lawrence, and there are times on these runs when you're sure the bottom is going to be on the shores. With 49 different trails of varying levels it has something for everyone.

HOTELS

The stone-clad, 30-room inn **Maison Otis** (23 rue St-Jean-Baptiste, 418/435-2255, www.maisonotis.com, $120–260) in Baie-Saint-Paul has its own sort of cozy charm with wood furniture, floral bedding, and stone walls. Slightly more modern but still with that floral country vibe, **Auberge La Muse** (39 rue St-Jean-Baptiste, 800/841-6839, www.lamuse.com, $120–400) is ideally located on a tree-lined street in the center of town, and the rooms are tastefully decorated and have a feminine touch.

Though available in the high season only, Isle-aux-Coudres's **L'Hôtel Cap-aux-Pierres** (444 chemin la Baleine, 888/222-3308, www.dufour.ca, $84–250) has 46 rooms, tastefully decorated with wood floors, antique-style furniture, and a country feel. Each room has

© FAIRMONT HOTELS

the majestic Fairmont le Manoir Richelieu in La Malbaie

classic views of both the river and the garden. The hotel also has an outdoor pool.

In La Malbaie, one of the area's biggest draws is the romantic ◖ **Fairmont le Manoir Richelieu** (181 rue Richelieu, 866/540-4464, www.fairmont.com/richelieu, $140–350). Built in 1899, in a similar style as the Château Frontenac, it sits atop the Pointe-au-Pic overlooking the St-Lawrence River. Destroyed by fire and rebuilt in 1929, the hotel today is a luxury resort with an adjoining 18-hole golf course and an on-site spa, as well as five different restaurants. The rooms are elegant and tastefully decorated and aim for a comfortable instead of sleek luxury.

Sitting on the Baie de Tadoussac, **Hôtel Tadoussac** (165 rue Bord-de-l'Eau, 800/561-0718, www.hoteltadoussac.com, $150–250) stands out on the horizon with its red copper roof and white clapboard siding. Opened in 1864, it's one of the oldest hotels in the region and maintains its historic feel (it has no air-conditioning in summer, but then again you don't really need it). The rooms have recently been modernized and have a nice, airy quality about them. Also on the property you'll find the Tadoussac chapel. Built by Jesuit missionaries, it is the oldest wooden church in North America and still has some of its original artifacts.

INFORMATION AND SERVICES

Before you go, check out the website **www.tourisme-charlevoix.com** for all the necessary tips and information. When you've made it to the region, **Baie-Saint-Paul Tourist Office** (800/677-2276, daily 9 A.M.–4 P.M. and till 7 P.M. in summer) is just off the highway on a hill over looking the city below; it's a great view but the turnoff is sharp. **La Malbaie Tourist Office** (495 blvd. de Comporté, Route 362, 800/667-2276, daily 8:30 A.M.–4:30 P.M.) is right on the water looking out over the river and has a nice park in front in which to take a break.

The **Tadoussac Tourist Office** (197 rue des Pionniers, 866/235-4744, www.tadoussac.com, May–late Oct. Mon.–Sat. 9 A.M.–5 P.M. and Sun. 10 A.M.–4 P.M.) is in the center of town and hard to miss. It has loads of information on the region as well as a few historical exhibits to give you more of an idea about the place, its culture and history.

GETTING THERE AND AROUND
By Bus

Intercar (320 Abraham Martin, 888/861-4592, www.intercar.qc.ca) coaches leave from Québec City's Gare du Palais bus terminal heading toward Baie Comeau three times a day Mon.–Sat. and once on Sunday. The same bus runs all along the Charlevoix coast. A round-trip ticket to Baie-Saint-Paul costs $39 and the ride takes one hour and 15 minutes; La Malbaie costs $56 and takes two hours; and a return ticket to Tadoussac costs $89 and the trip takes four hours and 10 minutes.

By Car

Follow Autoroute 440 out of Québec City and continue past Côte-de-Beaupré on Route 138. From there you'll have a couple of options; you can follow Route 138 into Baie-Saint-Paul and continue on the same route all the way to La Malbaie, or you can take Route 362 instead, which is more scenic.

BACKGROUND

The Land

GEOGRAPHY

Québec is Canada's largest province and covers an area of 1,540,681 square kilometers, basically the size of France, Germany, Belgium, Spain, Portugal and couple of Switzerlands put together, all in all an enormous territory. For the most part it is filled with boundless forests and innumerable lakes (some say more than 400,000), vestiges of the huge Sea of Champlain that flooded the area 10,000 years ago.

Québec's geography can be divided into three main regions. The Canadian Shield goes from the extreme north down to the plain of St-Lawrence River and includes the Laurentian mountains, said to be the oldest mountain range in the world. The Appalachians, at the south of that plain, turn the landscape into a green and hilly area characteristic of the Eastern Townships region and extend down to the United States. A rift valley between these two antediluvian geological formations, the St-Lawrence is a 1,200-kilometer-long river that takes its source from the Great Lakes and ends up in the world's largest estuary. Most of Québec's residents live along the banks of the river, and it's also the center of Quebec's development. Looking out over the landscape from the window of a plane, along with sprawling cities of Montréal and Québec you can see the rural landscape divided into narrow

© TOURISME MONTRÉAL

rectangular tracts of land extending from the river: These patterns denote the seigneurial land system and date back to the settlement of 17th-century Nouvelle France (New France).

Montréal

The second largest and second most populated city in Canada (after Toronto) and the largest in Québec, Montréal has a population of about two million. Standing at the confluence of the St-Lawrence and Ottawa Rivers, it is set on an island of 500 square kilometers, 50 kilometers long and 15 kilometers wide at its widest. North of the island is the suburb of Laval, and beyond that the Laurentian mountains; south of it, across the St-Lawrence, you'll find the south shore cities of Longueil and Brossard. Smaller islands surround Montréal, such as Île des Sœurs or Île Bizard; most of the islands are now suburban communities. South of the Vieux-Port, what used to be several little islands were consolidated into Île Sainte-Hélène for the Expo 67. Next to it, Île Notre-Dame was built from scratch with the 15 millions tons of rocks excavated from the construction of the Métro in 1965.

The most prominent geographical feature of the island, from which it takes its name, is the triple-peaked hill Mount Royal. Though locals like to call it a "mountain," its highest point is only 232 meters high. Except for the plateau surrounding the diminutive peak, the rest of the city is flatter than flat. The opening of the Lachine Canal in 1824 and its enlargement over the 19th century permitted ships to bypass the unnavigable Lachine Rapids, making Montréal a major port and linking the St-Lawrence to the Great Lakes, all of which turned the city into a booming economic center.

As in most North American cities, one of the biggest problems facing Montréal is traffic. The city's two main bridges off the island, Pont Jacques-Cartier and Pont Champlain, are chronically congested, a problem that worsens each year. Administratively, it's important to note that the City of Montréal does not include all the boroughs located on the island. In fact, five boroughs, including Hamstead, Montréal West, and Westmount, refused to merge with the rest of the city at the beginning of the 21st century and remain politically independent. This fact can sometimes get in the way when dealing with topics like city infrastructure.

Québec City

Located 240 kilometers northeast of Montréal, Québec City, with a population of half a million, thrives on the north bank of the St-Lawrence near its meeting point with the St-Charles River and not far from the foothills of the Laurentian mountains. Built on top and around the 98-meter-high Cap-Diamant, it overlooks the dramatic narrowing of the river that takes place in the St-Lawrence after Île d'Orléans. It's from this narrowing that the city gets its name, taken from the Algonquin word *kebec,* which means "where the river narrows."

It's this particular position that made it, in the mind of the colonizers, a logical commercial port as well as a strategic military point. The ramparts surrounding Vieux-Québec's Upper Town, the only fortified city left in North America, have made it an architectural jewel and helped the city earn the name the "Gibraltar of North America." Near the southern edge of Cap-Diamant, the Plains of Abraham (Québec's version of Central Park) extend along the cliffs. It was on these rolling hills that North America's fate was sealed in the haze of a battle between the British and the French in 1759.

One of the main physical features of the city is its two-level construction. Cap-Diamant and its cliffs break the urban landscape in two, prompting significant opposition between Haute-ville (Upper Town) and Basse-ville (Lower Town). This opposition is as significant sociologically as it is topographically. Thus, Upper Town (with the exception of Faubourg Saint-Jean-Baptiste) is historically the home of the ruling bourgeoisie, while Lower Town (Limoilou, Saint-Roch, Saint-Sauveur), which developed along the shores of the St-Lawrence and St-Charles Rivers, was the home of seamen, dock workers, and factory workers. This antagonism is in flux nowadays as exemplified by Nouvo Saint-Roch's gentrification. Motivated by the 400th anniversary's celebrations, much urban redevelopment has been done, particularly along the banks of the rivers, making Québec City one of the most likable cities in the world.

CLIMATE

"Mon pays ce n'est pas un pays, c'est l'hiver" (My country is not a country, it's winter) sang Québec's premier *chansonnier,* Gilles Vigneault. Truer words have never been spoken, especially regarding the six months during which winter takes over, changing the landscape and affecting the mood of its resigned inhabitants. Yes, wintertime temperatures have an average of -10°C in Montréal and can drop down to -30°C. In Québec City, it is usually 2–3 degrees colder. However, the winters aren't as harsh, cold, and snowy as they used to be, thanks to global warming. But the freezing wind, blowing *poudreuse* (drifting snow) everywhere like a tempest in the desert, is probably the toughest thing about being here in the winter. When the temperatures dip to bone-chilling proportions, make sure to cover up everything from your nose to toes or you'll end up with painful frostbite (ears and nose are the usual victims).

Approximately three meters of snow fall every winter but sometimes there's more. In the winter of 2007–2008 up to five meters fell on the city, piling into huge snowbanks on the side of the streets. Snowstorms are frequent and can last up to a day if not more. Snow removal can be interesting to watch if you're a tourist and have never seen it before. Every snowstorm costs the city approximately $10 million in snow-removal operations. The sidewalk and road snowplows can also be deadly—they caused five deaths in the winter of 2010—so be careful, especially when walking at night.

Despite being harsh and long, winters in Québec are also sunny with a bright luminosity that can sometimes be blinding. Because of the length of the season, stoical locals have adopted a "if you can't beat 'em join 'em" attitude in order to survive, and you'll be surprised to see just how active Quebeckers can be in winter, putting on their skates and snowshoes after every snowstorm, sometimes going to work on cross-country skis and pulling their kids in toboggans along the sidewalks. There is no need to say that winter has had a major cultural impact on this society; its influence is apparent in everything from the architecture to the invention of the Underground City.

Of course, Québec isn't just about winter, and people are often surprised to see just how hot and humid the summers are, with temperatures often reaching 35°C. After having complained about the cold all winter, locals curse the heat and turn their air-conditioning on full blast.

Autumn and spring are shorter in Québec but in many ways they are the most impressive seasons. In spring, the snow melts away, revealing new blossoms (and the women of the city are known for quickly sloughing off their winter clothes), while autumn has a particular beauty as the trees change to a rainbow of colors before shedding their leaves.

Flora and Fauna

The best place to explore Québec's rich and diverse fauna and flora is in the national parks. No matter what part of the province you decide to explore, national parks offer interpretive materials and guides to help you understand just exactly what it is you're surrounded by.

Montréal and Québec being cities, you won't have much chance to run into a moose or a black bear while getting a pint of milk at the *dép* (corner store). But, these two cities both have parks with protected fauna and flora (Parc du Mont-Royal in Montréal and Parc des Plaines d'Abraham in Québec), where you might see animals that can be exotic for some: red and gray squirrels, chipmunks, and raccoons. If you're wandering through Mont-Royal you might also glimpse a fox.

Both cities are remarkably green for their size, with trees lining just about every side street. Originally part of the Laurentian forest ecosystem, the vegetation has changed over time due to urbanization. A good example of this is Mont-Royal, originally made up exclusively of red oaks and sugar maples. The introduction in the 1960s and '70s of the Norway maple, which is more resistant to city pollution, has considerably changed the face of the beloved mountain. And today, they've overtaken

Jardin Botanique in Montréal

© TOURISME MONTRÉAL

much of the sugar maple, the difference being most visible in the fall when, instead of turning bright red the way sugar maples do, the Norway maples turn yellow.

History

EARLY INHABITANTS

Long before its European takeover, the North American continent was home to the indigenous people for thousands of years. Historians date the population back to 12,000 years ago, when hunting tribes crossed the Bering Strait in pursuit of game from Siberia. Those tribes then scattered all over the land, developing diverse ways of life as they adapted to different environments. At the time explorers arrived, the area that would eventually become known as the St-Lawrence valley was populated by the

nomadic Algonquin and sedentary Iroquoian tribes who lived off game, fish, and crops, and were particularly well adapted to their environment.

EUROPEAN ARRIVAL

When it comes to the discovery of Canada, it's French explorer Jacques Cartier's name that usually pops up. But what's less known is that by the time he finally made it to Québec in 1534, Newfoundland's coastline was being periodically cruised by explorers and fishermen

ARCHITECTURE IN QUÉBEC

When settlers first arrived in Québec their main concern was with security; with that in mind all of the first towns started out as fortified enclosures. These were made of wood or stone and designed in the five-pointed Vauban style. By the end of the French regime New France closely resembled provincial towns in the old country, with hospitals, convents, colleges, and churches whose steeples peeked out over the walls.

Early-1700s inhabitants had trouble adapting their homes to the cold weather, and many froze to death before the colony got it right. The design was altered and structures were made of rubble stone instead of wood, with small casement windows that were few and far between. The number of rooms in the house matched the number of chimneys. In 1721, wooden houses with mansard roofs were banned after a devastating fire, and stone firewalls and attic floors covered in terracotta tiles became the standard.

Although the British conquest took place in 1759, it wasn't until the 1780s that English influence could be seen in architecture around the province. A few high-ranking officials started building homes in the popular Palladian and Regency styles, with open-air porticoes and Italian columns. The Regency balconies and windows allowed for a perfect mix between inside and out, while also stopping the snow from blocking windows and doors in winter. Roofs became less slanted so the snow no longer fell directly on your head as you closed the door on your way out. All buildings during this period, commercial or residential, resembled country homes. You can still get a sense of this today on rue St-Jean in Québec City. Commercial buildings were set up to look like homes in part because the Catholic Church disapproved of the expansion of commerce.

© TOURISME MONTRÉAL

traditional circular outdoor staircases in Montréal

The industrialization of the province led to an architectural style that would forever define Montréal: the duplexes and triplexes with circular exterior staircases. Built between 1900 and 1930, these economical structures were meant to accommodate large families. With outdoor staircases to save on heating and space, and balconies reminiscent of rural galleries, they also gave inhabitants the feel of a personal entrance. Covered in either limestone or brick, each had decorative touches like a cornice, Tuscan columns, or art nouveau-inspired windows. Over 100 years later, these unique staircases and multiple-family dwellings continue to thrive in the city and set it apart.

© SACHA JACKSON

A Martello tower on the Plains of Abraham is an example of Québec City's fortifications before the Citadelle was built.

from different nations and that Vikings had sailed its coast and even put down a few roots 500 years before.

What Jacques Cartier did first, though, before other Europeans, was explore the interior of the river, a river that he named in honor of the saint on the calendar the day he reached it: St-Lawrence. Sent by the king of France, Francis I, with the mandate of finding gold and—the typical request of the day—a passage to Asia, the sailor explored the region thoroughly, visiting Iroquoian villages Stadacona (Québec) and, further upstream, Hochelaga, which he rechristened Mont-Royal, in honor of the king. After many voyages, he found neither gold nor Asia, bringing home instead a bunch of made-up stories told by fabulist natives and a handful of rocks he thought were diamonds (a popular French saying of the time was *"faux comme un diamant du Canada"* (fake as a Canadian diamond). Deemed inhospitable and dull, the land of Canada would remain unvisited and almost forgotten for half a century.

NOUVELLE FRANCE (NEW FRANCE)

Two things rekindled the French interest in this part of the world: the fur trade and an appetite for colonial expansion. In addition to these two motives the Catholic Church saw an opportunity to spread the gospel to the Amerindian population and sent missionaries along on the expedition. Seeing promise in the new European fashion of fur hats and coats, trading companies quickly formed, including the Compagnie des Cent-Associés, which set up outposts around Québec where the Amerindians and French could trade.

In 1608, Samuel de Champlain set up the first permanent trading post in an abandoned Iroquoian village that Jacques Cartier had visited 80 years before, building a wooden fort he called l'Abitation de Québec (*kebec* in Algonquin means "where the river narrows"). That first winter, most of the settlers died of scurvy and harsh weather, but the colony continued even though it faced numerous difficulties and was slow to grow. In 1635 (the year Samuel de Champlain, the Father of New France, died), the population was slightly more than 300 settlers, a fair part of them Catholic missionaries. Some of these missionaries organized the Société Notre-Dame de Montréal and, in 1642, decide to establish an evangelizing mission near the deserted village of Hochelaga. Called Ville-Marie, it would eventually become Montréal.

While colonists cleared forests and cultivated the land, the thriving fur trade attracted a different kind of young explorer, daring enough to go farther and farther in to the continent seeking bearskins, mink furs, and, above all, the popular and coveted beaver pelts. Called *coureurs des bois* (woods runners, or woodsmen), these adventurers are legendary figures in Québec, since they represent a life of freedom and a particular connection with nature that characterized the colonization of the continent. These *coureurs* also paved the way for the explorers and voyageurs to whom we owe the exploration of the regions of the Great Lakes and the Mississippi Valley, much of which they claimed for the French. These explorers left their mark on places all over the United States, including Detroit, St. Louis, and Baton Rouge.

The commercial relations brought on by the trade helped the French secure alliances with the Hurons, who in exchange for the pelts received copper and iron utensils, alcohol, and rifles. This alliance put the French colony in the middle of a bloody war when the English-backed Iroquois Five Nations launched an offensive campaign to wipe out the Hurons, their long-time enemies. The war lasted 25 years and seriously affected the young colony.

TOWARD DEFEAT

The conflicting commercial and political interests of the French and the English caused a succession of inter-colonial wars. In 1713, following a military defeat in Europe, the Treaty of Utrecht resulted in France relinquishing control of Newfoundland, Acadia, and the Hudson Bay, something that considerably hurt the fur trade and jeopardized the colony. This date marks the beginning of the end for New France

even if it took another 50 years for the British to secure power, a takeover that seemed inevitable considering the difference in population. Indeed, on the eve of the final battle, there were 60,000 French living in a huge territory, surrounded by two million British colonists living in the narrow strip of the thirteen colonies.

The final showdown happened on September 13, 1759, on an open field by Cap-Diamant. After a two-month-long siege, the French Army, led by General Montcalm, was attacked by surprise early in the morning. General Wolfe and the British Army used a dried-up old creek to climb the cliff, something everyone thought was impossible. The Battle of the Plains of Abraham, which sealed the fate of French North America, was bloody, lasted barely 20 minutes, and cost the lives of both generals. One year after, Montréal capitulated and thus France lost all of its colonies in North America, leaving behind a small population of deeply rooted French Catholics in an ocean of British Protestants.

BRITISH REGIME

Though at first they tried to assimilate the French minority by imposing British Common Law and having them swear an oath to the British King, the victors decided it was wiser to accommodate the French, wanting to secure their allegiance as social unrest and rebellion smoldered in the south. In order to cement the support of the French-Canadians, England wrote up the Act of Québec in 1774, recognizing French language and French civil law, and granting them freedom of religion. These concessions succeeded in preventing the French-Canadians from joining the rebels in the south who started the American Revolution a year later.

At the end of that war, in 1783, 50,000 United Empire Loyalists (British Loyalists) had fled the United States for the province of Québec, many of them settling into the Eastern Townships region. To accommodate these Loyalists, who were an English minority in a French-speaking majority, a new Constitutional Act was signed in 1791, dividing the province in two: Upper Canada (which

COMING NORTH: UNITED EMPIRE LOYALISTS

When things started looking really bad for the British during the American Revolution, a number of colonists who wanted to remain loyal to the British crown were offered free land and passage to other – non-rebelling – parts of the British colonies.

Called United Empire Loyalists because of their unyielding devotion to King George III, many choose to escape north, settling in the regions of southern Ontario and Québec. So many immigrated to the province, close to 50,000, that it sent the Québécois into a breeding frenzy and kicked of the *revanche des berceaux*, the "revenge of the cradle."

By 1791 so many had arrived in the country that the government signed the Constitutional Act, dividing the province in two: Upper Canada, which would eventually become Ontario, and Lower Canada, the province of Québec.

Though many Loyalists and descendants of Loyalists eventually moved out of the province, their influence can still be seen in the Eastern Townships, where covered bridges, clapboard houses, and Victorian gingerbread moldings are the norm.

would eventually become Ontario) and Lower Canada (the province of Québec). The names Upper and Lower Canada were given according to their location on the St. Lawrence River.

The 19th century was marked by the power struggles between the Francophones and the Anglophones in Lower Canada. The elected French-Canadian representatives were constantly at odds with the colonial British executive and legislative powers. Over the years, the nationalist and reformist Parti Canadien denounced the untenable situation, ending up in an armed insurrection. The Patriots War (Guerre des Patriotes) of 1837–1838 was immediately crushed and an emissary was sent

from London to study the problems of this wayward colony. The solution proposed by Lord Durham was radical: make every effort to assimilate French-Canadians. This was the impetus behind the Union Act, laid down by the British government in 1840. Along with unifying Upper and Lower Canada and giving them an equal political power—despite the fact that Lower Canada was much more populated—it also made English the only official language, despite the fact that the vast majority were Francophone-speakers. These new laws and the constant arrival of English-speaking immigrants prompted a major exodus of Francophones, many of whom immigrated to the United States.

CONFEDERATION

The troubled politics of the subsequent years coupled with a dire economic situation prompted leaders of Upper and Lower Canada to unify. The British North America Act, signed in 1867, is the constitutional act that solidified Canada as an independent nation that would eventually stretch from the Atlantic to the Pacific.

It also created the two-level structure of government, in which power is split between the federal and provincial levels. Even though Québec's minority status was deepened by it, the new structure granted the province jurisdiction over certain aspects, like education, civil law, and culture. Québec maintained a central importance in the evolution of the country, and before long a French-Canadian, Wilfrid Laurier, became prime minister of Canada. Elected in 1896, he was the first of many Québécois, including Pierre Elliot Trudeau and Jean Chrétien, who would lead the country.

Faced with a prodigious period of economic growth at the beginning of the 20th century, Prime Minister Laurier declared it "Canada's century." The prediction fell short, though, when the Great Depression disrupted economic and social progress in Québec for many years. World War II finally put an end to the economic doldrums, and in fact Québec came out of the war economically stronger than ever before and ready for social change, as the anarchist manifest *Refus Global* (Total Refusal), signed by artists and writers, made clear.

Despite this exciting new energy and mindset, the province would remain under the spell of Maurice Duplessis and his conservative party (Union Nationale) for another 15 years. In spite of its considerable economic growth, this period is often referred as "La Grande Noirceur" (The Great Darkness), the last obstacle before real transformation.

A QUIET REVOLUTION AND CONTEMPORARY TIMES

After the death of Maurice Duplessis in 1959, Québec was ripe for change, and the Liberal Party government of Jean Lesage was elected the year after, kicking off what would be dubbed the Révolution Tranquille (Quiet Revolution), a wide range of bold economical and social reforms. The most important result of these reforms is the secularization of society, putting an end to the centuries-long overarching power of the church in every aspect of Québécois society. Education, health care, and social services were no longer under the control of the church as the state began to take over.

The most ambitious economic project of the time, the nationalization of the province's electric companies under Hydro Quebec is a powerful symbol of that new ambition. The Quiet Revolution also witnessed the rise of nationalism. Jean Lesage's Liberal government election slogan, *maîtres chez nous* (masters in our own home), meant to put a stop to the unbridled selling of the province's natural resources to foreign business interests.

Montréal hosted two major international events that still define its identity: the 1967 World's Fair (Exposition Universelle—Terre des Hommes) and the Summer Olympic Games in 1976. The sentiment of empowerment at the time exacerbated enthusiasm for the idea of a stronger autonomy within the Canadian federation, and more and more people became attracted by the idea of building a new country instead, some groups even falling into extremism. Thus, the Front de Liberation du Québec

(FLQ), founded in 1963, used terrorist tactics against the Québec and national governments and businesses with the aim of establishing a socialist independent country.

In 1970, during the October crisis, when the FLQ kidnapped Québec Labour Minister Pierre Laporte and eventually killed him, Pierre Elliot Trudeau, then Canadian prime minister, launched the War Measures Act against Québec dissidents, putting the country under martial law to much public controversy. After that, the FLQ declined drastically and eventually disappeared.

Despite these radical actions and a certain support the FLQ gained with the public, all in all, the majority of pro-sovereigntists preferred moderate nationalism. In 1967, René Lévesque, a rising star of the Liberal government, quit the party and founded the Parti Québécois (PQ). Soon after, in 1976, a stunning and unexpected victory brought the PQ to power, putting the question of sovereignty at the forefront of political and social life of Québec society for decades. Bill 101 in 1977 made French the only official language of Québec. In 1980 Lévesque's government launched a referendum on the issue of independence, losing when the "no" side won with 60 percent of the vote. In time, the tensions with the federal government became aggravated, mostly over constitutional matters and Québec's refusal to ratify the repatriated Canadian constitution in 1982.

In 1995, a second referendum campaign is launched. This time the results were extremely close, and Canada held its breath: 49.4 percent of Quebecers voted "yes" and 50.6 percent voted "no," underlining the deep division of the population over the issue.

However, the national question has faded in importance over the last 15 years, with public attention drifting toward other public matters like the environment and economy. In 2003, the PQ was ousted from power after 10 years, and the Québec Liberal Party, resolutely federalist, was elected. Led by Premier Jean Charest, they were voted in for a third term in 2009.

Government and Economy

POLITICS

Canada's political system is modeled after the British parliamentary system it historically inherited. Central in the government organization is the House of Commons, sitting in Ottawa, a democratically elected body consisting of 308 members known as Members of Parliament (MPs). Each MP in the House of Commons is elected by simple plurality in an electoral district, also known as a riding. Elections are called within four years of the previous election or when the government loses a confidence vote.

The leader of the party that won the most seats becomes the new prime minister and forms the new government. Canada being a federation, this political structure is reproduced for every province. Therefore each of them has its own parliament. In Québec, it is called the Assemblée Nationale, and its 125 elected members sit in Québec City. The Canadian Constitution divides the power between federal and provincial governments. For example, defense, postal services, and international relations are under federal jurisdiction while education, health, and natural resources are under provincial jurisdiction. Since the Constitution is not always clear about these divided powers, constitutional conflicts arise, a situation that has been particularly true between Québec and the federal government.

Canada is also a constitutional monarchy. People are often surprised to know that there is a queen in Canada: Queen Elizabeth II of England is the Canadian head of state. Actually, it is mostly a formal and symbolic title, although she does have a representative in Canada acting on her behalf: the governor general. She is represented by the lieutenant-governor in the provinces.

This type of governmental structure favors a two-party system, but in Canada's case, four parties make up the federal government: the right-leaning Conservative Party, centrist Liberal Party, left-leaning NDP (New Democratic Party), and the Bloc Québécois, the Québec sovereigntist party. In major political battles the Conservatives and Liberals are always the front-runners, but the NDP and Bloc parties are instrumental to how government is run and what bills are passed in the House of Commons.

As of 2010 the federal government is headed by Prime Minister Stephen Harper of the Conservative party, but the government only rules with a minority. The Conservatives have ruled with a minority government since their election in 2006. In 2009, they made a bid for a majority government with a snap election but couldn't pull it off. The province of Québec is largely responsible for the preservation of a minority government because of its overwhelming support to the Bloc Québécois. Despite trying to appeal to the province's population by symbolically recognizing Québec as a "distinct nation in a united Canada," the Conservatives have been unable to win over voters in Québec. Instead the population has remained loyal to the Bloc Québécois.

On the provincial stage, two parties have been exchanging power for half a century: the centrist, federalist Québec Liberal Party, and the sovereigntist Parti Québécois founded by René Lévesque. In the 1980s and '90s, the Parti Québécois (PQ) became the center of international attention when it organized two referendums on Québec sovereignty, the outcome of which threatened to break up Canadian unity. The consecutive defeats of the PQ in these referendums and in recent elections has laid the sovereigntist question aside for the time being, though 40 percent of the people still support the bid for sovereignty.

ECONOMY

Since the beginning, Québec's natural resources have been the major asset in the province's economy. Vast forests, mining resources, rich agricultural land, and a huge potential for hydroelectricity—because of all the lakes—make

© SACHA JACKSON

Québec City's City Hall in Vieux-Québec's Upper Town

this province a gift from the gods. Historically everything began with the fur trade, kicking off the European colonization of the territory and sustaining it for over a century. In the 19th and most of the 20th centuries, wood, pulp, and paper industries took the lead and are still, along with the mining sector and hydroelectricity production, the most important sectors of Québec's economy.

The government plays an important role in the economy and is the largest employer in the province. Despite the trend toward more privatization, this strong state involvement reaches a certain consensus in the population and is considered essential due to the small size of its economy. Government-owned Hydro Québec, the world's leader in hydroelectricity, remains a national pride, and dams and development projects in the north are thoroughly followed by the population. Another economic national jewel is aerospace and railway maker Bombardier, a world-class company started 70 years ago by Joseph Bombardier, the inventor of the snowmobile.

Montréal

Once the undisputed economic center of Canada, Montréal lost its predominance to Toronto 40 years ago and now plays second fiddle to "the city that works." Even if most of Montréal's defenders would say this relative decline was caused by the massive fleeing of Anglophone businesses after the PQ reached power in 1976, you have to admit that the demographic and economic trends were already on track at the time. The last episode in this rivalry between the two cities was the acquisition of the Bourse de Montréal (Montréal Stock Exchange) by the Toronto Stock Exchange in 2007.

Despite this relative decline, however, Montréal thrives with high-class industries like aerospace (Bombardier, Pratt & Whitney, etc.), and information technology companies. Ubisoft, a major French video game publisher, in 1997 opened (with government funds) a subsidiary in Montréal, establishing itself in the new hip area Mile End. This studio, responsible for developing games like *Prince of Persia* and *Assassin's Creed,* is now one of the world's largest, with over 1,700 employees, making the city a central hub for that industry.

Québec City

Economically outpaced by its provincial counterpart in the middle of the 19th century, Québec City has nevertheless discreetly developed into a very successful city, with one of the lowest unemployment rates in Canada at 4.5 percent. Most jobs in Québec City are found in public administration, services, and tourism, with a large proportion of civil servants, because it is the seat of the entire provincial political apparatus.

The past few years have seen a particularly sound growth rate and many urban development projects, probably prompted by the enthusiasm occasioned by the city's 400th anniversary. The result of this growth meant that Québec City virtually averted the economic crisis of 2008 and is constantly depicted as a model city, much to the irritation of decline-struck Montréalers.

People and Culture

FIRST NATIONS

Québec's first inhabitants were the Amerindians. Eleven different First Nations tribes, including the Inuit, called the province home before the early days of colonization. Today, they represent a small part of the population, and three-quarters of them live on reserves throughout the province: The Mohawk reserves Kahnawake and Kanesatake in the Montréal region and the Wendat-Huron reserve Wendake north of Québec City are some of the bigger ones in the province. Though some Amerindians live in areas where they can hunt and fish, many of them have lost their traditional way of life and endure social hardships.

One of the most important political events of the past 20 years was the Oka Crisis, when for two months in the summer of 1990 Mohawks barricaded one of the main bridges into Montréal, protesting land claims and issues of self-government. The incident forced native issues to the forefront, and in recent years many agreements have granted Amerindians more autonomy.

FRANCOPHONES

The vast majority of the Québécois people are descendants of the original settlers who arrived between 1608 and 1759. From the 60,000 French-Canadians in 1759 there are now seven

© SACHA JACKSON

one of the many churches that can be found throughout Québec City

million living in Canada. Part of the reason Québec has such a strong cultural and social heritage is because of the population's demographics. In the late 18th century with the arrival of the United Empire Loyalists the French-Canadians became nervous at the idea of being over-populated by the English-speaking contingent. One

JEWISH QUÉBEC

King Louis XIV of France might have banned Jews from entering the colony of Nouvelle France, but Québec's Jewish roots can still be traced for centuries.

The first Jewish people to settle in Québec were members of the British Army who arrived after the initial conquest. Several are thought to have been a part of General Jeffery Amherst's battalion, four of which were officers. Of those officers at least one, Aaron Hart, remained in Canada, settling in Trois-Rivières and eventually becoming a wealthy landowner. One of his sons, Ezekiel Hart, later became the first Jew to be elected to public office in the British Empire.

Though the Jewish community in Montréal numbered little more than 200, the Spanish and Portuguese Synagogue of Montréal opened its doors in 1768 and became the first non-Catholic house of worship in the province. In Québec City the first known Jewish inhabitant was Abraham Jacob Franks, who settled in the city in 1767, but it wasn't until 1892 that the Jewish population in Québec City had enough members to warrant a proper synagogue. In the interim, however, they had founded a number of institutions, including the Québec Hebrew Sick Benefit Association, the Québec Hebrew Relief Association for Immigrants, and the Québec Zionist Society. By 1905, Québec City's Jewish population numbered 350.

As anti-Semitism mounted in Europe, over 155,000 Jews resettled in Canada, many of them in Montréal, where they became store-keepers, tradespeople, and workers in the city's numerous garment factories. The history of one of the city's greatest streets, boulevard St-Laurent, can be traced back to the immigrant families who worked and lived along the Main or in the factories nearby. Jewish businesses left an indelible mark on the city, and many of Montéal's most recognizable symbols — the smoked-meat sandwich, the bagel — come from that strong Jewish lineage.

At the end of World War II approximately 40,000 Holocaust survivors came to Canada, and in 1947, the Workmen's Circle and Jewish Labour Committee started the Tailors Project, aimed at bringing Jewish refugees to Montréal in the needle trades. Jewish immigration continued to expand in Québec, especially in the 1950s when North African Jews fled the continent, settling in Québec City and Montréal where their French language would be an asset.

The community today is concentrated in Montréal, in areas such as Hamstead, Côte-St-Luc, and Outremont, with a large Hassidic community in the Mile End. Though Québec City still has a Jewish community the majority of the province's Jewish population lives in Montréal, and in fact, many of the city's most recognizable citizens come from this community, including literary giants Irving Layton and Mordecai Richler, poet and musician Leonard Cohen, psychologist and linguist Steven Pinker, and even American Apparel founder Dov Charney.

---

response to this immigration was something that would later be called the *revanche des berceaux* (revenge of the cradle), which saw the families of French-Canadians growing larger by the year. Of course, the province's Catholic background helped, and throughout the years Québécois families were typically large and women had an average of eight children (Celine Dion is from a family of 14 kids). In the 1970s, however, the birthrate dropped considerably, and it remains one of the lowest in the world.

Though today the province is experiencing a baby boom, it is a mere blip compared to numbers in the mid-20th century. Much of the growth to the province's Francophone population now comes from immigration.

ANGLOPHONES

The first Anglophone immigrants arrived after the British conquest in 1759. Most of them were well-to-do Protestant merchants forever forging the stereotype of the rich Anglophone.

BEST FRENEMIES: QUÉBEC VS. MONTRÉAL

Québec City and Montréal have a long, friendly rivalry. Québec was the site of the first settlement in the province, and for centuries the two cities were competing trading posts. Even as Montréal's population grew, Québec continued to be the center of economic and political power. Then in the 19th century, the tides changed and Montréal supplanted Québec as the province's economic center. Its location at the crossroads between Europe and North American turned it into one of the most cosmopolitan cities on the continent, and business boomed.

In the 20th century Montréal hosted Expo 67 and the 1976 Olympics, solidifying its prominence on the world stage. Then in the 1990s, Québec City's NHL franchise, the beloved Québec Nordiques, was moved to Denver and the city spiraled into emotional depression, a state it is just now recovering from. All seemed lost for the province's capital city, until preparations began for its 400th anniversary in 2008.

Suddenly Québec City was changing, old working-class neighborhoods were being revitalized, the waterfront got a needed face-lift, and, perhaps most important, the mayor vowed to bring the NHL back to the city – an election promise that will be hard to make good on.

For the time being the cities are on relatively equal footing, but that hasn't changed the way they view each other. Québec City still sees Montréal as a city of two solitudes, where the citizens feel like strangers in their own town, while Montréalers chide those in Québec for being from a "village" and having an inferiority complex. As with all healthy rivalries, it's this push and pull between the two cities that propels them forward.

However, this wasn't always the case; one of the most important groups of immigrants was the working-class Irish, who arrived in the province as early as the founding of New France. The biggest wave of Irish immigrants came 1815–1860, driven from Ireland by the potato famine. They came to the province by the boatload, disembarking at Grosse-Île, an island off the shores of Québec City that was set up as a reception center. During the summer of 1847, thousands died during a typhus epidemic, and the orphaned children were adopted by Québec families. It is estimated a staggering 45 percent of Quebeckers have Irish ancestry, even if most of them don't know it. In Québec City many immigrant families were relegated to the slum-like dwellings in Petite Champlain, while in Montréal they congregated in places like Griffintown and Point-St-Charles.

The arrival of the United Empire Loyalists between 1783 and the beginning of the 19th century shaped not only the Eastern Townships, where most of them settled, but also the future of the country. They fled the United States in such great numbers as to facilitate the division of the province into Upper and Lower Canada. The 19th century also saw the largest number of immigrants from the British Isles, many of whom would put down roots in Montréal and, in the case of the Scots, found McGill University.

In the 1970s, after the rise to power of the PQ and the October Crisis in particular, many English-speakers left Québec, many settling in Ontario. Nowadays, they make up only 10 percent of the total population of the province and live mostly in Montréal. The west end of the city has the most prominent English boroughs: Westmount, Notre-Dame-de-Grace (NDG), and Montréal-West. Of the English-speakers who did stay, some 60 percent of them are now bilingual.

QUEBECKERS OF OTHER ETHNIC ORIGINS

Immigration from countries other than Britain and France only started in the 20th century. This growing ethnic diversity is particularly obvious in Montréal, whose history has been defined by successive waves of immigrants.

After World War II, the majority of immigrants arrived from Italy, Greece, and Portugal, communities that continue to have a stronghold in neighborhoods like the Mile End and Little Italy. For the most part these immigrants aligned themselves with the Anglophone community, raising Quebec's perennial concerns over French language subsistence. In 1977, the Parti Québécois passed Bill 101 as a solution to that perceived threat, forcing new arrivals into French schools. Immigration demographics began to change in the latter part of the century, and the 1970s and '80s saw exiles from Vietnam and Haiti join the ranks, followed more recently by North African, Chinese, and Central European immigrants.

Québec also has a large Jewish community, whose roots can be traced all the way back to the British conquest, while a large Hassidic community can be found in Outremont.

LGBT COMMUNITY

The first recorded gay establishment in North America, Moise Tellier's apples and cake shop, opened in Montréal in 1869. You can't get a better picture of the city's attitude toward the gay, lesbian, bi, and trans community than that. Like all LGBT communities Montréal's has faced discrimination and hardships, one of the most crucial being a raid in October 1977, during which 144 men were arrested. Those arrests, however, led to a 2,000-person-strong protest the following day. It's this show of political support and acceptance that Montréal has become known for.

Though the Village is instrumental to gay life, there are queer establishments and events all over the city. There is also massive support both within the city and community for younger members of the LGBT community. The community is smaller and subtler in Québec City, but it's no less supported.

Divers/Cité and Celebrations de la Fierte Montréal (Montréal's Pride Celebrations) are the city's two pride festivals, which take place in the summer a few weeks apart. Montréal also hosts a number of dance parties throughout the year aimed at the gay community, including

Black and Blue, a weekend-long party that's been going strong for over 20 years.

Québec City hosts its own annual pride celebration; decorations go up all over rue St-Jean, and Place d'Youville turns into a street party.

RELIGION

There is no denying the influence of the Catholic Church on the history of Québec, and almost every street corner features a three-story high cathedral, though today many of them are now condos. Instrumental in the founding of the nation and throughout most of its history, the Catholic Church only really began to lose its prominence in the 1960s and '70s. For the most part Francophones remain Catholic (though most are non-practicing) and Anglophones are Protestant, but there are also diverse religions encompassing Muslims, Jews, Hindus, and Sikhs.

LANGUAGE

The language issue is arguably the most important for Québécois Francophones since it's really what makes them both distinct and recognizable. They can be very touchy about how other people view their language, be it toward other Francophones who consider *joual* a mere dialect, or toward people who obstinately refuse to make any efforts to speak French. Don't be afraid, though; they're usually not hard to please, and using a mere *bonjour* (hello) or *merci* (thank you) is the safest way to gain their respect. They will often switch to English (even broken English) if they see you struggling.

In order to understand this somewhat intransigent stand on Québécois you have to understand the history. After the British conquest in 1759, even though language, religion, and other rights were granted to the French community, they were barred from political and economical power for a long time. This linguistic exclusionism, in which access to the upper levels of business and power was barred to the French-Canadians, lasted well into the 20th century. In fact, until the 1970s, English-speakers were the minority that ran many of the businesses and held positions of power in the province.

The Quiet Revolution in the 1960s however, helped to change all that as it fostered nationalist sentiment, which reached a peak when the Parti Québécois was elected in 1976. In 1977, Bill 101 was passed, asserting the primacy of French on public signs across the province, and apostrophes were removed from store fronts in the 1980s to comply with French usage. English is allowed on signage as long as it's half the size of the French lettering. Despite the debate that surrounded the bill when it was first implemented, many believe it has helped to preserve the language.

Any one with a good ear will likely be able to tell that there's a big difference between the French spoken here and the French in France. The French here is said to be equivalent to the French spoken in the 17th and 18th centuries in France, preserved due to its geographical isolation. The language spoken in everyday life is very specific and somewhat entertaining, since it's full of funny expressions and syntax. Depending on where you are in the province, some accents are harder to understand than those in the cities.

Unlike in France where they've integrated English terms like "weekend" into regular usage, Québec is much more ardent about the preservation of the language. That's not to say English words aren't in common usage in Québec; there is simply a heightened awareness of them. The Office Québécoise de la Langue Française is an institution whose mandate is to translate new words, typically those related to IT or technology, into a French equivalent. For example, in Québec, email is *courriel,* the French contraction of electronic mail, and Québec's stop signs are also written in French, with the word *arrêt* at their center, though even in France the signs read "stop."

Montréal is the largest French-speaking city outside of Paris, and 57 percent of Montréalers speak both official languages. Young Montréalers are less concerned with language issues than past generations, and a large majority, especially those that come from immigrant families, speak more than two languages.

The Arts

MUSIC

Without a doubt the province's best-known recording artist is Celine Dion. Born in the small town of Charlemagne 30 kilometers from Montréal, she was a mega-star in Québec and France when she was just a teenager and well before she started signing in English. Although she was criticized at first by her Francophone fan base for "selling out," her worldwide success in now a huge source of pride for the province, and fans now love (and buy) her English albums just as much as her French ones.

The province's second biggest export, music-wise, is Montréal's Arcade Fire, who took over the airwaves in 2004 with their infectious indie rock anthems and haven't looked back. Despite their rock star status—they've shared the stage with everyone from David Byrne to David Bowie—they remain active in the community, and many of the group's members play in other Montréal bands. Their success in the early 2000s was also part of a bigger Montréal indie rock explosion, with bands like The Dears, Wolfe Parade, and the Unicorns, among others. The explosion has died down a bit since then, but there is still a huge music scene in Montréal that is constantly evolving. In recent years Francophone bands like Malajube, Radio Radio, and Karkwa—who won the 2010 Polaris Music Prize, Canada's largest for an "indie" band—have been gaining fans across the language divide.

Poet and singer/songwriter Leonard Cohen is one of the city's most-loved inhabitants, and many of his melancholy and soulful compositions were inspired by the city, including the song *So Long Maryanne.* Grammy Award–winning artist Rufus Wainwright is also from Montréal, though he now resides in New York. Mixing symphonic sounds with a pop mentality, his sweeping compositions are utterly unique and catchy. His sister, Martha Wainwright, also a musician, is somewhat less experimental in her style, but it is reminiscent of other forms of music, not just pop. On one of her more recent albums (*Sans Fusils, Ni Souliers, à Paris*) she sings the songs of Edith Piaf. Of course, it helps when you have good genes, and the Wainwrights have them in spades: Their father is American folk singer Loudon Wainwright III, and their mother is Kate McGarrigle; she and her sister Anna are two of the biggest folk singers in the province. Since the 1960s, the McGarrigle sisters have sung and written in both French and English.

It wasn't until the 1960s that modern music really started to hit its stride in the province. Québec held a festival of experimental music in 1961, and by the mid-1960s the symphony was starting to attract a larger audience. It was also the heyday of folk singers or *chansonniers* like Félix Leclerc and Gilles Vigneault. Leclerc in particular had been singing and writing for a long time, even finding success in Paris, before returning to find the same success at home. Singing about themes like nature and celebrations has made him one of the most revered musicians in the province.

CINEMA

After being under religious censorship during the first half of the 20th century, Québec cinema really kicked off in the 1960s, when a generation of directors formed the National Film Board (NFB). This film board gave them a platform, and they started to make movies mostly about the Québécois identity. Part of the enthusiastic social transformations that were happening in arts in this period, they shot documentaries and features that gained international recognition, despite their local flavor. Experiments in documentary film led to the Direct Cinema genre, which included Pierre Perreault's *Pour la Suite du Monde,* a vivid documentary about the ancestral beluga hunt in Isle-aux-Coudres, and Michel Brault's *Les Orders,* a rendition of the October crisis of 1971.

In the 1970s, a number of feature films gained wide critical acclaim and today are seen as part of a golden age in Québec cinema. Among these is *La Vraie Vie de Bernadette* by Gilles Carle (1972), *J.A. Martin Photographe* by Jean Beaudin (1977), and Frank Mankiewicz's *Les Bons Débarras* (1979). Most important of all is Claude Jutra's 1971 movie *Mon Oncle Antoine,* a coming-of-age story set in the rural Québec of the 1940s, which is considered to be the greatest Canadian film.

The Québec film industry is seen as the strongest in the country, and Québec films regularly win top accolades at the Genie Awards, which are the Canadian film industry awards. Québec's French cinema has a stronger character than its English counterpart, which often struggles to differentiate itself from American cinema.

With movies like *Le Déclin de l'Empire Américain* (1986) and *Jésus de Montréal* (1988), Denys Arcand is probably the best-known Québécois director. *Les Invasions Barbares* (2003), a poignant critique of the aging generation of the Quiet Revolution, won the Oscar for Best Foreign Film and was Best Screenplay at Cannes. Other stand-out directors and their work include: Jean-Marc Vallée's *C.R.A.Z.Y.* and François Girard's *32 Short Films about Glenn Gould* and *The Red Violon.* Twenty-something newcomer Xavier Dolan's *J'ai Tué Ma Mère* and *Les Amours Imaginaries* both won big at the Cannes Film Festival and have set the course for a new generation of filmmakers.

LITERATURE

After Paris, Montréal has the most French-language writers in the world, many of whom have been translated into English. Playwright and author Michel Tremblay wrote *Chroniques du Plateau,* which has made him one of the most prolific and well-recognized authors in the province. His stories about working-class French-Canadians in the 1960s, written almost entirely in *joual,* defined the writing of his generation. Other writers include Hubert Aquin, Dany Laferrière, Marie-Claire Blais, and Anne Hébert, whose *Kamouraska* looks at treachery and love in 19th-century Québec. Gabrielle Roy's *The Tin Flute* tells the tale of a young woman in working-class Verdun during the Depression.

English-language Montréal literature has pretty much been defined, and reigned over, by the acerbic wit of Mordecai Richler, who continues to be one of the strongest voices in Anglophone literature, even after his death in 2001. His novels *The Apprenticeship of Duddy Kravitz, Son of a Smaller Hero,* and *St-Urbain's Horseman* defined not only the city's Jewish population but the city itself.

The witty and poignant novels and short stories of Mavis Gallant continue to weave their way through Montréal, despite the fact that she's long since immigrated to France.

New writers include Rawi Hage, who moved to Montréal in 2001 and whose 2006 novel *De Niro's Game* was nominated for the Scotiabank Giller Prize. His second novel, *Cockroach,* is an intimate look at an immigrant's experience in Montréal.

VISUAL ARTS

Early-Québec art can be divided into two subject matters: landscapes and religion. The province's first painters were Catholic missionaries who used paintings and engravings to convert the Amerindians. Since many of the works were by priests and nuns, they have a particularly naïve quality, a trend that continues in Québécois art. The first great Québécois painters emerged in the 19th century and included Théophile Hamel, known for portraits of explorers; Dutch-born Cornelius Krieghoff, who depicted settlers and images of the wilderness; and Ozias Leduc, whose portrait *Boy with Bread* is one of the defining images of Québécois art.

Work continued to be defined by snowy city-scapes and bucolic farmland until the modern era of Canadian painting was ushered in by Paul-Émile Bourduas, John Lyman, and Alfred Pellan in the 1940s. Bourduas was the most prolific and outspoken of all three and developed a radical style of surrealism that came to be identified with a group called the Automatistes.

In 1948 Bourduas published the manifesto *Refus Global* (Global Refusal), rejecting traditional social, artistic, and psychological norms of Québécois society and the religious and bucolic art that defined it. The manifesto called instead for an untamed liberation of creativity and championed abstract art.

Canadian art and Québec's artistic community were never the same again. Automatiste artist Jean-Paul Riopelle would soon emerge as the movement's newest driving force, and his abstract works, called "grand mosaics," would become world-renowned.

The 1960s and '70s were defined by artists like Claude Tousignant and Guido Molinari, whose abstract works used hypnotic geometric shapes and unusual color combinations to almost psychedelic proportions.

Some of Québéc's biggest contemporary artists include David Altmejd, known for mixed-media pieces that incorporate various materials—everything from a decapitated werewolf head to shards of broken mirrors—into something cohesive and anthropomorphic. Valérie Blass also plays with a mix of materials and human yet non-human forms. Adnad Hannah's film and photographic works play with traditional art history. Two of the province's biggest artists are collectives: The work of BGL plays with conventional objects or pop culture icons in unconventional ways—a melted Darth Vader, or a motorcycle covered with snow in the middle of a gallery floor. Cooke et Sasseville play with similar ideas, and one of their works involves a giant flamingo laying its head down on train tracks.

DANCE AND THEATER

The established Québécois culture and the province's bohemian disposition help nurture a particularly diverse arts scene in both languages.

French theater is some of the best in the world, whether you're in Québec City or Montréal, while English theater struggles to keep the pace. The country's top performing arts educational institution, the National Theater School, is found in the Plateau, attracting Canada's most promising playwrights and stage actors in either language.

There is an innovative contemporary dance scene in the province that has fostered internationally recognized companies like La La La Human Steps, O Vertigo, and Fondation Jean-Pierre Perreault as well as the careers of dancers and choreographers Margie Gillis, Marie Chouinard, and Benoît Lachambre. A number of Montréal institutions, like Agora de la Danse, Tangante, and Studio 301, are dedicated exclusively to emerging dance artists. Québec also supports two classical ballet companies, Les Grands Ballets Canadiens and Le Ballet de Québec.

THE CIRCUS

Cirque du Soleil is undoubtedly the most famous Québécois circus, founded in Baie Saint-Paul in the early 1980s by a group of street performers. These stilt-walkers, jugglers, and fire-eaters banded together to create a performance platform, since the circus tradition didn't exist in the province at the time. In the years since then, they've become part of a rich circus culture they helped to create. There are now two schools dedicated to the circus arts: the National Circus School, established in 1981, and Tohu, established in 2004, are both located in Montréal.

Cirque d'Éloize, established in 1993, is another professional company situated in Montréal that is quickly following in the footsteps of Cirque du Soleil when it comes to pushing boundaries and innovation. They bring an edginess and dance sensibility to their shows, which can be seen throughout the world. This dedication to circus arts also means the province has some of the best street performers in the world, who are especially visible during festival season.

ESSENTIALS

Getting There

MONTRÉAL
By Air
All international and in-country flights to Montréal arrive at **Pierre Trudeau International Airport** (514/394-7377, www.admtl.com) in Dorval.

The cheapest way to get from the airport to downtown is to take the 747 Express. The ride on this elongated city bus costs $7 one-way, and the ticket can then be used on other STM buses and Métros throughout the city. The bus takes passengers from the airport to nine downtown intersections, including Berri-UQÀM, the largest Métro station in the city. It runs 24 hours a day, 365 days a year, and takes approximately 40 minutes depending on traffic. During rush hours and bad weather, give yourself an extra 90 minutes leeway.

Airport shuttle **L'Aérobus** departs from the main bus terminal (Gare d'Autocars, 505 blvd. de Maisonneuve E., 514/842-2281, www.stationcentrale.com) and Montréal Trudeau every 30 minutes 9:30 A.M.–9 P.M., after which it runs once every hour, 24 hours a day. One-way tickets cost $16 and can be bought at electronic kiosks at the bus station, at a regular kiosk at the airport, or on the bus. The ride takes about 30 minutes depending on traffic and weather.

A taxi from the airport to downtown will

© TOURISME MONTRÉAL

cost you $35 before tip. All taxis charge the same rate for destinations inside the downtown perimeter.

By Rail

Montréal's train station, **Gare Centrale** (895 rue de la Gauchetière W., 514/989-2626), is located in the downtown core and is a major hub for Canada's **VIA Rail trains** (888/842-7245, www.viarail.ca). **Amtrak** (800/872-7245, www.amtrak.com) has a daily train heading to and from New York City, and though the ride is long—it clocks in at approximately 10 hours—it a scenic one alongside the Hudson River.

By Bus

Montréal's central bus terminal, the **Gare d'Autocars** (505 blvd. de Maisonneuve E., 514/842-2281, www.stationcentrale.com), is located in the Quartier Latin and has a restaurant and an information booth, as well as electronic ticket dispensers, which are often faster than lining up at the ticket counter. It connects with the Berri-UQÀM Métro station, a major junction for the city's subway lines. Taxis are always lined up outside the exit on rue Berri.

By Car

Like most major Canadian cities Montréal is accessible via the Trans-Canadian Highway, which crosses the island with two parallel routes. The southern part of the island can be traversed on Route 20 (Route 720 leads to downtown), the northern part of the island on Route 40; both have exits leading to downtown, including St-Laurent and St-Denis.

Driving up from the United States there are a number of ways to cross the border; from New York State you can take I-87 or I-89 north. From Massachusetts via New Hampshire and Vermont take Route 55. At the border, all travelers must present a valid passport and drivers must show the car's registration.

QUÉBEC CITY
By Air

A number of major airlines fly directly into Québec City's teeny-tiny **Aéroport**

International Jean-Lesage de Québec (418/640-2600, www.aeroportdequebec.com). Most air traffic comes from Montréal though there are a few direct flights from within Canada as well as some international flights, mostly from France and from a few major U.S. cities, including Detroit, Chicago, Newark, and Cleveland.

The airport is about 15 kilometers from downtown; there is no bus or shuttle service available, so the only way to get downtown is by taxi, which will set you back about $35.

By Rail

Train passengers arrive at Québec City at the **Gare du Palais** (450 rue de la Gare-du-Palais, 418/525-3000) in Vieux-Québec's Lower Town. Depending on where you're staying and the amount of baggage you're carrying it might be wise to take a taxi. City buses are also available just outside the terminal to Upper Town, including bus 800, which will take you through Saint-Jean-Baptiste and up to the Grande-Allée, Parliament, and the Plains area. A single ride costs $2.75.

By Bus

Buses to Québec arrive at the same place as the trains at **Gare du Palais** (320 rue Abraham-Martin, 418/525-3000), near the Vieux-Port; most hotels will be a short cab ride or uphill walk away.

By Car

Like Montréal, Québec City can be reached by Autoroute 20 in the south and Autoroute 40 in the north. The drive from Montréal will take approximately two and a half hours, and though the drive along Route 40 is more scenic, it's also a little bit longer. From Toronto, Route 401 connects with Route 20, as do I-87 in New York and I-89 and I-91 in Vermont. Arriving on Route 20, follow the signs for Pont Pierre-Laporte, and once you've crossed the bridge, turn right onto boulevard Laurier, which becomes Grande-Allée. Route 40 turns into boulevard Charest as you approach the city.

TRAVELING BETWEEN MONTRÉAL AND QUÉBEC CITY
By Air

Short-haul 50-minute flights depart from both cities 12 times a day on **Air Canada** (800/247-2262, www.aircanada.com), though by time you go to the airport, check in, and collect your baggage afterwards, it might be just as fast to drive.

By Rail

The train is a fast and fairly efficient way to travel, though the costs can sometimes be prohibitive. **VIA Rail** (888/842-7245, www.viarail.ca) runs the only service between the two cities and offers four daily departures from both **Montréal's Gare Centrale** (895 rue de la Gauchetière W., 514/989-2626) and **Québec City's Gare du Palais** (450 rue de la Gare-du-Palais, 418/525-3000). Train times run anywhere from three to three and a half hours, and a regular one-way ticket costs $102 before taxes, though seat sales can bring the price as low as $60.

By Bus

Both cities are served by the **Orléans Express** (888/999-3977, www.orleansexpress.com), with hourly departures from both **Montréal's Gare d'Autocars** (505 blvd. de Maisonneuve E., 514/842-2281, www.stationcentrale.com) and **Québec's Gare du Palais** (320 rue Abraham-Martin, 418/525-3000). A round-trip ticket costs approximately $80 and the ride can take anywhere from three to five hours.

By Car

Driving between the two cities is often the quickest and easiest. Take Autoroute 20 or Route 40 out of either city and head in the direction of the opposite city. Arriving in Québec on Route 20, follow the signs for Pont Pierre-Laporte and then exit onto boulevard Laurier, which becomes Grande-Allée. If you're on Route 40, it will turn into boulevard Charest as you approach Québec.

Heading into Montréal on Route 20, follow the signs for Pont Jacques-Cartier, which will take you straight into the heart of the Plateau. From Route 40 exit on any number of southbound streets, including Papineau, St-Denis, and St-Laurent.

There are also a couple of ride-share companies that can help save costs for both drivers and passengers: **Allo Stop** (www.allostop.com) and **Amigo Express** (www.amigoexpress.com).

Getting Around

PUBLIC TRANSPORTATION
Montréal

Montréal's Métro and bus system is run by the **STM** (Société de Transport de Montréal, 514/786-4656, www.stm.info). The **Métro** is quick, safe, and efficient and consists of five lines. It is easy to navigate. A single fare on both bus and Métro is $2.75, 12 tickets will set you back $13.50, and a weekly pass costs $22 for unlimited access. If you're in town for a short stay and plan to take the Métro often in one day get the unlimited day pass for $7. Sales are cash only at the ticket booth, but you can use both debit and credit cards at the newly installed automated machines.

Individual tickets also count as your transfer, so if you're planning on getting off the Métro and hopping onto a bus make sure you keep the card with you. The Métro runs 5 A.M.–1 A.M.

Métro and bus tickets are interchangeable, but if you want to get on the bus and don't have a ticket, make sure you have exact change. Once you've paid for your bus ticket make sure to take a transfer, which will look a regular ticket, especially if you're heading to the Métro or want to take another bus. Buses run all night long on many major streets, including Sherbrooke, Mont-Royal, St-Laurent, St-Denis, and avenue du Parc, but the nightbus number is often different from the daytime the Métro at Square Victoria in Montréal

number so double-check with the driver before you hop on.

Québec City

Québec City buses (www.rtcquebec.ca) are fast and efficient, with three major bus lines, called **MétroBus**, that run frequently and cover all the major areas of the city—some will even take you as far out as Chute Montmorency. A single bus ticket costs $2.60 and also acts as a transfer if you're transferring lines; if you don't have a ticket the bus accepts exact change.

The city also has a few buses aimed at tourists. The **Navette Desjardins** runs from June to mid-October and carries passengers from Beauport and Domain des Maizrets, north of the city, through the Vieux-Port and Lower Town and out to the Aquarium du Quebec and Promenade de Samuel de Champlain. A ticket costs $3 for all-day unlimited use, and a child rides for $1.50. Carrying approximately 20 passengers at a time, the **Ecobus** costs $1 and takes you from Vieux-Québec Lower Town to Upper Town.

DRIVING

In Montréal it is illegal to make a right-hand turn on a red light. Once you're off-island, it is fair game, but not in the city. Full of one-way streets and busy boulevards, Montréal is an easy city to navigate by car. But traffic, especially during rush hours or during construction (most of the time), gets a little out of hand. Parking can also be a real pain in the city, especially on quiet residential streets where permits, usually for residents only, are required. Free parking downtown is especially hard to come by, but there are meters that start around $3 per hour. Most of the meters are now automated and each parking spot is given a specific number; you punch that number into the machine and then place the receipt on your dashboard. If you don't see a machine but see a number on the spot, you're not looking far enough; some machines can be half a block away.

For a city that gets such cold winters underground parking lots are hard to find, though the majority of them exist downtown and offer reasonable day rates. Parking, underground or otherwise, isn't always included with the price of your hotel, so double-check before you book. Overall, driving in the city can be a time waster; it's best to use a car just for side trips and excursions.

Though you *can* make a right on a red in Québec City, driving is not ideal, especially if you're heading into Vieux-Québec's Upper and Lower Towns. The small, winding streets make them difficult to navigate, especially if you're not used to that type of driving. In the summer many of the streets are blocked off to accommodate pedestrians, mainly during the day and into the night. In the winter it's these same streets that are covered in ice and snow. Though there is less traffic in general in Québec City, parking is still a problem, especially on streets with slopes of 45 degrees. And much like Montréal the city has very few underground parking lots.

The speed limit on Canadian highways is 100 kilometers per hour (kph), and it's 50 kph on city streets unless otherwise noted. U.S. citizens don't need an international license and neither do drivers from England or France. If your driver's license is in a language other than English or French, you need an International Driver's Permit; see the Québec government website (www.saaq.gouv.qc.ca) for more information. Members of AAA (American Automobile Association, www.aaa.com) are covered under the Canadian equivalent CAA (www.caa.ca). Gasoline is more expensive than in the United States so fill up before crossing the border.

Rental Cars
Many of the large rental companies (Avis, Budget, Discount) are available in Montréal and Québec City. The minimum age to rent a vehicle is 25, and rates run the gamut from $34 per day to $60 depending on time of year.

If you're renting from downtown to head out of the city on weekends, plan ahead; many Montréalers have the same idea.

TAXIS
Montréal and Québec City both have a ton of different taxi companies. **Taxi Champlain** (514/273-2435) and **Taxi Co-op** (514/725-9885) can be found in Montréal. Try **Taxi Coop Québec** (418/525-5191) in Québec City. The initial charge is $3.30, each kilometer adds $1.60, and each minute of waiting is $0.60. Tip is usually 10–15 percent. Some drivers know the city well, others not so much, so make sure you have your destination with the cross street written down to show the driver, especially if it's a word you're unsure how to pronounce.

BICYCLING
In Montréal between April and November **Bixi bikes** (www.bixi.com) are available around the city. These are one of the fastest ways to get around and are easy to use. Swipe your credit card to get a number code, then type that number code into the bike of your choice to unlock it, and you're ready to ride. When you get to your destination return the Bixi to a station and make sure it is locked in. A trip under 30 minutes will cost you $5; after that a charge of $1.50 to $6 for each subsequent 30-minute period will apply. A $28 per month plan is available through the website.

Unless you're an experienced biker and brought your own ride, biking in Québec City is not recommended; there are some seriously steep hills that aren't fun going up or down. That being said, if you're planning on staying exclusively, or at least mostly, in Lower Town or Upper Town, then renting a bike is a great way to get around, and will allow you to ride along the river and the Vieux-Port.

Visas and Officialdom

PASSPORTS AND VISAS

All visitors must have a valid passport or other accepted secure documents to enter the country, even those entering from the United States by road or train. Citizens of the United States, Australia, New Zealand, Israel, Japan, and most western European countries don't need visas to enter Canada for stays up to 180 days. U.S. permanent residents are also exempt. Travelers who travel regularly between Canada and the United States should consider getting a Nexus membership; details are available at www.cdp.gov.

Nationals from South Africa, China, and about 150 other countries must apply for a temporary resident visa (TRV) in their home country. Full details can be found at **Citizen and Immigration Canada** (888/242-2100, www.cic.gc.ca). Single-entry visitor visas are valid for six months and cost $75; multiple-entry visas last for two years, as long as a single stay doesn't last for longer than six months, and cost $150. A separate visa is required if you intend to work in Canada.

CUSTOMS

Depending on how long your stay in Canada is, you're allowed to take various amounts of goods back home without paying any duty or import tax. There is a limit on the amount of tobacco and liquor you can bring back duty-free, and some countries have a limit on perfumes. For exact amounts check with the customs department in your home country. Also check the **Canadian Border Services Agency** (505/636-5064, www.cbsa-asfa.gc.ca) for details on bringing in and taking home goods.

There are very strict rules on bringing plants, flowers, food, and other vegetation into the country, so it's not advisable to bring them. If you're 18 years or older you're allowed to bring into the country 50 cigars or 200 grams of tobacco, as well as 1.14 liters of liquor, 1.5 liters of wine, or 24 cans or bottles of beer. If you bring more, you'll face a hefty fine. Those traveling with their pets will need a health certificate and a rabies vaccination certificate. The vaccination must be carried out 30 days before your departure. Nonresidents can be refunded for the GST (government sales tax) paid on purchases made in Canada. If you want a refund, however, keep your receipts; to be eligible your receipts must add up to $200. Call 800/668-4748 for details.

Conduct and Customs

MOVING DAY

While the rest of the country celebrates Canada Day, the nation's national holiday, on July 1, Quebeckers move. It is the unofficial moving day for renters across the province—this is the day most leases change hands—and it is usually a hot, sweaty day with cars, vans, trucks, SUVs, and even bikes loaded to the hilt and headed for new digs. It's also not uncommon to see people simply schlepping their belongings by foot.

Don't even think about renting a car on this day, as there likely won't be any left. A thrifter's paradise, the aftermath of the move leaves sidewalks and alleyways littered with discarded belongings and unwanted junk, which may turn out to be your treasure.

ALCOHOL

As in all Canadian provinces, if you're looking for wine, beer, or spirits, you have to get it at the **SAQ** (Société des Alcools de Québec, www.saq.ca), the store run by the provincial liquor board. Found all over the city, they carry a wide selection of wine and spirits and a small selection of imported beer. Québec differs from most other provinces in that beer and wine can also be purchased in your local grocery and corner stores.

The selection of wine and beer varies from store

SWEARING IN QUÉBÉCOIS

In Québec, swearing is its own language. Instead of being derived from naughty sexual innuendo, however, swear words come from Catholicism and its practices. Originating in the early 19th century, many of the swear words or *sacres* developed out of a frustration at the church that seemingly controlled everything. The church is much less influential since the Quiet Revolution, and though the swear words are still in use they are no longer as powerful and have become part of common language. Even English-speakers get into the habit, especially when talking with Québécois friends.

Among the most popular *sacres* and the ones you'll likely hear the most are *crisse* (Christ), *tabarnak* (from tabernacle), *ostie* (from host), and *sacrement* (from sacrement). Like all good swear words, however, they work best when used together, as in *criss d'ostie de tabarnak*, which defies translation.

Another word you might hear is *fucké*, which, weirdly enough, has nothing to do with the English pejorative; instead it means strange or bizarre, as in "*ce film était vraiment fucké*," or "that film was really weird."

to store; if you're in an upscale neighborhood the selection of wine at both the *dépanneur* (corner store) and the grocery store will likely be of a higher caliber than what you'd find elsewhere. (Montréalers commonly use the term "*dép* wine" to denote over-priced cheap-quality wine—though that's not always the case.) If you're looking for beer, a *dép* is your best bet. If you don't find the brand you're looking for just step into the fridge yourself; it might look like just another display case but step through the camouflaged door and you're in beerville. Drinking age in Québec is 18, and stores stop selling alcohol at 11 o'clock at night.

STRIP CLUBS

Montréal is known for its strip clubs, a long and proud tradition that's been part of the city's landscape since the early 20th century. They are as out in the open as you can get, with many of them slotted in between shops on rue Ste-Catherine. In fact, Super Sexe, one of the larger clubs in the city, is hard to miss, since its facade is adorned with an illuminated mural of flying women in capes and bikinis.

There are over 40 strip clubs to choose from, both full-contact and non-contact. Full-contact dances are legal in Québec, and popular. Dancers work on a freelance basis, which allows them to work at any club they'd like, and some work at both full- and non-contact bars.

Embracing its position as a sex-positive city, in Montréal it's not unusual to see women in strip clubs, and one of the most popular clubs in town, for both men and women, is Café Cleopatra, which has a popular transvestite cabaret on the second floor. Québec City has far fewer strip clubs but the same ethos applies (though you won't find them along a main shopping strip).

TIPPING

Tips and service charges aren't covered in the bill; instead a 15 percent tip should be added to the total bill at restaurants and bars at which you run a tab. When you order a drink at a bar, you're usually expected to pay when the drink is brought to you; a $1–2 tip for drinks is the standard. Tip the same for a valet parking attendant, bellhops at the hotel, and coat-check attendants. Chambermaids should be tipped $3–5.

SMOKING

Since May 2006, smoking is illegal in bars, cafés, clubs, and restaurants and not permitted in enclosed public spaces. Outdoors on the sidewalk or on a restaurant's or bar's patio is fair game. Some hotels, however, still have smoking and non-smoking options, though it's becoming rarer. There are a few cigar bars, including Whisky Café in Montréal and Société Cigare in Québec City, where smoking indoors is allowed due to specialized ventilation systems. You must be 18 years or older to buy tobacco in Québec.

Tips for Travelers

TRAVELING WITH CHILDREN

There are a ton of kid-friendly activities in Montréal and Québec City, most of which will tucker any kid out by the end of the day. Top choices include ice-skating and tobogganing in winter, wading pools and bike rides along the canal in summer. Public parks with playgrounds can be found throughout both cities and are perfect for blowing off some steam. However, some of the sleeker, cooler boutique hotels might not be the most fun for the kids. Children are also given half-price or free entry to most museums and attractions, or they offer family rates. Hotels will recommend babysitting services if none are available in-house.

WOMEN TRAVELERS

Montréal and Québec are relatively safe cities and women should feel at ease traveling alone in both. Still, the usual rules apply; women should avoid walking alone on quiet streets and dimly lit areas, such as Mont-Royal, late at night. Violence is far less prevalent here than in the States, but if you are attacked or sexually assaulted call 911 or the **Sexual Assault Center** (514/934-4504 in Montréal and 418/522-2120 in Québec City).

LGBT TRAVELERS

Québec is one of the top destinations for gay travelers. In 1977 Québec became the second political entity (after Holland) to include a non-discrimination clause on the basis of sexual orientation in its charter of rights. Gay marriage is legal in Québec, and attitudes toward homosexuality in the province are open and tolerant.

Of the two cities, Montréal is the queer capital, and **Tourisme Montréal** (www.tourisme-montreal.org) even has a gay and lesbian mini-site with suggestions for hotels, restaurants, meet-ups, and beyond. There's even the **Village Tourism Information Centre** (249 rue St-Jacques #302, 888/595-8110, summer Tues.–Thurs., winter Mon.–Fri.), which offers information on everything from restaurants to

A bike ride along the Lachine Canal in Montréal is a fun kid-friendly activity.

WINTER ESSENTIALS

If you want to fit in among the locals during winter's deep freeze you need two things: a parka and a pair of Sorel boots.

- **The Parka:** When it comes to parkas there are two schools: The younger generation goes for a selection from Canada Goose, while many mature Quebeckers opt for the Kanuk. Both are made in Canada and offer that important balance of warmth without the puffiness. When buying a parka the goal is to avoid the "Michelin Man" look; don't buy white and stay away from anything that has a ringed effect. Make sure it's got a fur-trimmed hood and covers your bum – good coverage is essential, especially when you want to take a crazy carpet down Mont-Royal.

- **The Boots:** Made with a heavy insulated rubber sole and sturdy leather, Sorel winter boots have been a Canadian staple since 1959. Introduced to the market by Kaufman

Footwear of Kitchener, Ontario, the boots were an instant hit. Originally they were made in Canada, but the company was bought by Columbia Sports in 2000. Though the boots are no longer Canadian owned and made, there is still a strong connection to their Canadian heritage. The ingenious construction of a thermal, waterproof sole paired with a more stylish upper is ideal for city life when 99.9 percent of the time you're walking through freezing gray slush.

- **The Fur:** Another popular winter material in Québec is fur, and it's not unusual to see both men and women covered in fur from head to toe. If you find fur offensive try to suppress your inner activist and instead take a deep breath – see that? Your nose is now completely frozen. Fur in Québec is less about style and more about survival and heritage, and many of the furs have been passed down through family members.

places to workout and is run by the **Québec Gay Chamber of Commerce** (www.ccgq.ca). **CAEO Québec** (www.caeoquebec.org) offers services for Montréal's English-speaking LGBT community and is behind **Gay Line** (888/505-1010), a help line that offers information on accommodations, services, and events.

Though there are a number of LGBT publications, monthly magazine *Fugues* (www.fugues.com) is the most comprehensive and has information on everything from hotels to saunas and up-coming gay events. It's available for free at racks around the city.

TRAVELERS WITH DISABILITIES

Most public buildings, including tourist offices, museums, and sights, are wheelchair accessible. Métro stations in Montréal, however are not accessible; instead almost all major bus routes are serviced by NOVA LFS buses adapted for wheelchairs. See www.stm.info from full details about your journey.

Access to Travel (www.accesstotravel.gc.ca) is a guide to accessible transportation across the country.

Kéroul (514/252-3104, www.keroul.qc.ca) is an association that specializes in tourism for people with disabilities. It publishes *Québec Accessible,* which lists 1,000-plus hotels, restaurants, museums, and theaters that are accessible. For English speakers, there is *The Accessible Road,* which offers information on everything from the most accessible top sights to how to get a handicapped parking sticker. It can be downloaded for free from the website.

Health and Safety

HOSPITALS AND CLINICS

Canadians have free health care, but it's not free for visitors, so be sure to get travel insurance before you leave your home country. Montréal has a number of high-ranking hospitals, but the emergency room wait can be lengthy, and if you're not a Canadian citizen the treatment could be pricey (though not compared to U.S. hospitals).

Emergency rooms can be found in Montréal at **Montréal General Hospital** (1650 ave. Cedar, 514/934-1934, ext. 42190) and **Royal Victoria Hospital** (ave. des Pins W., 514/934-1934, ext. 31557). There's also the **Montréal Children's Hospital** (2300 Tupper, 514/412-4400). In Québec City head to the **Hôpital Laval** (2725 chemin Ste-Foy, 418/656-8711).

For minor maladies visit walk-in-clinic **CLSC** (514/527-2361, www.santemontreal. qc.ca); the one closest to downtown Montréal is at Guy-Concordia Métro station (1801 blvd. de Maisonneuve W., 514/934-0354), or call to find the closest one. In Québec City the closest clinic can be found by calling 418/529-4777 or checking online at www.csssvc.qc.ca. Though the clinics will be glad to help you, you will have to pay cash to see a doctor; they don't take debit or credit.

If you're feeling unwell and just want some advice, call the health hotline (811) from any land line to speak with a nurse 24 hours a day.

PHARMACIES

There are two big pharmacy chains in Montréal, Pharmaprix (www.pharmaprix.ca) and Jean Coutu (www.jeancoutu.com), both of which offer late-night services at various locations. **Pharmaprix** (1500 rue Ste-Catherine W., 514/933-4744, daily 8 A.M.–midnight) also has a 24-hour location north of Mont-Royal (5122 chemin de la Côte-des-Neiges, 514/738-8464). **Jean Coutu** (1675 rue Ste-Catherine W., 514/933-4221, Mon.–Sat. 8 A.M.–midnight, Sun. 9 A.M.–midnight) is another option.

In Québec City the largest pharmacy is **Jean Coutu** (110 blvd. René-Lévesque, 418/522-1235, Mon.–Sat. 9 A.M.–9 P.M., Sun. 10 A.M.–9 P.M.), near avenue Cartier.

EMERGENCY SERVICES

The fire department, police, and ambulance can all be reached by dialing **911.** When in doubt you can reach the operator by dialing **0.** There's also the **Poison Center** (800/463-5060) if you're worried about something you've ingested.

CRIME AND HARASSMENT

Both Montréal and Québec City are relatively safe and violent crime is rare. Tourists are more likely to be the targets of thieves, like pickpockets at crowded bars, markets, and Métro stations. Cars with out-of-province license plates are also targets so make sure not to leave anything of value in the car and remove your car registration and identification papers. Pedestrians in Montréal should be careful, especially late at night when drivers don't always heed stop signs.

Information and Services

MONEY

Prices quoted in this book are in Canadian dollars. Canadian coins come in 1-cent (penny), 5-cent (nickel), 10-cent (dime), 25-cent (quarter), $1 (loonie) and $2 (toonie) pieces. Paper money comes in $5 (blue), $10 (purple), $20 (green), $50 (red), and $100 (brown). Though the Canadian dollar's value was once much lower than the American dollar, it now trades at a few cents off par: www.xe.com has the most current rates.

ATMs

ATMs are all round the city, not just in banks. Though if you're getting money out from a foreign account the safest way is to get it from a proper bank machine, to avoid fraud. Most banks charge you an additional fee when you withdraw a currency different from that of your home country as well as the original transaction fee. Also, double-check your daily withdrawal limit, so you don't get caught short.

Changing Money

Counters dedicated solely to exchanging money are becoming rarer and rarer. It's much simpler just to head to the bank; you'll find plenty in Montréal on rue Ste-Catherine, boulevard St-Laurent, and rue St-Denis. Foreign-exchange desks can also be found at the main tourist office and at the airport. In Montréal there's **Calforex** (1230 Peel, 514/392-9100), and in Québec City try **Transchange International** (43 rue de Baude, 418/694-6906).

Credit Cards

Major international credit cards are accepted at most stores, hotels, and restaurants. Carrying a credit card means you don't have the worry of carrying cash and it also gives you excellent exchange rates. Visa and Mastercard are the most widely accepted, though certain places also accept American Express and Diners Club.

MAPS AND TOURIST INFORMATION

Airports have information offices open year-round. Information for Montréal can be obtained from **Tourisme Montréal** (877/266-5687, www.tourism-montreal.org). For Québec province info about Montréal, Québec City, and environs visit **Bonjour Québec** (www.bonjourquebec.com).

Montréal has two main tourist offices. **Centre Infotouriste** (1001 rue Square Dorchester, daily 9 A.M.–6 P.M.) will help you rent boats or cars, plan a city tour, and even reserve a hotel room. Though not as big, **Old Montréal Tourist Office** (174 rue Notre-Dame E., June–Oct. daily 9 A.M.–7 P.M., Oct.–June daily 9 A.M.–5 P.M.) is also helpful.

In Vieux-Québec's Upper Town there's **Centre Infotouriste** (12 rue Ste-Anne, 800/363-7777, late June–early Oct. daily 9 A.M.–7 P.M., Oct.–June daily 9 A.M.–5 P.M.), and backing on to the Plains of Abraham is another **Centre Infotouriste** (835 ave. Wilfrid-Laurier, 800/266-5687, late June–late Aug. daily 9 A.M.–7 P.M., late Aug.–mid-June daily 9 A.M.–5 P.M.).

COMMUNICATIONS AND MEDIA
Phones
TELEPHONES

Thanks to the massive popularity of cell phones, public pay phones are becoming almost impossible to find, but if you do manage to fine one, a single local call will set you back $0.50. Though many are coin operated, some also accept phone cards and credit cards. The main area code for Montréal is **514,** though some newer numbers have the **438** area code. Québec City's area code is **418.** When dialing local numbers you must include the area code.

Toll-free numbers begin with **800, 866,** or **888** and must be preceded by a 1. Most of these numbers work in both Canada and the United States, but some may only work in a specified province. Dialing **0** for the operator or **911** for emergency services is free of charge from land lines and public phones, but calling **411** for directory assistance will cost you.

CELL PHONES
Tribrand model cell phones working on GSM 1900 and other frequencies are the only foreign cell phones that will work in Canada. If your phone doesn't work, it might be worth picking up an inexpensive phone at an electronics store and getting a pay-as-you-go plan. Travelers from the United States will likely have service, though roaming charges will probably apply; check with your provider for details.

Internet Services
A number of cafés offer free Wi-Fi; you can register for free at **Île Sans Fil** (www.ilesansfil.org) and find out where the 150-plus places are where you can get online with your laptop. Visit www.zapquebec.org for free Wi-Fi in Québec. If you left your computer at home you can check your email, for around $5, at a few places in downtown Montréal, including **Chapters Bookstore** (1171 rue Ste-Catherine W., 514/849-8825, daily 9 A.M.–11 P.M.) and **Netopia** (1737 rue St-Denis, 514/286-5446, 24 hours). In Québec City head to **Centre Internet** (52 Côte-du-Palais, 418/692-3359, daily 9:30 A.M.–9:30 P.M.) in Upper Town.

In Québec City, a couple of libraries offer free Internet access to visitors. **Bibliothèque Saint-Jean-Baptiste** (755 rue St-Jean, 418/641-6798, Mon.–Tues. and Thurs. noon–5 P.M., Wed. noon–8 P.M., Fri. 10 A.M.–5:30 P.M., Sat. 1–5 P.M.), in the Faubourg Saint-Jean-Baptiste offers an hour of free access, and **Bibliothèque Gabrielle-Roy** (350 rue St-Joseph E., 418/641-6789, Mon.–Fri. 8:30 A.M.–9 P.M., Sat.–Sun. 10 A.M.–5 P.M.) in Saint-Roch offers two hours of free access.

In Montréal, the **Atwater Library** (1200 Atwater, 514/935-7344, www.atwaterlibrary.ca, Mon. and Wed. 10 A.M.–8 P.M., Tues., Thurs., and Fri. 10 A.M.–6 P.M., Sat. 10 A.M.–5 P.M.)

offers Internet services for $4 per hour as well as free Wi-Fi access.

Many hotels, though not all, offer free Wi-Fi access, and the majority also have public computers.

Mail Services
Montréal's main post office is at 1250 rue University, but there are a number of locations downtown and around. If you know the post code of where you're staying, you can look up the closest branch to you at www.canadapost.ca or call **Canada Post** (866/607-6301) for general information.

Québec City's main post office is at 5 rue du Fort in Upper Town and offers a number of services. Stamps can also be purchased at newsstands, convenience stores, and tourist shops. Standard first-class airmail postage for letters and postcards costs $0.54 to Canadian destinations and $0.98 to the United States. Other destinations cost $1.65.

Newspapers and Periodicals
Montréal's only English-language daily paper is the *Gazette* (www.montrealgazette.com), which covers local and national news as well as arts and politics. Alternative weeklies such as the Montréal *Mirror* (www.montrealmirror.com) and the *Hour* (www.hour.ca) cover local news and entertainment with a focus on arts, music, and film happenings in the city.

The Globe & Mail (www.globeandmail.com) and the *National Post* (www.nationalpost.com) are the country's two national papers, and while both cover national and international events as well as the arts, the *Globe* leans more to the center-left and the *Post* to the right.

For French readers there's the federalist *La Presse* and separatist-leaning *Le Devoir,* both of which cover the news and art of the entire province, not just the Francophone community (though that's a large part of it). There's also *Le Journal de Montréal,* a tabloid paper, whose writers and editors have been on strike for the past two years (though that hasn't stopped the paper's sales). And in Québec there's *Le Soleil,* a great little paper with a focus on events in the capital. There's also the Francophone alternative weekly *Voir* (www.voir.ca), in both a Montréal and Québec version, great for getting the latest scoop on what's going on in town or for scoping out their restaurant reviews.

L'actualité is the Québec monthly news magazine, and *Maclean's* is Canada's only weekly news magazine.

Television

The main public-radio and television stations are run by the Canadian Broadcasting Corporation. The CBC is the English-language component and Radio-Canada is the French-language component; both are revered for their long broadcast history. The other major English-language network is the Canadian Television Network (CTV), which broadcasts both Canadian and U.S. programs as well as nightly newscasts.

For Francophone audiences there's Télé-Québec (TVA) and Télévision Quatre-Saison (TQS), both of which broadcast news programs, movies, and shows from France as well as dubbed American sitcoms and dramas.

Radio

There are a number of Francophone and Anglophone radio stations in Montréal, but stations in Québec are mostly Francophone, with the exception of the English-language artists they play. Many young, English-speaking Montréalers are fans of CBC Montréal 1 (88.5 FM), sort of the area's version of NPR. It has educational and cultural programs, and CBF (95.1 FM) is its French counterpart. Fans of Led Zeppelin hear them on heavy rotation on CHOM (97.7 FM); though it also plays alternative music, it's primarily classic rock. CKUT (90.3) FM) is a nonprofit station that plays an eclectic mix of music and news stories. CISM (89.3 FM) is Université de Montréal's

station, with a focus on indie and Francophone tunes. CJFM (95.9 FM) is Virgin Radio playing top 40 hits all day long, and CKGM (990 AM) is your classic oldies station.

In Québec City, however, Anglophones can tune into CBC Québec 1 (104.7 FM streaming), the city's only English-language radio station for all their cultural, news, and educational programs. Tune into CHYZ (94.3 FM) to hear what the students at Université Laval are listening to. CHIK (98.9 FM) gives you top pop and Francophone hits, and Radio-Canada (106.3 FM) keeps you informed in French about news and culture.

WEIGHTS AND MEASURES
Electricity

Like the U.S. and Japan, Canada uses 110-volt, 60-cycle electrical power. Canadian electrical goods have a plug with two flat, vertical prongs and sometimes a third rounded prong. Travelers from outside North America should bring a plug adapter for small appliances.

Measurements

Canada uses the metric system of measurement. Distances are measured in kilometers, liquids in liters and milliliters, but height, strangely enough, is measured in feet.

Time

Montréal and Québec City are both on eastern standard time (EST/EDT), the same as New York and Toronto. Canada switches to daylight saving time (one hour later than standard time) from the second Sunday in March to the first Sunday in November. "Spring forward, fall back," is a simple way to remember how to set your clocks properly. In Québec the 24-hour clock is used for most schedules, including movies and trains.

RESOURCES

Glossary

l'Abitation the first settlement (habitation)

allongé a long espresso coffee, the French name for an Italian *lungo*

Anglophone a native English speaker

Bill 101 a Québec law that deals with French and English language issues

boîte à chansons a place where you can hear singer/songwriters *(chansonniers)* play

boreal the type of forest that is found in the province of Québec

branchée plugged in, which translates to hip, or cool, in the French vernacular

brasserie a brewery or pub

brioche a type of sweet French bread

cabane à sucre a sugar shack; this is where you go to see maple syrup tapped from trees and eat maple-drenched treats

café where you buy coffee as well as the drink itself; usually refers to an espresso

calèche a horse-drawn carriage

chansonnier a folk singer/songwriter

côte hill; so if a street has "côte" in its name it's on a hill

coureurs de bois early fur hunters and adventurers who helped explore North America

dépanneur meaning "to help out"; it's the name for convenience stores in Québec, which are commonly referred to as *"dép."*

First Nations the name for Canada's Amerindian population

frites French fries

joual a popular form of slang

loonie Canadian one-dollar coin

Nouvelle France the name given to Québec by the French; it also means New France

pâté chinois a meat, potato, and vegetable pie similar to shepherd's pie

patriotes the name given to patriots who led an uprising against the government in 1837; it's used today to denote those who are against federal rule

pont a bridge

poudreuse blowing snow

quai quay that juts out into the water

Quebecker English name for all native citizens of the province of Québec

Québécois the name for the Francophone population in the province as well as the language they speak

Refus Global (Total Refusal) a manifesto of a group of Québec artists that radically changed the face of modern Québec art

sacres the name for Québécois swear words

sandwicherie a place that makes sandwiches

sloche slush made from melted snow

sovereigntists those who want Québec to separate from the rest of Canada

stimés hot dog with a steamed bun

Sulpicians society of Catholic priests founded in Paris in 1641 who were part of the founding of Québec

table d'hôte a fixed-price meal

terrasse an outdoor patio

terroir food products that come from the area, as in "terroir" cooking

tire sur la neige maple syrup that has been frozen on snow, a popular treat during the sugaring-off season

toastés hot dog with a toasted bun

toonie a Canadian two-dollar coin

tourtière a meat pie made with everything from pork and beef to game

viennoiseries pastries and sweet breads usually eaten at breakfast

French Phrasebook

If you're uncomfortable about breaking out your rusty 10th-grade French, relax. You might not even crease the spine of this phrasebook since just about everyone in Montréal understands English, even if they're not adept at speaking it. In Québec City their English isn't as fluid, but those who work in tourism and hospitality speak it flawlessly. Even if you do feel confident with your French, the Québécois accent will take some getting used to, and the language you hear on the street won't have much to do with the words you read in this phrasebook. The Québécois also have a tendency to speak very fast, so don't be afraid to ask them to slow down if you're having trouble understanding.

As has been explained throughout the guide, language is a central issue in Québec, so a good rule of thumb is to be polite; the Québécois are especially receptive to people who are at least trying to speak a little French, and they're always encouraging. Throw in a few easy French words here and there like *bonjour* or *merci* and you'll soon earn a friend for life, or at least gain their respect.

PRONUNCIATION

French is known for being difficult to pronounce – and as payback for creating such a difficult language, French-speakers are unable to properly pronounce any other language. When it comes to phonetic pronunciation, French is as bad as English. Most of the spellings and the pronunciations don't have much in common, which can make learning French difficult. Here are a few guidelines to get you started.

Vowels

Vowels in French can be confusing for an English speaker: the 'a' is **e,** the 'e' is **i,** and the **u** is from outer space. Here is the secret:

a pronounced 'a,' as in "cat."

i pronounced 'ee,' as in "free."

y pronounced the same way as i.

o pronounced 'aw,' as in "dog," or 'o,' as in "bone."

u This vowel has always been a tough one for English-speakers. The closest you can get would be to put your lips and tongue in position to say 'oh' and try to say 'ee' instead. If you assume your non-Frenchness, something like the 'ew' in "stew" is not that far.

e pronounced 'uh,' as 'a' in "about." Before two or more consonants, it is pronounced 'eh' as in "set." At the end of a word, such as *chaise* (chair), **e** is silent, except in words of one syllable like *je* (I), where it is pronounced 'uh.'

Vowel Groups

To make things harder, French assembles these letters to produce new sounds.

ai pronounced 'e,' as in "set," as well as **ei.**

au pronounced 'o,' as in "bone," as well as **eau.**

eu pronounced 'uh,' as in "about." It is sometimes spelled **œu,** as in *œuf* or *sœur.*

oi pronounced 'wa,' as in "wagon."

ou pronounced 'oo,' as in "foot."

Nasal Vowels

A typical aspect of French speech is nasal vowels, vowels pronounced through both the mouth and nose. They are as difficult for English-speakers to reproduce as the **u** and will require quite a bit of phonetic gymnastics before you get it right.

an, am pronounced 'ahn,' as in "aunt."

en, em sounds pretty close to 'ahn' as well but with a twist toward the 'on' of "honk."

in where the 'a' of "bag" is nasalized as in "anchor." You'll find more or less the same sound in many different spellings, such as **im, un, um, yn, ym, ain, aim, ein,** and **eim!**

on, om is a nasalized **o** pronounced like the 'on' of "long."

Accents

French has five different accents that stick to vowels and make French as exotic to read as it is to hear: In French they are called *accent aigu* (´), accent grave (`), accent circonflexe (^), accent tréma (¨), and the cédille (ç), which is only used with the letter 'c.'

The circumflex and grave accents appear as **è, à, ù, ê, â, û, î,** and **ô.** Except for the **ê** and the **è,** which are pronounced 'eh' as in "set," and the **ô,** which always sounds like 'o' as in "bone," the accents don't change the pronunciation of the letters; they are mere decoration.

The acute accent, as in **é,** is pronounced 'ay' as in "day," but shorter. The little thing hanging down from the 'c,' the cedilla, makes 'c' sounds like 's' and is there every time you write *français.*

Last but not the least, the dieresis (*tréma*) separates two vowel sounds, such as **ï** in *naïve,* which is not pronounced 'nev' but as two separate syllables, 'na-ive.'

Consonants

Most French consonants are similar to their English equivalents, even if there are a few differences. For example, *some* final consonants are silent; rather than pronouncing *vous* as "vooz," you'd say "voo." In general the following consonants are usually silent: **b, d, g, m, n, p, t, x,** and **z. S** is always silent in plurals but often pronounced otherwise. Others are generally pronounced: **c, f,** and **l. R** is usually pronounced except in the endings **er** and **ier.** Differences between the consonants in English:

c pronounced 'k' as in "kick" before **a, o,** or **u,** and 's' as in "set" before **e, i,** or **y.** Combine a **c** and an **h,** as in *chance* (luck), and it is pronounced like 'sh' as in "ship."

g pronounced 'g' as in "god," except when placed before **e, i,** or **y,** when it is pronounced 'zh' as in "measure." Combine it with an **n,** as in *vigne* (vine), and it is pronounced like 'ny' in "canyon."

h is always silent.

j pronounced 'zh' as in "measure."

ll pronounced 'y' as in "yes," in words like *famille.*

r is emphasized more strongly than in English and comes from the far back of the throat.

BASIC EXPRESSIONS

Hello *Bonjour*
Hi *Salut*

Good-bye *Au revoir/Salut*
Good morning/afternoon *Bonjour*
Good evening *Bonsoir*
Good night *Bonne nuit*
How are you? (courteous) *Allez-vous?*
How are you doing? (colloquial) *Ça va?/ Vas-tu?*
Fine, thank you. *Ça va bien, merci.*
And you? *Et vous?*
See you later. *À plus tard/À bientôt.*
Nice to meet you. *Enchanté.*
Yes *Oui*
No *Non*
Please *S'il vous plaît*
Thank you *Merci*
You're welcome *Bienvenu/de rien*
Excuse me *Excusez-moi*
Sorry *Pardon/désolé*
What's your name? *Comment vous appelez-vous?*
My name is . . . *Je m'appelle . . .*
Where are you from? *D'où venez-vous?*
I'm from . . . *Je viens de . . .*
Do you speak English? *Parlez-vous anglais?*
I don't speak French. *Je ne parle pas français.*
I don't understand. *Je ne comprends pas.*
I don't know. *Je ne sais pas.*
Can you please repeat? *Pourriez-vous répéter?*
What's it called? *Ça s'appelle?*
Would you like . . . ? *Voulez-vous . . . ?*

TERMS OF ADDRESS

I *je*
you *tu*
he *il*
she *elle*
we *nous*
you (plural) *vous*
they *ils/elles*
Mr./Sir *monsieur*
Mrs./Madame *madame*
Miss *mademoiselle*
young man *jeune homme*
young woman *jeune fille*
child *enfant*
brother/sister *frère/sœur*

father/mother *père/mère*
son/daughter *fils/fille*
husband/wife *mari/femme*
friend *ami/amie*
boyfriend/girlfriend *copain/copine*
married *marié/mariée*
single *célibataire*
divorced *divorcé/divorcée*

QUESTIONS
When? *Quand?*
What? *Quoi?*
What is it? *Qu'est-ce que c'est?*
Who? *Qui?*
Why? *Pourquoi?*
How? *Comment?*
Where is . . .? *Où est . . .?*
What's it called? *Ça s'appelle?*
Would you like . . . ? *Voulez-vous . . . ?*

GETTING AROUND
Where is . . .? *Où est . . .?*
How far away is . . .? *À quelle distance est . . .?*
How can I get to . . .? *Puis-je aller à . . .?*
bus *bus*
car *voiture*
train *train*
bus station *la station d'autobus*
train station *la gare de trains*
airport *l'aéroport*
What time do we leave? *À quelle heure est le départ?*
What time do we arrive? *À quelle heure arrive-t-on?*
a one-way ticket *un aller simple*
a round-trip ticket? *un aller retour*
Can you take me to this address? *Pourriez-vous m'emmener à cette adresse?*
north *nord*
south *sud*
east *est*
west *ouest*
left/right *gauche/droite*
straight ahead *tout droit*
entrance *entrée*
exit *sortie*

first *premier*
last *dernier*
next *prochain*

ACCOMMODATIONS
Are there any rooms available? *Avez-vous des chambres disponibles?*
I'd like to make a reservation. *J'aimerais faire une reservation.*
I want a single room. *J'aimerais une chambre simple.*
Is there a double room? *Y a-t-il une chambre double?*
private bathroom *salle de bains privée*
key *clé*
one night *une nuit*
Can you change the sheets/ towels? *Pourriez-vous changer les draps/ les serviettes?*
Could you please wake me up? *Pourriez-vous me réveiller?*
Is breakfast included? *Est-ce que le petit déjeuner est inclus?*

FOOD
to eat *manger*
to drink *boire*
breakfast *déjeuner*
lunch *dîner*
dinner *souper*
Can I see the menu? *Puis-je voir le menu?*
We're ready to order. *Nous sommes prêts à commander.*
Can I have some more wine? *Puis-je avoir un peu plus de vin?*
Can you bring me the bill please? *Pourriez-vous apporter l'addition?*
Is the service/the tip included? *Est-ce que le service est compris?*
I'm a vegetarian. *Je suis végétarien.*
It was delicious. *C'était délicieux.*
hot *chaud*
cold *froid*
sweet *sucré*
salty *salé*
bread *pain*
rice *riz*
Enjoy! *Bon appétit!*

Meat and Fish
meat *viande*
beef *bœuf*
pork *porc*
lamb *agneau*
chicken *poulet*
ham *jambon*
fish *poisson*
salmon *saumon*
mussels *moules*
oysters *huîtres*
shrimp *crevette*
tuna *thon*
rare *saignant*
medium *à point*
well done *bien cuit*
roasted *rôti*
boiled *bouilli*
grilled *grillé*
fried *frit*

Eggs and Dairy
milk *lait*
cream *crème*
butter *beurre*
cheese *fromage*
ice cream *crème glacée*
egg *œuf*
hard-boiled egg *œuf dur*
scrambled eggs *œufs brouillés*
poached egg *œuf poché*

Vegetables and Fruits
vegetables *légumes*
carrot *carotte*
tomato *tomate*
potato *patate/pomme de terre*
cucumber *concombre*
pepper *poivron*
mushrooms *champignons*
eggplant *aubergine*
peas *petits pois*
cabbage *chou*
apple *pomme*
pear *poire*
banana *banane*
orange *orange*
lemon *citron*

grape *raisin*
strawberry *fraise*
blueberry *bleuet*
raspberry *framboise*

Seasoning and Spices
sugar *sucre*
salt *sel*
black pepper *poivre*
onion *oignon*
garlic *ail*
olive oil *huile d'olive*
vinegar *vinaigre*
cinnamon *cannelle*
basil *basilic*
parsley *persil*
mint *menthe*
ginger *gingembre*

Drinks
drinks *boissons*
beer *bière*
wine *vin*
wine list *la carte des vins*
cheers! *à votre santé!*
water *eau*
ice *glace*
juice *jus*
filtered coffee *café filtre*
coffee with milk *café au lait*
black coffee *café noir*

SHOPPING
money *argent*
ATM *guichet automatique*
credit card *carte de crédit*
to buy *acheter*
to shop *magasiner*
I don't have change. *Je n'ai pas de monnaie.*
more *plus*
less *moins*
a good price *un bon prix*
sales *soldes*
How much does it cost? *Combien ça coûte?*
That's too expensive. *C'est trop cher.*
discount *rabais*
Can I try it on? *Est-ce que je peux l'essayer?*
It's too tight. *C'est trop serré.*

It's too big. *C'est trop grand.*
Can I exchange it? *Est-ce que je peux l'échanger?*

HEALTH AND SAFETY
Can you help me? *Pouvez-vous m'aider?*
I don't feel well. *Je ne me sens pas bien.*
I'm sick. *Je suis malade.*
Is there a pharmacy close by? *Y a-t-il une pharmacie pas loin?*
Can you call a doctor? *Pouvez-vous appeler un docteur?*
I need to go to the hospital. *Je dois aller à l'hôpital.*
medicine *médicament*
condom *condom, préservatif*
Is this neighborhood safe? *Est-ce que ce quartier est sécuritaire?*
Help! *À l'aide!, Au secours!*
Call the police! *Appeler la police.*
thief *voleur*

COMMUNICATIONS
to talk, to speak *parler*
to hear, to listen *écouter, entendre*
to make a phone call *faire un appel téléphonique*
cell phone *cellulaire*
What's your phone number? *Quel est ton numéro de téléphone?*
What's your email address? *Quelle est ton adresse électronique?*
collect call *appel à frais virés*
Do you have Internet? *Avez-vous Internet ici?*
post office *bureau de poste*
letter *lettre*
stamp *timbre*
postcard *carte postale*

NUMBERS
0 *zéro*
1 *un*
2 *deux*
3 *trois*
4 *quatre*
5 *cinq*
6 *six*
7 *sept*
8 *huit*
9 *neuf*
10 *dix*
11 *onze*
12 *douze*
13 *treize*
14 *quatorze*
15 *quinze*
16 *seize*
17 *dix-sept*
18 *dix-huit*
19 *dix-neuf*
20 *vingt*
21 *vingt-et-un*
30 *trente*
40 *quarante*
50 *cinquante*
60 *soixante*
70 *soixante-dix*
80 *quatre-vingt*
90 *quatre-vingt dix*
100 *cent*
101 *cent un*
200 *deux cent*
500 *cinq cent*
1000 *mille*
2000 *deux mille*

TIME
What time is it? *Quelle heure est-il?*
It's 2 o'clock. *Il est deux heures.*
It's 2:15. *Il est deux heures et quart.*
It's 2:30. *Il est deux heures et demie.*
It's 2:45. *Il est deux heures quarante-cinq.*
in two hours *dans deux heures*
now *maintenant*
before *avant*
after *après*
late/early *tard/tôt*
When? *Quand?*

DAYS AND MONTHS
day *jour*
night *nuit*
morning *matin*
afternoon *après-midi*
yesterday *hier*

tomorrow *demain*
today *aujourd'hui*
week *semaine*
month *mois*
year *année*
Monday *lundi*
Tuesday *mardi*
Wednesday *mercredi*
Thursday *jeudi*
Friday *vendredi*
Saturday *samedi*
Sunday *dimanche*
January *janvier*
February *février*
March *mars*
April *avril*
May *mai*
June *juin*
July *juillet*
August *août*
September *septembre*

October *octobre*
November *novembre*
December *décembre*

SEASONS AND WEATHER
season *saison*
spring *printemps*
summer *été*
autumn *automne*
winter *hiver*
weather *temps/météo*
sun *soleil*
It's sunny. *Il fait soleil.*
rain *pluie*
It's raining. *Il pleut.*
snow *neige*
It's snowing. *Il neige.*
snowstorm *tempête de neige*
ice *glace/verglas*
It's hot. *Il fait chaud.*
It's cold. *Il fait froid.*

Suggested Reading

HISTORY AND GENERAL INFORMATION
Dickinson, John A., and Brian Young. *A Short History of Québec*. Montréal: McGill-Queen's University Press, 1993, revised 2008. Originally written in 1992, this book is now into its fourth edition and offers a comprehensive overview of the province's social and economic development from pre-European to modern times. This latest edition includes reflections on the Bouchard-Taylor Commission on Accommodation and Cultural Differences, which examined attitudes toward immigration and immigrants in the province.

Fox, Joanna. *Montréal's Best BYOB Restaurants*. Montréal: Véhicule Press, 2009. One of Montréal's greatest attributes is its bring-your-own-wine restaurants. Restaurant reviewer and food industry insider Joanna Fox gives readers the low-down on 60 of the city's best BYOBs, with a selection to suit all tastes and budgets.

Grescoe, Taras. *Sacré Blues: An Unsentimental Journey through Quebec*. Toronto: Macfarlane Walter & Ross, 2001. Montréal author Taras Grescoe's modern account of Québec explores the stranger side of the province's pop culture, takes readers to a Francophone country-and-western festival, meets up with UFO-obsessed followers of Raël, and, of course, deconstructs a Montréal Canadiens hockey game. The book won the Québec Writers' Federation First Book Award and the Mavis Gallant Prize for Nonfiction in 2001.

Jenish, D'Arcy. *The Montreal Canadiens: 100 Years of Glory*. Toronto: Doubleday Canada, 2008. Published to coincide with the hockey team's 100th anniversary, this is the definitive history of the team—from the days of their first Stanley Cup win to the return of former player Bob Gainey as general manager. Even if you're not a fan, this book provides an insider's look at one of the NHL's most storied teams.

Lacoursiè re, Jacques, and Robin Philpot. *A People's History of Québec.* Montréal: Baraka Books, 2009. First published in French, this concise book looks at the history of the province through the people that discovered, explored and inhabit it. The focus is on day-to-day life and offers little-known details like the despicable "mixed dancing" at times of celebration and early settlers' love of *charivari,* a loud, rambunctious party through the streets.

FICTION AND MEMOIRS

Carrier, Roch. *The Hockey Sweater.* Montréal: Tundra Books, 1979. This semi-autobiographical children's picture book is one of the most memorable Canadian stories. It tells the tale of a boy in small-town Québec who orders an Canadiens hockey sweater from the Eaton's catalogue only to receive a Toronto Maple-Leaf jersey. Full of subtle comments on Québec and the rest of Canada, it's a touching story that has been immortalized by an NFB film.

Cohen, Leonard. *The Favourite Game.* New York: Vintage, 1963. In this semi-autobiographical book, protagonist Lawrence Breavman wanders through the Montréal streets with his best friend and confidant, Krantz, reminisces about his years at summer camp, and tries to understand the death of his father. *The Favourite Game* jumps between the past and present.

Doucet, Julie. *365 Days: A Diary.* Montréal: Drawn & Quarterly, 2008. Born and raised in Montréal, comic artist Julie Doucet first gained recognition as an artist for her zine *Dirty Plotte,* a funny, demented take on her own life experiences. Though she's since moved away from comics and become a full-time artist and illustrator, *365 Days* offers an intimate look at the artistic community she surrounded herself with in her early days and the experience of an artist in Montréal.

Hage, Rawi. *Cockroach,* Toronto: House of Anansi Press, 2009. IMPAC-Dublin award-winner Rawi Hage's second effort, *Cockroach,* tells the tale of a struggling immigrant living in Montréal's underbelly. A former taxi driver, Hage, who is originally from Lebanon, brings a unique perspective and an adept eye to the Montréal experience.

MacLennan, Hugh. *Two Solitudes.* Toronto: McClelland & Stewart, 1945. The title of this book has become emblematic of the country's French/English cultural and linguistic divide. Set between World War I and 1939, the book takes place in Saint-Marc-des-Érables, a small Québec town, and the booming, predominantly English city of Montréal. Centered on Paul Tallard, a Québécois at home with both languages, the book follows him on a quest to find his own identity and a way of defining the Canadian experience.

O'Neill, Heather. *Lullabies for Little Criminals.* Toronto: Harper Perennial, 2006. Heather O'Neill was born and (mostly) raised in Montréal, and her debut novel tells the story of Baby, a 12-year-old girl growing up in the seedy area of lower St-Laurent with her young, well-meaning junkie father. There is a touching humanity to O'Neill's writing, and her depiction of Montréal in all its real, gritty glory is fascinating.

Proulx, Monique. *Les Aurores Montréales.* Toronto: Douglas & McIntyre, 1997. Twenty-seven short stories make up this collection that takes place in pre- and post-referendum Québec. Weaving in and out of Montréal, the stories look at the lives of Quebeckers and how they are or aren't affected by the changing times.

Richler, Mordecai. *Son of a Smaller Hero.* Paris: André Deutsch, 1955. From Mile End's Jewish ghetto to the bed of a downtown shishka, this book follows prodigal son Noah Adler as he searches to find his identity in the neighborhoods and communities that make up Montréal.

Tremblay, Michel. *Les Belles Sœurs.* Vancouver: Talonbooks, revised ed., 1992. Arguably the most important Québécois writer of his generation, Tremblay was only 23 years old when he wrote this play in 1965. First presented in 1968 at Théâtre du Rideau Vert, it ushered in a new era of Québécois theater. Written in *joual* (working-class slang), the play is set in the triplexes of Montréal's Plateau and follows the exploits of the extended family on one street.

Internet Resources

Bonjour Québec
www.bonjourquebec.com
The province's official tourism website has comprehensive information on anything and everything to do with the province, from national parks to kid-friendly fun.

An Endless Banquet
www.endlessbanquet.blogspot.com
This Montréal couple closely connected with the food scene—she's a pastry chef, he's a former restaurant critic—give readers the lowdown on restaurants and food happenings around the city. From the best late-night burger to the best place to blow $200 on a meal, they've got you covered.

Montréal Mirror
www.montrealmirror.com
The city's alternative English weekly covers everything from news stories to movies, music, art events, and restaurant reviews. It also has a comprehensive listing section.

Québec T'aime
www.quebectaime.com
This Québec City–based blog run by the hippest writers in the city offers information on everything from the 10 Best Ice Cream Shops to the latest art openings.

Said the Gramophone
www.saidthegramophone.com
Though not exclusively Montréal-based (one of the writers lives in Toronto), this music blog offers an interesting insider take on the Québec and Montréal music scenes.

Tourism Montréal
www.tourisme-montreal.org
The official tourism site for the city also has a number of bloggers dedicated to specific aspects of the city—gay, nightlife, girly things—that keep the site fresh and interesting.

Voir
www.voir.ca
The online component to the Francophone alternative weekly, Voir has event listings, restaurant reviews, and a weekly webcast that takes you behind the scenes of the weekly photo shoot and gives you a rundown of the week's biggest events.

Index

Restaurants Index

MONTRÉAL

Nightlife Index

Shops Index

MONTRÉAL

QUÉBEC CITY

Hotels Index

www.moon.com

DESTINATIONS | ACTIVITIES | BLOGS | MAPS | BOOKS

MOON.COM is ready to help plan your next trip! Filled with fresh trip ideas and strategies, author interviews, informative travel blogs, a detailed map library, and descriptions of all the Moon guidebooks, Moon.com is all you need to get out and explore the world—or even places in your own backyard. While at Moon.com, sign up for our monthly e-newsletter for updates on new releases, travel tips, and expert advice from our on-the-go Moon authors. As always, when you travel with Moon, expect an experience that is uncommon and truly unique.

MOON IS ON FACEBOOK—BECOME A FAN!
JOIN THE MOON PHOTO GROUP ON FLICKR

MAP SYMBOLS

▦ Expressway	◖	Highlight	✗	Airfield	⌕	Golf Course
Primary Road	○	City/Town	✕	Airport	▣	Parking Area
Secondary Road	◉	State Capital	▲	Mountain	◬	Archaeological Site
Unpaved Road	✪	National Capital	✛	Unique Natural Feature	♠	Church
Trail	★	Point of Interest			⚲	Gas Station
Ferry	•	Accommodation	⚐	Waterfall	◌	Glacier
Railroad	▼	Restaurant/Bar	▲	Park	░	Mangrove
Pedestrian Walkway	■	Other Location	◨	Trailhead	▨	Reef
Stairs	∧	Campground	✕	Skiing Area	▨	Swamp

CONVERSION TABLES

°C = (°F - 32) / 1.8
°F = (°C x 1.8) + 32
1 inch = 2.54 centimeters (cm)
1 foot = 0.304 meters (m)
1 yard = 0.914 meters
1 mile = 1.6093 kilometers (km)
1 km = 0.6214 miles
1 fathom = 1.8288 m
1 chain = 20.1168 m
1 furlong = 201.168 m
1 acre = 0.4047 hectares
1 sq km = 100 hectares
1 sq mile = 2.59 square km
1 ounce = 28.35 grams
1 pound = 0.4536 kilograms
1 short ton = 0.90718 metric ton
1 short ton = 2,000 pounds
1 long ton = 1.016 metric tons
1 long ton = 2,240 pounds
1 metric ton = 1,000 kilograms
1 quart = 0.94635 liters
1 US gallon = 3.7854 liters
1 Imperial gallon = 4.5459 liters
1 nautical mile = 1.852 km

MOON MONTRÉAL & QUÉBEC CITY

Avalon Travel
a member of the Perseus Books Group
1700 Fourth Street
Berkeley, CA 94710, USA
www.moon.com

Editor and Series Manager: Erin Raber
Copy Editor: Deana Shields
Graphics Coordinator: Kathryn Osgood
Production Coordinator: Tabitha Lahr
Cover Designer: Tabitha Lahr
Map Editor: Albert Angulo
Cartographers: Albert Angulo, Lohnes and Wright, Bernadette Dugtong, Chris L. Henrick, Kat Bennett, Kaitlin Jaffe

ISBN-13: 978-1-59880-758-5
ISSN: 1559-3479

Printing History
1st Edition – 2006
2nd Edition – July 2011
5 4 3 2 1

Text © 2011 by Sacha Jackson.
Maps © 2011 by Avalon Travel.
All rights reserved.

Front cover photo: Montréal Convention Center © Philippe Renault/Hemis/Corbis
Color front matter photos: Page 1, Château Frontenac in Québec City © citylights/123rf.com; Page 2, Place des Arts © Tourisme Montréal; Page 3, panoramic view of old Québec © Tourisme Montréal; Page 4 (left), Cathédrale Marie-Reine-du-Monde © Sacha Jackson; Page 4 (center), the towers at the Grand Séminaire de Montréal © Sacha Jackson; Page 4 (right), La Grande Bibliothéque © La Grande Bibliothéque, Bernard Fougéres; Page 5 (left), Québec City's Musée de la Civilisation © Musée de la Civilization; Page 5 (center), view of Vieux-Québec's Lower Town from the Funiculaire © Sacha Jackson; Page 5 (right), Grand Séminaire de Québec © Sacha Jackson; Page 30 (icon), skyline of Downtown Montréal © Tourisme Montréal; Page 30 (bottom left), Basilique-Cathédrale Notre-Dame-de-Québec in Québec City © Sacha Jackson; Page 30 (bottom right), ice-skating at Place D'Youville © Claudel Huot; Page 31 © Pointe à Callière Musée d'Archéologie et d'Histoire; Page 32 © Régie des Installations Olympiques; Page 33 © Sacha Jackson; Page 34 © Sébastien Larose; Page 35 © Tourisme Montréal; Page 36 © Tourism Montréal/ Denis Lauzon; Page 37 © Tourisme Montréal; Page 38 © Canadian Tourism Commission, Pierre St-Jacques; Page 39 © Tourisme Montréal; Page 40 © Montreal Museum of Fine Arts/Michel Dubreuil; Page 41 (left) © Sacha Jackson; Page 41 (right) © Sacha Jackson; Page 42 © Musée National des Beaux-Arts du Québec/ Michel Dubreuil; Page 43 © Michel Tremblay; Page 44 © Sacha Jackson; Page 45 © Sacha Jackson; Page 46 © Tourisme Montréal; Page 47 © Sacha Jackson; Page 48 Alessandro Russo/www.123RF.com

Printed in Canada by Friesens

KEEPING CURRENT

If you have a favorite gem you'd like to see included in the next edition, or see anything that needs updating, clarification, or correction, please drop us a line. Send your comments via email to feedback@moon.com, or use the address above.